SOCIAL AND SCIENTIFIC UNCERTAINTIES IN ENVIRONMENTAL LAW

The publication of this book was supported by

VINCI ENERGIES

Bournemouth University

European Environmental Law Forum Series, Volume 8

SOCIAL AND SCIENTIFIC UNCERTAINTIES IN ENVIRONMENTAL LAW

Edited by
Tilak GINIGE
Iain GREEN
Patrick VAN CALSTER
Alain SIMONS
Joseph McMULLEN

INTERSENTIA
Cambridge – Antwerp – Chicago

Intersentia Ltd
8 Wellington Mews
Wellington Street | Cambridge
CB1 1HW | United Kingdom
Tel: +44 1223 736 170
Email: contact@larcier-intersentia.com
www.larcier-intersentia.com

Distribution for the UK and
Rest of the World (incl. Eastern Europe)
NBN International
1 Deltic Avenue, Rooksley
Milton Keynes MK13 8LD
United Kingdom
Tel: +44 1752 202 301 | Fax: +44 1752 202 331
Email: orders@nbninternational.com

Distribution for Europe
Lefebvre Sarrut Belgium NV
Hoogstraat 139/6
1000 Brussels
Belgium
Tel: +32 (0)2 548 07 13
Email: contact@larcier-intersentia.com

Distribution for the USA and Canada
Independent Publishers Group
Order Department
814 North Franklin Street
Chicago, IL 60610
USA
Tel: +1 800 888 4741 (toll free) | Fax: +1 312 337 5985
Email: orders@ipgbook.com

Social and Scientific Uncertainties in Environmental Law

ISBN 978-1-83970-403-1
D/2024/7849/17
NUR 823

British Library Cataloguing in Publication Data. A catalogue record for this book is available from the British Library.

ACKNOWLEDGEMENTS

We are delighted and thankful for the generous engagement of the many friends, colleagues, students, family, and external reviewers who have agreed to participate in this international legal enquiry into environmental law's social and scientific uncertainties.

We are most appreciative of their active contributions and scholarship, which is reflected in the many chapters that make our Social and Scientific Uncertainty in Environmental Law Conference Book – it was a labour of love that started in the time of COVID-19.

We also want to thank our editor, Rebecca Moffat, and our publisher, Francesca Ramadan. We appreciate their advice and support throughout the creation of this book.

CONTENTS

Acknowledgements v
List of Authors xix

Introduction
Tilak GINIGE, Iain GREEN, Patrick VAN CALSTER, Alain SIMONS, Joseph MCMULLEN, Susan Phaustus MBAYUWAYU and Freya RUSSELL 1

1. The European Environmental Law Forum Conference in Bournemouth . . . 1
2. Social and Scientific Uncertainties in Environmental Law. 2

PART I. LEGAL AND SCIENTIFIC UNCERTAINTY

Legal Uncertainty in EU Environmental Law: The Battle for the Last Word
Ludwig KRÄMER 15

1. Introduction: Precaution as an Answer to Scientific Uncertainty 15
2. The Challenge from Member States 16
3. Primacy of EU Law and the EU Treaties 21
4. Possible Solutions in Law 27

Environmental Science, Innovation and Transactions: Wicked Problems for Science and Law
Carolyn ROBERTS 31

1. Introduction 31
2. "Wicked" Problems 32
3. The "Wicked", "Super Wicked" or "Hyper Wicked" Problem of Flooding 33
4. Brokering Solutions to Wicked Problems at Various Scales 35
5. The Roles of Lawyers in Brokering Innovation 35
6. Whole-System Changes 37
7. Conclusion 38

PART II. THE MARINE ENVIRONMENT

The Role of Marine Protected Areas in Enhancing Biodiversity and Ocean Sustainability
Naomi TOWNSEND 41

1. Introduction 41
2. Overview of the Factors which can Influence MPA Success. 45
3. Legal Basis 55
4. Factors Affecting the Ecological Success of MPAs. 67
5. Conclusion. 83

Navigating a Sea of Uncertainty in the EU Regulation of Marine Renewables: The Case for Hybrid Co-Regulation?
Nikolaos GIANNOPOULOS 87

1. Introduction 87
2. The Wait-and-See Approach of the EU Towards Regulating Marine Renewables: A Paradox? 89
3. Opportunities and Challenges in Recalibrating the Environmental Regulation of Marine Renewables 94
   3.1. Beyond Pure Voluntariness: Examples of EU-Supported Hybrid Regulatory Arrangements. 97
   3.2. The Call for Complementing EU Principled Meta-Regulation with Private Standards. 101
4. Conclusions: What Role for a Co-Regulatory Approach in Regulating Marine Renewables?. 104

Maritime RAS Techno-Regulatory Regime: Six Blocks of Dynamic Influence Towards Good Environmental Stewardship
Tafsir Matin JOHANSSON, Jon SKINNER, Dimitrios DALAKLIS, Thomas KLENUM and Aspasia PASTRA 107

1. Introduction 107
2. Why Remote Inspection Technologies (RIT) in Shipping? 110
3. RIT Implications on the Law of the Sea?. 112
4. RIT Class Survey: Common Minimum Standards 115
5. The Case for Harmonising RIT Requirements through International Guidelines 120
   5.1. First Block: Remote Inspection Technology v. Remote Survey. 122
   5.2. Second Block: Developing Definitions 122
   5.3. Third Block: Operational and Technical Standards Based on Variety 123
   5.4. Fourth Block: Determining the Degree of Autonomy 124

5.5. Fifth Block: Data Management and Security 125
5.6. Sixth Block: Reference to the National Liability Regime 127
6. Conclusions 129

PART III. THE ATMOSPHERE

Legal and Regulatory Framework of Air Pollution in India: Evolution, Development and Reforms
Kanak MISHRA 133

1. Introduction 133
2. The Concept of Air Pollution 134
2.1. The Formulation of the Air Act 134
2.2. Measurement of Air Pollution: Air Quality Index 135
2.3. Air Pollution in the 1990s 135
2.4. Air Pollution in the 2000s 135
3. Case Analysis 136
3.1. *Taj Trapezium* Case 136
3.2. *CNG Vehicles* Case 138
3.3. *Relocation of Industries* Case (1995) 139
4. The Role of the Supreme Court 141
4.1. SC Order, 10 December 2018 141
4.1.1. Study on "Health Impact Assessment of Firecrackers Bursting During Dussehra and Diwali" 141
4.1.2. Study on "Health Effects of Chronic Exposure to Smoke from Biomass Fuel Burning in Rural Households" 141
4.1.2.1. Recommendations of the Study 142
4.1.2.2. Strengths and Limitations of the Study 142
4.1.3. Study on "Ambient Air Quality, Respiratory Symptoms and Lung Function of Children in Delhi" 143
4.2. Recourse Undertaken for the Excessively High Pollution Levels in Delhi as Per GAP, Notification 2017 143
4.3. Odd-Even Scheme to Combat Delhi Air Pollution 144
5. Conclusion 144

PART IV. THE FRESH WATER ENVIRONMENT

Water Reuse: A Sustainable Concept for Europe?
Linda SCHÖNFELDER 149

1. Introduction 149
2. Content of the Regulation 150
2.1. Scope 150
2.1.1. Treated Urban Wastewater 151

2.1.2. Agricultural Irrigation 151
2.1.3. Further Uses. 152
2.1.3.1. Industry, Amenity and Environmental Purposes 152
2.1.3.2. Indirect Use. 153
2.2. Obligations of Addressed Parties. 154
2.2.1. Reclaimed Water Quality. 154
2.2.2. Risk-Management Plan 156
2.2.3. Permit Obligation 156
2.2.4. Compliance Check 157
2.3. End Users. 157
3. Coherence with Other EU Legislation. 159
3.1. Urban Wastewater Treatment Directive (UWWTD) 159
3.2. Waste Framework Directive 160
3.3. Water Framework Directive (WFD) 162
3.3.1. Improvement Requirements 162
3.3.2. Prohibition of Deterioration 162
3.3.2.1. Ecological Status of Surface Water Bodies 163
3.3.2.2. Chemical Status of Groundwater Bodies 163
3.4. Nitrates Directive 164
3.5. Legislation on Foodstuffs 165
4. Conclusion and Outlook 166

Grey Water Reuse in the EU: Legal Obstacles, Shared Solutions and Future Challenges
Marko Perišić. 169

1. Introduction 169
2. The Importance of Grey Water Reuse 173
3. Characteristics of Grey Water. 175
4. The Legal Context of Water Reuse 176
5. Reflection on the Current EU Law Position on Water Reuse and its Enforcement in the Member States. 179
6. Conclusions. 181

PART V. WASTE MANAGEMENT

The EU Policy and Legislative Framework on Plastics: A Comprehensive Approach to Tackle a Challenging Environmental Problem
Susanna Paleari. 185

1. Introduction 185
2. The EU Policy and Legislative Framework to Manage Plastics 188

3. Legislative and Policy Measures Addressing the Plastic Value Chain..... 191
3.1. Measures Affecting Plastic Production.......................... 191
3.2. Measures Affecting Plastic Consumption....................... 195
3.3. Measures Affecting Plastic Waste Management................. 197
4. Conclusions... 201

Illegal Landfilling in Romania: A Never-Ending Story?
Violeta Stratan 203

1. Prologue: Legislative Framework................................ 203
2. Action and Characters of the Story 205
3. Epilogue: In Search of Solutions for an End to the Story?............. 211

PART VI. THE ROLE OF THE GENERAL PUBLIC

"Individual Concern" in Climate Protection Matters in the Context of Different Legal Protection Regimes
Janna Ringena 215

1. Groups of Individuals Suing the Legislator......................... 216
1.1. *People's Climate Case* 216
1.2. German Constitutional Complaints 217
1.3. Interim Conclusion 218
2. The Handling of Standing by the Courts........................... 219
2.1. *People's Climate Case* 219
2.1.1. *Plaumann* Doctrine 219
2.1.2. Lack of Standing 220
2.2. German Constitutional Complaints 221
2.2.1. Present, Individual and Direct Concern 221
2.2.2. Standing Assumed 222
2.3. Interim Conclusion 223
3. What about the *Plaumann* Doctrine? 224
3.1. Open Wording 224
3.2. Changed Contexts of Jurisprudence 225
3.2.1. The *Plaumann* Case Itself.............................. 225
3.2.2. The *Plaumann* Case in Light of the *Van Gend & Loos*, *Costa/ENEL* and *Leberpfennig* Cases 226
3.2.3. Judicial Adaptions of the *Plaumann* Doctrine 227
3.2.4. Interim Conclusion..................................... 228
3.3. Effective Legal Protection 229
3.3.1. Near-End of the *Plaumann* Doctrine after Declaration of the EUCFR.. 229

3.3.2. The ECJ Sticks to *Plaumann* 230
3.3.3. Interim Conclusion.................................. 231
3.4. Constitutional Traditions of the Member States 231
3.5. Avoiding Incoherence 233
3.6. Avoiding Rampant Expansions of the Right of Action 234
3.7. Interim Conclusion 234
4. Adapting the Interpretation of "Individual Concern" at EU Level 235
4.1. Fundamental Rights-Oriented Interpretation (GFCC) 235
4.2. Interest-Based Interpretation 236
4.3. Safeguarding the Separation of Powers......................... 237
4.4. Added Value of Abandoning *Plaumann* 238
5. Summary and Outlook... 238

Access to Justice for NGOs to Challenge Climate Commitments under the European Climate Law: A Lost Hope?
Alessandra Accogli 241

1. Introduction 241
2. The European Climate Law and the Measures Member States are Required to Take to Achieve Climate Neutrality 243
3. Access to Justice under Article 9 of the Aarhus Convention and Legal Standing for NGOs to Challenge the Content of National Energy and Climate Plans.. 246
3.1. Can Article 9 of the Aarhus Convention be Applied to the NECPs Adopted under the ECL?............................. 246
3.2. Can NGOs Challenge Specific Measures Contained in the NECPs before National Courts under Article 9 of the Aarhus Convention? 250
3.2.1. Legal Standing... 251
3.2.2. Scope of Judicial Review 253
4. Conclusions.. 257

PART VII. CLIMATE CHANGE

Climate Change and the UK's Local Authorities: A Snapshot of their Actions and Perceived Challenges
Soraia Da Cas.. 261

1. Introduction 261
1.1. Climate Emergency Declaration: Scientific and Social Drivers..... 262
1.2. UK National Policies, Local Authorities and Community Roles.... 263
1.3. Climate Action: Plans and Challenges 265

2. Methods 266
3. Results 270
4. Discussion 278
5. Conclusion 285
Appendix 285

The Role of Regulation in Strengthening Climate Resilience and Food Security in Nigeria
Erimma Gloria ORIE and King James NKUM 289

1. Background 289
2. Nigeria's Experience with Climate Change Impact 291
3. Climate Change and Food Insecurity in Nigeria 293
4. Global Trend in Climate Change Regulation 296
5. Significance of the Nigerian Climate Change Act in Strengthening Climate Resilience and Food Security in Nigeria 300
6. Conclusion and Recommendations 304

PART VIII. BIODIVERSITY LOSS

The Programmatic Approach, Uncertainty and Monitoring in the Habitats Directive: The Precautionary Principle as a Pavlovian Reflex to Uncertainty?
Rogier KEGGE and Hidde KREMERS 309

1. Introduction 309
2. The Programmatic Approach 310
3. The Dutch Programmatic Approach to Nitrogen 312
4. The *PAN* Case 313
5. Monitoring and the Habitats Directive 315
6. Monitoring in the Case Law 316
7. Adaptive Management versus the Precautionary Principle? 317
8. Conclusion 319

Legal Challenges before English Courts under Ecosystem Services Protection
Merve ROBSON, Oliver J. JARVIS, Rina CINDRAK, Tilak GINIGE and Iain GREEN 321

1. Introduction 321
2. The Need for Protecting Ecosystem Services 323
3. Environmental Cases before Courts 324
   3.1. General Focus of the English and Welsh Courts 324
   3.2. Previous Cases with Reference to Ecosystem Services 327

4. Discussion and Recommendations 328
4.1. Discussion 328
4.2. Recommendations 331
5. Conclusion 335

Strategic Climate Change Litigation and the EU Habitats Directive: What Lessons can be Learnt from the Recent Case Law Developments in the United States?
Hendrik SCHOUKENS 337

1. Introduction 337
2. A Quick Peek into the Endangered Species Act and the EU Habitats Directive 340
2.1. Introduction 340
2.2. Overview of the ESA 341
2.3. Overview of the EU Habitats Directive 342
3. Exploring the Potential for Climate-Based Litigation under the EU Habitats Directive 345
3.1. Introduction 345
3.2. Does Climate Change Fall within the Realm of Biodiversity Law? 345
3.3. Listing Protected Species on the Basis of Climate Change? 349
3.4. Designating New Habitats for Species at Risk because of Climate Change? 355
3.5. Preventing Future Lock-Ins and New CO_2 Emissions? 358
4. Conclusion 365

PART IX. GREEN INFRASTRUCTURE

Uncertainty in Green Infrastructure Decision-Making: Types, Consequences and Available Legal Tools
Yelena M. GORDEEVA 371

1. Introduction 371
2. Understanding the "Green Infrastructure" Concept 372
3. Uncertainty in GI Decision-Making Processes: Typology and Consequences 379
3.1. Typology on Uncertainties in GI Decision-Making Processes 379
3.2. Consequences of Uncertainty in GI Decision-Making Processes 381
4. Concluding Remarks 383

PART X. BUSINESSES

Enhancing Environmental Sustainability through Reforming Czech Contract Law
Rita Simon 387

1. Introduction 387
2. Promoting Sustainability as a Binding Target 388
   2.1. International and European Obligations 388
   2.2. More Responsible Production in the EU, but Low Focus on Consumption 389
3. Best Practices Towards Repairability and Durability in Europe 391
4. Low Ambition to Promote Sustainability in the Czech Republic 393
5. Conclusions 396

Foreign Direct Liability as an Emerging Norm for the Accountability of Transnational Corporations: The European Experience
Ikechukwu P. Ugwu 399

1. Introduction 399
2. The Failure of Accountability 401
3. Examining Foreign Direct Liability 403
   3.1. The Possible Legal Basis for Foreign Direct Litigation Cases in European Courts 404
   3.2. Selected FDL Cases in the EU Member States 406
4. The Failing ATS and Lessons for FDL Cases in Europe 412
5. European Commission Proposal for a Directive on Corporate Sustainability Due Diligence 415
6. Conclusion 416

PART XI. ENVIRONMENTAL CRIMES

The Prosecution of Environmental Crimes through Restorative Justice: The "Criminal Settlement Procedure" in the Italian System
Matteo Riccardi and Paola Martino 421

1. Introduction 421
2. Environmental Criminal Law in the Italian System: Overview of the "Criminal Stair" 422
3. The Discipline of the Diversion Procedure for Environmental Crimes (Section Sixth-*Bis*, Legislative Decree No. 152 of 2006) 427
   3.1. Regulatory Framework 427

3.2. The CSP Procedure: Conditions for the Application 430
3.3. The Procedure: A "Bracket" in the Criminal Proceeding 432
4. Conclusions 438

PART XII. ENVIRONMENTAL LIABILITY

Scientific Uncertainties and Responsibility in Environmental Law in the Environmental Liability Directive
Mariusz BARAN 443

1. Introduction 443
2. Liability Regime under Directive 2004/35/EC 446
3. Exclusion and Waiver of Liability under Directive 2004/35/EC 448
4. Available Scientific and Technical Data, Precautionary and Preventive Principles and the Polluter-Pays Principle 451
5. "State of Science and Technology" as a Key Concept in Environmental Law 457
6. Summary 461

PART XIII. JUDICIAL REVIEW

Elaborating on the Scientific Evidentiary Requirements of the Precautionary Principle
Rhoda JENNINGS 465

1. Introduction 465
2. Defining the Precautionary Principle 466
3. Emphasis on Science and Scientific Data 468
4. Legitimating Precautionary Decision-Making 469
5. Judicial Review of the Scientific Element of Precautionary Decision-Making 471
5.1. Attributes of the Scientific Data 471
5.2. Availability and Temporal Quality of Data 473
5.3. Minority and Contradictory Science 474
5.4. Role of the Scientific Evaluation and the Scientific Committee 477
5.5. Member State Discretion and Variable Precaution 480
5.6. Scientific Evaluation and Policy 481
5.7. The Role of Science and Scientific Advisory Bodies in Defining the Principle 483
6. Conclusion 484

PART XIV. RUSSIAN ENVIRONMENTAL LAW

Legal Risks and Legal Uncertainties in Russian Environmental Law
Nikolay KICHIGIN 489

1. Introduction 489
2. The Concept of "Legal Uncertainty in Environmental Law" 490
3. The Concept of "Legal Risk in Environmental Law" 491
4. Features of Legal Uncertainties and Environmental Risks in Environmental Law 496
5. Identification and Assessment of Legal Risks at the Stage of Development of the Draft Regulatory Legal Act 497
   5.1. Conducting an Experiment (Legal Experiment) 498
   5.2. Development of a Legal Model for Future Legal Regulation 499
   5.3. Working Out the Effect of the Projected Regulatory Legal Act of Environmental Law 500
6. Identification and Assessment of Legal Uncertainties and Legal Risks in Environmental Law at the Stage of Implementation of a Regulatory Legal Act 501
7. Means of Minimising Legal Uncertainties and Legal Risks in Economic Activity 503
   7.1. Environmental Audit 503
   7.2. Environmental Insurance 505
   7.3. Environmental and Legal Consulting 507
   7.4. Assessment of the Impact of the Planned Activity on the Environment 507
   7.5. Environmental Expertise 508
   7.6. Judicial Practice 508
   7.7. Explanations of Public Authorities 508
   7.8. Project Financing 509
   7.9. The Use of the Concept "Acceptable Risk" in Environmental Law 509
8. Minimisation of Legal Risks in Environmental Law on the Correlation between State Land Supervision and Municipal Land Control 510
9. Conclusions 512

LIST OF AUTHORS

Alessandra Accogli is a PhD researcher at UCD Sutherland School of Law. Her research examines the intersections of climate change, ecosystem degradation and human rights impacts through the case study of peatlands in Ireland. Alessandra holds an LLM in public international law from Université Libre de Bruxelles (ULB), where she also completed a one-year Master's degree in political science, and a second-cycle Master's degree in law from the Università del Salento (UniSalento).

Mariusz Baran is assistant professor at the Environmental Law Center, at the Faculty of Law and Administration of the Jagiellonian University in Kraków. He is a member of the Research Network on EU Administrative Law and the European Environmental Law Forum; a laureate of scientific awards, *inter alia* winner in the Competition of the Minister of Science and Higher Education of the Republic of Poland for scholarships for outstanding young scientists in 2015; and author of many works in the field of environmental law and EU law.

Rina Cindrak is completing her PhD at Bournemouth University and is a Researcher at Bournemouth University's Environment & Threats Strategic Research Area. Her research is focused on comparative law, assessing air pollution legal regimes in the UK and Europe, using scientific data to inform legal and policy decisions across frameworks to identify the most effective approaches in addressing environmental and human populace health concerns. She has given lectures on a part-time basis at Bournemouth University and is currently working in ESG (Environment, Social, Governance) in the Financial Service sector using data, policy and legal developments to advise on ESG developments and concerns.

Soraia Da Cas is a Bachelor in Law (LLB), with a PGDip in public law, and an MSc in green economy. Currently, she works in Brazil as a legal analyst in labour law.

Dimitrios Dalaklis joined the World Maritime University (WMU) in 2014, upon completion of a 26-year distinguished career with the Hellenic Navy. His expertise revolves around the interrelated maritime safety and security domains. He is an associate fellow of the Nautical Institute (NI) and a member of the International Association of Maritime Economists (IAME). He is the author/co-author of many peer-reviewed articles, books and studies, in both the Greek and English languages, with a strong research focus on issues relating to the implementation of the SOLAS Convention, and especially electronic equipment/systems supporting the safety of navigation.

Nikolaos Giannopoulos is an assistant professor in public international and EU law at Utrecht University's Law Faculty. His research focuses primarily on legal and regulatory aspects of marine renewables within the context of the EU's energy transition, with a particular interest in the interplay between environmental and economic factors. Additionally, he is involved in research concerning the implementation of the EU Green Deal in European seas, and the coherence of EU marine policies and legislation, through the EU Horizon-funded "CrossGov" project, bringing with him practical experience as a qualified lawyer at the Athens Bar Association in the field of public administrative law.

Tilak Ginige is a senior lecturer in environmental law at Bournemouth University's Faculty of Science and Technology. His research interests include renewable energy, mining waste, the Water Framework Directive, environmental liability, rights to nature and sustainable development law. In the past, he has contributed to the Catalan government's environmental policy, as an advisor to the president of the Generalitat of Catalunya. His other research-related achievements include involvement in EU-funded research concerning the Water Framework Directive and the EU Mining Waste Directive. He has published in reviewed journals, including the *European Environmental Law Review*; the *Law, Environment and Development Journal* (LEAD); the *Journal of Water Law* and the *International Journal of Liability and Scientific Enquiry*. He is a proponent of the critical need for evidence-based information to guide environmental policy and law.

Yelena M. Gordeeva is currently a consultant on climate solutions to RUSAL, implementing some of the first nature-based solutions to climate change in Russia in the context of the 2015 Paris Agreement. This includes carbon-offset projects on aviation forest fire protection of 505 thousand hectares in the Krasnoyarsk Region, and on temperate drained peatlands rewetting in the Leningradsky Region. Yelena is also a part time assistant professor in public international law at the Vyatka State University. Prior to being a consultant, Yelena successfully defended her PhD, "European and Russian Forests under International Climate Change Law", at the Law Faculty of Hasselt University (Belgium), under the supervision of Professor Dr Bernard Vanheusden (Hasselt University), Professor Dr Marjan Peeters (Maastricht University) and Dr Stejn Verbiest (Hasselt University). Yelena conducted her postdoctoral research in environmental law as part of an interdisciplinary research project on landscape connectivity for forest species (WOODNET), co-funded by the European Commission (BiodivERsA), investigating the available legal tools to manage uncertainty in green infrastructure decision-making, under the supervision of Professor Dr Charles-Hubert Born, at the Catholic University of Louvain-la-Neuve (Belgium).

Iain Green has spent the last 30 years working in higher education, gaining his PhD in environmental biology in 2003. The main focus of his research is the environmental effects of pollution. This work has encompassed terrestrial, marine and freshwater ecosystems, covering all levels of biology, from the cell to communities. Iain is currently deputy head of the Department of Life and Environmental Sciences at Bournemouth University, and leads soil protection research in the Environment & Threats Strategic Research Group.

Oliver J. Jarvis completed his Bachelor's degree in law at Bournemouth University in 2021, obtaining a First-Class degree with honours. Oliver's dissertation focused on sustainable development and intergenerational equity as well as a case study on the UK's High Speed 2 rail network. Since completing his degree, Oliver has been working at a full-service international law firm specialising in property. Oliver's main research interests are in the legal enforceability of sustainable development and environmental protection in England and Wales and internationally.

Rhoda Jennings is an EPA/IRC Postgraduate Scholar at the School of Law, University College Cork. Her research investigates how science and scientific evidence are integrated into EU environmental legislation. Rhoda is an environmental lawyer with a background in the natural sciences.

Tafsir Matin Johansson is an assistant professor at the World Maritime University-Sasakawa Global Ocean Institute (GOI), in Malmö, Sweden. Tafsir is a techno-policy analyst with a PhD in maritime affairs from the World Maritime University. His duties at the GOI include ocean governance and policy research, teaching, and developing innovative policy models. Tafsir has published extensively on maritime and ocean issues, and has worked on, or led, a number of multidisciplinary projects funded by Transport Canada (Government of Canada). Currently Tafsir serves as a CO-PI in a European Union Horizon 2020 programme-funded project titled "Overcoming Regulatory Barriers for Service Robotics in an Ocean Industry Context".

Rogier Kegge is an assistant professor of administrative and environmental law at Leiden University, the Netherlands. He specialises in nature conservation law and spatial planning law.

Nikolay Kichigin is acting head of the Department of Environmental and Agricultural Legislation of the Institute of Legislation and Comparative Law under the Government of the Russian Federation, leading research fellow, candidate of legal sciences. His research interests are environmental law, natural resource law and urban law.

Thomas Klenum (FRINA, C.Eng, Eur.Ing) is executive vice president for the Liberian Registry, with a career spanning 30 years, from naval architect and principal surveyor to managing director, with extensive technical, managerial and leadership experience gained through long-term international assignments to China, the UK, Luxembourg, the US and Germany, in addition to extensive experience from the Nordic area, based in Denmark. He graduated in 1993 with a BSc in Naval Architecture and after a short period at A.P. Moller-Maersk's shipyard (Odense Steel Shipyard) in Denmark and worked for over 20 years for Lloyd's Register prior to taking up position as Managing Director for SeaNet Maritime Services and Technical Director for the Liberian Registry (both part of the YCF Maritime Group) in 2014.

Ludwig Krämer, now retired, is a German judge who worked for more than 30 years in the environmental department of the European Commission. He was also active in academic teaching in Europe and North America, and published extensively on EU environmental law.

Hidde Kremers was a lecturer at Leiden University, and is now a lawyer at the Council of State of the Netherlands.

Paola Martino is a lawyer and member of the Milan Bar Association. She specialises in environmental permits, waste management, transboundary shipments of waste, by-products and end of waste. She is the author of several publications on environmental law.

Susan Phaustus Mbayuwayu completed her LLM in International Commercial Law at Bournemouth University, the Department of Humanities & Law, Faculty of Media and Communication. Her Master's dissertation focused on scientific uncertainty in environmental law. Currently, she is working with the Ministry of Finance. Susan's main research interests lie in the legal aspects of scientific uncertainty and artificial intelligence in the environment.

Joseph McMullen is a lecturer in law at Bournemouth University. His research focuses on the legal regulation of particulate pollution, and the impacts of air pollution on human health and wellbeing.

Kanak Mishra is currently pursuing a Master's degree in law from the University of Birmingham, UK. Her area of research is international law. She worked as the assistant director for international collaborations at O.P. Jindal Global University, India, prior to her Master's study.

King James Nkum is a lawyer, senior lecturer/deputy Dean of Law at Taraba State University, Nigeria, and visiting law lecturer to various institutions. He has authored numerous books and academic articles published in reputable local and international journals.

Erimma Gloria Orie is a member of the academic staff of the Faculty of Law, National Open University of Nigeria, Abuja, Nigeria, and a fellow of several academic institutions. She has researched extensively in the area of climate change and renewable energy. She has several peer-reviewed articles to her credit, as well as contributed chapters to books on energy law and environmental law.

Susanna Paleari has, since 2011, been a researcher at the Institute on Sustainable Economic Growth (IRCrES, Milan) of the National Research Council of Italy. Her main fields of expertise are environmental policies, legislation and environmental institutions. As a researcher, she has contributed to the activities of the European Topic Centre, an international consortium supporting the work of the European Environment Agency, and she is the author of several papers published in peer-reviewed journals.

Aspasia Pastra is an associate research officer at the World Maritime University-Sasakawa Global Ocean Institute (GOI), in Malmö, Sweden. To date, she has been involved in a number of state-of-the-art regulatory projects in maritime policy, ocean technology, environmental protection, port governance and gender diversity in the maritime sector. Dr Pastra has published extensively in the fields of maritime policy and governance, maritime robotics and techno-regulatory advancements, global environmental change, and team dynamics and leadership.

Marko Perišić is a PhD researcher in environmental law at the Faculty of Law of Hasselt University, in Belgium, and a researcher on the Phy2Climate Project under the Horizon 2020 Framework. He is a member of the Specialist Group on the "Soil and Sustainable Agriculture Law" (SoilSAL SG) of the IUCN World Commission on Environmental Law (WCEL).

Matteo Riccardi is a criminal lawyer, member of the Milan Bar Association and of European Criminal Bar Association (ECBA). He specialises in environmental crimes, health and safety at work and corporate criminal liability under Legislative Decree no. 231/2001. In 2017, he was awarded the prize "Avvocato Serafino Famà", under the patronage of the Italian Criminal Chambers Union, for the best appeal on the theme of the *ne bis in idem* principle in environmental criminal matter. He is the author of several publications on criminal law and criminal procedure.

Janna Ringena is a former PhD student at the Universities of Münster and Greifswald, Germany. Her thesis about the prevention of single-use plastics in the circular economy laws of the EU, Germany and France was published in August 2023. Currently, she is a legal trainee at the Higher Regional Court of Celle, based in Hannover.

Carolyn Roberts is a water and environment consultant. Formerly an academic, most recently at the University of Oxford, she has a particular interest in minimising human impact on the water cycle, and the role of innovation. She was the first Professor of Environment at Gresham College, London, giving lectures to the public, and also has a long history of advising the police on the movement of dead bodies in rivers and canals.

Merve Robson completed her PhD at Bournemouth University, the Department of Life and Environmental Sciences, Faculty of Science and Technology. After obtaining her Bachelor's degree in law and practising law as a criminal defence lawyer in Istanbul, she moved to the UK for her Master's degree in international commercial law. After completing her Master's dissertation on European nature conservation law, she started working on her PhD thesis which focuses on the legal protection of soil and ecosystem services at UK level. Currently, she is conducting research as part of the Environment and Threats Strategic Research Group. Merve's main research interests lie in the legal aspects of soil protection and ecosystem services. She is also interested in the application of new technologies to environmental protection.

Freya Russell (BSc) completed her Bachelor's degree in the Faculty of Science and Technology, Department of Life and Environmental Sciences at Bournemouth University in 2021. Her first-class BSc in Geography enabled her to follow interests within the marine sector whilst also forming skills and knowledge in environmental law and Geographic Information Systems. Since graduating, she has begun her PhD research into mangrove conservation using Bayesian Belief Networks and public participation to form a science and law hybrid.

Linda Schönfelder was a predoctoral research fellow at the University of Leipzig (Chair of Environmental and Planning Law) and the "Network of Competence on Future Challenges of Environmental Law" (KomUR). In the context of her dissertation, she is working on the topic of water reuse and its classification under European and national law Currently, she is working as an environmental lawyer in Berlin.

Hendrik Schoukens is a professor of environmental law at Ghent University, and a solicitor at the Bar of Brussels, in which capacity he frequently litigates high-profile environmental cases. Hendrik is also an elected city councillor for environmental and planning matters, in the Belgian municipality of Lennik.

Rita Simon, Dr. iur, LL.M (both University of Cologne), has been a senior researcher at the Institute of State and Law at the Czech Academy of Sciences since 2017. Her research focuses on consumer protection and sustainable consumption from the comparative perspective. She has worked in the Centre for Comparative Law at Charles University in Prague, in the Institute of Eastern European and Comparative Law at the University of Cologne, and has served as an associate in the Bureau for Civil Law and Codification at the Hungarian Ministry of Justice. She is a Member of the European Law Institute, SCORAI and the International Association of Consumer Law.

Alain Simons is a senior lecturer in games programming, and a researcher in computer graphics and digital visualisation images. His main research is on novel techniques to reduce the file size of colourful images distributed over digital networks without the loss of image quality, therefore reducing their energy load and the ecologic footstep of, for example, the Internet.

Jon A. Skinner is a retired Commander, US Navy, and a long-time Alaskan resident. His PhD, from the University of Alaska Fairbanks, is interdisciplinary: Polar Geography and Strategic Studies. He also holds an MS (Intelligence) and an MA (Strategic Planning) from the Naval Postgraduate School, Monterey, California. He currently serves as an adjunct with the Mat-Su College (University of Alaska Anchorage), and as an instructor with the Graduate College of Professional Military Education (Air University).

Violeta Stratan is a senior lecturer at the Faculty of Law of the West University of Timişoara, where she has taught, since 2000, legal English, legal French, history of law and administrative law. She is a member of the European Centre for Legal Studies and Research, attached to the Faculty of Law of Timişoara, and a member of the Association Henri Capitant Romania. In 2014, she published a book, *Local Autonomy and Subsidiarity in French and Romanian Law*, as a result of a PhD thesis defended at Montpellier University, France.

Naomi Townsend has acquired an Honours degree in law, and a Master's by research in marine conservation law and science, from Bournemouth University. She presented her Master's research at IMCC5 in Borneo, in 2018, and has continued to review and update this research, in line with legislation changes. She now lives in Perth, Australia, where she continues to be passionate about marine conservation.

Ikechukwu Ugwu is a doctoral student at the University of Silesia in Katowice, Poland, where his research is on the accountability of multinational corporations, and the rights of indigenous peoples. The Polish National Science Centre funds his research, including his contribution to this book, under grant number UMO-2021/41/N/HS5/01227. He obtained his LLMs, in public international law and intellectual property rights, from Bournemouth University and the University of Nigeria, respectively.

Patrick Van Calster obtained his PhD from Huddersfield University (UK). He is a criminologist with roots in philosophy. His research is both applied-driven and theoretically sophisticated and broadly concerns three interconnected topics: crime governance and policing; critical criminology, with a focus on (the violation of) human rights and privacy, (social) media, (alternative) measures of punishment, precautionary societies, and inequality and the dynamics of inclusion and exclusion; and cultural criminology (such as lifestyle, edgework, language and images/symbols).

INTRODUCTION

Tilak GINIGE, Iain GREEN, Patrick VAN CALSTER, Alain SIMONS, Joseph McMULLEN, Susan Phaustus MBAYUWAYU and Freya RUSSELL

1. THE EUROPEAN ENVIRONMENTAL LAW FORUM CONFERENCE IN BOURNEMOUTH

The eighth EELF Annual Conference was held at Bournemouth University between 8 and 10 September 2021. The main objective of this conference was to improve the understanding of social and scientific uncertainties in environmental law, thus enabling environmental law scholars to employ the best available knowledge and expertise while addressing knowledge gaps about how to mitigate actual and potential modern environmental harm.

Due to the COVID-19 pandemic, it was decided that the conference should be held online and presented from a television studio at Bournemouth University. The 23 keynote speakers were invited live to the studio for their presentations, followed by Q & A sessions. In between the keynote presentations, approximately 100 video panel presentation sessions were held, and broadcast live to the 229 online participants. This was all possible thanks to a bespoke implementation of Zoom peer-to-peer software technology, which included the novel use of breakout rooms for the video presentation panel sessions. It is hoped that the technology and format used could be beneficial for future conferences, as it contributes to fewer GHG emissions and lessens the impact on the environment.

The aim of the conference was to present a multidisciplinary perspective on environmental issues. As a result, several disciplines were brought together during the conference; consequently, this book looks different to previous editions. Each study provides a fresh perspective on the understanding of uncertainty in the field of environmental law, and furnishes a valuable contribution to knowledge that, despite the fact that science cannot provide the level of certainty that we desire, science still has a significant role to play.

Allow us now to discuss the rationale for the conference, which supports the work produced by the esteemed contributors.

2. SOCIAL AND SCIENTIFIC UNCERTAINTIES IN ENVIRONMENTAL LAW

In today's individualistic society, we are driven by an emotional desire for security and certainty. However, the intrinsic uncertainty of modern society, economy and politics does not meet this need. As our world becomes increasingly complex, science is unable to provide us with the certainty we require. The understanding of the Earth as an interconnected matrix of communities, economies and ecosystems underpins a fundamental inability to quantify and address threats to the natural environment. In addition, attempts to regulate human behaviour on the basis of uncertain theories is, typically, unwelcome.[1] There is still a lack of certainty regarding the extent of the impact that transboundary pollution has on various ecosystems. In this desire for certainty, many still turn to science to provide definitive answers. Although science cannot provide all the answers, it can often explain why and how things occur, and assist us in making future predictions based on our understanding of the world around us.

Sadly, much of what we desire from science is unattainable, as it operates only with partial certainty, as findings are based on probabilities. New evidence can invalidate predictions and modify well-accepted theories. While there is often no absolute certainty in science, scientific research is still able to reduce uncertainty. In many cases, hypotheses have been tested, analysed and examined so thoroughly that their chances of being wrong are infinitesimally small. Sometimes, uncertainties persist despite intensive research. In those cases, scientists make it their job to explain how well something is known and the limitations of their approach. When gaps in knowledge arise, scientists qualify the evidence to ensure others do not form conclusions beyond what is known.

One also needs to appreciate that scientific uncertainty does not mean science is flawed. Instead, it means there is an absence of certainty from a scientific point of view. A scientific investigation does not expect that every finding will be definitive; rather, it is a link in a chain. Furthermore, knowledge gaps are fundamental to the development of science, and therefore uncertainties in science are essential, as they help to promote further investigation and research. However, from a social perspective, this lack of certainty is often a cause for concern when attempting to evaluate the future effects of new industrial or technological developments.

In the field of environmental law, lack of certainty is reflected in disputes where there are numerous voices with an abundance of arguments that, in turn, demonstrate an ongoing struggle, from both scientific and policy management perspectives. In addition, the varied anthropogenic activities impacting our

---

1 Osman M., "Controlling uncertainty: A review of human behavior in complex dynamic environments", (2010) 136(1) *Psychological Bulletin* 65.

natural world means that nation-states are faced with having to manage multiple regulatory standards and levels of accountability which often need more coordination.[2] However, this then leads to uncertainties in terms of whether the scientific or technological solutions should be focused more on the intrinsic ecological value of the environmental medium or on its economic value to humankind.[3] Consequently, policymakers need clarification about the most appropriate way to balance the multiple views and reasonings presented in these disputes. Social and scientific uncertainties promote the development of several strands of scientific evidenced-based judgements that can be highly politicised and further complicate decision-making. The complications of employing science in policy were clearly seen during the COVID-19 pandemic, in the form of decisions made by the UK government, whereby decision-makers overruled scientific evidence presented to them. The customary separation between policymakers and scientists delivering evidence-based solutions to the policymakers became blurred. Scientists became policymakers suggesting definitive solutions, despite numerous social and scientific uncertainties.[4]

In an attempt to achieve certainty, we turn to science for help in evaluating the scale and impact of some of these specific anthropogenic activities labelled as environmental harm. Thus, science validates decision-makers' positions regarding environmental policy and laws. Nonetheless, the application of science in environmental law is not without complications, for example the judiciary have a limited scientific background to understand issues such as error margins, which are rarely considered in legal cases. Broadly speaking, science is the systematic study of the physical and natural world through observations, experimentation and testing of theories against obtained evidence. On the other hand, the law attempts to achieve a semblance of predictability and certainty[5] in a kaleidoscopic world of unpredictability and uncertainty.[6]

Scientific research is at the heart of identifying environmental harm, pushing humankind to produce relevant policy and legal responses. This link with science is what makes environmental law unique within the legal field. Science has a fundamental role in the validation of environmental policy and

2 Jones J. "Regulatory Design for Scientific Uncertainty: Acknowledging the Diversity of Approaches in Environmental Regulation and Public Administration," (2007) 19(3) *Journal of Environmental Law*, 347–365.

3 Weiss E., "Rule of law for nature in a kaleidoscopic world", in Voigt C. (ed.), *Rule of Law for Nature: New Dimensions and Ideas in Environmental Law* (Cambridge University Press, 2013), 27–45.

4 Choi B.C., Pang T., Lin V., Puska P., Sherman G., Goddard M., Auckland M.J., Sainsbury P., Stachenko S., Morrison H. and Clottey, C., "Can scientists and policy makers work together?", (2005) 59(8) *Journal of Epidemiology & Community Health* 632–7.

5 Houck O., "Tales from a troubled marriage: science and law in environmental policy", (2003) 302(5652) *Science* 1926–9.

6 Weiss E., above n. 3.

regulations, for example scientific advances continuously challenge our existing knowledge of the current environmental regulatory framework, and scientific data analysis has led to the creation of operational environmental rules.[7] It has been suggested that we are at that "90 seconds to midnight" moment[8] where scientists are being called upon to bring scientific evidence-based opinions to policymakers, to make these regulations just.

Various scholars have attempted to characterise scientific uncertainty[9] from a legal perspective, which has led to risk determination associated with the following categories: conceptual uncertainty; uncertainties related to measurement; uncertainties in sampling; modelling; and causal links uncertainties.[10]

Moreover, uncertainty at this point may be taken to describe the situation where the key system factors are known but not the probability of an adverse occurrence.[11] The need for regulatory processes in relation to greenhouse gases and climate change are good examples of how scientific evidence in the face of uncertain data sets has demonstrated the role that carbon dioxide has in maintaining homeostasis with regard to the Earth's temperature.[12] The wide-ranging factors that impact on the Earth's climate are known, yet the complex interactions between factors and numerous feedback mechanisms acting on them are not fully understood. For this reason, there is considerable uncertainty about the exact effects of greenhouse gas accumulation in the atmosphere and the forthcoming impacts on the global climate.[13]

Furthermore, there is much ignorance on how to interpret knowledge and uncertainty.[14] A good illustration of this condition can be taken from the growing use of chlorofluorocarbons (CFCs), up until the 1980s, in spray cans and refrigerants.[15] Initially, these substances were regarded as appropriate for their

---

7 Laitos J.G., "How Science Has Influenced, But Should Now Determine, Environmental Policy" (2019) 43 *William & Mary Environmental Law and Policy Review* 759.

8 Banks M., "Doomsday clock edges closer to midnight", (2023) 36(3) *Physics World* 11ii.

9 Jones J. "Regulatory Design for Scientific Uncertainty: Acknowledging the Diversity of Approaches in Environmental Regulation and Public Administration" (2007) 19(3) *Journal of Environmental Law* 347; Wynne B., "Uncertainty and Environmental Learning: Reconceiving science and policy in the preventive paradigm" (1992) 2 *Global Environmental Change* 120; Weiss C., "Expressing Scientific Uncertainty" (2003) 2 *Law, Probability and Risk* 25.

10 Jones J., above n. 9; Walker V.R., "The Myth of Science as a 'Neutral Arbiter' for Triggering Precautions" (2003) 26 *Boston College International and Comparative Law Review* 197; Walker V.R., "The Siren Songs of Science: Toward a Taxonomy of Scientific Uncertainty for Decision makers" (1991) 23 *Connecticut Law Review* 567.

11 Harding R. (ed.), *Environmental Decision-making: The Roles of Scientists, Engineers and the Public* (Federation Press, 1998), 165.

12 Wynne B., above n. 9.

13 Harding R., above n. 11.

14 Cooney R. and Dickson B., *Biodiversity and the Precautionary Principle: Risk, Uncertainty and Practice in Conservation and Sustainable Use* (Earthscan, 2005), 161.

15 Harding R, above n. 11, 166; Wynne B., above n. 9.

purposes, due to their stability. Science was lacking the technology to understand the full potential of these substances to damage the environment until the invention of the electron capture detector, by James Lovelock, in the 1960s. Lovelock's use of this technology demonstrated that all the CFCs produced up to that time (the early 1970s), were still in existence. Unfortunately, scientists had not anticipated the possibility that these CFCs would be transported into the stratosphere, where photodegradation would release chlorine. Chlorine in the stratosphere enters a chain reaction with ozone molecules, depleting the stratospheric ozone layer that acts as the planet's natural ultraviolet B radiation (UVB) filter.[16]

Ultimately, the success of any policy depends on how it is applied in the existing social context. For example, current knowledge about climate change effects may be used to inform policy decisions about the regulation of carbon emissions. However, this policy could be overturned by future decision-makers.[17] In reality, assumptions on risk connected to the circumstances are conditional.[18]

Overall, it is proposed that risk and uncertainty are inherent aspects of ignorance and indeterminacy. This is illustrated by the examples of CFCs and per- and polyfluoroalkyl substances (PFAS), which demonstrate that even when a problem or issue is thought to be fully comprehended, unexpected environmental issues can still arise.[19]

Sources of scientific uncertainty are argued to be incorrect measurements of the state of natural systems and their variability, leading to a fundamental misunderstanding of the use of such variables in predicting the future. Interpretation of incomplete data leads to abstract and simplified models to predict the response of managed systems to management actions.[20] Indeed, it is from the need for clarification of uncertainty that integration between science and law can be observed.[21]

Scientific uncertainty can be measured using scales, which helps to clarify precision and reasonableness in the face of controversial uncertainty.[22] It is suggested that several decisions and policies on environmental issues, as well as the foundation of the underlying scientific evidence and rationale, are formed from such scales.[23] Nonetheless, scientific knowledge may have natural prejudices and restrictions on providing a trustworthy source for decision-making.[24] It is

---

16 Ibid.

17 Ibid.

18 Ibid.

19 Harding R., above n. 11, 167; Wynne B., above n. 9.

20 Brosnan D.M., "Science, Law, and the Environment: The Making of a Modern Discipline" (2007) 37(4) *Environmental Law* 999.

21 Ibid., 1000.

22 Weiss C., above n. 9, 25.

23 Ibid.

24 Alder J. and Wilkinson D., *Environmental Law & Ethics* (Macmillan Press Ltd., 1999), 20.

worth noting that no scale can eliminate variances of scientific uncertainty, but such scales can help to make these variances more precise and accurate.[25]

An example of the scale of scientific uncertainty is best observed in the second report of the Inter-Governmental Panel on Climate Change (IPCC) 1995.[26] The report was heavily criticised for the presence of contradictions with regard to scientific uncertainty.[27] The IPCC's third report, of 2001, made the decision to include scientific uncertainty, in the sense that the report evaluated and allocated values to the uncertainty in connection with various statements of scientific facts contained therein.[28] In addition, the scales enable stakeholders, decision-makers and researchers to better communicate amongst themselves with clarity and much greater precision, concerning the extent of certainty and uncertainty in relation to scientific evidence; this, ultimately, helps them to make far-reaching environmental regulatory decisions.[29] Furthermore, there is an 11-point scale, which is based on standards of proof and is applied to various circumstances, to help with interpretation for the lay public, because it sets different levels of certainty or uncertainty that the law considers consistent with involvement in a wide variety of circumstances.[30]

It is acknowledged that protecting the environment and reducing environmental harm are essential. In so doing, stakeholders have reacted by creating and executing experiments, assembling and examining data, and developing and describing models, in order to improve understanding and provide estimates regarding the nature of environmental and ecological systems.[31] Nevertheless, most of these attempts face hurdles of uncertainty and, therefore, fail to fully accomplish their goals; it goes without saying that challenges of uncertainty must be met to guarantee effective environmental management.[32]

Starting with the difficulty of making future decisions, uncertainty is a hindrance to the process. This is because, most of the time, uncertainty will not be determined in a useful time frame.[33] Moreover, it is essential that policymakers, and indeed the general public, pursue the articulation, with some accuracy, of the degree of scientific uncertainty associated with a given scientific statement, and the degree of reaction to that uncertainty imposed by alternative methods of precaution.[34]

---

25 Weiss C., above n. 9, 26.

26 Ibid., 141.

27 Weiss C., above n. 9.

28 Ibid.

29 Ibid.

30 Ibid.

31 Ascough J., Maier H., Ravalico J. and Strudley M., "Future research challenges for incorporation of uncertainty in environmental and ecological decision-making" (2008) 219(3–4) *Ecological Modelling* 383–9.

32 Ibid.

33 Pollack H.N., *Uncertain Science ... Uncertain World* (Cambridge University Press, 2003), 188.

34 Weiss C., "Expressing Scientific Uncertainty" (2003) 2 *Law, Probability and Risk* 25.

Consequently, it does not matter which stages of the environmental decision-making process are deliberated for the reason of enabling decisions to be made with confidence or a known level of certainty; there should be transparency when dealing with various sources of uncertainty.[35] Therefore, the possible sources of uncertainty in environmental decision-making should be identified.[36] Furthermore, the standard of proof required in scientific evidence in policymaking is based on the fact that decisions must unavoidably be made under conditions of uncertainty. The degree of this uncertainty, in addition to the strategies to address that uncertainty, are crucial contributions to the risk assessment process.[37]

In recent years, there has been a decline in public confidence regarding decisions wholly based on scientific evidence,[38] as has been seen in vaccine hesitancy[39] that came from the UK-wide mass COVID-19 vaccination programme that took place in December 2020.[40] Scientific uncertainty creates difficulty in the interpretation of information concerning the uncertainties linked with risk analysis. Furthermore, it has been observed that presenting information on scientific uncertainty will damage public trust in science.[41] This can be evidenced by public reactions to genetically modified plants and the use of pesticides in agriproduction, in which there are several controversial viewpoints.[42] Some scientists also believe that if the public is exposed to information on scientific uncertainty, there is the possibility of a negative impact on public risk understanding.

The use of science in environmental law is of great importance,[43] as it not only functions in helping to understand and inform the regulatory process, through the creation of legislation, but also enables the development of science.[44] Scientific insights help to promote different types of understanding, and therefore evidence-based environmental law enables policymakers and lawyers to understand the underlying reasons why these laws are worth implementing.

It is further argued that, instead of attempting to promote the integration of these two disciplines (science and environmental law), it would be better, from the outset, to concentrate on the development of multidisciplinary

---

35 Ascough J. and others, above n. 31.

36 Ibid.

37 Weiss C., above n. 34.

38 Frewer L., Hunt S., Brennan M., Kuznesof S., Ness M. and Ritson C., "The views of scientific experts on how public conceptualize uncertainty", (2003) 6(1) *Journal of Risk Research* 75–85.

39 Rosenbaum L., "Escaping Catch-22 – Overcoming Covid Vaccine Hesitancy", (2021) 384(14) *New England Journal of Medicine* 1367–71.

40 Mavron N., *COVID-19 vaccine refusal, UK: February to March 2021: Exploring the attitudes of people who are uncertain about receiving, or unable or unwilling to receive a coronavirus (COVID-19) vaccine in the UK* (Office for National Statistics, 2021).

41 Frewer and others, above n. 38.

42 Ibid.

43 Brosnan, above n. 20, 988.

44 McEldowney J. and McEldowney S., *Environmental Law* (Pearson Longman 2010).

environmental law.[45] In a sense, this new discipline will possess features of science, law and policy.[46] Moreover, science is useful for the management of the environment, as an effective tool to understand a problem's origins and effects leads to more operative and strong policies and programmes.[47] However, creating science that is useful for decision-making, and which is technically reliable, relevant to decision-makers, and considered legitimate by stakeholders, is complicated.[48] Moreover, as discussed above, the science behind environmental problems is often uncertain; in other words, it does not promote one straightforward solution for decision-makers to apply.[49]

One of the dangers of scientific uncertainties is that they can lead to unverified, biased perspectives. This is best exemplified by the work of Bjørn Lomborg (Copenhagen Consensus Center), the author of works such as *The Skeptical Environmentalist*,[50] *Cool It*[51] and *False Alarm*.[52] In his work, he downplays the risks of global warming, understates the potential economic impacts of climate change and exaggerates the costs of cutting greenhouse gases. It is further argued that his misuse of outdated and misinterpreted numbers is central to his lukewarm arguments, which are helping to fuel the proverbial fire, by enabling climate change sceptics to challenge current global climate change policies and laws.[53]

In addition, a difficulty of conducting multidisciplinary research is that the disciplines involved do not necessarily share a common language, for example the mathematical language used by a physicist may not always be readily understood by a social scientist or law scholar. Thus, science produced by research bodies may not directly address the wants and needs of decision-makers, making it necessary for other organisations to help interpret the science to policymakers and connect the needs of decision-makers to scientists.[54]

---

45 Edwards G.I., "Multidisciplinary Approach to Environmental Problems and Sustainability", in Leal Filho W. (ed.), *Encyclopedia of Sustainability in Higher Education* (Springer 2019), 1.

46 Brosnan, above n. 20, 1005.

47 Ulibarri N., "Collaborative model development increases trust and use of scientific information in environmental decision-making" (2018) 82 *Environmental Science & Policy*, 136–42.

48 Ibid.

49 Ibid.

50 Lomborg B., *The Skeptical Environmentalist: Measuring the Real State of the World* (Cambridge University Press, 2003).

51 Lomborg B., *Cool It: The sceptical environmentalist's guide to global warming* (1st American ed., Alfred a Knopf Inc, 2008) 77–78.

52 Lomborg B., *False Alarm: How Climate Change Panic Costs Us Trillions, Hurts the Poor, and Fails to Fix the Planet* (Hachette UK, 2020).

53 Ward B., "A closer examination of the fantastical numbers in Bjorn Lomborg's new book" (*LSE News & Commentaries*, 10 August 2020), https://www.lse.ac.uk/granthaminstitute/news/a-closer-examination-of-the-fantastical-numbers-in-bjorn-lomborgs-new-book; Halley J.M., (2022), "Three visions of environmental apocalypse, or Not" (2022) 36 *Conservation Biology* e13923.

54 Ulibarri N., above n. 47.

Decisions are frequently made under uncertainty when probabilistic evidence is not clearly specified. Therefore, it follows, from adjustment of preferences in respect of a particular risk, that when a given decision is made, it is the application of an adaptive choice under uncertainty.[55]

Furthermore, complete scientific certainty is very unlikely to exist with respect to environmental and health risks. As a result, environmental and health decision-makers will never have all the scientific facts and information they would like to have, for any given regulatory decision.[56] To address this problem, decision-makers could adopt a precautionary stance when confronted with the prospect of harm to the environment or human health in the face of inadequate knowledge.[57] By the time the effects of some of these risks have been fully scientifically established, it will be too late to make an effective response; the damage will already have occurred, and reversing the harm will have become impractical or extremely difficult. Even though precaution is a crucial element of virtually every domestic regulatory system in the world for protecting human health and the environment,[58] cases like the mad cow disease outbreak in the UK demonstrate weaknesses in its application.[59]

It has been argued that the control of risk, under conditions of scientific uncertainty, cannot be left to scientists alone, and that such control requires political and epistemic perspectives.[60] The findings show the necessity for more research into the subject of the ideal design of transnational risk management under situations of scientific uncertainty. However, the research must consider the deep connections between science and politics, in addition to the ways in which these linkages have already become established in current supranational institutions.[61]

Furthermore, it is important to consider the principles outlined in the Stockholm Declaration when designing these regulatory structures. This places an emphasis on the need for a global perspective on environmental issues, and the Declaration calls for international cooperation to address these challenges. By incorporating the principles in the Declaration into the effort to develop these structures, a framework that is both effective and just can be created.[62]

55 Leuker C., Pachur T., Hertwig R. and Pleskac T., "Exploiting risk-reward structures in decision making under uncertainty" (2018) 175 *Cognition* 186–200.

56 Ibid.

57 Ibid.

58 Bernasconi-Osterwalder N., Magraw D., Oliva M.J., Orellana M. and Tuerk E., *Environment and Trade: A Guide to WTO Jurisprudence* (Earthscan, 2006).

59 Lanska D.J., "The Mad Cow Problem in the UK: Risk Perceptions, Risk Management, and Health Policy Development" (1998) 19(2) *Journal of Public Health Policy* 160–83.

60 Perez O. and Snir R., "Global Environmental Risk Governance under Conditions of Scientific Uncertainty: Legal, Political and Social Transformations" (2013) 2(1) *Transnational Environmental Law* 7–13.

61 Ibid.

62 Ibid., 69.

The multi-perspective approach permits the attainment of a comprehensive and clear picture of the scope and scale of the uncertainty. The conceptual framework needs to be aimed at practical decision-making situations, and it needs to enable decision-makers to acquire a more complete picture of the uncertainty. Currently, the focus in environmental law is on uncertainty as perceived by a single decision-maker as this is the level at which uncertainty is considered to be applied. This approach can lead to oversimplification, and it means that uncertainties specific to the group decisions of concerned parties may be overlooked. Thus, the decisions being made may not be representative of the group consensus.[63]

Furthermore, environmental governance that embraces scientific information in decision-making could be promoted by incorporating stakeholder collaboration into the process of interpreting and applying scientific findings. However, there is anecdotal evidence of the tendency for stakeholders to weaken the application of the research findings.[64]

The application of the precautionary principle[65] enables the identification of limits to scientific and technical data. This enables regulatory action to prevent or avoid environmental harm before it occurs, in situations where there is a lack of evidence of a cause-and-effect relationship. It has been further suggested that, in the Anthropocene epoch, society has been required to use science to comprehend anthropogenic impacts on the environment, and as a tool of risk assessment in reaction to resource limitations and societal needs.[66] We opine that there is a need to establish a regulatory culture which promotes a wider and more involved debate on the relative benefits, costs and uncertainties of policies and decisions, particularly those relating to ecosystem protection and risks to human health.[67]

Despite this fact, policymakers are almost always required to make decisions in the face of considerable uncertainties. In this regard, it should be noted that, although scientific investigations and interpretations provide information, uncertainties and indeterminacies will always exist.[68] Thus, as the planet becomes more inhabited, human burdens upon dwindling resources multiply, and the relationship between decisions and their effects becomes more complicated. Consequently, it is vital to make decisions that are grounded in the understanding that there is a level of scientific uncertainty that society must accept.[69]

---

63 Ibid.

64 Ulibarri N, above n. 47.

65 Santillo D., Stringer R.L, Johnson P.A. and Tickner J., "The precautionary principle: Protecting against failure of scientific method and risk assessment" (1998) 36(12) *Marine Pollution* 939–50.

66 Ibid.

67 Ibid.

68 Ibid.

69 Walker V.R., "The Siren Songs of Science: Toward a Taxonomy of Scientific Uncertainty for Decisionmakers", (1991) 23 *Connecticut Law Review* 567.

As Edith Brown Weiss noted,[70] uncertainty is an unfortunate reality of the Anthropocene epoch in a kaleidoscopic world. Climate change is one of the most evident manifestations of this reality, resulting in disastrous interactions between land, ice-covered areas, atmosphere, oceans, and marine and terrestrial biodiversity.

To survive the Anthropocene epoch as *Homo sapiens*, it is imperative not only that we enable decision-makers to appreciate scientific uncertainties, and to factor them in alongside trade-offs between multiple and equally legitimate societal values,[71] but also that we consider these trade-offs to promote tangible results from an ecologically sustainable perspective.

70 Brown Weiss E., "International Law in a Kaleidoscopic World" (2011) *Georgetown Law Faculty Publications and Other Works* 1622.

71 Ulibarri N., above n. 47.

PART I

LEGAL AND SCIENTIFIC UNCERTAINTY

LEGAL UNCERTAINTY IN EU ENVIRONMENTAL LAW

The Battle for the Last Word

Ludwig Krämer

1. INTRODUCTION: PRECAUTION AS AN ANSWER TO SCIENTIFIC UNCERTAINTY

Technical and scientific uncertainty play a significant role in EU environmental law and policy. They influence policy decisions and impact significantly on the orientation of environmental policies. A good example is a discussion on climate change. Here, global, EU-wide and national measures were adopted well before a scientific consensus was reached on the reality of emissions from human-influenced greenhouse gases and their effect on the warming-up of the atmosphere; indeed, even today, there are scientists and politicians who contest that man-made greenhouse gas emissions have any significant influence on climate change.

Yet, decisions by the EU on issues of scientific and technical uncertainty have gone well beyond climate change issues. Thus, the EU adopted an export ban for British beef, though, at the time of the decision, it had not been proven that there was a risk to human health from the "mad cow disease" which existed among British cattle;[1] it prohibited the realisation of plans or projects within protected natural areas, as long as it could not be excluded that the plan or project might have significant effects on the protected site.[2] It held that waste had to be classified as hazardous waste, and be subject to considerable restrictions, as long as it was not clear whether or not it was hazardous.[3] Additionally, the EU prohibited the use of the active substance "oxasulfuron" in pesticides, because it was not certain that its use was unproblematic for human health or the environment.[4] In all these cases, the precautionary principle, laid

1 CJEU, Case C-180/96, *United Kingdom v. Commission*, ECLI:EU:C:1998:192.

2 CJEU, Case C-127/02 *Waddenzeevereniging*, ECLI:EU:C:2004:482.

3 CJEU, Case C-487/17–C-489/17, *Verlezza*, ECLI:EU:C:2019:270.

4 CJEU, Case C-374/20P, *AgrochemMaks v. Commission*, ECLI:EU:C:2021:990.

down in Article 191 of the Treaty on the Functioning of the European Union (TFEU), played a decisive role. The principle was subject to a communication by the Commission in 2000,[5] and has been used by the Court of Justice of the European Union (CJEU) in settled case law, and by other EU institutions to decide on questions of scientific or technical uncertainty.

This contribution will describe a situation of *legal* uncertainty in EU and national environmental law, where the precautionary principle does not play a role. In section 2, the problem will be described. Section 3 will indicate the consequences which follow from the present situation of legal uncertainty, for EU law and its application within the Member States. Section 4 will discuss possible solutions to the problem.

2. THE CHALLENGE FROM MEMBER STATES

According to Article 19(1) of the Treaty on European Union (TEU), "(t)he Court of Justice of the European Union … shall ensure that in the interpretation and application of the Treaties the law is observed". This attribution of functions to the CJEU is general, and is not limited by any condition, or to specific sectors of Union law. Further, it does not mention any constitutional or supreme court of any of the EU Member States also having to ensure the interpretation and application of Union law. Thus, the CJEU has, by virtue of Article 19 TEU, a sort of monopoly to decide on the interpretation and application of EU law.

However, in May 2020, the German Constitutional Court (Bundesverfassungsgericht or BVerfG) issued a judgment in which it challenged this understanding of Article 19 TEU.[6] It argued that Article 19 TEU applied "in principle", and that, normally, judgments of the CJEU were to be followed EU-wide, as Article 19 provided for the general primacy of EU law over national law. This primacy had to be recognised by the (German) public authorities, including the BVerfG, in normal cases, even when judgments by the CJEU contained errors, or were, seen from a national German perspective, "wrong": "the mandate conferred upon the CJUE by Article 19 … TEU, to ensure that the law is observed in the interpretation and application of the Treaties, necessarily entails that the CJEU be granted a certain margin of error".[7]

5 European Commission, "Communication on the precautionary principle", COM(2000) 1: "whether or not to invoke the precautionary principle is a decision exercised where scientific information is insufficient, inconclusive, or uncertain and where there are indications that the possible effects on the environment, or human, animal or plant health may be potentially dangerous and inconsistent with the chosen level of protection."

6 Bundesverfassungsgericht, Case 2BvR 859/15, judgment of 5 May 2020, ECLI:DE:BVerfG:2020rs20200505:2bvr085915.

7 Ibid., para. 112.

However, according to the BVerfG, the primacy of EU law as interpreted by the CJEU is not unlimited. The BVerfG concluded that, according to Article 5(2) TEU, the EU could act only within the limits of the competences conferred upon it by the Member States (the principle of conferral).[8]

Based on this provision, it identified three areas where, according to German constitutional law, Article 19 TEU did not apply in full: (1) cases where judgments of the CJEU significantly impaired the protection of fundamental rights of German citizens; (2) cases where the CJEU ruled outside the competences which had been conferred on the Union (*"ultra vires"*); and (3) cases where a judgment of the CJEU affected the "constitutional identity" of Germany, as laid down in the German Constitution (the Grundgesetz). Where, in one of these three types of case, a judgment of the CJEU was "not comprehensible and must thus be considered arbitrary from an objective perspective", Article 19 TEU becomes inapplicable, and the decision on the interpretation of EU law falls back on the national (German) authorities. According to the BVerfG, it is that court which must ensure that the CJEU's decisions remain within the boundaries drawn by the three types of case mentioned above, and thus that they comply with German constitutional law. And before the BVerfG can argue that the limits of Article 19 TEU have not been respected by the CJEU, it must submit to that court a request for a preliminary ruling according to Article 267 TFEU.

The BVerfG's judgment of 5 May 2020 concerned decisions taken by the European Central Bank (ECB) for the purchase of government bonds, taken in the context of a public sector purchase programme. According to the BVerfG, the ECB had ignored the economic policy effects which these decisions might have; it concluded that these decisions were *ultra vires*, and thus not binding. Moreover, the CJEU, in its preliminary judgment under Article 267 TFEU,[9] given at the request of the BVerfG, had not correctly interpreted the proportionality principle, by failing to examine the effects of the ECB measures.[10] Its decision was thus objectively arbitrary, and did not bind the BVerfG and other German institutions and bodies.

When one leaves aside the ideological ballast constituted by the more theoretical considerations of the BVerfG, it remains that the judgment of the CJEU had been declared objectively arbitrary, and thus inapplicable, because the CJEU had, in the opinion of the BVerfG, wrongly applied the proportionality principle by not examining the effects of the ECB measures. The BVerfG did not discuss the argument of the CJEU in earlier judgments, in which the CJEU

---

8 TEU, Art. 5(2): "[u]nder the principle of conferral, the Union shall act only within the limits of the competence conferred upon it by the Member States in the Treaties to attain the objectives set out therein. Competences not conferred upon the Union in the Treaties remain with the Member States."

9 CJEU, Case C-593/17, *Weiss*, ECLI:EU:C:2018:1000.

10 TEU, Art. 5(4): "[u]nder the principle of proportionality, the content and form of Union action shall not exceed what is necessary to achieve the objectives of the Treaties."

declared that a decision had to be assessed according to its aim and content, but not according to its effects. Indeed, such effects were, in the opinion of the CJEU, too uncertain to be taken into consideration.[11]

If one follows the BVerfG's contention that a specific interpretation of the proportionality principle may make a judgment of the CJEU objectively arbitrary, and therefore inapplicable, there is no reason to limit such an interpretation to the proportionality principle. Rather, in the same way, other procedural or substantial principles – such as the right to be heard, the right to effective judicial protection, the principle of precaution, or the polluter-pays principle – may also lead a national court to consider a judgment of the CJEU arbitrary and not binding.

Even more relevant are the messages that the BVerfG judgment of 5 May 2020 sent out, which include the following indications:

- Article 19 TEU, which gives the CJEU the exclusive right to interpret EU law, is not to be interpreted according to its wording; national (constitutional) courts may also interpret EU law.
- The extent to which such an interpretation of EU law through national courts is possible depends on the national constitution of the Member State in question, and not on Article 19 TEU.
- It is the national law which decides whether a judgment of the CJEU is "erroneous" but must be accepted, or is "objectively arbitrary" and does not have to be accepted.
- When a national court is of the opinion that the proportionality principle was not correctly applied, it may consider a decision by an EU institution to be inapplicable.

The BVerfG did not explicitly decide on the question of whether it is only a national (constitutional) court which may declare a judgment of the CJEU inapplicable, or whether other national public authorities – national, regional or local governments, public agencies, etc. – could also take such a decision. However, as the BVerfG is of the opinion that national law, and in particular the national constitution, determines this question, the answer may be different from one Member State to another.

---

11 CJEU, Case C-5/16, *Poland v. European Parliament and Council*, ECLI:EU:C:2018:483, paras. 42 and 43: "[g]iven that, in order to know the real and specific effects of a legislative measure, it is necessary to analyse these effects after its entry into force, the legislature's choice would have to be based on assumptions as to the likely impact of that measure, which, by their nature, are speculative and are in no way objective factors amenable to judicial review … Consequently, it must be found that the effects of an EU measure … is not a factor that must be assessed in addition to the aim and content of that act, or its derogation therefrom." See also the earlier cases of CJEU, Case C-269/97, *Commission v. Council*, ECLI:EU:C:2000:183; and Case C-36/98, *Spain v. Council*, ECLI:EU:C:2001:64.

The BVerfG judgment of 5 May 2020 was quickly used in another context, this time in the environmental sector. In early 2021, Czechia applied to the CJEU because Poland had extended the permit for an open-air lignite mine in Turów (Poland) from 2020 to 2026 without making an environmental impact assessment. Czechia argued that the activity of the mine, which was situated close to the Czech border, led to a constant flow of groundwater from Czechia to the mine, and thus to a significant decline of the groundwater level in the Czech border region. The supply of drinking water to the local population, about 10,000 people, had become more and more difficult, and the land subsidence had caused damage to buildings in Czechia. Czechia asked, as an interim measure, that the mine be closed. Poland objected, but the CJEU ordered this closure.[12]

Poland refused to close the mine. The Polish government considered the interim order unfair, unjust and arbitrary. It argued that such closure would lead to the loss of several thousand jobs, and to the inundation of the lignite mine. As the lignite was transported to a nearby power plant, for which it was the main source of energy, more jobs would be lost in that plant. And as the plant provided electricity to some 7 per cent of the Polish population – about 3.7 million people – following the Court's order would cause an environmental and energy catastrophe, and be incompatible with the provisions of the Polish Constitution. The CJEU then fixed, at Czechia's demand, a penalty payment of 500,000 euros for each day of Poland's non-compliance with the interim order.[13] Poland again refused to comply with that order, raising the same objections as before. Poland then paid Czechia compensation of 45 million euros, and Czechia withdrew its application.

The substance of case C-121/21 and the two interim orders will not be discussed here; what is relevant for the discussion on legal uncertainty is the fact that the Polish government referred to the Polish Constitution in order to refuse compliance with the CJEU's (interim) decisions. This understanding of the relationship between Polish law and EU law in Poland was confirmed by a further judgment of the Polish Constitutional Court of 7 October 2021, in which the court affirmed that Polish constitutional law prevailed over EU law.

The parallelism between the arguments of the Polish government in case C-121/21R and the judgment of the BVerfG of 5 May 2020 is obvious: in both cases, the decisive argument is that the national constitution has primacy over EU law. Under Polish constitutional law, the public authorities have to protect the environment and the rights, freedom and security of Polish citizens.[14] Based on these provisions, the Polish government might well have argued that the closure

---

12 CJEU, Case C-121/21R, *Czechia v. Poland*, Order of 21 May 2021, ECLI:EU:C:2021:420.

13 CJEU, Case C-121/21, *Czechia v. Poland*, Order of 20 September 2021, ECLI:EU:C:2021:752.

14 Constitution of Poland, Art. 74(2): "[p]rotection of the environment shall be the duty of public authorities"; Art. 5: "The Republic of Poland shall safeguard … the freedoms and rights of persons and citizens, [and] the security of the citizens".

of the lignite mine would lead to an ecological catastrophe (inundation of the mine), and that the interruption of electricity supply for more than 3 million people would threaten their fundamental rights and security. Its arguments are not of a different quality to the arguments of the German BVerfG.

The fact that the BVerfG argued that a decision not to accept a CJEU judgment could only be taken by the Constitutional Court, and only after having asked the CJEU for a preliminary judgment, is not relevant. Indeed, this reasoning was the consequence of an interpretation, by the BVerfG, of German constitutional law, in particular Article 23 of the Grundsegetz. The Polish Constitution contains different provisions than the German Constitution,[15] and these may be subject to a different interpretation by the Polish Constitutional Court. The decisive element in both cases is that it is not the judgment of the CJEU under Article 19 TEU which has the last word on the interpretation of EU law, but rather the decision which flows out of the interpretation of the national constitution by a national authority, and in this regard the German and the Polish authorities – the BVerfG and the Polish government – agree.

According to the BVerfG, under German constitutional law, the decision whether or not to follow a judgment of the CJEU must be taken by the BVerfG. However, this cannot mean that, under the Polish Constitution, the Polish Constitutional Court must take such a decision. The interpretation of the BVerfG refers to German law, and has no effect on Polish constitutional law. Whether a Polish public authority or court could decide on the non-application of Article 19 TEU is a question of interpretation of the *Polish* Constitution, which might well allow the Polish government to decide that a judgment of the CJEU should not be followed.

In conclusion, both Germany (the BVerfG) and Poland (the Polish government) are of the opinion that the last word on the primacy of EU law lies with the national authorities (courts or executive authorities). The position of public authorities, governments and courts in the other EU Member States is not altogether clear,[16] though courts may be tempted to follow the German or Polish constitutional courts and grant primacy to national constitutional law.[17] The different understandings of the relationship between national law and Article 19 TEU raise a considerable number of legal uncertainties, as will be demonstrated below.[18]

---

15 See, e.g. ibid., Art. 90(1): "[t]he Republic of Poland may by virtue of international agreements, delegate to an international organisation or an international institution the competence of organs of State authority in relation to certain matters."

16 European Commission, "The Rule of Law Report 2021: The rule of law situation in the European Union", COM (2021)700.

17 See, on this, Franz C. Mayer, "Verfassungsgerichtsbarkeit" in A. von Bogdandy and J. Bast (eds.), *Europäisches Verfassungsrecht: Theoretische und dogmatische Grundzüge* (2nd ed.), 2009, p. 560 ff.

18 On 7 October 2021, the Polish Constitutional Court delivered a judgment, according to which Arts. 1, 2 and 19(1) TEU, which establish the primacy of EU law over national law, are incompatible with the Polish Constitution (case K 3/21). This judgment will not be discussed

3. PRIMACY OF EU LAW AND THE EU TREATIES

The primacy of EU law over national law is laid down nowhere in the EU treaties. An attempt to codify this primacy was made during the negotiations on a European constitution. When the Lisbon Treaty was adopted, all EU Member States signed and agreed to a declaration on primacy which stated:

> The Conference recalls that, in accordance with well settled case law of the Court of Justice of the European Union, the Treaties and the law adopted by the Union on the basis of the Treaties have primacy over the law of the Member States, under the conditions laid down by the said case law.[19]

The CJEU has maintained, in settled case law since 1964, that EU law has primacy over national law,[20] and has, since 1970, confirmed that this primacy also pertains to national constitutional law.[21]

The first legal uncertainty stems from the very existence of judgments such as that of the German BVerfG of 5 May 2020, and of the Polish Constitutional Court of 7 October 2021. Are the decisions taken by the ECB (in the German case) applicable or inapplicable in Italy, Greece, Finland or Estonia? The BVerfG only declared that they were inapplicable in Germany, but did not decide, and had no competence to decide, that they were inapplicable in all EU Member States. Subsequent to the judgment of the BVerfG, the ECB undertook some measures to assess the effects of its measures. It is, at present, still unclear whether these measures satisfy the BVerfG, as the case is still pending before that court. Neither is it at all clear whether other Member States had similar problems with the original ECB measures, and would now be satisfied with the supplementary measures. And even should the national government of another EU Member State be satisfied with the original and supplementary measures taken by the ECB, this would not necessarily mean that the national constitutional court of that Member State – which is legally supposed to be independent from government – would share this evaluation.

The BVerfG argued that it is the competence of the German Constitutional Court to determine whether a CJEU judgment is *ultra vires* and thus inapplicable.

---

further here. See also European Parliament, "Resolution of 21 October 2021 on the rule of law crisis in Poland and the primacy of EU law" (2021/2035(RSP)).

19 Declaration 17, annexed to the Treaties on European Union, OJ 2008, C 115, p. 344.

20 CJEU, Case 6/64 *Costa v. ENEL*, ECLI:EU:C:1964:66: "the law stemming from the Treaty, an independent source of law, could not, because of its special and original nature, be overridden by domestic legal provisions, however framed, without being deprived of its character of Community law and without the legal basis of the Community itself being called into question".

21 CJEU, Case 117/70, *Internationale Handelsgesellschaft*, ECLI:EU:C:1970:114. See, most recently, CJEU, Case C-357/19 and other cases, *PM, RO and Others*, ECLI:EU:C:2021:1034, paras. 244 ff, and in particular para. 251.

However, this refers to the situation in German law. The *Turów* case shows that, in Poland, the government assumes the right to decide whether a decision by the CJEU is to be applied or not. Following the logic of the BVerfG, one would have to admit that it is the national constitutional law of the 27 EU Member States which determines the body – whether a national, regional or local government, a constitutional or ordinary court, an agency, or another public authority – which may declare a CJEU judgment to be *ultra vires*. Inevitably, this will lead to a huge mess, as the CJEU judgment might be applicable in some states or regions but not in others.

The next aspect of legal uncertainty concerns the content of any CJEU judgment. The BVerfG argued that the CJEU enjoyed, in its decisions, a certain tolerance with regard to a margin of error: not all CJEU judgments which were considered "wrong" or erroneous by a national court or other body could be considered *ultra vires* or otherwise inapplicable. Such a characterisation was reserved only for serious errors.

The question, then, is who draws the borderline between significant and tolerable errors by the CJEU. A national constitutional court and a national government might come to different solutions on this question. A court in Member State A might assess the CJEU judgment differently to a court in Member State B, depending on the different economic, industrial, social or environmental circumstances in the two Member States. As there are 27 EU Member States, such discrepancies might lead to further diversified application of EU law.

Both the judgment of the BVerfG, and of the Polish government in the *Turów* case, referred to judgments of the CJEU. However, the problem is not limited to judgments. Indeed, when the EU adopts a legislative Act – a directive or a regulation – such a measure might also be considered *ultra vires* by a national court or executive body. When the primacy of EU law is accepted, the matter can be clarified by a decision of the CJEU. However, when this primacy is not recognised, it will be up to a national authority – an executive body or a court – to decide whether or not the legislative Act was *ultra vires*; and such a decision could even be adopted when an earlier CJEU judgment had confirmed the compatibility of the EU legislation (secondary law) with the EU treaties' primary law.

The difficulties become even greater when administrative decisions taken by the EU institutions in a specific case are in question. The Commission and the Council, and also public agencies such as the Chemicals Agency (ECHA) or the Food Safety Authority (EFSA), often have to decide whether a specific substance or product is toxic, carcinogenic or otherwise harmful to human health or the environment. The consequences of such decisions are laid down in EU legislation: the substance or product might be prohibited; be subject to a specific authorisation; be allowed to be marketed only in specific products, and in certain limited quantities; or be required to be properly packed and labelled, etc. Such decisions by EU institutions are numerous, and only some of them are tackled before the EU General Court of the CJEU. When the last word on whether or not a substance or a product is harmful lies with a national public authority or a national court, this might create a situation where the substance or product in question is declared to be harmful in one Member State, but without harmful properties in another Member State.

The impact of such diverging decisions between the different Member States, and between Member States and the EU level, is obvious: there cannot be a free circulation of goods within the EU, as each Member State would have to install border controls in order to ensure that its national legislation or jurisprudence is respected. Producers and traders would have to align the classification, packaging and labelling of substances and products to the different national requirements. Even such aspects as the spring hunting of birds, or their hunting with non-selective means, such as glue, prohibited under EU law, could be subject to different interpretations and applications by Member State courts, legislatures or public authorities, as national interpretations of the national constitutions might lead to different results.

It was mentioned above that the BverfG based its judgment of 5 May 2020 on the fact that the ECB and the CJEU had not properly interpreted the proportionality principle. The proportionality principle is a principle of general law which plays a very considerable role in EU law and policy. For example, whether a substance must be classified as toxic, or as being an endocrine disruptor, depends on the evaluation of available scientific data, studies or other findings. The weighing of this material and the reaching of a conclusion requires expertise, and administrative decisions are subject to judicial control. A national authority or court might, relatively frequently, assess the weight of the different studies etc. in a different way from the EU authorities or courts. Should a "wrong" interpretation or application of the proportionality principle allow a national authority to disregard the decision taken by the EU institutions? This is the opinion of the German BVerfG: the uniform application of EU law within the EU would be eliminated. Member States would be treated differently under the same legal EU provision.

In the Swedish case C-203/12, the CJEU decided that the level of negligence of an enterprise that had not timeously reduced its greenhouse gas allowances was not to be taken into consideration, and that the enterprise had to pay the full amount of the penalty which had been laid down in EU law.[22] In another case, a national court from Luxembourg asked the CJEU to review this decision, as the Luxembourg court was of the opinion that paying the full penalty was disproportionate when the negligence of the company was small or non-existent. The CJEU, though, confirmed its earlier decision.[23]

---

22 CJEU, Case C-203/12, *Billerud*, ECLI:EU:C:2013.664.

23 CJEU, Case C-113/19, *Luxaviation*, ECLI:EU:C:2020:228.

When the last word on the correct application of the proportionality principle is with a national court, constitutional or otherwise, these two CJEU judgments would be inapplicable, and the full penalty would probably not have to be paid in Sweden or in Luxembourg. In other Member States, where the issue in question was not subject to a court decision, the EU law provision would apply in full. Different applications from one Member State to another would be the inevitable consequence.

The German BVerfG limited itself to arguing that the proportionality principle had not been properly applied, and that, therefore, the CJEU judgment was inapplicable. However, there would be no reason to limit such arguments to the proportionality principle. Similar arguments would have to apply to the subsidiarity principle, and to the procedure concerning the rights of persons, such as the right to effective judicial protection, the right to be heard, the right to be represented by a lawyer, etc., and also to the precautionary principle, and other principles or human rights. If one were following the BVerfG, where rights of a natural or legal person had been impaired, a national constitutional court could declare such a decision or judgment by an EU institution to be objectively arbitrary, and therefore inapplicable. Which kinds of error would be declared irrelevant and arbitrary would depend on the interpretation of the individual national constitution by the national authority. And, as mentioned above, the constitutional law may also be interpreted to allow such decisions to be taken by national, regional or even local public authorities.

The Treaty on the Functioning of the European Union (TFEU) contains a number of provisions which are incompatible with the opinions expressed by the German and Polish Constitutional Courts. One example is Article 288 TFEU, which provides that regulations adopted by the EU are of general application, are binding in their entirety, and are directly applicable in all Member States. Therefore, should a national authority be entitled to declare an EU regulation to be objectively arbitrary, and thus inapplicable, this would be incompatible with Article 288 TFEU.

Under Article 114 TFEU, the EU may adopt measures for the establishment and functioning of the internal market. When such a measure is taken, any Member State who wishes to maintain national provisions in order to protect one of the "major needs" referred to in Article 36 TFEU, such as human health, the environment, etc., must inform the Commission of its intention.[24] The Commission shall approve or reject the Member State's measure (Article 114(6) TFEU). The provisions of Article 114(4) would be superfluous if a Member State could unilaterally decide that a specific EU measure would be contrary to its "major needs", and thus declare it inapplicable.

---

24 Art. 114(4) TFEU.

A similar observation applies as regards Article 114(5) TFEU.[25] This provision allows a Member State to introduce new national measures which deviate from an EU measure adopted under Article 114(1) TFEU. Such measures may be taken only in order to protect the environment or the working environment, and must comply with some other conditions. Again, the intended national measure needs to be approved by the European Commission. When a Member State, following the reasoning of the BVerfG, has the possibility to invoke a major need of its national constitution, and adopts, on that basis, new measures which deviate from the EU measure adopted under Article 114(1) TFEU, the provisions of Article 114(5) and (6) TFEU would again be superfluous. In particular, the EU procedure – notification of the new national measure to the Commission; proof of new scientific evidence; a situation which is specific to the acting Member State; authorisation by the Commission; the necessity for the Commission to examine the need of adaptation of the measure under Article 114(7) TFEU – would make no sense, as every Member State could act unilaterally.

On application of the Commission, the CJEU may declare, on the basis of Article 258 TFEU, that a Member State has infringed EU law. In such a case, Article 260(1) TFEU provides that the Member State has to take the necessary measures in order to comply with the CJEU judgment. If it does not do so, the Commission may request that the CJEU impose a financial penalty (Article 260 (2) and (3) TFEU). The CJEU fixes such a penalty, taking into account the seriousness of the infringement, the duration of the non-compliance, and the economic capacity of the Member State in question to pay the penalty.

If the last word on the compliance or non-compliance of a Member State with EU law rests with the Member States, the procedure of Article 260 TFEU would lose all its sense. Indeed, the national – constitutional or other – court may declare that the first judgment of the CJEU was *ultra vires* and did not comply with national constitutional law, and was therefore irrelevant. As the fixing of a financial penalty requires an evaluation of how serious the infringement was, how long the non-compliance lasted, and the economic–financial capacity of the Member State in question, a national court might relatively easily come to the conclusion that the proportionality principle had not been properly interpreted, and declare a judgment of the CJEU under Article 260 TFEU objectively arbitrary.

Under Article 263(6) TFEU, court action against the validity of a measure adopted by an EU institution must be introduced within two months. Apparently, this provision is intended to ensure legal security, and to avoid an EU measure being challenged in court several months or years after its adoption. Nothing is said in this regard in the BVerfG's judgment of 5 May 2020. Rather, its procedural

25 Art. 114(5) TFEU.

statements indicate that natural or legal persons in Germany may introduce proceedings before the Constitutional Court without observing the two-month period specified in Article 263(6) TFEU. In this way, that provision is no longer able to ensure the degree of legal security which it intends to grant.

The interim orders by the CJEU, and the refusal by Poland to comply with them, show that similar considerations apply to interim decisions by the CJEU under Article 279 TFEU. This procedure is, therefore, also likely to become meaningless, and without useful effect, when the last word on the interpretation of EU law is in the hands of national authorities or courts.

When the EU negotiates an international agreement, any Member State, the Council, the Commission, or the European Parliament, may ask the CJEU for an opinion on whether the envisaged agreement is compatible with the EU treaties. When the opinion of the court is positive, the agreement may be concluded. When the opinion is adverse, either the agreement is amended or the treaties are revised (Article 218(11) TFEU).

This provision would also lose its useful effect should a national court have the final word on the compatibility of the envisaged agreement with the EU treaties. Such a national decision could intervene even after the CJEU has declared the envisaged agreement compatible with the treaties. In such a case, the judgment of the BVerfG, followed to its logical conclusion, would mean that the Member State in question would have to vote against the conclusion of the envisaged agreement, and should the agreement be concluded nevertheless, the public authorities of that Member State would not be allowed to participate in the application of the agreement.

According to Article 216(2) TFEU, agreements concluded by the EU are binding on the EU institutions and on Member States. Should a national court be entitled to decide on the binding character of the concluding decision concerning an international agreement, the provision of Article 216(2) would become meaningless.

Finally, another horizontal aspect needs to be mentioned. The judgments by the German and Polish Constitutional Courts, which explicitly or implicitly give the last word to national courts, are silent on the question of what happens when national courts of different Member States reach different results on the legality of an EU measure. For example, should an EU institution – the Commission or the CJEU – declare a specific chemical substance to be carcinogenic, and prohibit it from circulation within the EU, and then three Member States' courts decide that it is not carcinogenic, while five other national courts decide that it is, what is the final decision as regards the EU? May the substance circulate freely, or is its circulation prohibited? Obviously, in such a case, the internal market for goods would no longer be functioning, as border controls would be inevitable, and this situation would not be limited to the internal market for goods, but would also influence the internal market for services, then transport, energy, competition, consumer, and environmental policy and law.

4. POSSIBLE SOLUTIONS IN LAW

The judgments of the BVerfG of 5 May 2020, and of the Polish Constitutional Court of 7 October, do not stand alone. On the one hand, they had been preceded by several other judgments of these two courts, pointing in the same direction. On the other hand, the Romanian Constitutional Court found, in a judgment of 8 June 2021, that:

> Article 148 of the [Romanian] constitution does not confer on Union law priority of application over the constitution of Romania. The obligations [flowing out of Decision 2006/928][26] cannot be incumbent on the courts, State bodies that are not authorised to cooperate with a political institution of the European Union.[27]

In view of this evolution and, in view of less clearly marked similar tendencies in a number of other EU Member States until recently, some reflections on the question of how this conflict on the priority of EU law or of national (constitutional) law might be solved seem appropriate.

Giving priority to national constitutional law over EU law, be it in certain areas only, would mean, in substance, an amendment of Article 19 TEU, which attributes to the CJEU the task of interpreting and applying EU law. As indicated above, such a decision would also mean that EU law would be interpreted and applied differently from one Member State to another, according to the respective constitutional court decisions in the different Member States. The CJEU, quite rightly, indicated that Article 4(2) TFEU requires the EU to "respect the equality of Member States before the Treaties", and that this legality of treatment could not be ensured if different national decisions on the interpretation of EU law were validly applied.[28]

To this argument must be added that the *Turów* case (C-121/21) demonstrates well that, once the priority of national constitutional law has been claimed, such a primacy is not limited to decisions by the constitutional or the ordinary courts of Member States. Rather, other public authorities, and even private natural or legal persons, may at any time argue that a specific provision of EU law is contrary to national constitutional law, and need not, therefore, be followed. It might take years, if not decades, for this kind of dispute on the legal meaning of EU law to be solved before the courts, should the executive bodies in Member States feel the necessity to pursue such attitudes.

---

26 Commission Decision 2006/928 establishing a mechanism for cooperation and verification of progress in Romania to address specific benchmarks in the area of judicial reform in the field of corruption, OJ 2006, L 354, p. 56.

27 Romanian Constitutional Court, Decision 390/321 of 8 June 2021, quoted from D. Calin, "The priority of the EU law in Romania: between reality and Fata Morgana", *UNIO EU Law Journal Official Blog*, 20 September 2021.

28 CJEU, Case C-357/19 (n. 21), para. 249.

Overall, the primacy of national law over EU law would mean the end of the European Union in its present form. There would not be equality of Member States before EU law, nor would there be harmonised or uniform rules of law, in practically all sectors of Union policy. The EU would have a status similar to that of the United Nations (UN) or the Organisation for Economic Co-operation and Development (OECD), the application of whose law depends on the goodwill of the Member States, and is more often disregarded than respected.

An amendment of the national constitutional law of Member States to explicitly accept the primacy of EU law does not appear to be a realistic solution. First, such an approach would require the amendment of 27 national constitutions. It might take years before such amendments were adopted everywhere. Second, a number of political forces in the Member States would see such an amendment as a further transfer of national sovereignty to the EU, which should be opposed for reasons of principle, of power balance, and of the maintenance of national identity. They might find support among the judiciary, including the constitutional or supreme courts, which would see such a change as a loss of their judicial power.

The EU could try to enforce the judgments of the CJEU by conducting infringement procedures against Member States which do not recognise the primacy of EU law. Such proceedings were started by Czechia against Poland in Case C-121/21R, because Poland had not executed an interim order by the CJEU. A financial penalty of 500,000 euros per day of non-compliance was fixed against Poland. Yet, when the CJEU closed the case in February 2022, Poland had neither paid that penalty nor executed the order of the CJEU to close the lignite mine until the delivery of the judgment in case C-121/21. In view of the war in Ukraine, it is unclear whether the Commission will insist on having the financial sanction against Poland executed. In another case, the CJEU fixed a penalty of 1 million euros per day against Poland, because it had not executed an interim order concerning the disciplinary measures taken against judges.[29] Also in that case, Poland had not paid the penalty by May 2022.

The Commission had launched a procedure under Article 258 TFEU against Germany, because the judgment of the BVerfG of 5 May 2020 infringed, in its assessment, the principles of autonomy, primacy, effectiveness and uniform application of EU law.[30] However, in December 2021, it ended this procedure:

> [F]or three reasons. First in reply to the letter of formal notice, Germany has provided very strong commitments. In particular, Germany has formally declared that it affirms and recognises the principles of autonomy, primacy, effectiveness and uniform

---

29 CJEU, Case C-204/21R, *Commission v. Poland*, Order of 27 October 2021, ECLI:EU:C:021:878. See also the Order of 6 October in this case, ECLI:EU:C:2021:834.

30 European Commission, "The Rule of Law Report, country report on the rule of law situation in Germany", SWD (2021) 706, p. 16.

> application of Union law as well as the values laid down in Article 2 TEU, including, in particular, the rule of law. Second, Germany explicitly recognises the authority of the Court of Justice of the European Union, whose decisions are final and binding. It also considers that the legality of acts of Union institutions cannot be made subject to the examination of constitutional complaints before German courts, but only be reviewed by the Court of Justice. Third, the German government, explicitly referring to its duty of loyal cooperation enshrined in the Treaties, commits to use all the means at its disposal to avoid, in the future, a repetition of the "ultravires" finding and take an active role in that regard.[31]

The "commitment" of Germany to respect the primacy of EU law has to be nuanced, though, for two reasons. First, the independence of courts, a principle of EU as well as of German law, has the consequence that the German government cannot make any commitment which would commit the BVerfG. Rather, this court decides *itself* on the content and the interpretation of its judgments.

The second reason is even more relevant. The judgment of 5 May 2020 links the right and the duty of the BVerfG to the content of the German Constitution itself. The BVerfG interprets this constitution in the sense that it is part of the German democratic system to allow decisions by EU institutions to be challenged as *"ultra vires"* decisions. Article 79 of the German Constitution does not allow the democratic system of Germany, as established by the German Constitution, to be amended through amendments of the Constitution. It follows from this that the "power" of the BVerfG to declare measures by EU institutions *"ultra vires"* decisions cannot be put in question by measures of the German legislature or executive, even if they were trying to amend the German Constitution.

When both the national constitutional courts and the CJEU maintain their interpretation of Article 19 TEU and the primacy of EU law, there is thus a stalemate, unless legal provisions are applied. Such legal provisions can be found in the UN Vienna Convention on the Law of the Treaties of 1969 ("Vienna Convention"). This Convention is generally interpreted as regulating customary international law. It applies to treaties between states, though some of its provisions also refer to international organisations.

Article 19 of the Vienna Convention declares that a state may, when signing or ratifying a treaty, formulate a reservation with regard to specific provisions of that treaty. The reservation must be formulated in writing, and communicated to the contracting states (Article 23(1)), and "[w]hen a treaty is a constituent instrument of an international organization … a reservation requires the acceptance of the competent organ of that organization" (Article 20(3)).

---

31 European Commission, "Press release of 2 December 2021", ec.europa.eu/commission/presscorner/detail/en/inf_21_6201.

The EU has not ratified the Vienna Convention.[32] However, the EU treaties contain a number of "reservations" which Member States made during the elaboration of the EU treaties. These are laid down in the different Protocols, which are part of the treaties,[33] and are annexed to their text. These concern, for example, the non-participation of Denmark in the euro as a national currency (Protocol no. 16), specific monetary rules of France with regard to its overseas territories (Protocol no. 18), specific rules for Ireland with regard to the free movement of persons (Protocol no. 20), and second homes in Denmark (Protocol no. 32). In all these cases, the generally applicable provisions of the EU do not apply to the Member State in question, under the conditions laid down in the respective Protocol.

When the Lisbon Treaties on European Union (TEU and TFEU) were negotiated, signed and ratified, no Protocol was elaborated as regards a limitation of the primacy of EU law, and no Member State made any reservation as regards Article 19 TEU or the primacy of EU law over national law, though the corresponding jurisprudence of the CJEU had existed since 1964 and 1970 respectively. Neither is such a reservation to be found in the accession acts of Poland, Romania or any other Member State. Legally, it is thus unacceptable that a Member State should now be able to affirm that it had, at the moment of ratifying the Lisbon Treaties, a mental reservation, according to which national (constitutional) law prevailed, generally or in certain cases, over EU law. *Legally*, the situation is thus clear: EU law has primacy over national law.

Politically, the power struggle between Member States and the EU is ongoing, with uncertain results. All EU citizens will thus have to continue to live with this legal uncertainty. In this power struggle, the rule of law, laid down in Article 2 TEU as one of the fundamental values of the EU, is not really accepted as a common denominator. The discussions on the future of the EU, marked also by Russia's war against Ukraine, will hopefully lead to some reorganisation of the continent to allow, finally, an ever-closer union to be reached, despite some national thinking preferring a different outcome.

---

32 As of January 2024, all EU Member States have ratified the Convention, except France and Romania.

33 TEU, Art. 51.

ENVIRONMENTAL SCIENCE, INNOVATION AND TRANSACTIONS

Wicked Problems for Science and Law

Carolyn ROBERTS

1. INTRODUCTION

The future is creeping up on us fast, insofar as environmental challenges are unfolding, as thousands of academic papers and government publications testify. Average global temperatures have been rising since the 1950s, and mathematical modelling now gives a clear indication of how this is likely to manifest itself, at high spatial resolution and over the next century or so, under various scenarios about reduced carbon emissions. Respected scientists are now united in their views on the shocking implications of this change, even if politicians continue to prevaricate.[1] Alongside this, there are impending biodiversity catastrophes, problems of deforestation and loss of wildlife,[2] and massive release of microplastic particles into the natural environment, as far away from populated areas as Antarctica,[3] and embedded in human and animal tissues. Air pollution is estimated to kill over 4 million people every year, and 99 per cent of the global population breathes air that exceeds World Health Organization recommended limits for contaminants such as nitrogen dioxides and fine particulates.[4] Moreover, within the UK, sewers discharged raw sewage

---

1 *United Nations Environment Programme*, "Adaptation Gap Report 2022", United Nations, November 2022; *Intergovernmental Panel on Climate Change: H.-O. Pörtner, D.C. Roberts, M. Tignor, E.S. Poloczanska, K. Mintenbeck, A. Alegría, M. Craig, S. Langsdorf, S. Löschke, V. Möller, A. Okem and B. Rama (eds.)*, "Climate Change 2022: Impacts, Adaptation and Vulnerability. Contribution of Working Group II to the Sixth Assessment Report of the Intergovernmental Panel on Climate Change", Cambridge University Press, 2022.

2 *Royal Society*, Climate Change and Biodiversity Interlinkages and Policy Options, Royal Society, 2021.

3 *A.R. Aves., L. E Revell, S. Gaw, H. Ruffell, A. Schuddeboom, N.E. Wotherspoon, M. LaRue and A.J. McDonald*, "First evidence of microplastics in Antarctic snow", The Cryosphere Discussions (preprint), https://doi.org/10.5194/tc-2021-385, in review, 2022.

4 *World Health Organisation*, "Fact Sheet on Air Pollution", https://www.who.int/news-room/fact-sheets/detail/ambient-(outdoor)-air-quality-and-health; *K. Cromar and N. Lazrak*,

into English rivers 373,000 times in 2021,[5] despite the technology for treating these discharges being readily available. The evidence of these problems is widely reported in the press and media by environmental scientists, and is very worrying.

Simultaneously, the UK population is told by UK Research and Innovation, the government agency responsible for allocating funding for university and business-related research and development, that we are at the forefront of a new, "green" industrial revolution. They note that "research, innovation and partnership continue to underpin the UK's commitment to achieving a (carbon) net zero economy by 2050, responding to the challenges of climate change and living more sustainably".[6] However, in order to effect changes, organisations, including businesses and universities, need to tackle some genuine challenges. Overlain onto the explicitly environmental challenges are societal shifts, such as ageing populations, city growth, failing infrastructure, developments in technology, as well as resource depletion. One wonders what is happening, since most of these problems have technological or societal solutions, but we fail to address them, and in some cases shy away from action.

2. "WICKED" PROBLEMS

The types of environmental problems we are experiencing are sometimes referred to as "wicked problems",[7] a phrase first articulated by American town planners Horst Rittel and Melvin Webber, in 1973. Wicked problems have particular characteristics, such as complexity and poor formulation, interconnected human or sociological and environmental dimensions, many different stakeholders in public and private domains, and a lack of agreement about what is important. When one of these stakeholders intervenes in the situation, the implications of what they do are often manifest at other locations, and at different times. Moreover, they use terminology in different ways, and may not agree as to when an appropriate solution has been reached.

"Risk Communication of Ambient Air Pollution in the WHO European Region: Review of Air Quality Indexes and Lessons Learned", World Health Organisation Regional Office for Europe, 2023.

5 *Environment Agency*, "Water and Sewerage Companies in England: Environmental Report 2021", updated 22 July 2022, Environment Agency, 2022.

6 *UK Research and Investment*, "Responding to Climate Change", https://www.ukri.org/news-and-events/responding-to-climate-change/, UKRI, 2022.

7 *H. Rittel and M. Webber*, "Dilemmas in a general theory of planning", *Policy Sciences*, 1973 (4), pp. 155–169.

3. THE "WICKED", "SUPER WICKED" OR "HYPER WICKED" PROBLEM OF FLOODING

Consider the issue of flooding in the UK, estimated in 2002 to be costing some £2.2 billion per year to manage and recompense or recover.[8] Since 2002, the estimates have increased and decreased in the face of intermittent flood events, but the financial costs are recognised to be likely to increase under most climate change scenarios. Even this figure largely ignores the mental health issues associated with flooding, as the stress plays out amongst those directly affected by inundation, and those affected in other more distant ways.[9] Flooding is a natural phenomenon whereby high rainfall or sudden snowmelt, or sea incursion, leads to areas of land that are normally dry being inundated. Rivers overtop on to their floodplains (they rarely "burst their banks", regardless of press reporting), low-permeability pavements and roofs generate sudden surface run-off that enters houses and commercial premises, and coastal structures such as railway tracks are inundated and eroded. Everyone is affected, by direct loss or damage to property and belongings, loss of industrial and commercial capacity, disruption to transport and other infrastructure, damage to children's educational progress, insurance claims and increased premiums, and increased demands on social and medical services. Some people die in floods, often not by drowning, but from electrocution or crushing injuries, and many people suffer from deteriorating mental health. The police, local authorities, the Environment Agency, water companies, central government, fire and rescue services, and residents in affected areas argue, and attempt to apportion or offload blame for what happened, and offer different opinions on what should be done to prevent future occurrences. Scientists whisper that flooding is an inherent natural characteristic of rivers and ocean margins, and that it cannot be controlled; statistically, unusual events will always occur, and probably at increasing frequency with climate change. Others frequently suggest that planners or house builders are culpable, and should be better "controlled" in some way, to prevent building on floodplains, or on areas that will generate excess run-off. They talk of "flash flooding", "overland flow" and "sewer surcharging", without a clear understanding of their various causes and characteristics.

Actual solutions to the problem of flooding include interventions that will physically reduce water entering areas perceived as inappropriate, such as dredging river channels; erecting flood barriers, walls and drains; constructing retention basins; and specifying porous paving in new developments. Others

---

8 *Office of Science and Technology*, "Foresight Future Flooding", Office of Science and Technology, Department for Farming and Rural Affairs, 2002.

9 *J. Finlay and P. Bolton*, "Flood Risk Management and Funding", House of Commons Library, 22 June 2022.

suggest that the priority is reducing the cost of the damage, rather than the actual levels of water, and propose insurance-based or financial compensation schemes for those affected. For others, mental resilience, and better education on what to do in the event of an imminent flood, are key; today's political focus is largely on flood "resilience" rather than prevention. However, all these apparent solutions raise other issues. Construction or installation of flood barriers simply routes water further downstream, flooding previously unaffected areas – protecting Tewkesbury adds to inundation in Gloucester when the River Severn floods, for example – a good example of an intervention in one place subsequently creating havoc in another, later. And who should pay for the insurance claims of those inundated?

Decision-making by authorities often also reflects short time horizons: the issuing of sandbags during a flood, or dredging a channel afterwards, for example, despite the fact that these are largely ineffective. Such measures reflect a desire for local and central authorities and the military to be seen to be doing something – anything – immediately. The time until the next local or national election is also, undoubtedly, a consideration when politicians don their wellington boots and "go walkabout", shaking hands and pontificating.

In 2012, Levin et al. developed the "wicked" concept further, into "super wicked problems", where time is running out, those who are largely responsible for creating the problem are also charged with providing a solution, and the central authority required to bring stakeholders together is weak or non-existent.[10] Many international problems manifest themselves as "super wicked", climate change being a prime example. The UK's flooding problem is also "super wicked", at least.

We might also add a further category of wickedness, namely "hyper wicked events", where some or all stakeholders are economical with the truth, for personal or professional gain. Suggestions of structural responses to flooding, by building bypass channels, enlarging drainage pipes, or constructing new dams are almost always made by engineers seeking new commissions, whereas investment in upstream controls by adjusting land uses high in river basins receives scant attention, as relatively few people would reap direct reward from the necessary rewilding, and the wider impacts have proved challenging to model. And again, coal mine owners frequently overstate the challenges and uncertainties associated with renewable energy, as a reason for increasing government investment in relatively expensive fossil fuel production. Even supposedly neutral scientists have some interests in securing further research funding to find innovative new approaches, and hence are prone to a degree of exaggeration.

---

10 *K. Levin, B. Cashmore, S. Bernstein and G. Auld*, "Overcoming the tragedy of super wicked problems: constraining our future selves to ameliorate global climate change", *Policy Sciences*, 2012 (45), pp. 123–152.

4. BROKERING SOLUTIONS TO WICKED PROBLEMS AT VARIOUS SCALES

All wicked problems demand new and more fluid ways of thinking, which frequently defy the linear approaches whereby teams of "experts" straightforwardly identify the problem and the solution, and steer the project through to a predetermined conclusion. In practice, solving wicked problems, whether "super" or "hyper" wicked, requires decision-taking in the light of uncertainty, and a great deal of negotiation, to arrive at solutions that may not be absolutely perfect, but are at least better than the alternatives. There are instances where this has been largely successful: international agreement on addressing the growing holes in the polar ozone layer, largely created by the use of hydrochlorofluorocarbons in refrigerants and packaging, for instance, was reached and captured in the 1987 Montreal Protocol, in which 197 countries agreed to phase out their use. Technological innovation developed replacement products. The problem has not been solved completely, and, indeed, a new sudden thinning has recently been alleged to have been detected over the tropics,[11] but despite some annual variability, and occasional violations of the international protocol, the polar ozone holes seem now to be slowly closing, and human exposure to harmful ultraviolet radiation is falling. Similarly, the UK's exports of coal-burning-derived acidic rainfall across the North Sea, in the 1970s and 1980s, to the detriment of Scandinavian forests, was also eventually addressed through a mixture of innovative technical and societal adjustments, following heated debate between scientists, foresters, energy companies, farmers and politicians. But despite these successes, scientists and technologists are often not forefronted in today's decision-making processes, despite their pleas for "evidence-based" decisions rather than political expediency.

5. THE ROLES OF LAWYERS IN BROKERING INNOVATION

Brokering these wicked debates, and representing the different local, national or international cases honestly, despite their complexity, is the job of lawyers. Naturally, lawyers also have a role in drafting and subsequently interpreting such agreements. In the UK, environmental law is facing a rapid phase of adjustments, following Britain's withdrawal from the European Union (EU). Until 2016, the EU was effectively responsible for generating most of the environmental legislation to which the UK was bound. EU directives emerged

11 *Q.-B. Lu*, "Observation of large and all-season ozone losses over the tropics", *AIP Advances* 2022 (12), 075006; doi: 10.1063/5.0094629.

out of international agreements, and although the implementation process was slow, and in some cases flawed (the Common Agricultural Policy is responsible for swathes of environmental damage across Europe, for instance), genuine progress in many areas of the environment was engendered. Conversely, in the 2020s, the UK remains in a period of considerable uncertainty. Whereas some EU legislation has proved relatively easy to pull across into UK legal and administrative systems, other issues are proving very problematic. Contaminated land law, industrial emissions limits, and product regulations relating to electronic waste, for instance, are changing minimally, and have mostly been adopted across. Conversely, net-zero emissions trading, fisheries protection and biodiversity enhancement should be shifting rapidly in the UK, as new bills have passed through Parliament: the Agriculture and Fisheries Acts of 2020, and the Environment Act 2021, for instance. Innovation in flood and water management legislation is another area where, despite the 2021 Act, progress remains sluggish, and is the subject of ongoing debate, reflecting its hyper wickedness, and the huge number of vested interests, each with their own opinion.

The UK requires a high level of innovation in technology, services and applications in tackling some of its environmental challenges. Bringing in something new can be a complex business. The American forecasting specialist Gartner produces an excellent annual analysis of innovation trends, particularly for digital technology, that is worth consulting. For several years, they have highlighted rapidly developing innovation, such as the growth in use of big data and artificial intelligence, increasingly "smart", connected and remotely controlled buildings, and monitoring and tracking technologies associated with the Internet of Things. The exploration of the potential of new material mixes in batteries, and the prospects of quantum computing allowing better forecasting of climate change, are, despite the hype often found in tech circles, now very real too.

Looking back over the last decade, technological innovations in solar power, global positioning systems and satellite imagery, the growing use of drones for monitoring, and the democratisation of information flows created by smart phones, have started to revolutionise the environmental sector. Drones, for example, now monitor crop growth and health, and, in theory, allow better, more targeted use of pesticides and fertilisers, which can be applied from robotic sprayers. New types of batteries enhance the ranges of electric cars to a level not previously envisaged. Tiny embedded sensors allow pipelines to be monitored, and flows in mains water networks to be controlled, to reduce pipe bursts and leakage. Robots pick strawberries, and will soon pick apples and mushrooms, optimising the yields and reducing the costs without sacrificing quality. And smartphones allow residents to exchange information about flooding threats or actualities with those managing the deluges, at least until their electricity runs out. There are hundreds of other examples where individual technology elements may need legal protection through patents. However, genuinely innovative solutions for wicked environmental challenges require negotiation between the stakeholders, and cannot be solved through technology alone.

6. WHOLE-SYSTEM CHANGES

What is often needed is wholesale changes to complete systems. A simple example concerns farming methods that integrate food production with water management and reutilisation of waste products, particularly dirty water, as "free" sources of nutrients and energy. Sometimes, fish or insects are added into the cycle, although that element of a circular economy is less well developed so far. These innovations are increasingly common, and the owners and customers of small urban farms in London, and large Scottish whisky distilleries, have already been beneficiaries. The technology is relatively straightforward, but the developments occur at the intersections between these systems: water, energy, waste and food. This requires discussion and agreement between the suppliers of the energy, the water and the raw materials, and new ways of distributing to consumers. Collaboration is crucial.

At a larger scale, substantial new residential developments are attempting to manage low-impact housing with exceptionally low water and energy use, recovery of water and energy from wastewater, and zero-emission heating systems. These require very careful planning of layouts, landscapes and ecology, and social settings in order to function – the domain of town planners. Integration of different themes is a prerequisite for solving the challenges, or at least arriving at better solutions than we have managed so far. Developers can, if appropriately incentivised, generate attractive places to live, where emissions of greenhouse gases and running costs are low, water consumption is minimised through the use of low-water-use appliances and grey water recycling, and biodiversity thrives. Residents' access to green space is particularly important in maintaining mental health. As a side effect, community interactions and mental health seem to improve, too, where environmental footprints are minimised, although hard evidence has proved challenging to tie down.[12] However, these "whole systems" innovations require complex negotiations, and a commensurate amount of sophisticated and aware input from legal teams, to ensure they work effectively. Not only do the systems have to be resource-efficient, but they need to be well integrated with other systems, such as transport for the people, the goods and the wastes, otherwise environmental gains made in production will be lost in distribution. Such systems must be long-lasting, in both physical and

---

12 *S. Lewis*, "Mental Health and Town Planning: Building in Resilience", Royal Town Planning Institute Practice Advice, October 2020.

human terms, but also sufficiently flexible to withstand sudden shocks, such as disruptions in supply chains, or weather and climate emergencies. They need to have "bouncebackability", or resilience from catastrophes.

7. CONCLUSION

What the new, environmentally more benign, systems described above have in common is a need for collaboration and partnership amongst stakeholders: the planners, scientists, technologists, energy supply companies, local authorities, water companies, transport logistics specialists and food retailers. Wicked environmental challenges inevitably require this approach. The associated transactions require careful brokering, to ensure that they are resilient, and do not fail at the first hurdle. That is where well-informed lawyers must act, to ensure fairness and resilience. At the "March for Science" demonstration in Westminster, in April 2017, protesters about government's lack of scientific judgement being used in decision-making were holding up placards about climate change, biodiversity loss and unliveable cities. One, illustrated with the obligatory chemical flasks and test tubes, read, "[i]f you're not part of the solution, you're part of the precipitate". Lawyers do need to join the solution, broker transactions, and foster collaboration for innovation, urgently.

PART II
THE MARINE ENVIRONMENT

THE ROLE OF MARINE PROTECTED AREAS IN ENHANCING BIODIVERSITY AND OCEAN SUSTAINABILITY

Naomi Townsend

1. INTRODUCTION

The marine environment is facing a number of threats which are damaging fauna and flora at an unsustainable rate, causing irrevocable damage.[1] The damage occurring is causing risk not only to the oceans' survival, but to that of humankind and all living organisms.[2] Predominantly, the destruction of the world's oceans and seas is instigated by the pressures of human activity, comprising but not limited to pollution, climate change, fishery undertakings, tourism and coastal advances.[3] These acts are resulting in the deteriorating health of most marine ecosystems, and diminishing marine biodiversity.[4] It is causing harm at levels which will inevitably cause endangerment of marine species, and therefore immediate action is necessary.[5] The consequences of inaction will be extreme, not just for the marine environment, but for the earth as a whole.[6]

Fishing eradicates billions of fish each year from the ocean.[7] Unsustainable fishing, or harmful fishing practices, such as certain methods of bottom trawling, not only cause targeted fish numbers to deplete, but also depletion of by-catch, as well as damage to the seabed and supporting marine habitats.[8] Trawling depletes

1 Boris Worm et al., "Impacts of biodiversity loss on ocean ecosystem services" [2006] 314(5800) *Science* 787–790.
2 UK Government, "2010 to 2015 government policy: marine environment" (*GOV.UK*, 8 May 2015) <https://www.gov.uk/government/publications/2010-to-2015-government-policy-marine-environment/2010-to-2015-government-policy-marine-environment>.
3 Joachim Claudet, *Marine Protected Areas: A Multidisciplinary Approach* (Cambridge University Press, 2011), foreword.
4 Jeremy Jackson et al., "Historical Overfishing and the Recent Collapse of Coastal Ecosystems" [2001] 293(5530) *Science* 629–637.
5 Philippe Sands et al., *Principles of International Environmental Law* (3rd ed., Cambridge University Press 2012), 351.
6 Ibid.
7 Terence Hughes et al., "Adaptive Management of the Great Barrier Reef and the Grand Canyon World Heritage Areas" [2007] 36(7) *A Journal of the Human Environment* 586–592.
8 WWF, "Overfishing" (*WWF*) <https://www.worldwildlife.org/threats/overfishing>.

fish numbers, by tearing up the seabeds and other fragile habitats.[9] At present, over 93 per cent of the world's fisheries are now fully or over-exploited.[10] The oceans and seas make up approximately 71 per cent of the Earth's surface, holding around 96.5 per cent of all water on Earth, and producing 50 per cent of the world's oxygen.[11] Numbers like this enforce the oceans' importance and scale. Major disasters would occur on a global scale without a successful biodiverse marine environment. The seas and oceans provide an assured and healthy food resource, but without a healthy and biodiverse marine environment, this would not exist.[12] A severe crash in the economy could also occur, due to trade and work loss,[13] as well as diminished tourism.[14] We therefore need a robust protection policy in place, to facilitate the recovery of biodiversity, and to help repair and prevent damage.

This contribution will discuss the variables that affect areas of the marine environment, and how legal designation policy systems are being put in place to ensure protection for the ocean.[15] These are known as Marine Protected Areas (MPAs). MPAs are a tool which have been established to help ensure healthy ecosystems and enhance fish stocks. The definitive goal of MPAs is to work with other strategies to ensure that the ocean's environment, as a whole, functions in a sustainable manner.[16] Sustainability, as defined by the *Brundtland Report*, argues for "development that meets the needs of the present without compromising the ability of future generations to meet their own needs".[17] With reference to the marine environment, the aim is to have a successful biodiverse environment status upheld at an optimum level, while forestalling depletion.[18] However, an optimum level has not been clearly defined.

MPAs are frequently used as a means to protect and promote the increase of ocean health and biodiversity.[19] In the last few decades, international policy and

---

9 Oceana, "Mounting evidence shows Danish sand dredging destroys cod and plaice habitat in the Sound" (*Oceana*, 22 June 2016) <http://oceana.org/press-center/press-releases/mounting-evidence-shows-danish-sand-dredging-destroys-cod-and-plaice>.

10 Food and Agriculture Organization of the United Nations Fisheries Department, "*The State of World Fisheries and Aquaculture 2018*" Meeting the sustainable development goals, Rome, 2018, Licence: CC BY-NC-SA 3.0 IGO.

11 USGS, "How much water is there on, in, and above the Earth?" (The USGS Water Science School, 2 December 2016) <https://water.usgs.gov/edu/earthhowmuch.html>.

12 UK Government (n. 2).

13 Steven Murawski, "Definitions of overfishing from an ecosystem perspective" [2000] 57 *ICES Journal of Marine Science* 649–658.

14 Ibid.

15 John Morelli, "Environmental Sustainability: A Definition for Environmental Professionals" [2011] 1(1) *Journal of Environmental Sustainability* 1–9.

16 Ibid.

17 Gro Harlem Brundtland, "What is sustainable development?", *Our Common Future* 8–9.

18 Ibid.

19 Utrecht Law Review, "Protected areas in environmental law introduction" [2009] 5(1) *Utrecht Law Review* 1–4.

legislation has influenced an increase in the establishment of MPAs on a global scale.[20] However, spatial management measures for marine environments are often being accounted for by several legal instruments, and the legal definition of an MPA varies from country to country.[21] Consequently, different opinions of MPAs, as a management tool, are held by different stakeholders, resulting in some instances of MPAs benefiting the marine environment, and others causing little, or even no, successful ecological outcomes.[22]

Some MPAs constrain or prevent damaging activities, to ensure conservation goals are met. This is important to achieve, as, ultimately, we desire our marine waters to be healthy and rich in biodiversity, preventing population collapse and extinction. However, with there being over 2 million known marine species globally,[23] this creates a challenge when designating and managing an MPA to cater to the needs of these species, due to their array of complex characteristics. To enable MPAs to protect biodiversity as much as possible, it is necessary to factor these needs into the management strategies at the design stage, and to ensure connectivity of MPAs as a network.

Furthermore, varied approaches and levels of protection can leave the definition of MPAs seeming "unclear".[24] Nonetheless, the International Union for Conservation of Nature (IUCN) defines an MPA as "a clearly defined geographical space, recognised, dedicated and managed, through legal or other effective means, to achieve the long-term conservation of nature with associated ecosystem services and cultural values".[25] Contrastingly, there are two predominant classifications for protected areas, the other being from the Convention on Biological Diversity (CBD).[26] In contrast to the IUCN definition, the CBD defines an MPA as "a geographically defined area which is designated or regulated and managed to achieve specific conservation objectives".[27] In international law, the CBD definition is binding, while several countries have adopted the IUCN's definition, and built it into their national laws.[28] The difference between the definitions is that the IUCN focuses on conservation as a whole, and association

20 Ibid.

21 Patricia Breen, "Temperate Marine Protected Areas and highly mobile fish: A review" [2015] 105 *Ocean & Coastal Management* 75–83.

22 Ibid.

23 Camilo Mora et al., "How Many Species Are There on Earth and in the Ocean?' [2011] 9(8) *PLoS Biology*.

24 Natalie Bown et al., *Contested Forms of Governance in Marine Protected Areas: A Study of Co-Management and Adaptive Co-Management* (Routledge 2013), 2.

25 IUCN, "When is a Marine Protected Area really a Marine Protected Area" (IUCN, 8 September 2012) <www.iucn.org/content/when-a-marine-protected-area-really-a-marine-protected-area>.

26 Paul Goriup, *Management of Marine Protected Areas: A Network Perspective* (John Wiley & Sons 2017), 71.

27 United Nations, Convention on Biological Diversity, 1992, IPCC-XVIII Doc. 4 (f) (14.VIII.2001).

28 Paul Goriup (n. 26), 71.

with cultural values and ecosystem services, whereas the CBD emphasises specific conservation objectives, which could be more open to interpretation.

Issues arise with MPAs that exist outside of national jurisdictions, as they pose fundamental questions with regard to the application and enforcement of international law.[29] At present, there are only a few MPAs situated wholly outside of national jurisdiction. The Ross Sea reserve, which was established by the Commission for the Conservation of Antarctic Marine Living Resource,[30] is by far the largest MPA outside of national jurisdiction. All other MPAs exist within the territorial waters and/or exclusive economic zones of coastal states,[31] which should help to ensure their optimum management, and enforcement of the laws. However, enforcement of the policies and laws in place to ensure MPAs achieve their goals varies greatly, meaning enforcement effectiveness does not have a definite standardisation. Without standardisation, constructive management cannot be achieved, potentially making MPAs ineffective.

A high-profile study has suggested that MPA success appears to rely on several influencing factors. These factors are: no take, effective enforcement, old, large, and isolated – also referred to as the NEOLI factors.[32] However, there is also much evidence suggesting that tourism can cause ecological decline, especially if poorly managed, as discussed below. There are, of course, other factors that influence success, such as the initial ecological state at the time of designation, and its potential biodiversity level (i.e. sandy areas vs. coral reefs), but the above-listed factors appear to be the most valuable.

MPAs vary enormously between countries, especially between those that are economically developed and those that are undeveloped.[33] Countries which are more economically developed tend to have more MPA coverage, with less developed countries being "left behind in the race to build a comprehensive global MPA network".[34] Throughout this contribution, a diverse, global range of 27 case studies will, therefore, be referred to throughout, and be the basis of the research.

This research encompasses the results of MPAs through a scientific definition of success (measurable ecological benefits). Accordingly, scientific methods to review MPAs' success in enhancing biodiversity and being effective are reviewed through science as well as law. A Bayesian belief network (BBN) was used to

29 Kamrul Hossian and Kathleen Morris, "Protecting Arctic Ocean Marine Biodiversity in the Area Beyond National Jurisdiction" [2017] *The Future of the Law of the Sea* 105–126.

30 Peter Sand, "Marine protected areas and ocean stewardship: a legal perspective" [2018] *Biodiversity* 1–3.

31 Ibid.

32 Graham Edgar et al., "Global conservation outcomes depend on marine protected areas with five key features" [2014] 506(7487) *Nature* 216.

33 Peter Jones, *Governing Marine Protected Areas* (Routledge 2014), 12.

34 Sophie Marinesque et al., "Global implementation of marine protected areas: Is the developing world being left behind?" [2012] 36(3) *Marine Policy* 727–737.

analyse 27 MPAs over a global scale, in both developed and developing regions, which varied greatly in terms of their different success factors (for example, enforcement levels, fishing restrictions). These MPAs were selected to cover a wide range of geographical areas, as well as to incorporate a wide range of sizes, ages, enforcement levels, fishing intensity and tourism intensity. A BBN is a method of integrating different data types, in this case to define the probability of the success of the MPA: they work by defining beliefs of the strength of connections between nodes in the network, which can, and should, be based, where possible, on real data or evidence. In this case, they allow expert opinion to be combined with detailed literature analysis from different MPAs, to define the ecological success of the MPA.[35]

Furthermore, this research uses environmental law methodology to assist in the incorporation of external factors and non-legal factors into the legal reasoning.[36] The project incorporates desk-based research throughout, to analyse the different marine laws in protecting and conserving ocean territory and life, both within different nations, and at an international level.

2. OVERVIEW OF THE FACTORS WHICH CAN INFLUENCE MPA SUCCESS

There are six factors which, upon review and analysis, appear to hold the most power when influencing the success of an MPA. This contribution will review and explain how each factor affects MPA status, and the role of each in enhancing biodiversity and sustainability.

Tourism is one of the younger factors, but is rapidly increasing its status to be a highly operative influence. Tourism can pose a great threat, not just for MPAs, but for sustainability and biodiversity on a global scale. Construction of tourist infrastructure can demolish habitats; affect water quality; cause disruption to the environment and its wildlife; and damage communities, through overdevelopment and disturbance of local culture.[37] However, ecotourism can promote conservation. Ecotourism is defined by the IUCN as, "[e]nvironmentally responsible travel to natural areas, in order to enjoy and appreciate nature

35 The connections and relative strengths of these connections are given for each BBN used, where values above 0.5 mean an increase in the affecter node will lead to a likely increase in the affected node, and a value less than 0.5 means an increase in the affecter node is likely to lead to a decrease in the affected node.

36 Aðalheiður Jóhannsdóttir, "The significance of the default: A study in environmental law methodology with emphasis on ecological sustainability and international biodiversity law", PhD dissertation, Universitetsbiblioteket, 2009.

37 Clevo Wilson and Clem Tisdell, "Conservation and Economic Benefits of Wildlife-Based Marine Tourism: Sea Turtles and Whales as Case Studies" [2003] 8(1) *Human Dimensions* of Wildlife 49–58.

(and accompanying cultural features, both past and present) that promote conservation, have a low visitor impact and provide for beneficially active socio-economic involvement of local peoples."[38] Tourism is one of the greatest global industries, bringing in high income, with the market continuing to grow.[39] It is necessary to distinguish between, on the one hand, sustainable tourism, which is purposely planned from the start to conserve natural resources, educate local residents and tourists, and respect and support local culture, and, on the other hand, conventional tourism, the intention of which is not necessarily to improve conservation or to educate, and which can promptly impair an environment.[40]

Where tourism is developed with the focus of maintaining pristine natural environments, it can have many benefits, creating an income to maintain and aid conservation work,[41] alongside benefiting local communities through employment and revenue generation.[42] With true ecotourism, the main goal is to sustain the environment and traditional cultures, unlike conventional tourism, where financial profit is the focus.

Tourism can have many positives in promoting sustainability and conservation for MPAs, but, equally, can cause negative impacts. The Great Barrier Reef (GBR), in Australia, has approximately 1.6 million tourists each year, and portrays both positives and negatives of tourism.[43] Tourism on the GBR is currently worth over £2.25 billion a year, with over 47,000 employees.[44] It provides work and income for locals, and, therefore, benefits its community and economy.[45] A key tool in the management and protection of the GBR is the tourism industry, raising approximately 8 million Australian dollars each year from tourists, and fees paid by operators. These funds contribute directly to the management of the GBR, from the Australian Government, through the environmental management charge.[46] Tourism operators have been acting as stewards of the GBR for nine years, through voluntary actions and the high-standard tourism programme set.[47] The tourism community is progressively working to incorporate best practice for the marine environment.[48]

---

38 Hector Ceballos-Lascurain, *Tourism, ecotourism, and protected areas: the state of nature-based tourism around the world and guidelines for its development* (Island Press 1996).

39 K.V.S.N. Jawahar Babu, "Sustainable Tourism: Benefits and Threats for MPA's" [2012] *Social Science Research Network*.

40 Ibid.

41 Clevo Wilson and Clem Tisdell (n. 37).

42 K.V.S.N. Jawahar Babu (n. 39).

43 Vicki Harriott, "Marine Tourism impacts on the Great Barrier Reef" [2004] 1(1) *Tourism in Marine Environments* 29–40.

44 Ibid.

45 Great Barrier Reef Marine Park Authority, *Great Barrier Reef Outlook Report 2014* (Great Barrier Reef Marine Park Authority 2014).

46 Ibid.

47 Ibid.

48 Ibid.

Yet, tourism vessels can cause great environmental impacts: they can physically disrupt the ocean's fauna and habitats (for example, through noise pollution, as discussed below, or poor anchoring practices), as well as disperse chemical pollutants into the ocean.[49] The GBR, in particular, is vulnerable to damage due to high levels of tourism,[50] as it suffers from induced damage from boats, due to ship grounding, anchoring, and waste discharge, which causes great disturbance to marine life.[51] Disturbance effects an MPA's effectiveness, by creating a change in the ocean fauna's living pattern, causing disruption to breeding, living and emigration.[52] Tourists can also trample on sensitive intertidal habitats, particularly when snorkelling and swimming. This disruption to habitats can cause several other consequences aside from instantaneous damage, such as species depletion, as well as longer-lasting elusive changes, such as altering the eating patterns and reproduction of marine species.[53]

The factor of age has been proposed as highly influential in the success of an MPA, as the longer an MPA has been established, the longer the ecological community should have had to recover.[54] The older an MPA is, the closer it should be to achieving its targets, but MPAs do vary, as some populations may take decades to recover.[55] Furthermore, and more precisely, older MPAs should have higher fish density than younger ones.[56] However, enforcement of an MPA can have an effect on whether age is a successful influencer: for example, if the MPA is older, but there is no enforcement, then it is possible that it could be less successful than a younger MPA with high enforcement.

When reviewing the factor of size, evidence suggests that the bigger the MPA, the more likely it will be to succeed in enhancing biodiversity and sustainability in that area, particularly where the MPA is established to help fish populations recover, and to restore coral reefs.[57] There is a particular focus on size, at present, which stems from the Convention on Biological Diversity, 10th Conference of

---

49 Jan Warnken and Troy Byrnes, "Impacts of tour boats in marine environments" *Environmental Impacts of Ecotourism* (2004) 99–123.

50 Leon Zann, "The State of the Marine Environment Report for Australia (SOMER): process, findings and perspectives" [1996] 33(1-3) *Ocean & Coastal Management* 63–86.

51 Troy Byrnes et al., "Environmental management of boating related impacts by commercial fishing, sailing and diving tour boat operators in Australia" [2016] 111 *Journal of Cleaner Production* 383–398.

52 Ibid.

53 Jean Holder, "Pattern and impact of tourism on the environment of the Caribbean" [1988] 9(2) *Tourism management* 119–127.

54 Philip Molloy et al., "Effects of marine reserve age on fish populations: a global meta-analysis" [2009] 46(4) *Journal of Applied Ecology* 743–751.

55 Ransom A. Myers et al., "Maximum population growth rates and recovery times for Atlantic cod, *Gadus morhua*" [1997] 95(4) *Fishery Bulletin* 762–772.

56 Phillip Molloy et al. (n. 54).

57 Benjamin Halpern, "The Impact of Marine Reserves: Do Reserves Work and Does Reserve Size Matter?" [2003] 13(1) *Ecological Applications* 117–137.

the Parties (COP10) in 2010.[58] COP10 has had a global influence on the size of MPAs, whereby a 2020 target was set which asked for at least 10 per cent of coastal and marine areas to be designated as protected areas,[59] extended from the original target date of 2010.[60] COP15 has now adapted this to 30 per cent by 2030.[61] As mentioned previously, influencing factors need the cooperation of each other, to help influence their success. A deficiency of "large MPAs" is that they may still allow for a wide range of human activities to take place there. This means that size is not actually as effective as intended,[62] due to human activities damaging the ecosystems that are meant to be conserved.[63]

Since COP10, there has been a clear trend towards the designation of larger MPAs, with several being in the millions of square kilometres. The Ross Sea MPA, designated in 2016, is vast at 1,550,000 square kilometres,[64] making it the world's second-largest MPA. The largest MPA is the Terres Australes MPA, which although created in 2006, was expanded greatly to 1,600,000 square kilometres in 2016.[65] President Barack Obama quadrupled the Papahanaumokakea Marine National Monument MPA in 2016, making it 1,508,870 square kilometres.[66] With the world's three largest MPAs being established in the seven years following COP10, it raises concerns that we are just making MPAs to reach percentage coverage targets. However, it could be that we have realised how effective MPAs are as a management tool, and, therefore, that these should be of a larger size, to achieve desired results and a sustainable future.

Isolation is a powerful factor when it comes to MPA success, due to less human activity taking place. However, the reason an MPA is established is due to that specific area needing protection, often from fishing, which in many cases can be more prevalent closer to shore, or to human settlements.

---

58 Convention on Biological Diversity, "Aichi Biodiversity Targets" (Convention on Biological Diversity 2010) <https://www.cbd.int/sp/targets/>.

59 Ibid.

60 Convention on Biological Diversity (CBD) (Rio de Janeiro, 5 June 1992), "Strategic Plan: future evaluation of progress".

61 Convention on Biological Diversity, "COP15: Nations Adopt Four Goals, 23 Targets for 2030 in Landmark UN Biodiversity Agreement" (Convention on Biological Diversity, 19 December 2022) <http://www.cbd.int/article/cop15-cbd-press-release-final-19dec2022>.

62 Benjamin Halpern et al., "A Global Map of Human Impact on Marine Ecosystems" [2008] 319(5865) *Science* 948–952.

63 Ibid.

64 Antarctic and Southern Ocean Coalition, "Ross Sea Region MPA", <https://www.asoc.org/campaign/ross-sea-mpa/>.

65 Overseas Countries and Territories Association, "The French Southern Territories National Nature Reserve becomes the second largest marine protected area in the world" <https://www.overseas-association.eu/the-french-southern-territories-national-nature-reserve-becomes-the-second-largest-marine-protected-area-in-the-world/>.

66 Papahānaumokuākea Marine National Monument, "About Papahānaumokuākea", <https://www.papahanaumokuakea.gov/new-about/>.

Of the 27 MPAs examined in this contribution, some are highly isolated, such as the Ross Sea protected area in Antarctica, which, as a result, escapes heavy fishing and shipping pressures.[67] Due to its isolation, Ross Sea is largely untouched by humans, with recent analyses of anthropogenic impacts showing that the Ross Sea is the least-affected stretch of ocean,[68] thus influencing the nutrient-rich waters.[69] Conversely, Bunaken National Park, located off the coast of Indonesia, is highly populated, with 22 villages inside the park, comprising approximately 30,000 people.[70] Most locals work as fishermen, and a number are employed in tourism involving boats.[71] This has caused the park to suffer from a slow but continuous degradation, owing to coral mining, anchor damage, diving, trash pollution, and harmful fishing methods.[72] The Bird Island Group MPA in South Africa, although located close to the busy Port Elizabeth, is surrounded by buffer zones and other protected areas on land and sea, to help achieve its goals, preventing further interference from human activity.[73] Recent studies have shown that the benefits of near-shore MPAs may be greater than isolated MPAs for enhancing fish stocks, although isolated MPAs have a greater ability to protect more mobile species, such as large predators.[74]

Scientists have now discovered that coral-reef fish larvae determine which reef they choose to make their home by listening to the reef,[75] as well as using acoustic cues, to navigate, locate prey, avoid predators, and find mates.[76] However, in some areas of the ocean, the reef may not be heard at all, due to large levels of anthropogenic noise.[77] This noise pollution is caused by several interfering activities, such as boats and tourism. With the growing exploitation and exploration of the ocean, this is significantly affecting

---

67 Brian Clark Howard, "World's Largest Marine Reserve Created Off Antarctica" (*National Geographic*, 27 October 2016) <https://news.nationalgeographic.com/2016/10/ross-sea-marine-protected-area-antarctica/>.

68 David Ainley, "A history of the exploitation of the Ross Sea" [2010] 46(3) *Antarctica* 233–243.

69 Brian Clark Howard (n. 67).

70 Pieter Van Beukering et al., "Case study 3: Bunaken National Marine Park (Indonesia)", *The Role of Marine Protected Areas in Contributing to Poverty Reduction* (Yumpu 2007).

71 Patrick Christie, "Marine Protected Areas as Biological Successes and Social Failures in Southeast Asia" [2004] 42 *American Fisheries Society Symposium* 155–164.

72 Patrick Christie, "Observed and perceived environmental impacts of marine protected areas in two Southeast Asia sites" [2005] 48(3–6) *Ocean & Coastal Management* 252–270.

73 Lorien Pichegru et al., "Industrial fishing, no-take zones and endangered penguins" [2012] 156 *Biological Conservation* 117–125.

74 Joshua E. Cinner et al., "Gravity of human impacts mediates coral reef conservation gains" [2018] 13 *Proceedings of the National Academy of Sciences* 6116–6125.

75 John Montgomery et al., "Sound as an orientation clue for the pelagic larvae of reef fish and crustaceans" [2006] 51 *Advances in Marine Biology* 143–196.

76 Rob Williams et al., "Quiet(er) marine protected areas" [2015] 100(1) *Marine Pollution Bulletin* 154–161.

77 S.D. Simpson et al., "Attraction of settlement-stage coral reef fishes to reef noise" [2004] 276 *Marine Ecology Progress Series* 263–268.

marine life.[78] During the last century, noise pollution from cargo ships, holiday ships, seismic testing, and drilling has increased, and continues to grow.[79] Therefore, isolation and location can also influence success by having minimal disturbances.

When the factor of no-take zones (NTZs) is implemented in an MPA, it can deliver a significant outcome with regard to sustaining and enhancing biodiversity.[80] NTZs provide limitations to fishing within an MPA, or completely prevent it. The influence of NTZs protects the habitats and locations of targeted marine species, in order to safeguard their populations, thus restoring the integrity of marine ecosystems.[81] NTZs can improve fisheries in several ways. These include: decreasing fishing for susceptible species; influencing the growth of abundance of over-fished stocks; streamlining enforcement, and therefore compliance; and lessening incidental fishing and by-catch.[82] As can be seen, NTZs are highly influential in the success of MPAs, as they promote enhancing biodiversity, allowing MPAs to attain targets. The issue that occurs, however, is that NTZs are only able to reach their maximum effect for success if there is enforcement supporting them.[83] Without enforcement, fishing may continue, due to there being a low risk of being caught, and no "personal" consequence.

Another issue faced when establishing an MPA as an NTZ is disrupting local communities by removing traditions and livelihoods. Many undeveloped countries, particularly smaller ones and islands, rely on fishing to bring in an income, and as a stable food resource.[84] This will demotivate locals to support conservation, due to job losses and shortages in supply of food.[85] To ensure that this does not occur, MPAs need to establish a way to either limit fishing, thus making certain areas no-take, or with restrictions, for example no trawling or dynamite fishing, or to involve and support the community within its establishment, such as by getting them involved, and supplying jobs like being a conservation ranger or researcher.[86] The Galápagos Marine Reserve is

---

78 Chao Peng et al., "Noise in the Sea and Its Impacts on Marine Organisms" [2015] 12(10) *International Journal of Environmental Research and Public Health* 12304–12323.

79 Aril Slotte et al., "Acoustic mapping of pelagic fish distribution and abundance in relation to a seismic shooting area off the Norwegian west coast" [2004] 67(2) *Fisheries Research* 143–150.

80 Brock Bergseth, "Effective marine protected areas require a sea change in compliance management" [2017] 75(3) *ICES Journal of Marine Science* 1178–1180.

81 L. Pichegru et al., "Marine no-take zone rapidly benefits endangered penguin" [2010] 6(4) *Biology Letters* 498–501.

82 Michael Lockwood et al., *Managing Protected Areas: A Global Guide* (Routledge 2012), 614.

83 Stuart Campbell et al., "Weak compliance undermines the success of no-take zones in a large government-controlled marine protected area" [2012] 7(11) PLoS One e50074.

84 Andy Thorpe et al., "Fisheries and poverty reduction" [2007] 2(085) *CAB Reviews: Perspectives in Agriculture, Veterinary Science, Nutrition and Natural Resources* 1–12.

85 Neil Andrew et al., "Diagnosis and management of small-scale fisheries in developing countries" [2007] 8(3) *Fish and Fisheries* 227–240.

86 Daniel Pauly et al., "Towards sustainability in world fisheries" [2002] 418(6898) *Nature* 689.

partially an NTZ, and has demonstrated an effective way to monitor fishing.[87] By involving the fishermen, and training them in how to fish sustainably, they feel involved, and motivated to help conservation. Fishermen work alongside the scientists, helping them monitor the health of the fish and crustacean population.[88]

The Chagos Islands have, through their NTZ status, helped to reinstate the bigeye tuna, which was registered as vulnerable by the IUCN, due to overfishing.[89] The Chagos MPA has helped maintain biodiversity and enhance population size, as well as helping to avert millions of accidental catches: for example, prior to the designation, approximately 10,000 sharks were caught by mistake each year.[90] At the opposite end of the size spectrum, Lundy Island is also a designated NTZ, and as a success measure it has achieved a 127 per cent increase in the abundance of legal-sized lobsters,[91] with the population and size of both crabs and lobsters, outside as well as inside the NTZ, increasing.[92] MPAs that have been established as an NTZ can be more successful, specifically with the increased likelihood of enhancing biodiversity.[93] Enforcement, as a factor, does not just influence MPAs, but also affects how all the other factors operate. As discussed above, MPAs can be designated and created with legislation and enforcement, to help improve and protect areas from their stressors.[94] There are laws which could be used to prevent harmful activities, such as fishing and tourism, as well as to restrict those activities causing unintentional disruption. However, while it can appear that laws are lacking, in many cases there could simply be other inherent defects, such as a lack of enforcement and structural management, making them ineffective.[95] As such, laws may be adequate in some instances, but ineffectively implemented. If laws were successfully enforced, they

87 G.J. Edgar et al., "Bias in evaluating the effects of marine protected areas: the importance of baseline data for the Galapagos Marine Reserve" [2004] 31(3) *Environmental Conservation* 212–218.

88 National Geographic Education Staff, "Case Study: Galápagos Marine Reserve" (*National Geographic*, 29 January 2011) <https://www.nationalgeographic.org/news/case-study-galapagos-marine-reserve/>.

89 Chagos Conservation Trust, "Fish" (Chagos Conservation Trust, 2017) <http://chagos-trust.org/chagos/biodiversity>.

90 Ibid.

91 Evan Moland et al., "Lobster and cod benefit from small-scale northern marine protected areas: inference from an empirical before–after control-impact study" [2013] 280(1754) *Proceedings of the Royal Society B: Biological Sciences*.

92 Miles G. Hoskin, Ross A. Coleman and Liz von Carlshuasen, "Ecological effects of the Lundy No-take Zone: The first five years (2003–2007)", (2009, Natural England, DEFRA and WWF-UK).

93 Mark Costello and Bill Ballantine, "Biodiversity conservation should focus on no-take Marine Reserves: 94% of Marine Protected Areas allow fishing" [2015] 30(9) *Trends in Ecology and Evolution* 507–509.

94 Rob Williams et al. (n 76).

95 Angela Haren, "Reducing Noise Pollution from Commercial Shipping in the Channel Islands National Marine Sanctuary: A Case Study in Marine Protected Area Management of Underwater Noise" [2007] 10(2) *Journal of International Wildlife Law & Policy* 153–173.

may allow for more MPAs to achieve their targets. With legislative frameworks in place, enforcement of MPAs has the potential to be the most powerful influencing factor; improved management allows for conservation targets to be achieved more efficiently.

However, one issue is that MPA law can appear vague.[96] The framework surrounding MPAs lacks a clear and sufficiently detailed definition of what a "successful" MPA is, leaving uncertainty as to what aims and objectives should be, and when "MPA success" has actually been achieved.[97] Even in England, where the success of Marine Conservation Zones is clearly defined in law (to the EU standard of Good Environmental Status, for certain species or habitat types), the definition is confusing and scientifically obtuse. It essentially indicates that the species or habitat should not decline, but provides no legal guidance on magnitudes of change.[98]

MPAs require an effective enforcement mechanism, because the absence of one might simply create a "paper park".[99] Some MPA networks are managed through different regional or international scales of management, depending on the type of MPA.[100] This does not promote consistency, and could cause MPAs not to achieve their maximum potential. For example, where an MPA focuses on a mobile species, it may need to be managed at several spatial scales,[101] as some species may cross international boundaries, meaning the MPA may be of such a large size, due to covering migratory paths, that it is in multiple national jurisdictions.[102] This can cause complications if an MPA is not enforced through international legislation, but only national legislation, meaning that protection may be ineffective once the species has migrated across the national borders. Therefore, the IUCN places much importance on ensuring that different countries have similar legislation and objectives, especially when focusing on crucially important species that require protection.

Effective enforcement does not just involve the legal basis, but also how the MPA is maintained and monitored: for example, the Statia National Marine Park is patrolled regularly, to ensure park regulations are being abided by.[103] Other MPAs

---

96 Tom Appleby and Peter Jones, "The marine and coastal access act – A hornets' nest?" [2012] 36(1) *Marine Policy* 73–77.

97 J Gallacher et al., "Evaluating the success of a marine protected area: A systematic review approach" [2016] 183(1) *Journal of Environmental Management* 280–293.

98 Rick Stafford et al., "Simple, policy friendly, ecological interaction models from uncertain data and expert opinion" [2015] 118 *Ocean & Coastal Management* 88–96.

99 Alexis N. Rife et al., "When good intentions are not enough … Insights on networks of 'paper park' marine protected areas" [2013] 6(3) *Conservation Letters* 200–212.

100 William Gladstone et al., "Development and management of a network of marine protected areas in the Red Sea and Gulf of Aden region" [2003] 46(8) *Ocean Coast Management* 741–761.

101 Ibid.

102 Patricia Breen (n. 21).

103 St. Eustatius National Marine Park, "Nature" (Statia Tourism) <https://statia-tourism.com/about-statia/nature/>.

are more technologically advanced, such as the Galápagos Marine Reserve in Ecuador, where they use satellite-based GIS technology to monitor activities, to ensure tourists observe and obey the regulations set out.[104] The Galápagos MPA also trains locals on how to fish sustainably, using encouragement and education as enforcement, in addition to scientists conducting surveys and monitoring the MPA frequently.[105] With the enforcement that the Galápagos MPA has, it challenges prohibited activities, and less damage is occurring, thus continuing to promote biodiversity and sustainability. Fines and charges for violations of MPA rules are also a strong enforcer. Bunaken National Park has heavy fines and, potentially, jail sentences for those who breach the most rigorous rules governing the activities.[106] The breach of fishing in the NTZ areas of the Bunaken MPA can be punishable with a jail sentence of ten years, alongside a fine of up to 2 million rupiahs.

Effective enforcement for the ocean and its habitats can, however, sometimes appear to outbalance the needs of humanity. A key example is the uproar caused during the designation of the Chagos Islands, a British Indian Ocean Territory since 1965.[107] The British government, on 1 April 2010, declared the Chagos Islands as an MPA,[108] measuring 640,000 square kilometres, making it over twice the size of the UK.[109] In the 1960s and 1970s, the archipelago removed all Chagossian inhabitants – approximately 1,500 people – from its islands.[110] The absence of human intervention and activities allows for the MPA to be uncorrupted and pristine, making it a highly biodiverse and sustained environment.[111] However, the issue was raised that this enforcement was unjust;[112] evicting Chagossians from their home and not allowing them to return, in pursuit of conservation, appeared to be a huge balancing issue.[113] There has been a persistent legal battle between the Chagossians and

104 National Geographic Education Staff (n. 88).

105 Ibid.

106 M.V. Erdmann, "Who's minding the reef? Corruption and enforcement in Indonesia" [2001] 8 *SPC Live Fish Information Bulletin* 19–20.

107 Charles Sheppard, *Coral Reefs of the United Kingdom Overseas Territories* (Springer 2013), 7.

108 Stephen Allen, *The Chagos Islanders and International Law* (Bloomsbury Publishing 2014), 284.

109 Chagos Conservation Trust, "Chagos Marine Reserve" (Chagos Conservation Trust) <https://chagos-trust.org/chagos/overview>.

110 Owen Bowcott, "Chagos islanders cannot return home, UK Foreign Office confirms" (*The Guardian*, 16 November 2016) <https://www.theguardian.com/world/2016/nov/16/chagos-islanders-cannot-return-home-uk-foreign-office-confirms>.

111 Heather Koldewey et al., "Potential benefits to fisheries and biodiversity of the Chagos Archipelago/British Indian Ocean Territory as a no-take marine reserve" [2010] 60(11) *Marine Pollution Bulletin* 1906–1915.

112 Ibid.

113 Ibid.

the UK.[114] It appears that the inhabitants returning would jeopardise the marine environment within this MPA, and they are, therefore, forbidden to return.[115] Chagossians value fishing as a key source of employment and food,[116] and so would they really be able to enjoy a sustained society and future within an NTZ? The answer is most likely no, although they do support the MPA, but disagree with the NTZ.[117] The alternative of removing the NTZ would allow damage to occur to the biodiversity, and marine life numbers to plummet within the MPA, ruining its sustainability.[118] Hence, enforcement, although it may appear brutal and unjust, is a highly important factor in regard to creating a successful MPA.

Some MPAs have little enforcement: although the rules are set out, they are not abided by, due to the lack of implementation. The Cabo Pulmo National Marine Park has endured and suffered pressures from commercial fishing in the past ten years, due to a lack of enforcement.[119] Both Mexican and American residents desire that the MPA has restricted fishing regulations, and promotes sustainable fishing practices, but without the required government support and implementation this is proving a difficult undertaking.[120] Conservation efforts are being assisted in the right direction, but the financial aid and federal enforcement is currently scarce,[121] and needs dramatic improvement.

Looking beyond the management and enforcement of an MPA, the wider environment also needs to be considered. MPAs are effective in conserving and enhancing nature; however, we also need to focus on management for biodiversity across the wider seascape for them to be effective. Isolation, when viewed as a method for "management", for other factors such as tourism and NTZs, can appear indolent, as less focus will need to be placed on enforcement and the surrounding environment.

The six factors discussed above, although the most influential, are not the only factors that affect MPAs. Several other factors can be considered in discussion and analysis. However, these have not been contemplated in the BBN that was

---

114 Press Association, "Chagos islanders go to supreme court in battle to be allowed home" (*The Guardian*, 22 June 2015) <https://www.theguardian.com/world/2015/jun/22/chagos-islanders-supreme-court-battle-return-home>.

115 Sandra Evers and Marry Kooy, *Eviction from the Chagos Islands: Displacement and Struggle for Identity Against Two World Powers* (Brill 2011).

116 Ibid.

117 David Hughes, "Chagos marine reserve decision 'ignored exiled islanders'" (*Independent*, 6 April 2010) <http://www.independent.co.uk/news/world/africa/chagos-marine-reserve-decision-ignored-exiled-islanders-1937297.html>.

118 Press Association (n. 114).

119 Baja Life Online, "Welcome to Cabo Pulmo National Marine Park" (Cabo Pulmo National Marine Park) <http://www.cabopulmopark.com>.

120 Ibid.

121 Baja Life Online, "The Reef" (Cabo Pulmo National Marine Park) <http://www.cabopulmopark.com/thereef>.

carried out. This is due to such factors either not being an occurring element in all MPAs, or being problematic to measure. Other factors that influence an MPA's success include: the state the MPA was in when it was designated, such as an unspoiled reef with rich biodiversity; climate change; coral bleaching occurring there; and education – where a society is well educated about the MPA and conservation, it is more likely to succeed.[122] However, those MPAs where there is no education or awareness are overlooked and more likely to be ignored, as people are unaware of the existence and motive, as well as the importance of conservation, causing ineffectiveness.

3. LEGAL BASIS

MPAs are an instrument requiring strong foundations to operate effectively, and this starts with the legal basis. The designation of MPAs, and the legislation surrounding them, revolve around maintaining a balance between maximising ecological conservation goals and allowing limited human activities, such as tourism and fishing.[123] MPAs are working to achieve an international goal, and therefore, as well as national laws, international legislation is at the core of enforcement.[124] Having a plethora of laws can prove to be confusing, although international legislation does act as a base for all laws, promoting a level of consistency. This allows for a more strategic approach, where nations can learn and build from each other, to ensure success in sustainability and biodiversity in our marine environment. The world, as a whole, is focusing on resolving the issues of the depletion of natural resources and losses of biodiversity within our oceans, and MPAs are the renovating tool, repairing the loss.[125] This shows how important it is that we focus on the management and designation that surrounds MPA legislation.

Currently, there is no international convention wholly devoted to marine spatial planning. However, in 1994, the United Nations (UN) Convention on the Law of the Sea 1982[126] (UNCLOS) expanded to encompass relevant regulations.[127] The majority of MPAs already established are built on geographical principles,

122 Timothy McClanahan et al., "A Comparison of Marine Protected Areas and Alternative Approaches to Coral-Reef Management" [2005] 16(14) *Current Biology* 1408–1413.

123 Peter Jones et al., *Governing Marine Protected Areas: Getting the Balance Right* (UNEP 2011).

124 B.C. O'Leary et al., "The first network of marine protected areas (MPAs) in the high seas: The process, the challenges and where next" 36(3) (2012) *Marine Policy* 598–605.

125 Ibid.

126 United Nations Convention on the Law of the Sea (Montego Bay) 10 December 1982, in force 16 November 1994; 21 ILM 1261 (1982) (1982 UNCLOS).

127 Myron Nordquist and Satya Nandan, *United Nations Convention on the Law of the Sea 1982, Volume VII: A Commentary* (Martinus Nijhoff Publishers 2011).

within jurisdictional borders founded on UNCLOS,[128] which allows for MPAs to be more easily managed, due to having a clear set location in which national laws can be followed. It provides clear definitions and differentiations between zones of the ocean that are under national jurisdiction, and those areas beyond it. An agreement was established, in 2023, under UNCLOS: a new treaty, which was reached by the Intergovernmental Conference on Marine Biodiversity of Areas Beyond National Jurisdiction (BBNJ).[129] This allows for areas beyond national jurisdictions, which are often designated as the "high seas", to have stronger protection, and to resolve the lack of precision and jurisdiction with which they were previously faced.[130]

UNCLOS is often referred to as the constitution for the oceans,[131] and it defines the different marine districts, in which different coastal states can exercise jurisdiction.[132] The BBNJ Treaty focuses on the high seas, with the objective of ensuring that these areas beyond national jurisdiction conserve and provide sustainable use of marine biological diversity, through international coordination and cooperation, implementing the Convention effectively for the present and long term.[133] The BBNJ Treaty will allow for large MPAs to be established, with the aim of preventing biodiversity loss and tackling environmental degradation; it will allow for gaps in the current establishment of high seas MPAs to be filled.[134] Although it is currently a new agreement, not exhaustive in regard to elaborating tools and mechanisms for marine conservation, and it focuses on the high seas and not the ocean as a whole, it has provided a strong framework and global goal. By having states agreeing on such measures, it allows for MPA management and designation to run as smoothly as possible, with less confusion than if it was uncoordinated. Coordination also allows for targets and strategies to be comparable, allowing for improvements and MPA system updates to be made more efficient and suitable. We are constantly learning about new factors, and what influences success, helping us to factor this learning into the management process strategy, by making a practical adaption.

---

128 Paul Goriup (n. 26), 55.

129 General Assembly resolution 72/249, "The rule of law at the national and international levels", A/RES/67/97 (14 December 2012), <undocs.org/en/A/RES/67/97>.

130 United Nations Convention on the Law of the Sea (New York) 20 February–3 March 2023, "Intergovernmental Conference on an international legally binding instrument under the United Nations Convention on the Law of the Sea on the conservation and sustainable use of marine biological diversity of areas beyond national jurisdiction", Resumed fifth session.

131 Tommy Koh, President of UNCLOS III, "A Constitution for the Oceans" (1982) <https://www.un.org/depts/los/convention_agreements/texts/koh_english.pdf>.

132 Paul Goriup (n. 26), 89.

133 United Nations Convention on the Law of the Sea (n. 130).

134 WWF, "WWF: Landmark High Seas Treaty agreed, ushering in new rules for two-thirds of the ocean" (WWF, 4 March 2023) <https://wwf.panda.org/?7913966/landmark-high-seas-treaty-agreed>.

UNCLOS manages the maritime activities of countries, which must respect the marine environment, in order to ensure that biodiversity is not depleted, thus achieving MPA targets. Furthermore, UNCLOS also promotes the protection of "rare or fragile ecosystems", along with areas where marine species and resources are "depleted, threatened or endangered", safeguarding their habitats.[135] This emphasises how a diverse range of protection is needed.

The aforementioned CBD implemented an international 2020 objective,[136] which reinforced the concept that, globally, MPAs are seen as a long-term instrument, enforcing the idea that they should be used and respected to repair and sustain our oceans' biodiversity. These targets allowed for MPAs to be recognised internationally, and to be considered a key legislative tool that should be abided by globally once established. The effectiveness of legislation helps to ensure that MPAs cause the oceans to be healthy, abundant and sustainable, as well as increasing the health of the oceans' inhabitants. By enforcing MPAs, this could allow not only for the ocean itself to be sustained, but also for an efficient and healthy worldwide environment to be generated.

The IUCN is a highly important governing body with both state and non-governmental members, allowing for diverse opinions, to help ensure the highest MPA success rate possible. Designation and management are carried out by the IUCN for MPAs, giving it a highly significant status in the MPA sector, and thus making the IUCN highly respected on a global scale, influencing all countries to manage MPAs at identical levels, and through similar strategies. The IUCN also enables the legal aspect of an MPA to be recognised at an international level. Policies are set through voting at episodic conferences of the World Conservation Congress, and by resolution.[137] The voting system provides an overall consensus from those who have a vested interest, and are knowledgeable in nature conservation.[138] This creates precision when designating the correct category and management approach, meaning MPAs can meet their targets more efficiently. By coming to international unanimous decisions, it allows for all governmental and national parties to become a part of the ocean protection movement, motivating their input, and allowing for more MPAs to be established, enhancing global biodiversity and sustainability.

---

135 Art.194, UNCLOS (n. 126).

136 Convention on Biological Diversity (n. 58).

137 Nigel Dudley and Marc Hockings, "Marine protected area governance and effectiveness across networks" [2017] *Management of Marine Protected Areas* 69–87.

138 Ibid.

Table 1. IUCN categories for MPAs[139]

Category	Characteristics	Primary Objective
Ia Strict Nature Reserve	Strictly set aside safeguarded areas that are established to protect and enhance biodiversity, as well as geological/geomorphological qualities. Human visitation is limited, to guarantee protection of the conservation principles. These protected areas can act as crucial indication areas for monitoring and scientific research.	To ensure protection of species, ecosystems and geodiversity features on a regional, national or global scale. These elements will have been produced entirely or predominantly by non-human dynamics, and will be damaged when exposed to all but very precautious human impact.
Ib Wilderness Area	Frequently large unmodified or marginally modified protected areas. They preserve their natural influence and character, with no enduring human habitation. Protected to reserve their natural condition.	To ensure current and future generations have the prospect to experience such areas they are to safeguard natural areas and their long-term ecological integrity. They are free from modern infrastructures, undisrupted by substantial human activities and where natural energies and progressions are dominating.
II National Park	An area that is set aside to protect large scale environmental procedures which is a large natural or near natural site. It is established to also safeguard ecosystems and species with the characteristic of the area. Thus providing an establishment for culturally and environmentally scientific, spiritual, recreational and educational visitor opportunities.	To promote recreation and education, whilst protecting the natural biodiversity and the fundamental ecological structure, supporting the environmental progressions.
III Natural Monument of Feature	Areas that are generally quite small and have a high visitor value. Set to protect a certain natural monument, which can be a sea mount, geological feature such as a cave, land mount, submarine cavern or a living feature such as an ancient grove.	To protect the natural monument/feature and the associated habitats and biodiversity surrounding it.

139 Nigel Dudley, *Guidelines for Applying Protected Area Management Categories*, Best Practice Protected Area Guidelines Series No. 21, IUCN (Gland 2008).

IV Habitat/Species Management Area	In order to sustain habitats or achieve the necessities of certain species, many protected areas need frequent and active interventions. However, it is not a requirement of category IV. The management of these areas reflect the priority of protecting a specific habitat or species.	To sustain, conserve and reinstate species and habitats.
V Protected Landscape/Seascape	An area which has developed a distinctive character with a significant biological, ecological, scenic and cultural value over time due to the interaction with people and nature. Also, where protecting the integrity of this interaction is fundamental to sustain and safeguard the area, and the nature conservation and values associated with it.	By using traditional management processes, it is priority to sustain and protect significant seascapes and landscapes, alongside the associated nature conservation and other principles created by the interactions with humans.
VI Protected area with sustainable use of Natural Resources	A normally large protected area, where majority is in a natural condition, and a part being under sustainable natural resource management. These areas conserve habitats and ecosystems, using traditional natural resource management systems and associated cultural values.	To sustain and protect the natural ecosystems alongside the use of natural resources, allowing for sustainable and conservation use to be mutually beneficial.

The IUCN classifies protected areas using one of six protected area management categories. MPAs are all designated for different reasons, so have different management objectives which influence which category they fall into (see Table 1 above).[140] By establishing different categories, it helps ensure a better management system, and when an MPA is established, the most related category is associated with it, implementing the most suitable management. This allows for MPA protection to be efficient, and designated goals to be achieved.[141] The UN, several national governments, and other international bodies, all recognise these categories as the global standard for recording and defining MPAs, and are incorporating them into legislation.[142] Such global recognition allows for a clear process to be followed, allowing us to work on reaching the best management system possible on a worldwide scale. Global recognition enables the majority of MPA processes to be similar and, therefore, uncomplicated. By having this straightforward management system, it influences a more conscious effort to establish more MPAs, and protect a higher percentage of the world's oceans, enhancing biodiversity and sustainability.

What is apparent is that setting these categories allows for a consensus as to what MPA significances are likely to be, and provides accommodation for multiple MPA objectives.[143] This system allows categorisation of MPAs to be an easier task, helping inform and guide management appropriately, to achieve the desired results.[144]

To help decide the category most suited for an MPA, the 75 per cent rule has been established. This rule establishes that the primary management aims should apply to at least three-quarters of the MPA. Several MPAs could encompass specific zones which could be used for other uses, such as fishing or tourism, in what is otherwise a strictly safeguarded MPA.[145] Within certain MPAs, the remaining 25 per cent can be movable, meaning that designated zones can be adjusted: for example, where a fishing zone might be accessible can be moved occasionally, in order to avoid over-fishing, allowing stocks and biodiversity to replenish in the previously fished-in area.[146] If an MPA which is nested within a larger MPA is managed differently, a different category may be better suited, and therefore that encompassed MPA can have its own category.[147]

140 Jon Day et al., *Guidelines for applying the IUCN protected area management categories to marine protected areas* (IUCN 2012).
141 Nigel Dudley (n. 139).
142 Ibid.
143 Nigel Dudley and Marc Hockings (n. 137).
144 Nigel Dudley (n. 139).
145 Nigel Dudley and Marc Hockings (n. 137).
146 Nigel Dudley (n. 139).
147 Michael J. Emslie et al., "Expectations and Outcomes of Reserve Network Performance following Re-zoning of the Great Barrier Reef Marine Park" [2015] 25(8) *Current Biology* 1–10.

Similarly, different zones within an MPA can have their own categories, as long as the zones are fixed, and described in law.[148]

Research conducted by Costello and Ballantine established that the IUCN management categories may not be followed as expected, due to 94 per cent of MPAs still allowing for fishing to take place within them.[149] This shows that few MPAs actually ban all types of fishing, implying that the IUCN categories are being followed as a guideline, and not as strictly as intended, meaning that they are being misapplied. This suggests that a management programme is yet to be established that successfully applies and works for all countries, especially where culture may value and rely on certain aspects, such as fishing.

The IUCN have also established a typology of governance types as to who governs an MPA, i.e. who has the responsibility and authority for the protected area in question (See Table 2 below). This can help cater to the management system and requirements an MPA needs, as well as allowing for the needs of the potential governors, such as stakeholders and the community. The involvement of those with a vested interest in an MPA, such as local fishermen etc., ensures promotion and support for enhancing its effectiveness, and achieving objectives such as the need for biodiversity, and for reefs and habitats to be sustained.[150]

Table 2. Governance categories for MPAs[151]

Type	Name	Description
A	Governance by government	• National or federal agency/ministry in charge • Sub-national agency/ministry in charge • Government-delegated management
B	Shared governance	• Diverse influences, collaborative management • Pluralist management, joint management • Several levels over frontiers – transboundary management
C	Private governance	• By a non-profit organisation e.g. university or NGO • By an individual owner • By a profitable organisation such as a corporate company
D	Governance by indigenous peoples and local communities	• Native and local persons conserved territories • An area declared and run by local the community e.g. community conserved areas

148 Ibid.

149 Mark Costello and Bill Ballantine (n. 93).

150 Nathan Bennett and Philip Dearden, "Why local people do not support conservation: Community perceptions of marine protected area livelihood impacts, governance and management in Thailand" [2014] 44 *Marine Policy* 107–116.

151 Nigel Dudley (n. 139).

The six management categories established by the IUCN allow for an internationally recognised MPA management system to be in place, giving a clear representation of the types of MPAs in a country, and how they are being managed. By having this clear picture, it allows for all countries to maintain a similar level for their MPAs, and adapt, compare and review other MPAs. Albeit that this is a logical operation, information provided in 2014 established that the IUCN management categories were not yet in full force, with only half of the world's MPAs having a management category assigned by government.[152] Therefore, this management tool is only going to work at full effectiveness if all countries abide by the system, to achieve the best outcome in enhancing MPA management and sustainability. Otherwise, if each country follows a different management process, lines will become blurred, and the system ineffective.

In the absence of internationally recognised standards for MPAs in regard to quality management and enforcement practices,[153] there are the globally recognised ratings of the International Organization for Standardization (ISO), which is a highly valued international leader[154] for quality (ISO 9000), and environmental management standards (ISO 14000).[155] Therefore, it is argued that countries should apply the ISO 14001 standard, which is for environmental enforcement and management systems.[156] The environmental management standards (14000) have been enhanced and changed, based upon considerations and agreements from an extensive base of stakeholder groups, and are accepted and highly valued by both private sectors and the public around the globe.[157] Primarily, these are applied to terrestrial parks, but, if applied to MPAs, the system can provide an adaptive system, which allows integration with prevailing practices.[158] The precedent already set in these standards being applied to a natural environment could, logically, be applied to MPAs.

Having an effective management system like the ISO 14000 would encourage a constant cycle of planning, implementing, reviewing and improving the procedures undertaken to meet the MPA environmental objectives. This should lead to sustainability and enhanced biodiversity,[159] with the system

152 D Juffe-Bignoli et al., *Protected Planet Report 2014* (UNEP-WCMC 2014).

153 Myles Thompson et al., "ISO 14001: Towards international quality environmental management standards for marine protected areas" [2008] 51(11) *Ocean & Coastal Management* 727–739.

154 T. Rotherham, "Raising standards: IUCN and the future of ISO 14001, Issues and options" [2001] (09-01) *Biodiversity Economics* 88.

155 Myles Thompson et al. (n. 153).

156 Ibid.

157 Paula Murray, "International Environmental Management Standard, ISO 14000: A Non-Tariff Barrier or a Step to an Emerging Global Environmental Policy" [1997] *Journal of International Economic Law* 577.

158 Myles Thompson et al. (n. 153).

159 K. McKinley et al., *The ISO 14000 essentials: a practical guide to implementing the ISO 14000 standard* (Canadian Standards Association 1996), 97.

allowing for continuous improvement, meaning that occurring problems can be resolved. Thompson et al. have suggested adapting the ISO 14001 standard when it comes to MPA management.[160] MPAs are unique in terms of water being a moving body, and with many migratory species. If an adaption was put in place, providing international standards for MPAs, it would likely enhance success rates in national reserve networks, but mainly allow for a more connected transnational approach for MPA enforcement and management.[161] This would allow for MPAs to enhance sustainability and biodiversity at a more significant rate.

Furthermore, the application of the new clause 4 of the ISO 14001 to MPAs would promote the factoring in of environmental impacts and changes.[162] The clause does this by stating that, when establishing an environmental management system, an organisation should start by defining the scope of management, which wholly depends upon an organisation's environmental policy, the conditions in which it operates, and the nature of the activities that occur there.[163] When looking at using the ISO 14001 for MPAs, it should be adapted so that the MPA is considered the organisation, providing services such as tourism and habitat protection, and goods such as fishery resources. Flora, fauna, fisheries and tourism are examples of the operation units an MPA goes through, which all have diverse activities occurring within and surrounding the MPA.[164] To define the MPAs' management scope, activities that occur there will have to be evaluated, alongside the broadness of the range of those activities. The legislation behind the MPA and authority in place should also be considered, as well as the restrictions the MPA has.[165] By looking at the core influencing factors, this can help complement the plan with the needs and attributes of the MPA, causing an effective system to be in place. The structure is already in place, and, therefore, could be implemented and adapted to apply to all MPAs.

The CBD entered into force in 1993,[166] with the aim of protecting global biodiversity,[167] setting the key target that "at least 10% of each of the world's ecological regions will be effectively conserved (CBD Decision VII/30, Target 1.1)" by 2010.[168] This target could be viewed as vague, as there was no

160 Myles Thompson et al. (n. 153).
161 Patricia Breen (n. 21).
162 International Organization for Standardization, *ISO 14001: Environmental management systems – specifications with guidance* (ISO 2004), 31.
163 Ibid.
164 Myles Thompson et al. (n. 153).
165 Graeme Kelleher and Richard Kenchington, *Guidelines for Establishing Marine Protected Areas* (vol. 3, IUCN 1991).
166 CBD (n. 60).
167 Patricia Breen (n. 21).
168 CBD (n. 60), division VII/30, 20 February 2004, in *Report of the Seventh Meeting of the Conference of the Parties to the Convention on Biological Diversity.*

definition of what "effectively conserved" meant. COP10 then adapted this target, as it had not been achieved, to be reached by 2020; however, this also was not achieved.

These targets have been criticised, in that they result in the designation of large MPAs to help meet percentage targets, rather than designating an MPA for a specific purpose, and focusing on those areas that need help.[169] Our oceans appear to be full of large, young MPAs. However, it could also be argued that this is a positive result of MPA success: we have learnt the importance and power of MPAs, and are, therefore, designating them bigger than ever before. By the CBD setting these objectives, it allows for all countries to be working towards the same target, meaning marine protection on a global scale. However, have the CBD and COP10 set a standard? The targets have been clear, but have lacked guidance. With the 10 per cent target not being achieved, we need to look at management when focusing on the new 2030 target, rather than just setting it and leaving countries to deal with it themselves. The BBNJ Treaty states that countries will need to assess the environmental impact of activities (EIA) in the oceans; however, it is noted that countries will conduct their own scoring, and make the ultimate decision on the environmental impact an activity would cause.[170] Article 205 states the requirement to provide assessment and monitoring reports to competent international organisations; however, it does not elaborate on how these should be carried out.[171] Standardisation appears to be lacking before the Treaty has even begun, and so we should combine the management systems we have in place to ensure that designated MPAs are being managed and monitored efficiently. If the management systems of the ISO 14001 were combined with the targets of the CBD and COP10, a clear structure would be set in place to help make these targets achievable. Instead, we appear to just keep setting bigger targets, for example 30 per cent of the oceans to be protected by 2030,[172] when we have not even reached the original target.[173]

Although all countries have been influenced by international law, each country's laws will still vary from one to another.[174] The reason that the national

---

169 P.J.S. Jones and E.M. De Santo, "*Viewpoint* – Is the race for remote, very large marine protected areas (VLMPAs) taking us down the wrong track?" [2016] 73 *Marine Policy* 231–234.

170 Kahlil Hassanali, "Internationalization of EIA in a new marine biodiversity agreement under the Law of the Sea Convention: A proposal for a tiered approach to review and decision-making" [2021] 87(106554) *Environmental Impact Assessment Review*.

171 Ibid.

172 United Nations, "UN delegates reach historic agreement on protecting marine biodiversity in international waters" (United Nations, 5 March 2023) <https://news.un.org/en/story/2023/03/1134157>.

173 Ibid.

174 Suzanne J. Boyes and Michael Elliott, "Marine legislation – The ultimate 'horrendogram': International law, European directives and national implementation" [2014] 86(1–2) *Marine Pollution Bulletin* 39–47.

laws vary is due to each country having different stressors and factors influencing their laws and enforcement methods, at different levels and strengths.[175] With all these different legislations in place, it makes establishing and managing MPAs a difficult task. The contrasting legal barriers and designations mean the lines of the legal map are blurred and confusing. The EU alone has adopted more than 200 pieces of legislation that have direct effects on marine management,[176] so when considering the global scale of legislation, it is overwhelming. There are so many overlapping laws, and there are questions as to which ones we should follow, and which ones should we ignore.[177] Furthermore, it has been suggested that there are gaps in the legislation which cause the legal perspective to appear unclear.[178]

International legal requirements stemming from international and EU law can be presented in complex structures, known colloquially as the "horrendogram".[179] The horrendogram[180] illustrates the complexity of legislation currently being used to conserve and manage our marine, coastal and transitional waters. The horrendogram is a diagram created to map out the international, European and national laws currently set out and proposed, to protect our marine environment.[181] This diagram was created by S Boyes and M Elliott to display the complex nature of the legislation in place.[182] The centre of the horrendogram displays the international treaties, protocols and conventions which, on a worldwide scale, have been signed by many countries, who have all agreed to uphold them.[183] The horrendogram[184] is a complex structure, but here it establishes the vast amount of legislation in place on a global scale, and explains why it is viewed as being so complex. It shows the vast amount of legislation, illustrating how overwhelming it is. The authors of the horrendogram[185] have not elaborated on the fact that, once these laws are unpicked, one can then see that they do not promote high levels of protection, and have left room for gaps and confusion. These gaps represent lack of detail, which result in MPAs not being able to reach their full potential of success when conserving the oceans. There is even such a lack of detail that it does not define the basics of what effective conservation is; this needs to be the starting point of all laws surrounding MPAs, to ensure the promotion of high level of biodiversity.

---

175 Michael Elliott, "Integrated marine science and management: Wading through the morass" [2014] 86(1–2) *Marine Pollution Bulletin* 1–4.

176 Suzanne J. Boyes and Michael Elliott (n. 174).

177 Raoul Beunen et al., "Implementation and Integration of EU Environmental Directives. Experiences from the Netherlands" [2009] 19(1) *Environmental Policy and Governance* 57–69.

178 Suzanne J. Boyes and Michael Elliott (n. 174).

179 Ibid.

180 Ibid.

181 Ibid.

182 Ibid.

183 Ibid.

184 Ibid.

185 Ibid.

Each country has to adapt to its surroundings and stressors, in order to achieve the most sufficient outcome, and allow MPAs to achieve their goals more efficiently.[186] More developed countries may focus on factors such as tourism, whereas underdeveloped countries may focus on methods of fishing, due to their reliance on it for income, and as a food source; the focus could be to ensure only sustainable methods of fishing are used, deterring harmful extractions such as trawling and dynamite fishing.[187] This is where the CBD is, unfortunately, weak and lacking in guidance.[188] We need clear guidance if we are to have sufficient MPAs. It is, therefore, suggested that a globally-recognised management standard like the ISO 14001 might offer leadership and clarity, if it is adapted to promote a standardised but bespoke MPA process.

UNCLOS remains one of the most fundamental conventions, if not *the* most fundamental, and it provides a definition for the obligations and rights of coastal and other states in the differentiated marine legal areas.[189] Without UNCLOS providing the foundation it does, legislation and enforcement would be unclear compared to what it is now.[190] Obligations and rights would be blurred and, therefore, could be non-existent or weakly enforced, causing MPAs to be an ineffective tool, diminishing ocean biodiversity and making the ocean an unsustainable environment.[191] Therefore, ISO 14001 should take the basis of UNCLOS to help establish its management system. UNCLOS helps to define the legal lines between jurisdictions, and work on a basis where legislation is identical, because if stripped back to basics, all jurisdictions appear to want the same outcome: sustainability, biodiversity, and protection of the marine environment, thus making the combination of ISO 14001 and UNCLOS best suited for a global scale.

The idea of adapting the ISO 14001 would not only allow for effective management, but establish continuous improvement.[192] It would help to codify the current MPA management guidelines, providing the paramount practices internationally. Having this level of international similarity would mean awareness could be raised, communication increased, and public and community engagement in the planning process improved. By including the public, it would encourage positive behaviour in following the management system

186 Nathan Bennett and Philip Dearden, "From measuring outcomes to providing inputs: Governance, management, and local development for more effective marine protected areas" [2014] 50(A) *Marine Policy* 96–110.

187 Mimi Lam, "Of Fish and Fishermen: Shifting Societal Baselines to Reduce Environmental Harm in Fisheries" [2012]17(4) *Ecology and Society* 18.

188 Kerry ten Kate, "Science and the Convention on Biological Diversity" [2002] 295(5564) *Science* 2371–2372.

189 Bleuenn Guilloux, "Which International Law for Ocean and Climate?" [2016] 2(2) *Ocean and Climate Scientific Notes* 79–88.

190 Ibid.

191 Ibid.

192 K. McKinley et al. (n. 159).

set out, acting as the system's enforcer, reducing potential disagreements, and eliminating the confusion of multiple global systems. Accordingly, an efficient system would be in place for restoring our oceans, and helping to reverse the damage to them. If there was an internationally-recognised management system applied globally to all MPAs, the knock-on effect from this standardisation would be an increase in the abundancy of flora and fauna,[193] thus generating positive impacts on the health of the marine environment,[194] and, ultimately, promoting the sustainability of our oceans.[195]

One of the key causes of "failure" in management is the mismatch between the enforcement to be put in place, the measures needing to be taken to ensure an MPA achieves its objectives, and the exact goals the MPA has been established to achieve.[196] If each MPA had a clear management plan which outlined its objectives, it would allow targets to be achieved, and biodiversity to increase abundantly at a more efficient speed, ensuring that objectives would be achieved.[197]

When reviewing the influence and role of management and legislation within MPAs, what is apparent is the complexity of factoring in scientific and legal concepts, which at times seems like "mixing water and oil".[198] To remedy this problem, standardisation needs to be in place for MPAs to have an effective management system.[199] ISO 14001, with the influence of UNCLOS and the targets of CBD and COP, could be the standardisation that will ensure that our MPAs are managed sustainably, thus promoting greater biodiversity, and reaching their targets. Once an effective system with clear guidelines is in place, this will allow a real difference in the way MPAs are viewed, and shorten the length of time it takes for their targets to be met.

4. FACTORS AFFECTING THE ECOLOGICAL SUCCESS OF MPAs

Ocean ecosystems are under pressure from a variety of anthropogenic sources, notably overfishing and climate change.[200] MPAs can be a scientifically proven

193 Patrick Christie, "Marine Protected Areas as Biological Successes and Social Failures in Southeast Asia" [2004] 42 *American Fisheries Society Symposium* 155–164.

194 Boris Worm et al. (n. 1).

195 Daniel Pauly et al. (n. 86).

196 Carolyn K. Robb et al., "Commercial fisheries closures in marine protected areas on Canada's Pacific coast: The exception, not the rule" [2011] 35(3) *Marine Policy* 309–316.

197 Ibid.

198 Oliver Houck, "Tales from a Troubled Marriage: Science and Law in Environmental Policy" [2003] 302(5652) *Science* 1926–1929.

199 Myles Thompson et al. (n. 153).

200 Annette C. Broderick, "Grand challenges in marine conservation and sustainable use" [2015] 2 *Frontiers in Marine Science* 11.

and legally enforceable method to manage the marine environment,[201] and one of the key methods is recommended by the CBD, which currently has targets for 30 per cent of the world's oceans to be protected by 2030.[202]

While there are many conservation success stories from MPAs,[203] other studies have demonstrated that poorly managed MPAs may have no ecological benefit,[204] and in many cases ecological data can be lacking in demonstrating successful outcomes.[205] Furthermore, there is often a divide in how data is collected for MPAs, with some focusing on management and governance, and some providing ecological data, but few providing both.[206]

Edgar et al. provide a comprehensive overview of the most important factors for creating an ecologically successful MPA,[207] commonly known as the NEOLI factors (no take, enforced, old, large and isolated). However, trends indicate that more MPAs are being designated, to help meet CBD targets,[208] several of which have been large, but due to their recent designation, relatively young.

There is considerable confusion about what should constitute an MPA. For example, the CBD definition suggests an MPA should be "managed to achieve specific conservation objectives".[209] Yet, the IUCN definition suggests that MPAs should "achieve the long-term conservation of nature with associated ecosystem services and cultural values".[210] As such, it is unclear exactly how, and to what extent, social conservation benefits should be considered, as part of evaluating an MPA's success. While this contribution will define success solely in ecological terms (likelihood of increasing biodiversity, population sizes or sizes of individuals), it will also include tourism, as a potential social

---

201 Marija Sciberras, "Evaluating the biological effectiveness of fully and partially protected marine areas" [2013] 2 *Environmental Evidence* 4.

202 Convention on Biological Diversity (n. 61).

203 Fiona R. Gell and Callum M. Roberts, "Benefits Beyond Boundaries: The Fishery Effects of Marine Reserves" [2003] 18 *Trends in Ecology and Evolution* 448–455; M. Sciberras (n. 201); David A. Gill et al., "Capacity shortfalls hinder the performance of marine protected areas globally" [2017] 543 *Nature* 665–669; Mark Costello and Bill Ballantine (n. 93); Benjamin Halpern et al. (n. 62).

204 Graham Edgar et al. (n. 32); David A. Gill et al. (n. 203); Richard Stafford et al., "An integrated evaluation of potential management processes on marine reserves in continental Ecuador based on a Bayesian belief network model" [2016] 121 *Ocean & Coastal Management* 60–69.

205 Richard Stafford et al., "Lack of evidence that governance structures provide real ecological benefits in marine protected areas" [2018] 152 *Ocean and Coastal Management* 57–61; David A. Gill et al. (n. 203).

206 Ibid.

207 Graham Edgar et al. (n. 32).

208 Derek P. Tittensor et al., "A mid-term analysis of progress toward international biodiversity targets" [2014] 346 *Science* 241–4; Callum M. Roberts et al., "Marine reserves can mitigate and promote adaptation to climate change" [2017] 114(24) *Proceedings of the National Academy of Sciences* 6167–6175.

209 United Nations Convention on Biological Diversity (n. 27).

210 Nigel Dudley (n. 139).

and economic benefit, but likely ecological hindrance to the ecological success of an MPA.[211]

There are clear potential conflicts between the "success" factors of an MPA. For example, without more resources and staff, larger-sized and isolated MPAs will be more difficult to enforce than a small MPA in full view from land. Indeed, a lack of resources has been identified as a key factor in MPAs not achieving their potential.[212] For many MPAs, economic viability must be considered, especially within the local community, if local fishing practices will be displaced.[213] As such, designation, governance and enforcement of MPAs is a delicate task, especially if multiple stakeholders are included in these processes.[214]

This contribution will re-evaluate the factors causing success of MPAs, using data from MPAs around the world. It will consider the NEOLI factors, as well as tourism (see Table 3), to predict the ecological success of MPAs using a BBN.[215] It will also consider the effects of interactions between the six factors, as well as the effects on factors including fish catch and overall local economic income, on the success scores of the MPAs.

Table 3. Factors which can contribute to the success of MPAs

Influencing factor	Why is this factor influential and important?
Size	Size influences MPAs in achieving their targets. The bigger the MPA, the more likely it is to be successful in enriching biodiversity and sustainability in that area, predominantly where MPAs are established to recover from overfishing, and restore and repair coral reefs.[216]
Age	Age impacts on, and enhances, the benefits an MPA provides.[217] The older an MPA, the more likely it is to be nearer to achieving its objectives. However, each MPA differs: for example, some populations may take decades to recover[218] – this could be due to the condition it was in before it was designated. Furthermore, older MPAs should have greater fish density than younger ones.[219]

(continued)

211 Marco Milazzo et al., "The Impact of Human Recreational Activities in Marine Protected Areas: What Lessons Should Be Learnt in the Mediterranean Sea?" [2002] 23 *Marine Ecology* 280–290; P.F.M. Lopes et al., "Fisheries, tourism, and marine protected areas: Conflicting or synergistic interactions?" [2015] 16 *Ecosystem Services* 333–340.

212 David A. Gill et al. (n. 203).

213 Paige West et al., "Parks and Peoples: The Social Impact of Protected Areas" [2006] 35 *Review of Anthropology* 251–277; Richard Stafford et al., "Lack of evidence that governance structures provide real ecological benefits in marine protected areas" (n. 205).

214 Estelle Jones et al., "Are fisheries-dependent communities in Scotland really maritime-dependent communities?" [2014] 95 *Ocean & Coastal Management* 254–263.

215 Rick Stafford et al. (n. 98).

216 Benjamin Halpern et al. (n. 62).

217 Phillip Molloy et al. (n. 54).

218 Ransom A. Myers et al. (n. 55).

219 Phillip Molloy et al. (n. 54).

Table 3 *continued*

Influencing factor	Why is this factor influential and important?
Tourism	Tourism is a great threat to the oceans, and causes biodiversity and sustainability to plummet. This is due to human disturbance through diving, swimming, using boats, pollution, and many other activities. These undertakings effect the water quality, demolish habitats, and consequently cause huge disruption to the environment.[220] Therefore, the more tourism, the more human disturbance, leading to disruption of biodiversity. Tourism can be beneficial, however, if done in the correct manner and monitored, raising awareness and money to help enforcement in sustaining the MPA.
NTZ or fishing restrictions?	MPAs that are not NTZs can bring a lot of disturbances with them, with several methods of fishing not only destroying habitats but extracting fish, and involving the crossing of boats. All of this can reduce biodiversity, and deter fish from their usual routines and breeding patterns. NTZs allow for MPAs to recover more quickly and efficiently, with habitats staying intact, and ocean life undisturbed, encouraging biodiversity to upsurge.
Location	An MPA's location will dramatically affect its success. Those MPAs that are isolated away from land do not face all the stressors that those closer to land do. Being isolated, and at a distance, prevents a lot of human disturbance, such as tourism and fishing. However, this factor cannot be controlled, an MPA is an area that requires to be established to be conserved and protected, and therefore cannot change location.
Enforcement	Without enforcement, an MPA would not be of any value; there would be no promotion of objectives. The status will become pointless, and rules will not be abided by. With no enforcement, MPAs will not achieve their goals, and will be ineffective and lack biodiversity.

Source: Compiled by the author.

Twenty-seven MPAs from across the world were considered in this study, including ones from developed and underdeveloped countries (please note data collected is from 2018). The MPAs considered in this study spanned a wide range of the different success factors (Figures 1 and 2), and a detailed analysis of the importance of these factors for each MPA was conducted from scientific literature and appropriate web sources. A small sample of MPAs were selected, and although these were varied, the view can be taken that being self-selected was a limitation when reviewing the probabilistic values. A BBN (fully described in Stafford et al.)[221] was used to convert values allocated to each factor to an overall success score.

220 Clevo Wilson and Clem Tisdell (n. 37).
221 Rick Stafford et al. (n. 98).

The BBN model developed by Stafford et al.[222] is based on previous BBNs (reviewed by Grover;[223] see Hammond and Ellis[224] for an ecological example applied to species interactions). The model used has several important differences, making the application of the networks much more intuitive for application to reciprocal interactions. While this method does not produce results that are fully quantitative, they can be considered "ordinal" when ranking the effectiveness for better protection for biodiversity.[225] The model provides "a convenient way of analysing complex systems"[226] and data, although figures should be viewed with an ordinal and not a literal approach.[227] The BBN provides "an enhanced conceptual awareness"[228] of the relationships between influencing factors and areas that have been established as an MPA.[229]

The BBN model used in this study was constructed using Microsoft Excel 2010, with the use of VBA programming to perform many of the calculations (see mpamanagement.net for copies of the spreadsheet). For each node in the network, a "prior" value between 0 and 1 is given, to indicate the belief that a given node may increase or decrease ($P(X_i)$ and $P(X_d)$, respectively). A node is only ever considered as increasing or decreasing, and the probability gives a clear indication of the likelihood of this. In this belief network, the sum of the probability of a species increasing and decreasing must equal 1. The parameters of node interactions are provided in a series of interrelated matrices. Each interaction is independent of any others, and only direct effects between nodes are modelled – indirect effects are emergent properties of the network. The belief network draws on four sets of parameters for each node interaction:

1. Probability of node b decreasing, given node a is increasing.
2. Probability of node b increasing, given node a is increasing.
3. Probability of node b increasing, given node a is decreasing.
4. Probability of node b decreasing, given node a is decreasing.

---

222 Ibid.

223 Jeff Grover, "A Literature Review of Bayes' Theorem and Bayesian Belief Networks (BBN)" [2012] 9 *Strategic Economic Decision-Making* 11–27.

224 T.R. Hammond and Jim Ellis, "A meta-assessment for elasmobranchs based on dietary data and Bayesian networks" [2002] 1(3) *Ecological Indicators* 197–211.

225 Richard Stafford et al., "Evaluating optimal solutions to environmental breakdown" [2020] 112 *Environmental Science and Policy* 340–347.

226 James R Sokolnicki et al., "Assessing Environmentally Effective Post-COVID Green Recovery Plans for Reducing Social and Economic Inequality" [2022] *Anthropocene Science* 375–383.

227 Ibid.

228 Richard Stafford et al., "Evaluating optimal solutions to environmental breakdown" (n. 225).

229 Ibid.

In most cases, these are highly related parameters, where parameter 2 above is equal to 1 – parameter 1, parameter 3 is equal to parameter 1, and parameter 4 is equal to parameter 2. However, they do not have to follow the above rules, and can be set independently if needed. Given these parameters, intermediate probabilities of each node increasing given node interactions are calculated using the following Bayesian equation:

$$P\left(X_i \mid Y\right)=\left[P\left(X_i \mid Y_i\right)*P\left(Y_i\right)+P\left(X_i \mid Y_d\right)*P\left(Y_d\right)\right],$$

Where X is the MPA under consideration, and Y are the interacting success nodes and success scores, subscripts i and d indicate increasing or decreasing MPA success.

Where no knowledge of a change in node exists (i.e. the prior probability of change is 0.5), then this node is not included in the above equation (however, such inclusion might occur in the second iteration of the model: see below for details).

At this point, no "prior" information on node X is included in the calculation. To ensure that any prior knowledge available is maintained in the network, the overall posterior probability for each species is calculated in two ways, with the first ensuring that additional information on node interactions adds to the certainty provided by the prior; the second will ignore prior values, if information on node interactions provide more certain information than the prior:

(1) $$\text{Post}\left(X_i\right)=P\left(X_i\right)+\mid 1-P\left(X_i\right)\mid *\left[\Sigma 1-n\left(P\left(X_i\right)*\left(P\left(X_i \mid Y\right)-0.5\right)\right)/n\right],$$

And

(2) $$\text{Post}\left(X_i\right)=\left[\Sigma 1-n\left(P\left(X_i \mid Y\right)\right)\right]/n$$

where n is the number of interactions with node X. The final value of $\text{Post}(X_i)$ is given by the value displaying the most certainty (i.e. furthest in magnitude from 0.5). The model is then repeated for a second iteration, but with updated prior probabilities such that:

$$P(X_i) = \text{Post}(X_i).$$

Three iterations of the model are performed, to ensure that data propagate fully through the network.

Figure 1. Ordinal representation of size of the 27 MPAs used in the study

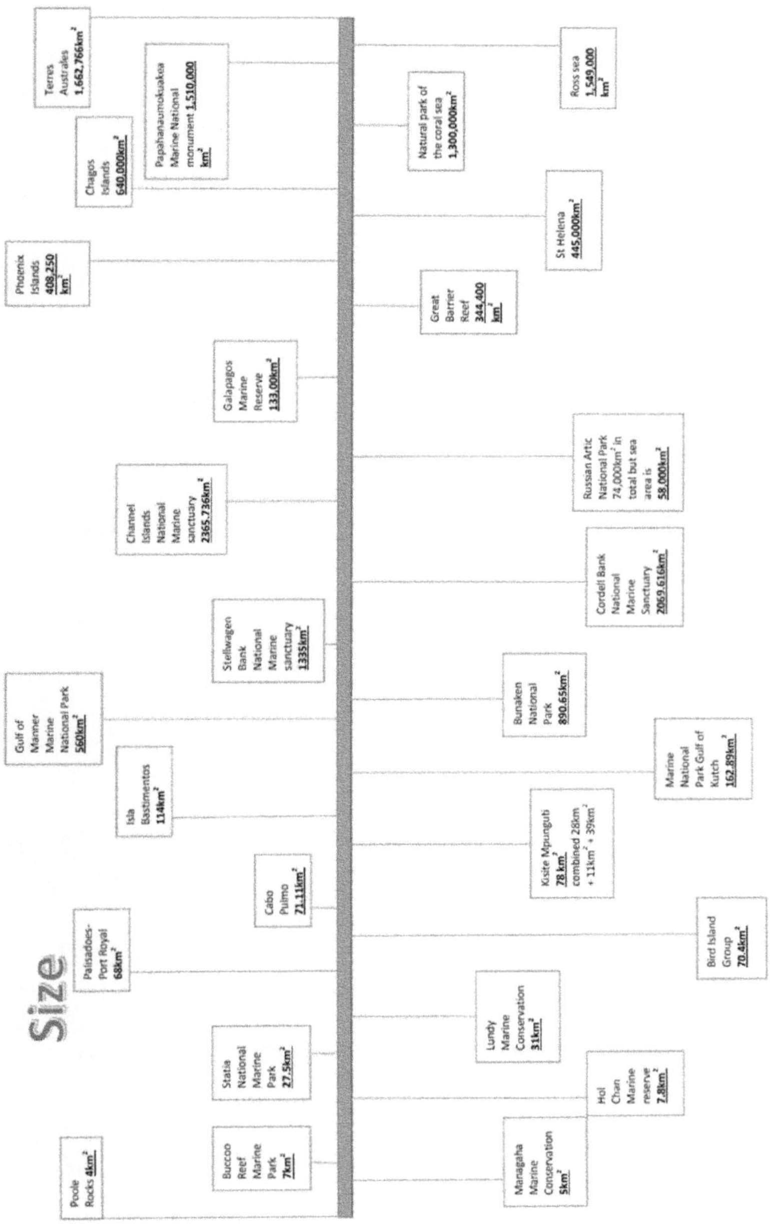

Source: Produced by the author.

Figure 2. Age line showing age difference of the 27 MPAs

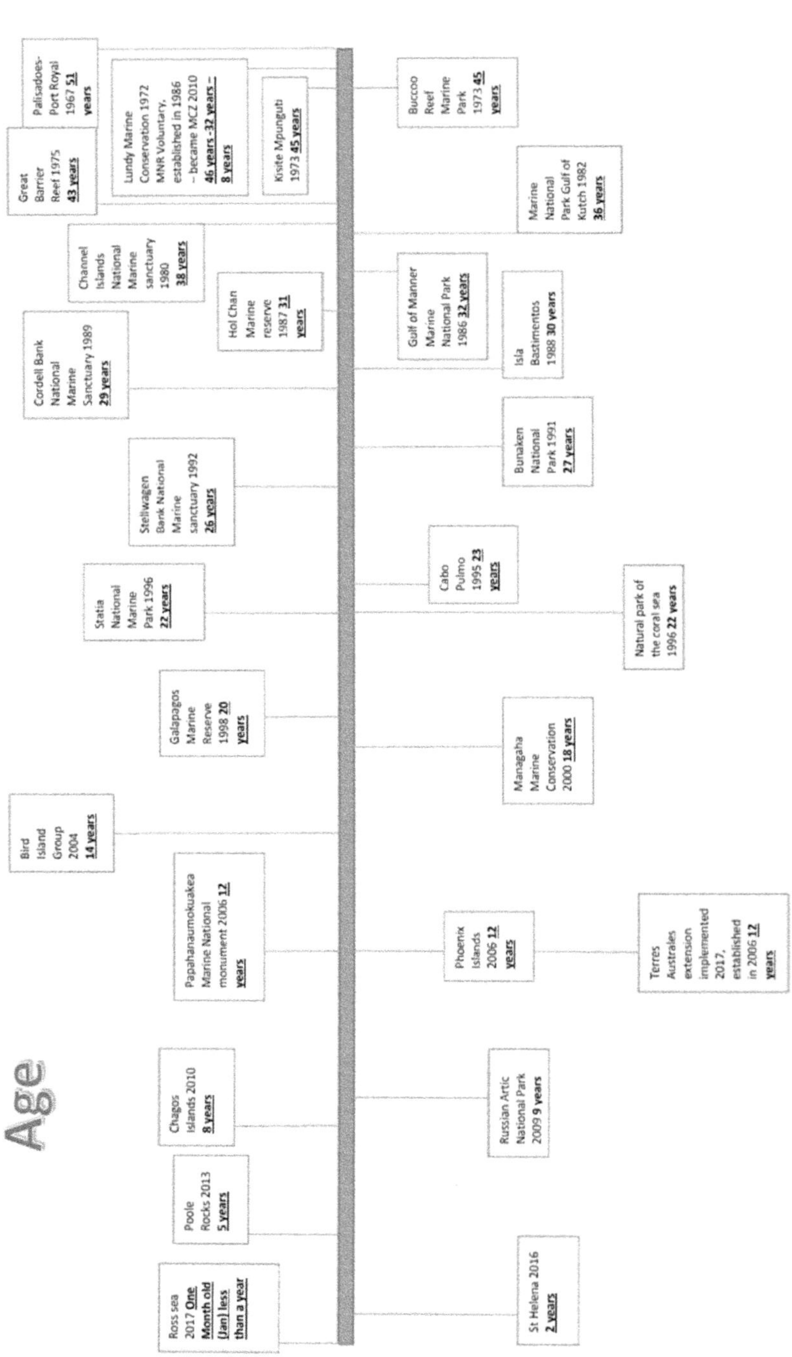

Source: Produced by the author.

Figure 3. Diagrammatic representations of Bayesian belief networks used to determine success

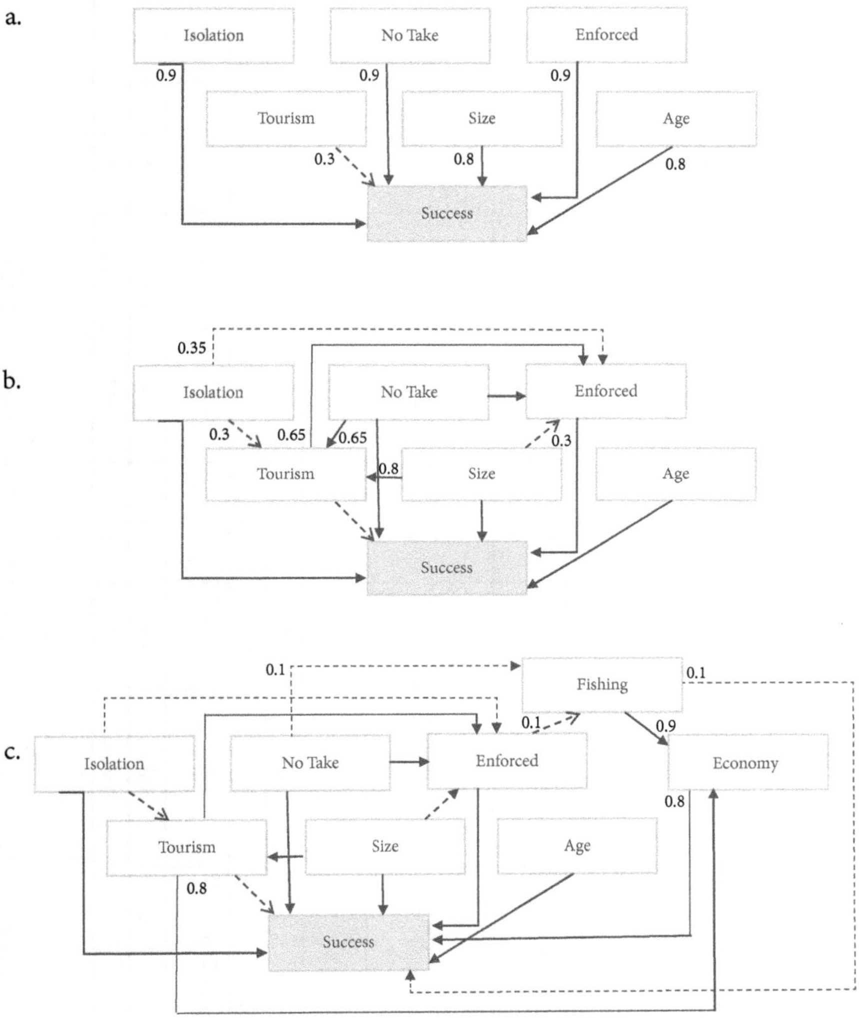

Note: White rectangles represent key success factors, and shaded rectangles represent the success node in the network. Edges joining nodes indicate connections between the nodes, with dotted lines indicating a negative interaction (if input node increases, it is likely that target node will decrease, and connection strength < 0.5), and solid lines indicating positive interactions (if input node increases, it is likely that target node will also increase, and connection strength > 0.5). Numbers indicate connection strengths, with 0 indicating highest certainty of a negative interaction from input to target node, and 1 indicating the highest certainty of a positive interaction: (a) Basic model; (b) considering interactions between the input nodes; (c) inclusion of factors which directly influence fishing and economic success.

Source: Produced by the author.

Table 4. Input values and success for each of the MPAs considered in this study

	MPA	Success Score 1	Tourism	No take	Isolation	Size	Age	Enforcement
1.	Chagos Islands (Indian Ocean) (UK territory)	0.85	0.01	0.99	0.96	0.76	0.14	0.97
2.	The Great Barrier Reef (Australia)	0.49	0.74	0.34	0.21	0.67	0.77	0.71
3.	Papahanaumokuakea Marine National Monument (Hawaii)	0.76	0.13	0.81	0.91	0.92	0.22	0.86
4.	Galapagos Marine Reserve (Ecuador)	0.69	0.39	0.84	0.72	0.64	0.36	0.92
5.	Ross Sea Protected Area (Antarctica)	0.74	0.06	0.68	0.98	0.95	0.01	0.87
6.	Terres Australes Francaises (France)	0.74	0.09	0.58	0.98	0.98	0.22	0.81
7.	Lundy Marine Conservation zone (United Kingdom)	0.44	0.77	0.54	0.15	0.17	0.83	0.82
8.	Managaha Marine Conservation Area (Saipan)	0.42	0.22	0.99	0.12	0.06	0.32	0.39
9.	St Helena (South Atlantic Island) (UK territories)	0.38	0.18	0.10	0.18	0.73	0.04	0.62
10.	Palisadoes-Port Royal (Jamaica)	0.40	0.34	0.27	0.09	0.20	0.92	0.56
11.	Poole Rocks (United Kingdom)	0.25	0.64	0.24	0.12	0.03	0.09	0.76
12.	Isla Bastimentos National Marine Park (Panama)	0.34	0.70	0.22	0.38	0.31	0.54	0.28
13.	Cabo Pulmo National Marine Park (Mexico)	0.44	0.26	0.28	0.64	0.25	0.41	0.44
14.	Kisite Mpunguti (Kenya)	0.50	0.75	0.42	0.62	0.28	0.81	0.57

15.	Gulf of Mannar Marine National Park (India)	0.31	0.68	0.24	0.29	0.36	0.58	0.08
16.	Marine National Park, Gulf of Kutch (India)	0.30	0.72	0.15	0.19	0.34	0.65	0.22
17.	Bunaken National Park (off the coast of Indonesia)	0.35	0.85	0.18	0.18	0.39	0.49	0.71
18.	Natural Park of the coral sea (New Caledonia)	0.45	0.63	0.26	0.38	0.90	0.40	0.28
19.	Statia National Marine Park (Netherlands Antilles)	0.44	0.43	0.52	0.41	0.14	0.40	0.70
20.	Buccoo Reef Marine Park (Trinidad and Tobago)	0.39	0.88	0.26	0.67	0.08	0.81	0.50
21.	Phoenix Islands Protected Area (Republic of Kiribati)	0.61	0.14	0.31	0.96	0.70	0.22	0.62
22.	Channel Islands National marine sanctuary (California)	0.67	0.87	0.86	0.83	0.48	0.68	0.84
23.	Cordell Bank National Marine Sanctuary (USA-Northern California)	0.57	0.17	0.39	0.75	0.45	0.52	0.61
24.	Stellwagen Bank National Marine Sanctuary (Massachusetts)	0.36	0.59	0.47	0.24	0.42	0.47	0.13
25.	Bird Island Group MPA (South Africa)	0.62	0.16	0.99	0.76	0.22	0.25	0.71
26.	Russian Artic National Park (Russia)	0.57	0.43	0.38	0.80	0.62	0.16	0.83
27.	Hol Chan Marine Reserve (Belize)	0.31	0.91	0.33	0.31	0.11	0.56	0.44

Source: Compiled by the author.

Figure 4. Locations of the MPAs used in this study

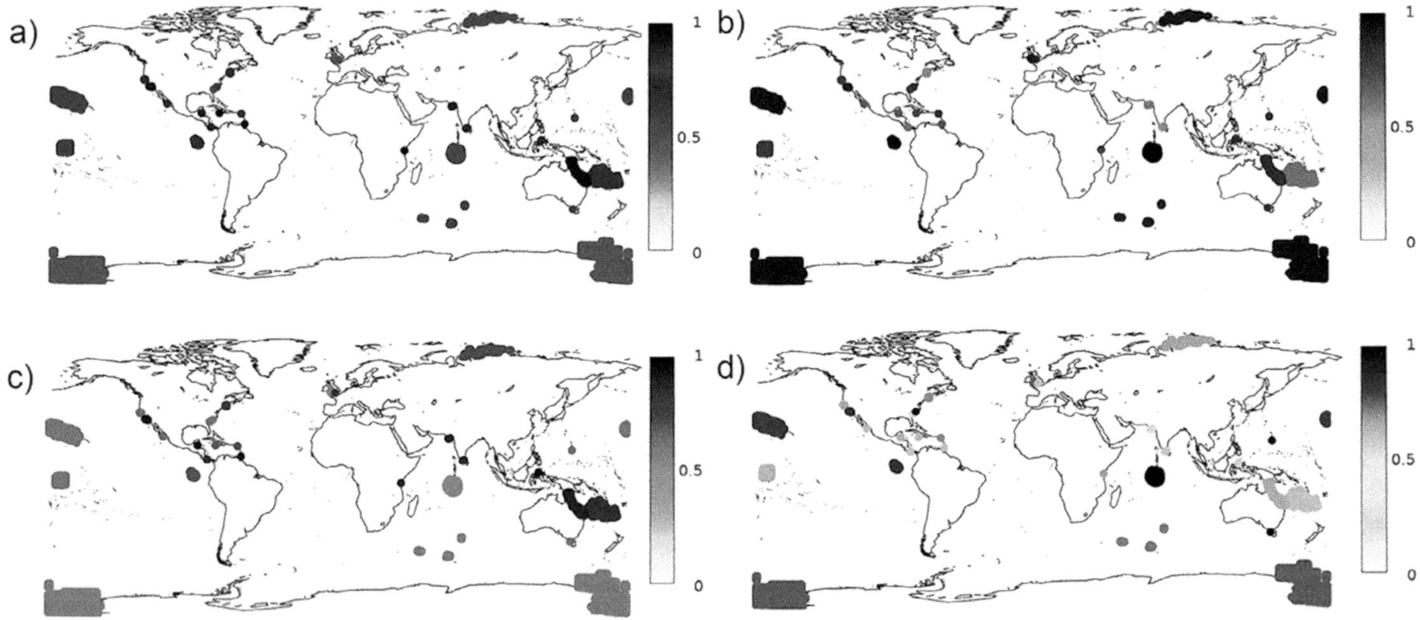

Note: Heat maps are colour representations of input values for the BBN for: (a) age; (b) enforcement; (c) tourism intensity; and (d) fishing restriction. The filled colour, not the border, is representative of the input. value.

Source: Produced by the author.

Figure 5. Locations and heat map of the success scores for the MPAs used in this study

Note: The filled colour, not the border, is representative of the success score.

Source: Produced by the author.

Figure 6. Relationships between each of the input factors and predicted MPA success

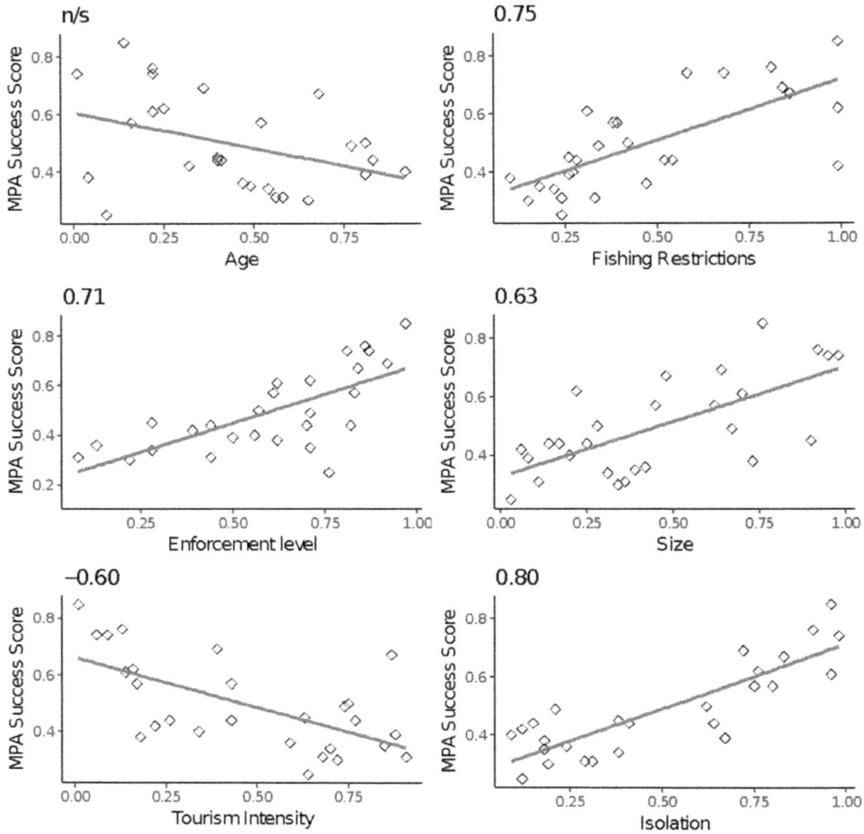

Note: Where correlations are significant, the r value is given.
Source: Produced by the author.

The predicted ecological success of MPAs varied considerably (graph 1; Figure 6), with no clear geographical trends, other than more isolated MPAs generally being more successful than those close to land (see below). The comparison of different models involving interaction between factors, or inclusion of fishing and economic factors, resulted in almost no change to success scores (maximum difference of 3 per cent from any MPA); as such, the results presented are only for the original model described in Figure 3a.

While success scores have been calculated using predictive methods, it is, nevertheless, useful to consider correlations between influencing factors and success, to determine the importance of the effect of each factor on success. While this is a somewhat circular argument, a lack of correlation provides good evidence that the factor can, in some cases, be replaced or superseded by other factors, to ensure (or prevent) success.

Figure 7. Relationships between different input factors which show significant correlations

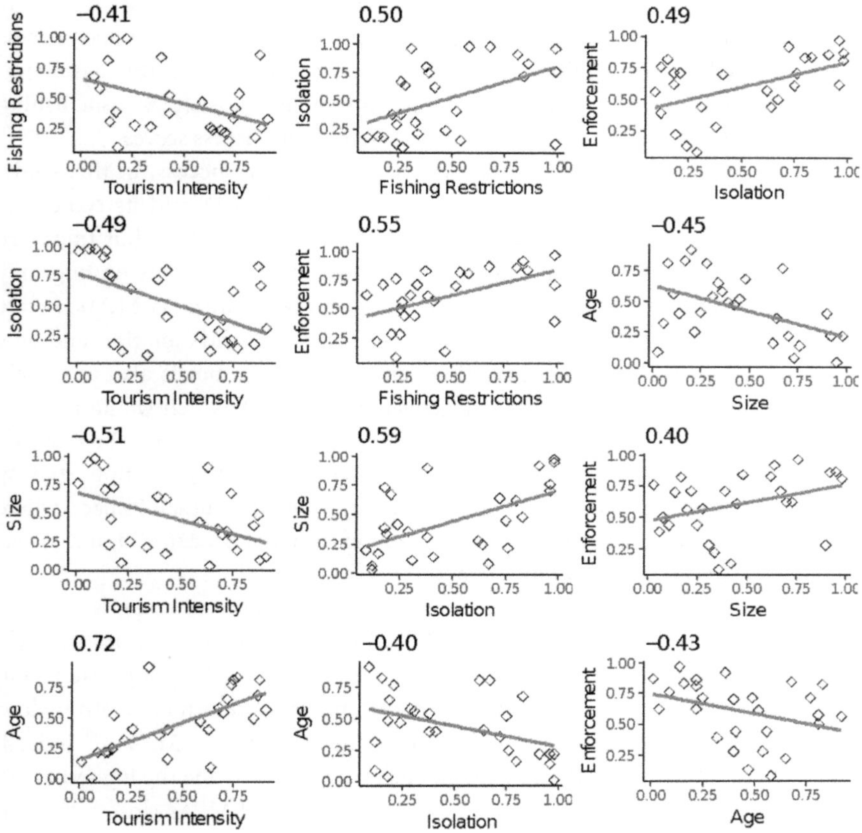

Note: Where correlations are significant, the r value is given.
Source: Produced by the author.

By considering magnitude of the r values of the correlations, isolation demonstrates the best fit with success, although most of the other factors (excluding age) show moderately strong correlations with r values > 0.6 (Figure 6; all are highly significant $p < 0.001$). Age shows a non-significant but negative correlation with success. There are also some significant correlations between different influencing factors, although these are mainly only of moderate strength (Figure 7).

The 27 MPAs studied showed a wide range of success scores, from low to high. Examining the role of each influencing factor in success demonstrated that the current study largely agreed with that of Edgar et al.[230] for most of the factors which

230 Graham Edgar et al. (n. 32).

may determine MPA success, but that tourism also played a significant role in the current study, with increased levels of tourism causing a decline in ecological effectiveness. Age of MPA was found to be less important than what had previously been proposed, and in this case a negative relationship between age and success was identified, despite the positive relationship specified in the BBN. Isolation was found to be the most important factor in establishing success. Establishing feedback between the factors provided little difference in success scores.

Given the use of predictive algorithms to determine success, in this study, the lack of a positive relationship between the age of MPA and its ecological success is unexpected, and contrary to much previous work;[231] but there are studies that also support this conclusion.[232] To some extent, this finding may be driven by the recent trend to allocate large isolated areas as MPAs, hence the negative relationships found between size and age, and isolation and age. Isolation showed the strongest relationship with success, but is also positively related to many other factors (and negatively to tourism), which would indicate that isolated MPAs may also fulfil many of the other roles which may be required for ecological success. The beneficial role of isolation is largely supported by recent studies on the role of MPAs in areas of high and low human impact, where the ecological success of the MPA, especially in terms of predator biomass, was higher in areas far from human impact.[233]

Creating isolated offshore MPAs is a controversial topic, however, with many people questioning whether they provide real ecological benefit, or are simply a mechanism to meet targets.[234] Questions have been raised as to how much benefit the MPAs really provide, as factors such as fishing pressure can be relatively low, or even absent, in some areas recently designated as offshore MPAs.[235] Indeed, Cinner et al.[236] also show that, although offshore MPAs provide the highest levels of fish, and especially predator biomass, it is non-isolated MPAs close to human activity which provide the greatest improvement in fish stocks, when compared with similar reference areas.

---

231 Ransom A. Myers et al. (n. 55); Simon Jennings, "Patterns and predictions of population recovery in marine reserves" [2001] 10 *Reviews in Fish Biology and Fisheries* 209–231; Phillip Molloy et al. (n. 54); Graham Edgar et al. (n. 32).

232 Benjamin S. Halpern and Robert R. Warner, "Marine reserves have rapid and lasting effects" [2002] 5 *Ecology Letters* 361–366.

233 Joshua E. Cinner et al. (n. 74).

234 Derek P. Tittensor et al. (n. 208); Enric Sala et al., "Assessing real progress towards effective ocean protection" [2018] 91 *Marine Policy* 11–13.

235 Vinicius J. Gigilo et al., "Large and remote marine protected areas in the South Atlantic Ocean are flawed and raise concerns: Comments on Soares and Lucas (2018)" [2018] 96 *Marine Policy* 13–17; Luiz A. Rocha, "Bigger Is Not Better for Ocean Conservation" (*The New York Times*, 20 March 2018) <https://www.nytimes.com/2018/03/20/opinion/environment-ocean-conservation.html>.

236 Joshua E. Cinner et al. (n. 74).

Large, isolated MPAs, however, if well enforced, are useful in preventing expansion of further offshore fishing in the high seas. In the tropics, MPAs have appeared to create coral reef systems more resilient to climate change, and less prone to diseases, than those in other areas.[237] They can also be relatively simple to designate when they lie in a single nation's waters, perhaps because of the lack of commercial fishing in the area, and the economic inefficiency of fishing in these isolated areas.[238] Indeed, the issues of establishing no-take zone MPAs in coastal waters can be difficult, due to the reduction in fish yield which can occur, and, as such, many non-isolated MPAs are multi-use.[239] Encouraging tourism is often seen as a way of offsetting loss of fishing income,[240] yet it can have detrimental effects on the ecological efficiency of the MPA. As such, while isolated MPAs may be the most ecologically beneficial, research on how to balance effective ecological protection alongside fishing income and less harmful measures of tourism, in coastal areas, is also needed.[241]

The results from this study predict that large, isolated, well enforced no-take MPAs, which limit tourism and damage, provide the greatest ecological benefits. However, many consider that MPAs have recently been designated to meet CBD targets. This study confirms the view that, to ensure the best possible protection for the marine environment, more large and isolated MPAs will require to be designated. For this to happen, we need to designate outside of national jurisdictions. However, at present, only one MPA exists outside of national jurisdiction waters. Further study on the legal and policy mechanisms to both create and enforce MPAs which cross, or fall outside of, national boundaries is clearly needed.

5. CONCLUSION

This contribution has reviewed ecological, social and legal issues around the implementation of MPAs. Through a predictive modelling approach, it has

---

237 Elizabeth McLeod et al., "Designing marine protected area networks to address the impacts of climate change" [2009] 7 *Frontiers in Ecology and the Environment* 362–370; Peter J. Mumby et al., "Reserve design for uncertain responses of coral reefs to climate change" [2011] 14(2) *Ecology Letters* 132–140; C.R.C. Sheppard et al., "Reefs and islands of the Chagos Archipelago, Indian Ocean: why it is the world's largest no-take marine protected area" [2012] 22 *Aquatic Conservation* 232–261.

238 Enric Sala et al., "The economics of fishing the high seas" [2018] 4(6) *Science Advances*.

239 Estelle Jones et al. (n. 214).

240 Enrique Oracion et al., "Marine Protected Areas for Whom? Fisheries, Tourism, and Solidarity in a Philippine Community" [2005] 48(3–6) Ocean & Coastal management 393–410; K.V.S.N. Jawahar Babu (n. 39); Richard Stafford et al., "Lack of evidence that governance structures provide real ecological benefits in marine protected areas" (n. 205).

241 Richard Stafford et al., "Lack of evidence that governance structures provide real ecological benefits in marine protected areas" (n. 205).

largely supported the work of previous studies (such as Edgar et al.)[242] in identifying the importance of different elements or factors which influence an MPA's success, although its results also show the importance of reducing tourist-inflicted damage, and the limited importance of the age of an MPA in establishing its ecological success.

Fishing, while disruptive, may not be the most harmful action to the marine environment; it is the methods that are used which can cause the most impairment,[243] damaging marine habitats, and causing species to have no liveable environment, and therefore depleting and dying out.[244] However, some societies and cultures rely on fishing, to make a living, for cultural reasons, and because fish is a cheap and protein-rich food source. These pressures can cause conflict when trying to implement conservation measures.[245]

Looking at the key influencing factors for ecologically successful MPAs, in the previous section, an MPA "should" be isolated to help it maximise being successful in attaining biodiversity and effectiveness. Isolation proved to be the most important factor from the BBN results, and, as such, it is promising to see more isolated MPAs being established recently. However, many of these recent MPAs may not have had much fishing effort initially, and the designation may add little to their effectiveness. Thus, although isolation creates a greater standard of biodiversity for an MPA, an isolated MPA would not achieve the same level of "improvement" of an MPA that is close to land and human activity. When an MPA is isolated, it is often too far away for activities such as tourism and fishing, automatically making it more effective than MPAs closer to land. It could also be that large and isolated MPAs are being created to portray the idea of environmental awareness, and to meet targets.[246] However, it could just be that we are operating proactively, instead of reactively, to the damage that may occur in the future, ensuring that our present pristine ocean areas are maintained, and abundant in biodiversity, thereby avoiding impairment completely.

Although the BBN results displayed isolation as being the most influential factor, without enforcement and management, isolated MPAs may not be effective. Without legislation, MPAs would not be designated, and would, therefore, be non-existent. For the influencing factors to be beneficially effective on an MPA, in enhancing biodiversity and overall marine sustainability, the legislation and management behind it plays a highly significant role. Without strong management and standardised designation, enforcement of factors could be lacking, which would cause MPAs to be inadequate. However, without being isolated, an MPA can still be effective. Although isolation is a great influence

242 Graham Edgar et al. (n. 32).
243 Daniel Pauly et al. (n. 86).
244 Oceana (n. 9).
245 WWF (n. 8).
246 Enric Sala et al., "Assessing real progress towards effective ocean protection" (n. 234).

in effectiveness for an MPA, as being further away from human activity allows high levels of biodiversity, improvements closer to land are just as important and greater.[247] We need MPAs close to land, as this is where the greatest damage is caused. Therefore, when reflecting on the factors that influence an MPA, although isolation is the most influential factor for an MPA being effective, it is not a necessity for a successful MPA when measuring improvement and success.

A key question to consider now is, "how are we going to adopt large MPAs?". With several of the world's biggest MPAs being established in the last seven years, we need to consider that the new MPAs designated will cover multiple national jurisdictions, or be in the high seas.[248] The new BBNJ Treaty, if successfully implemented and governed, could be highly successful, but management and standardisation will need to be observed and critiqued, to ensure that MPAs are effective in ensuring conservation and sustainability. EIAs will need to be stringently reviewed, ensuring the main focus is on the environment and biodiversity, and not any other beneficial outcome, such as monetary value. A concern could be that, although this greater agreement is a step in the right direction, it is lacking effective management, and provides a loophole for companies to establish themselves with countries that lack the resources to conduct comprehensive evaluations for EIAs, resulting in a more flexible environmental review.

An elegant solution to ensure minimal tourist and fishing damage, and to create long-lasting and well-enforced MPAs, would be to introduce the ISO 14001 and apply it to marine environments, specifically MPAs. With the influence of UNCLOS, and the targets of CBD and COP, this could be the groundbreaking standardisation needed. It will ensure that our MPAs are managed sustainably, thus promoting greater biodiversity and the reaching of their targets, instead of constantly postponing these to a future date, as happens at present. Once we have an effective system in place, with clear guidelines, it will allow a real difference in the way MPAs are viewed, and how long it takes for their targets to be met will reduce considerably.

From an international view on how we can manage MPAs, if we adopt the ISO 14001 as a standard, it would be sufficient, due to MPA management needing to fit minimum standards. The ISO 14001 caters to most of the influencing factors, instigating for overall effective MPA enhancement. MPAs need a minimum enforcement standard behind them, giving them a backbone and structure, to help enforce and manage them effectively. The ISO 14001, however, provides not only minimum standards, but is also a work in progress, with multiple improvement goals over time. This not only promotes establishment

247 Joshua E. Cinner et al. (n. 74).

248 High Seas Alliance, "Treaty Tracker" (4 September 2018) <http://highseasalliance.org/treatytracker/>.

of long-term MPAs, but means that the older an MPA, the more efficient it would be. This can be beneficial, as MPAs would be constantly improving and, therefore, not taking any steps backwards. Fishing and tourism would need to meet certain standards to be accredited, as these are services that an MPA provides.[249] As such, again, the levels of responsible tourism and fishing should continually improve towards a better system. Enforcement would also need to be improved and adapted, in order to meet the standards set. This would help to allow for MPA management to have an internationally recognised management system, rather than each national jurisdiction having their own system. This would allow MPAs outside of national jurisdiction, or those that cross borders, to be enforced and managed effectively. We could then focus on the MPA itself, and what management it needs to be most effective in achieving its goals, unlike the present, where the focus surrounds the confusion management is currently bringing, which is taking away the true focus and meaning of MPAs.

The world is now viewing MPAs as a key tool to help reverse damage and maintain the pristine habitats and biodiversity in certain areas of the ocean. Accordingly, MPA numbers are going to grow, with more being designated. We are still learning what makes a good MPA, and improving and working on the ones currently established, thus meaning that MPA effectiveness, and biodiversity success, should be reviewed again, to see where improvements can occur, so we can help to sustain and repair our oceans. If we did not have a mechanism such as ISO 14001 added to the enforcement system, to constantly re-evaluate MPA progress, MPAs would just be lines on a map; is this really what we want for our marine environment?

---

249 Myles Thompson et al. (n. 153).

NAVIGATING A SEA OF UNCERTAINTY IN THE EU REGULATION OF MARINE RENEWABLES

The Case for Hybrid Co-Regulation?

Nikolaos Giannopoulos

1. INTRODUCTION

Against the backdrop of heated debates about fully integrating sustainability across European Union (EU) policies, and motivated by the EU's obligations under the Paris Agreement, the European Green Deal set out ambitious goals towards achieving zero-pollution climate neutrality by 2050.[1] To that end, the EU has pledged to adopt *ad hoc* instruments, such as the European Climate Law,[2] as well as to review and, where necessary, revise EU energy and environmental rules. The generation of renewable energy at sea, as an infinite source which does not – at least directly – contribute towards carbon emissions, is projected to play a key role in the energy transition.[3] In that regard, the 2020 EU Offshore Renewable Energy Strategy stressed that private investments in marine renewables are indispensable for the EU to meet its climate commitments, safeguard energy security, and improve the competitiveness of the EU energy market.[4] Considering the lack of clear baseline information about the environmental status of European seas, and the ensuing environmental, scientific and technological uncertainty, the EU purports to establish a flexible, technology-neutral legal framework that can adapt to novel developments, to facilitate the clean energy transition.[5]

---

1 EU Commission, "The European Green Deal", COM (2019) 640 final.

2 Regulation (EU) 2021/1119 of 30 June 2021 establishing the framework for achieving climate neutrality and amending Regulations (EC) No. 401/2009 and (EU) 2018/1999 [2021] OJ L 243/1.

3 EU Commission, "Transforming the EU's Blue Economy for a Sustainable Future", COM (2021) 240 final, 3.

4 EU Commission, "An EU Strategy to harness the potential of offshore renewable energy for a climate neutral future", COM (2020) 741 final.

5 EU investors have raised concerns that the investment climate within the EU has been deteriorating: see EU Commission, Public Consultation Document, "An Intra-EU Investment Protection and Facilitation Initiative", 5.

At the same time, the regulatory framework needs to guarantee predictability and transparency, and prevent the potential "risk-shifting" in terms of environmental protection.[6]

Considering the EU's wait-and-see approach, and its reliance on non-binding instruments, this contribution examines the relevance of hybrid co-regulation in tackling the vexed challenges posed by unknown risks concerning the proliferation of marine renewables. Uncertainty in this emerging sector manifests in various forms, such as in terms of cumulative environmental effects, technological and scientific developments, and changing climate conditions, which influence both the regulators and the regulatees. Against this background, this contribution discusses how underlying considerations, such as regulatory complexity, uncertainty, the precautionary principle, and the calls for technology neutrality and innovation, test the limits of a binary approach to law, and call on us to reorientate our understanding of co-regulation. Considering the opportunities and challenges in recalibrating the environmental regulation of marine renewables, this contribution further argues that a hybrid regulatory arrangement, which transcends the pigeonholing distinction between public and private regulation, can overcome the constraints of command-and-control regulation in the face of rapid technological and scientific developments, and offer future-proof environmental solutions.

The EU's co-regulatory approaches in the field of renewable biofuels, as well as on the safety of offshore oil and gas activities, are assessed against their capacity to meet their respective policy objectives to imply best practices. Drawing lessons from the achievements and weaknesses of these examples of co-regulation within the multilevel EU legal order, and integrating the input of related economic and empirical research, this contribution proposes an inclusive framework combining principle-based EU "meta-regulation", the development of techno-normative standards by specialised agencies, the role of Member States as regulatory intermediaries, and private sector initiatives. Yet, the contribution does not underestimate or conceal the "dark side" of the suggested regulatory paradigm. On the contrary, bearing in mind the limitations of private regulation, it suggests that the design of hybrid arrangements and the establishment of oversight and compliance mechanisms play a key role in both their input and output legitimacy. The contribution concludes by highlighting the need for more empirical and economic research, to determine whether the marriage of the diverse expertise of these poles-apart "captains", in the context of co-regulation, can help them navigate a sea of uncertainty in the regulation of a dynamic and technically complex sector.

---

6 Rakhyun Kim and Harro van Asselt, "Global Governance: Problem Shifting in the Anthropocene and the Limits of International Law" in Elisa Morgera and Kati Kulovesi (eds.), *Research Handbook on International Law and Natural Resources* (Edward Elgar Publishing 2016), 473–495.

2. THE WAIT-AND-SEE APPROACH OF THE EU TOWARDS REGULATING MARINE RENEWABLES: A PARADOX?

Oceans are at the heart of EU-wide debates on the necessity to improve coherence and harness synergies between climate change mitigation, on the one hand, and biodiversity conservation and restoration, on the other.[7] Oceans operate as natural sinks for carbon emissions and regulate the climate, and can, thus, function as crucial allies in tackling both the climate and biodiversity crises.[8] At the same time, it is undeniable that the marine environment and economy are intrinsically linked. Healthy oceans and the sustainable blue economy they support are indispensable to achieving the transformation set out in the European Green Deal.[9] Marine renewable energy is a prominent example of the financial and social benefits resilient oceans could offer. With a higher average output than land-based renewable energy generation, it is expected to materially contribute to the EU's legally binding targets of reducing greenhouse gas (GHG) emissions by at least 55 per cent of their 1990 levels by 2030, and becoming climate-neutral by 2050. To that end, the EU's offshore renewable energy strategy builds on an increased momentum for the expansion of marine renewables, and aims to multiply their capacity fivefold by 2030, and thirtyfold by 2050.[10]

It is estimated that the necessary investments to achieve that unparalleled capacity of renewable energy generation at sea will be up to 800 billion euros.[11] At present, the EU industry is among the global leaders in ocean energy technologies, primarily in the form of wind, wave and tidal energy, but other technologies, such as algal biofuels, ocean thermal energy conversion, and floating photovoltaic installations, are projected to develop at a commercial scale in the near future.[12] Even though the invisible hand of the European market, and innovative technological developments (i.e. digitalisation), are expected to continue driving the growth of the sector, there is a need for greater regulatory intervention by the EU and its Member States to establish a credible long-term framework for investors.[13] For instance, pilot projects on multi-use platforms,

---

7 Intergovernmental Panel on Climate Change, "Special Report on the Ocean and the Cryosphere in a Changing Climate" [2019].

8 EU Commission, "EU Biodiversity Strategy for 2030", COM (2020) 380 final, 3.

9 EU Commission, "The European Green Deal" (n. 1).

10 EU Commission, "An EU Strategy to harness the potential of offshore renewable energy for a climate neutral future" (n. 4).

11 Joint Research Centre, 'Facts and figures on Offshore Renewable Energy Sources in Europe' [2020], JRC121366.

12 EU Commission, "Progress of clean energy competitiveness", SWD (2020) 953 final.

13 Based on the Member States' national energy and climate plans, current policies would only lead to an installed capacity of approx. 90GW in 2050, which is way below the EU's goal for 400GW, <https://ec.europa.eu/energy/topics/energy-strategy/national-energy-climate-plans_en#final-necps>.

which enable the creation of artificial reefs around installations, or the combination of aquaculture and energy exploitation, are promoted to minimise the potential impacts on marine species and their habitats, and reconcile the placement of new energy infrastructures with other economic activities.[14]

The EU's strategy regarding the expansion of marine renewables exemplifies the paradigm shift in the EU's conception of environmental and climate objectives as co-drivers of the sustainable blue economy.[15] Yet, there are currently remarkable implementation and regulatory gaps which must be overcome to scale up environmental protection and meet the targets of zero pollution and climate neutrality.[16] The deployment of marine renewable energy infrastructure is often associated with negative environmental impacts, such as acoustic disturbance, habitat loss of marine wildlife, and contamination by chemical emissions and organic compounds.[17] In addition, there remains considerable scientific uncertainty about the cumulative environmental externalities of large-scale deployment of offshore renewables.[18] To turn the EU's ambitious decarbonisation plan into a success, the regulation of marine renewables should live up to fundamental constitutional principles of the EU legal order, in particular sustainable development, the achievement of a high level of protection, and the improvement of the quality of the environment.[19] In that regard, the question remains whether the current EU environmental legal framework is fit to address the challenges posed by the rapid expansion of energy installations in European seas.

Given the potential environmental impacts of marine renewables, the EU has emphasised its responsibility to ensure the protection of the marine environment from the risks they pose.[20] Having regard to the transboundary nature of marine biodiversity, EU intervention and regional cooperation for the coordination of marine environmental approaches and standards within each marine region are necessary to avoid regulatory fragmentation.[21] Adopting different approaches and timelines for tackling the key pressures created by marine renewables would result in ineffective protection of marine ecosystems in European seas. In that

---

14 Nathalie Steins et al., "Combining Offshore Wind Farms, Nature Conservation and Seafood: Lessons from a Dutch Community of Practice" (2021) 126 *Marine Policy* 1, 2.

15 Ludwig Krämer, "Planning for Climate and the Environment: the EU Green Deal" (2021) 17 *Journal of European Environmental & Planning Law* 267, 268.

16 Ruven Fleming and Romain Mauger, "Green and Just? An Update on the 'European Green Deal'" (2021) 17 *Journal for European Environmental & Planning Law* 164, 164–180.

17 EU Commission, "Impact Assessment, Blue Energy Communication", SWD (2014) final 15–16.

18 Catherine Ann Caine, "The Race to the Water for Offshore Renewable Energy: Assessing Cumulative and In-combination Impacts for Offshore Renewable Energy Developments" (2020) 32 *Journal of Environmental Law* 83, 84.

19 Art. 3(3), Consolidated Version of the Treaty on European Union [2008] OJ C115/13 (TEU).

20 Decision 1386/2013/EU of the European Parliament and of the Council on a General Union Environment Action Programme to 2020, Annex, paras. 21–22.

21 Nikolaos Giannopoulos, "Regionalism and Marine Environmental Protection: The Case of Offshore Energy Production" (2021), <https://ssrn.com/abstract=3770726>.

respect, EU institutions have repeatedly called for the stepping-up of efforts to keep offshore energy activities compatible with achieving the goal of the good environmental status of European seas:[22] "offshore renewable energy will only be sustainable if it does not have adverse impacts on the environment".[23] Nonetheless, marine pollution, and other disturbances of marine ecosystems, by the emerging deployment of marine renewables remain virtually unregulated under EU law.[24] Although there are no international rules with direct implications for the environmental regulation of offshore renewables, the lack of specific EU rules and standards appears somewhat paradoxical.

In practice, EU environmental law instruments address selected issues related to offshore energy activities.[25] Some, however, do not focus particularly on, nor directly apply to, marine renewables. For instance, the Marine Strategy Framework Directive (MSFD) was adopted with the ambition of maintaining marine ecosystems in a healthy and resilient condition.[26] Nonetheless, the report on its first implementation cycle revealed that the EU and its Member States had failed to achieve the good environmental status of European seas. As conceded in the European Green Deal, the EU has not met Aichi Target 11 under the UN Biodiversity Convention, which required that 10 per cent of coastal and marine areas were conserved by 2020.[27] Instead, an estimated quarter of the EU's coastal area has lost its seabed habitats, due, among other things, to renewable energy activities.[28] Marine biodiversity loss largely continues in the EU, as marine ecosystems in European seas remain at a "vulnerable" status, and the "good" state of habitats and species is not secured.[29] Certain marine populations and groups of species remain under threat of extinction, including seabirds, elasmobranches and cetaceans.[30] Impulsive underwater noise produced by renewable energy platforms has been identified as one of the main pressures affecting marine ecosystems. Even though such noise is currently, before the anticipated proliferation of marine renewables, spatially restricted to approximately 8 per cent of the EU's marine area, it is still present in large areas of European seas.[31]

---

22 EU Council, Conclusions on Blue Growth of 26 June 2017, 10662/17, para. 24.

23 EU Commission, "An EU Strategy to harness the potential of offshore renewable energy for a climate neutral future" (n. 4), 11.

24 Krämer (n. 15), 277.

25 Suzanne Boyes and Michael Elliot, "Marine Legislation: The Ultimate 'Horrendogram': International Law, European Directives and National Implementation" (2014) 86 *Marine Pollution Bulletin* 39, 39.

26 Directive 2008/56/EC establishing a framework for community action in the field of marine environmental policy [2008] OJ L 164/19.

27 EU Commission, "The European Green Deal" (n. 1), 10.

28 EU Commission, "EU Biodiversity Strategy for 2030" (n. 8), 16.

29 EU Commission, "Combined Evaluation Roadmap/Inception Impact Assessment of the MSFD" [2021] 3.

30 EU Commission, "Report on the Implementation of the MSFD", SWD (2020) 60 final, 16.

31 Ibid., 21.

In particular, the lack of sector-specific rules appears inconsistent with the zealous goals of EU environmental policy instruments, which highlight the commitment to integrating sustainability requirements into the regulation of offshore economic activities, to streamline them with EU's international commitments. For instance, the EU Biodiversity Strategy for 2030 envisaged the restoration of damaged marine ecosystems, and proclaimed that, *inter alia*, 30 per cent of EU seas should be classified as protected areas, and at least one-third of those – representing 10 per cent of European seas – should be strictly protected (up from 1 per cent today).[32] On that matter, the EU Commission simply argues that the scaling-up of the offshore wind industry is estimated to require less than 3 per cent of the European maritime space, and can, therefore, be compatible with the biodiversity goals.[33] Yet, the Commission admits that there is a considerable degree of uncertainty about the cumulative environmental externalities of the projected expansion of marine renewables, and thus "the situation must be monitored and our scientific knowledge updated as capacity is scaled up and new technologies are developed".[34] The existing EU legislation does not contain an obligation for Member States to adopt biodiversity restoration plans, and there are no binding targets or timelines for the adoption of implementing measures to deliver the objectives of the 2030 Biodiversity Strategy. The need for stronger action at the EU level is becoming even more acute as marine biodiversity loss is exacerbated by climate change.[35]

Overall, the relevant EU legislation and policy appear to be overly preoccupied with economic considerations, such as removing the barriers for technological innovation, and attracting investments by harmonising the national support schemes, to ensure energy security and the functioning of the internal EU energy market.[36] That is probably the case because this is a sector where market penetration is lagging, with competitors finding themselves at a disadvantage, and the degree of competition is currently considered insufficient to deliver the desired efficiencies. National support schemes, such as feed-in tariffs, tax exemptions, and other economic incentives, have conferred an economic advantage upon the producers of electricity from renewable sources: one that they would not have obtained under normal market conditions. In particular, the Member States' practice of providing fixed electricity prices has sheltered the renewable energy sector from price signals, leading to market distortion. The Commission has strongly supported the view that support schemes must be

32 EU Commission, "EU Biodiversity Strategy for 2030" (n. 8), 5.

33 EU Commission, "An EU Strategy to harness the potential of offshore renewable energy for a climate neutral future" (n. 4), 2.

34 Ibid., 10.

35 IPCC (n. 7).

36 EU Commission, "An EU Strategy to harness the potential of offshore renewable energy for a climate neutral future" (n. 4).

adapted to respond to the falling production costs of maturing renewable energy technologies, such as wind energy generation.[37] Even though the Renewable Energy Directives afford broad discretion to Member States to design support schemes in order to reach the EU's renewable energy targets, the Commission has stressed that these schemes must comply with EU internal market rules. In that respect, the 2014 Environmental and Energy Guidelines adopted a strict approach to the various interventions in the energy sector, to limit them to what is necessary.[38]

This liberal economic approach of the Commission is vividly illustrated in the 2030 Biodiversity Strategy, which puts remarkable emphasis on the economic benefits of nature protection measures, and the compelling business case for biodiversity conservation to contribute towards Europe's economic recovery.[39] On the other hand, the EU has been somewhat reluctant to lay down binding environmental obligations.[40] In particular, the EU has, so far, waited to see how technology unfolds, and has developed only non-binding instruments[41] which aim to foster innovation and not hamper competition in the internal market. The primary disadvantage of this approach is the voluntary nature of EU guidelines, which may be disregarded by EU courts, in the event of legal disputes.

Postponing the adoption of preventive measures at the EU level appears to be inconsistent with the precautionary principle.[42] Yet, the current wait-and-see approach does not necessarily equate to regulatory paralysis, as the EU is actively monitoring related developments before adopting more concrete environmental rules.[43] It echoes the fast pace of technological developments in the sector; if the EU adopted hard-binding rules immediately, they could quickly become obsolete. However, in the absence of sector-specific instruments, ocean energy projects are only subject to the existing sectoral EU (marine) environmental directives.[44] The lack of specificity, and the heterogeneity of the existing instruments, increase the risks posed to the marine environment, because Member States retain broad discretion in formulating their domestic protection measures, and are enabled to prioritise economic interests. According to economic theories, the ensuing

---

37 EU Commission, "Renewable Energy Progress Report", COM(2013) 175 final, 9–10.

38 EU Commission, "Guidelines on State Aid for Environmental Protection and Energy 2014–2020" [2014] OJ L 200/1.

39 EU Commission, "EU Biodiversity Strategy for 2030" (n. 8) 4, 15–18.

40 Anna Cudennec, "The European Legal Framework for Marine Renewable Energies" (2016) 30 *Ocean Yearbook* 488, 495.

41 EU Commission, "Guidance Document on Wind Energy Developments and EU Nature Legislation", COM (2020) 7730 final.

42 Art. 191(2), Consolidated Versions of the Treaty on European Union and the Treaty on the Functioning of the European Union (TFEU) [2016] OJ C202/1 (TFEU).

43 Steins et al. (n. 14).

44 Ronán Long, "Harnessing Offshore Wind Energy in Europe: Legal Challenges and Policy Conundrums in the European Union" (2014) 29 *International Journal of Marine and Coastal Law* 690, 702–703.

regulatory competition, and the correlated uncertainty, send negative signals to the industry, and can negatively affect technological innovation in the EU market.[45]

3. OPPORTUNITIES AND CHALLENGES IN RECALIBRATING THE ENVIRONMENTAL REGULATION OF MARINE RENEWABLES

In the context of reviewing the MSFD, the EU is exploring avenues to tackle challenges in the regulation of offshore economic activities.[46] Among other things, the Commission has stressed the need to complement the MSFD with more specific legislation where there are gaps, as in the case of marine renewables.[47] The plans for an unparalleled transformation of the blue economy have triggered debates about how to and who should regulate offshore renewables to achieve a competitive energy market, safeguard innovation (which is deemed important for energy security and consumer welfare), and, at the same time, protect the marine environment while navigating a sea of uncertainty. Indeed, while the offshore energy sector has taken an impressive stride forward by advancing technologies, with an improved result in terms of electricity capacity, significant knowledge gaps remain regarding the status of the marine environment in different regions, as well as the cumulative and long-term impacts of the rapid rise of marine renewables on biodiversity.[48] Besides the extensive knowledge, assessment and reporting needed, the main challenges for the proper regulation of marine renewables are related to the implementation of the EU instruments, which suffers due to lack of expertise, resources, and political will, at the domestic level.[49]

Traditionally, the identification of public interests, and the ensuing regulation for their realisation, was considered to be a state monopoly. However, considering the challenges of regulating highly dynamic markets, the assumption that top-down regulation is a panacea for safeguarding public interests is being put to the test. Member States often lack the capacity and data to keep abreast of technological and scientific developments, and the implementation of technical rules is costly and burdensome. At the same time, EU free movement and state

---

45 Michèle Finck, "Blockchains: Regulating the Unknown" (2018) 19 *German Law Journal* 665, 676.

46 Art. 23, Marine Strategy Framework Directive (n. 26).

47 EU Commission, "Report on the Implementation of the MSFD" (n. 30), 26–29.

48 Bastien Taormina et al., "A Review of Potential Impacts of Submarine Power Cables on the Marine Environment: Knowledge Gaps, Recommendations and Future Directions" (2018) 96 *Renewable and Sustainable Energy Reviews* 380, 380–381.

49 EU Commission, "Report on the Implementation of the MSFD" (n. 30), 29.

aid rules shape the discretion of Member States to intervene and regulate markets for the sake of public interests. Even though the relevant EU rules provide for exceptions to accommodate public interest considerations,[50] the EU is pushing for the liberalisation of markets, and sector-specific rules usually aim to narrow down state intervention to the minimum, to avoid regulatory fragmentation and the resulting distortion of competition.[51]

The shift of the role of the state, as a source of regulation within the EU, has resulted in the proliferation of soft-law instruments and mixed forms of regulation, which purport to involve the industry and other stakeholders in the lawmaking and implementation processes. Parallel to the several national self-regulatory initiatives, private regulation is gaining momentum, and is often part of the regulatory strategies of the EU to address novel challenges, in cases of regulatory uncertainty and technical complexity, in many sectors, such as food security, sports and Internet regulation.[52] Such private regulation has taken various forms, including voluntary regulation to address the particular interests of an industry, morally motivated self-regulation (voluntary corporate social responsibility initiatives), and private regulation that is explicitly endorsed by states or the EU, in order to achieve certain public purposes (for example, the EU code of conduct on countering illegal hate speech online). In addition, private regulation may be the result of pressure exerted by non-governmental organisations (NGOs) or lobby groups. Even without state intervention, private regulation can have (quasi-)binding effects, and can be enforced through various market mechanisms (for example, reputational mechanisms).[53] Although private regulation has gained momentum, due to its flexibility in cases of regulatory uncertainty and technical complexity, it has been criticised as an ineffective alternative to public regulation, *inter alia* due to the risks for regulatory capture, and the lack of robust enforcement mechanisms.[54] That critique is partly based on empirical evidence supporting the view that private (self-)regulation does not always prioritise the protection of public interests.[55] Nonetheless, pure

50 See, for instance, the exception for services of general economic interest under Art. 106(2) TFEU (n. 42).

51 See, for instance, EU Commission, "Guidelines on State Aid for Environmental Protection and Energy 2014–2020" (n. 38), which call for the gradual reduction of support schemes and the shift from feed-in tariffs to feed-in premiums.

52 Vassilis Hatzopoulos and Sofia Roma, "Caring for Sharing? The Collaborative Economy under EU Law" (2017) 54 *Common Market Law Review* 81, 81.

53 Reviews have a considerable impact as an enforcement mechanism against users who do not comply with the relevant guidelines of the platforms: see the case of Airbnb "community guidelines", described in Michèle Finck, "Digital Regulation", LSE Law, Society and Economy Working Paper 15/2017, 9.

54 Study for the Assessment of the Implementation of the Code of Practice on Disinformation, SMART 2019/0041 [2020].

55 John Infranca, "Intermediary Institutions and Sharing Economy" (2016) 90 *Tulane Law Review* 29, 35–36.

self-regulation is rare; there is often some sort of delegation or endorsement by the Member States or the EU.[56] For instance, the incorporation of private standards within EU or national regulatory regimes results in their becoming *de facto* mandatory.[57] Furthermore, private standards are often associated with public norms and international (environmental) rules, to gain legitimacy and increase their uptake by the industry.[58] Therefore, the public–private division of regulation distorts the more nuanced reality, and is used only as a heuristic concept for this contribution.

In light of the rapid pace with which the marine renewable sector is projected to progress to deliver the European Green Deal, one major concern is that the regulatory framework needs to be flexible and quickly adaptable.[59] Regulatory experimentation, potentially in the form of sandboxes that allow innovators to test their technologies and business models in an environment that temporarily exempts them from cumbersome administrative procedures, could reduce legal uncertainty, and bring innovation to the market more quickly, while safeguarding public interest considerations.[60] For instance, pilot projects are taking place to assess the impacts of multi-use, nature-inclusive offshore energy platforms.[61] Due to technological complexity and regulatory uncertainty, co-regulation,[62] as a hybrid model of public–private regulation, could lead the way forward and offer future-proof solutions, by combining the benefits of both regulatory paradigms.[63] Such hybrid regulatory arrangements can strike a balance between legal stability and predictability, while at the same time fostering innovation and

---

56 Arts. 40 and 41, Regulation (EU) 2016/679 of 27 April 2016 on the protection of natural persons regarding the processing of personal data and on the free movement of such data, and repealing Directive 95/46/EC OJ L119/1.

57 Eric Lambin and Tannis Thorlakson, "Sustainability Standards: Interactions between Private Actors" (2018) 43 *Civil Society, and Governments, Annual Review of Environment and Resources* 369, 379.

58 Axel Marx, "The Public–Private Distinction in Global Governance: How Relevant is it in the Case of Voluntary Sustainability Standards" (2017) 3 *The Chinese Journal of Global Governance* 1, 12–15.

59 In the context of the digital market, the EU Commission has suggested a model of co-regulation, which would combine the establishment of procedural obligations on digital platforms with private industry standards, and the drawing-up of codes of conduct by providers of intermediation services: Study for the Assessment of the Implementation of the Code of Practice on Disinformation, SMART 2019/0041 [2020].

60 Esther Van der Waal, Alexandra Das and Tineke van der Schoor, "Participatory Experimentation with Energy Law: Digging in a 'Regulatory Sandbox' for Local Energy Initiatives in the Netherlands" (2020) 13 *Energies* 458, 458.

61 TNO Project on Energy Islands and Green Production Platforms <https://www.tno.nl/en/sustainable/renewable-electricity/system-integration-wind/energy-islands-conversion-transport/>.

62 This refers to a broad spectrum of regulatory initiatives between pure voluntary self-regulation and pure state regulation: Tinne Heremans, *Professional Services in the EU Internal Market – Quality Regulation and Self-regulation* (Bloomsbury Publishing 2012), 81–82.

63 Fabrizio Caffagi, "Rethinking Private Regulation in the European Regulatory Space", EUI Working Paper LAW 2006/13.

competition in the internal market.[64] In particular, this contribution suggests the endorsement of a co-regulatory approach at the EU level, where goal-based regulation would dictate objectives, allowing private regulators some discretion in selecting the necessary measures to achieve them, and at the same time enabling the regulator to benefit from the expertise of relevant stakeholders in highly specialised sectors.[65] Effectively, this contribution suggests drawing on an existing regulatory approach, since co-regulation already forms part of the EU's regulatory toolbox, albeit mostly limited to the implementation stage.[66]

3.1. BEYOND PURE VOLUNTARINESS: EXAMPLES OF EU-SUPPORTED HYBRID REGULATORY ARRANGEMENTS

The co-regulatory approach in the field of product safety offers an illustrative example of an EU-supported hybrid regulatory arrangement.[67] According to that approach, EU directives only establish essential product safety requirements, and leave the technical details to be developed by European standardisation bodies.[68] Compliance with these private standards means that products conform with safety and health requirements set by the EU rules.[69] The advantage of using such standards is that they offer consumers and businesses legal certainty, and, at the same time, their flexibility does not hamper innovation. Another example of EU delegated co-regulation is found in the Unfair Commercial Practices Directive, Article 5 of which suggests that general EU rules should be complemented by forms of self-regulation.[70] Its general clauses were drafted to ensure that the Directive is future-proof, and contains safeguards in case self-regulation fails

64 EU Commission, "Online Platforms and the Digital Single Markets: Opportunities and Challenges for Europe", COM (2016) 288 final, 5.

65 Interinstitutional Agreement on Better Law-Making, OJ L 123/1, para. 18.

66 European Economic and Social Committee on Self-Regulation and Co-regulation in the EU legislative framework, Opinion of 22 April 2015, C291/29.

67 The Discussion Draft on Online Intermediary platforms, which proposes the transplant of this mode of co-regulation to digital platform regulation. The draft includes several suggestions and requirements to improve the integrity of online quality reputation systems (online ratings and reviews). See also EU Parliament Think Tank, "Reform of the EU liability regime for online intermediaries" [2020].

68 See also the example of the European Standardization Committee, which has drafted a set of horizontal voluntary standards for services, EU Commission, "Guidelines on the applicability of Article 101 of the Treaty on the Functioning of the European Union to horizontal co-operation agreements" C (2023) 3445 final.

69 That presumption of compliance is partly associated with the institutional framework under which these standards are promulgated, as they ensure transparency and participation of relevant stakeholders. The situation might be slightly different where standards are formulated by independent private standard-setting bodies.

70 Hans-W. Micklitz, "A General Framework Directive on Fair Trading" in Hugh Collins (ed.), *The Forthcoming EC Directive on Unfair Commercial Practices* (Kluwer Law International 2004), 62.

to achieve the goals pursued.[71] The need for such a layered regulatory approach also became apparent in the case of the digital market.[72] Public regulation needs to be technologically neutral,[73] and has to be complemented by an intermediate normative layer, such as specialised "techno-legal standards" which can translate legal rules and objectives into technical specifications.[74] The essential role of digital platforms as regulatory intermediaries is also illustrated in the recent EU Platform to Business (P2B) Regulation.[75] The P2B Regulation follows the co-regulation approach, combining a principle-based regulatory framework with self-regulation, by means of encouraging the development of codes of conduct by providers of intermediation services.[76]

As far as the regulation of marine renewables is concerned, the MSFD Impact Assessment considers strengthening the Directive's implementation by adopting implementing Acts to address problems such as administrative burden.[77] Similarly, the 2030 EU Biodiversity Strategy calls for a hybrid approach to regulating economic activities, referring to the establishment of a European biodiversity governance framework, which will include a set of agreed indicators, and will enable regular assessment and corrective action when necessary. This element of oversight could address the systemic limitations of unrestrained self-regulation by establishing safeguards in case private regulation fails to achieve the goals set. In addition, a co-regulatory approach can promote inclusivity and foster the EU's democratic legitimacy.[78] For instance, the Commission

---

71 Jan Trzaskowski, "Interpretation and Assessment under the Unfair Commercial Practices Directive: ICC Code for Advertising and Marketing and the Commission's Staff Working Document" in Ulf Bernitz and Caroline Heide-Jorgensen (eds.), *Marketing and Advertising Law in a Process of Harmonisation* (Bloomsbury 2017), 85.

72 The Offshore Safety Directive (2013/30/EU) is an example of such layered co-regulation at the EU level for the realisation of public interests. The EU legislature, under the pressure of the industry and certain Member States, opted for a goal-based approach, which allows significant leeway for self-regulation.

73 The Unfair Commercial Practices Directive is an example of technologically neutral rules, as it applies irrespective of the device used to implement a certain commercial practice.

74 Cristoph Busch, "Self-Regulation and Regulatory Intermediation in the Platform Economy" in Marta Cantero Gamito and Hans-W. Micklitz (eds.), *The Role of the EU in Transnational Legal Ordering: Standards, Contracts and Codes* (Edward Elgar 2020), 127–129.

75 Regulation (EU) 2019/1150 of 20 June 2019 on promoting fairness and transparency for business users of online intermediation services OJ L 186/57. *Inter alia*, this Regulation provides that terms and conditions need to be drafted in plain and intelligible language, sets out grounds for delisting business users, and obliges intermediaries to establish a system to deal with complaints in a timely manner. For a relevant discussion, see Katerina Maniadaki, "Net Neutrality Regulation in the EU: Competition and Beyond" (2019) 10 *Journal of European Competition Law and Practice* 479, 479–488.

76 Friso Bostoen and Daniel Mandrescu, "Assessing Abuse of Dominance in the Platform Economy: A Case Study of App Stores" (2020) 16 *European Competition Journal* 431, 476–477.

77 EU Commission "Combined Evaluation Roadmap/Inception Impact Assessment of the MSFD" (n. 29), 4.

78 Michèle Finck, "Digital Regulation: Designing a Supranational Framework for the Platform Economy", LSE Legal Studies Working Papers No. 15, 2017.

has suggested promoting a polycentric, collaborative approach, which entails dialogues with stakeholders and improving participatory governance, to address complex regulatory challenges and act as a counterbalance for safeguarding the proper functioning of private regulation.[79] This approach goes beyond the two-way consultations between Member States and individual maritime sectors under the Maritime Spatial Planning Directive (MSPD). Specifically, the Commission has proposed the establishment of "communities of practice", where the industry, social partners, NGOs and scientists can exchange ideas, share experiences, and work on joint projects relating to multipurpose offshore installations.[80] The Community of Practice in the Dutch part of the North Sea could serve as an example of an informal participatory tool, which may assemble the necessary evidence for data-driven decision-making in regulating emerging technologies.[81]

A co-regulatory approach can ensure co-responsibility and co-ownership by all relevant actors in meeting the relevant environmental commitments. Making the industry responsible for its own regulation can improve the implementation of EU law on the ground, by facilitating less costly implementation/enforcement, as well as continuous review and adaptation of the regulatory framework.[82] This strategy can tap in to the decentralised expertise of the industry, to react to the particularities of the sector.[83] Importantly, private regulation is not limited by political and territorial constraints.[84] Instead, it can foster regulatory competition between transnational companies in promoting public interests, and could, therefore, lead a race to the top, in terms of environmental standards, instead of merely seeking compliance with minimum harmonised standards under EU directives.[85] Economic theory holds that the industry will invest in environmental protection if market competitiveness requires it, or if it is in fear of stricter regulatory action by governments.[86] It has, therefore, been suggested

---

79 EU Commission, "EU Biodiversity Strategy for 2030" (n. 8), 15.

80 EU Commission, "An EU Strategy to harness the potential of offshore renewable energy for a climate neutral future" (n. 4), 10.

81 Steins et al. (n. 14), 2.

82 Molly Cohen and Arun Sundararajan, "Self-Regulation and Innovation in the Peer-to-Peer Sharing Economy" (2015) 82 *University of Chicago Law Review* 116, 129–132.

83 Maximilian Grafenstein, "Co-regulation and the Competitive Advantage in the GDPR: Data Protection Certification Mechanisms, Codes of Conduct and the 'State of the Art' of Data Protection-by-Design", <https://papers.ssrn.com/sol3/papers.cfm?abstract_id=3336990>.

84 Mehdi Piri Damagh and Michael Faure, "Self-Regulation versus Public Regulation: An Analysis of Environmental and Safety Standard Setting in Oil and Gas Pipeline Sector" in Niels Philipsen et al. (eds.), *Market Integration: The EU Experience and Implications for Regulatory Reform in China* (Springer 2016), 287.

85 Michael Fehling, "Energy Transition in the European Union and its Member States: Interpreting Federal Competence Allocation in the Light of the Paris Agreement" (2021) 10 *Transnational Environmental Law* 339, 359–360.

86 Damagh and Faure (n. 84), 297.

that market-based coercion, and the diffusion of best practices, can replace the need for sanctions, in ensuring enforcement of the applicable environmental standards.[87]

The design of a hybrid governance approach may determine its effectiveness in delivering sustainability goals.[88] For co-regulation to work, clear goals need to be set out, as well as the conditions under which co-regulation might apply, and what effects it might generate. Under the Renewable Energy Directive, voluntary schemes became the main tools for producers to demonstrate their compliance with the EU sustainability criteria.[89] The Commission recognised these schemes, as long as they contained the minimum environmental criteria set in the Renewable Energy Directive, and provided for competent, independent and fraud-free auditing and certification that verified companies' claims of compliance at least once a year. Reliance on voluntary sustainability standards promised to increase flexibility, and to benefit from innovation and best practices on the ground. These voluntary schemes were expected to function both as secondary regulators – by providing further sustainability criteria – and as monitoring and verification mechanisms.

However, this expectation did not materialise, because of the minimal requirements set by EU sustainability standards, as well as the absence of monitoring, enforcement and sanctioning mechanisms.[90] In particular, the lax EU meta-regulation enabled the proliferation of competing voluntary schemes, which in turn led to a lack of incentive on the part of producers to be certified against the best available sustainability practices.[91] Even though multi-stakeholder schemes, including NGOs, purported to enhance the sustainability standards, moving beyond the minimum requirements under the Renewable Energy Directive, concurrent industry-based initiatives adhered to those baseline minimum requirements, initiating a "race to the bottom". Pressure for low-cost production seems to have led to "commoditized, low-quality auditing".[92] Under the Directive, the Commission is not tasked with supervising the operation of the various private schemes, making it impossible for it to gather the necessary evidence to control potential infringements of the sustainability requirements for certification.[93] The EU Parliament's decision

---

87 Michelle Reese, "Nanotechnology: Using Co-Regulation to Bring Regulation of Modern Technologies into the 21st Century" (2013) 23 *Health Matrix* 537, 563.

88 Axel Marx, "Public-Private Partnerships for Sustainable Development: Exploring their Design and Its Impact on Effectiveness" (2019) 11 *Sustainability* 1087.

89 EU Commission, "Renewable Energy Progress Report", COM (2019) 225 final, 13.

90 Yoshiko Naiki, "Trade and Bioenergy: Explaining and Assessing the Regime Complex for Sustainable Bioenergy" (2016) 27 *European Journal of International Law* 129, 141.

91 See critique by the European Court of Auditors, *Special Report: The EU System for Certification of Sustainable Biofuels* (Publications Office of the EU 2016), 27.

92 Tim Bartley, *Rules without Rights: Land, Labor, and Private Authority in the Global Economy* (OUP 2018), 264.

93 European Court of Auditors (n. 91), 28.

to propose an end to the use of palm oil illustrates the lack of trust in the effectiveness of this hybrid approach to preventing the negative externalities of biofuel production.[94] Further explanations for the failure of this hybrid approach in delivering sustainability may be the absence of a counterbalancing power, in terms of consumer involvement in the formulation and use of biofuels standards, as well as the lack of transparency, and lack of involvement of NGOs, which could apply pressure by "naming and shaming" lax voluntary schemes. In practice, this example illustrates that there are deeply rooted structural problems that necessitate a more active involvement of both the public and the EU in the design and implementation of private standards, as well as in mandatory rules, to safeguard public interest considerations.[95]

3.2. THE CALL FOR COMPLEMENTING EU PRINCIPLED META-REGULATION WITH PRIVATE STANDARDS

Drawing on the existing experiences with the EU's involvement in hybrid regulatory arrangements, this contribution argues that, under certain conditions, private regulation of environmental and safety aspects of marine renewables can operate in a complementary manner with EU principled meta-regulation.[96] The EU can be assisted in implementing the legal framework by regulatory surrogates (standard-setting bodies, external audit firms), while simultaneously exerting influence over their substance and procedures. Co-regulation needs to be controlled by a third party, which is either an official body or an independent regulatory authority, normally with oversight and monitoring power, and, in some instances, the power to impose sanctions. Specifically, the EU rules should operate as principled meta-regulation of private regulatory initiatives, setting specific environmental objectives for the activities of the marine renewables sector, and closely overseeing their performance, while leaving the technical details to be developed by competent bodies, such as European standardisation bodies.[97] To better orchestrate private regulatory capacity towards delivering

94 Sarah Stattman et al., "Toward Sustainable Biofuels in the European Union? Lessons from a Decade of Hybrid Biofuel Governance" (2018) 10 *Sustainability* 4111.

95 Christine Moser and Sina Leipold, "Toward 'hardened' accountability? Analyzing the European Union's hybrid transnational governance in timber and biofuel supply chains" (2021) 15 *Regulation and Governance* 115, 128.

96 Enrico Partiti, "The Place of Voluntary Standards in Managing Social and Environmental Risks in Global Value Chains" (2021) 13 *European Journal of Risk Regulation* 114, 117.

97 The EU Regulation on fairness and transparency in the platform economy (EU 2019/1150) follows the co-regulatory approach sketched out above, combining a principle-based legal framework with industry standards, while encouraging the drawing-up of codes of conduct by providers of intermediation services. In particular, the providers of these services must draft their terms and conditions in plain and intelligible language, set out the grounds based on which the platform may demote or delist its business users, and set up internal systems to handle complaints from business users in a timely manner.

public interests, the proper selection of these regulatory intermediaries is essential.[98] For example, harmonised European standards would have some advantages, compared with industry-based instruments, as they are elaborated in a tested and trustworthy institutional setting which ensures transparency and participation by relevant stakeholders. Therefore, public authorities should distinguish between schemes established and managed by the industry, and those under mobilised by more inclusive multi-stakeholder initiatives.

At the same time, effective orchestration of private regulation depends on the substantive and procedural requirements established by the public authorities, and their monitoring and verification. EU meta-regulation, in the form of precise substantive and procedural requirements, is needed to ensure that private and public interests are balanced.[99] In other words, meta-regulation is not envisaged as a way to reduce the level of regulatory oversight (as in the case of the Renewable Energy Directive), but, rather, implies a reorientation of regulatory activity from direct regulation towards setting guidelines for the design of private regulation. Depending on the design of the regulatory arrangement, proper orchestration of the capacity of private regulators by the EU can improve procedural inclusiveness and transparency, and initiate a "race to the top".[100] For example, the Commission has often used soft-law instruments, such as guidelines, to support voluntary initiatives, and encourage the adoption of private standards and codes of conduct by the business sector, in cooperation with other relevant stakeholders.[101]

To maintain the technological neutrality of EU rules, they must be supported by an intermediate normative layer, such as specialised "techno-legal standards", which can translate the environmental objectives into technical specifications.[102] The advantage of using such standards is that they offer businesses the necessary legal certainty to invest in expanding the sector, while their flexibility allows for market innovation.[103] Fostering innovation is especially crucial at a time when economic stability and energy security, in the context of a raging pandemic, are at stake, and regulatory burdens could prove too costly for the industry to

98 Rebecca Schmidt, "Protecting the Environment through Sports? Public-Private Cooperation for Regulatory Resources and International Law" (2018) 28 *European Journal of International Law* 1341, 1341.

99 Axel Marx and Jan Wouters, "Competition and Cooperation in the Market of Voluntary Sustainability Standards", UNFSS Discussion Paper No. 135, 19.

100 Enrico Partiti, "Orchestration as a Form of Public Action: The EU Engagement with Voluntary Sustainability Standards" (2019) 25 *European Law Journal* 94, 96.

101 With regard to EU-sponsored self-regulation, see the EU's guidelines to support voluntary self-regulation, such as the Memorandum of Understanding regarding the sale of counterfeit goods on the Internet, and the Code of Conduct on countering illegal hate speech online (last evaluation June 2020).

102 Busch (n. 74), 127–129.

103 Theo van den Hoogen et al., "The Emergence and Use of Self-Regulation in the European Decision-Making Process: Does it Make a Difference?" (2010) 4 *Legisprudence* 343, 343–383.

bear. Yet, these standards need to meet certain conditions to be trustworthy and legitimate. In that regard, the EU Parliament has requested that the Commission establish criteria to evaluate the credibility of private standards, such as independence from industry, the inclusion of social and environmental interests in standard-setting, independent auditing and transparency.[104]

The layered co-regulatory approach adopted by the EU in the context of offshore oil and gas activities can serve as a model for the regulation of marine renewables.[105] The Offshore Safety Directive assigns an exceptional position to the industry, which plays an instrumental role in shaping lawmaking and implementation processes. There is a significant amount of (sometimes *de facto*) delegated regulation by the private industry, which defines its own operational standards. In particular, the operators of offshore oil and gas installations are under an obligation to prepare, and submit to the competent domestic authority, a series of documents relating to the management of risks associated with those activities.[106] The Directive also contains provisions for stimulating public consultation in the decision-making process. Once offshore oil and gas activities have commenced, operators are required to ensure that their corporate prevention policies apply throughout the life cycle of the installations, by taking all necessary measures, including setting up appropriate monitoring mechanisms, to ensure effective implementation.[107]

Instead of imposing prescriptive standards for the operation of offshore installations, the Directive calls for the adoption of a series of procedural measures to reduce the risks of offshore oil and gas activities. Under this goal-oriented approach, the offshore industry becomes primarily responsible for the safety of its operations. Moreover, the Directive contains ample references to "best practices and standards".[108] These norms regularly follow a performance-based approach rather than being based on rigid prescriptive requirements imposed by the Member States.[109] To disseminate such best regulatory practices, reinforce the exchange of information, and enhance cross-border cooperation among the Member States, the Commission has created the European Union

104 Partiti, "Orchestration as a Form of Public Action" (n. 100).

105 Even though further monitoring is needed, the implementation report on the Offshore Safety Directive provides that it has largely been effective in improving the response to possible emergencies in the sector: see EU Commission "Report assessing the implementation of Directive 2013/30/EU of the European Parliament and the Council of 12 June 2013 on the safety of offshore oil and gas operations and amending Directive 2004/35/EC", COM/2020/732 final.

106 Art. 11, Offshore Safety Directive (n. 72).

107 Ibid., Art. 11(1)(h), (i) and (j). See also Arts. 15 and 16.

108 EU Commission, "Best Available Techniques Guidance Document on Upstream Hydrocarbon Exploration and Exploitation" 27 February 2019.

109 Myron Nordquist and Aimee Fausser, "Offshore Drilling in the Outer Continental Shelf: International Best Practices and Safety Standards in the Wake of the Deepwater Horizon Explosion and Oil Spill" in Michael W. Lodge and Myron Nordquist (eds.), *Peaceful Order in the World's Oceans: Essays in Honor of Satya N. Nandan* (Brill 2014), 115–145.

Offshore Oil and Gas Authorities Group.[110] Importantly, compliance with best practices does not give rise to a presumption of conformity with the substantive environmental requirements of the Directive, and hence does not affect the liability of operators. Conformity with best practices can serve as rebuttable proof, but operators need to demonstrate the continuous performance of due diligence.

Although the Directive places significant responsibility upon the industry, state supervision of the industry's normative developments, and monitoring of their implementation, are indispensable. One of the most significant lessons learned from the *Deepwater Horizon* blowout is that the existence of binding rules cannot safeguard the safety of operations and prevent major accidents. Instead, it is the rigorous compliance with those rules by the industry that plays the biggest role.[111] To that end, Member States must take all measures, and show constant vigilance, to ensure that operators fully comply with the regulatory framework, and with their commitments undertaken in the documents mentioned above, such as the major hazards report.[112] Additionally, the Directive envisages independent verification and continuous inspection of offshore installations, before the commencement of their operation, and periodically after the start of their activities, to assess whether the operator is complying with the major hazards report and all other documents submitted for the licensing.[113] Third-party auditing, and the use of new technologies such as satellite images and remote sensing, can contribute to better compliance. In juxtaposition to the "hands-off" approach regarding monitoring and enforcement in the context of the Renewable Energy Directive, the accident confirms that effective monitoring and enforcement mechanisms must be in place to guarantee the good functioning of private complements to legislation.

4. CONCLUSIONS: WHAT ROLE FOR A CO-REGULATORY APPROACH IN REGULATING MARINE RENEWABLES?

Although existing EU environmental instruments apply to certain aspects of the operation of marine renewables in European seas, many essential issues are falling between the cracks. This emerging sector can serve as an important laboratory to assess the viability of a co-regulatory approach in the context of regulatory uncertainty and technical complexity. Uncertainty manifests itself in various

---

110 EU Commission, Decision of 19 January 2012 on setting up of the European Union Offshore Oil and Gas Authorities Group, OJ L2012/C.

111 Sergei Vinogradov, "The Impact of the Deepwater Horizon: The Evolving International, Legal Regime for Offshore Accidental Pollution Prevention, Preparedness and Response" (2013) 44 *Ocean Development & International Law* 335, 350.

112 Art. 8(1), Offshore Safety Directive (n. 72).

113 Ibid., Arts. 17 and 21(3).

forms, such as environmental effects, technological and scientific developments, and changing climate conditions, all of which influence both the regulators and the regulatees. In light of the precautionary principle, the EU's ambitious commitments to achieve biodiversity conservation and zero pollution, and the high rate of innovation in the sector, the EU should not wait until emerging technologies are fully mature before conversing with the relevant stakeholders. This contribution argues that, instead of greenwashing the environmental externalities of marine renewables, a hybrid regulatory model that transcends the pigeonholing distinction between public and private regulation could already, at this stage of development, facilitate innovation, address the unknown risks of the expansion of the sector, and offer future-proof solutions.[114] Therefore, the anticipated regulation of marine renewables could serve as the quintessential testing ground to examine the feasibility and limits of a co-regulatory approach which can, arguably, reconcile the need for legal stability and predictability with the requirements of innovation and competition in the internal energy market.

Nonetheless, one cannot overlook the "dark side" of co-regulation. Besides the potential frictions between hybrid regulatory arrangements and EU competition law, there are plenty of challenges in achieving a truly inclusive and transparent regulatory framework, in light of the discrepancies of power, among diverse groups of stakeholders, to leverage their positions. Even if enabling the participation of affected communities would safeguard procedural legitimacy, there is little evidence that this would also improve output legitimacy – in other words, whether more inclusive regulatory frameworks can bring about more effective marine environmental protection.[115] In addition, the co-regulatory framework tests the limits of the EU's constitutional framework, by raising issues of authority delegation and the application of competition law to private environmental agreements.[116] In terms of legitimacy and accountability, co-regulation triggers discussions about the extent of (judicial) control of private environmental standards in the EU legal order.[117] For instance, the lack of control over the proliferation of voluntary sustainability standards for biofuels, under the Renewable Energy Directive, has attracted heavy criticism regarding potential greenwashing at the EU level.[118]

114 Caffagi (n. 63).

115 Suzanne Kingston and Edwin Alblas, "Of the People, by the People, for the People? The European Union's Experience with Private Environmental Regulation and Enforcement" in Madeleine de Cock Buning and Linda Selden (eds.), *Private Regulation and Enforcement in the EU: Finding the Right Balance from a Citizen's Perspective* (Hart 2020), 189.

116 Megi Medzmariashvili, "Delegation of Rulemaking Power to European Standards Organizations: Reconsidered" (2017) 44 *Legal Issues of Economic Integration* 353, 353–366.

117 Mariolina Elantonio, "Alternative Forms of Regulation: Are They Really Better Regulation" (2017) 19 *European Journal of Law Reform* 141, 155–161.

118 ISEAL Alliance, "Private Sustainability Standards and the EU Renewable Energy Directive", <https://www.isealalliance.org/impacts-and-benefits/case-studies/private-sustainability-standards-and-eu-renewable-energy>.

The design of hybrid arrangements plays a key role in both their input and output legitimacy, as effective co-regulation requires an active role on behalf of the public and the EU, to prevent merely shifting the responsibility for achieving sustainability to private actors. Unless meticulously designed and overseen by public regulators, private environmental standards can raise significant questions about their compatibility with the EU's constitutional principles. The question thus remains as to what extent traditional regulatory tasks of the EU and its Member States can be delegated to the market; and even then, to what extent should the EU and its Member States intervene and create safeguards, in case private regulation fails to protect public interest considerations? When an important environmental target is not met by means of private standards, direct regulation should take over. Bearing these concerns in mind, this contribution posits that we need to further explore the advantages and limitations of co-regulation, instead of merely questioning the effectiveness and legitimacy of private regulatory instruments. These convoluted issues cannot be answered by legal research alone; it is necessary to build upon other research theories, concepts and methodologies. In that regard, further empirical and economic research is needed, to shed further light on the effectiveness of a hybrid regulatory approach in regulating marine renewables within the multilevel EU legal order.

MARITIME RAS TECHNO-REGULATORY REGIME

Six Blocks of Dynamic Influence Towards Good Environmental Stewardship

Tafsir Matin JOHANSSON, Jon SKINNER, Dimitrios DALAKLIS, Thomas KLENUM and Aspasia PASTRA*

1. INTRODUCTION

Breakthrough innovation followed and enhanced by revolutionary technology has brought the maritime regulatory community the transformative promise of "Robotic and Autonomous Systems (RAS)" – but what is needed to allow RAS to best be embraced?[1] One of the unique aspects of applying RAS-configured service robots is the potential to acquire unique data and information on the ocean and marine environment, to enhance current research in remote exploration. Like other dynamic robotic developments, these RAS service robots have advanced from single applications, like remote exploration and data gathering, to a wide range of more holistic services. Within the maritime domain, technological innovations have led to effective integration of RAS, gradually transforming – and, in niche areas, replacing – human-presence-based operations. Dubbed as a by-product of the Fourth Industrial Revolution, remote inspection techniques (RIT), utilising RAS-oriented service robotics, are now being tested and

* This contribution derives from the findings of project BUGWRIGHT2: Autonomous Robotic Inspection and Maintenance on Ship Hulls and Storage Tanks (Task 1.4), funded by the European Union's Horizon 2020 research and innovation programme under grant agreement No 871260. The authors would like to thank the Nippon Foundation, the World Maritime University and the World Maritime University-Sasakawa Global Ocean Institute, Matanuska Susitna College (University of Alaska) and the Liberian Registry.

1 *T. Johansson*, "International Standards for Hull Inspection and Maintenance of Robotics and Autonomous Systems" in *J. Kraska and Y. Park* (eds.), *Emerging Technology and the Law of the Sea*, Cambridge University Press, 2022. See also *D. Dalaklis et al.*, "The port of Gothenburg under the influence of the fourth stage of the industrial revolution: Implementing a wide portfolio of digital tools to optimize the conduct of operations", *Maritime Technology and Research (MTR)*, 2022 4(3).

deployed to survey critical areas, such as enclosed spaces of commercial vessels, that are prone to damage and deterioration, and are otherwise difficult to access and monitor.

On the external front, outer-hull inspections require upkeep through annual surveys, intermediate surveys and special (or renewal) surveys, and enhanced surveys, which are unavoidable obligations for ship owners and operators, under international law. The principal regulations for outer-hull survey and maintenance are covered in the 2011 International Maritime Organization (IMO) Guidelines for the control and management of ships' biofouling to minimize the transfer of invasive aquatic species. The Guidelines call for two specific actions: the monitoring of the biofouling status of a vessel, and the mitigation of both imminent and potential threats to vessel safety and the marine environment. Traditionally, these surveys have been human-centric, requiring much time and effort. Classification societies, licensed by flag states to survey and classify ships, and issue certificates, have laid down significant, and at times onerous, conditions that must be met at the preliminary, inspection and post-inspection stages. Since inception, RIT have been a preferred alternative to human-centric regulatory tasks that pose a risk to human life.

The novel aspect of the application of RIT to climate change mitigation benefits derived from hulls with a better environmental footprint has garnered widespread attention in the maritime regulatory and policy communities, and there are clear indicators that the paradigm shift has begun.[2] National flag state authorities, and classification societies and ship owners, have all been steadily adapting to RIT-based solutions, especially during the COVID-19 pandemic and its special challenges, and limitations on human presence on board ships. But though the market growth of new service robotic solutions is promising, the non-standardised assortment of RIT, built with varying technical specifications, designed to perform the very same inspection and maintenance tasks, will likely slow market growth and, ultimately, hinder mass deployment. Standardisation is an international concern. It is clear that service robots should not be developed in isolation.[3] Unfortunately, manufacturers initially moved from developing industrial robots with a single use, to polyfunctional RIT, without clearly established common standards. Moving forward, though, all stakeholders would benefit from embracing and adhering to critical safety, quality, performance and

---

2 Remote Survey, Det Norske Veritas: https://www.dnv.com/oilgas/remote-survey/index.html; Survey by Remote Inspection Techniques – Use of Approved Service Suppliers, Det Norske Veritas: https://www.dnv.com/news/survey-by-remote-inspection-techniques-use-of-approved-service-suppliers-144572; Remote Technology Points to Cost Efficiency and Quality Gains, Det Norske Veritas: https://www.dnv.com/oilgas/perspectives/remote-technology-points-to-cost-efficiency-and-quality-gains.html.

3 *G. S. Virk et al.*, "ISO Standards for Service Robots", Advances in Mobile Robotics – The Eleventh International Conference on Climbing and Walking Robots and the Support Technologies for Mobile Machines, 2008, 1–6, pp. 1, 2.

efficiency standards, developed in a cooperative and common effort; and the earlier in the life cycle the better. Otherwise, achieving good environmental stewardship may prove unnecessarily slow, cumbersome and costly.

Good environmental stewardship is intrinsically linked to the responsible use and protection of the environment through sustainable and resilience-based conservation practices.[4] Those practices consist of interlocked "approaches, activities, behaviors, and technologies to protect, restore, or sustainably use, the environment".[5] Specifically, innovation has provided the opportunity to apply emerging technologies or new applications to achieve positive results across the marine transport domain, which also requires good environmental governance.

The current reality is that the international maritime RIT governance framework is fragmented and shrouded with grey areas that impede the integration of RIT alternatives at both the regional and national levels. Harmonisation efforts are at an embryonic stage, and this is acknowledged at the European Union (EU) level. Noteworthy in this milieu is a 2021 working document, issued by the General Secretariat of the Council of the EU, which focuses on harmonising international guidance for remote survey.[6] Its authors assert that there are outstanding issues that call for the common minimum standards developed by the International Association of Classification Societies (IACS) to be revisited with a view to harmonising the core steering mechanisms for effective and efficient operation of RIT on a global scale. This working paper embraces and underlines the need to bring consistency among the different classification societies' techno-regulatory provisions and practices. The need for such harmonisation is reinforced by the unique proposition tabled by the EU High-Level Expert Group on Artificial Intelligence (AI), which calls attention to a number of elements that constitute lawful, ethical and trustworthy AI, through the creation of a robust horizontal regulatory foundation (see Figure 1).[7]

---

4 *F. S. Chapin et al.*, "Ecosystem Stewardship: Sustainability Strategies for a Rapidly Changing Planet", *Trends in Ecology & Evolution*, 2010, 25(4), 241–249; Further insights can be gathered from the following publications: *N. Belelfontaine and T. Johansson*, "Effective and Efficient Maritime Administration and Corporate Social Responsibility" in *L. Froholdt* (ed.), *CSR in the Maritime Industry*, Springer, 2018; *L. Hildebrand, N. Belelfontaine and T. Johansson*, "The International Maritime Organization and Oil Pollution in the Mediterranean Sea" and *N. Belelfontaine and T. Johansson*, "The Role of the International Maritime Organization in the Prevention of Illegal Oil pollution from Ships: North Sea Special Status Area", both in A. Carpenter (ed.), *Oil Pollution in the Mediterranean Sea (The Handbook of Environmental Chemistry)*, Springer, 2016.

5 *N.J. Bennett et al.*, "Environmental Stewardship: A Conceptual Review and Analytical Framework", *Environmental Management*, 2018, 61, 597–614; See *A. Christodolou et al.*, "Four Spheres of Influence: The Critical Role of Ports in Global Decarbonization Efforts", *Ocean Yearbook*, 2021, vol. 35, 148–172.

6 *Council of the European Union*, Working Document: Non-paper from the Commission drafted to Facilitate EU Coordination, 1178/20, ADD 1, Annex, Brussels, 29 October 2020 (OR. en): https://data.consilium.europa.eu/doc/document/ST-11781-2020-ADD-1/en/pdf.

7 Report of the High-Level Expert Group on Artificial Intelligence, 2019, COM, pp. 1–36.

It is also worth noting that underwater hull-cleaning via RAS is likely to be introduced primarily to comply with the requirements necessary for the issuance of mandatory IMO anti-fouling systems (AFS) certification by flag states. However, with the adoption of the new International Convention for the Prevention of Pollution from Ships (MARPOL), Annex VI, Regulation 28 requirement for a Carbon Intensity Indicator (CII) rating to be calculated and assigned to a ship each year (since 2023), coupled with increasingly stricter CII values, underwater hull-cleaning using RAS may well emerge as the new CII standard, replacing current AFS certification. Also projected under stricter environmental requirements is that RAS will become a central component of a ship's underwater hull maintenance and environmental optimisation. An inherent benefit of complying with these requirements is reduced fuel consumption, which renders a financial incentive for ship owners and operators. RAS and related RIT stand to benefit ship owners and operators, as well as RIT manufacturers and developers, inspection companies, classification societies, and other RAS and RIT stakeholders, and – most importantly – the environment and society at large.

In the setting of good environmental stewardship, and with EU practices as a focus, the use of progressive technologies in the surveying and maintenance of vessels' outer hulls will be assessed in this contribution. The underlying importance of RIT for shipping, as well as its implications for the United Nations Convention on the Law of the Sea, 1982 (UNCLOS), as a governance framework pertaining to safety and, especially, environmental protection, will be discussed. Subsequently, RIT common minimum standards will be delineated, followed by a first-hand insight into the building blocks for a RIT regulatory blueprint (developed under the World Maritime University's BUGWRIGHT2 project). Finally, concluding remarks will highlight the need for policy harmonization, to allow for seamless integration of RIT, to foster good environmental stewardship.

2. WHY REMOTE INSPECTION TECHNOLOGIES (RIT) IN SHIPPING?

Considering the extent of the maintenance executed through required statutory and classification tasks, and performed by major carriers of a world fleet comprising nearly 10,000 "large ships" (between the age range of 0 to more than 25 years), and nearly 5,000 "very large ships" (over the age of 5 years), the advantages of utilising RIT are manifold.[8] The principal types of ships involved in this commercial shipping include tankers, bulk carriers, containerised traders,

[8] UNCTAD/RMT/2019/Corr.1, Review of Maritime Transport: 2019, United Nations, Geneva, 1–132 (31 January 2020), p. 4 (ships by age and size). See also Electronic Quality Shipping

and residual general cargo ships. On the increase are the number of bulk trade shipments.[9] Dry bulk commodities account for 40 per cent of total dry cargo shipments (as of 2018).[10] In its 2019 statistics report, the European Maritime Safety Agency (EMSA) estimated a total of nearly 12,000 bulk carriers trading internationally in 2018.[11] According to the EMSA estimates for the same year, there were a total of 16,250 general cargo ships with a gross tonnage of 59,206, and 13,757 oil and chemical tankers with a gross tonnage of 345,545.[12]

Shipping performance at the highest level of efficiency is the principle that drives the world fleet's operation. But constraints highlighted by researchers indicate "hull resistance", which negatively impacts hull performance, and hinders a ship's optimal performance.[13] Among many subfactors affecting hull performance, hull fouling, or biofouling most significantly contributes to increased global shipping emissions.[14] In technical terms, hull fouling increases water resistance, and in so doing also increases energy usage, a very significant concern for the shipping industry, while also impacting on scheduling and maintenance costs.[15] Preliminary findings from a Global Industry Alliance (GIA) report stressed the importance of "maintaining a smooth and clean hull free from biofouling", to avoid an increase in greenhouse gas (GHG) emissions.[16]

Information System, "The World Fleet in 2018: Statistics from Equasis", European Maritime Safety Agency (2019): http://www.emsa.europa.eu/equasis-statistics/items.html?cid=95&id=472, p. 9, Table 3.

9 UNCTAD/RMT/2019/Corr.1, supra note 8, p. 5: see Fig. 1.1.

10 Ibid., at 5: see Fig. 1.1. See also Electronic Quality Shipping Information System, supra note 8, at p. 6.

11 Electronic Quality Shipping Information System, supra note 8, p. 8, Table 1 (ships by type and size) and Table 2 (ships by gross tonnage). See also Statista, "Number of Ships in the World Merchant Fleet as of January 1, 2019, by type": https://www.statista.com/statistics/264024/number-of-merchant-ships-worldwide-by-type/.

12 Electronic Quality Shipping Information System, supra note 8, p. 8, Table 1 (ships by type and size) and Table 2 (ships by gross tonnage).

13 *P. Deligiannis*, "Ship Performance Indicator", (2017) *Marine Policy* 75, 204–209, p. 205 *et seq*.

14 Ibid., p. 204. See *R. Adland et al.*, "The Energy Efficiency Effects of Periodic Hull Cleaning", (2008) *Journal of Cleaner Production* (178), 1–13, p. 2.

15 *T. McClay et al.*, "Vessel Biofouling Prevention and Management Options Report", UNCLAS// Public, CG-926 R&DC 2015, 1–54, p. (v). See *M.P. Schultz et al.*, "Economic Impact of Biofouling on a Naval Surface Ship", (2011) *Biofouling*, 27:1, 87–98, pp. 87, 88, 89 *et seq.*; *H. Wang and N. Lutsey, Long-Term Potential for Increased Shipping Efficiency Through the Adoption of Industry-Leading Practices*, International Council on Clean Transportation, 2013, White Paper, 1–26, pp. 3, 4, 5, 6, 7 and 8.

16 *Global Industry Alliance*, "Preliminary results: Impact of Ships' Biofouling on Greenhouse Gas Emissions", 2021, GEF-UNDP-IMO GloFouling Partnerships project: https://wwwcdn.imo.org/localresources/en/MediaCentre/Documents/Biofouling%20report.pdf.

Service providers specialising in niche areas are reaping the benefits of RAS, which are changing the traditional image of inspection and maintenance. Noteworthy expanded applications involve close-up surveys; thickness measurements of structures; and biofouling cleaning of commercial vessels, using micro aerial vehicles (MAVs), magnetic crawlers and remotely operated vehicles (ROVs). The introduction of the above types of uses into survey and maintenance practices "alleviate[s] the need for humans to work in … dangerous or dirty environments but also improve [their] image into one with productive and cost saving elements requiring the need for highly skilled, tech-savvy engineers".[17]

3. RIT IMPLICATIONS ON THE LAW OF THE SEA?

Implications on UNCLOS, brought by RIT, are best assessed by reviewing the legal status of RIT, and secondly, and distinctly, the impact harmonised standards governing new technology will have on UNCLOS.

To assess the first strand, Part XIII of UNCLOS, which regulates marine scientific research-related activities, is the key section.[18] Although the term "marine scientific research" remains undefined in Part XIII, the term itself is central to all work related to preservation of the marine environment.[19] Both the scale and extent of marine scientific research is grounded not only on an in-depth assessment of the detrimental effects of ocean pollutants, but also on the exploration of science-based solutions.[20] Assessment of data sets gathered through surveys acquired via technology is now common practice in the world of marine scientific research. Ocean exploration, ocean floor mapping, and aggregation of oceanographic data, using floaters, drifters and underwater gliders or autonomous underwater vehicles (AUVs) are examples of this trend. However, the deployment of these technologies has not always been free from debate. Questions have been raised by policy analysts as to whether the legal

17 *M.J. Farnsworth et al.*, "Autonomous Maintenance for Through-Life Engineering" in *L. Redding and R. Roy* (eds.), *Through-life Engineering Services*, Springer International Publishing, 2014, 395–419, p. 397.

18 United Nations Convention on the Law of the Sea, adopted 10 December 1982, UNTS 1833 (entered into force 16 November 1994) (UNCLOS), Part XIII. An authoritative definition is found in *A.H.A Soons*, *Marine Scientific Research and the Law of the Sea*, TMC Asser Instituut, 1982, p. 6: "any study or related experimental work designed to increase man's knowledge of the marine environment".

19 *T. Davenport*, "Submarine Communications Cables and Science: A New Frontier in Ocean Governance?" in *H.N. Scheiber, J. Kraska and M. Kwon* (eds.), *Science, Technology and New Challenges to Ocean Law*, Brill Nijhoff, 2015, p. 226. This statement is based on *A.H.A Soons*, supra note 18, p. 14.

20 *T. Davenport*, supra note 19.

status of gliders and floaters constitutes "operational oceanography", due to the fact that they are tied to the geographic territory, which invokes the labyrinthine principles of the "consent regime".[21]

In the current context, debate can be set aside on the ground that RIT, although bearing a subtle connection to marine scientific research, are fundamentally and primarily for a different purpose: to provide both statutory and classification alternatives to human-centric surveys on vessels that are berthed, anchored or moored within internal waters, or dry-docked in a structured area. Notwithstanding the absence of a point of reference that determines the legal status of professional RIT, UNCLOS's "safety at sea" provisions are applicable, and require adherence. Taking the necessary measures under UNCLOS for ensuring "safety at sea" is a vital responsibility of the flag state. Explicitly covered under "safety at sea", in Article 94, are provisions for both vessel "construction" and "seaworthiness", with an expectation that flag states conduct services on vessel structures, in support of good operation and performance.

"Intention" is a nuance critical to understanding the applicability of RIT. Specifically, *intentionality*, in the modern technological environment, occurs when operational objectives are aligned with international objectives obliging service suppliers and end users of innovative equipment to remain compliant. To determine whether this can be termed "improved compliance" can be ascertained by comparing vessel performance and energy efficiency levels between two different bulk carriers: one that has been surveyed manually, and one that has benefited from RIT.

Indicators of "intention" or "intentionality" include *writing*, *sensing* and *shaping*: subsets that combine to structure and regulate the objectives of an anticipated environment.[22] Techno-regulatory standards mirror the *writing* subset that defines the dynamics of "environing technology".[23] Published techno-regulatory standards, developed by international organisations, are objective-specific, and impact on the modern technological environment. In many ways,

21 *T. Hofman and A. Proelss*, "The Operation of Gliders under the International Law of the Sea", (2015) *Ocean Development and International Law*, 46:3, 167–187, p. 168. See also *K. Bork, Johannes Karstensen, M. Visbeck and A. Zimmermann*, "The Legal Regulation of Floats and Gliders – In Quest of a New Regime?", (2008) *Ocean Development & International Law*, 39:3, 298–328, pp. 307, 311.

22 *S. Sörlin and N. Wombs*, "Environing Technologies: A Theory of Making Environment", (2018) *History and Technology*, 34, 101–125, pp. 5, 6, 7 and 8.

23 Ibid., p. 7. As indicated by scholars Sörlin and Wombs, "often these technologies are also connected to writing, as documenting is intrinsic to many activities, especially those which are circulated in society and over time. The United Nations Convention on the Law of the Sea, UNCLOS, or the IPCC Fifth Assessment Report are examples of writing (documents) that environ".

regional and national objectives are deeply ingrained in the environmental objectives of UNCLOS, which, in turn, endorses harmonised international standards – the next discussion.

Part XII of UNCLOS highlights *good environmental stewardship*, and requests Member States (MS) to undertake:

> individually or jointly as appropriate, all measures … that are necessary to prevent, reduce and control pollution of the marine environment from any source, using … the best practicable means at their disposal and in accordance with their capabilities, and … [to] endeavor to harmonize their policies in this connection.[24]

Here, strong emphasis is placed on mitigating vessel-source pollution, by regulating vessel design, construction and equipment.[25] Furthermore, Part XII lays the foundation for a global and regional cooperative regime, with reference to "competent international organizations", to establish "international rules, standards and recommended practices and procedures" on vessel-source pollution.[26]

UNCLOS views general accepted international rules and standards (GAIRS) as a pathway for a symbiotic, compatible and reciprocal nexus for existing international treaties.[27] Markedly, GAIRS allows for "new concepts, such as precaution and biodiversity to become part of UNCLOS normative structure", and helps move the trajectory of the cooperation regime towards good environmental stewardship.[28] To that end, GAIRS endorses competent international organization-developed standards, provided that the standards so developed resonate with the central objectives of UNCLOS.[29] Openness, and complementarity to other regimes tied to good environmental stewardship, stand as the cruxes of Article 211 and 237 UNCLOS, and both bolster support to this rule of reference.[30] In that vein, GAIRS not only regulates consistency

---

24 UNCLOS, supra note 18, Part XII, Art. 194; see also Code for the Implementation of Mandatory IMO Instruments, IMO Resolution A. 973(24), adopted on 1 December 2005, at s. 4 (General).

25 UNCLOS, supra note 18, Part XII, Art. 194(3).

26 Ibid., Part XII, Art. 197.

27 Ibid.

28 *R.A. Barnes*, "The Continuing Validity of UNCLOS" in *J. Barrett and R.A. Barnes (eds.), The United Nations Convention on the Law of the Sea: A Living Instrument*, British Institute of International and Comparative Law, 2016, 459–489, p. 472, citing *D. Freestone*, "International Fisheries Law Since Rio: The Continued Rise of the Precautionary Principle" in *A. Boyle and D. Freestone* (eds.), *International Law and Sustainable Development: Past Achievements and Future Challenges*, Oxford University Press, 1999, p. 135.

29 UNCLOS, supra note 18, Arts. 21(2), (4); 39(2)(a)–(b); 41(3); 53(8); 60(3),(5), and (6); 94(2)(a); 94(5); 211(2), (5), and (6)(c); 226(1)(a); and 271.

30 UNCLOS, supra note 18, Arts. 22; 39; 41(4)–(5); 53(9); 60(3), (5); 61(2), (5); 119(2); 197–202; 204–205; 207(4); 208(5); 210(3); 211(1)–(6); 212–214; 216; 217(1), (4), (7); 218(1); 220(7);

with IMO-promulgated instruments, but also elucidates a broad scope for accommodating IMO Recognized Organizations (RO), and their rules and requirements.

4. RIT CLASS SURVEY: COMMON MINIMUM STANDARDS

IACS is the key international body that comes into play in all discussions related to RIT international rules and requirements. Serving in the capacity as an RO on behalf of maritime administrations, IACS is composed of 11 members that set international classification standards covering "90% of the world's cargo-carrying ship tonnage".[31] Taken together, IACS rules and requirements apply to both *statutory* (subject to the flag states' agreement) and *classification* surveys, the successful completion of which result in the issuance of statutory and classification certificates, respectively. Suffice to note that the same *statutory* survey and certification procedures that were attached to a plethora of IMO instruments are now harmonised, through IMO's Harmonized System of Survey and Certification (HSSC), with the objective of standardising survey procedures and timelines.[32] Within the harmonised texts, the HSSC provides direct reference to classification society standards, to strengthen uniformity that will enhance MS compliance with good environmental status.[33]

Significantly, IACS advocates for the integration of RIT platforms under specified conditions. Those conditions are detailed in Recommendation 42, titled "Guidelines for Use of Remote Inspection". At the outset, Recommendation 42 stipulates that unmanned robot arms, remotely operated vehicles (ROV), climbers, drones and other acceptable means may be deployed to "facilitate the required external and internal examinations, including close-up surveys and gauging", subject to approval and consultation among the RIT technician, the owner's

---

222–223; 238–239; 242–244(2); 246(3), (5), (5)(d); 248–249; 251–253(1)(b), (4), (5); 254(1)–(4); 256–257; 262–263(3); 265; 266(1); 268–273; 275(1)–(2); 276(1); 278; 297(1)(c); 319(2)(a). See also Report of the Secretariat of the International Maritime Organization, Implications of the United Nations Convention on the Law of the Sea for the International Maritime Organization, U.N. Doc. LEG/MICS.8, p. 8.

31 *International Association of Classification Societies*, "About IACS – Introduction": https://www.iacs.org.uk/about/.

32 Survey Guidelines under the Harmonized System of Survey and Certification (HSSC), 2017, A 30/Res. 1120, adopted on 18 December 2017. *NB* the 2017 HSSC was amended and updated in 2019, to reflect amendments to BWM Convention, MARPOL and 1974 SOLAS. No survey-specific changes were made in these amendments. The amendments are set out in Annex XX to IMO Document III 6/15.

33 *T. Johansson*, supra note 1.

representative, and the attending surveyor.[34] Restrictions on RIT platform usage are also in place where there is a likelihood of severe damage or deterioration being observed in structures, in which case manual close-up surveys and thickness measurements may be initiated.[35]

IACS Unified Requirement (UR) Z17, titled "Procedural Requirements for Service Suppliers", embodies a theoretical extension of Recommendation 42.[36] Composed of RIT-led standards, UR Z17 is aimed at firms providing *statutory* surveys (where flag states reserve the right to conduct their own assessment and approval of service suppliers for statutory surveys) and *classification* surveys. In this document, there are detailed procedural as well as special requirements to be followed for the use of ROVs to carry out in-water surveys on ships and mobile offshore units (s. 3), as well as the use of RITs as an alternative means for close-up surveys of the structure of ships and mobile offshore units (s. 4) (see Table 1 below).[37]

Notably, while Recommendation 42 notes ROV as a division of RIT, ROV has, nevertheless, received specific attention, through the formulation of a separate section under UR Z17. If this placement is guided by the rationale that ROVs operate underwater, or on water surfaces, which is different from navigating RITs in the air, or on steel hulls, then perhaps the methodology, as well as external disruption factors (strong water currents, ice infestation during winter, etc.), should have been highlighted. Moreover, the deployment of ROVs by service providers in in-water cleaning operations invokes the question whether section 3 of IACS UR Z17 should enshrine a caveat within the texts, referring to precautionary measures when removing heavy metal and coating flakes from vessels' hulls (for environmental benefits). Turning to section 16, which covers requirements specifically only where RITs serve as an alternative means for close-up surveys, it is noteworthy that section 16.1 has adopted two terms: "Unmanned Aerial Vehicles (UAV)" and "Drones", under two distinct bullet points. But what are the differences between the two, if any? Several other questions also remain unanswered, leaving the task of building beyond minimum standards to individual classification society members.

---

34 IACS, Recommendation 42 Guidelines for Use of Remote Inspection Techniques for surveys – Rev.2 June 2016 (Recommendation 42), downloaded from the official homepage of IACS: https://www.iacs.org.uk/resolutions/recommendations/41-60/rec-42-rev2-cln.

35 Ibid., s. 2.1.

36 IACS UR Z17, Procedural Requirements for Service Suppliers: https://www.irclass.org/media/5751/2-relevant-sections-of-ur-z17-rev16.pdf.

37 Ibid.

Table 1. Overview of IACS UR Z17 Procedural and Special Requirements

Procedural Requirements for Service Suppliers					
Principal Building Blocks				**Principal Focus**	**Governing the Scope of Suppliers that Provide RIT Services**
Procedures for Approval and Certification	*Conditions for Issuance of Certificate*	*Cancellation of Approval*	*Approval of Service Providers by the Concerned Authority Where the Society is Authorized by Flag Administration*	**Actors**	**S. 3:** Manufacturers, Service Providers, Agent, Subsidiary and Subcontractor
Application by Manufacturers Endorsing Agents or Subsidiaries	*ISO 9000 Quality System*	*Conditions for Certification*		**Mechanisms**	**S. 4:** Permissible in Statutory Services and Classification Services except non-ESP ships <500 Gross tonnage (GT) and all Fishing vessels
	Auditing the Supplier	*Service Suppliers Relation with Equipment Manufacturer*		**Tools**	**S. 4.1.3:** Verification and Accountability of Work Done by Third Party; **S. 4.2:** Approval of Service Provider by the Concerned Society; **S. 4.3:** Approval of Service Provider by the Concerned Society where the Society is Authorized by Flag Administration; **S. 5.1:** Procedures for Approval and Certification; **S. 5.2.1 to S. 5.2.10:** General Requirements for Suppliers; **S. 5.3:** Auditing the Supplier; **S. 5.4:** Conditions for Certification; **S. 5.5.1:** Supplier to Demonstrate Documented System Pertaining to Quality Management in accordance with ISO 9000 Series; **S. 5.5.3:** Application by Manufacturers' Endorsing Agents or Subsidiaries; **S. 5.6.1:** Service Suppliers Relations with the Equipment Manufacturer; **S. 6.1:** Conditions for Issuance of Certificate of Approval to Supplier and Content of Certificate; **S. 8.1 to S. 8.4:** Cancellation of Approval; **S. 5.2.11:** Reporting by Suppliers; **S. 5.2.12:** Documented Procedures and Instructions on Recordings by Suppliers

(continued)

Table 1 *continued*

Special Requirements (for ...): Annex 1		
Firms Engaged in Statutory and Classification Surveys	**ROV Special Requirements Pursuant to S. 4**	
S. 3: Firms carrying out an in-water survey on ships and mobile offshore units by diver or Remotely Operated Vehicle (ROV).	**The Human Element**	**Supervisor:** qualified according to national or international industrial NDT standard **Operator:** qualified according to national or international industrial NDT standard **Training of Personnel:** Supplier is responsible for training of operator, supervisor with respect to training on handling equipment. Must have knowledge on: -Ship's underwater structure and appendages, propeller shaft, propeller, rudder and its bearings, etc.; -Non-destructive testing in accordance with a recognized national or international industrial NDT standard; - Certification as a thickness measurement firm when conducting thickness measurements under water; -Bearing clearance measurements on rudders and propeller shaft; -Under-water video monitoring with TV-monitors on deck, as well as still picture work; -Operation of under-water communication system; -Any special equipment necessary for the work carried out. **Verification:** The supplier must have the Surveyor's verification of each separate job, documented in the report by the attending Surveyor(s) signature.
	Reporting System	A plan for training of personnel in the reporting system, minimum Rule requirements for relevant ship or unit types, ship's or unit's underwater structure, measuring of bearing clearances, the recognition of corrosion damage, buckling and deteriorated coatings, etc. shall be included.
	Procedures & Guidelines	Operational procedures and guidelines for firms carrying out in-water survey by ROV shall also include: -Guidance for the operation and maintenance of the Remotely Operated Vehicle, if applicable; and -Methods and equipment to ensure the ROV operator can determine the ROV's location and orientation in relation to the vessel.

S. 16: Firms engaged in survey using Remote Inspection Techniques (RIT) as an alternative means for Close-up Survey of the structure of ships and mobile offshore units	**RIT Special Requirements Pursuant to S. 16**	
	The Human Element	Supervisor & Operator: Similar to the former Training of Personnel: – Marine and/or offshore nomenclatures. – The structural configuration of relevant ships types and MOUs, including internal structure. – The remote inspection equipment and its operation. – Survey plans for examination of hull spaces of various configurations, including appropriate flight plans if using a UAV. – Thickness measurement ™ and non-destructive examination (NDE), in accordance with a recognized National or International Industrial NDE Standard when these are part of the service.
	Training Plan	Same as s. 4 (except the title here is training plan)
	Documentation & Records	The supplier shall maintain: -Records of training; -Operator statutory and regulatory licences – Equipment register for UAVs, Robots, data collection devices, data analysis devices etc.; -Equipment maintenance manuals and records/ logbook; -Records of calibration; and -UAV/Robot operation logbook
	Verification	The supplier must have the Surveyor's verification of each separate job, documented in the report by the attending Surveyor(s) signature.

Source: Adapted IACS UR Z17, Procedural Requirements for Service Suppliers (Rev. 15 October 2020).

5. THE CASE FOR HARMONISING RIT REQUIREMENTS THROUGH INTERNATIONAL GUIDELINES

The task of achieving environmental compliance excellence is difficult and complex, and its complexities are exacerbated even further by the plurality of classification rules. Presently, there are more than 50 classification societies that have specific procedural standards. For example, rules and requirements developed by the American Bureau of Shipping (ABS), China Classification Society (CCS), Bureau Veritas (BV), Det Norske Veritas (DNV) and Lloyd's Register (LR), to name just a few, indicate that much effort has been placed on the outlining of rules and requirements, in order to keep pace with maritime innovation. However, not all societies have developed relevant operational and technical standards. IACS's ability to establish common minimum standards with the necessary degree of regulatory symmetry has been hindered by the unfortunate development of multiple sets of rules governing the same technology.

Conceiving sound and effective regulations at the EU level requires that specific methods and principles be embedded across all classification societies that promulgate rules. Recalling Articles 42, 43(2), 91(1), 100(2), 173(3), 175, 188, 192(1), 194(2) and 195(2) of the Treaty on the Functioning of the European Union, the European Association of Classification Societies (EurACS) notes that: "[a]n 'all embracing' maritime policy where synergy between the various fields of expertise is exploited will strengthen the competitiveness of the EU maritime sector".[38] In reality, what is absent is an EU integrated RAS policy that delineates the basic elements or principles which could serve as a foundation for attaining RIT regulatory symmetry.

To illuminate the elements that would best constitute a harmonised RIT regulatory blueprint, the authors of this contribution have delved into *de lege lata* ("the law as it exists"), taking into account the rules of major classification societies (both members and non-members of IACS and EurACS). The findings from these analyses indicate inconsistencies. On a positive note, there also emerges a unique outline of six building blocks that could help facilitate the harmonisation process. Additionally, the initial findings were explored in detail by the authors during semi-structured interviews of 32 officials based in the United States of America (US), the Netherlands, Canada, Norway, China and Singapore. The respondents represented national administrations (5), classification societies (7), service suppliers or agents (9), industry stakeholders (4), and academia (7), in their official capacities.[39] It is important to note that some respondents

---

38 EurACS – European Association of Classification Societies, BV – DNV – GL – LR – RINA, Towards a Future Maritime Policy of the Union, Contribution by EurACS: https://europa.eu/documents/comm/green_papers/pdf/com_2006_0275_en_part2.pdf.

39 Interviews were conducted between March and June 2021, as a part of the research methodology under project BugWright2 work package 1.4.2, titled "National Comparative Analysis".

(about 10 per cent) voiced concerns regarding the integration of service robotics to satisfy regulatory obligations, and noted the fallacy of regulatory symmetry. Others confirmed that achieving alignment through a top-down approach, led by the IMO and IACS, in consultation with the International Organization for Standardization (ISO), as well as industry and academia (collectively known as the triple helix), was a crucial ingredient of achieving global environmental and other objectives within the maritime domain. All in all, the expository responses helped carve out ways forward, considering the six building blocks that will have an important bearing on the rules that will emerge, should an international guidance be developed in response to an MS request (*de lege ferenda* – on the basis of new law) (see Figure 1 below).

Figure 1. Six Building Blocks of Influence

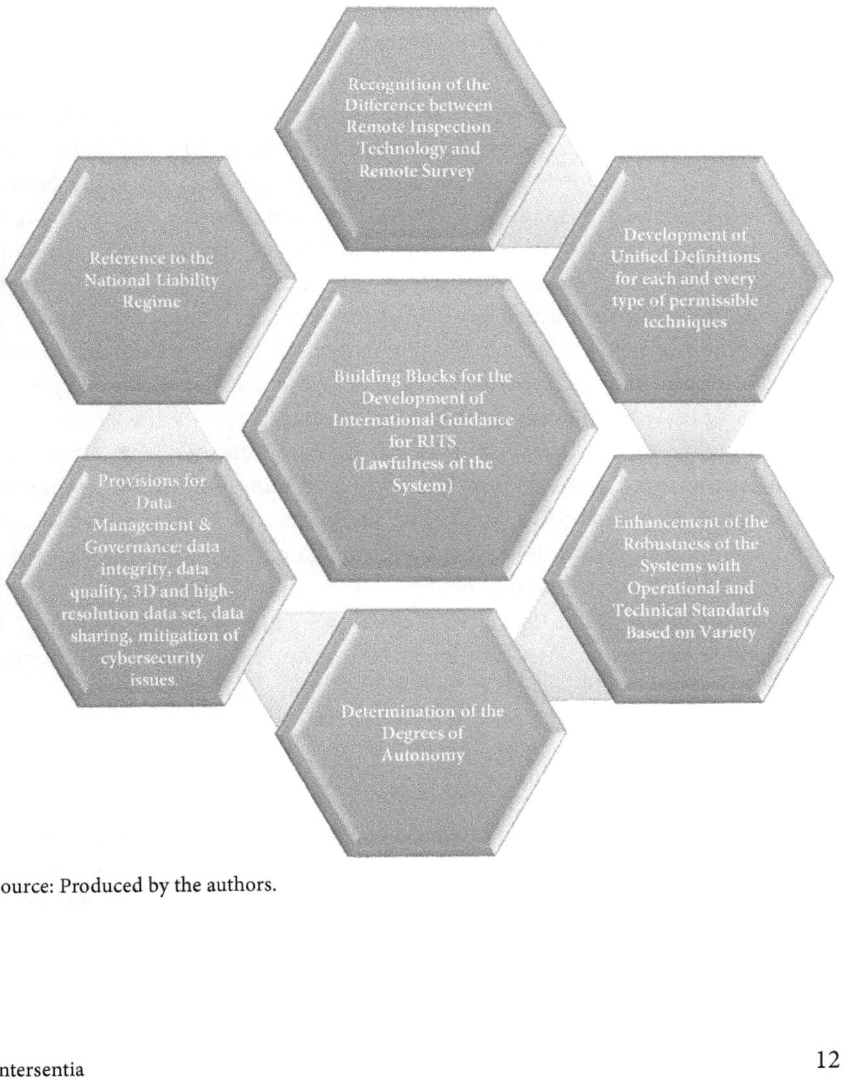

Source: Produced by the authors.

5.1. FIRST BLOCK: REMOTE INSPECTION TECHNOLOGY v. REMOTE SURVEY

To set the scene, it will help to start with a general observation: the inherent difference between the terms "RIT" and "remote survey" cannot be determined from the texts of IACS common minimum standards, as these do not reference remote surveys. The former term (RIT) refers to acceptable technologies or techniques that could be used when carrying out prescribed surveys, either *in situ* or off site. The term "remote survey", on the other hand, denotes a survey conducted via remote technology off site, without requiring the physical presence of the surveyor concerned. This difference must be preserved, in theory and in practice, to avoid using the two terms interchangeably.

5.2. SECOND BLOCK: DEVELOPING DEFINITIONS

IACS makes an effort, in section 1.1 of Recommendation 42, to list equipment types, and this list currently serves as the minimum standard definition of RIT. Considering the evolving nature of innovation, these types will, inevitably, branch out into other expeditious complex systems, necessitating the development of unified definitions for each and every type of permissible technique. The authors of this contribution further assert that the procedural rules and requirements ought to be founded on concrete product definitions.

No two techniques are built following a standard pattern, although certain tangible components may be the same. It is also observed that different types of techniques operate in different environments. Techniques also differ in terms of tasks and outcomes. However, for all types, the common trait is incorporating innovation towards full autonomy. Depending on how innovation progresses in relation to each individual acceptable technique, technological and other differences will stay discernible, despite the amalgamated placement of all types under the common term "remote inspection techniques".

Notable template definitions already exist, and can be found in sections 1.1, 1.3 and 1.5 of Guidance Notes developed by the American Bureau of Shipping (ABS):

> **1.1 Unmanned Aerial Vehicles (UAVs)**
>
> An unmanned aerial vehicle (UAV), commonly known as a drone, is an aircraft without a human pilot onboard. A UAV can be a tethered or wireless vehicle designed to fly in or around a structure. The UAV can be remotely controlled or programmed to fly a predetermined route using the information on a specific asset's condition to target known areas of concern. It can collect visual data (e.g., still images, live-stream, and recorded video), perform Nondestructive Testing (NDT), and measure plate thickness from difficult to-reach structures and areas.

1.3 Remotely Operated Underwater Vehicles (ROVs)

An ROV is an unmanned unit designed for underwater observation, survey, inspection, construction, intervention, or other tasks. Like UAVs, an ROV can be remotely controlled or programmed to travel a predetermined route using the information on a specific asset's condition to target known areas of concern. It can collect visual data, perform Nondestructive Testing (NDT), and measure plate thickness in difficult to-reach areas.

1.5 Robotic Crawlers

A robotic crawler, commonly referred to as a "crawler", is a tethered or wireless vehicle designed to "crawl" along a structure using wheels or tracks. Crawlers are often equipped with magnets to operate on a vertical or inclined surface or hull structures in air or underwater.[40]

5.3. THIRD BLOCK: OPERATIONAL AND TECHNICAL STANDARDS BASED ON VARIETY

As discussed earlier, individual RIT are marked by operational and technical differences. Therefore, this requires the introduction of operational and technical standards that complement mandatory procedural requirements. Operational and technical standards are beyond the purview of IACS, hence their exclusion from the scope of UR Z17.[41] Such standards, however, are important for setting a baseline for determining operational limitations, to establish timelines for the initiation of "confirmatory surveys" (where surveyors proceed to examine abnormal damage and deterioration manually, pursuant to section 1.3 of IACS Recommendation 42). Fortunately, however, classification societies, such as ABS, for example, have developed operational standards for UAV, ROV and robotic crawlers (which are termed as Remote Inspection Vehicles (RIV), as opposed to the common minimum standard term "RIT" that is used widely at the EU level).

Given an inherent vulnerability to risk, "risk assessment" is an important feature of operational standards. It is worth noting that surveys using aerial drones, unlike those using crawlers and ROVs, can easily be compromised, due to humidity, lighting and air turbulence. Furthermore, hybrid RITs, which have the potential to conduct biofouling cleaning in addition to survey operations, require limiting all possible risks prior to their deployment. The ABS-promulgated Guidance Notes also include sound methodologically construed categories of risk assessments, founded on operational standards, for the three

40 American Bureau of Shipping (2022), "Guidance Notes on the Use of Remote Inspection": https://ww2.eagle.org/content/dam/eagle/rules-and-guides/current/other/242-gn-remote-inspection-tech-dec-2022/rit-gn-dec22.pdf.

41 Recommendation 42, supra note 34.

preferred types of RITs: explosion risks in hazardous areas, dropped object risks, collision risks (for example, with other RIVs), lost link risks (for example network compromise), and other risks, consisting of high-risk working areas, and risks associated with other parallel operations and emergency situations.

The CCS, in its document titled "Guidelines for Use of Unmanned Aerial Vehicles", describes in detail the technical standards for UAVs.[42] These standards focus on safety performance, operation performance, enduring capacity, data transmission and communication, data storage (for example, video and image resolutions and video and photo formats), and requirements for airborne cameras.[43] Technical standards, according to the authors of the present contribution, close the circle of procedural rules and requirements, in so far as they ensure safety and reliability, and enable interoperability, by providing a common language to evaluate performance.

5.4. FOURTH BLOCK: DETERMINING THE DEGREE OF AUTONOMY

Vocabularies found in the document titled "ISO 8373: 2012 (en) Robots and Robotic Devices – Vocabulary", developed by the Technical Committee ISO/TC 184, set out a number of useful definitions relevant to both industrial and service robots. In defining the term "robots", ISO keeps the performance facet open-ended, appreciating "the degree of autonomy", loosely translated as the level of a system's reliance on human intervention in the execution of predetermined tasks, when operating within the programmed pathway.[44] It is important to note here that, while the definition of "operator" acknowledges the integration of human intervention to "start, monitor and stop the intended operation", it does not proffer any further clarification on what the term "monitor" entails.[45]

Professional service robots, or RITs, have built-in image sensors that convert photons into electrical signals that are then viewed and analysed by operators engaged in commercial inspection activities. Therefore, according to section 2.12 ("professional service robot"), when read together with section 2.17 ("operator"), monitoring intended operations could be viewed as pertaining to the "inspection function" being undertaken, or "inspected", through the service robot's image sensors. In other words, the current system portrays a

42 China Classification Society, "Guidelines for Use of Unmanned Aerial Vehicles for Surveys, 2018": https://www.ccs.org.cn/ccswzen/articleDetail?id=201910000000003817.

43 Ibid., s. 2.6.

44 ISO 8373: 2012 (en) Robots and Robotic Devices – Vocabulary (2012), International Organization for Standardization: https://www.iso.org/obp/ui/#iso:std:iso:8373:ed-2:v1:en, s. 2.6.

45 Ibid., s. 2.17.

model built on semi-autonomy or supervised autonomy. Bearing in mind the aims of realising full autonomy, the RIT systems today could undergo strategic recategorisation in a fashion similar to what has been accomplished in relation to maritime autonomous surface ships (MASS).[46] It is necessary to emphasise that such a categorisation, from the outset, could help keep track of many graduations towards autonomy, and thereby assist classification societies with future revisions.

Table 2. Categorisation of RIT Based on MASS Degree of Autonomy

Degree/Level of Autonomy	MASS	RIT
First Degree	Ship with automated processes and decision support with seafarers on board to operate and control the systems. Systems are partially automated and unsupervised, with seafarers on board ready to assume control.	RIT-survey conducted in the presence of the attending surveyor. This degree aligns explicitly with IACS Recommendation 42 and IACS UR Z17.
Second Degree	Remotely controlled ship with seafarers on board.	Remote class survey with the possibility of surveyor to intervene, if necessary.
Third Degree	Remotely controlled ships without seafarers on board.	Remote class survey without attending surveyor.
Fourth Degree	Fully autonomous ship.	RIT with automated processes and artificial intelligence-based machine learning operating systems to support decision-making.

Source: Adapted from IMO Doc. MSC 100/20/Add. 1, Annex 2.

5.5. FIFTH BLOCK: DATA MANAGEMENT AND SECURITY

Data acquisition is the heart of all RIT interventions.[47] Stakeholders involved in this process include non-human actors, for example technological tools and

---

46 IMO Doc. MSC 100/20/Add. 1, Annex 2, Framework for the Regulatory Scoping Exercise for the Use of Maritime Autonomous Surface Ships (MASS), 7 Dec. 2018, ¶ 1 and IMO, MSC 99th Briefing (2018): http://www.imo.org/en/MediaCentre/PressBriefings/Pages/08-MSC-99-MASS-scoping.aspx.

47 *T. Johansson, D. Dalaklis and A. Pastra*, "Maritime Robotics and Autonomous Systems Operations: Exploring Pathways for Overcoming International Techno-Regulatory Data Barriers", (2021) *Journal of Marine Science and Engineering* 9(6), 594; see also *T. Johansson, R. Long, and D. Dalaklis*, "The role of WMU-sasakawa global ocean institute in the era of big data" (2019), *The Journal of Ocean Technology*, 14(4), 22–29.

infrastructure, and human actors, i.e. service providers, classification societies and ship owners (end users).[48] Those in the latter category are, aptly, known as the "human-in-the-loop", with supervisors, operators and surveyors remaining engaged during data storage, and verification of data collected through RIT-based visual inspection and close-up surveys. In essence, the RIT infrastructure communicates data to the "human-in-the-loop" via five independent layers: hardware, network, Internet, infrastructure and application.[49]

Within the RIT multi-stakeholder landscape, "control of data" has received due attention in section 5.2.6 of IACS UR Z17, which, unfortunately, dwells only on service suppliers' duty to confirm computer software's ability to acquire, record, report, store, measure and monitor data, and does not do justice to its title.[50] Corroborated by interview respondents, the *status quo* inadequacy does not create any privacy contentions for EU Member States, since non-personal data, such as ones that are acquired by RIT, fall outside the scope of EU's Regulation 2016/679 on the General Data Protection Regulation (GDPR).[51] That being said, RIT-acquired data is attached to the vessel history, as it informs surveyors (conducting periodical surveys) about maintenance tasks previously completed. As such, asset-related information in shipping has, traditionally, been treated with utmost confidentiality, to protect ship owners from unforeseen threats caused by breaches in cybersecurity.

Individual efforts to govern non-personal data management and data security are noted in various guidelines articulated by individual classification society members. For example, data calibration and analytics has received attention in the RIT-specific document titled "Remote Inspection Technique Systems (RITS) Assessment Standard for use on LR Class Surveys of Steel Structure", issued by LR.[52] Data capture and treatment considerations have also been prioritised in "Guidance Notes for Inspection using Unmanned Aircraft Systems", issued by the same society.[53] In this document, key provisions on data, encapsulated in section 8, entitled "Inspection Data", cover important recommendations on "data security principles, standards and methods" against "manipulation or unwanted distribution".[54] DNV has also advanced rules and requirements in the document

48 *D. Loshin*, *Master Data Management*, 1st ed., Kaufmann, 2008.

49 *T. Johansson, D. Dalaklis and A. Pastra*, supra note 47. See *P.P. Ray*, "Internet of Robotic Things: Concept, Technologies, and Challenges", (2017) *IEEE Access*, 4, 9489–9500.

50 IACS UR Z17, supra note 36, s. 5.2.6.

51 European Union, Regulation (EU) 2016/679 of the European Parliament and of the Council of 27 April 2016 on the Protection of Natural Persons with Regard to the Processing of Personal Data and on the Free Movement of Such Data, and Repealing Directive 95/46/EC (General Data Protection Regulation).

52 Lloyd's Register, "Remote Inspection Technique Systems (RITS) Assessment Standard for Use on LR Class Surveys of Steel Structure", 2018.

53 Lloyd's Register, "Guidance Notes for Inspection Using Unmanned Aircraft Systems", 2016.

54 Ibid.

titled "Approval of Service Supplier Scheme", which illustrates a concrete effort to regulate RIT data storage.[55] Section 16.1.4 of Appendix A obliges service suppliers to store data in an orderly fashion whereby the files should be made available upon request for a duration of five years.[56] This provision is quite unique, as common minimum standards do not address questions such as who should be responsible for data and image preservation, and how long individual survey data and images need to be preserved for.

Criteria for RIV post-operation data review and processing tasks are a striking feature of the "Guidance Notes on the Use of Remote Inspection Technologies", developed by the ABS.[57] Also in this document, all essential elements integral to the data decision domain are infused in sections 4.9 and 4.11. A strong emphasis on "data security policies and procedures" can be found in section 4.11.1.1(h).[58] On the Asian front, the CCS have provided a similar emphasis on data acquisition, data processing and data security, in section 3 of their "Guidelines for Use of Unmanned Aerial Vehicles for Surveys".[59] Collectively, all of the provisions briefly discussed above provide a settled discourse on non-personal data integrity for a semi-autonomous system.

5.6. SIXTH BLOCK: REFERENCE TO THE NATIONAL LIABILITY REGIME

Legal scholars dealing with RAS issues have concluded that there are no philosophical or legal grounds to refer to technology as a "subject" or a "being", from an ontological standpoint.[60] From a producer standpoint, both industrial robots and service robots are manufactured through an action or a process, and refined for sale. Focusing on the keyword "manufacture", it is posited that all RAS, whether autonomous vessels, autonomous vehicles or RIT, are merely "products" that are offshoots of a cascade of applied science-related innovations. The functional approach is to apply a legal framework to govern the usage of products.[61] This is perhaps because service robots need to possess a high degree

55 Det Norske Veritas-Germanischer Lloyd, "Approval of Service Supplier Scheme", 2019.

56 Ibid., s. 16.1.4.

57 American Bureau of Shipping, supra note 40.

58 Ibid.

59 China Classification Society, "Guidelines for Ship Remote Surveys", 2019.

60 *A. Bertolini*, "Robotic Prostheses as Products Enhancing the Rights of People with Disabilities: Reconsidering the Structure of Liability Rules", (2015), *International Review of Law, Computers & Technology*, 29:2–3, 116–136, p. 117.

61 *V. Alexandropoulou et al.*, "Maritime remote inspection technology in hull survey & inspection: A synopsis of liability issues from a European Union context", (2021), *Journal of International Maritime Safety, Environmental Affairs, and Shipping*, 5:4, 184–195. See also *A. Pastra et al.*, "Building a trust ecosystem for remote technologies in ship hull inspections", (2022), *Journal of Law, Innovation and Technology*, 14(2), 474–479.

of autonomy, because their *modus operandi* takes place in an "unconstrained, human-centered environment".[62]

Safety and liability are interrelated concepts. As noted by the European Commission, higher levels of safety symbolise a minimal risk of harm, while ensuring adequate compensation for damages.[63] Existing and emerging applications of complex varieties of RIT (as discussed earlier) will demand a concrete safety net that could protect end users from third-party liability. Consequently, the authors of this contribution do not consider it feasible to include a new RIT liability provision within common minimum standards, but instead submit the proposition that a reference, in brief, be made to the national liability regime, within the scope of the MS-requested international guidelines. Off-site remote surveys bear risks of damage to physical assets. Risks ranging, *inter alia*, from dropped objects, and collisions or lost digital links, to defective products, create the need to solve RIT-induced liability issues through existing regional or national policies, so as to remove a major barrier that could potentially inhibit the market growth of RIT.

The above nexus would prove to be advantageous for EU MS, given that this proposition would allow liability incurred from the usage of RIT to be governed by EU Product Liability Directive 85/374/EEC.[64] RIT used in remote inspections are operated using (battery-produced) electricity, which is viewed as a product, pursuant to Article 2 of Directive 85/374/EEC. The producer or manufacturer could resort to the defence mechanism found in Article 7, to the effect that:

> [H]aving regard to the circumstances, it is probable that the defect which caused the damage did not exist at the time when the product was put into circulation by him or that this defect came into being afterwards; or … that the state of scientific and technical knowledge at the time when he put the product into circulation was not such as to enable the existence of the defect to be discovered.[65]

Alternatively, in the case of strict product liability, the manufacturing company will most likely acquire insurance, and manage to exploit the economies of

62 *T. Haidegger et al.*, "Applied ontologies and standards for service robots", (2013), *Robotics and Autonomous Systems*, 61(11), 1215–1223.

63 European Commission, "2020 Report on the Safety and Liability Implications of Artificial Intelligence, the Internet of Things and Robotics. Report from the Commission to the European Parliament, the Council and the European Economic and Social Committee".

64 EU Product Liability Directive 85/374/EEC, 1985, Council Directive 85/374/EEC of 25 July 1985 on the approximation of the laws, regulations and administrative provisions of the Member States concerning liability for defective products, OJ L 210, 7.8.1985, 29–33. See also *A. Ozturk*, "Lessons Learned from Robotics and AI in a Liability Context: A Sustainability Perspective" in *A. Carpenter, T. Johansson and J.A. Skinner* (eds.), *Sustainability in the Maritime Domain: Towards Ocean Governance and Beyond*, Springer Sustainability Series, 2021.

65 EU Product Liability Directive 85/374/EEC, supra note 64, Art. 7.

scale by distributing costs along the value chain.[66] The liability circle for RIT will, thus, be closed.

6. CONCLUSIONS

RAS service robots are now being effectively integrated into surveys of critical areas which are difficult to access and monitor, providing a safe alternative to human-centric tasks.[67] Furthermore, the application of RIT allows for ship hulls with a better environmental footprint.[68] Though new service robotic solutions are promising, RIT built with non-standardised technical specifications will likely hamper mass deployment. Unfortunately, the current RIT governance framework also impedes integration across all levels of the maritime community. On a positive note, efforts are under way, particularly within the EU, to harmonise international guidance for remote surveys. There is a clear need to review and update common minimum standards, to effectively integrate RIT into the global maritime sector.

The surge of RIT deployment in the maritime world embodies a visionary prospectus: enhanced performance in ocean affairs, and maintenance of good environmental stewardship. Whatever the merits of this vision, state-of-the-art equipment-governing class rules and requirements do little beyond lightweight standards. Common minimum standards have resulted in a duplication of efforts, to say the least.

Recent years have seen unique developments at the international level, such as the introduction of the goal-based standards (GBS) into IMO initiatives. GBS are a clear and feasible way forward for a regulatory framework covering RAS and RIT. Notably, IMO applied the GBS concept through IMO Resolution MSC.287(87), titled "Adoption of the International Goal-Based Ship Construction Standards for Bulk Carriers and Oil Tankers" (2010). Subsequently, IMO's audit

---

66 *M.C. Rodríguez-Villalobos et al.*, "Economies of Scale and Minimization of the Cost: Evidence from a Manufacturing Company", (2018), *Journal of Eastern Europe Research in Business and Economics*, 1–16.

67 *K. Hey Chu, M.G. Papaioannou, Y. Chen, X. Gon, and I.H. Ibrahim*, "Techno-regulatory challenges for Remote Inspection Techniques (RIT): The Role of Classification Societies", *D. Knukkel*, "Remote Inspection Schemes: Past, Present & Future", and also *A. Kartsimadakis*, "Remote Inspections Scheme on Tanker Vessels during Covid-19 Pandemic", all in *T. Johansson et al.* (eds.), *Smart Ports & Robotic Systems: Navigating the Waves of Techno-Regulation and Governance (vol. 2)*, Palgrave Macmillan, 2022.

68 Remote Survey, Det Norske Veritas: https://www.dnv.com/oilgas/remote-survey/index.html; Survey by Remote Inspection Techniques – Use of Approved Service Suppliers, Det Norske Veritas: https://www.dnv.com/news/survey-by-remote-inspection-techniques-use-of-approved-service-suppliers-144572; Remote Technology Points to Cost Efficiency and Quality Gains, Det Norske Veritas: https://www.dnv.com/oilgas/perspectives/remote-technology-points-to-cost-efficiency-and-quality-gains.html.

and verification process was finalised and approved, in July 2016, demonstrating that IACS' Common Structural Rules have been successfully implemented into each of the 12 IACS member classification societies' rules and requirements, in accordance with the GBS concept for bulk carriers and oil tankers. GBS is now being implemented into a variety of other IMO instruments, to include the International Convention for the Safety of Life at Sea (SOLAS) and the International Code of Safety for Ships using Gases or other Low-flashpoint Fuels (IGF Code). The GBS concept would also be highly suitable for a common global regulatory framework covering RAS and RIT.

Finally, the IMO is cognisant that strategies and standards need to be aligned through the development of a common methodology, through internationally harmonised guidelines. This has become even more evident during the COVID-19 pandemic, as ship owners have turned to RIT mode for remote surveys. In light of these challenges, six strategic blocks have been proposed which can enable national regulators to sustain a regulatory regime shared with other stakeholders, to best keep pace with a technological environment in flux. Crafting these fundamental blocks is a task that is well overdue from members of EurACS. Regardless of the eventual direction international guidance takes, members of EurACS will need to coordinate their efforts for uniformity, to ensure that the EU RIT stakeholders can thrive in this paradigm shift. Both EU and non-EU classification societies need to stay synchronised, and adhere to future international guidance. Much work lies ahead to keep innovation coordinated for the common good, in mankind's epic battle with negative impacts of climate change.

PART III

THE ATMOSPHERE

LEGAL AND REGULATORY FRAMEWORK OF AIR POLLUTION IN INDIA

Evolution, Development and Reforms

Kanak MISHRA

1. INTRODUCTION

This contribution has three sections, in order to comprehensively understand how the legal and regulatory framework of air pollution in India has spun out over the years. Section 1 discusses the concept of air pollution in detail. Section 2 delves further into air pollution, by historically tracing the legislative jurisprudence on the issue, through the famous *Taj Trapezium* case (1987),[1] the *CNG Vehicles* case (1985),[2] and the *Relocation of Industries* case (1995).[3] This section also attempts to analyse the dynamic role the Supreme Court has played by indulging in "judicial governance". Section 3 deals with the general framework of air pollution, as adopted by the Supreme Court's gathering of suggestions from all stakeholders and formulation of relevant committees. This section also sets out the Apex Court's plans and orders on Delhi smog, and the odd-even scheme.

The Indian Supreme Court has, time and again, relied on the term "sustainable development" as a means to widen its "judicial governance" on environmental law and policy issues. While such governance has sometimes been mistaken for judicial activism, this dynamic approach of the Court, in consonance with the executive's regulatory framework, has carved out a unique framework for understanding and dealing with air pollution in India.

Air pollution has been a growing cause of concern for environmentalists across the globe for quite some time now. The Supreme Court's jurisprudence to curb air pollution began with a very narrow approach of heavily regulating pollution-causing transportation, which subsequently transformed into a risk-assessment approach. Acting on several public interest litigations filed by noted

1 1987 AIR 1086.
2 Writ Petition (civil) 13029 of 1985.
3 Writ Petition (civil) 4677 of 1995.

environmentalist M.C. Mehta, the Court, in the *Taj Trapezium* (1987), *CNG Vehicles* (1985) and *Relocation of Industries* case (1995) cases, assumed itself as the *parens patriae* of the environment, by imbibing both the "precautionary" principle and the "polluter-pays" principle.

The aftermath of these three monumental cases saw the Supreme Court assume the role of a "protector". The Court not only rebuked the lacuna, on the part of governmental agencies, in implementing existing environmental legislation, but also issued several orders to both the Central and State Pollution Control Boards, and other environmental authorities, to come up with a transparent mechanism of curbing air pollution through modern-day instrumentalities, such as the Graded Action Plans (GAPs).[4]

By undertaking a holistic and all-imbibing analysis of air pollution in India, from the 1990s onwards, the aim of my research project was to reach a conclusion as to whether the role of the Apex Court has been adequate or excessive in shaping a concrete air pollution discourse in India, considering that India follows the doctrine of separation of powers, whereby the judiciary ought not to intervene in the actions of the executive. Being fully aware of the expanse of literature available on air pollution, I followed a three-pronged approach towards my research project, which would hinge on an understanding of the existing legislation on air pollution, such as the Air (Prevention and Control of Pollution) Act of 1981 and the Environment (Protection) Act 1986 (EPA), analysis of important Supreme Court judgments on air pollution, and the working of regulatory agencies in this domain. I would, further, review the changing approach of the Court in being a regulator, through its introduction of the GAP to monitor Delhi's smog. In the course of this contribution, I hope to historically map the legal and regulatory discourse on air pollution in India, along with understanding the roles of the judiciary and the executive in shaping a sustainable development discourse in the country.

2. THE CONCEPT OF AIR POLLUTION

2.1. THE FORMULATION OF THE AIR ACT

The Air (Prevention and Control of Pollution) Act of 1981[5] was enacted by invoking the Central Government's power under Article 253 of the Indian Constitution. The preamble to the Air Act states that the Act represents an implementation of the decisions made at the United Nations Conference on the Human Environment, held in Stockholm in 1972. Although it is a central statute,

4 Supreme Court Order dated 25.11.2016 in *M.C. Mehta v. UOI* (2016) 4 SCC 269.

5 The Air (Prevention and Control of Pollution) Act, 1981.

executive functions under the Air Act are carried out, in the states, by state pollution control boards; this delegation of executive functions is permitted by Article 258(2) of the Constitution.

2.2. MEASUREMENT OF AIR POLLUTION: AIR QUALITY INDEX

An air quality index (AQI) is used by government agencies to communicate, to the public, how polluted the air currently is, or how polluted it might get. Public health risks increase as the AQI rises. Computation of the AQI requires an air pollutant concentration over a specified averaging period, obtained from an air monitor or model. Taken together, concentration and time represent the dose of the air pollutant, on the basis of which the health risks are analysed. AQI values are typically grouped into ranges.[6] Each range is assigned a descriptor, a colour code, and a standardised public health advisory. During a period of very poor air quality, such as an air pollution episode, when the AQI indicates that acute exposure may cause significant harm to public health, agencies may invoke emergency plans that allow them to order major emitters (such as coal-burning industries) to curtail emissions until the hazardous conditions abate.

2.3. AIR POLLUTION IN THE 1990s

'Death is in the Air', reported the famous magazine *Down To Earth* on 15 November 1997.[7] The magazine's report said that number of people dying in urban India due to deteriorating air quality was rising every year, and that very little was being done to deal with pollution in Indian cities. The rise in air pollution reached up to 28 per cent in the 1990s. The rise in air pollution contributed to 66 per cent of total premature deaths in India. The number of air pollution-related ailments requiring medical treatment and hospital admissions had sky-rocketed to 25 million cases, when the estimate in 1991–92 was 19 million.

2.4. AIR POLLUTION IN THE 2000s

A large share of the Indian population is exposed to pollution levels that do not conform to global and national air quality standards. Globally, Indian cities rank

6 Central Pollution Control Board (CPCB) Final Report 2014-15, India, https://app.cpcbccr.com/ccr_docs/FINAL-REPORT_AQI_.pdf.

7 Down to Earth, "Death is in the air", 15 November 1997, https://www.downtoearth.org.in/coverage/death-is-in-the-air-24804.

poorly in terms of air pollution.[8] Numerous monitoring sites across India report high concentrations of PM2.5, which exceed the benchmark limit (of 40 $\mu g/m^3$) suggested by the National Ambient Air Quality Standards (NAAQS).[9] In 2015, more than half the Indian population – about 670 million people – were exposed to ambient PM2.5 concentrations that did not comply with India's NAAQS.[10] Further, fewer than 1 per cent enjoyed air quality that met the global World Health Organization (WHO) benchmark limit of 10 $\mu g/m^3$. About one-quarter of the population lived in areas where the WHO guideline was exceeded by more than nine times. Exposure to air pollution poses a severe health burden in India. Available health impact assessments suggest that several hundred thousand cases of premature deaths annually are attributable to pollution.[11]

3. CASE ANALYSIS

3.1. *TAJ TRAPEZIUM* CASE

This case was about the presence of a significant amount of sulphur dioxide in the air, which was resulting in the corroding and yellowing of the white marble of the Taj Mahal. The amount of sulphur dioxide had increased in the air near the Agra region because of the presence of two coal power plants.

The Court applied the principle of sustainable development in this case, observing that there needs to be a balance between economic development and environmental protection. The Court indicated that relocation of the industries from the Taj Trapezium Zone (hereinafter referred to as TTZ) was to be resorted to only if natural gas was not acceptable or available, by or to the industries, as a substitute for coke/coal. The Court relied on *Vellore Citizens Welfare Forum v. Union of India and Ors.*, to define two principles: the "precautionary principle" and the "polluter-pays principle".[12]

The polluter-pays principle means that, if a hazardous activity is carried out by any person, then such person is liable to make good for the loss caused to

---

8 "World Air Quality Report: 35 Indian cities in top 50 of world's most polluted list", *The Indian Express*, 23 March 2022, https://indianexpress.com/article/lifestyle/health/35-indian-cities-50-world-most-polluted-air-pollution-quality-aqi-pm-levels-7832341/.

9 Ibid.

10 Council on Energy, Environment and Water (CEEW), "More than 670 million Indians would breathe poor quality air in 2030 despite compliance with pollution control policies: CEEW-IIASA study", 29 March 2019, https://www.ceew.in/press-releases/more-670-million-indians-would-breathe-poor-quality-air-2030-despite-compliance.

11 Council on Energy, Environment and Water (CEEW), *Report: Pathways to Achieve National Ambient Air Quality Standards (NAAQS) in India*, March 2019, https://www.ceew.in/publications/pathways-achieve-national-ambient-air-quality-standards-naaqs-india.

12 *Vellore Citizens' Welfare Forum v. Union of India* 1996(5) SCC 647.

the individual person, irrespective of whether the polluter took reasonable care while carrying on their activities.[13] Remediation of the damaged environment is part of the procedure of "sustainable development" and, as such, the polluter would be liable to compensate the individual sufferers, as well as for the cost of reversing the damage to the ecology.

The emissions generated by the coke/coal-consuming industries are air pollutants, and had a damaging effect on the Taj and the people living in the TTZ. The atmospheric pollution in TTZ had to be eliminated at any cost. Not even a 1 per cent chance can be taken when – human life apart – the preservation of a prestigious monument like the Taj is involved. The 292 industries were, as per the schedule given out by the court order, required to change over to the natural gas as an industrial fuel. The industries which were not in a position to obtain gas connections, for any reason, were to stop functioning with the aid of coke/coal in the TTZ and must relocate themselves as per the directions given the court. Hence, the court, by order dated 10 May 1996, stopped the operation of all brick kilns in the TTZ, with effect from 15 August 1996.

Subsequently, the Supreme Court again upheld the protection of Taj and its environs, in the order dated 8 December 2017.

In 2018, an article by written by Adrian Higgins, in the *Washington Post*, regarding the work being done by the Aga Khan Foundation for the conservation of the Taj, was published on their official website.[14] The Aga Khan Foundation had decided to carry out certain work, in order to restore this wonder of the world, and bring it back to its original glory. They are restoring the massive red sandstone and marble pavilion, its garden, and 10 smaller mausoleums dating to the sixteenth century. The restorations have been led by the Aga Khan Development Network, whose agencies provide cultural, medical, educational and other aid in developing countries. Shubham Borkar opines that

> These monuments gradually lose their significance in the budding wretchedness of urbanization … They lose their architectural significance disconnecting people from their history … This system of preservation of only 'protected monuments' creates a bias towards other monuments and distorts the history of important facts and facets of valuable legacy. Therefore, an urgent and stringent call for action is necessary to prevent destruction and vandalism of not only the recognized and protected monuments but also the unknown remainders of the sublime past.[15]

---

13 Ibid.

14 Adrian Higgins, "The Real Magic of Taj Mahal", *The Washington Post*, 15 March 2018, https://www.washingtonpost.com/lifestyle/home/the-real-magic-of-the-taj-mahal/2018/03/15/23e972ba-eb41-11e7-b698-91d4e35920a3_story.html.

15 Shubahm Borkar, "Protecting the Unprotected: The Struggle to Save India's Neglected Monuments: Archeology Laws in India", 15 July 2019, https://www.linkedin.com/pulse/protecting-unprotected-struggle-save-indias-neglected-borkar.

3.2. *CNG VEHICLES* CASE

The purpose of understanding the *CNG Vehicles* case is to narrate the role of the Supreme Court in controlling air pollution in Delhi, in the face of political contestation and government reluctance in implementing what had already long been on the statute books.

In the *Delhi Vehicular Pollution* case, M.C. Mehta's public interest litigation, filed in 1985, concerning air pollution in Delhi and the surrounding region, saw no action being taken till 1990, when a series of directions were passed as continuing mandamuses. The Court justified monitoring of the case to ensure compliance with Articles 39(e), 47, and 48-A of the Constitution, making authorities realise their obligations under statutory provisions, and preventing the frustration of legislative intent. It ordered periodic vehicle emission checks, with the power of cancellation of registration certificates of faulty vehicles. It directed the Ministry of Environment to establish an expert committee (the Bhure Lal Committee, constituted under section 3 of the Environment Act, 1986) to review technological, legal, and administrative solutions to curb pollution, and around 30 reports were submitted to this committee between 1991 and 1997.

The Supreme Court regretted that the Union of India had showed an indifferent attitude to the conversion of commercial vehicles to compressed natural gas (hereinafter referred to as CNG), and had discredited CNG as a proper fuel, as the government had delayed the setting-up of adequate dispensing stations, and had represented to the Court that CNG was in short supply. The recommendations made by the Bhure Lal Committee, being statutory, continued to remain in force. The Court did not accept the plea of the government that CNG was in short supply, and that it was unable to supply an adequate quantity, and termed the plea of the government as a deliberate attempt to frustrate the orders passed by the Court. The Court stated that there was no shortage of CNG, and even if there was a shortage of an essential commodity, the priority must be given to public health, as opposed to the balance sheet of a company. The Court added that to enable industries to cut their losses or make more profit at the cost of public health would not be a sign of good governance, and would be contrary to the constitutional mandate of Articles 39(e), 47, and 48-A. The Court took into account the concept of sustainable development and its two essential features, namely the "precautionary principle" and the "polluter-pays principle", and observed that the increase in respiratory diseases, especially amongst children, should be a cause of concern for any responsible government; the precautionary principle would give rise to the expectation that the government and health authorities would take appropriate measures to handle the air pollution.

The Court relied on the following Articles of the Constitution:

> Article 39(e): that the health and strength of workers, men, and women, and the tender age of children are not abused and that citizens are not forced by economic necessity to enter avocations unsuited to their age or strength.
>
> Article 47: The State shall regard the raising of the level of nutrition and the standard of living of its people and the improvement of public health as among its primary duties and, in particular, the State shall endeavour to bring about prohibition of the consumption except for medicinal purposes of intoxicating drinks and of drugs which are injurious to health.
>
> Article 48A: The State shall endeavour to protect and improve the environment and to safeguard the forests and wild life of the country.[16]

The rules framed under the EPA prescribe emission norms for specific industries. General standards apply, in the absence of industry-specific norms. Thus, the Court emphasised the implementation of existing emission norms rather than making new ones. The *CNG* case is relevant to understanding how and where the statutory agencies abdicate their responsibilities, compelling judges to fill the regulatory vacuum. Several reasons contribute to the ineffective functioning of the pollution control boards. Corruption, lack of independence, and diffused responsibilities among regulators are some of the reasons for administrative sloth.

The Court, then, can be seen as a "protector". This is also clear in the environmental cases where the Court establishes itself as the main protector of the environment, and undertakes tasks that go far beyond the judicial function. For example, in the Delhi vehicular pollution case,[17] the Court not only ordered the entire city bus fleet to convert to CNG, but also considered the issue of CNG pricing. Thus, in many cases where formal legislation is lacking, the Court has no problem with making law, for example by defining guidelines to prevent sexual harassment in the workplace. These examples show that, in practice, the Supreme Court goes far beyond the traditional competencies of a judiciary, violating the separation of powers, which raises fundamental questions of legitimacy and accountability.

3.3. *RELOCATION OF INDUSTRIES* CASE (1995)

M.C. Mehta v. Union of India and Ors.[18] was a prolonged case that questioned the presence of hazardous and non-conforming (to zoning rules under Delhi's

---

16 The Constitution of India, 1949.

17 *M.C. Mehta v. UOI*, (1991) SCR (1) 866.

18 Writ Petition (civil) 4677 of 1985.

Master Plan) industries in residential areas. It started as a public interest litigation (PIL), filed by M.C. Mehta, demanding the closure of industries operating in residential zones. In 1995, India's Supreme Court ruled in favour of Mehta, directing hundreds of hazardous and small-scale industries operating in "non-conforming areas" to relocate outside the metropolitan region, to the periphery of the larger National Capital Region (NCR). Under this order, 168 hazardous industries were relocated from the capital. The ruling appeared to be more about depopulating the city (of its urban poor) than it was about improving air and water quality. This was evident from the following passage, in which the court noted that:

> The city has become a vast and unmanageable conglomeration of commercial, industrial, unauthorized colonies, resettlement colonies and unplanned housing with a total lack of open spaces and green areas. Once a beautiful city, Delhi now presents a chaotic picture. The only way to relieve the capital city from the huge additional burden and pressures is to deconcentrate the population, industries and economic activities in the city and relocate the same in various priority towns in the NCR.[19]

Then came the order of 12 September 2000, in which 27 industries, said to be "undisputedly polluting" ones, including those producing acids or chemicals, involved in dyeing and bleaching, electroplating, or making glass products, plastic dye, polythene and PVC compounds, among other things, were listed to be shut down. It followed up this order with yet another one on 25 January 2001, wherein "it decreed that all 'potentially polluting industries' will be targeted"!

The Supreme Court passed the following directions, in its judgment dated 7 May 2004, regarding relocation of industries:

> All Industrial Units that have come up in Residential/non-conforming areas in Delhi on or after 1st August 1990 shall close down and stop operating as per the following schedule:
>
> (a) Industrial Units pertaining to extensive industries ('F' category) within a period of four months.
> (b) Industrial Units pertaining to light and service industries (category 'B' to 'F') within five months.
> (c) Impermissible household industries (category 'A') within six months.
> (d) 6,000 industrial units on the waiting list for allotment of industrial plots within 18 months.[20]

19 Ibid., para. 5 (2001.01.03).
20 Writ Petition (civil) 4677 of 1985.

4. THE ROLE OF THE SUPREME COURT

In acting as a protector, the Supreme Court has looked at various studies and reports regarding the impact of environmental pollution on health and economy (since 2010), as per its order dated 10 December 2018.[21]

4.1. SC ORDER, 10 DECEMBER 2018

In compliance with the Supreme Court order, the Central Pollution Control Board (CPCB) uploaded studies on the impacts of pollution on health. The order, passed by Justices Madan B. Lokur and Deepak Gupta, observed that, even though studies had been conducted on the impact of air pollution on health and the economy, they were not available in the public domain. The bench raised the possibility that the government was spending more on treatment than it was on controlling pollution.

4.1.1. Study on "Health Impact Assessment of Firecrackers Bursting During Dussehra and Diwali"[22]

The most recent of the studies was on the health impact of bursting firecrackers during Diwali and Dussehra, published in 2017. The study was carried out by Maulana Azad Medical College, in four areas in Delhi. People in these areas were interviewed two days before and after Dussehea, and again three days before and after Diwali. The findings showed that there was not much difference in the functioning of their respiratory systems before and after Dussehra, and during Diwali. There was some increase in coughs and breathlessness, but this did not translate into any significant illness requiring immediate medical attention. However, there were cases of excessive watering, redness, and burning sensations in the eyes post-Diwali, in some areas. The results of the study, even though air pollution levels were high, can be termed inconclusive, since it was carried out after the Supreme Court banned the sale of firecrackers, and limited the time for bursting them.

4.1.2. Study on "Health Effects of Chronic Exposure to Smoke from Biomass Fuel Burning in Rural Households"[23]

The women in rural households in India prepare breakfast, lunch, dinner and tea for the whole family, using biomass as the cooking fuel. Biomass is a cheaper

---

21 Writ Petition (civil) 13029 of 1985.

22 DHNS, "Air quality did worsen during Deepavali: CPCB", *Deccan Herald*, 5 January 2018, https://www.deccanherald.com/archives/air-quality-did-worsen-during-1914256.

23 T. Lahiri et al., "Health effects of chronic exposure to smoke from Biomass Fuel burning in rural areas", 2007, https://www.researchgate.net/publication/317286203_Health_effects_of_chronic_exposure_to_smoke_from_Biomass_Fuel_burning_in_rural_areas.

alternative source of energy for poor people who cannot afford cleaner fuel. Liquefied petroleum gas (LPG) users are few in rural India, and in many cases they also use biomass to reduce fuel costs. A large section of these women will have been chronically exposed to biomass smoke since their early teens, before their marriages, when they started assisting their mothers in the kitchen. Also, the study showed that the consequences of sustained biomass smoke exposure could be detrimental to their reproductive health, because it may change their menstrual cycle length, and could enhance the possibility of spontaneous abortions, stillbirths, and underweight babies. Other topics included in the study were respiratory symptoms, lung function, anaemia, susceptibility to infection, platelet hyperactivity, hypertension and increased risk of CVD – cardiovascular diseases, change in immunity, Reproductive toxicity, Neurotoxicity (smoke alters circulating levels of neurotransmitters) and Altered cell signalling and increased Cancer risk.

4.1.2.1. Recommendations of the Study

It is recommended that there is intensive public awareness and education programs, especially among the rural womenfolk informing them about the health risks associated with biomass fuel use. There should also be the inclusion of education and training for improved kitchen hygiene as part of the primary health care training for rural health professionals. There is a need to develop monitoring instruments designed to address pollution, stove efficiency, and other technical parameters under Indian conditions. Therefore, there should be an investment in Research and Development for the production of relatively low-cost devices that would facilitate monitoring on a broader set of households. Efforts should be made to provide clean fuels to biomass users. Intense research on the development of biomass-based clean household fuels that will be greenhouse-gas neutral and health-promoting in the line of generation of biogas from anaerobic digestion of animal dung. In the meantime, the authority may consider the supply of cleaner fuels like LPG and kerosene to the rural people, and incentives may be given to households below the poverty line in the form of the stove and fuel subsidies.

4.1.2.2. Strengths and Limitations of the Study

The major strengths of the present study are the large sample size, identified human cohorts, and their focused and detailed examination of a multitude of health parameters. Yet, the study has its limitations:

1. Biomass smoke contains hundreds of pollutants. Still, they only measured PM10 and PM2.5 levels in cooking areas, CO in exhaled breath, and t-MA

in urine, leaving emission of gaseous pollutants such as oxides of nitrogen and sulphur, transition metals and polycyclic aromatic hydrocarbons (PAHs) undetected. Thus, their possible impact on biological parameters is unknown.

2. the study did not attempt to identify potential toxic components responsible for these biological changes. For example, physicochemical.
3. Indoor measurements and biological sampling were carried out for a limited number of days. Therefore, seasonal variation and climatic changes could have influenced the measured parameters.

4.1.3. *Study on "Ambient Air Quality, Respiratory Symptoms and Lung Function of Children in Delhi"*[24]

The study on children reported that they had 1.8 times more upper respiratory symptoms such as sinusitis, running or stuffy nose, sneezing, sore throat, and common cold with fever. These children also had twice as much lower respiratory symptoms such as frequent dry cough, sputum-producing cough, wheezing breath, breathlessness on exertion, chest pain or tightness, and disturbed sleep due to breathing problems. This report emphasized the higher prevalence of underlying respiratory diseases. The study also showed that the issues were more prevalent in children from low socio-economic backgrounds.

4.2. RECOURSE UNDERTAKEN FOR THE EXCESSIVELY HIGH POLLUTION LEVELS IN DELHI AS PER GAP, NOTIFICATION 2017[25]

The GAP under section 3 of the EPA, 1986, enables the power of the Central Government to take measures to protect and improve the environment. Subject to the provisions of this Act, the Central Government has the power to take all such measures as it deems necessary or expedient for protecting and improving the quality of the environment, and preventing, controlling and abating environmental pollution.

---

24 Central Pollution Control Board, Ministry of Environment & Forests, "Study on Ambient Air Quality, Respiratory Symptoms and Lung Function of Children in Delhi", October 2012, https://www.cpcb.nic.in/uploads/healthreports/Study-Air-Quality-health-effects_Children-2012.pdf.

25 Central Pollution Control Board, Ministry of Environment & Forests, "Graded Response Action Plan for Delhi & NCR", https://cpcb.nic.in/uploads/final_graded_table.pdf.

Figure 1. Notification[26]

MINISTRY OF ENVIRONMENT, FOREST AND CLIMATE CHANGE

NOTIFICATION

New Delhi, the 12th January, 2017

S.O. 118(E).—Whereas high level of air pollution in Delhi and National Capital Region of Delhi has been a matter of serious concern and requires urgent measures to address the issue, particularly with reference to episodic rises in pollution levels;

And whereas a Graded Response Action Plan and appropriate measure to address different levels of air pollution as per National Air Quality Index (AQI) adopted by Government of India was submitted by the Central Pollution Control Board on the 25th November, 2016 before the Hon'ble Supreme Court which was further modified;

And whereas the Hon'ble Supreme Court in its order dated the 2nd December, 2016 has directed the Central Government to examine the Graded Response Action Plan and issue appropriate notification under sub-section (1) of section 3 of the Environment (Protection) Act, 1986 (29 of 1986);

And whereas the matter has been examined, and after due consideration the Central Government considers it appropriate to entrust the task of implementing the Graded Response Action Plan as a measure under sub-section (1) of section 3 of the Environment (Protection) Act, 1986 (29 of 1986) to the Environment Pollution (Prevention and Control) Authority (hereinafter referred to as 'EPCA') in compliance of the aforesaid orders;

Now, therefore, in pursuance of sub-section (1) of section 3 of the Environment (Protection) Act, 1986 (29 of 1986), the Central Government hereby assigns the task of implementation of the Graded Response Action Plan to the EPCA established under sub-section (3) of section 3 of the said Act vide notification number S.O.93 (E), dated the 29th January, 1998 and re-constituted from time to time by the Central Government.

[F. No. Q-18011/13/2000-CPA]

ARUN KUMAR MEHTA, Jt. Secy.

4.3. ODD-EVEN SCHEME TO COMBAT DELHI AIR POLLUTION

The scheme was based on the last digit of the vehicle's registration number. Under this scheme, odd and even-numbered vehicles would be allowed on the roads on alternate days. This flagship scheme of Delhi's AAP government was aimed at combating pollution, and was first implemented in 2015, in furtherance of the GAP.

5. CONCLUSION

This contribution explained how institutional interventions to combat air pollution in India began with judicial governance during the 1990s, through a prominent *CNG Vehicles* case. This case was among the first public interest litigations (PILs) filed by noted environmentalist M.C. Mehta. The *locus standi* for

[26] Ministry of Environment, Forest and Climate Change, "Notification", 12 January 2017, https://ismenvis.nic.in/Database/Notification_12th_January_2017-SO118E_14091.aspx.

filing a PIL in India witnessed a considerable broadening of its scope over time, and this eventually became the reason for the Court to assume itself the protector, guardian and *parens patriae* of the environment. Key environmental principles borrowed from the Stockholm Conference, like sustainable development, and its subthemes, such as intergenerational equity, the precautionary principle, the polluter-pays principle and the public trust doctrine, formed the core part of most judgments. With a brief stint of judicial activism, the judiciary decided to govern the growing air pollution in the country, with the aid of the existing substantive provisions of the law, as an alternative to introducing new legislation. The EPA was amended to introduce the GAP, as a measure for the National Ambient Air Quality (NAAQ) Standard. The Air (Prevention and Control of Pollution) Act of 1981 was also revamped, and the ambit of executive power was deliberately and carefully expanded.

The contribution also expanded on the role of the Indian executive in the failure of specialised regulatory mechanisms, such as the Environmental Impact Assessment (EIA). In the name of a technocentric perspective on environmental development, the Government of India has managed to dilute the EPA, leading to the erosion of the ecocentric environmental jurisprudence crafted by the Supreme Court over the years.

In a country where environmental issues have largely been governed by the judiciary, the contribution has stressed the need for increased public participation in decision-making, especially by involving environmental victims, and the most vulnerable, such as the indigenous communities. To enable the same, there needs to be strong environmental leadership and a robust policy framework, to enable "environmental incentives". The author believes that these two suggestions have immense potential to drive environmental reform in India.

The shifting focus of the Supreme Court, in the air pollution jurisprudence, from a transport regulatory approach, to a more general air pollution framework which involves the formulation of a Graded Response Action Plan (GRAP), a GAP and delving into more extensive and systematic issues, such as smog, is a testament to the Supreme Court's "judicial governance". From the implementation and enforcement perspective, the Government of India has already implemented emission controls for large stationary sources and road vehicles. While these measures help decouple air pollutant emissions and economic growth, their positive impact on ambient air quality is limited by the rapid expansion of commercial activities. These measures will be insufficient for halting a further deterioration in air quality, given the tenfold increase in gross domestic product (GDP) that is expected by 2050.

PART IV

THE FRESH WATER ENVIRONMENT

WATER REUSE

A Sustainable Concept for Europe?

Linda SCHÖNFELDER

1. INTRODUCTION

In the last 30 years, the number of droughts in the EU has increased by about 20 per cent,[1] resulting in one-third of its territory now suffering from water stress.[2] For this reason, there is a need to generate alternative water supplies, especially for agriculture, which exerts the most significant pressure on renewable water resources.[3] However, the potential of the "*resource*" wastewater is seldom recognised, and mostly left unexploited.[4] Water reuse, unfortunately, did not receive any attention in European environmental policy for a long time. It was first acknowledged in the 2012 Commission Communication *A Blueprint to Safeguard Europe's Water Resources*,[5] which refers to the political obligation to implement decisive agreements under international law.[6] Due to its Regulation (EU) No. 2020/741 of 25 May 2020 on minimum requirements for water reuse ("Water Reuse Regulation" or "WRR"),[7] valid since 26 June 2023, the EU has finally placed particular emphasis on the protection of freshwater resources by reusing water for agricultural irrigation, with reference to the Sustainable Development Goals of the United Nations,[8] and other international standards

1 COM (2007) 414 final from 18.07.2007, p. 2; COM (2012) 672 final from 14.11.2012, p. 2 *et seq.*; cf. *European Drought Observatory*, "Animation of Combined Drought Indicator maps during last year (Status: June 2022)", www.edo.jrc.ec.europa.eu.

2 See COM (2018) 337 final, 28.05.2018, p. 1; see Recital 7 of the Regulation (EU) 2020/741 of the European Parliament and of the Council of 25 May 2020 on minimum requirements for water (WRR), below n. 7.

3 See. *European Environmental Agency (EEA)*, "Indicator Assessment: Use of freshwater resources in Europe", CSI 018, WAT 001 Published 23.12.2019, last modified 22.11.2021, www.eea.europa.eu.

4 See COM (2018) 337 final, 28.05.2018, p. 2.

5 COM (2012) 673 final, 14.11.2012, pp. 16, 24.

6 Ibid., p. 21.

7 Regulation (EU) 2020/741 of the European Parliament and of the Council on minimum requirements for water reuse, OJ 2020 L 177/22 (hereinafter "WRR").

8 Recital 14 of the WRR, above n. 7; See *European Commission*, "Reflection Paper: Towards a Sustainable Europe by 2030", p. 63.

on water reuse.[9] However, the WRR is not the only set of rules that must be consulted, since agricultural water reuse needs to comply with other relevant EU legislation.[10] In this context, scientific remarks and different regional environmental conditions must be considered, to ensure a high level of environmental protection, as set out in TFEU Article 191(2). It is also debatable whether the Regulation fits into the concept of the overriding principle of "Integrated Water Resources Management", as set out in WRR Article 1, as it is not enough to set minimum requirements. In addition to legal integration, a concept for financing, allocation, and all needed infrastructure for production, supply and irrigation are also desirable.[11]

2. CONTENT OF THE REGULATION

The WRR describes a five-tier water reuse system that contains all the technical elements from production to irrigation.[12]

"Urban wastewater" is first treated in a wastewater treatment plant (step 1), and then undergoes further treatment in the plant itself, or, as set out in the definition of a reclamation facility in WRR Article 3(5), in another facility that further treats wastewater (step 2). This water is delivered to the end user through a delivery infrastructure (step 3). The reclaimed water can then be temporarily stored in a storage infrastructure, if necessary (step 4). Using water for irrigation represents "*reuse*", in the narrower sense (step 5).[13] The core of the WRR lies in its requirements for permits and risk management, in conjunction with the minimum standards for the quality of reclaimed water and its monitoring, described in Annex I, and the risk-management framework, set out in Annex II.

2.1. SCOPE

The WRR does not provide for a mandatory application of water reuse for Member States.[14] According to Article 2(1), the WRR applies only when treated urban wastewater is reused, in accordance with Article 12(1) of Directive 91/271/EEC, for agricultural irrigation, as specified in section 1 of Annex I to the WRR.

---

9 Recital 10 of the WRR, above n. 7.

10 See ibid., Recital 27.

11 See *M. van Rijswick et al.*, "Ten building blocks for sustainable water governance: an integrated method to assess the governance of water", *Water International* 39/2014 (725), p. 727 *et seq.*

12 WRR, above n. 7, Art. 3(15).

13 See *M. Spieler, L. Muffler and J. E. Drewes*, "Wasserrechtliche Rahmenbedingungen der Wasserwiederverwendung in Deutschland (Teil 1)", UWP 4/2020 (176), p. 181.

14 Ibid., p. 184.

2.1.1. *Treated Urban Wastewater*

In the catalogue of definitions in WRR Article 3(3), the Regulation refers to the definition of "urban wastewater", contained in Article 2(1) of the Urban Wastewater Treatment Directive 91/271/EEC (UWWTD).[15] According to this, urban wastewater means "domestic wastewater or the mixture of domestic wastewater with industrial wastewater and/or run-off rainwater". According to UWWTD, Article 2(2), domestic wastewater means "wastewater from residential settlements and services which originates predominantly from the human metabolism and from household activities", while industrial wastewater, according to UWWTD Article 2(3), means "any wastewater which is discharged from premises used for carrying on any trade or industry, other than domestic wastewater and run-off rainwater". WRR Article 2(1) continues to refer to "treated" urban wastewater. It can be deduced from the definition of "reclaimed water" in WRR Article 3(4) that "treated" urban wastewater is, first of all, urban wastewater that meets the requirements of the UWWTD, before it requires further treatment in the sense of section 2 of Annex I of the WRR. Furthermore, WRR Article 2(1) refers to UWWTD Article 12(1), where the original water reuse requirement is standardised, and accordingly, establishes the reference to the requirements standardised in the UWWTD. Therefore, it is "treated" urban wastewater if it meets the requirements of the UWWTD.

2.1.2. *Agricultural Irrigation*

According to Article 2(1), the scope of the WRR covers only "agricultural irrigation", which is described in more detail in Annex I, section 1, regarding various crop categories. The term "irrigation" has not yet been defined in any EU regulation, or in the WRR itself. Only Table 1 in section 2 of Annex I of the WRR refers to the permissible irrigation methods for specific crop categories. At this point, the question also arises as to what extent the Union legislature has included the supply of water to agricultural fields, with an additional fertilising effect, in "irrigation", since the potential for a fertilising effect of reclaimed water is mentioned in the recitals of the WRR.[16] The scope of application must also extend to fertilising irrigation, since the affected parties could otherwise evade the minimum requirements of the WRR by using reclaimed water for fertilising uses, and not only for pure irrigation. Although there are no particular parameters, in the WRR itself, for limiting nutrients. The WRR is linked to the UWWTD, which contains nutrient requirements for discharges of

---

15 Council Directive 91/271/EEC concerning urban wastewater treatment, OJ 1991 L 135/40 (hereinafter "UWWTD").

16 Recital 11 and 12 of the WRR, above n 7.

treated urban wastewaters in sensitive areas,[17] and to the Groundwater Directive (Directive 2006/118/EC)[18] and the Nitrates Directive (Directive 1991/676/EEC),[19] both of which set out limits for the content of nitrogen in groundwater bodies (50 mg/l).[20] The WRR, in conjunction with other relevant EU laws, thus covers the protection of the environment from nutrient inputs.

2.1.3. *Further Uses*

Further evidence that the European legislature has also recognised the potential of water reuse for other purposes can be found in the WRR.

2.1.3.1. Industry, Amenity and Environmental Purposes

The last paragraph of section 1 of Annex I of the WRR states that Member States may use "reclaimed water" for other purposes, namely "industrial water reuse" and "amenity-related and environmental purposes", without prejudice to relevant EU environmental and health legislation. The scope of the WRR does not cover those uses. The Committee of the Regions has already noted that an extension of the scope of the WRR to the areas of industry and the energy sector would mean a complete change of the entire text structure,[21] but did not exclude an extension of the scope to "irrigation of green spaces in urban areas, parks, gardens and ground for public use (e.g. recreation, sport)", because the same minimum requirements as for agricultural irrigation could be applied here.[22] The European Parliament and the Council, nevertheless, decided to extend the scope of the WRR only to the reuse of treated urban wastewater for agricultural irrigation.[23] In this respect, WRR Article 2(1) refers to the term "agricultural irrigation" in section 1 of Annex I of the WRR, for which minimum requirements

---

17 Table 2 of Annex I of the UWWTD, above n. 15.

18 Directive 2006/118/EC of the European Parliament and of the Council on the protection of groundwater against pollution and deterioration, OJ 2006 L 379/12 (hereinafter "Groundwater Directive"): No. 1 of Annex I of the Groundwater Directive sets out quality standards for nitrates.

19 Council Directive 91/676/EEC concerning the protection of waters against pollution caused by nitrates from agricultural sources, OJ 1991 L 375/1 (hereinafter "Nitrates Directive"): Point A No. 2 of Annex I of the Nitrates Directive, sets out criteria to designate "nitrate vulnerable zones".

20 Para. 5(b) of Point (A) of Annex II of the WRR, above n. 7.

21 Opinion of the Committee of the Regions on "Proposal for a Regulation of the European Parliament and of the Council on minimum requirements for water reuse", OJ C 86, 07.03.2019, pp. 353 *et seq.*, Point II.11.

22 Ibid., Amendment 8.

23 Position of the Council at first reading with a view to the adoption of a Regulation of the European Parliament and of the Council on minimum requirements for water reuse, 07.04.2020 (ST 15301 2019 REV 2 ADD 1), p. 4.

are laid down in section 2 of Annex I of the WRR. The subparagraph referring to other uses, which was inserted in the context of the first reading by the European Parliament,[24] intends only to take into account the great potential of water reuse for other purposes,[25] which Member States may allow if it is deemed necessary due to local conditions and requirements.[26] When doing so, other relevant EU laws on health and environmental protection must be observed ("without prejudice"). It can also be noted that there was no consensus in the legislative process about which concrete activities should be assigned to which area of water reuse. Depending on which terms are used, there may also be overlaps. Accordingly, it is up to the Member States to allocate concrete water reuse activities to the areas of "environment"[27] or "amenity".[28] However, according to WRR Article 12(3)(a), the Commission shall, as part of the evaluation set out in Article 12(1), assess the feasibility of extending the scope of the Regulation to reclaimed water intended for further specific uses, including reuse for industrial purposes.

2.1.3.2. Indirect Use

Pursuant to WRR Article 12(3)(b), the Commission should also examine whether the scope of application of the Regulation should be extended to the "indirect use of treated wastewater". "Indirect use" could be used to address groundwater recharge, which is otherwise not addressed at all by the WRR, though in the preliminary work on the WRR, aquifer recharge was identified as an important field of application of water reuse.[29] Ultimately, EU provisions on aquifer recharge were not considered appropriate, "due to a strong local dimension".[30] During the first reading, the European Parliament proposed that the Commission include the assessment of laying down minimum requirements for the purpose of "aquifer recharge" in its review programme.[31] In addition, it

24 Legislative resolution on the proposal for a regulation of the European Parliament and of the Council on minimum requirements for water reuse, 12.02.2019 (P8_TA-PROV(2019)0071), Amendment 105.

25 Recital 29 of the WRR, above n. 7; Position of the Council at first reading, above n. 23, p. 4.

26 Recital 29 of the WRR, above n. 7.

27 See Draft Report on the proposal for a regulation of the European Parliament and of the Council on minimum requirements for water reuse, 28.09.2018 (PE628.362), Amendment 72.

28 Cf. ibid., Amendment 71; Draft Report, Amendments 114–310, 06.11.2018 (PE629.751), Amendment 152; Draft Report, Amendments 311–479, 06.11.2018 (PE630.372), Amendment 423.

29 See *L. Alcalde Sanz and B. Gawlik, JRC Science for Policy Report: Minimum quality requirements for water reuse in agricultural irrigation and aquifer recharge – Towards a legal instrument on water reuse at EU level*, Publications Office of the EU, 2017, p. 34.

30 COM (2018) 337 final, 28.05.2018, p. 9.

31 Legislative resolution (2019), above n. 24, Amendment 101; see also Draft Report on minimum requirements for water reuse (2018), 28.09.2018, above n. 28, Amendment 65, pp. 76 *et seq.*

proposed that the Commission should examine whether the expansion of the requirements of the Regulation for the "indirect use" of treated wastewater was necessary.[32] Indirect use was, thus, not initially equated with aquifer recharge, for which the European Parliament considered a far more differentiated legal framework necessary.[33] However, the text of the WRR, which was reached in the course of institutional negotiations, deleted this assessment programme of the Commission.[34] A footnote in the Commission's position on the adopted text of the European Parliament in the first reading now states that the indirect use of wastewater is seen as equivalent to the discharge of treated wastewater into water bodies for the purpose of its reuse.[35] Aquifer recharge can, thus, be considered a subcase of indirect water reuse.

2.2. OBLIGATIONS OF ADDRESSED PARTIES

According to WRR Article 1(1), the Regulation lays down "minimum requirements for water quality and monitoring and provisions on risk management, for the safe use of reclaimed water in the context of integrated water management". These are addressed to the responsible parties, especially the reclamation facility operator,[36] and the competent authority.[37]

2.2.1. Reclaimed Water Quality

The Regulation sets minimum quality requirements to guarantee that reclaimed water is safe. WRR Article 4 addresses the obligation to ensure the water quality standard to the reclamation facility operator, meaning a natural or legal person who operates or supervises a reclamation facility.[38] The operator is a responsible party, as set out in WRR Article 3(14).[39] The reclamation facility operator's

---

32 Ibid.

33 Ibid.

34 Provisional Agreement Resulting from Interinstitutional Negotiations, 21.01.2020 (PE646.828), Art. 12(3)(b).

35 Commission response to the text adopted in plenary, 16.04.2019 (SP (2019)354), fn. 1: "Indirect reuse means the discharge of treated wastewater back into surface or groundwater bodies, from where it is then abstracted to be used again."

36 *M. Spieler, L. Muffler and J.E. Drewes*, above n. 13, p. 183.

37 *S.R. Laskowski*, "Unionsrechtliche Mindestanforderungen für die (Ab-)Wasserwiederverwendung in der Landwirtschaft – ein Beitrag zum Gewässerschutz?, *ZUR* 2020 (321), p. 322.

38 WRR, above n. 7, Art. 3(6).

39 Ibid., Art. 3(14): "responsible party means a party carrying out a role or activity in the water reuse system, including the reclamation facility operator, the urban wastewater treatment plant operator where different from the reclamation facility operator, the relevant authority other than the designated competent authority, the reclaimed water distribution operator or the reclaimed water storage operator responsible".

responsibility ends at the "point of compliance", namely the point where the treated water is delivered to the next actor in the chain (for example, distribution operator, storage operator or end user).[40] Up to this point, the operator is responsible for the minimum water quality, as set out in section 2 of Annex I (Table 1), as well as for complying with the additional conditions laid down in the permit of the competent authority, according to WRR Article 6(3)(c) and(d).[41] To ensure this, the water quality is to be monitored in accordance with Article 4(2), section 2 of Annex 1 of the WRR, and the additional conditions set by the permit of the competent authority.[42]

Table 1. Minimum requirements for the quality of reclaimed water

<table>
<tr><th rowspan="2">Reclaimed water quality class</th><th rowspan="2">Indicative technology targets</th><th colspan="5">Quality requirements</th></tr>
<tr><th>E. Coli (number/ 100 ml)</th><th>BOD$_5$ (mg/l)</th><th>TSS (mg/l)</th><th>Turbidity (NTU)</th><th>Other</th></tr>
<tr><td>A</td><td>Secondary Treatment, filtration, disinfection</td><td>≤ 10</td><td>≤ 10</td><td>≤ 10</td><td>≤ 5</td><td rowspan="4">Legionella spp.: < 1000 cfu/l, where there is a risk of aerosolisation
Intestinal nematodes (helminth eggs): ≤ 1 egg/l for irrigation of pasture and forage</td></tr>
<tr><td>B</td><td>Secondary treatment and disinfection</td><td>≤ 100</td><td rowspan="3">In accordance with Directive 91/271/EWG
(Annex I Table 1)</td><td rowspan="3">In accordance with Directive 91/271/EWG
(Annex I Table 1)</td><td>-</td></tr>
<tr><td>C</td><td>Secondary treatment and disinfection</td><td>≤ 1000</td><td>-</td></tr>
<tr><td>D</td><td>Secondary treatment and disinfection</td><td>≤10 000</td><td>-</td></tr>
</table>

Source: Table 2 of Section 2, Annex I of the WRR.

Section 2 of Annex I of the WRR divides reclaimed water into the quality classes A to D. Requirements for purification technology and water quality are specified for each of the different quality classes. With regard to the targets for the technology, secondary treatment and disinfection are prescribed for each quality class, and there is an additional requirement for filtration for quality class A. Limit values and deviation tolerances for E. coli, BOD$_5$ (biochemical oxygen demand), TSS (total suspended solids), turbidity, legionella spp., and intestinal nematodes (helminth eggs) are then standardised for the various quality classes.

These minimum requirements should take into account the objective of WRR Article 1, which intends to reach a high level of environmental protection.

---

40 Ibid., Art. 3(11).

41 See *M. Spieler, L. Muffler and J. E. Drewes*, above n. 13, p. 183.

42 Monitoring requirements are not covered in this contribution, but see Tables 3 and 4 of s. 2, Annex I of the WRR, above n. 7.

Therefore, the European legislature must be guided by the best available scientific guidance.[43] In the legislative process of the Regulation, the European legislature took its cue from the technical reports of the Joint Research Centre (JRC), which had already played a significant role in the Commission's legislative initiative.[44] This was expressed mainly by giving scientific considerations priority over political considerations.[45] The scientific assessments of the JRC thus had a major impact on the Regulation.

2.2.2. Risk-Management Plan

Pursuant to the second sentence of WRR Article 6(3), the risk-management plan is the necessary admission requirement for obtaining a production permit from the competent authority, since it constitutes the basis for the permitting process.[46] It must contain all elements as set out in Annex II of the WRR, and identify the responsibilities of the reclamation facility operator and other responsible parties. The competent authority must ensure that a water reuse risk-management plan is established, and this may cover one or more water reuse systems.[47] Along with other responsible parties and end users, as appropriate, the reclamation facility operator prepares the risk-management plan according to Article 5 and Annex II of the WRR.

2.2.3. Permit Obligation

According to WRR Article 6(1), the production and supply of reclaimed water intended for agricultural irrigation shall be subject to a permit that is applied for, by the responsible parties and, where relevant, the end users according to national law, from the competent authority of the Member State in which the reclamation facility operates, or is planned to operate.

The minimum content of the permit is prescribed in WRR Article 6(3). This includes, *inter alia*, the obligations of the reclamation facility operator and other responsible parties; the quality class(es); the agricultural use, according to Table 1 of Annex I of the WRR; the conditions for water quality and monitoring, as specified in section 2 of Annex I of the WRR; additional requirements that are set out in the risk-management plan; the validity period of the permit; and the point of compliance.

---

43 *B. Arndt*, *Das Vorsorgeprinzip im Unionsrecht*, Mohr Siebeck, 2009, p. 199.

44 *L. Alcalde Sanz and B. Gawlik*, above n. 29, p. 5; COM (2018) 337 final, 28.05.2018, pp. 8 and 13.

45 Position of the Council at first reading above n. 23, p. 6; Recital 10 of the WRR, above n. 7.

46 General approach of the Council on the proposal for a Regulation of the European Parliament and of the Council on minimum requirements for water reuse, 17.06.2019 (ST 10278 2019 INIT), p. 4.

47 WRR, above n. 7, Art. 5(1).

The Regulation does not specify any details regarding the authorisation procedure. Rather, it is left to the Member States to apply already-existing authorisation procedures to water reuse, provided that these are adapted to the minimum requirements of the Regulation.[48] Pursuant to WRR Article 6(5), the competent authority usually decides on granting the permit "without delay". However, if, due to a complex application, the decision will take more than 12 months, the competent authority must inform the applicant of the expected date of the decision.

2.2.4. *Compliance Check*

Pursuant to WRR Article 7(1), the competent authority shall verify whether the conditions set out in the permit are being complied with, *inter alia* through "on-the-spot checks"; and, pursuant to WRR Article 7(5), whether the responsible parties are complying with the measures and tasks set out in the risk-management plan. If this is not the case, the competent authority may request the responsible parties to immediately take all necessary measures to restore compliance, and to inform the end users (WRR Article 7(2)). If there is a significant risk to the environment and health as a result, the operator must stop the supply of reclaimed water, in accordance with WRR Article 7(3).

2.3. END USERS

End users, meaning natural/legal persons who use water for agricultural irrigation,[49] are not responsible parties within the meaning of WRR Article 3(14). According to WRR Article 5(2), it is now only envisaged that the end users, who are to be consulted by the responsible parties, be involved in the preparation of the risk-management plan as appropriate. They may also apply for a permit, if provided for by national law (WRR Article 6(2)); however, due to WRR Article 7(2), the conditions laid down in the permit cannot be enforced against the end users.[50] WRR Article 7(2) stipulates that, in the event of non-compliance with the conditions by the responsible parties, the end users be informed immediately.

In the legislative process, there were some proposals to extend the responsibility of end users beyond the position of mere consumers,[51] but these

48 See ibid., Recital 23.

49 Ibid., Art. 3(2).

50 *M. Spieler, L. Muffler and J.E. Drewes*, above n. 13, p. 183.

51 Opinion of the Committee of the Regions on "Proposal for a Regulation of the European Parliament and of the Council on minimum requirements for water reuse", OJ C 86, 07.03.2019, p. 353 *et seq.*, Point II.13, Amendment 2 (Art. 6(4) and (5)), Amendment 3 (Art. 7(5)); see also Amendment 4 (Art. 8(5)), Legislative resolution (2019), above n. 24, Amendments 58 and 71.

did not prevail in the trilogue negotiations.[52] In the end, the Union legislature probably considered the obligations of end users to be covered by Union food law.[53] However, it is presupposed that responsible parties and end users will cooperate to ensure that the supply of reclaimed water meets the needs of the end users regarding crop categories (Table 2).[54] Furthermore, information campaigns for end users, set up by the Member States, are considered a basic measure to ensure an optimal and safe reuse of water, for a high level of environmental, human and animal protection.[55]

Table 2. Permitted agricultural use and irrigation method

Minimum reclaimed water quality class	Crop category (*)	Irrigation method
A	All food crops consumed raw where the edible part is in direct contact with reclaimed water and root crops consumed raw.	All irrigation methods.
B	Food crops consumed raw where the edible part is produced above ground and is not in direct contact with reclaimed water, processed food crops and non-food crops including crops used to feed milk- or meat-producing animals.	All irrigation methods.
C	Food crops consumed raw where the edible part is produced above ground and is not in direct contact with reclaimed water, processed food crops and non-food crops including crops used to feed milk- or meat-producing animals.	Drip irrigation (**) or other irrigation method that avoids direct contact with the edible part of the crop.
D	Industrial, energy and seeded crops.	All irrigation methods (***).

Source: Table 1 of Section 2 Annex 1 of the WRR.

(*) If the same type of irrigated crop falls under multiple categories of Table 1, the requirements of the most stringent category shall apply.

(**) Drip irrigation (also called trickle irrigation) is a micro-irrigation system capable of delivering water drops or tiny streams to the plants and involves dripping water onto the soil or directly under its surface at very low rates (2–20 litres/hour) from a system of small-diameter plastic pipes fitted with outlets called emitters or drippers.

(***) In the case of irrigation methods which imitate rain, special attention should be paid to the protection of the health of workers or by standers. For this purpose, appropriate preventive measures shall be applied.

---

52 Provisional Agreement Resulting from Interinstitutional Negotiations, above n. 34.

53 See Recital 28 of the WRR, above n. 7.

54 Ibid., Recitals 18 and 21.

55 Ibid., Art. 9(2); See Recitals 22 and 32.

However, according to WRR Article 6(7), the Member States are free to require a further specific permit, *inter alia* for the use of reclaimed water in order to apply additional requirements and barriers identified in the risk-management plan.

3. COHERENCE WITH OTHER EU LEGISLATION

Water reuse can hardly be assigned to one branch of law. It combines elements of circular economy law, water law, agricultural law and food law. Moreover, the Water Reuse Regulation complements other relevant EU legislation regarding health and environmental risk that must be considered,[56] especially within water reuse risk management.[57]

Foremost, the following interfaces need to be considered (Figure 1).

Figure 1. EU legislative Acts that are met by agricultural water reuse

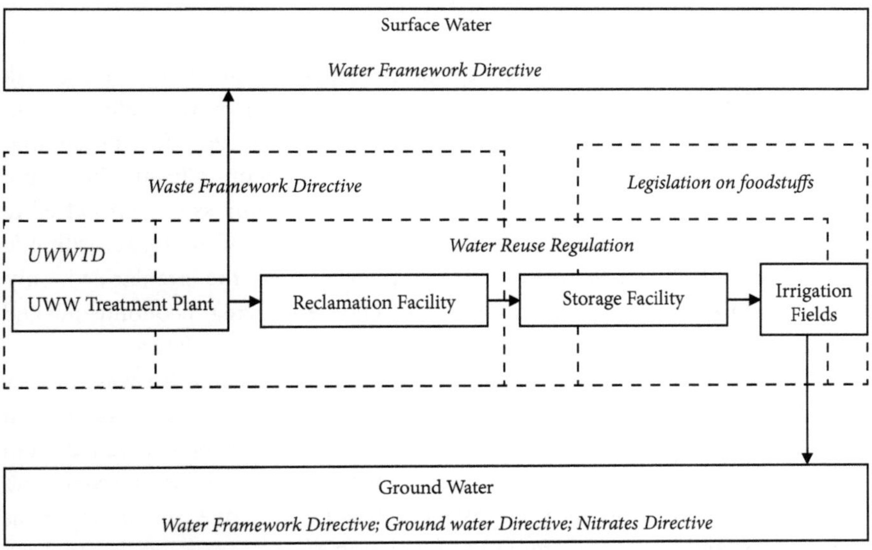

Source: See also European Commission, Guidelines to support the application of Regulation 2020/741 on minimum requirements for water reuse (2020/C 298/18); Modifications made by the author.

3.1. URBAN WASTEWATER TREATMENT DIRECTIVE (UWWTD)

The Regulation supplements the UWWTD, which establishes minimum quality and monitoring requirements, especially for the collection, treatment and

56 Ibid., Recital 27.

57 Ibid., para. 5 of Annex II.

discharge of urban wastewater, in the Member States. However, an obligation to discharge treated wastewater into water bodies is not provided. Article 12(1) of the UWWTD even stipulates a requirement for the reuse of wastewater whenever it is appropriate, which is specified by the WRR in Article 2(1). The WRR also explicitly refers to the UWWTD in several provisions (Article 3(3); Tables 2 and 3 of Annex I). The minimum requirements of the WRR consider the requirement according to the second sentence of UWWTD Article 12(1): the water must be treated in such a way that it does not pose a harmful risk to the environment. Due to UWWTD Article 5, it should be noted that the requirements for wastewater in "sensitive areas", in agglomerations of 10,000 inhabitants or more, also apply to wastewater intended for reuse, unless it is demonstrated that the reuse of water does not contribute to the pollution of the sensitive areas.[58]

3.2. WASTE FRAMEWORK DIRECTIVE

The WRR does not contain an explicit reference to the Waste Framework Directive (Directive 2008/98/EC),[59] in either Annex II or the definitions in Article 3. However, the WRR is part of the Union's strategy for the circular economy.[60] In its Communication of 2 December 2015 on "Closing the loop – An EU action plan for the circular economy",[61] the Commission committed to developing a legislative framework for water reuse.[62] Furthermore, according to WRR Article 1(2), the Regulation also aims to promote the circular economy. It is, therefore, surprising that the interface between circular economy law and water law has not been addressed more clearly by the EU legislature.

The scope of application of the Waste Framework Directive was initially open, since the Union legislature wanted to regard wastewater as "waste" within the meaning of the Waste Framework Directive. This can be concluded from Waste Framework Directive Article 2(2)(a), which states that "wastewaters" are excluded from the scope of the Waste Framework Directive, "to the extent as they are covered by other Community legislation".[63]

---

58 See Common Implementation Strategy for the Water Framework Directive and the Flood Directive: Guidelines on Integrating Water Reuse into Water Planning and Management in the context of the WFD, 10.06.2016, pp. 49 *et seq.*

59 Directive 2008/98/EC of the European Parliament and of the Council on waste and repealing certain Directives, OJ 2008 L 312/3.

60 COM (2020) 98 final, 11.03.2020, Point 3.7.

61 COM (2015) 614 final, 02.12.2015.

62 Ibid., p. 3.

63 ECJ Judgment: Case C-252/05, *Thames Water Utilities* [2007] ECLI:EU:C:2007:276, para. 26; ECJ Judgment: Case C-629/19, *Sappi Austria* [2020] ECLI:EU:C:2020:824, para. 34.

As a condition for the full exclusion of wastewater of the scope of the Waste Framework Directive, it is required that the more specific Community legislation contains precise provisions on the management of waste, and ensures at least an equivalent level of environmental protection.[64] It can be said that the UWWTD contains special or supplementary provisions to the Waste Framework Directive regarding the *disposal* of treated wastewater,[65] while the WRR, by referring to UWWTD Article 12, contains provisions for the *recovery* of wastewater. This also corresponds to the lists in Annex I and Annex II of the Waste Framework Directive, which give concrete indications for the classification of disposal or recovery operations. Thus, according to Annex I, D 6 of the Waste Framework Directive, the release into a water body is a "disposal operation". According to Annex II, R 10 of the Waste Framework Directive, the use of a substance for agricultural purposes is a "recovery operation". These complementary legislative Acts can be regarded as *lex specialis* to the Waste Framework Directive, with regard to the specific areas regulated therein.[66]

Therefore, the provisions of the Waste Framework Directive can be used for the interpretation of the WRR.[67] This concerns specifically the transmission of the hierarchy of waste (Article 4, Waste Framework Directive); however, because of special considerations for the environmental outcome, due to the principle of a high environmental protection level – and as also set down in Waste Framework Directive Article 4(2) – certain provisions for "waste" cannot always be transferred to "wastewaters". Orientation towards the waste hierarchy (i.e. (1) prevention; (2) preparing for reuse; (3) recycling; (4) other recovery; and (5) disposal) is already not required, due to the value ascribed in the Water Framework Directive (Directive 2000/60/EC)[68] to maintaining the water ecology as a whole. This can also be inferred from the WRR, since, according to Article 6(6)(d), the permit must be reviewed and updated in any instance where the ecological status of surface waters has been significantly affected by climatic changes or other conditions. According to the end-of-waste-status provisions (Article 6) of the Waste Framework Directive, with the complementary question of when wastewater turns into water again,[69] the point where wastewater meets

---

64 ECJ Judgment to Directive 75/442/EEC: Case C-114/01, *AvestaPolarit Chrome* [2003] ECLI:EU:C:2003:448, paras. 52 and 61; *Thames Water Utilities* above n. 63, para. 34; *Sappi Austria*, above n. 63, para. 36.

65 Arg. Ex. ECJ Judgment, *Thames Water Utilities*, above n. 63, paras. 39 *et seq.*; see *Kropp*, in *Lersner/Wendenburg/Versteyl* (eds.), *Recht der Abfallbeseitigung des Bundes der Länder und der Europäischen Union, Erich Schmidt Verlag*, 2nd ed., 2015, No. 7460, Art. 2, para. 29.

66 See *Thames Water Utilities* above n. 63, para. 39 *et seq.*; see *Sappi Austria*, above n. 63, para. 37 et seq.; see ECJ Judgment: Case C-444/00, *Mayer Parry Recycling* [2003] ECLI:EU:C:2003:356, para. 57.

67 See *Mayer Parry Recycling*, above n. 66, paras. 53 *et seq.*

68 Directive 2000/60/EC of the European Parliament and of the Council establishing a framework for Community action in the field of water policy, OJ 2000 L 327/1.

69 See *M. Spieler, L. Muffler and J.E. Drewes*, above n. 13, p. 179.

a specific purpose is of significant importance. It can be derived from the WRR itself that wastewater, after its further treatment in a "reclamation facility", can be called "reclaimed water".[70] The definition of the "point of compliance", in WRR Article 3(11), simultaneously makes it clear that the operations of supply and use already involve "reclaimed water", and not "wastewater".

3.3. WATER FRAMEWORK DIRECTIVE (WFD)

According to its Article 1(2), the WRR shall contribute to the objectives of the WFD, by addressing water scarcity in the Member States; it therefore overlaps with the goals of the WFD, to promote sustainable water use (WFD Article 1(b)), and to mitigate the effects of floods and droughts (WFD Article 1(e)). However, it might also conflict with some of the environmental objectives in WFD Article 4.

3.3.1. Improvement Requirements

Water reuse could especially contribute to limiting water abstraction from groundwater bodies, and is intended to reduce the effects of discharging treated wastewater into water bodies.[71] This corresponds, in particular, with the improvement requirement in Article 4 of the WFD. As stated in Article 11(4), in conjunction with Annex VII, Part B, of the WFD, water reuse can, in any case, be included as a "supplementary" measure in the Member States' programme of measures. Through the analysis required by WFD Article 5, it can be determined where the reuse of reclaimed water is a viable option.[72] If a Member State decides to introduce water reuse, this becomes mandatory for the respective river basin districts, when it is included in the programme of measures.[73] However, according to WRR Article 2(2), Member States may also decide to exclude water reuse for certain river basin districts, or parts thereof.

3.3.2. Prohibition of Deterioration

Water reuse might also conflict with some environmental objectives set out in WFD Article 4. This particularly applies to the "prohibition of deterioration", pursuant to which the status of all bodies of surface water and groundwater must not deteriorate. Water reuse could, in particular, have effects on the ecological status of surface water bodies, and the chemical status of groundwater bodies.

---

70 WRR, above n. 7, Art. 3(4); Legislative resolution (2019), above n. 24, Amendment 42; *M. Spieler, L. Muffler and J.E. Drewes*, above n. 13, p. 179.

71 Recital 2 of the WRR, above n. 7.

72 See *Bio by Deloitte, Optimising Water Reuse in the EU: Public consultation analysis report*, European Commission, 2014, p. 43.

73 *M. Spieler, L. Muffler and J.E. Drewes*, above n. 13, p. 184.

3.3.2.1. Ecological Status of Surface Water Bodies

The reduced disposal of water into rivers, caused by water reuse, could lead to a deterioration of the ecological status of surface water bodies. According to WFD Article 2(21), the "ecological status" of surface water bodies means "the quality of the structure and functioning of aquatic ecosystems associated with surface waters, classified in accordance with Annex V". The quality components in Annex V of the WFD are divided into biological elements, supported by hydromorphological, chemical and physicochemical elements. Since the hydromorphological quality elements (i.e. dynamics of water flow, river continuity, river depth) and physicochemical elements (i.e. temperature, oxygen content, salinity, nutrient conditions) only have a supporting function, they are not directly relevant to the question of deterioration.[74] However, these elements, in turn, can have negative consequences for the relevant biological quality elements, set out in paragraph 1.1.1 of Annex V of the WFD (i.e. the composition, abundance, and age structure of fish fauna).[75]

The EU legislature has provided instruments, in the WRR, to take account of the quality elements at the national and regional levels. According to WRR Article 2(2)(c), Member States may decide that the reuse of water, in certain river basin districts or parts of river basin districts, is not appropriate, due to pressures on the status of surface water bodies. Also, at the regional level, the competent authorities are responsible for monitoring the ecological status of surface water bodies, and updating the permit in the event of a change in climatic conditions (WRR Article 6(6)(d)).

3.3.2.2. Chemical Status of Groundwater Bodies

The deterioration of the chemical status of groundwater bodies could occur, due to the percolation of reclaimed water, and the enrichment of groundwater with the nutrients and pollutants contained therein. According to paragraph 2.3.1 of Annex V of the WFD, the parameters for determining the chemical status of the groundwater body are its conductivity and its concentration of pollutants, for which the quality elements "good" or "poor" are defined for assessment.

The WRR itself lacks substance-related limit values for reclaimed water that relate to groundwater protection. Still, the risk of groundwater degradation needs

---

74 *W.-D. Dallhammer and C. Fritzsch*, "Verschlechterungsverbot – Aktuelle Herausforderungen an die Wasserwirtschaftsverwaltung", *ZUR* 2016 (340), p. 343; *K. Faßbender*, "Das Verschlechterungsverbot im Wasserrecht – aktuelle Rechtsentwicklungen", *ZUR* 2016 (195), p. 201.

75 *K. Faßbender*, in: *R. von Landmann and E. Rohmer* (Founder), *Umweltrecht Kommentar*, 97. EL Dezember 2021, WHG, § 33, para. 6, with further references; *W.-D. Dallhammer and C. Fritzsch*, above n. 74, p. 343.

to be eliminated as part of the risk management in accordance with Annex II of the WRR, with the relevant time for assessment being the mixing of reclaimed water with the groundwater.[76] Requirements for reclaimed water regarding heavy metals, pesticides, disinfection by-products, pharmaceuticals, micropollutants, microplastics and antimicrobial resistance must first be determined through risk assessment, and included as additional or stricter conditions in the risk-management plan. This shifts a large part of the environmental protection to the regional level, which is to be welcomed, since, due to different ecological conditions, it ensures better coordination of groundwater protection than regulation on the EU level.

Furthermore, reclaimed water does not have to be completely free of pollutants, which follows from WFD Article 11(3)(f), and Groundwater Directive Article 6(3)(1)(d). In particular, irrigation water from bank filtrate or surface waters – for which minimum requirements do not yet exist at the European level – cannot be considered of a higher quality than "reclaimed water", as defined by the WRR.[77] Here, residual risks are socially acceptable, and groundwater cannot be certified as completely free of pollutants either.[78] Furthermore, the guarantee of a "zero risk" is also unnecessary for legal system reasons, because the obligation to respect the environmental precautionary principle, as set out in TFEU Article 191(2), does not require that every risk must be eliminated.[79]

3.4. NITRATES DIRECTIVE

The requirements of the Nitrates Directive need to be observed in the context of risk assessments. Certain provisions of the Nitrates Directive refer to the term "fertilizer". A "fertilizer", in the context of Article 2(e) of the Nitrates Directive, means any substance containing one or more nitrogen compounds, applied on land to enhance vegetation growth. Reclaimed water in the scope of the WRR is not meant as a "fertilizer" in the sense of the Nitrates Directive, though it can have a fertilising side effect.[80] Member States may include in their code(s) of good agricultural practice, *inter alia*, measures to prevent water pollution caused by the infiltration of water from irrigation systems.[81] Furthermore, according to Article 5(5) of the Nitrates Directive, Member States shall take additional measures in their action programmes, if it becomes apparent that the objectives of the Nitrates Directive cannot be achieved by the steps taken up to that point.

---

76 *M. Spieler, L. Muffler and J. E. Drewes*, "Wasserrechtliche Rahmenbedingungen der Wasserwiederverwendung in Deutschland (Teil 2)", *UWP* 1/2021 (21), p. 25.

77 Ibid. at p. 27.

78 Ibid.

79 Ibid.; see Groundwater Directive, above n. 18, Art. 6.

80 See Recitals 11 and 12 of the WRR.

81 Annex II, (B)(10) of the Nitrates Directive, above n. 19.

3.5. LEGISLATION ON FOODSTUFFS

The WRR refers to the European food law, in Article 2(4), and within the element keys of risk assessment in Point B of Annex II.[82] Hygienic requirements, especially for end users who can be considered "food business operators"[83] for "primary production",[84] result from the General Food Law Regulation (Regulation 178/2002/EC),[85] as well as from the Regulation on Hygiene of Foodstuffs (Regulation 852/2004/EC).[86] Food business operators are responsible for ensuring that foods comply with the requirements of food law.[87] Irrigation water has to be "clean water",[88] which means water that does not contain microorganisms or harmful substances in quantities capable of directly or indirectly affecting the health quality of food.[89] Food business operators must also comply with other European and national laws that contain requirements for the prevention of food contamination.[90]

According to Article 4(3) of the Regulation on Hygiene of Foodstuffs, food business operators must operate in compliance with microbiological criteria. Microbiological criteria for foodstuffs can be found in the Regulation on Microbiological Criteria (Regulation 2073/2005/EC).[91] According to Article 3(1) of the Regulation on Microbiological Criteria, food business operators must ensure that the microbiological criteria for food, contained in Annex I of the Regulation, are complied with at all stages of production, processing and distribution. Annex I of the Regulation on Microbiological Criteria includes E. coli criteria for vegetables and fruits.[92]

Also relevant for primary crop production is the "Commission notice on guidance document on addressing microbiological risks in fresh fruits

---

82 See also Recital 28 of the WRR, above n. 7.

83 See Art. 3(3) of the General Food Law Regulation, below n. 85.

84 See ibid., Art. 3(17).

85 Regulation (EC) No. 178/2002 of the European Parliament and of the Council laying down the general principles and requirements of food law, establishing the European Food Safety Authority and laying down procedure in matters of food safety, OJ 2002 L 21/1 ("General Food Law Regulation").

86 Regulation (EC) No. 852/2004 of the European Parliament and of the Council on the hygiene of foodstuffs, OJ 2004 L 139/1 (hereinafter "Regulation on the Hygiene of Foodstuffs").

87 See Art. 17(1) of the General Food Law Regulation, above n. 85; see Art. 4(1) of the Regulation on the Hygiene of Foodstuffs, above n. 86.

88 Art. 2(1)(i), Regulation on the Hygiene of Foodstuffs, above n. 86; para. 5(c) of Point A.II of Annex I, Regulation on the Hygiene of Foodstuffs, above n. 86.

89 See *A. Meisterernst and O. Sosnitza*, in *W. Zipfel and K.-D. Rathke* (eds.), *Lebensmittelrecht: Loseblatt-Kommentar*, 181. EG November 2021, EG-Lebensmittelhygiene-Verordnung, Art. 2, para. 27.

90 No. 3 lit. a of Annex I of the Regulation on the Hygiene of Foodstuffs.

91 Commission Regulation (EC) No 2073/2005 on microbiological criteria for foodstuff, OJ 2005 L 338/1.

92 See Chapter 2.5 of Annex I of the Regulation on Microbiological Criteria.

and vegetables at primary production through good hygiene" (Commission Guidance Document),[93] which is intended to help users comply with the hygiene requirements for fresh fruits and vegetables. Appendix II of the Commission Guidance Document provides a matrix that agricultural food business operators can use for primary production, for the risk assessment of water.

Particular attention must be paid to the Regulation on Maximum Levels for Contaminants in Foodstuff (Regulation 1881/2006/EC),[94] which sets standards for the maximum content of specific contaminants in food. Contaminants are all substances that are not intentionally added to food.[95] According to Article 1 of this Regulation, the edible part of the foodstuffs listed in the Annex may not be placed on the market if they exceed the maximum levels for contaminants specified therein. Reclaimed water must, therefore, not cause these crops to exceed the established maximum contaminant levels.

4. CONCLUSION AND OUTLOOK

The WRR intends to provide a regulatory framework for water reuse for agricultural irrigation. However, it does not refer to all components of the water reuse system, as defined in WRR Article 3(15). The focus is mainly on the obligations of reclamation facility operators, while the obligations of the end users, which played a controversial role in the legislative process, were considered by the Union legislature to be covered by food law. However, the question of whether the established minimum requirements meet a high level of environmental protection should consider the scientific basis of the legislation. In this context, it should be mentioned that the European legislature referred to the scientific studies of the JRC, and that adaptation to scientific and technical progress is possible by amending the Regulation at several levels (see WRR Articles 5(5) and 12).

Moreover, the WRR fits into the complex framework of European legislation which must be observed in the risk assessment of the responsible parties, and ultimately by the competent authority, before granting a permit. Environmental protection is thus shifting primarily to the regional level, but the WRR also contains specific provisions to consider the value enshrined by other legislative Acts, in particular the Water Framework Directive. Furthermore, even if the

93 Commission notice on guidance document on addressing microbiological risks in fresh fruits and vegetables at primary production through good hygiene, OJ 2017 C 163/1.

94 Commission Regulation (EC) No 1881/2006 setting maximum levels for certain contaminants in foodstuffs, OJ 2006 L 364/5.

95 *K.-D. Rathke and M. Edelhäuser*, in: *W. Zipfel and K.-D. Rathke* (ed.), *Lebensmittelrecht: Loseblatt-Kommentar*, 181. EG November 2021, EU-Kontaminanten-Höchstgehalte-Verordnung, Art. 1, para. 3.

WRR does not explicitly refer to the Waste Framework Directive, it is relevant for the interpretation and classification of the WRR, and should be considered in relation to certain legal questions (water hierarchy, end of wastewater status).

In its different enforcement and implementation elements, the WRR takes into account the different ecological circumstances of the Member States. The use of water reuse technologies will also become more harmonised, but further support mechanisms are only rarely available at the EU level. For financial matters, at least, the new Common Agricultural Policy contains specific financial provisions for irrigation, in Article 74 of Regulation 2021/2115/EU.[96] According to Article 74(5) of that Regulation, Member States may grant support for investments in the use of reclaimed water as an alternative water supply, if the provision and use of such water is compliant with the WRR.

Finally, attention should be paid to the fact that Member States that are inexperienced in reusing water, and which currently have no legal provisions dealing with water reuse, have an enormous need for adaptation and implementation. The Commission was, in consultation with the Member States, required to draw up guidelines, by 26 June 2022, to improve the practical implementation of the WRR.[97] Whether these guidelines will be helpful remains to be seen. In the end, of the total water abstraction in the EU of around 247,020 million m^3/year,[98] 20 per cent could be saved just by using the resource water more appropriately.[99] Let us see if we get there.

---

96 Regulation (EU) 2021/2115 of the European Parliament and of the Council establishing rules on support for strategic plans to be drawn up by Member States under the common agricultural policy (CAP Strategic Plans) and financed by the European Agricultural Guarantee Fund (EAGF) and by the European Agricultural Fund for Rural Development (EAFRD) and repealing Regulations (EU) No. 1305/2013 and (EU) No. 1307/2013, OJ 2021 L 435/1.

97 European Commission, Guidelines to support the application of Regulation 2020/741 on minimum requirements for water reuse (2020/C 298/01).

98 *T. Dworak, M. Berglund and C. Laaser, EU Water saving potential (Part 1 – Report)*, Ecological Institute, 2007, p. 15.

99 COM (2007) 414 final, 18.07.2007, p. 4, with further references.

GREY WATER REUSE IN THE EU

Legal Obstacles, Shared Solutions and Future Challenges

Marko Perišić

1. INTRODUCTION

According to certain data, less than 1 per cent of global water resources are actually fresh and renewable.[1] Except for in the most developed countries, the vast majority of wastewater is discharged directly into the environment without adequate treatment.[2] Pollution will be driven by higher populations and economic growth, and the lack of wastewater treatment will result in an additional reduction in water resources.[3] After it has been used, water is all too often seen as a burden to be disposed of, or a nuisance to be ignored.[4] As Emmerson claims, "[p]eople commonly say we 'use' water, however, it is more accurate to say we dirty it."[5]

The lack of fresh water is one of the world's main problems, and results from overpopulation, urbanisation and climate change: each of these factors will be considered below.

When we think about these three factors, we can also recall the words of Italo Calvino, who, writing about Marco Polo's visit to Kublai Khan, says:

> Hell, if there be such a thing – is not tomorrow. Hell is right here, and today we live in it; together we make it up. There are only two ways to avoid suffering in this Hell. The first way out is easy for most people: Let Hell be, live it up, and stop noticing it.

---

1 *D. Brooks, O. Brandes and S. Gurman*, *Making the Most of the Water We Have: The Soft Path Approach to Water Management*, London: Earthscan, 2009, pp. 4–20.

2 *UNESCO World Water Assessment Programme*, *The United Nations World Water Development Report 2017: Wastewater, the untapped resource*, Paris: UNESCO 2017, Executive Summary, pp. 1–12.

3 *A. Boretti and L. Rosa*, "Reassessing the projections of the World Water Development", *npj Clean Water*, pp. 2, 15, 2019, p. 3.

4 *UNESCO*, *World Water Assessment Programme*, supra note 2.

5 *G. Emmerson*, "Every Drop is Precious: Greywater as an Alternative Water Source", Queensland Parliamentary Library, Research Bulletin no. 4/98, Brisbane, 1998, p. 11.

> The second way is risky. It demands constant attentive curiosity to find out who and what in midst of this Hell is not part of it, so as to make it last by giving space to it.[6]

The situation in the world will be aggravated by unequal population growth in various geographical areas, unrelated to local resources. Many regions and countries in the world will face problems arising from the increase in their populations. This will lead to the phenomenon of overpopulation, which will stretch current water resources to their limits, cause an increase in water pollution, and, potentially, lead to the danger of civil and international conflicts, especially over existing water supplies. One of the main consequences of overpopulation is the pressure on available water resources used to supply the population. It is necessary to prepare for the future thoroughly and rationally. According to Food and Agricultural Organization (FAO) data, in addition to the agricultural sector, which is responsible for 70 per cent of water abstraction worldwide,[7] large increases in water demand for industry and energy production are projected.

One definition of urbanisation is that it is "a complex socio-economic process that transforms the built environment, converting formerly rural into urban settlements, while also shifting the spatial distribution of a population from rural to urban areas".[8] According to expectations and certain estimates, if the current trend continues, the twenty-first century will be the century when the world's population becomes predominantly urban.[9] The global urban population exceeded the global rural population in the year 2007, for the first time in history.[10] Taking into account that, by 2018, half of the world's population lived in cities, it is estimated that, by end of this decade, that percentage will increase to 60 per cent, and one in every three people will live in cities with at least half a million inhabitants.[11] The expansion of municipal water supply, sanitation systems and urbanisation contributes to the rising demand for water. The regulation of the relationship between humanity and water is closely linked to how political power is exercised. The structure of the powers within the community is also conditioned by the bond that is established between people and the water resource.[12] As the urban population grows, increasing quantities of water are diverted to cities; however, those diversions require

---

6 *I. Calvino, Le città invisibili*, Milan: Mondadori, 2020, p. 160.

7 *FAO, Water pollution from agriculture: a global review*, Rome: UN, 2017, p. 2.

8 *United Nations, World Urbanization Prospects 2018*, New York: Department of Economic and Social Affairs, Population Division, 2019, p. 1.

9 *A. Gregory and M. Hall, Urban water sustainability*, Clayton, Australia: CSIRO, 2011, p. 75.

10 *United Nations, World Urbanization Prospects 2018*, supra note 8, p. 5.

11 *United Nations, The World's Cities in 2018 – Data Booklet*, Department of Economic and Social Affairs, Population Division, New York: UN, 2018.

12 *R. Louvin, Aqua Æqua Dispositivi giuridici, partecipazione e giustizia per l'elemento idrico*, Torino: G. Giappichelli Editore, 2018, p. 68.

massive infrastructure, and affect aquatic ecosystems from which water is taken. Moreover, water conveyance requires substantial energy inputs. Supplying the increasing urban demand thus has major implications for energy use, and consequently for greenhouse gas emissions.

Climate change has become an inevitable phenomenon in recent years and is expected to gain momentum in the coming period. The most significant force that drives climate change is anthropogenically released greenhouse gases.[13] According to scientists, dry regions will become drier, and wet regions wetter.[14] In other words, evaporation may dry out some areas and cause water to fall as excess precipitation on others. As water is a common component of the entire climate system (i.e. the atmosphere, hydrosphere, cryosphere and biosphere), any change in the climate impacts on water through different means.[15] Thus, more and more solar energy will be trapped, which will lead to the intensification of the hydrological cycle, resulting in changes of the precipitation pattern. Such changes will worsen the situation with floods and droughts, and will have a drastic impact on the availability of fresh water.[16] Furthermore, a warmer temperature increases the rate of evaporation of water into the atmosphere, and thus increases the atmosphere's capacity to hold water.[17] Consequently, as temperatures rise, more water is needed for people and animals to maintain their health and thrive, but also for diverse economic activities, such as growing food crops, raising livestock and producing energy for power plants. A higher temperature can reduce the toxic levels, facilitating biodegradation of chemicals, but may also increase toxicity.[18] In areas that are experiencing increases in rainfall, diverse types of problems can emerge. Some of these concern water infrastructure, sewer systems, water treatment plants, etc.[19]

Changing climate events, such as extreme weather ranges, will lead to more untreated wastewater. Emerging needs, accompanied by climate change, consist of adaptation of wastewater management. Namely, there is considered to be a vicious cycle involving climate change and wastewater management, with each problem intensifying the other. During wastewater treatment, the emission of greenhouse gases occurs, contributing to the problem of climate change.[20]

---

13 *International Panel for Climate Change*, *Fifth assessment report for climate change*, Geneva: WMO, UNEP, 2013, pp. 13–14.

14 *R.P. Singh A.S. Kolok and S.L. Bartelt-Hunt* (eds.), *Water Conservation, Recycling and Reuse: Issues and Challenges*, Singapore: Springer, 2019, p. 204; See also *M.G. Donat et al.*, "More extreme precipitation in the world's dry and wet regions", *Nature Climate Change*, 2016, pp. 508–513.

15 *R.P. Singh, A.S. Kolok and S.L. Bartelt-Hunt*, supra note 14, p. 207.

16 Ibid.

17 *FAO*, supra note 7.

18 *R.P. Singh, A.S. Kolok and S.L. Bartelt-Hunt*, supra note 14, p. 206.

19 *Ibid.*, pp. 205–206.

20 *Ibid.*, p. 203.

Therefore, it can easily be said that the influence is mutual and reciprocal. Various issues are associated with climate change and wastewater treatment operations. Climate change not only affects freshwater resources, but also affects wastewater treatment, through an overabundance of water or a lack of water, and through poor water quality. The impacts on the wastewater infrastructure can be directly or indirectly associated with climate change. The indirect impacts are reflected in the decreasing usage of water that flows into the wastewater transmission and treatment systems. Further, this implies a decrease in the overall water volume, but not the waste load.[21]

In reality, numerous urban water systems are already under pressure, and may face additional challenges, while associated structures and facilities are vulnerable to the adverse effects of climate change.[22] Floods, whether they are the result of increased rainfall or are created during storms, affect wastewater treatment plants' efficiency. Significant damage can be caused to the environment and people by floods, which have a strong potential to release untreated waste into the ecosystem, if they affect wastewater facilities.[23] Damage caused to wastewater treatment plants can take some time to repair, further implying a possible release of untreated waste. The rise in temperature may also impose certain unwanted effects on wastewater treatment plants, reflected in a rising likelihood of sewer corrosion and odour problems.[24] Warmer temperatures may indirectly cause grave weather conditions, exacerbated by urban heat islands, which could, in turn, result in additional convective thunderstorms, hail, cyclonic events, and higher winds, that may exceed the design capacity of the infrastructure.[25] Moreover, a higher temperature may reduce the quality of wastewater. Facilitating the growth of algal bloom in wastewater will reduce the dissolved oxygen concentration. With a higher temperature, organic matter decomposition could increase, releasing the nutrients (nitrogen and phosphorus) into water, thereby increasing the eutrophication of wastewater.[26]

Given all the above facts, contributing to higher water stress, ever-increasing water demand, and a growing gap between water supply and demand, it is no surprise that global water demand is projected to increase significantly over the coming decades.

If current trends continue, water quality will continue to deteriorate over the coming decades, especially in resource-poor countries, endangering human health and ecosystems, contributing to water scarcity, and limiting sustainable

---

21 *A. Zouboulis and A. Tolkou, Effect of Climate Change in Wastewater Treatment Plants: Reviewing the Problems and Solutions*, Cham: Springer, 2015, p. 10.

22 *R.P. Singh, A.S. Kolok and S.L. Bartelt-Hunt*, supra note 14, p. 209.

23 *A. Zouboulis and A. Tolkou*, supra note 21, p. 7.

24 *R.P. Singh, A.S. Kolok and S.L. Bartelt-Hunt*, supra note 14, p. 207.

25 *A. Zouboulis and A. Tolkou*, supra note 21, p. 6.

26 *R.P. Singh, A. S. Kolok and S.L. Bartelt-Hunt*, supra note 14, p. 107.

economic development.[27] The question of quality entails the no less important question of quantity, from which emerges the concern of whether we will have enough water to meet our needs. Moreover, humanity's bad habits, combined with his lifestyle, play a significant part in an irrational relationship with water.

2. THE IMPORTANCE OF GREY WATER REUSE

> Unless one merely thinks the man was intended to be an all-conquering and sterilising power in the world, there must be some general basis for understanding what it is the best to do. This means looking for some wise principle of co-existence between man and nature.[28]

The economic value and environmental importance of grey water are often underestimated. Grey water should be viewed as a valuable resource, not as waste. Grey water, with its nutrients, has the potential to replace commercial fertilisers. Its reuse could result in various benefits, such as reduced water and fertiliser costs, reductions in water bills, etc.[29] The benefits of water reuse are economic, social and environmental, such as:

a) increased availability of drinking water, by using drinking water for drinking and reclaimed water for other purposes;
b) reduced production costs for the use of high-quality reclaimed water;
c) reduced energy consumption, which would be consumed by using deep groundwater;
d) increased agricultural production;
e) reduced nutrient loads to receiving waters;
f) reducing water imports or the need for desalination;
g) enhanced environmental protection by restoration of streams, wetlands and ponds;
h) increased employment and local economy;
i) integrated and sustainable use of water resources.[30]

Grey water management is gaining more and more attention, because improper wastewater management is one of the most important causes of environmental

[27] *D.A. Caponera, Principles of Water Law and Administration*, Rotterdam: Brookfield, 1992, pp. 14–15.
[28] *C.S. Elton, The Ecology of Invasions by Animals and Plants*, Chicago: University of Chicago Press, 1958, p. 145.
[29] *A. Morel and S. Diener, Greywater Management in low and middle-income countries, review of different treatment systems for households or neighbourhoods*, Dübendorf: Swiss Federal Institute of Aquatic Science and Technology (Eawag), 2006, p. 7.
[30] *L.A. Sanz and B. M. Gawlik*, Water Reuse in Europe – Relevant guidelines, needs for and barriers to innovation, Luxembourg: JRC Science and Policy Reports, 2014, pp. 9–10.

pollution and diseases. Although less contaminated than other wastewater sources, untreated grey water contains pathogens, salts, solid particles, fat, oil and chemicals.[31] Hence, the two main risks are the presence of pathogenic microorganisms and toxic heavy metals. The microbial risk implies two abilities: one is the ability to reproduce in the environment; the other is to survive, and to be transmitted to humans directly via contact with grey water, or indirectly via insect vectors. A long-term risk for humans and animals is a concentration of heavy metals in grey water.[32] Grey water management is a precondition for clean and healthy living conditions.[33] If reuse practices are inappropriate, the substances described above may potentially cause harm to human health, and to soil and groundwater quality.[34] Using untreated grey water for irrigation purposes is highly inadvisable.[35] Its harmful effects on soil can include changing the soil's hydrochemical characteristics.

One potential alternative means of mitigating water insecurity is grey water treatment, to provide sufficient quantities and reserves of fresh water in the future, while not endangering the environment. If given the necessary attention, this practice could help reduce overreliance on freshwater resources, and reduce pollution caused by the discharge of untreated grey water into freshwater resources.

An alternative source of water, including safe wastewater management, could be of enormous help to protect ecosystems, energy, nutrients and other renewable materials.[36] Compared with rainwater harvesting, which is dependent on hydrological conditions, grey water reuse has been considered a reliable method of ensuring water security.[37] In any case, discharging grey water into the sewer is a missed opportunity to save resources.

Therefore, there is a need for proper and harmonised European legislation that will address different types of water reuse. To achieve this, it is necessary, first, to set out a common understanding/definition of grey water, and to recognise its different grades, and its distinction from black water.

---

31 *A. Morel and S. Diener*, supra note 29, p. 6.

32 *R.M.S. Mohamed, A.A. Saeed Al-Gheethi and A.H.M. Kassim*, *Management of Greywater in Developing Countries: Alternative Practices, Treatment and Potential for Reuse and Recycling*, Cham: Springer, 2019, p. 46.

33 *B. Imhof and J. Mühlemann*, *Greywater treatment on household level in developing countries – a state of the art review*, Zurich: Swiss Federal Institute of Technology, 2005, p. 35.

34 *L.A. Sanz and B. M. Gawlik*, supra note 30, pp. 9–10.

35 Ibid.

36 *B. Dabić, E. Mladenović and J. Grabić*, "Potencijali sive vode za navodnjavanje urbanog zelenila: Osvrt na stanje u Republici Srbiji", *Glasnik Šumarskog fakulteta Univerziteta u Banjoj Luci*, 2018, p. 104.

37 *M. Oteng-Peprah, M. Agbesi Acheampong and N.K. deVries*, "Greywater Characteristics, Treatment Systems, Reuse Strategies and User Perception – a Review", *Water Air Soil Pollution*, 2018, p. 225.

3. CHARACTERISTICS OF GREY WATER

In general terms, grey water is a type of wastewater that is generated from household activities.[38] As it is less polluted than sewage, grey water also represents one of the best sources of potable water. "Grey water" can be defined as "untreated wastewater from washbasins, baths, showers and laundry facilities that excludes WC, urinal, bidets, soiled laundry water, cleaner's sinks, kitchen sinks and dishwashers or other wastewater which is of non-domestic origin".[39] It is called grey water because, if stored for even short periods, the water will often cloud, turning a grey colour.[40] Various different countries have different definitions of grey water: some of these include water sourced from the kitchen and dishwasher, but other countries do not include wastewater from the washing machine.[41] However, there is a consensus on the distinction between grey water and black water. Both can be reused, after different levels and methods of treatment. The separation of grey water from black water is considered a critical step for proper management aimed at facilitating the treatment process. Grey water has a lower quality than potable water, and a higher quality than black water (toilet wastewater). Grey water contains its own division: there is light grey water and dark grey water. Whereas light grey water includes wastewater from the bathroom, showers and tubes, dark grey water includes more contaminated waste, from laundry facilities, dishwashers and kitchen sinks.[42]

The characteristics of grey water depend on several factors. Important roles are played by customs, lifestyles, chemical household products and other household activities. No less important is the distribution link of drinking water or grey wastewater, and the quality of supply.[43] Grey wastewater has different characteristics depending on where it is generated:[44] whether it originates from the bathroom, laundry, kitchen, or is of mixed origin. It follows that different types of grey wastewater will have different pre-treatment needs, but will also be suitable for different types of reuse. The analysis of grey water characteristics in the different categories shows that kitchen grey water and laundry grey water are higher in both organics and physical pollutants, compared with bathroom

---

38 *R.M.S. Mohamed, A.A. Saeed Al-Gheethi and A.H.M. Kassim*, supra note 32, p. 3.

39 *D.T.K. James et al.*, "Grey water reclamation for urban non-potable reuse – challenges and solutions a review", 2016, p. 4.

40 *G. Emmerson*, supra note 5, p. 8.

41 *WHO, Overview of greywater management health considerations, Discussed and approved at the regional consultation on national priorities and plans of action on management and reuse of wastewater, Amman, Jordan* (Report WHO-EM/CEH/125/E), Geneva: WHO, 2006, p. 8.

42 *A. Albalawneh and C. Tsun-Kuo*, "Review of the Greywater and Proposed Greywater Recycling Scheme for Agricultural Irrigation Reuses", *International Journal of Research – Granthaalayah*, 2015, p. 17.

43 *E. Eriksson et al.*, "Characteristics of grey wastewater", Environment & Resources DTU, Technical University of Denmark, Lyngby, 2002, p. 86.

44 Ibid.

and mixed grey water.[45] Bathroom grey water is deficient in both nitrogen and phosphorus, due to the exclusion of urine and faeces.[46] Also deficient in nitrogen are laundry grey water and mixed grey water. Kitchen grey water features high levels of organic substances, suspended solids, turbidity and nitrogen.[47] Kitchen grey water does not lack nitrogen and phosphorus. Due to its lower quality, many grey water reuse standards prohibit the use of kitchen effluent.[48] However, to maintain an optimal COD:[49] N:P ratio in the biological treatment process of grey water, it is suggested that a small amount of kitchen grey water should be collected with other streams.[50] Either way, bathroom and laundry grey water are less contaminated by microorganisms than kitchen grey water.[51] Storage is also an important element. Grey water should not be stored for longer than about 48 hours, but to improve its quality, it is best for it to be stored for at least 24 hours.[52]

4. THE LEGAL CONTEXT OF WATER REUSE

Water reuse has been practiced for a long time. Its potential and importance as a valuable resource have been recognised. The European continent is characterised by different legislations, both within its largest part, which consists of the European Union (EU) Member States, and within its smaller part, which consists of non-EU countries. Concerning the EU, Directive 91/271/EEC (the Urban Waste Water Treatment Directive) requires treated wastewater be reused whenever appropriate.[53] The Urban Waste Water Treatment Directive has played an important role: its implementation has contributed to obtaining treated wastewaters of quite high quality, which can be reused for specific applications.[54]

---

45 *F. Li, K. Wichmann and R. Otterpohl*, "Review of the technological approaches for grey water treatment and reuses", *Science of The Total Environment*, 2009, p. 3440.

46 *S. Vinitha*, "Effect of Greywater Characteristics on its Chemical Coagulation", *International Journal Of Engineering Technology and Management Sciences [IJETMS]*, 2020, p. 1; See also *I. Bodnar et al.*, "Qualitative characterization of household greywater in the northern great plain region of Hungary", *Environmental Engineering and Management Journal*, 2014, pp. 11-19; *S. N. Abed and M. Scholz M.*, "Chemical simulation of greywater", *Environmental Technology*, 2016, pp. 1631-1646.

47 *F. Li, K. Wichmann and R. Otterpohl*, supra note 45.

48 *A. Maimon, E. Friedler and A. Gross*, "Parameters affecting greywater quality and its safety for reuse", *Science of The Total Environment*, 2014, p. 21.

49 Chemical oxygen demand.

50 *F. Li, K. Wichmann and R. Otterpohl*, supra note 45.

51 *A. Maimon, E. Friedler and A. Gross*, supra note 48, p. 18.

52 *A. Dixon et al.*, "Measurement and modelling of quality changes in stored untreated grey water", *Urban Water*, 2000, p. 292.

53 Art. 12 of Council Directive 91/271/EEC of 21 May 1991 concerning urban waste-water treatment, OJ L 135, 30/05/1991.

54 *N. Voulvoulis*, "Water reuse from a circular economy perspective and potential risks from an unregulated approach", *Current Opinion in Environmental Science & Health* 2018, p. 33.

Furthermore, the non-exclusive list of supplementary measures provided for in Part B of Annex VI to Directive 2000/60/EC[55] contains, among other things, water reuse measures.[56] Since directives are legislative Acts that require EU countries to achieve a certain goal or a specific result, but leave them free to choose how to do so,[57] each Member State was free to establish its own standards for water reuse. The outcome is, for example, that the French criteria are based on the revised World Health Organization (WHO) criteria and Australian guidelines, whereas, on the other hand, the Greek and Italian regulations are based on Californian regulations.[58] In addition to the most usual standards on water reuse from the EU Member States (e.g., France, Greece, Italy), Cyprus, Portugal and Spain also have their own standards.[59] The reality is that only a small number of Member States are practicing water reuse, and have adopted national legislation or standards in that regard. It can be noted that, while the standards of Cyprus, France, Greece, Italy and Spain are regulations within national legislation, in Portugal the standards on water reuse are merely guidelines.[60] Further, not all standards have the same purpose, parameters, limit values, water quality levels, monitoring requirements, etc. It follows that national legislations are uneven, and may lead to the creation of barriers and obstacles, and differences in health standards, in relation to products irrigated with reclaimed water, as well as endangering public confidence in the reuse of water. Since water problems are multidimensional, multisectoral and multiregional, the sensible opinion is that this can be resolved only through multi-institutional coordination and cooperation. As water is multidimensional, the approach to dealing with these problems must be the same, and help must be sought from the results of several scientific disciplines. By harmonising requirements for safe water reuse, better protection of the environment, and of human and animal health, will be achieved.

As one of the main elements in the transformation towards a circular economy is providing more sustainable practices for resources and waste management,[61] the EU has included reclaimed water as part of the circular

55 Directive 2000/60/EC of the European Parliament and of the Council of 23 October 2000 establishing a framework for Community action in the field of water policy, OJ, 22/12/2000.

56 Recital 8 of Regulation (EU) 2020/741 of the European Parliament and of the Council of 25 May 2020 on minimum requirements for water reuse, OJ L 177, 05.06.2020 (Regulation 2020/741/EU).

57 *M. Cini and N. Pérez-Solórzano Borragán*, *European Union Politics* (6th ed.), Oxford: Oxford University Press, 2016, p. 195.

58 *Water Board of Oldenburg and East Frisia (OOWV)*, "Methodology to collect successful practices in monitoring and assessing and ensuring compliance with water reuse standards", *Aquares Interreg Europe*, 2018, p. 11.

59 *L.A. Sanz and B.M. Gawlik*, supra note 30, p. 22.

60 Ibid.

61 *M. Smol, C. Adam and M. Preisner*, "Circular economy model framework in the European water and wastewater sector", *Journal of Material Cycles and Waste Management*, 2020, p. 682.

economy. Water reuse in the EU is influenced by strategic documents, such as the Commission Communication on Water Scarcity and Droughts,[62] the Blueprint for Safeguarding European Waters,[63] and the Circular Economy Strategy.[64] Regarding the transition to a circular economy, the overall sustainability of water reuse is of vital importance. An important step toward harmonisation within the EU has been made by Regulation 2020/741/EU on minimum requirements for water reuse.[65] Considering the low effect of national regulations on this important matter, the idea is to stimulate safe reuse of wastewater for irrigation by harmonising minimum quality requirements. Regulation 2020/741/EU represents a cornerstone in the implementation of reclaimed water for agricultural irrigation; it establishes minimum requirements for water quality and monitoring, and contains provisions on risk management, and for the safe use of reclaimed water, in the context of integrated water management. Pursuant to Article 3(4) of the Regulation, reclaimed water is defined as "urban wastewater that has been treated in compliance with the requirements set out in Directive 91/271/EEC and which results from further treatment in a reclamation facility in accordance with Section 2 of Annex I to this Regulation". Said Regulation is based on two communications of the European Commission:

1. The 2012 Blueprint to Safeguard Europe's Water Resources.
2. The 2015 EU Action Plan for the Circular Economy.

The 2012 Blueprint to Safeguard Europe's Water Resources aimed to remove obstacles to greater use of alternative water supply options, and thus to reduce water shortages and the vulnerability of supply systems, and also proposed instruments to regulate water reuse standards.[66]

The 2015 EU Action Plan for the Circular Economy concerned the Commission's obligations to promote the reuse of treated water, as well as to take steps on legislative proposals concerning minimum requirements for the reuse of water.[67]

Regulation 2020/741/EU contributes to the achievement of the Sustainable Development Goals of the United Nations 2030 Agenda for Sustainable Development, in particular Goal 6 on the availability and sustainable management of water and sanitation for all, and Goal 12 on sustainable consumption and

---

62 *European Commission*, Water Scarcity and Drought-Environment. Available at: https://environment.ec.europa.eu/topics/water/water-scarcity-and-droughts_en.

63 *European Commission*, Water Blueprint-Environment. Available at: https://environment.ec.europa.eu/topics/water_en.

64 *E. Mesa-Pérez and J. Berbel*, "Analysis of Barriers and Opportunities for Reclaimed Wastewater Use for Agriculture in Europe", *Water*, 2020, p. 2.

65 Regulation (EU) 2020/741 supra note 56.

66 Recital 3 of Regulation 2020/741/EU, supra note 56.

67 Ibid., Recital 6.

production.[68] However, the importance of this Regulation lies not only in its application to the reuse of treated wastewater for agricultural irrigation, but also in relation to the use of reclaimed water for other purposes, for example environmental purposes.

5. REFLECTION ON THE CURRENT EU LAW POSITION ON WATER REUSE AND ITS ENFORCEMENT IN THE MEMBER STATES

For too long, the lack of EU-level standards on water reuse represented a problem. The previous regulatory framework was not directed towards regulating the reuse of treated wastewater.[69] The new Regulation on Minimum Requirements for Water Reuse took almost 30 years to be adopted, after the Urban Waste Water Treatment Directive, and 20 years after the Water Framework Directive (WFD). Of course, this cannot be without consequences; the result is that most Member States do not practice water reuse, and have not developed national legislation or standards. Establishing minimum standards, and thus unifying the rules for water reuse at the EU level, will undoubtedly be an ambitious solution for some Member States. The enforcement of the Regulation itself will probably take place at several speeds, where particular needs, and the development of technology, will play important roles.

However, an important point of the Regulation is that, in addition to caring for the environment and human health, it also introduces care for animal health. Further, harmonising standards on minimum requirements for water reuse will not only contribute to the replacement of freshwater resources, which are already limited, but will also enhance sustainable agricultural production.

The Regulation itself does not prohibit water reuse for other purposes, for example environmental purposes.[70] This gives the Member States greater freedom in choosing for which purposes, other than agriculture, water reuse could be used. Nevertheless, this approach also represents a risk of not using the full potential of water reuse. The potential of grey water does not lie exclusively in its use for agricultural purposes, i.e. in rural areas; it could also be used to advantage in urban areas, such as for athletics fields, lawns, cemeteries, parks, golf courses, car washing, domestic gardens, etc.[71] The definition of urban

---

68 Ibid., Recital 14.

69 *J. Fawell, K. Le Corre Pidou and P. Jeffrey*, "Common or independent? The debate over regulations and standards for water reuse in Europe", *International Journal of Water Resources Development*, 2016, pp. 559–572.

70 Annex I, s. 1 of Regulation 2020/741/EU, supra note 56.

71 *E. Eriksson et al.*, supra note 43, p. 85; See also *D.A. Okun*, "Distributing reclaimed water through dual systems", *American Water Works Association Journal*, 1997, pp. 52–64.

wastewater in the Regulation follows the definition provided in Article 2(1) of Directive 91/271/EEC,[72] thereby missing a chance to address wastewater of different origins. Therefore, acknowledgement of different types of water reuse followed by the guidelines is necessary to provide various options in more detail, and give the Member States the possibility to make decisions according to their own particular needs. Initiatives for harmonisation should also be strengthened for water reuse applications other than agricultural ones. Otherwise, Member States may practice water reuse only in order to comply with the minimum requirements set in the Regulation.

Investment in wastewater treatment also depends on the administrative barriers in individual countries. As long as fresh water is economically more profitable, in terms of its use for agricultural purposes, the justifications for not using treated wastewater will be more robust. For water reuse to become more attractive and widely used, and, at the same time, to address the direct costs of water reuse to farmers, it is necessary to develop economic initiatives, such as stimulants, i.e., subventions. In addition to investments in, and funding for, more sustainable methods of performing agricultural activities, placing products irrigated with treated wastewater on the market creates an additional burden for farmers: how the "yuck" factor can be overcome. To address the market, eco-labelling of such products is one of the possible options.[73] Additionally, the "yuck" factor is certainly less prominent in the case of grey water than in the case of black water. On the other hand, consumers of such products are interested, among other things, on the safety of their use. Concerns may arise regarding E. coli levels, as one of the measurements that reclaimed water needs to meet for safe irrigation,[74] since it has already been established not to be a reliable factor, because of its rapid decay outside its natural environment.[75]

Regarding the countries not yet practising wastewater reuse, it remains unclear how to deal with this. The high level of investment needed to upgrade wastewater treatment plants, and lack of funding, are indicated among the main reasons for the low uptake of water reuse in the EU.[76] Possible solutions could be found on site, or in source treatment practices, also known to be less costly and

---

72 "Urban wastewater" means domestic wastewater or the mixture of domestic wastewater with industrial wastewater and/or run-off rainwater.

73 *A. B. Suman and A. Toscano*, "Public Acceptance of Water Reuse for Agriculture in the Wake of the New EU Regulation: Early Reflections", *Journal for European Environmental & Planning Law* 18, 2021, p. 234.

74 Annex 1, s. 2 of Regulation 2020/741/EU, supra note 56.

75 *EU Water Directors, Guidelines on Integrating Water Reuse into Water Planning and Management in the context of the WFD: Common Implementation Strategy for the Water Framework Directive and the Floods Directive*, Amsterdam: European Environment Agency, 2016, p. 39.

76 Recital 13 of Regulation 2020/741/EU, supra note 56.

more effective, decreasing the pressure on local wastewater treatment plants in their daily operations.[77]

However, the impact of politics should not be ignored; the extent to which the water reuse concept takes off will depend on political prioritisation and support. It is not known what impact the new Regulation will have on third countries, namely on candidate countries to the EU, and on the obligation to harmonise national legislation with EU law.

6. CONCLUSIONS

Various pressures on freshwater resources have forced today's humanity to think about alternative solutions that, ultimately, concern their survival. As previously described, freshwater resources are unevenly and irregularly distributed, and some regions of the world are experiencing an extreme shortage of water.[78] Deteriorating water quality, as well as shortages caused by unpredictable weather conditions, climate change and droughts, have not left the EU immune from these pressures.

One potential source to mitigate water insecurity is grey water treatment, to provide sufficient quantities and reserves of freshwater in the future while not endangering the environment. If given the necessary attention, this practice could help reduce overreliance on freshwater resources, and reduce pollution caused by the discharge of untreated grey water into freshwater resources. However, the economic value of grey water often remains underestimated. Grey water should be viewed as a valuable resource, not as waste. The potential of reusing grey water is, undoubtedly, great, mainly because of its ability to replace freshwater uses in various contexts.

As previously described, the attitude of the EU towards water can clearly be seen, based on directives, strategies, plans and other documents that preceded Regulation 2020/741/EU, which was published on 25 May 2020, in the midst of the coronavirus pandemic. The EU is an essential factor in international relations, but at the same time it exerts both a direct and indirect influence with its decisions, on both Member States and non-Member States. This implies a great responsibility, and an outstanding obligation, because it will be subject to the judgement of history about what could have been done, and what was actually done.

Although there are initiatives to harmonise standards on a critical issue, such as water reuse, the possibility of barriers along the way should not be underestimated. The kind of future that awaits water reuse is very uncertain to

---

77 *R.M.S. Mohamed, A.A. Saeed Al-Gheethi and A.H.M. Kassim*, supra note 32, p. 118.

78 *P.H. Gleick*, "Water and Conflict: Fresh Water Resources and International Security", *International Security*, 1993, p. 79.

at this point, as it is uncertain whether there will be a general acceptance of the idea. Science should provide the final word on that, and in applying scientific achievements, politics should not have any interest narrower than human interest. Numerous factors will probably influence the general application of the idea of water reuse shortly. Barriers could be political, economic or cultural; they could arise in social attitudes and public support, or depend on the diversity of situations from country to country, and region to region.

As analysed in this contribution, Regulation 2020/741/EU lacks general definitions of diverse types of treated wastewater. Providing definitions with clear distinctions, divisions and subdivisions would further contribute to a stronger acceptance of the idea of water reuse. Indeed, further investments in wastewater management are needed, to separate wastewater of different origins. In the long term, this would have a positive effect on wastewater treatment plants that are already under pressure. At the same time, the challenges that may arise during the enforcement of the new Regulation must also be considered, along by possible solutions.

Finally, as the finite nature of clean drinking-water supplies begins to reach into national and worldwide consciousnesses more deeply, the rational incentives for reusing grey water will continue to be strengthened.[79]

Grey water reuse is a large, ambitious and significant project of the future. Every day, in the world, vast amounts of drinking water are used for technical uses, from industry to domestic households and various services (for example, car washing), and irretrievably lost. In addition, this pollutes the environment, which harms nature, human health and animal health.

To build more rational relationships between humanity and nature, and between humanity and itself, the idea of grey water reuse requires overcoming the existing situation, for which there are at least two prerequisites: the removal of legal obstacles – that is, the achievement of the necessary level of national legislation and its standardisation – and, on the other hand, economic investment in infrastructure.

Today's world is faced with overpopulation in certain regions, increased urbanisation, and climate change. All three factors affect humanity's need to solve the problems described above, according to people and their living environments. It is about factors which must be taken care of or taken into account, and rational solutions must be sought. The path to those solutions also leads through the idea of grey water reuse, and the path to such reuse leads through stronger efforts to remove legal obstacles and unify national legislation. The investments required are big, but the result will be significant. Today's human needs to think about the condition in which they will leave the planet to their descendants.

---

[79] *S. Charlesworth, C.A. Booth and K. Adeyeye, Sustainable Water Engineering*, Amsterdam: Elsevier, 2021, p. 49.

PART V
WASTE MANAGEMENT

THE EU POLICY AND LEGISLATIVE FRAMEWORK ON PLASTICS

A Comprehensive Approach to Tackle a Challenging Environmental Problem

Susanna PALEARI

1. INTRODUCTION

Plastic plays an essential role in the modern economy, since it is a cheap, light and versatile material, which can be combined with many chemical additives to improve its performance and functionality. It has a wide range of different applications (packaging, vehicles, textiles, electrical and electronic equipment, construction materials, etc.) and delivers unquestionable societal and environmental benefits (for example, plastics widely contribute to food preservation, healthcare, the growth of renewable energy sources, etc.).

In 2020, plastic production in the EU27+3 (the European Union plus Norway, Switzerland and the United Kingdom) reached 55 million tonnes, equal to 15 per cent of world's plastics production. In the same year, the EU plastic industry, with almost 52,000 companies (including plastics raw materials producers, plastics converters, plastics recyclers, and plastics and rubber machinery manufacturers) had a turnover of almost €330 billion, giving direct employment to more than 1.5 million people. The European plastics industry ranked eighth in Europe in terms of value added, standing at a similar level as electrical equipment, and close to the level of the pharmaceutical industry.[1]

There are hundreds of types of plastics (also called polymers), which can be grouped into two main families, namely thermoplastics and thermosets. Most of the demand from European converters of virgin plastics (about 85 per cent) is related to thermoplastics (like polyethylene, polypropylene, polystyrene, polycarbonate, PVC, etc.), which are used mainly in single-use items, and can repeatedly be melted when heated, and hardened when cooled. The remaining

1 *Plastics Europe*, *Plastics – The Facts 2021*, Plastics Europe 2021, pp. 8 *et seq*.

fraction of plastic demand concerns thermosets (like polyurethane or silicone), which are used mainly in durable consumer products (for example, in the building and automotive sectors) and which, once they have been heated and formed, cannot be remelted and reformed again.[2]

While delivering many benefits, plastic has, however, significant environmental drawbacks throughout its life cycle. Plastic production worldwide has increased almost continuously, from 1.8 million tonnes in 1950 to 348 million tonnes in 2017,[3] and it is expected to double in the next 20 years, in a business-as-usual scenario.[4] The global average use of plastics is 45 kilogrammes per person per year.[5] Plastic goods are almost entirely produced from virgin fossil feedstocks (accounting for approximately 7 per cent of oil consumption), with the attendant greenhouse gases (GHGs) and pollutants emissions. Data from the European Environment Agency (EEA)'s GHG Inventory shows that annual emissions related to plastic production in the EU amount to around 13.4 million tonnes of CO_2, which is about 20 per cent of the chemicals industry's emissions EU-wide.[6]

At the global level, packaging is the largest end-use market segment for plastics, with over 40 per cent of total usage, 95 per cent of which is single-use.[7] Many chemicals that can be found in plastic products raise concerns about potential impacts on human health and the environment, also due to their combined effect.[8] Especially during the first use of plastic products, consumers and users can be exposed to toxicity, through the migration of particles, additives, impurities and degraded chemicals.

In 2020, 65 per cent of plastic waste collected in Europe (EU27+3) was destined for energy recovery and landfilling, while only 35 per cent was recycled,[9] with an attendant loss of valuable resources to the economy, and a huge cost to the environment (again in terms of pollution and GHG emissions). A lot of plastic escapes collection systems, with negative impacts on human health and the environment: each year, at least 8 million tonnes of plastics leak into the ocean, where, in a business-as-usual scenario, there will be, by weight,

---

2 *Deloitte Sustainability*, *Blueprint for plastics packaging waste: Quality sorting and recycling – Final report*, Deloitte Sustainability 2017, p. 8.

3 *Pew Charitable Trusts*, *Breaking the Plastic Wave*, Pew Charitable Trusts 2020, p. 17.

4 *L. Lebreton and A. Andrady*, "Future scenarios of global plastic waste generation and disposal", *Palgrave Communications* 5, Art. 6, 2019, p. 2.

5 *European Environment Agency*, *Plastics, the circular economy and Europe's environment – A priority for action*, EEA Report No. 18/2020, 2020, p. 15.

6 *Ibid.*, p. 36.

7 *Changing Markets Foundation*, *Talking Trash: The corporate playbook of false solutions to the plastic crisis*, Changing Markets Foundation 2020, p. 20.

8 See, e.g. *L. Zimmermann et al.*, "Benchmarking the in Vitro Toxicity and Chemical Composition of Plastic Consumer Products", *Environmental Science and Technology*, 2019, (53), pp. 11467–11477.

9 *Plastics Europe*, *supra*, note 1, p. 26.

more plastics than fish by 2050.[10] Abundant levels of microplastics have been found from the Arctic to the Alps, in the air, soil, rivers, and even in the deepest oceans around the world. According to a recent study,[11] the average person eats at least 50,000 particles of microplastic a year, and breathes in a similar quantity.

All of this explains why plastic has become a hot topic, both at the international level and on the EU agenda.

The objective of the present contribution is to provide an overview of the main elements of the EU policy and legislative framework addressing the environmental impacts generated by plastic products throughout their whole life cycle. The focus is not only on the current measures, but also on the wide range of initiatives planned by the 2020 Circular Economy Action Plan (CEAP)[12] and the other relevant policy documents that are part of the European Green Deal (EGD)[13] strategic package. This analysis shows the complexity of the framework, which consists of many interlinked policy tools, belonging to various policy areas, which often (directly or indirectly) affect multiple stages of the plastic value chain. It also highlights that the measures in place are not equally effective in changing the behaviour of socio-economic actors (particularly producers and consumers) and, hence, contributing to solving the plastic problem. Finally, it suggests which further measures might be introduced, and how the policy design of selected current measures can be improved to increase the effectiveness of the framework.[14] The overview, which is updated to March 2022, may serve as a good starting point for further analytical work to be performed in the future.

The remainder of the contribution is structured as follows: section 2 briefly outlines the EU policy and legislative framework on plastic, from a historical perspective. It shows that EU environmental legislation started, from the 1960s and 1970s onwards, to regulate the use of chemicals in plastic production and plastic waste management (with a set of provisions that has been progressively extended), while measures to reduce pollution and GHG emissions in production processes, and to promote sustainable plastic consumption on a voluntary basis, were introduced later. Section 3 critically analyses the main elements of the policy and legislative framework, by grouping them based on the phase of the plastic value chain they mainly affect. In particular, it highlights the need to better address selected issues that play a key role in solving the plastic

10 *WEF – Committee to Improve the State of the World*, *The New Plastics Economy: Rethinking the future of plastics*, WEF 2016, p. 7.

11 *K.D. Cox et al.*, Human Consumption of Microplastics, *Environmental Science and Technology*, 2019, 53(12), pp. 7068–7074.

12 European Commission Communication, "A new Circular Economy Action Plan For a cleaner and more competitive Europe", COM(2020)98 final.

13 European Commission Communication, "The European Green Deal", COM(2019)640 final.

14 For an analysis of the different definitions of legal effectiveness, see *S. Maljean-Dubois*, "The Effectiveness of Environmental Law: A Key Topic", in *S. Maljean-Dubois* (ed.), *The Effectiveness of Environmental Law*, Intersentia 2017, pp. 1–12.

problem (such as eco-design, or the extension of products' lifetime), through the introduction of new measures, or by improving the policy design of existing ones. Section 4 concludes the contribution. Most of this work is related to the activities of the European Topic Centre on Waste, Materials and the Green Economy (ETC/WMGE), funded by the European Environment Agency.

2. THE EU POLICY AND LEGISLATIVE FRAMEWORK TO MANAGE PLASTICS

Since the late 1960s, the EU has adopted several pieces of legislation addressing plastics and, in particular, chemical substances used in plastic products and plastic waste. The first EU legal text in the field of chemical products was the 1967 Directive on the Classification, Labelling and Packaging (CLP) of dangerous substances,[15] which required suppliers to classify their products, before placing them on the market, according to 15 hazard categories. The Directive was repeatedly amended, and two different regimes were shaped for "new" and "existing" chemicals, based on the cut-off date of 1981. While "new chemicals" had to be tested by national authorities before they were placed on the market, manufacturers and importers were required to submit specific information on "existing chemicals" directly to the European Commission, providing the basis for risk assessment. The latter process, however, was extremely slow, and failed to deliver the expected results. New comprehensive legislation (the REACH Regulation)[16] was therefore issued, to create a single system for the registration, evaluation, restriction and authorisation of both "new" and "existing" chemicals. Plastic, as it moves from its monomer and additive constituents, through the polymer, mixture and finished article, as well as when it leaves the waste status by being recycled, is subject to the various requirements established by both the REACH and CLP Regulations.[17] Further relevant requirements have been set by the chemicals legislation applying to selected materials (for example, food

---

15 Council Directive 67/548/EEC on the approximation of laws, regulations and administrative provisions relating to the classification, packaging and labelling of dangerous substances; OJ 196 (no longer in force).

16 Regulation (EC) No. 1907/2006 of the European Parliament and of the Council concerning the Registration, Evaluation, Authorisation and Restriction of Chemicals (REACH), establishing a European Chemicals Agency, amending Directive 1999/45/EC and repealing Council Regulation (EEC) No. 793/93 and Commission Regulation (EC) No. 1488/94 as well as Council Directive 76/769/EEC and Commission Directives 91/155/EEC, 93/67/EEC, 93/105/EC and 2000/21/EC, OJ L 396.

17 *Ibid.*; Regulation (EC) No. 1272/2008 of the European Parliament and of the Council on classification, labelling and packaging of substances and mixtures, amending and repealing Directives 67/548/EEC and 1999/45/EC, and amending Regulation (EC) No. 1907/2006, OJ L 353.

contact materials)[18] and articles (for example, toys or plastic articles treated with biocides)[19] containing plastics. The use of chemicals in plastic products is also regulated by the waste legislation (see, in particular, the rules on chemical substances in electric and electronic equipment (EEE)).[20]

With regard to plastic waste, EU legislation was, firstly, passed to regulate some waste treatment options (incineration[21] and landfilling),[22] waste shipment,[23] and packaging waste.[24] The range of waste streams addressed by legislation was then extended to include several end-of-life products containing plastics, such as vehicles,[25] waste electrical and electronic equipment (WEEE),[26] construction and demolition (C&D) waste,[27] textiles,[28] and single-use plastic (SUP) items.[29] The extension of the relevant legislation was the result of an increased European Commission policy focus on plastic, which has been reflected, *inter alia*, in the adoption of the European Strategy on Plastic Waste in the Environment;[30] the first Circular Economy (CE) Action Plan, which identified plastic as a priority area of intervention;[31] the 2018 EU Plastic Strategy;[32] and the new CE Action

---

18 Regulation (EC) No. 1935/2004 of the European Parliament and of the Council on materials and articles intended to come into contact with food and repealing Directives 80/590/EEC and 89/109/EEC, OJ L 338.

19 Directive 2009/48/EC of the European Parliament and of the Council on the safety of toys, OJ L 170; Regulation (EU) No. 528/2012 of the European Parliament and of the Council concerning the making available on the market and use of biocidal products, OJ L 167.

20 Directive 2011/65/EU of the European Parliament and of the Council on the restriction of the use of certain hazardous substances in electrical and electronic equipment, OJ L 174.

21 Council Directive 89/369/EEC on the prevention of air pollution from new municipal waste incineration plants, OJ L 163 (no longer in force); and Council Directive 94/67/EC on the incineration of hazardous waste OJ L 365 (no longer in force), later replaced by subsequent legislation.

22 Council Directive 1999/31/EC on the landfill of waste, OJ L 182.

23 Council Regulation (EEC) No. 259/93 on the supervision and control of shipments of waste within, into and out of the European Community, OJ L 30 (no longer in force), later replaced by subsequent legislation.

24 European Parliament and Council Directive 94/62/EC on packaging and packaging waste, OJ L 365.

25 Directive 2000/53/EC of the European Parliament and of the Council on end-of-life vehicles, OJ L 269.

26 Directive 2012/19/EU of the European Parliament and of the Council on waste electrical and electronic equipment (WEEE), OJ L 197.

27 Directive 2008/98/EC of the European Parliament and of the Council on waste and repealing certain Directives, OJ L 312.

28 *Ibid.*

29 Directive (EU) 2019/904 of the European Parliament and of the Council on the reduction of the impact of certain plastic products on the environment, OJ L 155.

30 European Commission Green Paper on a European Strategy on Plastic Waste in the Environment, COM(2013)123 final.

31 European Commission Communication, "Closing the loop – An EU action plan for the circular economy", COM(2015)614 final.

32 European Commission Communication, "A European Strategy for Plastics in a Circular Economy", COM(2018)28 final.

Plan (CEAP), which again lists plastics (along with selected items containing plastics) as a key product value chain.[33]

Following the initial legislation on chemicals and waste, the environmental impacts generated by plastic throughout its life cycle have been addressed by EU directives and regulations belonging to other policy areas. Plastics and chemicals are among the materials used by the industrial sectors covered by the Industrial Emissions Directive (IED),[34] which also regulates waste incineration (along with the Directive on Medium Combustion Plants).[35] Oil refining, the manufacturing of bulk chemicals, and plastics conversion (differently from waste incineration and the production/use of plastic products) are included in the current emission trading system (ETS),[36] which is a cornerstone of the EU's policy to combat climate change. The EU Ecolabel,[37] and the Green Public Procurement (GPP) criteria developed by the European Commission,[38] which are aimed at stimulating, on a voluntary basis, the purchase of green products by consumers and public authorities, apply to many plastic items (furniture, EEE, detergents, etc.). The Own Resource Decision,[39] applicable since 1 January 2021, has introduced a national contribution to the EU budget, based on the amount of non-recycled plastic packaging waste.

As emerges from the above, the overall EU policy and legislative framework to regulate plastics is broad and complex, since the measures it sets address a wide range of products and waste streams containing plastics (for example, packaging, EEE, vehicles, C&D waste, etc.), pertain to several policy areas (for example, waste, chemicals, air pollution, climate change, etc.), have different natures (regulatory, economic, voluntary tools), impact on different parts of the plastic value chain (production, consumption and waste management, even if, as shown above, consumption has, traditionally, been under-regulated compared with the other phases of the value chain), and are rapidly evolving, since new policy and legislative initiatives are continuously being taken by the EU.[40]

---

33 European Commission Communication, "A new Circular Economy Action Plan For a cleaner and more competitive Europe", *supra*, note 12.

34 Directive 2010/75/EU of the European Parliament and of the Council on industrial emissions (integrated pollution prevention and control), OJ L 334.

35 Directive (EU) 2015/2193 of the European Parliament and of the Council on the limitation of emissions of certain pollutants into the air from medium combustion plants, OJ L 313.

36 Directive 2003/87/EC of the European Parliament and of the Council establishing a scheme for greenhouse gas emission allowance trading within the Community and amending Council Directive 96/61/EC, OJ L 275.

37 Regulation (EC) No. 66/2010 of the European Parliament and of the Council on the EU Ecolabel, OJ L 27.

38 *European Commission*, "Green Public Procurement Criteria and Requirements", https://ec.europa.eu/environment/gpp/eu_gpp_criteria_en.htm.

39 Council Decision (EU, Euratom) 2020/2053 on the system of own resources of the European Union and repealing Decision 2014/335/EU, Euratom, OJ L 424.

40 The EU legislative and policy framework on plastics is continuously evolving; the cut-off date of this research work was 15 March 2022.

These features of the EU plastics measures turn out also to be potential criteria that can be used in order to classify the measures. The following subsections present and critically analyse some of the most important EU plastics measures (both current and planned), grouping them, as a first step, based on the phase of the value chain (i.e. production, consumption or waste management) they mainly affect. As will be clarified below, these three phases (as well as the measures addressing them) are closely interrelated.

3. LEGISLATIVE AND POLICY MEASURES ADDRESSING THE PLASTIC VALUE CHAIN

3.1. MEASURES AFFECTING PLASTIC PRODUCTION

The way in which a plastic product is manufactured directly affects both its consumption and end-of-life phase, and may contribute significantly to waste prevention. For instance, according to the Ellen MacArthur Foundation,[41] without fundamental redesign and innovation, about 30 per cent of plastic packaging will never be reused or recycled. Design for the environment (DfE) encompasses at least four different dimensions: the selection of low-impact materials (for example, avoiding hazardous substances or using recycled resources); the reduction of material (for example, tackling overpackaging); the optimisation of initial lifetime (for example, increasing durability or reuse of components); and the optimisation of the end-of-life system (for example, design for disassembly, or producing mono-material goods that can easily be recycled).[42]

Many EU measures currently in place are aimed at stimulating eco-design. Firstly, several legislative requirements address the presence of chemicals in plastic products. Pursuant to the REACH Regulation,[43] the manufacture, placing on the market, or use of chemicals can be restricted (for example, banned or limited) where they pose unacceptable risks to human health or the environment, while the authorisation regime applies to substances of very high concern (SVHC), to prompt their substitution with less dangerous ones. Obviously, the lists of restricted chemicals, and of SVHCs, need to be continuously updated. For instance, an initiative has recently been launched by the European Chemicals Agency to restrict intentionally added microplastics

---

41 *Ellen MacArthur Foundation, The New Plastics Economy: Rethinking the future of plastics & catalysing action*, Ellen MacArthur Foundation 2017, p. 36.

42 *Organisation for Economic Co-operation and Development (OECD), Extended Producer Responsibility: Updated Guidance for Efficient Waste Management*, OECD Publishing 2016, p. 162.

43 Regulation (EC) No. 1907/2006, *supra*, note 16, Titles VII and VIII.

in products, such as detergents or cosmetic products, which is projected to prevent the release of 500,000 tonnes of microplastics into the environment over 20 years.[44] Based on the Chemicals Strategy for Sustainability,[45] the REACH Regulation will be comprehensively revised in 2022, to, *inter alia*, extend the duty of registration to certain polymers of concern (polymers are currently exempted from registration), better address the combined effect generated by several substances (which is very relevant to plastics, given their chemical complexity), and ensure that consumer products (such as toys, furniture and textiles) do not contain harmful chemicals. The Strategy also suggests that the EU should support the transition to safe and sustainable-by-design chemicals, including sustainable bio-based chemicals. Along with chemicals legislation, many EU directives covering waste streams containing plastics (like packaging or EEE) also establish provisions banning or limiting the use of certain dangerous substances.

Secondly, most waste streams containing plastics (packaging, WEEE, end-of-life vehicles, and certain SUP items) are subject to extended producer responsibility (EPR).[46] The Commission also plans to introduce EPR for textiles.[47] EPR is an economic tool which, in compliance with the "polluter-pays" principle, makes producers responsible for the environmental impacts of their products throughout their whole life cycle. Producers are, thus, required to cover the costs of managing the waste generated by their products, and this, besides increasing waste collection and recycling (see section 3.2. below), was expected to stimulate DfE. In principle, indeed, the cost of managing environmentally friendly products, once they reach their end-of-life status, is lower than that associated with the treatment of waste that contain hazardous substances, or which cannot be recycled. The effectiveness of EPR with respect to DfE is, however, disputed, and in any case low.[48] One of the main reasons is that producers generally comply with their EPR obligations collectively, by taking part in producer responsibility organisations (PROs), and most PROs allocate the costs of waste management to member producers in accordance with their market shares (i.e. the number or

---

44 European Chemicals Agency (ECHA), "Microplastics", https://echa.europa.eu/hot-topics/microplastics.

45 European Commission Communication, "Chemicals Strategy for Sustainability – Towards a Toxic-Free Environment", COM(2020)667 final.

46 European Parliament and Council Directive 94/62/EC, *supra*, note 24; Directive 2000/53/EC, *supra*, note 25; Directive 2008/98/EC, *supra*, note 27; Directive 2012/19/EU, *supra*, note 26; Directive (EU) 2019/904, *supra*, note 29.

47 European Commission Communication, *supra*, note 33, p. 10.

48 *A. Massarutto*, "The long and winding road to resource efficiency – an interdisciplinary perspective on extended producer responsibility", *Resource, Conservation and Recycling* 2014 (85), p. 14; *S. Paleari*, "Extended Producer Responsibility in the EU – Achievements and future prospects", in *B. Pozzo and V. Jacometti* (eds.), *Environmental Loss and Damage in a Comparative Law Perspective*, Intersentia 2021, p. 140 *et seq.*

weight of products placed on the market), without any eco-modulation. The eco-modulation of fees, based on product criteria, such as recyclability and material choices, is not strictly mandatory pursuant to the EU legislation in force.[49] Another relevant problem is that design requirements eventually incorporated into modulated fees applied by PROs need to be harmonised at the international level (or at least at the EU level) when products are globally traded. For example, financial incentives from one local EPR scheme will not be taken into account for the design of mobile phones that are sold on the global market.[50] There is a need, therefore, not only to extend EPR to more products, but also to improve its ability to promote DfE, by supporting a better and more widespread eco-modulation of PROs' recycling fees.

Apart from EPR, there is not currently a comprehensive approach, at the EU level, to ensure that all products placed on the EU market become increasingly sustainable. The 2020 CEAP[51] has announced a "sustainable product policy initiative" to revise the Eco-design Directive,[52] which defines minimum eco-design requirements for energy-using products. The scope of the Directive will be widened (to include, for example, textiles and furniture), and the Commission will consider the introduction of overarching product sustainability principles.

In addition to chemicals legislation, the Eco-design Directive and EPR, a wide range of EU measures are aimed at stimulating the eco-design of specific products. For instance:

- The Packaging Waste Directive[53] establishes a set of essential requirements on the composition and reusable and recoverable nature of packaging that must be met by all packaging placed on the market. These requirements have been operationalised through EU standards. The Commission[54] has announced that both the requirements and the standards will be revised, since they have been criticised for being too vague.[55]
- The SUP Directive[56] bans several plastic items (for example, plates, cutlery, straws, food containers and expanded polystyrene cups, etc.) for which more

---

49 Directive 2008/98/EC, *supra*, note 27, as amended by Directive (EU) 2018/851 of the European Parliament and of the Council amending Directive 2008/98/EC on waste, OJ L 150, Art. 8a.

50 *OECD*, *supra*, note 42, p. 176.

51 European Commission Communication, "A new Circular Economy Action Plan For a cleaner and more competitive Europe", *supra*, note 33, pp. 3 *et seq.*

52 Directive 2009/125/EC of the European Parliament and of the Council establishing a framework for the setting of ecodesign requirements for energy-related products, OJ L 285.

53 European Parliament and Council Directive 94/62/EC, *supra*, note 24, Art. 9.

54 European Commission Communication, "A new Circular Economy Action Plan For a cleaner and more competitive Europe", *supra*, note 33, p. 8.

55 *Eunomia et al., Effectiveness of the Essential Requirements for Packaging and Packaging Waste and Proposals for Reinforcement: Final Report and Appendices*, EU Publications 2020.

56 Directive (EU) 2019/904, *supra*, note 29, Arts. 5 and 6.

sustainable alternatives are readily available. The Directive also provides for a minimum recycled content of drinks bottles and containers up to three litres (which is very relevant to boosting plastic recycling – see section 3.3. below) and, in order to prevent plastic litter, it requires that caps and lids remain attached to plastic beverage containers during their entire intended use stage.

- GPP and EU Ecolabel criteria,[57] which apply to many plastic products, stimulate DfE, as they are both largely based on eco-design criteria. Their impact is, however, reduced, due to the limitations of voluntary approaches. The Commission will, therefore, consider the introduction of binding GPP criteria and targets in sectoral legislation, along with the more systematic integration of recyclability and recycled content principles into the EU Ecolabel criteria.[58]

Another interesting aspect relating to plastic manufacturing concerns the use of carbon. Since, currently, only 1 per cent of carbon used in the EU economy is of recycled origin, the Commission intends to progressively replace fossil carbon with more sustainable streams of recycled carbon, from waste, sustainable biomass, and directly from the atmosphere. In particular, an aspirational objective has been established that at least 20 per cent of the carbon used in chemical and plastic products should be from sustainable non-fossil sources by 2030.[59]

Finally, when looking at production processes, both GHG and pollutants emissions, as stated above, are regulated by EU legislation.[60] The planned revision of the IED[61] may result in the inclusion of further installations in current sectors (for example, in the textile sector)[62] that are just below the existing thresholds. In relation to GHG, the reform of the EU ETS[63] will align the cap with the new net emissions-reduction target by 2030 (a decrease of

57 *European Commission*, "Green Public Procurement Criteria and Requirements", *supra*, note 38; Regulation (EC) No. 66/2010, *supra*, note 37.

58 European Commission Communication, "A new Circular Economy Action Plan For a cleaner and more competitive Europe", *supra*, note 33, p. 5.

59 European Commission Communication, "Sustainable carbon cycles", COM(2021)800 final, p. 17.

60 Directive 2010/75/EU, *supra*, note 34; Directive 2003/87/EC, *supra*, note 36.

61 Directive 2010/75/EU, *supra*, note 34; European Commission Communication, "Pathway to a Healthy Planet for All – EU Action Plan: Towards Zero Pollution for Air, Water and Soil", COM(2021)400 final.

62 *Client Earth, Revision of the Industrial Emissions Directive – Client Earth's response to the Targeted Stakeholder Survey*, 18 June 2021, p. 18.

63 European Commission Proposal for a Directive of the European Parliament and the Council amending Directive 2003/87/EC establishing a system for greenhouse gas emission allowance trading within the Union, Decision (EU) 2015/1814 concerning the establishment and operation of a market stability reserve for the Union greenhouse gas emission trading scheme and Regulation (EU) 2015/757, COM(2021)551 final.

55 per cent, compared with 1990s levels), providing industries with a greater incentive to limit their exposure to the carbon price. To this end, however, it will also be key to addressing the problem of the free allocation of emissions allowances to petrochemicals plants, which, until now, have been granted to prevent the risk of carbon leakage.

Finally, the Commission intends to develop a specific policy framework on bioplastics, as well as on biodegradable/compostable plastics.[64] This initiative is relevant both to cutting GHG emissions from plastic production (as bioplastics fully or partially derive from biological renewable resources rather than from fossil raw materials), and to designing plastics that can be composted, instead of being landfilled or incinerated. It is also a very sensitive issue because, although these bio-based and biodegradable polymers may positively impact on the environment,[65] they are not currently exempted from the SUP Directive.[66] It is crucial that, within this context, the Commission clarifies the meaning of various terms (which are often misleading), and assesses where the use of these materials will lead to genuine environmental benefits throughout their whole life cycle.

3.2. MEASURES AFFECTING PLASTIC CONSUMPTION

EU measures regulating plastic production also affect plastic consumption. For instance, restricting the use of dangerous chemicals in plastic products contributes to preventing or minimising their impacts on human health and the environment during consumption, and the optimisation of initial lifetime is one of the main objectives of DfE. The benefits of a longer product life include the reduction of waste generation.

There are also other EU requirements directly addressing plastic consumption. Some directives covering waste streams containing plastic encourage the reuse of discarded products and their components (as in the case of packaging and vehicles),[67] or set targets which jointly apply to reuse and recycling/recovery (as in the case of end-of-life vehicles (ELVs),[68] C&D waste,[69] plastic household waste,[70] and WEEE).[71] Moreover, the Packaging Waste Directive,[72] as amended

64 European Commission Communication, "A new Circular Economy Action Plan For a cleaner and more competitive Europe", *supra*, note 33, pp. 9 *et seq.*

65 *S. Lambert and M. Wagner*, "Environmental performance of bio-based and biodegradable plastics: the road ahead", *Chemistry Society Review* 2017 (46), pp. 6855–6871.

66 Directive (EU) 2019/904, *supra*, note 29.

67 European Parliament and Council Directive 94/62/EC, *supra*, note 24, Art. 5; Directive 2000/53/EC, *supra*, note 25, Art. 7.

68 Directive 2000/53/EC, *supra*, note 25, Art. 7.

69 Directive 2008/98/EC, *supra*, note 27, Art. 11.

70 *Ibid.*

71 Directive 2012/19/EU, *supra*, note 26, Art. 11.

72 European Parliament and Council Directive 94/62/EC, *supra*, note 24.

in 2015,[73] requires Member States to take measures to achieve a sustained reduction in the consumption of lightweight plastic carrier bags (i.e. plastic carrier bags with a wall thickness below 50 microns) on their territory, such as national reduction targets, economic instruments (for example, fees or taxes) and marketing restrictions. Pursuant to the SUP Directive,[74] Member States must achieve a measurable quantitative reduction in the consumption of drinks cups and food containers by 2026, relative to 2022.

Plastic consumption is currently under-regulated from a circular perspective, compared with plastic production and, especially, the end-of-life phase. The 2020 CEAP[75] plans a set of initiatives to enhance the participation of consumers in the CE and extend the lifetimes of products. To support sustainable consumption, in addition to the EU Ecolabel criteria,[76] the Commission will propose minimum GPP criteria and targets in sectoral legislation, and will revise EU consumer law to ensure that consumers receive trustworthy and relevant information on products at the point of sale (for example, on their lifespan, the availability of repair services and spare parts, and repair manuals). Consumers will also be better protected against greenwashing and premature obsolescence, through minimum requirements for sustainability labels and logos. The Commission will establish a new "right to repair", to encourage consumers to use consumer goods for a longer time, by repairing defective products, and by purchasing more second-hand and refurbished ones (textiles and electronics/information and communication technology have been selected as pilot sectors). Other specific measures scheduled to improve the consumption of plastic products include the following:[77]

- A legislative initiative on reuse, to substitute reusable products for single-use packaging, tableware and cutlery, in food services.
- Regulatory measures on chargers for mobile phones and similar devices, such as the introduction of a common charger, improving the durability of charging cables, and incentives to decouple the purchase of chargers from the purchase of new devices.
- Making drinkable tap water accessible in public places, to prevent packaging waste and promote the use of reusable water bottles.

---

[73] Directive (EU) 2015/720 of the European Parliament and of the Council amending Directive 94/62/EC as regards reducing the consumption of lightweight plastic carrier bags, OJ L 115, Art. 2.

[74] Directive (EU) 2019/904, *supra*, note 29, Art. 4.

[75] European Commission Communication, "A new Circular Economy Action Plan For a cleaner and more competitive Europe", *supra*, note 33, pp. 5 *et seq.*

[76] Regulation (EC) No. 66/2010, *supra*, note 37.

[77] European Commission Communication, "A new Circular Economy Action Plan For a cleaner and more competitive Europe", *supra*, note 33, pp. 7, 9 and 12.

The adoption and implementation of these initiatives is fundamental to enhancing the sustainable consumption of plastics. To this end, it might also be useful to require a stricter application of the waste hierarchy (according to which, prevention and reuse are the most-preferred options) by EPR schemes, and to establish a policy framework on remanufacturing, refurbishing and reconditioning (currently, there is no commonly accepted legal definition of these terms in the EU).

3.3. MEASURES AFFECTING PLASTIC WASTE MANAGEMENT

As noted above, a lot of plastic waste escapes the European collection system, and most of the plastic waste collected is destined for energy recovery and landfilling (65 per cent, in 2020),[78] with a significant loss of valuable resources to the economy, and a huge cost to the environment. Therefore, there is a strong need to tackle plastic litter and support plastics recycling, by boosting both the supply of – and, especially, the demand for – recycled plastics. Indeed, the market for recycled plastic shows a low degree of maturity compared to those for other secondary raw materials (such as paper, metals or glass), which is mainly due to a low and unstable demand for plastic recyclates, driven, *inter alia*, by their low quality.[79]

On the supply side, there is, in the first place, a wide range of EU measures aimed at improving the amount and quality of collected and recycled plastic waste. Pursuant to the Waste Framework Directive,[80] Member States must set up a separate collection for plastic, and, by 1 January 2025, for textiles. Other collection obligations apply to WEEE[81] and plastic drinks bottles (by 2025–29).[82] The CE Action Plan[83] sets out several initiatives to improve collection and sorting, such as the introduction (if feasible) of EU-wide labelling that facilitates the correct separation of packaging waste at source; an EU-wide take-back scheme, to return or sell back old mobile phones, tablets and chargers; and solutions for high-quality sorting of, and removing contaminants from waste.

Recycling targets are in place for most waste streams containing plastics (packaging,[84] end-of-life vehicles,[85] WEEE,[86] C&D waste,[87] plastic household

---

78 *Plastics Europe*, *supra*, note 1, p. 26.

79 ETC/WMGE (2021), "Overcoming barriers to step-up secondary raw materials markets" (unpublished research report).

80 Directive 2008/98/EC, *supra*, note 27, as amended by Directive (EU) 2018/851 of the European Parliament and of the Council amending Directive 2008/98/EC on waste, OJ L 150, Art. 11.

81 Directive 2012/19/EU, *supra*, note 26, Art. 7.

82 Directive (EU) 2019/904, *supra*, note 29, Art. 9.

83 European Commission Communication, *supra*, note 33, pp. 7 and 9.

84 European Parliament and Council Directive 94/62/EC, *supra*, note 24.

85 Directive 2000/53/EC, *supra*, note 25, Art. 7.

86 Directive 2012/19/EU, *supra*, note 26, Art. 11.

87 Directive 2008/98/EC, *supra*, note 27, Art. 11.

waste, and certain SUP items).[88] These imply a collection obligation, and are often implemented through EPR schemes. These targets stimulate an increase in plastic recycling rates, even if they also include, in their scope, non-hazardous plastic waste shipped for recycling within and outside the EU (which is counted as "recycled" by the exporting country). The EU's exportation of plastic waste outside its territory has dropped in recent years (down by 16 per cent in 2020, relative to 2018, in EU27+3),[89] following the progressive introduction of rigid waste importation policies by non-OECD (Organisation for Economic Co-operation and Development) countries, often culminating in bans on imports.[90] For its part, the EU, by amending the Waste Shipment Regulation (WSR),[91] in 2020,[92] has established that plastic waste that is hard to recycle can no longer be exported from the EU to non-OECD countries. A new revision process has recently been launched by the European Commission, to further restrict the exportation of waste that has harmful environmental and health impacts in third countries, or which can be treated domestically within the EU.[93] Another shortcoming of EU recycling targets is that, since they are weight-based, they do not reward high-quality recycling, and, when applied to multi-material products (such as ELVs), they tend to penalise plastics, compared with heavier and more easily recyclable materials (for example, metals). The low quality of recycled plastics, however, makes their use uneconomic, and is one of the reasons for their weak demand. To address the problem, the Commission[94] will consider extending the use of material-specific recycling targets (currently applied to packaging waste) to further waste streams, such as C&D waste.

Along with collection and recycling targets, EPR has also proved effective in creating and consolidating recycling markets. For instance, among the different types of EPR schemes, deposit-and-refund schemes[95] for polyethylene terephthalate bottles have usually succeeded in combining high recycling

---

88 Directive (EU) 2019/904, *supra*, note 29, Art. 9.

89 *Plastics Europe*, *supra*, note 1, p. 26.

90 A. D'Amato et al., *Plastics waste trade and the environment*, Eionet Report ETC/WMGE 2019/5, 2019, pp. 27 *et seq*.

91 Regulation (EC) No. 1013/2006 of the European Parliament and of the Council on shipments of waste, OJ L 190.

92 Commission Delegated Regulation (EU) 2020/2174 amending Annexes IC, III, IIIA, IV, V, VII and VIII to Regulation (EC) No. 1013/2006 of the European Parliament and of the Council on shipments of waste, OJ L 433.

93 European Commission Proposal for a Regulation of the European Parliament and the Council on shipments of waste and amending Regulations (EU) No. 1257/2013 and (EU) No. 2020/1056, COM(2021)709 final.

94 European Commission Communication, "A new Circular Economy Action Plan For a cleaner and more competitive Europe", *supra*, note 33, p. 11.

95 A deposit-and-refund scheme is a collection scheme whereby consumers pay a small amount of money (deposit fee) for their packaging at the point of purchase, and are reimbursed upon the return of the empty packaging to a specific collection point.

rates (typically over 80 per cent) with economic efficiency.[96] By shifting the responsibility for waste management from municipalities and taxpayers to producers, EPR has mobilised technical and managerial skills, and relevant financial resources, from the private sector, which have resulted in infrastructure development and technological innovation.[97] However, in the case of plastics, these positive effects are less evident than in other recycling markets. For instance, with regard to recycling technologies, the most common method for recycling plastic waste is mechanical recycling, which is currently applied to a few plastic polymers. Innovative solutions for advanced sorting, environmentally friendly chemical recycling, and an expanded role of mechanical recycling, are needed if the EU wants to ensure, as stated by the EU Plastic Strategy,[98] that by 2030 more than half of plastics waste generated in Europe is recycled.

Another potentially powerful economic instrument that could boost plastic recycling (as well as waste prevention) is the new EU plastic tax, which has been in place since January 2021.[99] It consists of a national contribution (with a uniform rate of 0.80 euros per kilogram), based on the amount of non-recycled plastic packaging waste produced by each Member State, which Member States pay into the EU budget.

According to the 2020 CEAP,[100] the Commission will assess the scope for shaping further EU-wide end-of-waste criteria for certain (unspecified) waste streams. Unlike other materials, such as selected metals and glass, there are no current EU-wide end-of-waste criteria for plastics. The introduction of such criteria might stimulate plastic waste recycling, by reducing the administrative burden associated with managing plastic waste.

Other EU measures scheduled by the 2020 CE Action Plan,[101] and by the Chemicals Strategy for Sustainability,[102] are aimed at improving the quality of recycled plastics. A first point of interest concerns chemicals. The Commission intends to create harmonised systems to track and manage information on substances (at least on SVHCs, which are often contained in plastics, and which stay in material streams for a long time when recycled mechanically) along the plastic value chain, and to develop methodologies to minimise the presence of chemicals that pose problems to health or the environment in recycled materials and articles made thereof. Secondly, the Commission will enhance the role of

96 *Reloop, Global Deposit Book 2020*, Reloop 2020.

97 *S. Paleari*, *supra*, note 48, p. 144.

98 European Commission Communication, "A European Strategy for Plastics in a Circular Economy", *supra*, note 32, p. 5.

99 Council Decision (EU, Euratom) 2020/2053, *supra*, note 39, Art. 2.

100 European Commission Communication, "A new Circular Economy Action Plan For a cleaner and more competitive Europe", *supra*, note 33, p. 14.

101 *Ibid.*, pp. 13 *et seq.*

102 European Commission Communication, Chemicals Strategy for Sustainability – Towards a Toxic-Free Environment", *supra*, note 45, pp. 6 *et seq.*

standardisation. A general need to shape quality standards has been reported in the plastics sector, regarding both input for recycling and recyclates.[103]

Policy tools that address the demand side of plastics recycling have mainly been of a voluntary nature, apart from recycling content obligations. These obligations fall under the concept of DfE, as they require manufacturers to shift from using virgin to recycled plastic feedstock. They have been introduced by the SUP Directive,[104] for plastic bottles, and their application will probably be extended, in the next future, to key products, such as packaging, construction materials and vehicles.[105] Similar incentives are provided, on a voluntary basis, by GPP and EU Ecolabel criteria, which also stimulate the consumption of sustainable products (including those made of recycled plastics). As noted above (in section 3.2.), the Commission intends to overcome the voluntary nature of GPP, by proposing minimum GPP criteria and targets in sectoral legislation,[106] which could increase its effectiveness.

Finally, the environmental impacts generated by the different plastic waste treatment options (landfilling, incineration and recycling) are also regulated by EU legislation.[107] Although, according to the waste hierarchy, recycling (including composting) is considered generally preferable to energy recovery, the latter represents the predominant plastic waste treatment in the EU (with a rate of 42 per cent in EU27+3, in 2020),[108] due to the high calorific value of certain polymers, and to the limited availability of recycling solutions. Plastic waste incineration leads to significant CO_2 emissions, but is excluded from the EU ETS. Moreover, recycling requires fuel consumption, to collect, sort and process plastic waste, but by reducing raw material extraction to produce virgin plastics, results in lower net GHG emissions.[109] With regard to the different recycling methods, chemical recycling is more energy-intensive than mechanical recycling, and its environmental impacts have not yet been fully investigated. Chemical recycling has, therefore, traditionally been seen by the Commission as a last-resort option, after prevention, reuse and mechanical recycling. Interesting insights emerge, however, from the EU Taxonomy Climate Delegated Act,[110]

103 European Commission Communication, "A European Strategy for Plastics in a Circular Economy", *supra*, note 32, pp. 8 *et seq.*

104 Directive (EU) 2019/904, *supra*, note 29, Art. 6.

105 European Commission Communication, "A new Circular Economy Action Plan For a cleaner and more competitive Europe", *supra*, note 33, pp. 4–5, 8–11, 13–14.

106 *Ibid.*, p. 5.

107 Council Directive 1999/31/EC, *supra*, note 22; Directive 2010/75/EU, *supra*, note 34.

108 *Plastics Europe*, *supra*, note 1, p. 26.

109 *EEA*, *supra*, note 5, p. 47.

110 Commission Delegated Regulation (EU) 2021/2139 of 4 June 2021 supplementing Regulation (EU) 2020/852 of the European Parliament and of the Council by establishing the technical screening criteria for determining the conditions under which an economic activity qualifies as contributing substantially to climate change mitigation or climate change adaptation and for determining whether that economic activity causes no significant harm to any of the other environmental objectives; C/2021/2800, OJ L 442, Annex I (3.1.7).

which, in order to help the EU to scale up sustainable investment, provides a classification system to establish a list of environmentally sustainable economic activities. The final text excludes waste to energy from that list and changed from considering chemical recycling as sustainable "where mechanical recycling is not possible", to "where mechanical recycling is not technically feasible or economically viable". It also deleted the stipulation that, to pass the sustainability test, chemical processes must produce at least 27 per cent fewer life-cycle GHG emissions than manufacture from virgin feedstock. Emissions from chemical recycling must now simply be lower than the life-cycle GHG emissions of the equivalent plastic in primary form, manufactured from virgin material.[111] These criteria provide incentives for the development of chemical recycling technologies, but with less stringent GHG emissions requirements.

4. CONCLUSIONS

Plastic plays an essential role in our economy, and represents a very important European industry, both in terms of value added and job creation. The consumption and production of plastic, however, have both grown exponentially since the 1950s, resulting in huge adverse environmental impacts throughout its whole life cycle. The EU has devoted increasing attention to the "plastic problem", and is continuously working to update and expand the legislative and policy framework, to tackle the related environmental challenges. The analysis of this framework, provided by the present contribution, shows its high complexity: several regulatory, economic and voluntary tools, belonging to various policy areas, address the environmental impacts generated by plastics, with multiple and interrelated effects.

Although the framework is extensive, and addresses the whole plastic value chain, there is still room for improvement. With regard to plastic production, there is a need to develop a comprehensive approach to better support DfE, which is crucial to making plastic products more durable, and replacing virgin plastic with secondary raw materials; to shape a favourable legal regime for bioplastics and biodegradable/compostable plastics only when they are beneficial to the environment throughout their whole life cycle; and, within the EU ETS, to greatly incentivise petrochemical plants to reduce their GHG emissions. Plastic consumption, which is currently under-regulated, compared with the other stages of the value chain, is at the heart of many initiatives planned by the 2020 CEAP. It will be especially important to establish and enforce a right to repair,

111 Euractive, "Last minute EU taxonomy changes water down sustainability criteria for waste, NGOs say", 23 April 2021, https://www.euractiv.com/section/circular-materials/news/last-minute-eu-taxonomy-changes-water-down-sustainability-criteria-for-waste-ngos-say/.

for consumers, and to exploit the potential of the Ecolabel and GPP criteria to promote sustainable consumption. In the end-of-life phase, the EU policy and legislative framework, which is already very articulated, should support the transition towards a more mature plastic recycling market, by extending, where appropriate, EPR (for example, to textiles), shaping targets that reward high-quality recycling, enhancing the role of standardisation, and improving the traceability of chemicals.

Finally, along the whole plastic value chain, a higher level of integration between the measures in place (especially when they belong to different policy areas) should be achieved, to leverage synergies, and to solve any contradictions or inconsistency among them. Voluntary instruments may become more effective when they are connected to regulatory or economic instruments. For instance, the EU Ecolabel criteria could be used to better operationalise the essential requirements of the Packaging Waste Directive,[112] or as basis to eco-modulate recycling fees paid by producers to PROs. Working on the interfaces between chemicals, products and waste legislation to make them more coherent is another crucial issue. Although traditionally perceived as being in opposition to one another, the objective of enabling recycling and improving the uptake of SRMs (stemming from waste policy), and that of substituting dangerous or problematic substances, or, where this is not possible, restricting their use (stemming from the chemical policy) are both key to increasing plastics recycling within non-toxic material cycles.[113]

---

112 European Parliament and Council Directive 94/62/EC, *supra*, note 24.

113 European Commission Communication on the implementation of the circular economy package: options to address the interface between chemical, product and waste legislation, COM(2018)32 final.

ILLEGAL LANDFILLING IN ROMANIA

A Never-Ending Story?

Violeta STRATAN

1. PROLOGUE: LEGISLATIVE FRAMEWORK

The never-ending story to which the title of this contribution refers could begin any time before Romania's accession to the EU in 2007. It could go back to 1973, when Act no. 9[1] on the protection of the environment was adopted, echoing the *travaux* of the first World Conference on the Environment (Stockholm, 1972). This Act, *inter alia*, prohibited waste from being dumped in watercourses (Art. 13), or in unauthorised places (Art. 19), in order to avoid environmental pollution.[2] However, this framework regulation, and the other special regulations adopted during the totalitarian regime in the field of environment protection, had a rather declarative character, and could not be properly enforced, due to a lack of correlation with the legal provisions in other branches of law (administrative, criminal and civil law), and a lack of interest, on the part of the public authorities, in enforcing the legislation or applying administrative sanctions to environmental polluters. Despite the official declarations, the ecological dimension of the country's economic development was neglected.[3] Another starting point of the story could be Act no. 137/1995[4] on environment protection, some provisions of which[5] established that waste is to be dumped only in authorised areas, with a view to preventing any damage to the environment (soil, water, air, etc.) or hazards to human health. Such obligations were incumbent upon both local authorities and the natural and legal persons. In 1999, a decade after the revolution, Romania's first sustainable

---

1 Act no. 9 of June 20, 1973, on the protection of the environment, published in the Official Journal no. 91 of 23 June 1973, https://legislatie.just.ro/Public/DetaliiDocumentAfis/311.

2 *Ibid.*, Arts. 13 and 19.

3 Mircea Duțu, *Dreptul mediului*, C.H. Beck, 2008, pp. 6–9.

4 Act no. 137 of December 29, 1995, on the protection of the environment, published in the Official Journal no.304 of 30 December 1995, https://legislatie.just.ro/Public/DetaliiDocument/6385?isFormaDeBaza=True&rep=True.

5 See *ibid.*, Arts. 25 and 40.

development strategy was drafted. The aim of this strategy – the promotion of the continuous improvement and preservation of the well-being of the population, in correlation with the requirements of a sensible use of natural resources and the conservation of the ecosystem – took, as a premise, the idea that the benefits of economic development should outweigh its costs, including those relating to the conservation and the improvement of the environment.[6] With a view to fulfilling the obligations assumed prior to its EU integration, Romania reformed its environmental regulation again, in 2005, with the adoption of the Government Ordinance no. 195 on environmental protection. This emergency ordinance, which has since been amended many times, with a view to meeting EU requirements, represents the current framework regulation on environmental protection in Romania. One year later, the municipal sanitation services were conferred a unitary legal framework, through Act no. 101/2006, currently in force.

Then, in 2007, when the country became a member of the EU, its national priorities changed. The new sustainable development strategy, adopted in 2008, aimed at reducing the socio-economic gap vis-à-vis the other Member States, and, at the same time, improving the country's environmental performance to comply with EU standards. Special regulations were subsequently adopted for the same purpose. Until the autumn of 2021, the waste regime was governed by Act no. 211/2011,[7] which transposed Directives 1999/31/EC and 2008/98/EC into domestic law. The new regulation in the field, Emergency Government Ordinance no. 92/2021,[8] transposes EU Directive 2018/851.[9] However, 15 years after these strategic goals were set, Romania is still facing many challenges with regard to the implementation of EU environmental policies in several areas, one of which is waste management.

At this point in the story, wherever we place its beginning in time, the hero seems to be the Romanian legislator, whose last decades' activity produced legislation accurately reflecting the environmental requirements agreed at EU level. However, like most stories, this one also has some bad characters, responsible for the obvious "implementation gap on the ground": the lack of administrative capacity and coordination, the lack of appropriate funding, low rates of recycling and resource efficiency, and an undeveloped circular

[6] Romania's Sustainable Development Strategy 2030, available at http://dezvoltaredurabila.gov.ro/web/wp-content/uploads/2019/03/Romanias-Sustainable-Development-Strategy-2030.pdf, p. 17.

[7] Act no. 211/2011 on waste, republished in the Official Journal of Romania no. 220 of 28 March 2014, currently abolished by EGO no. 92/2021 on waste, https://legislatie.just.ro/.

[8] Emergency Government Ordinance no. 92/2021 on waste, published in the Official Journal of Romania no. 820 of 26 August 2021, https://legislatie.just.ro/.

[9] Directive (EU) 2018/851 of the European Parliament and of the Council of 30 May 2018 amending Directive 2008/98/EC on waste, https://eur-lex.europa.eu/legal-content/EN/TXT/?uri=celex%3A32018L0851.

economy.[10] Are there any others? Can they be changed? Can the illegal dumping story have a (happy) ending? These are some of the questions that the following pages shall try to answer.

2. ACTION AND CHARACTERS OF THE STORY

The first *Environmental Implementation Review* reached the following conclusion: "environmental policy developments in Romania are mainly driven by EU Regulations and Directives. … The legislation is generally correctly transposed and when instances of non-conformity occur, the country cooperates and amends its legislation accordingly".[11] Nevertheless, the implementation of the legislation remains "a real challenge", as indicated by the fact that "Romania, although a new Member State, is among the countries with the highest number of environmental infringements, mainly in the areas of waste management (e.g., operation of substandard landfills)".[12]

The problems caused by the numerous substandard landfills in Romania are quite notorious. Cases like those of the landfills in Măldăreşti (Vâlcea), Pata Rât (Cluj) or Mestecăniş (Suceava) have made headlines more than once.[13] Non-compliant landfills, representing real dangers for the environment (huge quantities of waste disposed *in situ*, for a much longer period than initially authorised, bad odours, infested waters), have destroyed landscapes as a result of a number of factors. These include bad administrative decisions, inspections being carried out without any visible result in the field, decision-making and control authorities passing responsibility to each other, local authorities allegedly unable to solve the situations, tonnes of waste being carried needlessly for hundreds of kilometres because of "wars" between waste management operators, non-operational ecological landfills, and corrupted tender procedures. Such incidents have become all too common subjects in the mass media.

Romania has been warned many times to solve its landfill issues, and dispose of waste in a manner that does not endanger human health and the environment, through prohibiting the abandonment, dumping or uncontrolled disposal of waste. Thus, in October 2020, having benefited from a transitional period,

10 The EU Environmental Implementation Review 2017, *Country Report – Romania*, p. 4, https://www.eumonitor.eu/9353000/1/j9vvik7m1c3gyxp/vkbjdak1yfy5; The EU Environmental Implementation Review 2019, *Country Report – Romania*, p. 3, https://ec.europa.eu/environment/eir/pdf/report_ro_en.pdf.

11 Commission Staff Working Document, The EU Environmental Implementation Review, *Country Report – Romania*, Brussels, 03.02.2017, SWD(2017) 55 final, https://ec.europa.eu/environment/eir/pdf/country-reports-archive/report_ro_en.pdf, p. 26.

12 *Ibid.*

13 See the documentary *România, te iubesc!*, available at https://www.youtube.com/watch?v=4pM2gS0t7nc.

according to its Accession Treaty, that should have been closed by July 2019, the European Commission called on Romania to close, seal and ecologically restore 15 illegal landfills out of 101 dumping sites. On that occasion, it emphasised that waste must be treated without risk to water, air, soil, plants or animals, without causing a nuisance through noise or odours, and without adversely affecting the countryside or places of special interest.[14] In November 2021, and following a similar warning issued on 14 May 2020, the Commission again urged Romania "to close, seal and ecologically restore 48 illegal landfills and to comply with the judgment of the Court of Justice of the EU of 18 October 2018".[15] Indeed, Romania should have closed and rehabilitated those substandard landfills by 16 July 2009, and, due to slow progress, the Commission had referred the matter to the Court of Justice of the EU, in 2017.[16] The action concerned Romania's failure to fulfil its obligations under Article 14(b), in conjunction with Article 13, of Directive 1999/31/EC, regarding the 68 then-existing landfill sites which had not been granted a permit to continue to operate, and which, accordingly, should have been closed, pursuant to Articles 7(g) and 13 of that Directive. The Commission maintained that Romania, in justifying the failure to meet the obligations arising under the Directive, could not rely on purely domestic situations, such as the bankruptcy of operators, disputes relating to property law, the conduct of administrative proceedings, or the responsibility of local authorities.

The numerous substandard landfills represent only one side of the illegal landfilling story this contribution is about to tell. Another side becomes visible through the media and the reports of the environmental control authorities, mainly those of the National Environmental Guard:[17] it is the story of the illegal dumping sites, much too present in Romanians' everyday lives. According to the National Environmental Guard's report for 2018, out of the 31,661 inspections on environmental pollution, 2,323 aimed at checking the municipal and thoroughfare sanitation status. These led to the discovery of 2,716 illegal waste dumping sites, with a total surface area of 4,062,268 square metres. Subsequently, 313 warnings and 611 fines were issued. Most fines (595) were issued to local administrations, with the remaining 16 being directed towards municipal sanitation agents, other economic agents, or natural persons. The inspections also revealed that, out of the 2,263 local administrations subject to control,

---

14 October infringements package: key decisions, https://ec.europa.eu/commission/presscorner/detail/EN/INF_20_1687.

15 Landfills: Commission refers ROMANIA to the Court of Justice of the European Union over its failure to comply with the Court judgment, https://ec.europa.eu/commission/presscorner/detail/EN/IP_21_5354.

16 Case C-301/17, *European Commission v. Romania*, https://curia.europa.eu/juris/liste.jsf?num=C-301/17.

17 Available at https://www.gnm.ro/note.php.

701 had not implemented a selective waste collection system, and, therefore, 69 fines and 131 warnings were issued to them. A year later, 2,512 inspections regarding local sanitation services were carried out, from a total number of 31,194 environmental pollution inspections. The number of uncontrolled illegal dumping sites discovered climbed to 3,837 (with the surface of affected soil amounting to 1,384,980 square metres). As in the previous year, corrective measures were established, and administrative sanctions applied as follows: for failure to selectively collect waste, local administrations were punished with 68 warnings and 135 fines, and economic agents with 3 warnings and 20 fines; for failure to meet selective waste collection targets, local administrations were also sanctioned, with 18 warnings and 4 fines. Additionally, 3,024 localities and 2,588 watercourses were subject to controls aimed at checking the watercourses' sanitation status. On this occasion, 1,908 mixed waste dumping sites were discovered along the shores of the inspected watercourses, for which 77 warnings and 11 fines were consequently issued. In 2020, 2,850 inspections were performed at the local sanitation services level, entailing 451 warnings and 408 fines for local administrations and municipal sanitation agents. The annual check on watercourses' sanitation status resulted in 54 warnings and 14 fines applied for illegal waste dumping and improper waste management. In 2021, at national level, 2,845 inspections were carried out by Environmental Guard representatives on municipal sanitation status, resulting in 620 warnings and 552 administrative sanctions being applied for non-compliance with waste management requirements. For the first time, the National Environmental Guard (NEG) report expressly referred to sanctions other than warnings and fines, such as the suspension of the activity of economic agents, or the confiscation of vehicles involved in the offences, which were predominantly the transporting and dumping of illegal waste.

Who is responsible for such infringements on environmental legislation? First, the central authorities are accountable for some drawbacks in the legislation. A relevant example is that of the old landfill tax – currently called the circular economy tax – which was introduced through Romanian legislation in 2013. It should have been applied since 2014, but has been postponed twice: first until 2017, and then until 2019. The government ordinances postponing the landfill tax were adopted when landfilling was obviously preferred in Romania, due to its low cost. For quite a long period of time, until 2018, the legislation also lacked other relevant instruments to divert waste from landfills (for example, mandatory recycling targets for municipalities, accompanied by penalties for non-compliance, performance indicators in the sanitation services public contracts). Even where the legislation was in accordance with the EU standards, it was not accompanied by guidelines for its implementation, or by efficient economic instruments to promote its provisions (for example, recycling, pay-as-you-throw schemes, relevant investment instruments). Another drawback was represented by the belated publication of the National Waste Management Plan currently in force: it dates from 28 April 2017, four years later than it should have been adopted, and one day after the EC announced that it had referred Romania to the Court of Justice, for failure to comply with the requirements of Articles 28–30 of Directive 2008/98/EC on Waste.

Second, local administrations are liable. Too often, media headlines refer to tens of tonnes of waste illegally dumped in various municipalities,[18] but waste management-related offences are sometimes committed under the closed eyes of, or even by, the institutions subordinated to certain local authorities.[19] The low desire of local administrations to apply penalties to the population, in cases of failure to comply with the sanitation regulations, is reflected in the absence of a comprehensive and decisive enforcement action against illegal landfilling at their level of competence, in the very low recycling rates of municipal waste, and in the very high landfilling rates repeatedly reported, the belated adoption of county waste management plans (in 2019, the majority of such planning instruments were still under preparation), etc. Moreover, case law shows that local administrations have frequently been found liable in court. Some of these decisions are illustrative of their lack of diligence against, or even complicity in, waste management regulation infringements. Thus, in 2018, a local authority appealed the decision of a first-instance court, seeking to change it, annul the notice of contravention, and, subsidiarily, replace the fine with a warning. The local administration had been fined for the failure to clean up land owned by it, as previously directed by officers of the NEG (in breach of Art. 96 of EGO 195/2005),[20] as well as for the failure to keep the evidence of collected and transported waste (infringing Art. 25 of Government Decision 1061/2008).[21] Indeed, an illegal waste dumping site had been discovered on the municipality's land after a previous inspection with a similar finding. The mayor claimed, *inter*

18 Ministrul Mediului: Am găsit zeci de mii de tone de deşeuri depozitate ilegal în Bucureşti, https://www.digi24.ro/stiri/sci-tech/natura-si-mediu/ministrul-mediului-am-gasit-zeci-de-mii-de-tone-de-deseuri-depozitate-ilegal-in-bucuresti-doar-in-februarie-1461670; https://www.banatulazi.ro/timisoara-murdara-deseuri-abandonate-peste-tot-santiere-neconforme-si-noroi-pe-strazi/; https://www.monitorulcj.ro/actualitate/88082-este-sau-nu-cluj-napoca-orasul-cu-cel-mai-mult-gunoi-aruncat-ilegal-plin-de-deseuri-la-periferiile-metropolelor.

19 Garda de Mediu a amendat cu 50.000 de lei două instituţii ale Primăriei Capitalei pentru că depozitau ilegal deşeuri, https://www.wall-street.ro/articol/Social/285780/garda-de-mediu-a-amendat-cu-50-000-de-lei-doua-institutii-ale-primariei-capitalei-pentru-ca-depozitau-ilegal-deseuri.html#gref; https://cursdeguvernare.ro/seful-garzii-de-mediu-in-fiecare-zi-descoperim-cate-o-primarie-care-ingroapa-deseuri-ilegal.html; https://www.libertatea.ro/stiri/video-o-masina-a-primariei-alexandria-arunca-gunoaie-pe-un-camp-chiar-sub-privirile-prefectului-care-facea-curatenie-4091400.

20 Emergency Government Ordinance no. 195/2005 on the protection of the environment, published in the Official Journal of Romania no. 1196 of 30 December 2005, https://legislatie.just.ro/.

21 Government Decision no. 1061/2008 on the transport of waste on the Romanian territory, published in the Official Journal of Romania no. 672 of 30 September 2008, https://legislatie.just.ro/.

alia, that the illegal waste dumping entailing the administrative sanctions was accidental: the land had been cleaned in compliance with the NEG directions, but the inhabitants of the village had subsequently dumped waste there again, because all the landfills in the area were either closed or unauthorised. The Court of Appeal upheld the decision of the first-instance court, stating that the failure to clean up a significant quantity of waste illegally dumped on the land owned by it, contrary to the obligations it was established to have during several previous inspections by the NEG, amounted to a continuous, repeated contravention, for which the penalties had been correctly individualised.[22] Another case involved a local administration that had been fined after a large waste dumping site had been identified near the City Hall, facts amounting to the offence described in Article 19 of Act 211/2011. Here, again, the court denied the local administration's petition to annul the notice of contravention and, subsidiarily, to replace the fine with a warning. The main reason underlying the decision consisted in the fact that the petitioner's failure to carry out an efficient waste management process, by allowing large amounts of waste to accumulate directly on the soil, served as a bad example to the inhabitants of the community, for whom the City Hall must represent a standard of conduct. Furthermore, the impact of this method of waste collection on the environment was obvious, as the waste that had accumulated on the soil was not degradable. Therefore, in the judges' opinion, replacing the fine with a warning would only encourage the future repetition of the petitioner's contravention of environmental protection legislation.[23] An analysis of the case law on environment protection legislation infringements *lato sensu* (based on various legal provisions applicable to waste management, including the most recently adopted ones) reveals, however, that Romanian courts have been rather willing to accept petitioners' claims to replace the fines applied to them with warnings, the less severe sanctions prescribed by law. Thus, in a case involving a local administration fined for an illegal waste dumping site found on its territory, the court referred to the "well known difficulties that the authorities generally face, in trying to comply with environmental rules, difficulties engendered both by the citizens who infringe them and by the lack of objective (material, financial, administrative, etc.) possibilities to manage the waste collection in accordance with the environmental legislation in force".[24] It further stated that the maximum fine applied by the environmental authorities represented a significant amount of money for a relatively small community, being likely to unbalance the local budget, with negative effects on the population. This large sum of money

---

22 Vâlcea Court of Appeal, Decision no. 784/04.09.2018, in G. Manu, *Jurisprudența contravențională de mediu*, Universul Juridic, 2021, pp. 103–109.

23 Horezu Court, Decision no. 639/14.09.2020, www.rolii.ro.

24 Dărăbani Court, Decision no. 559/11.10.2021, www.rolii.ro.

could be otherwise used for ensuring the town's sanitation, especially since the new legislation, EGO 92/2021, imposes much more restrictive and costly rules, including those for selective waste collection, which requires significant financial resources from the local administration. For these reasons, the court considered that a warning was a sufficient sanction for the local authority, and that the fine would have been particularly burdensome for the community's budget, and disproportionate to the concrete social danger of the offence, as well as to the subsequent conduct of the local authorities. Indeed, the land eventually being cleaned up proved, in the judges' opinion, that no "resistance" to environmental education had been met, and that the corrective purpose of the sanction had been accomplished.

A third group of responsible parties consists of all waste producers who do not willingly comply with the legislation, and who fail to understand the real stakes behind the waste management rules: that of ensuring for us, and for the future generations, a fair chance to live on this planet.

In 2018, certain legislative improvements were made: the Act governing waste management at that time was amended by a government ordinance[25] establishing increased fines applicable to waste management-related offences, and local authorities' obligations to include performance indicators in their sanitation service contracts, with penalties for the failure to meet such indicators, as well as to implement the PAYT (pay-as-you-throw) instrument (on criteria such as the volume, the collection frequency, the weight, or the customised bags used for waste collection), to apply distinct tariffs to the population for the residual and recyclable waste collected by sanitation agents, and sanctions for non-compliance with the requirements to collect waste separately, to include the contribution to the circular economy in the above tariffs, and to inform their communities on the waste management systems, and on the location of the separate waste collection centres, whose functioning they must ensure. In 2021, the waste management legislation was reformed again, by EGO no. 92/2021 on waste, transposing EU Directive 2018/851. This regulation maintains the prior improvements, and introduces new ones. It sets a new sanction for illegal waste dumping: the obligation to remove waste dumped in unauthorised places, to clean the soil, and to eliminate the waste in accordance with the legislation in force.[26] Its annexes provide the necessary and long-awaited guidelines relating to the economic instruments meant to stimulate the implementation of the waste hierarchy, to minimal performance indicators to be included in sanitation services contracts, and to waste prevention measures.

---

25 Emergency Government Ordinance no. 74/2018, published in the Official Journal of Romania no. 630 of 19 July 2018, https://legislatie.just.ro/.

26 In its Art. 63.

3. EPILOGUE: IN SEARCH OF SOLUTIONS FOR AN END TO THE STORY?

While never-ending stories might be appreciated in fantasy, they are inappropriate in relation to illegal landfilling and environmental pollution. Our story must find an end. First and foremost, this might be achieved through a change of mentality; a mindset shift towards environment protection, induced in the population, perhaps by increasing the number of awareness campaigns and educational projects aiming at familiarisation with the stakes of environmental protection and sustainable development. This might include encouraging the public to participate in decision-making processes in relation to such matters. Some steps forward have already been made. The Ministry of Environment has launched the project "Let's clean up Romania!", whereby local authorities all over the country get financial help for cleaning up illegal dumping sites in their areas. Cleaning-up campaigns also call on the voluntary participation of the public. Another step forward consists in the amendment of the National Education Act,[27] at the beginning of this year: the new provisions blow the winds of change needed for environmental education to be brought into Romanian schools. Article 65 of the Act set out an obligation, incumbent upon both the Ministry of Environment and the Ministry of Education, to draft a strategy on environmental education by 31 December 2022. This strategy is to be transposed into school curricula, starting with the school year 2023–24. Further, Article 68 includes environmental competences among the eight key competence fields for primary and secondary education. In March this year, the Minister of Education issued an order[28] providing for a new optional subject to be introduced within the secondary education curriculum – Ecological and Environment Protection Education – for the fifth, sixth and seventh grades. This formal educational programme aims to drive long-awaited societal change in Romania, and, in the long run, to bring an end to the never-ending story of illegal landfilling.

The problem remains, however, regarding the necessary change of mentality in the Romanian adult population, which has not benefited from such formal environmental education. Adequate infrastructure and relevant financial instruments to stimulate waste prevention, recycling and reuse might be a solution to this. Enhancing local authorities' accountability for waste management, making them pre-eminently responsible for it by law, is likely to motivate them to properly enforce the existing legal provisions, to make supplementary efforts

27 Act no. 1/2011 of national education, published in the Official Journal of Romania no. 18 of 10 January 2011, last amended by Act no. 14/2022, published in the Official Journal of Romania no. 29 of 10 January 2022.

28 Order no. 3.446 relating to the curriculum for the optional subject entitled Ecological and Environment Protection Education, published in the Official Journal of Romania no. 343 of 7 April 2022.

to compel the performance of contractual sanitation services clauses, and to stimulate the population's compliance with waste management rules, by both preventive and punitive means. For instance, higher tariffs should be imposed on citizens failing to collect waste selectively than on those who are compliant. An important step forward was taken in 2021,[29] when the deposit-refund scheme became operational in Romania.

Increasing the number of planned and unplanned inspections by all the controlling authorities, and on all players involved in waste management, is also part of the answer to the problem. Inspections also need to be accompanied by more effective administrative sanctions. The present author agrees totally with the Romanian authors who consider that the applicability of the warning as an administrative sanction for environmental offences should be limited to less serious environmental offences,[30] since it is not an effective deterrent against the most serious ones. In fact, fines themselves seem to lack efficiency, since case law shows that they no longer deter certain economic agents operating in the field of waste management. Opinions have been expressed regarding the need to establish the legal limits of fines, not in fixed sums of money, but in percentages of turnover.[31] On the other hand, by virtue of the general regulation on administrative offences,[32] community service is only applicable to natural persons, and no special regulation provides for its applicability to environmental offences. According to the Romanian legal literature, community service might constitute an efficient punishment for offences committed by legal entities whose professional activities relate to environment protection (for example, public institutions subordinated to local authorities in charge of public spaces maintenance, waste management contractors), and should be *de lege ferenda* applicable in such cases.[33]

These are only some things that are likely to put an end to the illegal landfilling story briefly presented here. Yet the – perhaps longer term – expectation is great: to improve the conclusions of the report for Romania in future editions of the *Environmental Implementation Review*, and to accomplish the purpose of the campaign launched in April this year: "a country free from illegally dumped waste!" The reader is invited to contribute to the drafting of a happy ending to this tale.

---

29 https://www.colectaredeseuri.ro/garantie-pentru-ambalaje-si-pet-uri/.

30 O. Podaru and R, Chiriță, *Ordonanța Guvernului nr. 2/2001 privind regimul juridic al contravențiilor, comentată și adnotată*, Sfera Juridică, 2006, p. 52; G. Manu, above n. 22, p. 35.

31 G. Manu, above n. 22, p. 38.

32 Government Ordinance no. 2/2001 on the legal regime of administrative offences, published in the Official Journal of Romania no. 410 of 25 July 2001.

33 G. Manu, above n. 22, pp. 40–41.

PART VI

THE ROLE OF THE GENERAL PUBLIC

"INDIVIDUAL CONCERN" IN CLIMATE PROTECTION MATTERS IN THE CONTEXT OF DIFFERENT LEGAL PROTECTION REGIMES

Janna RINGENA*

Recent jurisprudence within the European Union (EU) and abroad makes apparent that the design of legal standing is a bottleneck in helping climate protection concerns succeed in court.[1] This becomes particularly clear when comparing the European Court of Justice (ECJ)'s decision on the *People's Climate Case*[2] with the decision of the German Federal Constitutional Court (GFCC) on four complaints against the Federal Climate Protection Act.[3] In both cases,

* The author would like to thank Victoria Lacis, Lucas Hennicke and Julian Albrecht for helpful feedback on an earlier draft. The author would also like to thank Dr Dominik Römling for a continuous professional exchange on legal standing in environmental cases. This contribution is based on a presentation given at EELF in September 2021 and was written in May 2022.

1 See *P. Toussaint*, "Loss and damage and climate litigation: The case for greater interlinkage", *RECIEL* 2021 (30), pp. 16, 20, who designates a lack of standing as a "key obstacle" to succeeding in court. Cf. also *O. Kelleher*, "Systemic Climate Change Litigation, Standing Rules and the Aarhus Convention: A Purposive Approach", *Journal of Environmental Law* 2022 (34), pp. 107, 108; *B.J. Preston*, "The Influence of the Paris Agreement on Climate Litigation: Causation, Corporate Governance and Catalyst (Part II)", *Journal of Environmental Law* 2021 (33), p. 227, pp. 234–38, 248, 252.

2 ECJ Judgment: Case C-565/19, *Carvalho and Others v. Parliament and Council* [2021] ECLI:EU:C:2021:252.

3 Bundes-Klimaschutzgesetz (KSG) of 12/12/2019, BGBl. I, p. 2513, last amended by Art. 1 G of 18/08/2021, BGBl. I, p. 3905; GFCC Climate protection order: Case 1 BvR 2656/18 [2021] ECLI:DE:BVerfG:2021:rs20210324.1bvr265618. Besides, climate claims have also been successful in France, where legal protection before the administrative courts only requires an interest of any kind (see Conseil d'État Decision: Case no. 427301, *Grande Synthe and Others v. French Government* [2020] ECLI:FR:CECHR:2020:427301.20201119 and Tribunal administrative de Paris Decision: Cases no. 1904967, 1904968, 1904972, 1904976/4-1, *Oxfam France and Others v. French Government* [2021]), and in the Netherlands, where individuals, represented by the non-governmental organisation (NGO) Urgenda, could rely on a plausible impairment of their human rights, laid down in Arts. 2 and 8 ECHR (Hoge Raad Judgment: Case 19/00135, *Urgenda v. The Netherlands* [2019] ECLI:NL:HR:2019:2007). For an overview, see also *J. Ringena*, "Klimaschutz vor höchsten Gerichten – die Entscheidung des BVerfG im Vergleich zur Rechtsprechung des Conseil d'État und des EuGH", *JuWissBlog* no. 47-2021, 07/05/2021 (https://www.juwiss.de/47-2021/).

more than 30 individuals sued legislators for not having adopted sufficiently tight climate protection targets. The action before the ECJ failed because it lacked standing, while the complaint before the GFCC was admissible, and even partially well-founded.

Even though individual legal protection is designed differently at European level, and at German constitutional level, it is remarkable that the ECJ and the GFCC both require "individual concern" by a sovereign legal Act.[4]

This contribution starts with an overview of the above-mentioned procedures and judgments (section 1), before dealing with the divergent handling of standing by the courts, especially their divergent understanding of "individual concern" as a central requirement of standing (section 2). Thereafter, it asks whether the *Plaumann* doctrine is still an adequate means of establishing standing in actions for annulment raised by non-privileged applicants (section 3). Finally, it deals with possible adaptions of the interpretation of "individual concern", and addresses the question of how the German understanding could be an inspiration for EU case law (section 4).

1. GROUPS OF INDIVIDUALS SUING THE LEGISLATOR

The so-called *People's Climate Case*[5] before the ECJ, as well as the constitutional complaints that led to the GFCC's climate protection order, aimed at overwriting current climate protection law by means of strategic litigation. Both the appellants in the ECJ case and the complainants in the GFCC complaint referred to excesses in the carbon budgets allocated by the respective legislators.[6]

1.1. *PEOPLE'S CLIMATE CASE*

Thirty-seven EU citizens and foreigners[7] sued for the annulment of three European legal Acts concerning climate protection, which were in force at the time.[8] They acted as non-privileged applicants in the sense of Article 263(4) of

4 See below, and cf. Art. 263(4) TFEU and Art. 93(1) no. 4a Basic Law in conjunction with §90(1) Federal Constitutional Court Act.

5 ECJ Judgment: Case C-565/19, *Carvalho and Others v. Parliament and Council* [2021] ECLI:EU:C:2021:252.

6 Ibid., at para. 15; General Court Order: Case T-330/18 *Carvalho and Others v. Parliament and Council* [2019] ECLI:EU:T:2019:324, para. 18; GFCC Climate protection order: Case 1 BvR 2656/18 [2021] ECLI:DE:BVerfG:2021:rs20210324.1bvr265618. paras. 42, 60 *et seq.*, 72.

7 General Court Order: Case T-330/18 *Carvalho and Others v. Parliament and Council* [2019] ECLI:EU:T:2019:324, para. 1.

8 Directive (EU) 2018/410 of the European Parliament and of the Council of 14 March 2018 amending Directive 2003/87/EC to enhance cost-effective emission reductions and low-carbon investments, and Decision (EU) 2015/1814, OJ 2018 L 76/3; Regulation (EU) 2018/842

the Treaty on the Functioning of the European Union (TFEU). The opposing parties were the European Parliament and the Council, as the EU's legislative bodies.

The applicants worked in the touristic or agricultural sectors, and feared their professional activities being affected by the consequences of climate change, for example droughts and floods, in the near future.[9] Therefore, they considered themselves to be directly and individually concerned by insufficient legislation, and thus infringed in their fundamental rights.[10] They claimed certain legal Acts to be violating the Paris Agreement, as they permitted greenhouse gas emissions that would not adhere to the 1.5 degree Celsius limit specified in Article 2(1)(a) of the Paris Agreement. Consequently, they called for the relevant legal Acts to be annulled, but to remain in force until the legislators tightened the relevant legislative provisions, to ensure that climate protection legislation would not be reduced to zero until the legislators improved it.[11]

The action of annulment did not succeed, either at first or second instance: The General Court, as well as the ECJ, dismissed the action as inadmissible, for lack of "individual concern" and, therefore, lack of standing.[12]

1.2. GERMAN CONSTITUTIONAL COMPLAINTS

The complainants in the context of the German climate protection order were young (mostly under 30) and numerous (45 individuals from Germany, Bangladesh and Nepal, as well as 2 legal entities). Like the complainants in the *People's Climate Case*, they worked, or planned to work in the near future, in the

of the European Parliament and of the Council of 30 May 2018 on binding annual greenhouse gas emission reductions by Member States from 2021 to 2030 contributing to climate action to meet commitments under the Paris Agreement and amending Regulation (EU) No. 525/2013, OJ 2018 L 156/26; Regulation (EU) 2018/841 of the European Parliament and of the Council of 30 May 2018 on the inclusion of greenhouse gas emissions and removals from land use, land-use change and forestry in the 2030 climate and energy framework, and amending Regulation (EU) No. 525/2013 and Decision No 529/2013/EU, OJ 2018 L 156/1; For a brief overview of the procedure, see *Kelleher* (supra, note 1), pp. 128–29; *B.J. Preston*, "The Influence of the Paris Agreement on Climate Litigation: Legal Obligations and Norms (Part I)", *Journal of Environmental Law* 2021 (33), p. 1, pp. 23–24.

9 General Court Order: Case T-330/18 *Carvalho and Others v. Parliament and Council* [2019] ECLI:EU:T:2019:324, paras. 24 and 31.

10 Ibid., at paras. 30 *et seq*.

11 Ibid., at para. 18; cf. *G. Winter*, "*Armando Carvalho and Others v. EU*: Invoking Human Rights and the Paris Agreement for Better Climate Protection Legislation", TEL 2020 (1), p. 137, pp. 138–55; *G. Winter*, "*Armando Carvalho et alii versus Europäische Union*: Rechtsdogmatische und staatstheoretische Probleme einer Klimaklage vor dem Europäischen Gericht", *ZUR* 2019 p. 259, pp. 260–65.

12 General Court Order: Case T-330/18 *Carvalho and Others v. Parliament and Council* [2019] ECLI:EU:T:2019:324, paras. 33 *et seq*.; ECJ Judgment: Case C-565/19, *Carvalho and Others v. Parliament and Council* [2021] ECLI:EU:C:2021:252, paras. 35 *et seq*.

touristic or agricultural sectors, feared negative consequences on their work, or suffered diseases that would worsen due to climate change.[13]

As they considered the German Federal Climate Protection Act an insufficient contribution to reaching the 1.5 degree Celsius limit specified in the Paris Agreement and, therefore, insufficient to protect them from effects of climate change, they complained of being infringed in their fundamental rights by the legislative bodies of the Federal Republic of Germany.[14] The complainants, similarly to the approach taken by the appellants in the *People's Climate Case*, sought the annulment of the Federal Climate Protection Act, but asked for its continued existence until the legislator tightened climate protection goals and measures.[15]

The GFCC accepted the complaints of the individuals for decision and considered them to be partially well-founded, because of an infringement of intertemporal freedom rights in the sense of Article 2(1) of the Basic Law,[16] which protects the general freedom of action.[17]

1.3. INTERIM CONCLUSION

In both cases, a group of individuals who are likely to be affected by the consequences of climate change in the near future sued the legislator for not having adopted sufficient legislation to mitigate climate change.

Unlike the constitutional complaint, the European action for annulment within the meaning of Article 263(4) TFEU is not a type of action that is aimed primarily at challenging violations of fundamental rights by legislation or other state actions:[18] its focus is, rather, on the review of the legality of legal Acts of the EU in general.[19] Nevertheless, it opens up a possibility for individuals to complain if they are individually and directly concerned.[20] Therefore, it is

13 GFCC Climate protection order: Case 1 BvR 2656/18 [2021] ECLI:DE:BVerfG:2021:rs20210324.1bvr265618, paras. 43, 66, 83.

14 In German, Bundestag und Bundesrat; GFCC Climate protection order: Case 1 BvR 2656/18 [2021] ECLI:DE:BVerfG:2021:rs20210324.1bvr265618, paras. 1, 38 *et seq.*

15 Ibid., at paras. 1, 38 *et seq.*, 267 *et seq.*

16 Grundgesetz für die Bundesrepublik Deutschland (GG) of 23/05/1949, BGBl. III outline no. 100-1, last amended by Art. 1 *et seq.* G of 29/09/2020, BGBl. I., p. 2048.

17 GFCC Climate protection order: Case 1 BvR 2656/18 [2021] ECLI:DE:BVerfG:2021:rs20210324.1bvr265618, paras. 90, 142, 182 *et seq.* Cf., on this, *R. Krämer-Hoppe*, "The Climate Protection Order of the Federal Constitutional Court of Germany and the North-South Divide", *German Law Journal* 2021 (22), p. 1393, pp. 1399–400.

18 For the aims of the constitutional complaint, see *G. Morgenthaler, "Art. 93 GG", in V. Epping and C. Hillgruber* (eds.), BeckOK Grundgesetz, ed. 50, 2022, para. 49.

19 *W. Cremer*, "Art. 263 AEUV", in *C. Calliess and M. Ruffert* (eds.), EUV/AEUV, ed. 6, 2022, para. 1.

20 Art. 263(4) TFEU: "Any natural or legal person may … institute proceedings against an act … which is of direct and individual concern to them".

considered to be at least partially a functional equivalent to a constitutional complaint.[21]

Finally, in both the European and the German legal systems, individuals have the possibility to take action against laws that affect their fundamental rights. The applicants in both cases made use of this possibility: both lawsuits aimed at declaring climate protection law insufficient, due to a violation of fundamental rights and of superior international law (Art. 2(1)(a) of the Paris Agreement).

2. THE HANDLING OF STANDING BY THE COURTS

The General Court and the ECJ, on the one hand, and the GFCC, on the other, came to different conclusions concerning the admission of the actions.

2.1. *PEOPLE'S CLIMATE CASE*

With regard to legal standing, natural persons, according to Article 263(4) TFEU, need to be individually and directly concerned by the EU Act in question. It is not necessary to be affected in a legal sense.[22]

2.1.1. Plaumann *Doctrine*

The ECJ defined "individual concern", in the sense of Article 263(4) TFEU, as part of the *Plaumann* judgment.[23] The so-called *Plaumann* doctrine considers a person to be individually concerned only if the legal Act affects him or her because of certain personal characteristics or special circumstances which distinguish him or her from all other persons, and, therefore, individualises him or her in a similar way as the addressee.[24] Thus, individuality, in the sense of Article 263(4) TFEU, means exclusivity, according to the jurisprudence of the European courts.

---

21 *M. Borowski*, Die Nichtigkeitsklage gem. Art. 230 Abs. 4 EGV, EuR 2004 pp. 879, 908.

22 ECJ Judgment: Case 169/84, *Compagnie française de l'azote (Cofaz) SA and others v. Commission of the European Communities* [1986] ECLI:EU:C:1986:42, Reports of Cases 1986, 391, paras. 31; cf. *B.W. Wegener, Rechte des Einzelnen*, Nomos 1998, p. 158; *M. Ruffert, Subjektive Rechte im Umweltrecht der Europäischen Gemeinschaft*, UTR 1996, p. 190; *G. Winter*, "Not fit for purpose. Die Klagebefugnis vor dem Europäischen Gericht angesichts allgemeiner Gefahren", *EuR* 2022 (3), pp. 367, 370.

23 ECJ Judgment: Case 25/62, *Plaumann v. Commission of the EEC* [1963] ECLI:EU:C:1963:17, Reports of Cases 1963, 199. For a brief overview, see also *D. Medhurst, A Brief and Practical Guide to EU Law*, 3rd ed., Blackwell Science Ltd. 2001, p. 61.

24 "Persons other than those to whom a decision is addressed may only claim to be individually concerned if that decision affects them by reason of certain attributes which are peculiar to them or by reason of circumstances in which they are differentiated from all other persons

2.1.2. *Lack of Standing*

The applicants (at first instance) respectively appellants (at second instance) in the *People's Climate Case* argued that they were individually concerned, as the effects of climate change will affect them differently: for example, a farmer in northern Europe will have to deal with different difficulties from someone working in the touristic sector in southern Europe.[25] Subsidiarily, the appellants advocated a relaxation of the criterion of individuality.[26]

Nevertheless, they did not convince European judges: The ECJ stated that, "the fact that the appellants, owing to the alleged circumstances, are affected differently by climate change is not in itself sufficient to establish the standing of those appellants to bring an action for annulment of a measure of general application such as the acts at issue",[27] and that "the appellants had not established that the contested provisions of the acts at issue distinguished them individually from all other natural or legal persons concerned by those provisions just as in the case of the addressee".[28]

In summary, the appellants' plea of being affected differently by climate change, for example due to their different professions, was not sufficient to establish standing. As most people are probably going to be affected by climate change in the future, there was no individual concern, in the sense meant by EU primary law. This jurisprudence is, therefore, in line with the general finding that the more people who are affected, the less likely a particular person is to succeed in an action for annulment according to Article 263(4) TFEU, before the ECJ.[29] This ruling is one of many unsuccessful lawsuits, at EU level, in the environmental field.[30]

---

and by virtue of these factors distinguishes them individually just as in the case of the person addressed": ECJ Judgment: Case 25/62, *Plaumann v. Commission of the EEC* [1963] ECLI:EU:C:1963:17, Reports of Cases 1963, 199, p. 107.

25 General Court Order: Case T-330/18 *Carvalho and Others v. Parliament and Council* [2019] ECLI:EU:T:2019:324, paras. 30 *et seq.*

26 ECJ Judgment: Case C-565/19, *Carvalho and Others v. Parliament and Council* [2021] ECLI:EU:C:2021:252, paras. 54 *et seq.* For detail, see section 3 below. For an overview, also consult *M. Willers*, "Climate Change Litigation in European Regional Courts: Jumping Procedural Hurdles to Hold States to Account?", in *I. Alogna, C. Bakker and J.-P. Gauci* (eds.), *Climate Change Litigation: Global Perspectives*, Brill Nijhoff 2021, pp. 294–309, pp. 299–300.

27 ECJ Judgment: Case C-565/19, *Carvalho and Others v. Parliament and Council* [2021] ECLI:EU:C:2021:252, para. 40; cf. also General Court Order: Case T-330/18 *Carvalho and Others v. Parliament and Council* [2019] ECLI:EU:T:2019:324, para. 50.

28 ECJ Judgment: Case C-565/19, *Carvalho and Others v. Parliament and Council* [2021] ECLI:EU:C:2021:252, para. 50; cf. also General Court Order: Case T-330/18 *Carvalho and Others v. Parliament and Council* [2019] ECLI:EU:T:2019:324, para. 49.

29 Cf. *Kelleher* (supra, note 1), p. 131; *J.D. Braun and M. Kettner*, "Die Absage des EuGH an eine richterrechtliche Reform des EG-Rechtsschutzsystems", *DÖV* 2003 pp. 58, 66.

30 Cf. *L. Krämer*, "Access to Environmental Justice: the Double Standards of the ECJ", *JEEPL* 2017 (14), p. 159, pp. 163–66.

2.2. GERMAN CONSTITUTIONAL COMPLAINTS

According to Article 93(1)(4a) of the Basic Law, and §90(1) of the Federal Constitutional Court Act,[31] complainants must demonstrate sufficiently plausibly that their fundamental rights, or rights equivalent to fundamental rights, have been infringed by the public authority, so that such an infringement actually appears possible (the so-called "possibility doctrine").[32]

2.2.1. Present, Individual and Direct Concern

In addition to the above, the GFCC requires there to be a "present, individual and direct concern".[33]

First, the legal norm attacked by the complainant must be suitable, in structure and content, to interfere with fundamental rights, i.e. to *directly* change the position of the complainant protected by fundamental rights, to his or her disadvantage.[34] Additionally, the complainant's impairment of fundamental rights must be his or her own; he or she has to be *individually* affected.[35]

The complainant must either be addressed directly or *legally* affected; mere reflex effects or simple factual effects are insufficient.[36] In the case of indirect and *de facto* impairments, fundamental rights can also be affected individually and directly if these impairments are equivalent to imperative interventions, in terms of objective and effect.[37]

Further, the complainant's concern must occur *presently*, i.e. either now or concretely foreseeable in the near future, as complainants should be able to

31 Bundesverfassungsgerichtsgesetz (BVerfGG) of 11/08/1993, BGBl. I, p. 1473, last amended by Art. 4 G of 20/11/2019, BGBl. I, p. 1724.

32 Cf. *C. Hillgruber and C. Goos*, *Verfassungsprozessrecht*, 5th ed., C.F. Müller Verlag 2020 §3, paras. 231 *et seq.*, with further references.

33 Ibid., at §3, paras. 268 *et seq.*; see GFCC Order: Case 1 BvR 220/51 [1951], BVerfGE 1, 97, p. 101 *et seq.*; GFCC Order: Case 1 BvR 241/56 [1957], BVerfGE 6, 273, p. 277; GFCC Order: Case 2 BvR 386/63, 2 BvR 478/63 [1966], BVerfGE 20, 283, p. 290; GFCC Judgment: Case 2 BvF 1/69, 2 BvR 629/68, 2 BvR 308/69 [1970], BVerfGE 30, 1, p. 16; GFCC Judgment: Case 1 BvR 424/71, 1 BvR 325/72 [1973], BVerfGE 35, 79, p. 107; GFCC Order: Case 1 BvR 274/72, 1 BvR 209/72, 1 BvR 195/73, 1 BvR 194/73, 1 BvR 184/73, 1 BvR 247/72 [1975], BVerfGE 40, 141, p. 156; GFCC Order: Case 2 BvR 460/80 [1983], BVerfGE 64, 367, p. 375 *et seq.*; GFCC Judgment: Case 2 BvR 1387/02 [2005], BVerfGE 114, 258, p. 274.

34 GFCC Order: Cases 1 BvR 274/72, 1 BvR 209/72, 1 BvR 195/73, 1 BvR 194/73, 1 BvR 184/73, 1 BvR 247/72 [1975], BVerfGE 40, 141, p. 156.

35 GFCC Order: Case 1 BvR 222/51 [1951], BVerfGE 1, 91, p. 95 *et seq.*; GFCC Order: Case 1 BvR 220/51 [1951], BVerfGE 1, 97, p. 101 *et seq.*

36 *J. Wieland*, "Art. 93 GG", in *H. Dreier* (ed.), *Grundgesetz – Kommentar*, ed. 3, 2018, para. 95. See also GFCC Order: Case 1 BvR 241/56 [1957], BVerfGE 6, 273, p. 278; GFCC Order: Case 2 BvR 638/84 [1988], BVerfGE 78, 350, p. 354.

37 GFCC Order: Case 2 BvR 1371/13 [2018] ECLI:DE:BVerfG:2018:rk20180315.2bvr137113, para. 29, with further references.

prevent impairments in the future.[38] Therefore, they need to point out whether and how they are going to be concerned;[39] a "virtual" concern is insufficient.[40]

The present nature of a concern is also established if a further implementation step, for example an administrative act, is generally required to affect the complainant,[41] but the law attacked already changes his or her legal position.[42] In particular, if the complaint is directed against a legal norm, it is likely that the complainant will not yet be affected by the norm, but will be subject to its effects in the future. A present-day effect is assumed if a law currently forces the complainant to make a decision that will not be correctable later, or causes them to make a disposition that they will not be able to undo after the law has been implemented and applied.[43]

2.2.2. Standing Assumed

In a case before the Administrative Court of Berlin, in 2019, similar to the one before the GFCC, the judges rejected a "present, individual and direct concern" of fundamental rights, since the applicants' impairments due to climate change had not yet materialised,[44] and, at the time of realisation, everyone would be affected in some way. They referred to a lack of exclusivity, with reference to the General Court's order in the *People's Climate Case*.[45]

The GFCC, in 2021, nevertheless assumed legal standing: first, it considered the concern to be direct and present, as consequences of climate change can no longer be prevented once they have been realised:

> The complainants are presently affected in their own fundamental rights by the provisions governing the amount of greenhouse gas emissions allowed until 2030 in §3(1) 2 and §4(1) 2 KSG [Climate Protection Act] … Even provisions that only begin posing significant risks to fundamental rights over the course of their subsequent implementation can fall into conflict with the Basic Law … This is certainly the case where a course of events, once embarked upon, can no longer be corrected.[46]

38 GFCC Order: Case 1 BvR 385/77 [1979], BVerfGE 53, 30, pp. 48 *et seq.*

39 GFCC Order: Case 1 BvR 539/96 [2000], BVerfGE 102, 197, p. 207.

40 GFCC Order: Case 1 BvR 220/51 [1951], BVerfGE 1, 97, pp. 101 *et seq.*

41 GFCC Order: Cases 1 BvR 209, 269, 362, 420, 440, 484/83 [1983], BVerfGE 65, 1, pp. 36 *et seq.*

42 GFCC Order: Case 1 BvR 539/96 [2000], BVerfGE 102, 197, p. 207.

43 *Wieland* (supra, note 36), para. 95. See also GFCC Order: Cases 1 BvR 724/81, 1 BvR 1000/81, 1 BvR 1015/81, 1 BvL 16/82, 1 BvL 5/84 [1987] BVerfGE 75, 246, p. 263, with further references; GFCC Order: Case 1 BvR 539/96 [2000], BVerfGE 102, 197, p. 207.

44 Administrative Court of Berlin Judgment: Case 10 K 412.18 [2019] ECLI:DE:VGBE:2019:1031.VG10K412.18.00, para. 71.

45 Ibid., at paras. 72 *et seq.*, with reference to General Court Order: Case T-330/18 *Carvalho and Others v. Parliament and Council* [2019] ECLI:EU:T:2019:324, para. 50.

46 GFCC Climate protection order: Case 1 BvR 2656/18 [2021] ECLI:DE:BVerfG:2021:rs20210324.1bvr265618, para. 108 (official English translation).

Notably, the judges considered the complainants to be individually concerned in their fundamental rights, as the "mere fact that very large numbers of people are affected does not exclude persons from being individually affected in their own fundamental rights".[47] In this regard, the GFCC explicitly distanced itself from the General Court and ECJ's understanding of "individual concern".

2.3. INTERIM CONCLUSION

Both the courts of the EU and the GFCC require "individual concern", for the admission of a particular action. Within European law, any kind of individual interest is sufficient; the GFCC, however, requires an impairment of a legal position.

The General Court and the ECJ define "individual concern" with reference to the *Plaumann* doctrine, in a manner that equates individuality with exclusivity.[48] In contrast, the GFCC does not require such exclusivity, and takes the position that "individual concern" cannot be denied solely because many persons may be affected.[49]

This differentiation was decisive for the success (or otherwise) of the aforementioned climate actions in the courts. In the context of the German constitutional complaints, the understanding of "individual concern" as not necessarily "exclusive concern" led to an assumption of standing, and thereby paved the way towards a comprehensive judicial review of the Federal Climate Protection Act. By contrast, the ECJ's strict standing rules are the reason why EU legal Acts concerning climate change have not been judicially reviewed on a European level.[50]

Climate change will surely affect an enormous number of people, and will, therefore, probably never be able to ensure exclusive concern. Comprehensive and effective judicial review of climate protection Acts is, thus, only possible if exclusivity is not required within the framework of admissibility. Consequently, the question arises whether "individual concern", in the sense of Article 263(4) TFEU, necessarily means "exclusive concern", or whether this legal term also can be interpreted differently to establish legal standing.

---

47 Ibid., para. 110.

48 ECJ Judgment: Case C-565/19, *Carvalho and Others v. Parliament and Council* [2021] ECLI:EU:C:2021:252, paras. 40 *et seq.*; General Court Order: Case T-330/18 *Carvalho and Others v. Parliament and Council* [2019] ECLI:EU:T:2019:324, paras. 49 *et seq.*

49 See GFCC Climate protection order: Case 1 BvR 2656/18 [2021] ECLI:DE:BVerfG:2021:rs20210324.1bvr265618, para. 110. With this argumentation, the General Court of the EC also once deviated from the *Plaumann* doctrine, in 2002: see General Court Judgment: Case T-177/01, *Jégo-Quéré & Cie SA v. Commission of the EC* [2002] ECLI:EU:T:2002:112.

50 *S. Bogojević*, "Human rights of minors and future generations: Global trends and EU environmental law particularities", *RECIEL* 2020 (29), pp. 191, 192.

3. WHAT ABOUT THE *PLAUMANN* DOCTRINE?

Providing for the possibility that the ECJ would not accept the appellants' individual concerns, the appellants argued for a turn away from the *Plaumann* doctrine. In the following, their arguments will serve as a starting point for an examination and evaluation of to what extent the *Plaumann* doctrine is binding law for European courts, and to what extent it should be modified. In this context, the author is *not* shedding light on the extent to which the ECJ's ruling violates Article 9(3) of the Aarhus Convention.[51]

3.1. OPEN WORDING

First, the appellants argued that the wording of Article 263(4) TFEU does not cover the criterion of exclusive concern. The court has somewhat developed this criterion, and has already relaxed it in the past, to ensure effective legal protection.[52]

The ECJ instead considered any understanding of "individual" other than "exclusive" to be contradictory to Article 263(4) TFEU.[53] The judges upheld the jurisprudence of the General Court, as they found the appellants' demonstration of individual distinction insufficient.[54]

It became apparent that the ECJ took the understanding of individuality meaning exclusivity as being expressively laid down in Article 263 (4) TFEU:

> [T]he appellants cannot ask the Court of Justice to set aside such conditions, which are expressly laid down in the FEU Treaty, and, in particular, to adapt the criterion of "individual concern" as defined by the judgment in Plaumann, in order that they may have access to an effective remedy.[55]

However, this is not as clear as stated:[56] the wording of the provision says, "[a]ny natural or legal person may … institute proceedings against an act … which is of

---

51 For this, see, in detail, *Kelleher* (supra, note 1), pp. 130–32; *C. Poncelet*, "Access to Justice in Environmental Matters – Does the European Union Comply with its Obligations?", *Journal of Environmental Law* 2012 (24), p. 287, pp. 296–309; *J.H. Jans and H. Vedder*, *European Environmental Law*, 4th ed., Europa Law Publishing 2012, pp. 243–44.

52 ECJ Judgment: Case C-565/19, *Carvalho and Others v. Parliament and Council* [2021] ECLI:EU:C:2021:252, para. 54.

53 Ibid., para. 70.

54 Ibid., para. 73.

55 Ibid., para. 76.

56 Cf. also *Cremer*, "Art. 263 AEUV" (supra, note 19), para. 40; *C. Calliess*, "Kohärenz und Konvergenz beim europäischen Individualrechtsschutz", *NJW* 2002 pp. 3577, 3579; *C. Calliess and M. Lais*, "Anmerkung zu EuGH, Öffnung des europäischen Zugangs zum Gericht für Einzelne und (Umwelt-)Verbände", *ZUR* 2002, p. 344; *W. Cremer*, "Individualrechtsschutz gegen Rechtsakte der Gemeinschaft: Grundlagen und neuere Entwicklungen", in *C. Nowak and W. Cremer* (eds.), *Individualrechtsschutz in der EG und der WTO*, Nomos 2002,

direct and individual concern to them". It relates to the legal term of "individual" instead of "exclusive". The meaning of "individual", therefore, has to be judicially interpreted, and, theoretically, can also be understood less strictly.[57] Indeed, the *Plaumann* judges interpreted "individual" and formulated the requirement of exclusivity. The context of this interpretation is investigated in the following subsection.

3.2. CHANGED CONTEXTS OF JURISPRUDENCE

The *Plaumann* judgment's historical context must necessarily be taken into account when examining the requirement of "individual concern" and its current interpretation.[58]

3.2.1. The Plaumann *Case Itself*

Regarding the *Plaumann* case itself, it turns out that the doctrine's aim was to limit the judicial enforcement of individual economic interests. The Federal Republic of Germany applied for authorisation to set its own customs tariff for clementines. The Commission refused this authorisation, and the *Plaumann* company, an importer of clementines, appealed against this refusal.[59]

Within the procedure, an essential question was whether a company can take action against a decision of the Commission.[60] According to Article 173(2) TEEC, a predecessor provision to Article 263(4) TFEU, "any natural or legal person may ... institute proceedings against a decision ... which, although in the form of ... a decision addressed to another person, is of direct and individual concern to the former". As already mentioned, the ECJ stated that persons in these cases are individually concerned only if a decision "affects them by reason of certain attributes which are peculiar to them or by reason of circumstances in which they are differentiated from all other persons and by virtue of these factors distinguishes them individually just as in the case of the person addressed".[61]

The ECJ found the claim to be inadmissible, and dismissed it due to a lack of standing, because the commercial activity of the appellants could also be carried

pp. 27–45, p. 40; *M. Nettesheim*, "Effektive Rechtsschutzgewährleistung im arbeitsteiligen System europäischen Rechtsschutzes", *JZ* 2002 p. 928, p. 932; *Winter*, "Not fit for purpose" (supra, note 22), pp. 394–96.

57 Cf. GFCC Climate protection order: Case 1 BvR 2656/18 [2021] ECLI:DE:BVerfG:2021:rs20210324.1bvr265618, para. 110.

58 Cf. *U. Haltern, Europarecht: Dogmatik im Kontext (1)*, 3rd ed., Mohr Siebeck 2017, paras. 8 *et seq.*, 20 *et seq.*

59 ECJ Judgment: Case 25/62, *Plaumann v. Commission of the EEC* [1963] ECLI:EU:C:1963:17, Reports of Cases 1963, 199, p. 97.

60 Ibid., p. 98 *et seq.*

61 Ibid., p. 107.

out by anyone else. Since then, "individual concern" has been understood as "exclusive concern".[62]

The *Plaumann* judgment was a decision in the context of a bilateral relationship between the Commission and the *Plaumann* company, which had only a limited scope of application, as it dealt only with customs tariffs on clementines. The *People's Climate Case*'s range is a lot broader, as the applicants respectively appellants are attacking three main legal climate protection Acts. One could, therefore, argue that if the legal Act is even broader (such as the Union's climate targets), and its consequences affect even more people (climate change), individuality cannot be assumed *a fortiori*.

On the other hand, however, it is clear that the ECJ's aim, in 1963, was to avoid a flood of lawsuits in cases relatively insignificant to the public, and concerning only individual issues with European competition, or the mere fact of being affected as an economic operator.[63] In climate cases, however, the scope of the decision is far greater, and affects every EU citizen in some way. The interest at issue has a significant public dimension.[64]

The *Plaumann* criterion was developed for a purely economic context that is fundamentally different from the overarching environmental and climate contexts of the *People's Climate Case*.[65] In order to do justice to these interests, an interpretation in the sense of the *Plaumann* doctrine is insufficient.[66] In addition, a wider interpretation of "individual concern" would do justice to the significantly stronger anchoring of environmental and climate protection in European primary law today, compared with 1963.[67]

3.2.2. *The* Plaumann *Case in Light of the* Van Gend & Loos, Costa/ENEL *and* Leberpfennig *Cases*

The *Plaumann* judgment was one of several groundbreaking ECJ decisions during the 1960s.[68] During the same period, the judgments in *Van Gend &*

62 Cf. also *M. Pechstein*, *Entscheidungen des EuGH*, utb 11th ed., 2020, pp. 335–36.

63 *Ruffert* (supra, note 22), p. 191 See also below (section 3.2.2.).

64 *Jans and Vedder* (supra, note 51), p. 241.

65 Similarly, see ibid., pp. 239–41.

66 See ECJ Order: Case T-585/93, *Greenpeace and Others v. Commission* [1995] ECLI:EU:T:1995:147, paras. 32 *et seq.*; cf. also *N. Gérard*, "Access to the European Court of Justice: A Lost Opportunity", *Journal of Environmental Law* 1998 (10), p. 331, pp. 340–41; *D.L. Torrens*, "Locus Standi for Environmental Associations under EC Law – *Greenpeace* – A Missed Opportunity for the ECJ", *RECIEL* 1999 (8), p. 336, pp. 339–40; *Winter*, "Not fit for purpose" (supra, note 22), p. 373.

67 *Krämer*, "Access to Environmental Justice" (supra, note 30), pp. 182–85. For an overview of the current anchoring of environmental and climate protection in primary law, see *H. Vedder*, "The Treaty of Lisbon and European Environmental Law and Policy", *Journal of Environmental Law* 2010 (22), p. 285, pp. 287–95.

68 Cf. overview in *Pechstein* (supra, note 62).

Loos[69] and *Costa/ENEL*[70] dealt with the validity and applicability of European law in the Member States. In *Van Gend & Loos*, the judges found that treaties not only bind Member States, but also have an effect on national law, to the extent that primary law can create subjective public rights at a national level.[71] It led to a particular increase in the intensity of validity and applicability of European law.[72] In *Costa/ENEL*, the judges declared European law to be an autonomous legal order that takes precedence over national law. Consequently, later Member State law may not undermine European legal rights and obligations.[73] In the *Leberpfennig* judgment,[74] the ECJ, for the first time, recognised the direct effect of European secondary law: due to the *effet utile*, Member States could no longer invoke their defaults of non-implementation.[75]

Regarding these 1960s judgments, the main objective of European jurisprudence during this time becomes clear: in the first ten to fifteen years of European jurisprudence, European law was outlined and given more force. There was a high need for acceptance of European law by the Member States. If, during these times, individuals had been able to bring actions against legal Acts of the European Communities, it would have weakened the system as a whole.[76]

Today, this problem no longer exists, as EU law is accepted as an independent order of law.[77] In general, courts follow case law of the ECJ, and question the primacy of EU law's application only in individual cases *(ultra vires)*.[78] Therefore, the strict understanding of individuality as exclusivity is out of date.

3.2.3. *Judicial Adaptions of the* Plaumann *Doctrine*

The ECJ itself eventually determined the *Plaumann* doctrine to be too narrow, and therefore started extending its scope from the 1970s onwards: examples of

69 ECJ Judgment: Case 26/62, *Van Gend en Loos v. Administratie der Belastingen* [1963] ECLI:EU:C:1963:1, Reports of Cases 1963, 3.

70 ECJ Judgment: Case 6/64, *Costa v. ENEL* [1964] ECLI:EU:C:1964:66, Reports of Cases 1964, 1141.

71 ECJ Judgment: Case 26/62, *Van Gend en Loos v. Administratie der Belastingen* [1963] ECLI:EU:C:1963:1, Reports of Cases 1963, 3, p. 12; Cf. *Wegener*, *"Rechte des Einzelnen"* (supra, note 22), pp. 60–64.

72 *Pechstein* (supra, note 62), p. 97.

73 Cf., ibid, p. 1; ECJ Judgment: Case 6/64, *Costa v. ENEL* [1964] ECLI:EU:C:1964:66, Reports of Cases 1964, 1141, p. 594.

74 ECJ Judgment: Case 9/70, *Grad v. Finanzamt Traunstein* [1970] ECLI:EU:C:1970:78, Reports of Cases 1970, 825.

75 Ibid., at pp. 536 *et seq.*; cf. *Pechstein* (supra, note 62), pp. 143–44.

76 Cf. *Borowski* (supra, note 21), p. 893; *Nettesheim* (supra, note 56), p. 929; *Wegener*, *"Rechte des Einzelnen"* (supra, note 22), p. 159.

77 *Borowski* (supra, note 21), p. 893.

78 Cf. *G. Nicolaysen*, "Rechtsgemeinschaft, Gemeinschaftsgerichtsbarkeit und Individuum", *in C. Nowak and W. Cremer* (eds.), *Individualrechtsschutz in der EG und der WTO*, Nomos 2002, pp. 17–25, p. 20.

assumed "individual concern" include involvement in a previous administrative procedure,[79] and the significant impairment of a competitive position.[80] Two judgments from the 1990s[81] suggest that the ECJ even considered possible impairments of fundamental rights to be sufficient for standing to sue.[82]

However, the expectations raised were disappointed in the end: in the long term, European case law did not move away from the *Plaumann* doctrine.[83]

3.2.4. Interim Conclusion

Ultimately, it turns out that the good reasons for a narrow understanding of individuality in 1963 no longer hold today.

First, the *Plaumann* decision concerned a bilateral relationship of limited consequence for other individuals, whereas today it is common sense that consequences of climate change are going to have an impact on every individual, and thus have a broad range. As a result, judges should make a distinction between interests concerning the environment or climate protection, on the one hand, and economic interests, on the other.

Thus, within its historical context, the *Plaumann* doctrine was one component of a judicial strategy that aimed at establishing and strengthening European law. This is no longer necessary, because EU law is recognised as a legal order, and as taking precedence over national law in its application. Therefore, a strict understanding of "individual concern" is outdated. This will be underlined in the section 4 below.

Finally, wider interpretations of "individual concern" are legally possible, and have even been formulated by the ECJ itself.

---

79 E.g. ECJ Judgment: Case 169/84, *Cofaz v. Commission* [1986] ECLI:EU:C:1990:301, paras 23 *et seq*. For further references see *Cremer*, "Art. 263 AEUV" (supra, note 19), para. 41.

80 E.g. ECJ Judgment: Case 264/82, *Timex v. Council and Commission* [1985] ECLI:EU:C:1985:119, paras. 12 *et seq*. For further references, see *Cremer*, "Art. 263 AEUV" (supra, note 19), para. 44; *M.-P. Granger*, "Towards a liberalisation of standing conditions for individuals seeking judicial review of Community acts: *Jégo-Quéré et Cie SA v. Commission and Unión de Pequeños Agricultores v. Council*", *The Modern Law Review* 2003 (66), p. 124, pp. 126–27. See also, with specific criticism of the facilitation in favour of purely economic interests, *Krämer*, "Access to Environmental Justice" (supra, note 30), p. 175.

81 Joint inspection of ECJ Judgment: Case C-309/89, *Codorníu v. Council* [1994] ECLI:EU:C:1994:197, paras. 21 *et seq*.; ECJ Judgment: Case C-306/93, *SMW Winzersekt v. Land Rheinland-Pfalz* [1994] ECLI:EU:C:1994:407, paras. 24. Cf. also *Winter*, "Not fit for purpose" (supra, note 22), pp. 374–76.

82 Cf. *Cremer*, "Art. 263 AEUV" (supra, note 19), para. 45; *C. Nowak*, "Zentraler und dezentraler Individualrechtsschutz in der EG im Lichte des gemeinschaftlichen Rechtsgrundsatzes effektiven Rechtsschutzes", in *C. Nowak and W. Cremer* (eds.), *Individualrechtsschutz in der EG und der WTO*, Nomos 2002, pp. 47–79, pp. 55–57.

83 *C. Nowak*, "Zentraler und dezentraler Individualrechtsschutz in der EG im Lichte des gemeinschaftlichen Rechtsgrundsatzes effektiven Rechtsschutzes", in *C. Nowak and W. Cremer* (eds.), *Individualrechtsschutz in der EG und der WTO*, Nomos 2002, pp. 47–79, pp. 56–57.

3.3. EFFECTIVE LEGAL PROTECTION

In order to ensure effective legal protection, to which the EU is committed under Article 47 of the Charter of Fundamental Rights of the European Union (EUCFR),[84] the appellants in the *People's Climate Case* demand to be guaranteed access to a court proceeding.[85]

While some see effective legal protection in the interplay of European and Member State legal remedies as being safeguarded,[86] others see severe conflicts with Article 47 EUCFR, due to the narrow understanding of "individual concern".[87] This is particularly convincing when, as is the case in the *People's Climate Case*, a European legal Act and not Member State implementation Acts are the subject of the action: other proceedings under European law (such as the preliminary ruling, in the sense of Article 267 TFEU) are not applicable,[88] and alternative national judicial proceedings would not offer effective legal protection against European law.[89]

3.3.1. *Near-End of the* Plaumann *Doctrine after Declaration of the EUCFR*

After the EUCFR was declared, in 2000, a legal momentum arose that almost led to the abandonment of the *Plaumann* doctrine.

In *Jégo-Quéré v. Commission*, in 2002, the General Court deviated from the *Plaumann* doctrine, for reasons of effective legal protection:[90] in the absence of a legal remedy in the Member State, the Court acknowledged the obligation to guarantee an effective legal remedy, according to Article 47 EUCFR, before a

84 "Everyone whose rights and freedoms guaranteed by the law of the Union are violated has the right to an effective remedy before a tribunal": Art. 47 EUCFR.

85 ECJ Judgment: Case C-565/19, *Carvalho and Others v. Parliament and Council* [2021] ECLI:EU:C:2021:252, paras. 59 *et seq.*

86 *Nowak* (supra, note 83), pp. 78–79; *S. Lenz and S. Staeglich*, "Kein Rechtsschutz gegen EG-Verordnungen? – Europäische Rechtsschutzdefizite und ihr Ausgleich durch die Feststellungsklage nach §43 I VwGO", *NVwZ* 2004, p. 1421, pp. 1423–24.

87 (supra note 10) p. 259, p. 267; *W. Frenz and A.-M. Distelrath*, "Klagegegenstand und Klagebefugnis von Individualnichtigkeitsklagen nach Art. 263 IV AEUV", *NVwZ* 2010, p. 162, pp. 163; *Calliess* (supra, note 56), pp. 3580–81.

88 See the appellants' argumentation in ECJ Judgment: Case C-565/19, *Carvalho and Others v. Parliament and Council* [2021] ECLI:EU:C:2021:252, para. 60; *L. Krämer*, "Climate Change, Human Rights and Access to Justice", *JEEPL* 2019 (16), pp. 21, 31. On the unpromising preliminary ruling procedure in environmental matters in general, see *L. Krämer*, "Public Interest Litigation in Environmental Matters before European Courts", *Journal of Environmental Law* 1996 (8), pp. 1, 7.

89 See the appellants' argumentation in ECJ Judgment: Case C-565/19, *Carvalho and Others v. Parliament and Council* [2021] ECLI:EU:C:2021:252, paras. 59 *et seq.*; cf. *Granger* (supra, note 80), p. 131; *Winter*, "Not fit for purpose" (supra, note 22), pp. 377.

90 General Court Judgment: Case T-177/01, *Jégo-Quéré v. Commission* [2002] ECLI:EU:T:2002:112, paras. 47 *et seq.* Cf. *Cremer*, "Art. 263 AEUV" (supra, note 19), para. 50.

European court.[91] Therefore, the General Court not only adapted the *Plaumann* doctrine, but explicitly refrained from applying it: the Court did not require exclusive concern, but merely a concern in relation to a legal position that was not just a simple interest.[92]

In *Unión de Pequeños Agricultores v. Council*, also in 2002, Advocate General Jacobs argued in the same direction, opting for the reform of the right of action in order to guarantee legal protection if legal proceedings cannot be initiated in the Member States. To ensure the same legal protection within the Member States, which shall not be dependent on the structuring of legal proceedings in the Member States,[93] he opted for a new definition of "individual concern". In contrast to the General Court, he did not propose the assertion of a violation of rights, but of a measure, that has "substantial adverse effect on his interests".[94]

The argumentations of Advocate General Jacobs, as well as those of the General Court, are convincing, especially since the EUCFR entered into force as EU primary law in 2009. European courts are supposed to be the ones reviewing legal Acts of the Union with regard to their compatibility with European primary law.[95] Legal protection against EU legal Acts is the responsibility of the EU.[96] Furthermore, accepting complex detours via other procedures, for example preliminary ruling procedures, is not reasonable.[97]

3.3.2. *The ECJ Sticks to* Plaumann

Despite the above, the ECJ did not agree at the time, but required an amendment to the text of the TFEU, for a corresponding change in jurisprudence.[98] It did not even consider the arguments of Advocate General Jacobs or the General Court in its decision;[99] instead, it placed the responsibility for ensuring effective legal

---

91 General Court Judgment: Case T-177/01, *Jégo-Quéré v. Commission* [2002] ECLI:EU:T:2002:112, paras. 44 *et seq.*; cf. *Granger* (supra, note 80), pp. 130–31; *Calliess and Lais* (supra, note 56), p. 346.

92 General Court Judgment: Case T-177/01, *Jégo-Quéré v. Commission* [2002] ECLI:EU:T:2002:112, para. 51; cf. *Granger* (supra, note 80), pp. 132–33.

93 Opinion of Advocate General F.G. Jacobs in Case C-50/00 P, *Unión de Pequeños Agricultores v. Council* [2002] ECLI:EU:C:2002:197, paras. 50 *et seq.*

94 Ibid., at para. 60; cf. *Braun and Kettner* (supra, note 32), p. 61; *Granger* (supra, note 80), pp. 133–34.

95 Cf. Opinion of Advocate General F.G. Jacobs in Case C-50/00 P, *Unión de Pequeños Agricultores v. Council* [2002] ECLI:EU:C:2002:197, para. 49.

96 *Calliess* (supra, note 56), p. 3580; *Nettesheim* (supra, note 56), p. 934.

97 Opinion of Advocate General F.G. Jacobs in Case C-50/00 P, *Unión de Pequeños Agricultores v. Council* [2002] ECLI:EU:C:2002:197, paras. 54 *et seq.*

98 ECJ Judgment: Case C-50/00 P, *Unión de Pequeños Agricultores v. Council* [2002], ECLI:EU:C:2002:462, paras. 36 *et seq.*

99 *B. Lindner*, "Zur Klagebefugnis natürlicher und juristischer Personen für Nichtigkeitsklagen gem. Art. 230 IV EG gegen EG-Verordnungen", *NVwZ* 2003, pp. 569, 571; *Braun and Kettner* (supra, note 29), p. 64.

protection on the Member States.[100] Since the declaration and entry into force of Article 47 EUCFR, the ECJ has, ultimately, failed to adapt its case law.[101]

Neither did the ECJ change its jurisprudence in the *People's Climate Case*: the judges referred to the fact that Article 47 EUCFR does not guarantee a right of unlimited access to courts,[102] and that an interpretation other than that of the *Plaumann* doctrine would be contrary to the wording of primary law.[103] In this respect, there was hardly any discussion of the arguments presented or discussed by academics.

3.3.3. *Interim Conclusion*

After the declaration of the EUCFR, fundamental rights obtained a higher significance on the European level, which led to judicial developments that could have culminated in the abandonment of the *Plaumann* doctrine. The General Court, as well as an Advocate General, took the stance that the understanding of "individual concern" needed to be adapted, to uphold the right to an effective remedy in the sense of Article 47 EUCFR. Nevertheless, the ECJ stuck to its *Plaumann* doctrine, and did not even take into account the well-justified arguments in favour of its abandonment. In the context of the *People's Climate Case*, the ECJ continued this practice.

This is regrettable, especially since consequences of climate change could have a significant existential impact on the fundamental rights of those affected, and, ultimately, every applicant and appellant depends more on effective legal protection the higher the stakes are for him or her.[104]

3.4. CONSTITUTIONAL TRADITIONS OF THE MEMBER STATES

Additionally, the appellants in the *People's Climate Case* considered the criterion of exclusive concern not to be presupposed by the legal systems of the Member States, either in the context of administrative law actions, or in constitutional law actions.[105] However, according to Article 6(3) TEU,

---

100 ECJ Judgment: Case C-50/00 P, *Unión de Pequeños Agricultores v. Council* [2002] ECLI:EU:C:2002:462, paras. 41 *et seq.*; cf. *Nettesheim* (supra, note 56), p. 932.

101 *Krämer* "Access to Environmental Justice" (supra, note 30), p. 179.

102 ECJ Judgment: Case C-565/19, *Carvalho and Others v. Parliament and Council* [2021] ECLI:EU:C:2021:252, para. 77.

103 Ibid., para. 78.

104 *Borowski* (supra, note 21), p. 907.

105 ECJ Judgment: Case C-565/19, *Carvalho and Others v. Parliament and Council* [2021] ECLI:EU:C:2021:252, para. 55.

"constitutional traditions common to the Member States shall constitute general principles of the Union's law", meaning that the constitutional law of the Member States is supposed to be a source of legal information for the European courts.[106]

As already shown, an action for annulment by non-privileged applicants merely requires any individual interest to be concerned, not necessarily a legal position. Thus, it distinguishes itself from objective legal control (cf. the French *intérêt à agir*),[107] on the one hand,[108] and from the infringement action, which requires the infringement of a legal position, in the sense of the German judicial system, on the other.[109] The German right of action, as an outer limit of legal design, does not require exclusivity, which is why it seems to be contradictory that the European legislator would require mandatory exclusivity,[110] especially because an action for annulment not only aims at the protection of individual rights, but also at preserving higher-ranking law, and, therefore, should have lower barriers for judicial control.[111]

Moreover, no Member State of the EU requires exclusivity in this context: the requirement at the EU level thus has no connection to a constitutional principle in any of the Member States.[112]

106 ECJ Judgment: Case C-11/70, *Internationale Handelsgesellschaft mbH v. Vorratsstelle für Getreide- und Futtermittel* [1970] ECLI:EU:C:1970:114, para. 4. See also *E. Pache*, "Art. 6 GRCh", in *M. Pechstein, C. Nowak and U. Häde* (eds.), *Frankfurter Kommentar zu EUV, GRC und AEUV*, Mohr Siebeck 2017, para. 45.

107 On the French *"intérêt à agir"*, in comparison with "individual concern" within the meaning of Art. 230(4) TFEU old version, see *R. Colavitti*, "L'accès au juge en matière d'environnement, La délicate question de l'intérêt à agir" in *O. Lecucq and S. Maljean-Dubois* (eds.), *Le rôle du juge dans le développement du droit de l'environnement*, Bruylant 2008, pp. 45–59, pp. 45–53; see also *J.-M. Woehrling*, "Rechtsschutz im Umweltrecht in Frankreich", *NVwZ* 1999 pp. 502, 503; *J.-M. Woehrling*, "Die deutsche und die französische Verwaltungsgerichtsbarkeit an der Schwelle zum 21. Jahrhundert", *NVwZ* 1998, p. 462, pp. 463–64.

108 Cf. *J.C. Moitinho de Almeida*, "Le recours en annulation des particuliers (article 173, deuxième alinéa, du traité CE): nouvelles réflexions sur l'expression 'la concernent … individuellement'", in *O. Due, M. Lutter and J. Schwarze* (eds.), *Festschrift für Ulrich Everling (1)*, 1995, pp. 849–874, pp. 849–50; *L.-J. Constantinesco, Die unmittelbare Anwendbarkeit von Gemeinschaftsnormen und der Rechtsschutz von Einzelpersonen im Recht der EWG*, 1969, pp. 32–33.

109 ECJ Judgment: Case 169/84, *Cofaz v. Commission* [1986] ECLI:EU:C:1990:301, paras. 21 *et seq.*, with further references, commented on by *G. Nicolaysen*, "Ein neuer Weg der Konkurrentenklage", *EuR* 1986, pp. 261, 264.

110 *T. von Danwitz*, "Die Garantie effektiven Rechtsschutzes im Recht der Europäischen Gemeinschaft", *NJW* 1993, pp. 1108, 1115; cf. also *C.H. Ule, Empfiehlt es sich, die Bestimmungen des europäischen Gemeinschaftsrechts über den Rechtsschutz zu ändern und zu ergänzen? (1)*, Gutachten 46. dt. Juristentag 1966, pp. 21–22.

111 *Borowski* (supra, note 21), p. 880.

112 Cf. *M. Eliantonio et al.*, *A Comparative study on Legal Standing* (Locus Standi) *before the EU and Member States' Courts*, Intersentia 2012, pp. 74–81; *Winter*, "*Armando Carvalho and Others v. EU*: Invoking Human Rights and the Paris Agreement for Better Climate Protection Legislation" (supra, note 11), p. 157; e.g. France, cf. *Colavitti* (supra, note 107), p. 52.

3.5. AVOIDING INCOHERENCE

The appellants in the *People's Climate Case* argued that it would be incoherent to generally exclude the possibility of legal action for individuals,[113] because at the time of the *Plaumann* decision, Article 173 TEEC only granted remedies against decisions and regulations,[114] whereas nowadays a person can obtain legal protection against all legal Acts and measures, as per Article 263 TFEU.[115] This is convincing, especially as legal Acts, by their very nature, affect a large group of people. It would be paradoxical if the fact that a legal Act adversely affected a large number of individuals, causing widespread rather than limited harm, precluded the appellants' standing to bring an action.[116] In addition, the participation in an administrative procedure cannot be the only possible constellation of clear individual and direct concern, especially since it is not even provided for in all areas of EU law.[117]

Besides, there are even further dynamics concerning legal standing in European case law that contradict each other, and are ultimately incoherent.

On the one hand, the ECJ, especially in environmental law, is known for setting low requirements for the existence of subjective rights in European secondary law, and thus burdening Member State courts with providing effective legal protection.[118] According to the ECJ, subjective rights already exist if general interests entail a favour for individuals; a specifically individual-protecting function is not required.[119] In this way, the ECJ strengthens legal protection before Member State courts.

On the other hand, as already pointed out, high standards regarding "individual concern" are required in cases of action for annulment that are decided by the ECJ itself. This case law is somewhat contradictory: while the ECJ establishes broad rights of action at Member State level,[120] it severely restricts

---

113 ECJ Judgment: Case C-565/19, *Carvalho and Others v. Parliament and Council* [2021] ECLI:EU:C:2021:252, paras. 57 *et seq.*

114 Critised by *Constantinesco* (supra, note 108), pp. 33–34.

115 *Frenz and Distelrath* (supra, note 87), pp. 162.

116 See the appellants' argumentation in ECJ Judgment: Case C-565/19, *Carvalho and Others v. Parliament and Council* [2021] ECLI:EU:C:2021:252, para. 56; Opinion of Advocate General F.G. Jacobs in Case C-50/00 P, *Unión de Pequeños Agricultores v. Council* [2002] ECLI:EU:C:2002:197, para. 59. Cf. *Jans and Vedder* (supra, note 51), p. 241; *L. Allkemper*, *Der Rechtsschutz des einzelnen nach dem EG-Vertrag*, Nomos 1995, p. 87.

117 *Cremer*, "Individualrechtsschutz gegen Rechtsakte der Gemeinschaft: Grundlagen und neuere Entwicklungen" (supra, note 56), p. 45.

118 Cf. *Wegener*, *"Rechte des Einzelnen"* (supra, note 22), pp. 46–55.

119 Cf. ECJ Judgment: Case C-237/07, *Janecek* [2008] ECLI:EU:C:2008:447, para. 42; *C. Marxsen*, "Der subjektive Rechtsschutz nach klassischem Konzept und Tendenzen seiner Objektivierung", *Die Verwaltung* 2020 (53), pp. 215, 228; *Lenz and Staeglich* (supra, note 86), p. 1427; *J. Krüper*, *Gemeinwohl im Prozess*, Duncker & Humblodt 2009, p. 330.

120 Cf. *S. Schlacke*, "Zur fortschreitenden Europäisierung des (Umwelt-)Rechtsschutzes", *NVwZ*, 2014, p. 11, pp. 11–18; *F. Kirchhof*, "Der Richter als Kontrolleur, Akteur und Garant der Rechtsordnung", *NJW*, 2020, pp. 1492, 1495.

rights of action against Union legal Acts.[121] It thus demands far more from the Member State courts than it demands from itself, and consequently handles individual rights of action incoherently.[122]

3.6. AVOIDING RAMPANT EXPANSIONS OF THE RIGHT OF ACTION

Finally, the abandonment of the *Plaumann* doctrine could prevent a rampant expansion of the right of action and ensure effective legal protection.[123] This is underlined by the fact that the fear of a flood of lawsuits seems to be exaggerated, especially since strict requirements (direct concern and time limits) continue to exist,[124] and further, more legal protection-friendly, requirements could be created.[125]

3.7. INTERIM CONCLUSION

Ultimately, the case for abandoning the *Plaumann* doctrine is convincing for various reasons:

(1) First, the wording of Article 263(4) TFEU does not mandatorily require an exclusive concern, but allows a different interpretation. Judicial adaptations are possible, which European courts have themselves shown.
(2) Regarding the context in which the *Plaumann* doctrine was developed, this narrow understanding of "individual concern" is now outdated. Furthermore, its formulation was aimed at regulating a bilateral and pure economic case that is not comparable to the broad challenges faced due to the consequences of climate change.
(3) As legal protection cannot be obtained at national level, and consequences of climate change are able to cause widespread impairments of fundamental rights, due to non-compliance with legal obligations of the Paris Agreement, Article 47 EUCFR demands legal protection against European Acts at EU

121 See also *Calliess and Lais* (supra, note 56), pp. 346–47; *Calliess* (supra, note 56), p. 3579; *Eliantonio et al.* (supra, note 112), p. 25; *Frenz and Distelrath* (supra, note 87), p. 164.
122 *Frenz and Distelrath* (supra, note 87), p. 164; *Danwitz* (supra, note 110), p. 1114; *Jans and Vedder* (supra, note 51), p. 243.
123 Cf. the appellants' argumentation in ECJ Judgment: Case C-565/19, *Carvalho and Others v. Parliament and Council* [2021] ECLI:EU:C:2021:252, paras. 63 *et seq.*
124 *Lindner* (supra, note 99), p. 571; *Calliess* (supra, note 56), p. 3581; *Borowski* (supra, note 21), p. 903; *Gérard* (supra, note 66), p. 344.
125 See above (propositions of the General Court and of Advocate General Jacobs in 2002, in section 3.3.1); cf. *Granger* (supra, note 80), pp. 134–35.

level. Therefore, "individual concern" must be interpreted in a broader way, to justify standing, and thereby grant access to justice.

(4) Constitutional traditions of the Member States, which ought to be considered by European judges, as per Article 6(3) TEU, outline a broader understanding of "individual concern", since no national constitution demands exclusive concern, in order to establish a right of action.

(5) Besides, it would be systematically incoherent to limit the right of action to those exclusively concerned, as Article 263 TFEU opens the way for actions for annulment of European legal Acts: directives and regulations, by their very nature, address numerous individuals. Furthermore, the ECJ has strengthened legal protection on a Member State level by easing the requirements for standing, during recent years. By adhering to the strict requirements for standing before the ECJ, it fails to meet its own standards.[126]

(6) Finally, floods of lawsuits, in the event of a relaxation of the "individual concern"-requirement, seem unlikely, since strict preconditions continue to exist. Additionally, in no case is there an argument for abandoning the legal concept of "individual concern"; rather, there is an argument for a different understanding.

4. ADAPTING THE INTERPRETATION OF "INDIVIDUAL CONCERN" AT EU LEVEL

The *Plaumann* doctrine should, therefore, be abandoned, and a new interpretation of "individual concern" should be established.

4.1. FUNDAMENTAL RIGHTS-ORIENTED INTERPRETATION (GFCC)

In relation to the interpretation of "individual concern", the appellants in the *People's Climate Case* propose to assert a possibly significant encroachment of European fundamental rights, which runs the risk of affecting fundamental rights in their essence.[127] A similar legal concept, of interpreting "individual concern" in a different manner from "exclusive concern", could be found in the GFCC's interpretation of "individual concern" in the context of possible fundamental rights infringements. As already mentioned, the GFCC rules out

---

126 Cf. also *Krämer* (supra, note 30), "Access to Environmental Justice", p. 185; *Jans and Vedder* (supra, note 51), p. 243.

127 ECJ Judgment: Case C-565/19, *Carvalho and Others v. Parliament and Council* [2021] ECLI:EU:C:2021:252, paras. 63 *et seq.*

an *actio popularis* by requiring a "direct, individual and present concern" in relation to fundamental rights. The GFCC explicitly declares that individuality is not excluded by a lack of exclusivity.[128]

The GFCC already has a reputation for setting the pace within the EU,[129] which could be useful in this context. Furthermore, judges of the General Court, in the *Jégo-Quéré v. Commission* case, who did not require exclusive concern, but instead a concern in a legal position that is not just a simple interest,[130] already approximated the GFCC's standpoint. In addition, several academics, Advocate General Jacobs in particular, have proved that other forms of "individual concern" are not only conceivable options within the EU legal system, but also overdue, to uphold Article 47 EUCFR.[131]

The action of annulment in the sense of Article 263(4) TFEU is, as has already been pointed out, a partial equivalent to a constitutional complaint.[132] In conjunction with the fact that the European legislator has supplemented European primary law by means of fundamental rights laid down in the EUCFR, it seems evident that individuals should have an option to enforce their fundamental rights, especially with regard to Article 47 EUCFR.[133] Therefore, the GFCC's requirement of a possible infringement of fundamental rights that concern the complainant individually, but not in an exclusive sense, is a convincing approach to enabling the protection of fundamental rights without opening the doors to an *actio popularis*, and without disregarding separation of powers. The GFCC's way of handling the right of action can be transferred to Article 263(4) TFEU by way of a fundamental rights-oriented interpretation.

4.2. INTEREST-BASED INTERPRETATION

The fundamental rights-oriented interpretation is, ultimately, based on an interaction between the TFEU and the EUCFR. If it is assumed that the interpretation of "individual concern" must be limited to Article 263(4) TFEU,

---

128 Cf. GFCC Climate protection order: Case 1 BvR 2656/18 [2021] ECLI:DE:BVerfG:2021:rs20210324.1bvr265618, para. 110.

129 *T. Ellerbrok and R. Pracht*, "Das Bundesverfassungsgericht als Taktgeber im horizontalen Verfassungsgerichtsverbund", *EuR* 2021, p. 188; *A. Dyevre*, "Domestic Judicial Defiance in the European Union: A Systemic Threat to the Authority of EU Law?", *Yearbook of European Law* 2016 (35), pp. 106, 127.

130 However, the ECJ did not agree at the time, but required an amendment to the text of the treaty for a corresponding change in jurisprudence, cf. ECJ Judgment: Case C-50/00 P, *Unión de Pequeños Agricultores v. Council* [2002], ECLI:EU:C:2002:462, paras. 36 *et seq.*

131 See sections 3.3.1. and 3.7. above.

132 See section 1.3. above.

133 Cf. *Krämer*, "Climate Change, Human Rights and Access to Justice" (supra, note 91), pp. 32–34; *Kelleher* (supra, note 1), p. 130. See also Art. 263(2) TFEU, *Winter*, "Not fit for purpose" (supra, note 22), p. 387.

there are no explicit references to fundamental rights in its wording.[134] However, notwithstanding the above, it has been shown that the designation "individual" does not mandatorily need to be interpreted as "exclusive". This interpretation is outdated, and is not fit to deal with environmental and climate issues. Furthermore, Article 47 EUCFR commands a less severe interpretation.[135]

Another option, other than a fundamental rights-oriented interpretation, could be to retain the model of "individual concern" in a matter of interest, but to phase out the understanding of individuality as exclusivity. Instead, it could include a certain level of intervention, which could be specified by further case law.[136] Within the framework of this potential case law, the principle of separation of powers must, of course, be upheld.

4.3. SAFEGUARDING THE SEPARATION OF POWERS

Against all the doubts that are harboured regarding successful climate lawsuits, it is important to not forget that, in the context of separation of powers,[137] in addition to the legislative and executive branches, the judiciary also has a responsibility to mitigate the consequences of climate change in a way that preserves fundamental rights, and to mediate between different interests.[138] This becomes clear in so far as the interests of children and the unborn can only be represented to a limited extent in the actual parliamentary process, as they cannot express themselves.[139] This, moreover, distinguishes them from "living" minorities, who can be represented by Members of Parliament who do not belong to their group. Judicial control of this lack of representation within legislative bodies is, therefore, necessary.[140] This judicial control must be limited

---

134 ECJ Judgment: Case C-50/00 P, *Unión de Pequeños Agricultores v. Council* [2002] ECLI:EU:C:2002:462, paras. 41 *et seq.*; ECJ Judgment: Case C-565/19, *Carvalho and Others v. Parliament and Council* [2021] ECLI:EU:C:2021:252, paras. 78.

135 See section 3.3. above.

136 Cf. *Borowski* (supra, note 21), p. 907. See also Opinion of Advocate General F.G. Jacobs in Case C-50/00 P, *Unión de Pequeños Agricultores v. Council* [2002] ECLI:EU:C:2002:197, para. 60. See, in detail, *Winter*, "Not fit for purpose" (supra, note 22), pp. 388–91.

137 In contrast to other opinions, *B.W. Wegener*, "*Urgenda* – Weltrettung per Gerichtsbeschluss?", *ZUR* 2019, p. 3, pp. 10–13; *L. Friedrich*, "Gemeinwohl vor Gericht: Chancen und Risiken öffentlich-rechtlicher 'Public Interest Litigation'", *DÖV*, 2021, p. 726, pp. 731–33; Winter, on the other hand, points out that the separation of powers at the EU level is far more complex than at the national level, and its theorem, therefore, cannot be applied directly: cf. *Winter*, "Not fit for purpose" (supra, note 22), p. 382.

138 *Krämer* (supra, note 30), p. 183; *Preston*, "The Influence of the Paris Agreement on Climate Litigation" (supra, note 8), p. 15.

139 *F. Ekardt*, *Sustainability*, 2020, pp. 186–88, 199–202; *M. Niehaus*, "Gerichte gegen Gesetzgeber? – Der Klimawandel in den Gerichtssälen", in *B. Huggins et al.* (eds.), *Zugang zu Recht*, Nomos 2021, pp. 241–260, p. 249.

140 *Ekardt* (supra, note 139), pp. 186–88, 199–202; cf. also *Kelleher* (supra, note 1), p. 108.

to a review of the relevant legal Acts, without dictating the concrete measures that are to be taken by the legislator.[141]

In this way, case law can contribute significantly to developing the law, and is thus essential for adapting the legal system to the challenges of climate change.[142]

4.4. ADDED VALUE OF ABANDONING *PLAUMANN*

The benefit of a fundamental rights-oriented interpretation of "individual concern", or an extension of the interest-based interpretation, would be an undoubtedly effective legal protection under Article 47 EUCFR, and an adaption to actual contemporary challenges of case law that is currently stuck at the same level it was almost 60 years ago. In this manner, European courts would show self-reflection on the contexts of decisions that have prevailed until today, and demonstrate a constant willingness to question and improve the legal protection system without overturning its foundations and making it unstable. This might also increase general trust in the judicial system, as European courts would show that they are not arguing in a "that is how it has always been done" way.[143]

It is not a matter of turning the legal protection system on its head, but merely of expanding the understanding of "individual concern", and in this way adapting the legal system to actual challenges that are unique in the history of humankind.[144]

5. SUMMARY AND OUTLOOK

The *People's Climate Case* and the German constitutional complaints were both led by individuals whose fundamental rights were being, or in the near

---

141 *Ekardt* (supra, note 139), p. 188; *Niehaus* (supra, note 139), p. 251; see also GFCC Climate protection order: Case 1 BvR 2656/18 [2021] ECLI:DE:BVerfG:2021:rs20210324.1bvr265618, paras. 266 *et seq.*

142 *G.M. Colombo and L. Wegener*, *The Value of Climate Change-Impacted Litigation*, University of Strathclyde 2019, p. 7; cf. also *C. Franzius*, "Prävention durch Verwaltungsrecht: Klimaschutz", in VVDStRL (ed.), *Machtverschiebungen* (81), 2022, pp. 384–436, pp. 425–26; cf. *Preston*, "The Influence of the Paris Agreement on Climate Litigation" (supra, note 8), p. 14; *Preston*, "The Influence of the Paris Agreement on Climate Litigation (Part II)" (supra, note 1), p. 248. The *People's Climate Case* itself is also said to have helped raise the EU's climate targets, even though it was unsuccessful in court, see *Kelleher* (supra, note 1), p. 131.

143 In contrast to frustration among younger people, who feel they are not being heard in court, cf. *Krämer*, "Access to Environmental Justice" (supra, note 30), p. 183.

144 See also *Kelleher* (supra, note 1), p. 133; *Toussaint* (supra, note 1), p. 24; *C. Garofalo*, "The strategic role of courts in advancing climate policy", *JuWissBlog* no. 91/2020, 19/06/2020, (https://www.juwiss.de/91-2020/).

future would be, impaired by the consequences of climate change. Applicants and complainants sued their legislators, aiming to tighten up climate protection ambitions within the law. The GFCC assumed standing for reasons of "direct, individual and present concern", whereas the European Courts rejected standing, due to a lack of "individual concern" in the sense of the *Plaumann* doctrine. Consequently, only the GFCC judicially controlled climate protection law. European Courts, in sticking to the "exclusive" understanding of the *Plaumann* doctrine, missed this chance. The judges hardly dealt with criticism of the *Plaumann* doctrine. As long ago as the 1960s, academics demanded that being affected in relation to legally protected interests,[145] or a broadly understood directly injured interest,[146] should be sufficient to be regarded as individually affected, in the context of an action for annulment. The *Plaumann* doctrine has been criticised for almost 60 years, and criticism is not abating. Before the *People's Climate Case*, it experienced an upswing, after the ECJ did not follow Advocate General Jacobs in the *Unión de Pequeños Agricultores v. Council* judgment.[147] The appellants in the *People's Climate Case* picked those arguments up, and expressed them at the ECJ.

Finally, the abandonment of the *Plaumann* doctrine is politically and legally overdue. The context in which it was formulated was purely economic, and took place in a period where the European legal order was not as accepted in its primacy as it is today. Furthermore, the EUCFR was not yet in force, and today it demands effective legal protection, in the sense of its Article 47, that cannot be granted by court proceedings in the Member States where the subject matter of the action is pure EU secondary law. Besides, abandoning *Plaumann* is necessary to ensure a coherent judicial protection system that considers the constitutional traditions of the Member States, none of which require exclusive concern. Possible adaptions of the interpretation of "individual concern" are based on fundamental rights, or include a certain level of intervention that is to be concretised by means of case law. Rampant expansions of the right of action can thus be avoided, and the separation of powers safeguarded.

The pressure on the EU judiciary to change its jurisprudence is increasing,[148] and is not likely to abate in relation to future judgments dealing with the control of European (climate protection) legislation.

---

145 *Ule* (supra, note 110), pp. 20–21.

146 *Constantinesco* (supra, note 108), pp. 89–90.

147 See section 3.3. above. Cf. also *Granger* (supra, note 80), pp. 124–25, with further references.

148 *Bogojević*, "Human rights of minors and future generations" (supra, note 50), p. 200; *S. Bogojević*, "COVID-19, Climate Change Action and the Road to Green Recovery", *Journal of Environmental Law* 2020 (32), pp. 355, 358. Already made clear by Advocate General F.G. Jacobs' Opinion in Case C-50/00 P, *Unión de Pequeños Agricultores v. Council* [2002] ECLI:EU:C:2002:197, paras. 82 *et seq.*

Of course, it would be desirable for such court proceedings not to be necessary, due to successfully reduced emissions by means of the EU Fit for 55 package.[149] Nevertheless, the next environmental action is likely to be brought. Then, it will be overdue for the ECJ to finally deal with the arguments that have been put forward in detail, and to abandon the antiquated *Plaumann* doctrine.

---

149 *European Commission*, "Delivering the European Green Deal", 2021 (https://ec.europa.eu/info/strategy/priorities-2019–2024/european-green-deal/delivering-european-green-deal_en).

ACCESS TO JUSTICE FOR NGOs TO CHALLENGE CLIMATE COMMITMENTS UNDER THE EUROPEAN CLIMATE LAW

A Lost Hope?

Alessandra Accogli

1. INTRODUCTION

In June 2021, the European Climate Law ("ECL") was adopted.[1] The latter aims at enshrining into law the objective of climate neutrality by 2050, previously advanced in the European Green Deal.[2] However, a few months before its adoption, in April 2021, the negotiations between the Council and European Parliament ("Parliament"), on the European Commission ("Commission")'s proposal, resulted in the non-adoption of the Parliament's amendment on access to justice.[3] The amendment was meant to insert a new provision in the ECL, namely Article 11a, entitled "Access to justice". The provision foresaw the possibility for "members of the public concerned" to have access to a review procedure before a court of law, with a view to challenging actions or omissions of Member States in relation to climate neutrality.[4] Article 11a partially mirrored the provisions on access to justice of the Aarhus Convention,[5] which, having

1 Regulation (EU) No. 1119/2021 establishing the framework for achieving climate neutrality and amending Regulations (EC) No. 401/2009 and (EU) No 2018/1999, OJ 2021 L 243/1 ("European Climate Law").

2 Commission Communication (COM) No. 640, "The European Green Deal", 2019 ("European Green Deal").

3 *F. Simon and K. Taylor*, "Breakthrough as EU negotiators clinch deal on European climate law", *Euractiv*, 21 April 2021, <https://www.euractiv.com/section/climate-environment/news/breakthrough-as-eu-negotiators-clinch-deal-on-european-climate-law/>.

4 Parliament Amendments adopted by the European Parliament on 8 October 2020 on the proposal for a regulation of the European Parliament and of the Council establishing the framework for achieving climate neutrality and amending Regulation (EU) No. 1999/2018 (European Climate Law) (COM(2020)0080 – COM(2020)0563 – C9-0077/2020 – 2020/0036(COD)), 2020 ("Parliament's Amendments"), Amendment 92.

5 Convention on Access to Information, Public Participation in Decision-making and Access to Justice in Environmental Matters, Aarhus, 25 June 1998; in force 30 October 2001 ("Aarhus Convention").

been ratified by all Member States and the EU itself,[6] establishes procedural rights in the entire field of environmental law.

A similar provision in the ECL, in addition to enabling individuals and non-governmental organisations ("NGOs") to exercise the rights conferred on them by said law, would have been an important means of improving the implementation of EU climate commitments by Member States, since national courts have the power to review decisions that are incompatible with EU law.[7] Therefore, it would have achieved the twofold goal of pre-empting any discussions on the application of the Aarhus Convention to climate change measures and the frequent legal disputes regarding legal standing (or *locus standi*) and the scope of judicial review.

Despite the lack of an explicit provision on access to justice in the ECL, this contribution questions whether the Aarhus Convention may still play a role in enabling NGOs to challenge the measures that Member States are required to adopt under the ECL. The scope of the contribution is limited to the legal actions of NGOs before national courts. Issues concerning access to EU courts, for individuals or NGOs, to challenge acts adopted by EU institutions, will not be part of the analysis.

This contribution adds to the overall theme of the 8th EELF Annual Conference 2021, on "Social and Scientific Uncertainties in Environmental Law", by exploring how the climate change regime could be better equipped to deal with uncertainties at judicial level. On the one hand, it is now well recognised that climate change is caused by human activities that have unequivocally led to an unprecedented increase in greenhouse gas ("GHG") concentrations in the atmosphere, causing approximately one degree Celsius of global warming above pre-industrial levels,[8] and that a reduction of these emissions, "to limit the temperature increase to 1.5°C above pre-industrial levels", is crucial.[9] Consequently, action has been undertaken, at international, regional and national levels, to put in place a legal regime to deal with the problem.[10] On the

---

6 Council Decision 2005/370/EC on the conclusion, on behalf of the European Community, of the Convention on Access to Information, Public Participation in Decision-making and Access to Justice in Environmental Matters, OJ 2005, L 124/1.

7 Commission Notice C/2017/2616 on access to justice in environmental matters, OJ 2017 C 275/1 ("Commission Notice"), paras. 5, 17 and 31.

8 *Intergovernmental Panel on Climate Change*, "Summary for Policymakers", *Global Warming of 1.5°C, An IPCC Special Report on the impacts of global warming of 1.5°C above pre-industrial levels and related global greenhouse gas emission pathways, in the context of strengthening the global response to the threat of climate change, sustainable development, and efforts to eradicate poverty*, IPCC, 2018 ("IPCC 2018"), p. 4; *Intergovernmental Panel on Climate Change*, "Summary for Policymakers", *Climate Change 2021, The Physical Science Basis*, IPCC, 2021, p. 5 ("IPCC 2021").

9 Paris Agreement, adopted 12 December 2015, entered into force 4 November 2016, 55 ILM 740 ("Paris Agreement"), Art. 2(1)(a).

10 *E. Woerdman, M. Roggenkamp and M. Holwerda, Essential EU Climate Law*, Edward Elgar Publishing Limited, 2021, pp. 10–42.

other hand, the climate change regime is characterised by regulatory approaches involving the reduction of GHG emissions, including through promoting energy efficiency, energy saving and renewable energy.[11] Determining the type and scope of policy measures to be taken to achieve national and EU energy and climate goals is an overarching challenge for policymakers, due to scientific uncertainties surrounding the deployment of certain measures (for example, uncertainties concerning afforestation projects on peatlands), as well as their potential economic and social drawbacks (for example, issues relating to higher electricity prices, due to the phasing-out of fossil fuels, and the increase in the use of renewable energies in the industrial and transport sectors; and job losses and/or lower wages in sectors not benefiting from the deployment of renewables).[12] Therefore, uncertainty remains, especially for national authorities, as to the best means to achieve the climate targets, and how best to balance them with other national needs. NGOs, in light of their expert knowledge, should be given concrete opportunities to contribute to decision-making, and to bring claims with the view to challenging such decisions in matters of public interest such as climate change, where obstacles relating to social and scientific uncertainties remain.

The remainder of this contribution is structured as follows. Section 2 briefly discusses the main objectives of the ECL, questioning whether the measures that Member States are required to take in implementation of the law could, potentially, be challenged before national courts, and, if so, what those measures are. Section 3 then explores the scope of the provisions of the Aarhus Convention on access to justice for environmental NGOs, and whether, based on these provisions, NGOs should be granted legal standing to challenge Member States' lack of ambition towards climate neutrality. Finally, section 4 is devoted to the conclusions.

2. THE EUROPEAN CLIMATE LAW AND THE MEASURES MEMBER STATES ARE REQUIRED TO TAKE TO ACHIEVE CLIMATE NEUTRALITY

The ECL represents an important contribution to the EU climate regime, as it establishes a framework for the achievement of the EU's goal of becoming climate-neutral by 2050,[13] namely the goal of reaching a balance between GHG emission reductions by source, and their removal by sinks.[14] The law forms

11 *M. Peeters and S. Nóbrega*, "Climate Change-related Aarhus Conflicts: How Successful are Procedural Rights in EU Climate Law?", *RECIEL* 2014 (23), pp. 354, 366.

12 *K. Williges et al.*, "The potential for successful climate policy in National Energy and Climate Plans: highlighting key gaps and ways forward", *Sustainable Earth* 2022 (5) pp. 1, 3.

13 European Climate Law, *supra*, note 1, Arts. 1 and 2(1).

14 *K. Kulovesi and S. Oberthür*, "Assessing the EU's 2030 Climate and Energy Policy Framework: Incremental change toward radical transformation?", *RECIEL* 2020 (29), p. 151.

part of the European Green Deal, a package of measures announced by the Commission in December 2019,[15] and approved by the European Council in December 2019,[16] to foster the transition towards the common goal of a climate-neutral economy.[17]

The law also envisages an EU-wide net GHG emission reduction target of at least 55 per cent by 2030, compared with 1990 levels, and a climate target for 2040, to be proposed by the Commission "within six months of the first global stocktake" referred to in the Paris Agreement.[18] Another element of the law that is worth mentioning is the establishment of the European Scientific Advisory Board on Climate Change.[19] In the words of the regulation, the board "shall serve as a point of reference for the Union on scientific knowledge relating to climate change by virtue of its independence and scientific and technical expertise". Its main tasks include "considering the latest scientific findings of the IPCC reports and scientific climate data", and "providing scientific advice and issuing reports on existing and proposed Union measures, climate targets and indicative greenhouse gas budgets", while assessing their coherence with ECL and the Paris Agreement.[20] Finally, the ECL also aims at enhancing the EU adaptive capacity, in accordance with Article 7 of the Paris Agreement, through the adoption of a Union strategy on adaptation to climate change.[21]

Turning now to the question of the measures that Member States are required to take to achieve climate neutrality under the ECL, Article 2(2) foresees the obligation for Member States to "take the necessary measures … at national level … to enable the collective achievement of the climate-neutrality objective".[22] Article 5(4) substantiates Article 2(2), indicating that Member States are expected to "adopt and implement national adaptation strategies and plans".[23] However, besides the adaptation strategies and plans referred to in Article 5, the ECL does not require Member States to adopt any other Act whose adoption was not already foreseen in existing EU climate legislation.[24] The "necessary national measures" which Article 2(2) of ECL refers to, for the achievement of climate neutrality, form part of the National Energy and Climate Plans ("NECPs")[25] and

15 European Green Deal, *supra*, note 2.

16 European Council Conclusions, EUCO 29/19, 12 December 2019, para. 1.

17 *A. Sikora*, "European Green Deal – legal and financial challenges of the climate change", *ERA Forum* 2021 (21), pp. 681, 682.

18 European Climate Law, *supra*, note 1, Arts. 4(1) and (3).

19 *Ibid.*, Art. 3(1).

20 *Ibid.*, Art. 3(2).

21 *Ibid.*, Art. 5.

22 *Ibid.*, Art. 2(2).

23 *Ibid.*, Art. 5.

24 *S. Bechtel*, "The European Climate Law and Access to Justice", *ClientEarth*, 17 June 2020, <https://www.clientearth.org/projects/access-to-justice-for-a-greener-europe/updates/the-european-climate-law-and-access-to-justice/>.

25 Regulation (EU) No. 2018/1999 on the Governance of the Energy Union and Climate Action, OJ 2018 L 328/1 ("Governance Regulation"), Art. 3.

Long-Term Strategies ("LTSs")[26] that Member States had already committed to adopting, under the Regulation on the Governance of the Energy Union and Climate Action ("Governance Regulation").[27] This approach is evidenced in Article 7 of the ECL, on the assessment of national measures, where it is clarified that the ECL will complement the provisions of the Governance Regulation, by requiring the Commission to assess Member States' progress towards the climate-neutrality target for 2050, as well as the interim climate targets.[28]

Therefore, it is the NECPs and LTSs, as well as the measures therein, that could potentially be challenged in court, if found to be insufficient. The above-mentioned Parliament amendment on access to justice confirms this, since it would have been granted to members of the public "with a view to challenging the substantive or procedural legality of decisions, acts or omissions", subject to Article 10 of the Governance Regulation,[29] which in turn refers to public consultation requirements for NECPs and LTSs. While LTSs require Member States to develop a vision for 2050, and thus cover a period of at least 30 years, NECPs are interested in the short-term perspective, which covers periods of 10 years.[30] The NECPs for 2020–30 had to be submitted by December 2019, and are all available.[31] On the other hand, the submission of LTSs by January 2020 is experiencing delays from some states.[32] This contribution will focus mainly on the NECPs for 2020–30. These plans are expected to indicate the main national objectives for five dimensions of the EU's Energy Union Strategy, namely decarbonisation; energy efficiency; energy security; the internal energy market; and research and innovation and competitiveness, and, on this basis, describe current and planned policies and measures to meet these objectives.[33]

Based on this overview of the ECL, the following section examines whether the provisions of the Aarhus Convention on access to justice cover the NECPs, so as to allow NGOs to challenge them, and, if so, whether the scope of judicial review encompasses a content-wise judicial consideration of the plan.

---

26 *Ibid.*, Art. 15.

27 Governance Regulation, *supra*, note 25.

28 European Climate Law, *supra*, note 1, Art. 7. See also *Kulovesi and Oberthür*, *supra*, note 14, 156.

29 Parliament's Amendments, *supra*, note 4, Amendment 92.

30 *C. Zell-Ziegler et al.*, "Enough? The role of sufficiency in European energy and climate plans", *Energy Policy* 2021 (157), p. 112483.

31 *European Commission*, "National energy and climate plans (NECPs)", <https://energy.ec.europa.eu/topics/energy-strategy/national-energy-and-climate-plans-necps_en#national-long-term-strategies>. See also *Zell-Ziegler et al.*, *supra*, note 30.

32 *European Commission*, "National long-term strategies", <https://ec.europa.eu/info/energy-climate-change-environment/implementation-eu-countries/energy-and-climate-governance-and-reporting/national-long-term-strategies_en>. See also *Zell-Ziegler et al.*, *supra*, note 30.

33 *Zell-Ziegler et al.*, *supra*, note 30.

3. ACCESS TO JUSTICE UNDER ARTICLE 9 OF THE AARHUS CONVENTION AND LEGAL STANDING FOR NGOs TO CHALLENGE THE CONTENT OF NATIONAL ENERGY AND CLIMATE PLANS

The main provision of the Aarhus Convention devoted to access to justice is Article 9. In particular, Article 9(2) addresses the possibility to challenge decisions, acts or omissions concerning activities that are subject to public participation requirements,[34] while Article 9(3) requires that the challenged act or omission contravenes provisions of national law related to the environment.[35]

Section 3.1. will address the initial question of whether Articles 9(2) and 9(3) can be applied to the NECPs adopted under the ECL in accordance with the Governance Regulation. Section 3.2. will then question whether NGOs are entitled to have access to a judicial review procedure, to challenge specific measures included in the NECPs. In other words, both the question of legal standing for NGOs to challenge climate plans, and the scope of judicial review of such plans, will be addressed.

The analysis below will, in particular, rely on the 2017 Commission Notice on Access to Justice in Environmental Matters ("2017 Commission Notice"),[36] the 2014 Implementation Guide of the Aarhus Convention ("Aarhus Implementation Guide"),[37] the findings of the Aarhus Convention Compliance Committee ("Compliance Committee"),[38] and the relevant decisions of the Court of Justice of the European Union ("CJEU").

3.1. CAN ARTICLE 9 OF THE AARHUS CONVENTION BE APPLIED TO THE NECPs ADOPTED UNDER THE ECL?

Unlike the other procedural rights guaranteed under the Aarhus Convention, namely the right of access to environmental information, and the right of the public to participate in decision-making, which have been implemented through

34 Aarhus Convention, *supra*, note 5, Art. 9(2).

35 *Ibid.*, Art. 9(3).

36 Commission Notice, *supra*, note 7, paras. 9 and 11.

37 *UNECE, The Aarhus Convention: An Implementation Guide*, 2nd ed., UN, 2014.

38 The Aarhus Convention Compliance Committee is empowered to receive submissions on compliance issues directly from the public, other than from States Parties, and to draw up reports and recommendations, which are, however, non-binding and non-judicial in nature: *S. Kingston, V. Heyvaert and A. Čavoški, European Environmental Law*, Cambridge University Press, 2017, p. 171.

the adoption of specific EU directives,[39] a general directive providing an overall framework for access to justice in environmental matters does not exist.[40] Notwithstanding this, express access-to-justice provisions, mirroring Article 9 of the Aarhus Convention, can largely be found in EU secondary legislation requiring Member States to provide legal standing.[41] No EU climate change legislation contains explicit provisions on access to justice, especially after the failure to adopt the Parliament's amendment to the ECL.[42] However, the CJEU has already required Member States to grant access to justice in cases where it was not mentioned in any specific pieces of EU legislation.[43]

That being said, it is important to draw a distinction between Articles 9(2) and 9(3) of the Aarhus Convention. Article 9(2) requires parties to take legislative steps to ensure access to a review procedure to challenge "any decision, act or omission", in so far as it falls within the scope of Article 6, which regulates public participation requirements for specific activities, or within the scope "of other relevant provisions of [the] Convention".[44] The rationale behind Article 9(2) is that public participation requirements applicable to specific activities confer the right on those concerned to ask for a judicial review of the decision, act or omission at stake.[45] In order to extend the scope of the provision to the NECPs adopted under the ECL in accordance with the Governance Regulation, it is necessary to argue that the NECPs constitute decisions or acts under Article 9(2) of the Aarhus Convention.

On one hand, Article 6 of the Convention covers specific activities that require the participation of the public in their decision-making processes.[46] For the most part, this includes activities, listed in Annex I of the Convention, that must be preceded by the issuance of a permit by a public authority before they can commence (for example, spatial planning decisions or development

39 Directive 2003/4/EC on public access to environmental information and repealing Council Directive 90/313/EEC, OJ 2003 L 41/26 and Directive 2003/35/EC providing for public participation in respect of the drawing up of certain plans and programmes relating to the environment and amending with regard to public participation and access to justice Council Directives 85/337/ EEC and 96/61/EC, OJ 2003 L 156/17.

40 *Peeters and Nóbrega*, *supra*, note 11, 358.

41 Commission Notice, *supra*, note 7, para. 28, which refers, by way of example, to Art. 25 of the Industrial Emissions Directive, 2010/75/EU; Art. 11 of the Environmental Impact Assessment Directive, 2011/92/EU; and Art. 23 of the Seveso III Directive, 2012/18/EU.

42 See section 1 above.

43 See Case C-127/02, *Landelijke Vereniging tot Behoud van de Waddenzee and Nederlandse Vereniging tot Bescherming van Vogels v Staatssecretaris van Landbouw, Natuurbeheer en Visserij* [2004] ECR I-7405 ("C-127/02, *Waddenzee*"); Case C-237/07, *Dieter Janecek v. Freistaat Bayern* [2008] ECR I-6221 ("C-237/07, *Janecek*"); Case C-240/09, *Lesoochranárske zoskupenie VLK v. Ministerstvo životného prostredia Slovenskej republiky* [2011] ECR I-1255 ("C-240/09, *LZI*").

44 Aarhus Convention, *supra*, note 5, Art. 9(2); *UNECE*, *supra*, note 37, 173.

45 Commission Notice, *supra*, note 7, para. 65; *UNECE*, *supra*, note 37, 126.

46 Aarhus Convention, *supra*, note 5, Art. 6.

consents), but also other activities which, although not included in the Annex, have a significant impact on the environment.[47]

On the other hand, the wording "under any other provisions of the Convention" encompasses Article 7 of the Convention, which requires public consultation for plans and programmes relating to the environment.[48] The Convention does not define "plans and programmes", but legal definitions can be found in other legal instruments.[49] The Strategic Environmental Assessment ("SEA") Directive,[50] for instance, defines plans and programmes with reference to their adoption procedures (for example, "[plans and programmes] which are required by legislative, regulatory or administrative provisions").[51] The Aarhus Implementation Guide adds that plans and programmes under Article 7 may "include government initiatives to achieve particular policy goals ... such as incentive programmes to meet certain pollution reduction targets".[52] Furthermore, the 2017 Commission Notice states that "such plans and programmes which are mandatory under EU law but for which no explicit public participation provisions have been established, still need to include public consultation".[53] It follows that "mandatory consultation confers participation rights on those members of the public who are entitled to participate".[54] Therefore, access to justice, to challenge decisions, acts and omissions of public authorities regarding plans and programmes, is governed by Article 9(2) of the Convention, through Article 7.[55] There are, however, interpretations which only accept that Article 9(2) should be limited to challenging decisions on specific activities which need to be preceded by a permit.[56] For instance, in the case ACCC/C/2005/11 *(Belgium)*, concerning an area plan *("plan de secteur")* providing for a landfill, the Compliance Committee found that the crucial element to determine whether a decision can be challenged under Article 9(2) or 9(3) is whether the decision amounts to a permit to carry out the activity.[57] Since the area plan did not qualify as such, Article 9(2) was ruled out.[58] However, although the Committee did not consider the possibility that the area plan might qualify as a plan under Article 7

47 Commission Notice, *supra*, note 7, para. 65.
48 Aarhus Convention, *supra*, note 5, Art. 7.
49 *UNECE*, *supra*, note 37, 176.
50 Directive 2001/42/EC on the assessment of the effects of certain plans and programmes on the environment, OJ 2001 L 197/30.
51 *Ibid.*, Art. 2(a). See also *UNECE*, *supra*, note 37, 176.
52 *UNECE*, *supra*, note 37, 176.
53 Commission Notice, *supra*, note 7, para. 97.
54 *Ibid.*, para. 65.
55 *Ibid.*, para. 98.
56 *ClientEarth*, *Access to Justice in European Union Law – a legal guide on Access to justice in environmental matters*, 2nd ed., ClientEarth, 2021, p. 14 ("ClientEarth Guide").
57 Findings of the Compliance Committee on Communication ACCC/C/2005/11 *(Belgium)*, para. 29.
58 *Ibid.*, para. 31.

of the Convention, the wording of the Convention suggests that the application of Article 9(2) can be extended to plans and programmes.

Therefore, it can be concluded that the reference to plans and programmes in Article 7 of the Aarhus Convention may well cover the NECPs that Member States are required to adopt in order to achieve the climate-neutrality objective under the ECL. To reinforce the argument, Article 10 of the Governance Regulation requires public consultation in the adoption of the "national energy and climate plan ... as well as of the long-term strategies".[59] Since it is clear from the above that mandatory consultation confers participation rights, then access to a judicial review procedure to challenge the NECPs should be ensured under Article 9(2).

As clarified by the Aarhus Implementation Guide, the fact that Article 9(2) may be invoked to challenge decisions, acts or omissions relating to public participation does not affect the possibility that Article 9(3) may also apply.[60] Article 9(3) requires Parties to guarantee access to justice, "to challenge acts and omissions by private persons and public authorities which contravene provisions of its national law relating to the environment". Therefore, the right to challenge the NECPs should be considered covered by Article 9(3) of the Convention, to the extent that these amount to acts or omissions contravening provisions of national law relating to the environment.

Firstly, both the Aarhus Implementation Guide and the Compliance Committee acknowledge the "broad spectrum of acts and omissions" to which the provision is applicable.[61]

Secondly, as regards the requirement that acts and omissions must contravene provisions of national laws related to the environment, it is crucial that the provision in question concerns the environment, but it need not be a provision of environmental law; indeed, it could be a provision of any law concerning any policy.[62] Thus, even provisions found in planning laws may be covered by Article 9(3) if, for instance, they relate to the exploitation of natural resources, or environment-related issues.[63] Moreover, Article 2(3) of the Convention provides a broad and non-exhaustive definition of environmental information, which includes "plans and programmes, affecting or likely to affect the elements of the environment".[64] Furthermore, the concept of "acts" was interpreted to include plans and programmes, in the findings of the Compliance Committee

59 Governance Regulation, *supra*, note 25, Art. 10.

60 *UNECE, supra*, note 37, 193.

61 Findings of the Compliance Committee on Communication ACCC/C/2006/18 *(Denmark)*, para. 26; *UNECE, supra*, note 37, 197.

62 UNECE, *supra*, note 37, 197; ClientEarth Guide, *supra*, note 56, 33.

63 *Ibid.*

64 Aarhus Convention, *supra*, note 5, Art. 2(3)(b). See also Findings of the Compliance Committee on Communications ACCC/C/2013/85 & ACCC/C/2013/86 *(United Kingdom)*, paras. 70–71.

concerning a challenge to spatial plans, which "provide the framework for the future development of the respective areas".[65] Finally, the reference to "national law" also encompasses EU law applicable in the Member State.[66]

In light of the above, and of the findings of the Compliance Committee in ACCC/C/2011/58 *(Bulgaria)*, the NECPs fall within the broad definition of acts under Article 9(3) of the Convention, as they provide the framework for the measures that Member States intend to adopt to meet the climate targets. As such, in situations where they allegedly contravene provisions of national or EU law that relate to, or help to protect, or otherwise impact on, the environment, they can be challenged in line with Article 9(3). This could happen, for instance, if a Member State was to abandon any contribution to the climate-neutrality target, thus contravening the ECL.[67]

In conclusion, the analysis above shows that, despite the lack of a specific provision on access to justice in the ECL, both Articles 9(2) and 9(3) of the Aarhus Convention can be applied to the NECPs adopted in accordance with the Governance Regulation.

3.2. CAN NGOs CHALLENGE SPECIFIC MEASURES CONTAINED IN THE NECPs BEFORE NATIONAL COURTS UNDER ARTICLE 9 OF THE AARHUS CONVENTION?

This subsection questions whether NGOs are entitled to have access to a judicial review procedure to challenge specific measures included in the NECPs. In other words, both the question of legal standing for NGOs to challenge climate plans, and the scope of judicial review of such plans, are addressed.

The issues of legal standing and the scope of judicial review go hand in hand in ensuring effective justice. Legal standing refers to the entitlement to bring a legal challenge to a court of law, whereas the scope of judicial review concerns the possible grounds, in terms of areas of law and legal arguments, that may be raised, as well as the standard of scrutiny applied by the courts.[68]

In the following subsections, Articles 9(2) and 9(3) will be examined, in turn, to consider what possibilities each of these provisions offer to NGOs wanting to challenge actions or inaction of Member States in relation to climate neutrality.

---

65 Findings of the Compliance Committee on Communication ACCC/C/2011/58 *(Bulgaria)*, paras. 62–64.

66 ACCC/C/2006/18 *(Denmark)*, *supra*, note 61, para. 27.

67 ClientEarth, "Short Note: Access to justice under the EU Climate Law", 2 December 2020, <https://www.clientearth.org/media/iziosvmx/access-to-justice-under-the-climate-law.pdf> ("ClientEarth Short Note").

68 Commission Notice, *supra*, note 7, paras. 58 and 108.

3.2.1. *Legal Standing*

Concerning the first issue, NGOs often face the obstacle of having to prove legal standing, due to the existence of restrictive criteria at national level. National rules and conditions on legal standing constitute one of the main barriers to accessing justice in environmental matters, including climate action.[69]

Article 9(2) of the Aarhus Convention requires standing to be granted to "members of the public concerned" who either have "a sufficient interest" or maintain "impairment of a right".[70] The expression "members of the public concerned" is further defined under Article 2(5) of the Convention, which specifies that "non-governmental organizations promoting environmental protection and meeting any requirements under national law shall be deemed to have an interest".[71]

At the same time, Article 9(2) does not guarantee unconditional access to justice for members of the public, as Member States are still in a position to impose certain conditions, to avoid overly broad legal standing.[72] In line with the case law of the CJEU, the 2017 Commission Notice suggests some examples of requirements that would be consistent with the Aarhus Convention, for example that the NGO has the protection of the environment as its substantial objective, or that it has a reasonable number of members.[73] However, while it is true that states retain some discretion in limiting the scope of legal standing of NGOs, it is also true that they cannot use that discretion to "make it in practice impossible or excessively difficult to exercise rights conferred by EU law".[74]

It follows that environmental NGOs, provided that they fulfil national law requirements, enjoy a form of legal standing *de lege* under Article 9(2) of the Convention.[75] Furthermore, it is worth noting here that the CJEU has also

69 Germany constitutes an example, as rules on standing are based on rigid rights requirements. As does, to a lesser extent, Italy, with its traditional requirement for a legitimate interest. The Netherlands constitutes an exception, as NGOs are granted standing if the public interest they seek to protect is affected: *N. de Sadeleer, G. Roller and M. Dross, Access to Justice in Environmental Matters and the Role of NGOs: Empirical Findings and Legal Appraisal*, Europa Law, 2005. See also Case C-115/09, *Bund für Umwelt und Naturschutz Deutschland, Landesverband Nordrhein-Westfalen eV v. Bezirksregierung Arnsberg* [2011] ECLI:EU:C:2011:289 ("C-115/09, *Trianel*"), concerning the interpretation of the Environmental Impact Assessment Directive, and in which the CJEU clarified that NGOs can derive from the Directive the right to challenge a project "likely to have significant effects on the environment", even where national procedural law in Germany would not permit this (para. 60).

70 Aarhus Convention, *supra*, note 5, Art. 9(2); see also ClientEarth Guide, *supra*, note 56, 22.

71 Aarhus Convention, *supra*, note 5, Art. 2(5).

72 Commission Notice, *supra*, note 7, para. 72.

73 *Ibid.*, paras. 78–81, referring to Case C-263/08 *Djurgården*, where the Court found that a membership requirement of 2,000 members was not in line with the Convention.

74 "C-115/09, *Trianel*", *supra*, note 69, para. 43; see also *UNECE*, *supra*, note 37, 195.

75 Commission Notice, *supra*, note 7, para. 74.

recognised such *de lege* standing for NGOs in the context of EU legislation which does not contain specific provisions on access to justice.[76]

Contrary to Article 9(2), Article 9(3) does not refer to "members of the public concerned", but simply to "members of the public", which include "one or more natural or legal persons, and, in accordance with national legislation or practice, their associations, organisations or groups".[77] Thus, based on the definition of "public" in the Convention, the scope of legal standing in Article 9(3) is broader than in Article 9(2), as it does not refer to either the requirement to be affected or to have an interest.[78] However, in stating that members of the public have legal standing "where they meet the criteria, if any, laid down in its national law", the Convention allows parties to set certain criteria for access to justice, in a way that appears similar to Article 9(2), with the exception that the latter prescribes what these criteria should consist of (for example, sufficient interest or impairment of a right).

The facts that Article 9(3) does not contain any clear and precise obligation so as to directly regulate the legal position of the public, and that the provision is subject, in its implementation or effects, to the adoption of subsequent domestic measures, led the CJEU to declare that the provision has no direct effect.[79] In other words, this means that an applicant cannot rely on Article 9(3) of the Aarhus Convention to obtain standing to challenge an act or omission of a public authority in a national court.[80] It follows that, in the absence of specific EU rules implementing the obligations derived from Article 9(3) of the Convention,[81] it is left to the domestic legal systems of each Member State to lay down the procedural rules on standing.[82] However, the CJEU relied on the concept of "effective judicial protection", in accordance with Article 47 of the Charter of Fundamental Rights of the European Union, to call for an interpretation of national rules by the courts that is "to the fullest extent possible ... consistent with the objectives laid down in Article 9(3) of the Aarhus Convention".[83] Otherwise, the Court held, the right to bring proceedings under the provision would be deprived of all useful effect.[84] Similarly, the Compliance Committee

76 *Ibid.*, paras. 69–70, referring to Case C-243/15, *Lesoochranárske zoskupenie VLK v. Obvodný úrad Trenčín* [2016] ECLI:EU:C:2016:838 ("C-243/15, *LZII*").

77 Aarhus Convention, *supra*, note 5, Arts. 9(2) and 2(4).

78 Commission Notice, *supra*, note 7, para. 92.

79 C-240/09, *LZI*, *supra*, note 43, para. 45; Case C-664/15, *Protect Natur-, Arten- und Landschaftsschutz Umweltorganisation v. Bezirkshauptmannschaft Gmünd* [2017] ECLI:EU:C:2017:987, para. 45 ("C-664/15, *Protect Natur*").

80 ClientEarth Guide, *supra*, note 56, 40.

81 It has already been mentioned above that a general EU directive providing an overall framework for access to justice in environmental matters does not exist. See section 3.1 above.

82 C-240/09, *LZI*, *supra*, note 43, para. 47. See also *ClientEarth Guide*, *supra*, note 56, 40.

83 C-240/09, *LZI*, *supra*, note 43, paras. 49–51; C-664/15, *Protect Natur*, *supra*, note 79, para. 45.

84 C-664/15, *Protect Natur*, *supra*, note 79, para. 46.

reiterated that, although the Parties are not obliged to establish a system of *actio popularis* in their national laws, they cannot, at the same time, "take the clause 'where they meet the criteria, if any, laid down in its national law' as an excuse for introducing or maintaining so strict criteria that they effectively bar all or almost all environmental organisations from challenging act or omissions that contravene national law relating to the environment."[85]

In conclusion, the discretion accorded, under Article 9(3), to states, in establishing criteria for standing, should not ultimately preclude effective remedies for members of the public, and should be in line with the Convention's objective of ensuring access to justice.[86]

3.2.2. Scope of Judicial Review

Concerning the scope of judicial review, this often raises questions about the legal grounds that NGOs can raise before the courts to challenge certain acts, and, consequently, how far the scrutiny of the courts can go, i.e. whether it can extend to a complete review of the contested decisions, acts or omissions.

As to the possible grounds on which decisions, acts or omissions can be challenged under Article 9(2), the provision envisages that NGOs can challenge both their "substantive and procedural legality".[87] In the *Trianel* case, after clarifying that the provision in question, which mirrored Article 9(2), did not in any way limit the grounds that could be put forward in support of the action, the CJEU held that those grounds must "include the rules of national law implementing EU environment law and the rules of EU environment law having direct effect".[88] The Compliance Committee went even further than the CJEU, establishing that, although the Convention refers to environmental issues, the wording of Article 9(2) does not limit the scope of judicial review to alleged violations of legal provisions "serving the environment", "relating to the environment" or "promoting the protection of the environment", which means that the violation of legal provisions other than environmental ones can be invoked.[89]

As to the standard of scrutiny applied by judges in their assessment of the grounds raised, the Aarhus Convention does not specify the extent of the review of substantive and procedural legality that needs to be undertaken.[90] However, the CJEU did clarify that judicial review cannot be confined to the procedural

---

85 ACCC/C/2005/11 *(Belgium)*, *supra*, note 57, para. 35. See also *UNECE*, *supra*, note 37, 198.

86 ACCC/C/2005/11 *(Belgium)*, *supra*, note 57, para. 36.

87 Aarhus Convention, *supra*, note 5, Art. 9(2).

88 C-115/09, *Trianel*, *supra*, note 69, paras. 37 and 48.

89 Findings of the Compliance Committee on Communication ACCC/C/2008/31 *(Germany)*, para. 78. See also ClientEarth Guide, *supra*, note 56, 19.

90 Commission Notice, *supra*, note 7, para. 127.

legality of a decision, but should be extended to the merits of that decision.[91] Likewise, the Compliance Committee reiterated that parties to the Convention should not impose a very high threshold for review, so as to rule out *prima facie* substantive legality issues.[92] It follows that national courts are entitled to assess the substantive merits of the public authority's decision.[93]

Turning to analysis of Article 9(3) of the Convention, the provision does not contain any explicit reference to "substantive and procedural legality", but simply envisages the possibility "to challenge acts and omissions by private persons and public authorities which contravene provisions of its national law relating to the environment".[94] However, the Aarhus Implementation Guide is extremely clear in arguing that, despite the lack of an explicit reference, the scope of review under Article 9(3) cannot be limited to either procedural or substantive legality, but should cover both aspects.[95] Similarly, the Compliance Committee has interpreted the provision to mean that both substantive and procedural grounds can be invoked to challenge public authorities' acts or omissions.[96] What is important to underline, on the possible grounds under which an act or omission can be challenged under Article 9(3), is the limitation to contraventions of national law relating to the environment. The phrasing seems to exclude the rules of EU law that have not been transposed in the national legal system, but have direct effect, which instead fall within the scope of Article 9(2), as explained above.

As to the standard of review, in addition to reiterating the considerations already made pursuant to Article 9(2), which also apply to paragraph 3, it is worthwhile dwelling, in light of the purpose of this contribution, on some of the decisions of the CJEU on the substantive review of plans and programmes.

In cases concerning a requirement to prepare air quality plans, such as the *Janecek* and *ClientEarth* cases, the Court specifically addressed the issue of the content of the plans, but did so by referring to the detailed requirements (for example, the limit values of pollutants, or the duration of the excess pollution) contained in the directive in question, namely the Air Quality Directive,[97] requiring the adoption of such plans.[98] It did, however, also refer to "the broad logic of the directive [seeking] an integrated reduction of pollution", which limits

91 Case C-137/14 *European Commission v. Federal Republic of Germany* [2015] ECLI:EU:C:2015:683, para. 80 ("C-137/14, *Commission v. Germany*").

92 Findings of the Compliance Committee on Communication ACCC/C/2008/33 *(United Kingdom)*, paras. 125–127.

93 ClientEarth Guide, *supra*, note 56, 21.

94 Aarhus Convention, *supra*, note 5, at Art. 9(3).

95 *UNECE*, *supra*, note 37, 199.

96 ACCC/C/2008/33 *(United Kingdom)*, *supra*, note 92, paras. 124–125.

97 Directive 2008/50/EC on ambient air quality and cleaner air for Europe, OJ 2008 L 152/1.

98 C-237/07, *Janecek*, *supra*, note 43, paras. 43–44; Case C-404/13, *R (on the application of ClientEarth) v. The Secretary of State for the Environment, Food and Rural Affairs* [2014] ECLI:EU:C:2013:805, para. 53 ("C-404/13, *ClientEarth*").

the exercise of the Member States' discretion in adopting measures to those that are deemed adequate.[99]

In the joined cases known as *Stichting Natuur en Milieu*,[100] the Court dealt with the requirement for Member States to draw up air-pollution control programmes, to comply with ceilings on emissions of specific pollutants set by the National Emissions Ceiling Directive.[101] At first, the Court appeared determined to establish that wide flexibility is afforded to Member States in the adoption of specific measures, since imposing limits on the development of the programmes would interfere with the need for the states to strike a certain balance among the various interests involved.[102] However, subsequently, and in a similar way to the reasoning adopted in *Janecek*, the CJEU, referring to the aim of the directive to reduce national emissions of the pollutants, held that Member States have the task "of adopting or envisaging appropriate and coherent policies and measures capable of reducing, as a whole, emissions of those pollutants".

From the analysis of the Court's case law, it follows that the CJEU envisages that the scrutiny of the national courts extends to the adequacy of the measures contained in plans and programmes whose adoption is required by EU law.[103] The adequacy of these measures should be assessed with respect to the aims of the EU directives prescribing their adoption, which, in the cases considered, consist mainly in keeping emissions below certain limits set in the directives themselves.

The analysis of the issues of standing and the scope of judicial review, under Articles 9(2) and 9(3) of the Aarhus Convention, offers the tools to answer the aforementioned question of whether NGOs are entitled to have access to a judicial review procedure, to challenge specific measures included in the NECPs adopted under the ECL in line with the Governance Regulation.

Concerning legal standing, the interpretation of both Article 9(2) and Article 9(3) suggests that environmental NGOs should be granted legal standing to challenge the NECPs, in the same way as the CJEU held that members of the public should be able to challenge air quality plans and national air-pollution control programmes.[104] Therefore, the answer to the question seems

---

99 C-237/07, *Janecek*, *supra*, note 43, paras. 45–46; C-404/13, *ClientEarth*, *supra*, note 98, para. 57.

100 Joined Cases C-165 to C-167/09, *Stichting Natuur en Milieu and Others v. College van Gedeputeerde Staten van Groningen* (C–165/09) and *College van Gedeputeerde Staten van Zuid-Holland* (C–166/09 and C-167/09) [2011] ECR I-4599 ("C-165 to C-167/09, *Stichting Natuur en Milieu*").

101 Directive 2001/81/EC on national emission ceilings for certain atmospheric pollutants, OJ 2001 L 309/22.

102 *Ibid.*, paras. 88–89.

103 Commission Notice, *supra*, note 7, para. 146.

104 Respectively, C-237/07, *Janecek*, *supra*, note 43, and C-165 to C-167/09, *Stichting Natuur en Milieu*, *supra*, note 100.

quite straightforward, at least in theory, since Member States enjoy a certain discretion in establishing criteria for standing at national level. However, as clarified by the CJEU and the Compliance Committee, national criteria should not preclude effective remedies for NGOs, and should be in line with the Convention's objective of ensuring access to justice.

Concerning the scope of judicial review, the question comes down to how specific the provisions of the Governance Regulation are concerning the NECPs. As indicated above, the ECL relies on the adoption of the NECPs under the pre-existing Governance Regulation.

In principle, the jurisprudence of the CJEU appears to be uniform in deciding that the scrutiny of national judges may extend to the substantive merits of the acts or omissions of public authorities, and, more precisely with regard to plans, to the adequacy of the measures contained in such plans. It should, therefore, follow that NGOs should be able to argue that a NECP violates a substantive requirement of EU environmental law, under Article 9(2), or of national law relating to the environment, under Article 9(3). However, it is also true that the Court usually measures the adequacy of the content of the plans against the requirements contained in the directive in question, which are rather detailed in prescribing the objectives to be achieved. This presupposes that the EU law under consideration regulates the public authority's actions in a sufficiently precise manner.[105] However, the Governance Regulation, while not requiring a transposition Act at national level to be effective, leaves Member States considerable discretion as to the national objectives, targets and contributions to be indicated in the NECPs, as well as the planned policies and measures, thus limiting, in practice, the possibilities of substantive challenges to such measures.[106] On the upside, in declaring that Member States have the task of adopting measures that are appropriate, the CJEU has repeatedly referred to the need for such measures to be consistent with the general objective of the directives; that is, in the cases analysed, to reduce emissions of various pollutants. The ECL relies on the NECPs adopted under the pre-existing Governance Regulation, to achieve the GHG emission reductions necessary to bring the EU to net zero by 2050, including a reduction target of at least 55 per cent, compared with 1990 levels, to be achieved by 2030.[107] The adequacy of the measures adopted in the NECPs should, therefore, be assessed against these objectives, in cases where a Member State abandons any contribution to the climate-neutrality objective, or where their contribution is found to be insufficient.[108] Furthermore, while allowing a certain degree of discretion, the Governance Regulation nevertheless offers a detailed description concerning, *inter alia*, the setting-up of the Member

105 ClientEarth Short Note, *supra*, note 67.

106 *Ibid.*

107 *Ibid.* See also section 2 above.

108 *Ibid.*

States' objectives, targets and contributions,[109] as well as their contributions in the area of renewable energy.[110] Moreover, there may also be scenarios where a NECP violates provisions of EU law other than the ECL or the Governance Regulation – for example, where a measure conflicts with the obligations contained in other directives – or scenarios where the plan violates provisions of national law relating to the environment.

4. CONCLUSIONS

The analysis conducted above shows that, despite the non-adoption, in the ECL, of the Parliament's amendment on access to justice, the Aarhus Convention offers an enormous contribution to ensuring that environmental NGOs have legal standing to challenge the NECPs adopted by Member States under the Governance Regulation. The wording and the subsequent interpretation of both Articles 9(2) and 9(3) of the Aarhus Convention indicate that environmental NGOs should be granted legal standing to challenge the substantive legality of the plans. The jurisprudence of the CJEU is quite clear in stating that the scrutiny of national judges may extend to the adequacy of the measures contained in plans and programmes. It has also repeatedly referred to the need for such measures to be consistent with the general objective of the EU legislation, which, in the case of the ECL, is the achievement of climate neutrality by 2050. It therefore seems crucial to ensure that NGOs, in light of their level of expertise and knowledge, are guaranteed access to justice, to hold public authorities accountable if their contributions to the climate-neutrality objective are deemed insufficient or inadequate in view of the current science. This is all the more so considering the scientific and social uncertainty that remains, especially for national authorities, as to the best means of achieving the climate targets, and how to balance these with other national needs. NGOs should be given concrete opportunities to contribute to decision-making, and to bring claims with a view to challenging inadequate climate plans, thus strengthening climate ambition.

However, this is easier said than done. It does not follow from this that it is irrelevant whether or not an express provision on access to justice forms part of the ECL. Article 11a, as amended by the Parliament, would have offered a specific legal basis in the context of EU climate law, thus pre-empting any legal disputes concerning legal standing. Moreover, despite Article 9 and the interpretation of the provision given by the CJEU, Member States still adopt

[109] Governance Regulation, *supra*, note 25, Art. 4, which cross-references Annex I.

[110] *Ibid.*, at Art. 5, which cross-references measures contained in other EU directives.

rules and conditions limiting legal standing and the scope of judicial review. It is, therefore, hoped that Member States interpret national criteria on standing and the scope of judicial review, "to the fullest extent possible", consistent with the objectives laid down in the Aarhus Convention, as advocated by the CJEU. This would not only guarantee NGOs an effective judicial remedy, but would also ensure that the climate-neutrality objectives of ECL are more easily achieved.

PART VII

CLIMATE CHANGE

CLIMATE CHANGE AND THE UK'S LOCAL AUTHORITIES

A Snapshot of their Actions and Perceived Challenges

Soraia Da Cas*

1. INTRODUCTION

The international response to climate change began with the First World Climate Change Conference, in 1979, organised by the United Nations Environment Programme (UNEP) and the World Meteorological Organization (WMO).[1] A series of studies and conferences were conducted, to develop targets and strategies for limiting emissions of greenhouse gases (GHGs).[2] In 1992, 155 states signed the United Nations Framework Convention on Climate Change, a document with comprehensive scope. This was followed by the adoption of the Kyoto Protocol in 1997, which established higher commitments for developed countries.[3] The Kyoto Protocol goal was to reduce GHG emissions to 5 per cent below 1990 emission levels, between 2008 and 2012 (the "first commitment period").[4] Although the Protocol targets for developed countries regarding GHG emissions were met, many countries used carbon trading, a controversial

* Environment & Threats Strategic Research Group, Department of Life and Environmental Sciences, Faculty of Science & Technology, Bournemouth University, Talbot Campus. The author acknowledges Roxanne King for her contributions to the questionnaire development and Rick Stafford for discussions regarding data analysis.

1 *E. Morgera*, *The External Environmental Policy of the European Union: EU and International Law Perspectives*, Cambridge University Press, 2012, 118.

2 *Morgera*, supra, note 1, 119.

3 *P. Sands*, *Principles of International Environmental Law* (electronic resource) (2nd ed.), Cambridge University Press, 2003, p. 141; United Nations Framework Convention on Climate Change (UNFCC), 48th Sess., Supp. No. 49, UN Doc. A/RES/48/189 (1994), 1; Kyoto Protocol to the United Nations Framework Convention on Climate Change, 37 ILM 22 (1998), 2303 UNTS 148; UN Doc. FCCC/CP/1997/7/Add.1.

4 *S. Tsai*, "UNFCCC Technical Workshop on Mechanisms of the Kyoto Protocol", *Colorado Journal of International Environmental Law and Policy*, 2000, 220–221; *UNFCC*, Kyoto Protocol – Targets for the first commitment period, UNFCC, 2020, available at <https://unfccc.int/process-and-meetings/the-kyoto-protocol/what-is-the-kyoto-protocol/kyoto-protocol-targets-for-the-first-commitment-period>.

measure, allowing parties to obtain credits for GHG reductions from countries not obliged to reduce their emissions.[5] Consequently, overall global emissions continued to rise.[6] The next international document to be prepared was the 2015 Paris Agreement, aiming to stop the increase in global average temperature to below 2 degrees Celsius above pre-industrial levels, and trying to limit the temperature increase to 1.5 degrees Celsius.[7] To date, it has been ratified by 192 countries, and it was set to be applied from 2020, but the rule book and technicalities about its aims are still under negotiation. This should have happened in the United Nations Conference of the Parties 26 (COP26), but the event was delayed because of the COVID-19 pandemic.[8]

1.1. CLIMATE EMERGENCY DECLARATION: SCIENTIFIC AND SOCIAL DRIVERS

It has been established that climate change concerns are not a novelty in international politics. However, the subject has been gaining wider attention recently.[9] The 2018 Intergovernmental Panel on Climate Change (IPCC) Report sets a "net-zero" target for 2050 GHG emissions, in order to achieve the 1.5 degrees Celsius goal of the Paris Agreement, increasing the level of urgency regarding climate action.[10] Additionally, a series of social movements addressing the climate emergency have intensified their activities, particularly among young people, best exemplified by the activist Greta Thunberg,[11] but also by non-violent actions by Extinction Rebellion, denoting the "climate emergency momentum".[12] Data indicates that civil disobedience movements regarding climate change, as well as scientific reports, may contribute greatly to the growth

---

5 *Sands*, supra, note 3.

6 *N. Maamoun*, "The Kyoto protocol: Empirical evidence of a hidden success", *Journal of Environmental Economics and Management*, 2019 (95), 227–256.

7 *Conference of the Parties Decision*, 1/CP.21 (2016) UN Doc. FCCC/CP/2015/10/Add.1, 2.

8 *UNFCC*, "Paris Agreement – Status of Ratification", available at <https://unfccc.int/process/the-paris-agreement/status-of-ratification>; *UNFCC*, "COP 26 Postponed", available at <https://unfccc.int/news/cop26-postponed>.

9 *S.J. Thackeray et al.*, "Civil disobedience movements such as School Strike for the Climate are raising public awareness of the climate change emergency", *Global Change Biology*, 2020 (26), 1042–1044.

10 *V. Masson-Delmotte et al.* (eds.), Global warming of 1.5°C: An IPCC Special Report on the impacts of global warming of 1.5°C above pre-industrial levels and related global greenhouse gas emission pathways, in the context of strengthening the global response to the threat of climate change, sustainable development, and efforts to eradicate poverty, IPCC, 2018.

11 *A. Holmberg and A. Alvinius*, "Children's protest in relation to the climate emergency: A qualitative study on a new form of resistance promoting political and social change", *Childhood*, 2020 (27), 78–92; *Thackeray* et al., supra, note 9.

12 *K. Davidson et al.*, "The making of a climate emergency response: Examining the attributes of climate emergency plans", *Urban Climate*, 2020 (33), 100666.

of public awareness of, and engagement with, climate change.[13] Moreover, research also suggests that environmentally friendly laws and regulations are positively impacted upon by public opinion and environmental protest and advocacy.[14] Also, pro-environmentalism changes in public opinion facilitated the adoption of renewable energy policies in Europe.[15] Amidst this scenario, governments around the globe made climate emergency declarations,[16] public written resolutions from administrations, encouraging emergency actions to stop global warming.[17] In the United Kingdom (UK) specifically, the central government declared a climate emergency in May 2019, and 300 local authorities (LAs) have, to date, declared a climate emergency themselves.[18]

1.2. UK NATIONAL POLICIES, LOCAL AUTHORITIES AND COMMUNITY ROLES

In the UK, the Climate Change Act 2008 set the net UK carbon account for the year 2050 to be at least 80 per cent lower than the 1990 baseline; this was amended to 100 per cent, in 2019.[19] The legislation comprises carbon budgets for five-year periods, in order to achieve the "net-zero" target by 2050. The Wales Environment Act 2016 establishes the same carbon emissions target as the UK-wide legislation. The Climate Change (Emissions Reduction Targets) (Scotland) Act 2019 amends the Climate Change (Scotland) Act 2009, setting targets to achieve net-zero emissions by 2045.[20] Northern Ireland is the only region without specific legislation addressing the climate crisis. LAs are at the forefront of coping with the consequences of the climate crisis, and have also been

13 *Thackeray et al.*, supra, note 9.

14 *J. Agnone*, "Amplifying Public Opinion: The Policy Impact of the U.S. Environmental Movement", *Social Forces*, 2007 (85), 1593–1620; *S. Dasgupta and E. De Cian*, "The influence of institutions, governance, and public opinion on the environment: Synthesized findings from applied econometrics studies", *Energy Research & Social Science*, 2018 (43), 77–95.

15 *B. Anderson, T. Böhmelt and H. Ward*, "Public opinion and environmental policy output: A cross-national analysis of energy policies in Europe", *Environmental Research Letters*, 2017 (12), 1–10.

16 *Climate Emergency Declaration*, "Climate emergency declarations in 1,765 jurisdictions and local governments cover 820 million citizens", 2020, available at <https://climateemergencydeclaration.org/climate-emergency-declarations-cover-15-million-citizens/>.

17 *Davidson et al.*, supra, note 12.

18 *Climate Emergency Declaration*, "United Kingdom: Bipartisan UK Parliament declares a climate emergency", 2019, available at <https://climateemergencydeclaration.org/united-kingdom-bipartisan-uk-parliament-declares-a-climate-emergency/>; *Climate Emergency Network*, "List of Councils who have declared a Climate Emergency", 2020, available at <https://www.climateemergency.uk/blog/list-of-councils/>.

19 Climate Change Act 2008, s. 1(1).

20 Climate Change Act 2008, s. A1(2).

granted a leading role in GHG emissions-reduction efforts: they are responsible for implementing the aims recognised by nations in the Paris Agreement.[21] In the UK, LAs are considered crucial players in achieving the legislated carbon budgets.[22] They exercise substantial authority over matters such as land use, building, spatial planning, public housing, transport, and, in some cases, energy generation, all of which are related to GHG emissions.[23] However, even though LAs are nominally independent, they remain under considerable guidance from central government, being subject to a voluntaristic approach to environmental management, and mechanisms to lower costs, such as competitive tendering.[24] Furthermore, their propinquity to the community allows them to build a key function in the development of partnerships between the public, private and voluntary sectors.[25]

Research has been conducted on the progress of LAs in the UK in tackling climate change, regarding adaptation and mitigation issues (for example, Allman et al.; Heidrich et al.; Porter et al.; Tingey and Webb),[26] and the challenges they face (for example, Demeritt and Langdon).[27] Additionally, the role of community and social engagement in environmental policy and action has been an issue of discussion in previous works (for example, Milbourne; Holstead et al.).[28]

21 *O. Heidrich et al.*, "National climate policies across Europe and their impacts on cities strategies", *Journal of Environmental Management*, 2016 (168), 36–45; *V.C. Broto*, "Urban Governance and the Politics of Climate change", *World Development*, 2017 (93), 1–15; *C. Rosenzweig et al.* (eds.), *Climate Change and Cities: Second Assessment Report of the Urban Climate Change Research Network*, Cambridge University Press, 2018; *M. Wolfram et al.*, "Learning in urban climate governance: concepts, key issues and challenges", *Journal of Environmental Policy and Planning*, 2019 (21), 1–15.

22 *Committee on Climate Change*, "How local authorities can reduce emissions and manage climate risks", Committee on Climate Change, 2012; *House of Commons Science and Technology Committee*, "Clean Growth: Technologies for Meeting the UK's Emissions Reduction Targets, Twentieth Report of Session 2017–19", HC 1454.

23 *J.J. Porter, D. Demeritt and S. Dessai*, "The right stuff? informing adaptation to climate change in British Local Government", *Global Environmental Change*, 2015 (35), 411–422; *J. H. Armstrong*, "Modelling effective local government climate policies that exceed state targets", *Energy Policy*, 2019 (132), 15–26.

24 *D. Demeritt and D. Langdon*, "The UK Climate Change Programme and Communication with Local Authorities", *Global Environmental Change*, 2004 (14), 325–336; *J. Connelly et al.*, *Politics and the Environment: From Theory to Practice* (3rd ed.), Routledge, 2012, 358.

25 *Demeritt and Langdon*, supra, note 24; *Porter, Demeritt and Dessai*, supra, note 23.

26 *L. Allman, P. Fleming and A. Wallace*, "The Progress of English and Welsh Local Authorities in Addressing Climate Change", *Local Environment*, 2004 (9), 271–284; *O. Heidrich et al.*, "Assessment of the climate preparedness of 30 urban areas in the UK", *Climatic Change*, 2013 (120), 771–784; *Porter, Demeritt and Dessai*, supra, note 23; *M. Tingey and J. Webb*, "Governance institutions and prospects for local energy innovation: laggards and leaders among UK local authorities", *Energy Policy*, 2020 (138), 111211.

27 *Demeritt and Langdon*, supra, note 24.

28 *Milbourne, P.*, "Everyday (in)justices and ordinary environmentalisms: community gardening in disadvantaged urban neighbourhoods", *Local Environment*, 2012 (17), 943–957; *K. Holstead, G. Taylor Aiken, W. Eadson and S.T. Braunholtz*, "Putting community to use in environmental policy making: Emerging trends in Scotland and the UK", *Geography Compass*, 2018 (12), 1–15.

Nonetheless, such subjects demand deep institutional, social, technical and physical changes, being submitted to constant evolution.[29] Therefore, it is essential to monitor the progress of policies and the new challenges imposed on LAs.

1.3. CLIMATE ACTION: PLANS AND CHALLENGES

According to a survey led by the Local Government Association (LGA), in 2002, the majority of LAs in Wales and England (68 per cent) had not taken into consideration climate change in their areas, and just 4 per cent had climate change strategies.[30] In the work of Demeritt and Langdon,[31] 51.6 per cent of respondents advised that their LA was taking or planning to take climate actions, developing a climate change strategy, or integrating climate into local development planning, almost the same percentage recorded by the LGA research (52 per cent),[32] showing a broad disengagement from climate change. The Planning Act 2008 has established that, since 2008, LAs in the UK must include "policies designed to secure that the development and use of land in the local planning authority's area contribute to the mitigation of, and adaptation to, climate change"[33] in local planning papers. The work of Heidrich et al.[34] presents a possible change in relation to climate action: 25 of 30 urban areas analysed had established climate mitigation/adaptation strategies. More recently, Tingey and Webb[35] demonstrated that the majority of UK's LAs (82 per cent) were working on local energy/carbon plans and/or investments in energy projects.

Regarding the challenges faced during the process of Climate Action planning, lack of resources, little support from the government, and low levels of competence and political salience appeared as the main hurdles in previous research about LAs in the UK and Europe.[36] Adding a new layer of concern in relation to the global climate crisis, the current COVID-19 pandemic is impacting heavily on nations' economies, and disrupting everyday life and work.[37] Its consequences are likely to influence progress on climate change

29 *Wolfram et al.*, supra, note 21.

30 *Local Government Association, Climate Change: A Survey of Local Authorities*, LGA Publications, 2002.

31 *Demeritt and Langdon*, supra, note 24.

32 *Wolfram et al.*, supra, note 21.

33 Planning Act 2008, Part 9, ch. 2, s. 182.

34 *Heidrich et al.*, supra, note 26.

35 *Tingey and Webb*, supra, note 26.

36 *Demeritt and Langdon*, supra, note 37; *D. Reckien et al.*, "How are cities planning to respond to climate change? Assessment of local climate plans from 885 cities in the EU-28", *Journal of Cleaner Production*, 2018 (191), 207–219.

37 *R.D. Manzanedo and P. Manning*, "COVID-19: Lessons for the climate change emergency", *Science of the Total Environment*, 2020 (742), 140563.

strategies, although there are studies suggesting that the recovery phase of the COVID-19 response could represent an opportunity for policymakers to invest in long-term solutions focusing on climate change.[38]

Considering the importance of updated studies analysing UK LAs' current climate action strategies, and the challenges local governments face in trying to implement climate-directed policies, this contribution aims to offer a snapshot of the situation, taking into consideration recent events not yet considered by the literature, such as civil movements demanding action from governments, and the COVID-19 pandemic. Furthermore, the gap in assessing the role of public engagement in the development of such actions, and how the community is involved in UK local governments' plans to tackle climate change, will be analysed.

2. METHODS

A combination of desk-based study and a survey was chosen, with the aim of investigating, from a LA perspective, what the drivers are for climate emergency declarations, what their priorities are in the current stage of GHG emissions-reduction plans, and what perceived challenges have been encountered.

The desk-based approach consisted of a literature review and browsing climate change documents on selected UK LA websites. This was performed to better comprehend the evolution of the subject, supporting the creation of an analytic framework for understanding the data findings.[39]

Based on previous reports,[40] a questionnaire was employed to collect data from a large number of individuals, in a standardised process that better describes and compares their attitudes, seeking information for further analysis.[41] The questionnaire in this contribution contained both qualitative and quantitative elements, with closed and open questions, and was sent to 110 LAs in the UK. The questionnaire was designed to explore drivers for climate emergency declarations (CEDs), the stage of climate action plans and their priorities, perceptions about challenges in their application, and the role of the community. It was distributed, by email, to LAs in Scotland, Northern Ireland, England and Wales. The contact details for departments responsible for climate change were searched for in the LAs' websites. If it was not possible to find these, the email was sent to the

38 *C. Hepburn et al.*, "Will COVID-19 fiscal recovery packages accelerate or retard progress on climate change?", *Oxford Review of Economic Policy*, 2020 (36), S359–S381.

39 *A. Bryman*, *Social Research Methods* (4th ed.), Oxford University Press, 2012, 110.

40 *K.E. Warner and C. Ryall*, "Greener purchasing activities within UK local authorities", *Eco-Management and Auditing*, 2001 (8), 36–45; *A. Hull*, "Implementing Innovatory Transport Measures: What Local Authorities in the UK Say About Their Problems and Requirements", *European Journal of Transport and Infrastructure Research*, 2009 (9), 202–218.

41 *C. Robson and K. McCartan*, *Real World Research* (4th ed.), John Wiley & Sons, 93.

chief executive officer of the LA. Aiming to guarantee a higher rate of responses within a short time frame, the emails were sent through the Environmental Information Regulation (EIR), since previous contact with officers, in order to explain about the survey, was impaired due to the COVID-19 pandemic.

To ensure comparability, the LAs in England were selected from among unitary authorities and metropolitan boroughs/districts, with a few cities selected outside these parameters, only to obtain a proper geographical distribution (Table 1). Greater London Authority has a *sui generis* situation, but was included because it is the capital of England, and has a considerable percentage of the UK's population. In Scotland and Wales, the LAs were selected from among unitary authorities, on the basis of population size and geographical distribution. The selection criteria were inspired by a previous work,[42] which used the Eurostat Urban Audit Methodology, applying the following guidelines:[43] (1) at least 20 per cent of the national population; (2) national and regional capitals; (3) large (> 250,000 population) and medium-sized (>50,000 and <250,000 population) LAs; (4) LAs geographically spread within countries. Responses were obtained from 80 LAs' officers, from a total of 110, achieving a response rate of 72.72 per cent. This response rate compares well with other surveys of LAs (for example, Demeritt and Langdon 2004). The geographical distribution of responses was also homogeneous. Thus, non-respondent bias should not affect the results.

Descriptive analysis was carried out via IBM SPSS Statistics 26, to establish relationships and differences between variables, using cross-tabulation. Median and IQR were used for scaling ordinal data, and Spearman's Rank for correlations.[44] For open-ended questions, post-coding was used to observe data patterns, within a thematic approach, considering that such a method is appropriate for research questions that surpass an individual's experience.[45]

Table 1. Selected local authorities, region, country and type

Local Authority	Region	Country	Type
Cornwall +	South West	England	UA
Buckinghamshire +	South East	England	UA
Durham +	North East	England	UA
Wiltshire +	South West	England	UA
Bristol +	South West	England	UA
Bournemouth, Christchurch and Poole	South West	England	UA

(continued)

42 *Heidrich et al.*, supra, note 26.
43 *Eurostat, European Regional and Urban Statistics Reference Guide, Methodologies and Working Papers*, Eurostat, 2010.
44 *Manzanedo and Manning*, supra, note 37, 187.
45 *Ibid.*, 205.

Table 1 *continued*

Local Authority	Region	Country	Type
Cheshire East +	North West	England	UA
Dorset +	South West	England	UA
Leicester +	East Midlands	England	UA
East Riding of Yorkshire +	Yorkshire and the Humber	England	UA
Cheshire West and Chester +	North West	England	UA
Nottingham +	East Midlands	England	UA
Northumberland +	North East	England	UA
Shropshire	West Midlands	England	UA
Brighton & Hove +	South East	England	UA
Central Bedfordshire +	East	England	UA
South Gloucestershire +	South West	England	UA
Medway +	South East	England	UA
Milton Keynes	South East	England	UA
Plymouth	South West	England	UA
Hull +	Yorkshire and the Humber	England	UA
Derby	East Midlands	England	UA
Stoke-on-Trent	West Midlands	England	UA
Southampton	South East	England	UA
Swindon	South West	England	UA
Portsmouth +	South East	England	UA
Luton +	East	England	UA
North Somerset +	South West	England	UA
Warrington +	North West	England	UA
York +	Yorkshire and the Humber	England	UA
Peterborough +	East	England	UA
Stockton-on-Tees +	North East	England	UA
Herefordshire	West Midlands	England	UA
Bath and North East Somerset +	South West	England	UA
Southend-on-Sea +	East	England	UA
Telford and Wrekin +	West Midlands	England	UA
North Lincolnshire	Yorkshire and the Humber	England	UA
Thurrock +	East	England	UA
Bedford +	East	England	UA
Wokingham +	South East	England	UA
Reading +	South East	England	UA
North East Lincolnshire +	Yorkshire and the Humber	England	UA
West Berkshire	South East	England	UA
Windsor and Maidenhead +	South East	England	UA
Blackburn with Darwen +	North West	England	UA

(continued)

Table 1 *continued*

Local Authority	Region	Country	Type
Slough +	South East	England	UA
Isle of Wight	South East	England	UA
Middlesbrough +	North East	England	UA
Blackpool +	North West	England	UA
Redcar and Cleveland +	North East	England	UA
Torbay	South West	England	UA
Halton +	North West	England	UA
Bracknell Forest +	South East	England	UA
Darlington +	North East	England	UA
Hartlepool	North East	England	UA
Liverpool +	North West	England	MB
Knowsley +	North West	England	MB
St Helens	North West	England	MB
Sefton +	North West	England	MB
Wirral +	North West	England	MB
Manchester +	North West	England	MB
Bolton	North West	England	MB
Bury +	North West	England	MB
Oldham +	North West	England	MB
Rochdale	North West	England	MB
Salford +	North West	England	MB
Stockport +	North West	England	MB
Tameside +	North West	England	MB
Trafford	North West	England	MB
Wigan	North West	England	MB
Sheffield	Yorkshire and the Humber	England	MB
Barnsley	Yorkshire and the Humber	England	MB
Doncaster	Yorkshire and the Humber	England	MB
Rotherham +	Yorkshire and the Humber	England	MB
Newcastle upon Tyne +	North East	England	MB
Gateshead +	North East	England	MB
South Tyneside +	North East	England	MB
North Tyneside +	North East	England	MB
Sunderland +	North East	England	MB
Birmingham	West Midlands	England	MB
Coventry +	West Midlands	England	MB
Dudley +	West Midlands	England	MB
Sandwell +	West Midlands	England	MB
Solihull	West Midlands	England	MB

(continued)

Table 1 *continued*

Local Authority	Region	Country	Type
Walsall +	West Midlands	England	MB
Wolverhampton +	West Midlands	England	MB
Leeds +	Yorkshire and the Humber	England	MB
Bradford +	Yorkshire and the Humber	England	MB
Calderdale	Yorkshire and the Humber	England	MB
Kirklees +	Yorkshire and the Humber	England	MB
Wakefield +	Yorkshire and the Humber	England	MB
Norwich +	East	England	NMDC
Ipswich +	East Anglia	England	CT
Lincoln +	East Midlands	England	CT
Cambridge +	East	England	CT
Exeter	South West	England	CT
Carlisle	North West	England	CT
Greater London Authority +	London	England	SG
Glasgow +	–	Scotland	UA
Edinburgh	–	Scotland	UA
Aberdeen City	–	Scotland	UA
Highland +	–	Scotland	UA
Dundee +	–	Scotland	UA
Cardiff +	–	Wales	UA
Gwynedd	–	Wales	UA
Swansea +	–	Wales	UA
Wrexham +	–	Wales	UA
Belfast +	–	Northern Ireland	UA
Derry and Strabane +	–	Northern Ireland	UA
Mid Ulster +	–	Northern Ireland	UA

Note: The LAs that participated in the survey are marked with a +. UA = unitary authority; MB = metropolitan borough; NMDC = non-metropolitan district council; CT = county town; SG = *sui generis*.

Source: Compiled by the author.

3. RESULTS

From the 110 LAs that the survey was sent to, 80 responded, representing a population of around 31 million. Among the respondents were London, Glasgow, Belfast and Cardiff – England's, Scotland's, Northern Ireland's and Wales' largest LAs, respectively. The geographical distribution is displayed in Figure 1.

Figure 1. Geographical distribution of survey respondents

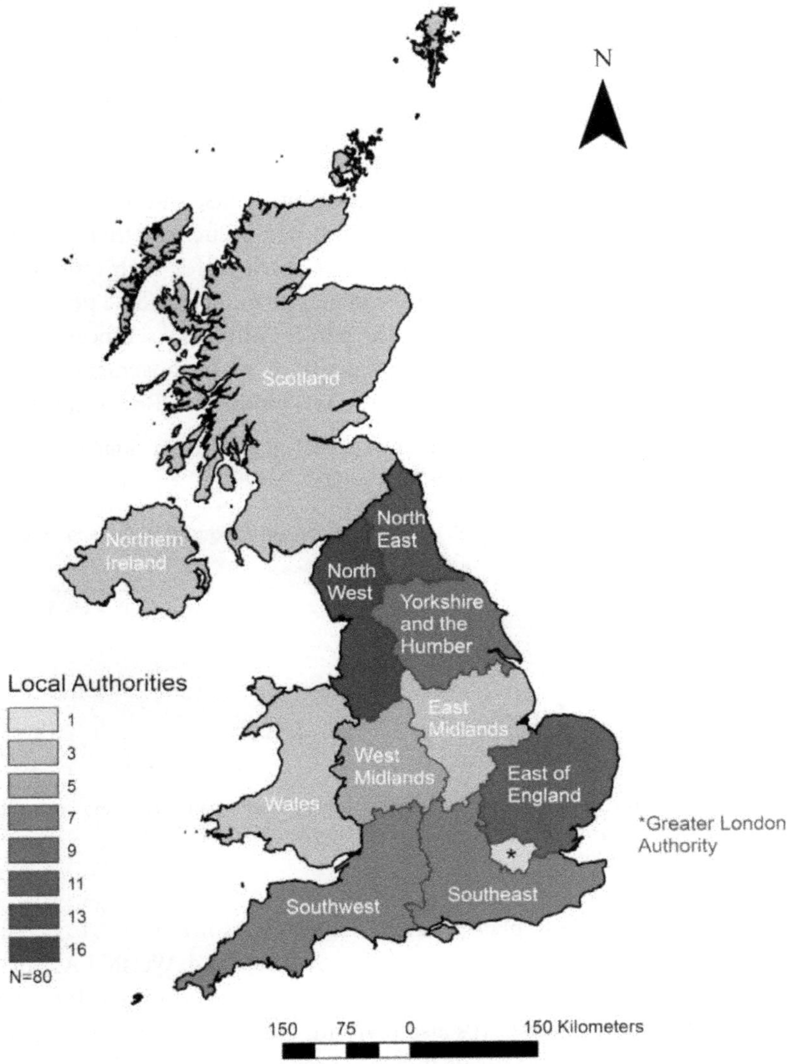

Note: The number of respondents is colour-coded from light to dark grey, divided by country in Scotland, Northern Ireland and Wales, and by region in England. Greater London Authority, marked with an asterisk, is not included in any specific region.

Source: Map created using QGIS (QGIS Development Team, 2020). Contains National Statistics data © Crown copyright and database right 2020. Contains NRS data © Crown copyright and database right 2020: www.nisra.gov.uk. Contains OS data © Crown copyright [and database right] 2020. Office for National Statistics; National Records of Scotland; Northern Ireland Statistics and Research Agency (2011). 2011 Census: boundary data (United Kingdom) 2020. UK Data Service. SN:5819 UKBORDERS: Digitised Boundary Data, 1840- and Postcode Directories, 1980- http://discover.ukdataservice.ac.uk/catalogue/?sn=5819&type=Data%20catalogue, retrieved from http://census.ukdataservice.ac.uk/get-data/boundary-data.aspx. Contains public sector information licensed under the Open Government Licence v3.

From the total of respondents, 95 per cent (N=76) had declared a climate emergency or similar initiative, and 67.5 per cent (N=54) had a designated department or officer dealing with climate action (in Northern Ireland, however, only one-third of the sample had a designated department), while 37.5 per cent (N=30) of the total were also signatories to the Covenant of Mayors. When asked about the influence of social movements (for example, school strikes and Extinction Rebellion) and specialists' reports (for example, IPCC reports) on CEDs, 34.7 per cent in relation to social movements, and 43.7 per cent in relation to specialists' reports, answered that it had influenced them to a great or very great extent. Similar percentages were reached, for each question, for answers stating it had had at least some or moderate influence (36.2 per cent and 45.1 per cent, respectively) (Figure 2). The perceptions of LAs' officers seem to be slightly more divided regarding the influence of social movements than the influence of specialists' reports (Mdn=4 IQR=3 and Mdn=4 IQR=2, respectively).

Figure 2. Influence of social movements and specialists' reports on climate emergency declarations (CEDs), according to survey respondents

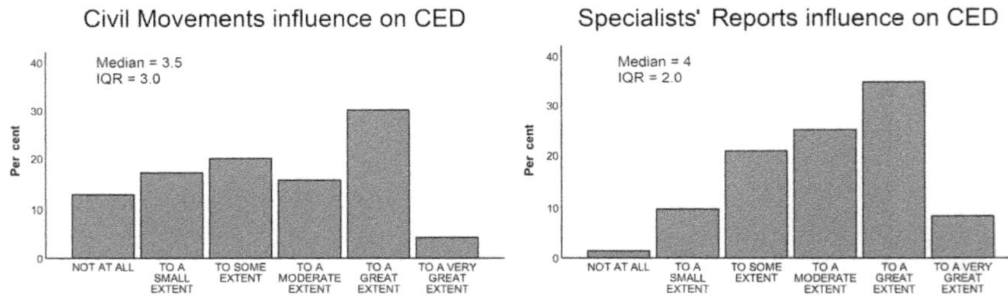

Notes: Options for answers varied from "not at all" (scoring value = 1) to "to a very great extent" (scoring value = 6), increasing by a value of 1 for each answer in the scale.

Source: Produced by the author.

Regarding climate action plans (CAPs) or similar initiatives, 70 per cent (N=56) of LAs had one (100 per cent for Scottish and Welsh LAs, in the sample), and from those that did not (N=24), all intended to develop a CAP, with 2 LAs that already had CAPs also planning to develop new updated ones. The percentage of LAs with CAPs increased among those that had a specific department dealing with climate change (77.8 per cent). From the LAs that had CAPs, 66 per cent had produced those plans recently – between 2019 and 2020. The dates of the CEDs and the phase of the CAPs – the majority either in discussion (42.5 per cent) or implementation (40 per cent) – are summarised in Figure 3.

Figure 3. Date of climate emergency declarations (CEDs) and phase of climate action plans (CAPs) of survey participants

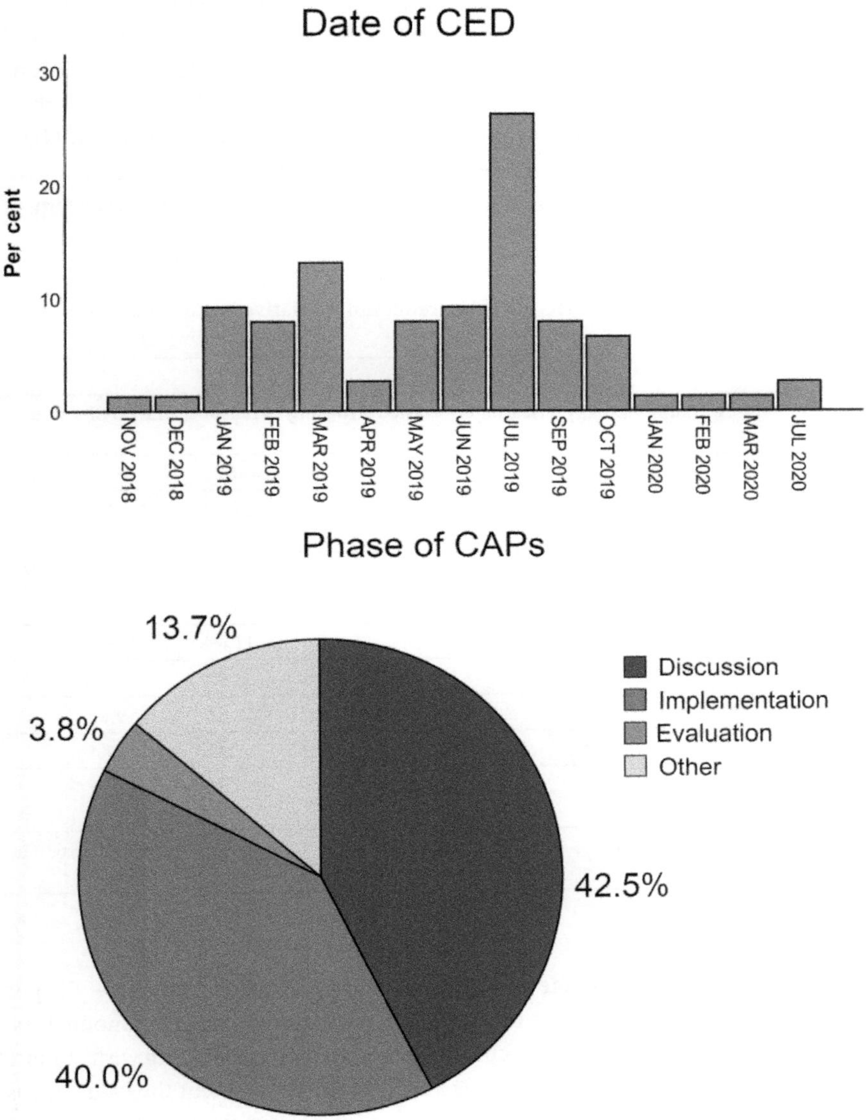

Notes: "Other" includes, for example, "between discussion and implementation", "revision", "waiting for publication" and "different phases concomitantly".

Source: Produced by the author.

The sectors presented in the questionnaire were included in most CAPs: building (both new buildings and existing ones) (93.3 per cent), energy (93.3 per cent), heating/cooling (90.7 per cent), waste (80 per cent), housing (76 per cent), transport (96 per cent), land use, land-use change and forestry (LULUCF) (68 per cent), and other (23.8 per cent). The additions by respondents for the category "other" included water, industry and carbon sequestration. Opinion seems to be divided with regard to priorities in GHG emissions reduction, showing that LAs do not follow a particular set of priorities, and that a considerable number (N=24) do not deem a system of priorities applicable at all. The distribution is presented in Table 2.

Table 2. Priorities in CAP/GHG emission reduction initiatives according to sectors

	Sectors							
	Building	Energy	Heating/ Cooling	Waste	Housing	Transport	LULUCF	Other
Valid answers	67	69	68	67	68	69	67	11
1=Least prioritised	20.9%	11.6%	13.4%	14.9%	19.4%	15.9%	10.4%	9.1%
2	1.5%	7.2%	5.9%	9%	1.5%	2.9%	4.5%	9.1%
3	7.5%	5.8%	5.9%	3%	6%	5.8%	4.5%	9.1%
4	7.5%	7.2%	5.9%	7.5%	9%	11.6%	4.5%	
5	6%	11.6%	13.2%	6%	3%	5.8%	9%	9.1%
6	6%	7.2%	7.4%	7.5%	9%	11.6%	9%	
7	11.9%	5.8%	7.4%	10.4%	7.5%	7.2%	10.4%	
8=Most Prioritised	3%	5.8%	2.9%	1.5%	3%	4.3%	1.5%	
Not Applicable	35.8%	37.7%	38.2%	40.3%	41.8%	34.8%	46.3%	63.6%

Source: Compiled by the author.

There was a high percentage of LAs with GHG emissions targets – 85 per cent (N=68). When analysing the presence of emissions targets among LAs, according to the presence of a specific department or officer dealing with climate change, among those that did not have a designated department the value drops to 69.2 per cent, and increases to 92.6 per cent among those with a specific department. Different target dates were presented, and the data was divided into four main categories: net zero by 2030 or earlier; net zero between 2031 and 2040; net zero between 2041 and 2050; and annual or other targets. The majority aimed to be net zero by 2030–61.6 per cent (N=45). The other targets amounted to 12.3 per cent (N=9) for net zero by 2040, 17.8 per cent (N=13) for net zero by 2050, and 8.2 per cent (N=6) for annual/other targets. Moreover, most of the targets of their CAPs included emissions from both the council's own operations and the whole council area (64.1 per cent).

In reference to hurdles in implementation of GHG emissions reduction (Figure 4), a lack of funding (67.5 per cent of valid answers ranked this between fourth and fifth, with fifth meaning the biggest hurdle), and lack of support from central government (47.3 per cent ranked this between fourth and fifth) were among the biggest issues, according to LAs' officers. Among Scottish LAs, the latter hurdle did not appear as a great concern, ranking either second (66.7 per cent) or third (33.3 per cent). Despite appearing in third, as an important hurdle in the whole data, when separated by England's regions (Table 4), LAs in the West Midlands indicated that lack of staffing and lack of expertise were great concerns, since 80 per cent of the answers in both categories fell into the two biggest hurdles range. The region also presented a lower percentage (40 per cent) of LAs with specific departments to deal with climate change than the UK average. For the majority of LAs in Yorkshire and Humber (83.3 per cent), lack of jurisdiction was cited among the two biggest hurdles. A similar result was seen for the Greater London Authority, which cited lack of jurisdiction as one of the biggest hurdles.

Figure 4. Perception of respondents in reference to hurdles in implementation of GHG emissions reduction

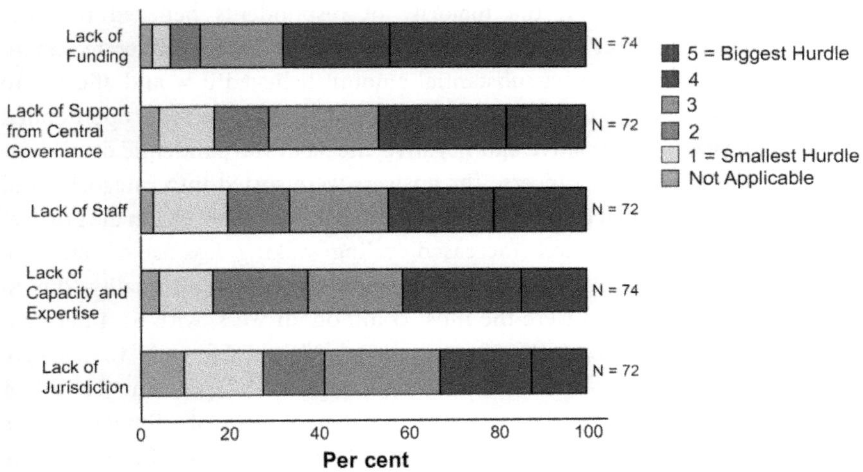

Notes: Frequency distributions (percentage) are coloured in shades of grey from 1=Smallest Hurdle to 5=Biggest Hurdle, including the category "Not Applicable".

Source: Produced by the author.

When asked about the sectors that presented most challenges, the answers were less homogeneous. However, heating/cooling, housing, waste and transport had the highest scores among the most challenging sectors (Table 3). When asked if these challenges were being addressed in CAPs, 52 LAs (73.2 per cent) responded positively.

Table 3. Local authorities' perceptions on challenges, divided by sectors

	Sectors							
	Building	Energy	Heating/ Cooling	Waste	Housing	Transport	LULUCF	Other
Valid answers	71	71	69	69	68	70	70	8
1=Smallest Challenge	7%	2.8%	1.4%	1.4%	1.5%	1.4%	14.3%	12.5%
2	4.2%	12.7%		17.1%	1.5%	1.4%	2.9%	
3	12.7%	7%	10.1%	10.1%	7.4%	10%	11.4%	
4	19.7%	21.1%	10.1%	21.7%	8.8%	10%	10%	
5	12.7%	18.3%	18.8%	23.2%	14.7%	20%	11.4%	12.5%
6	19.7%	18.3%	23.2%	10.1%	13.2%	21.4%	12.9%	12.5%
7	15.5%	11.3%	23.2%	7.2%	33.8%	27.1%	7.1%	12.5%
8=Biggest Challenge	4.2%	2.8%	7.2%	1.4%	5.9%	4.3%	2.9%	37.5%
Not Applicable	4.2%	5.6%	5.8%	7.2%	13.2%	4.3%	27.1%	12.5%

Source: Compiled by the author.

In relation to COVID-19, the majority of respondents believed that the pandemic would affect climate action at least to some/moderate extent (59.2 per cent, N=42), and a substantial amount believed it would affect it to a great or very great extent (32.4 per cent, N=23). Additionally, open-ended questions revealed the positive and negative effects of the pandemic on climate action, according to LAs' officers. The answers were sorted into categories and coded, according to what respondents had written down (Table 5). On the positive side, increases in active travel (increased cycling/walking, less use of vehicles), leading to a reduction of traffic, as well as improvements in air quality (due to a reduction in emissions) were the most common answers, with 61.4 per cent (N=43) and 41.4 per cent (N=29) respectively. With reference to negative effects, financial impacts were the main concern for 53.7 per cent (N=36) of respondents, followed by delay in the implementation of climate actions (31.3 per cent, N=21). The sectors believed to be the most affected by the COVID-19 pandemic were transport (82.8 per cent), building (53.1 per cent) and housing (35.9 per cent).

Finally, in relation to community engagement and climate change communication, 86.3 per cent (N=63) of respondents believed that the community should be involved in climate action to a great or very great extent. The remaining 13.7 per cent (N=10) believed that the community should be engaged to a moderate extent. Their perceptions regarding current community engagement indicated an intermediate level – 75 per cent (N=54) responded either "some" or "moderate". The community role since CEDs had increased to

Figure 5. Frequency distribution (shown as a percentage) of the communication channels used by local authorities (LAs) (top) and the actors they engage with (bottom)

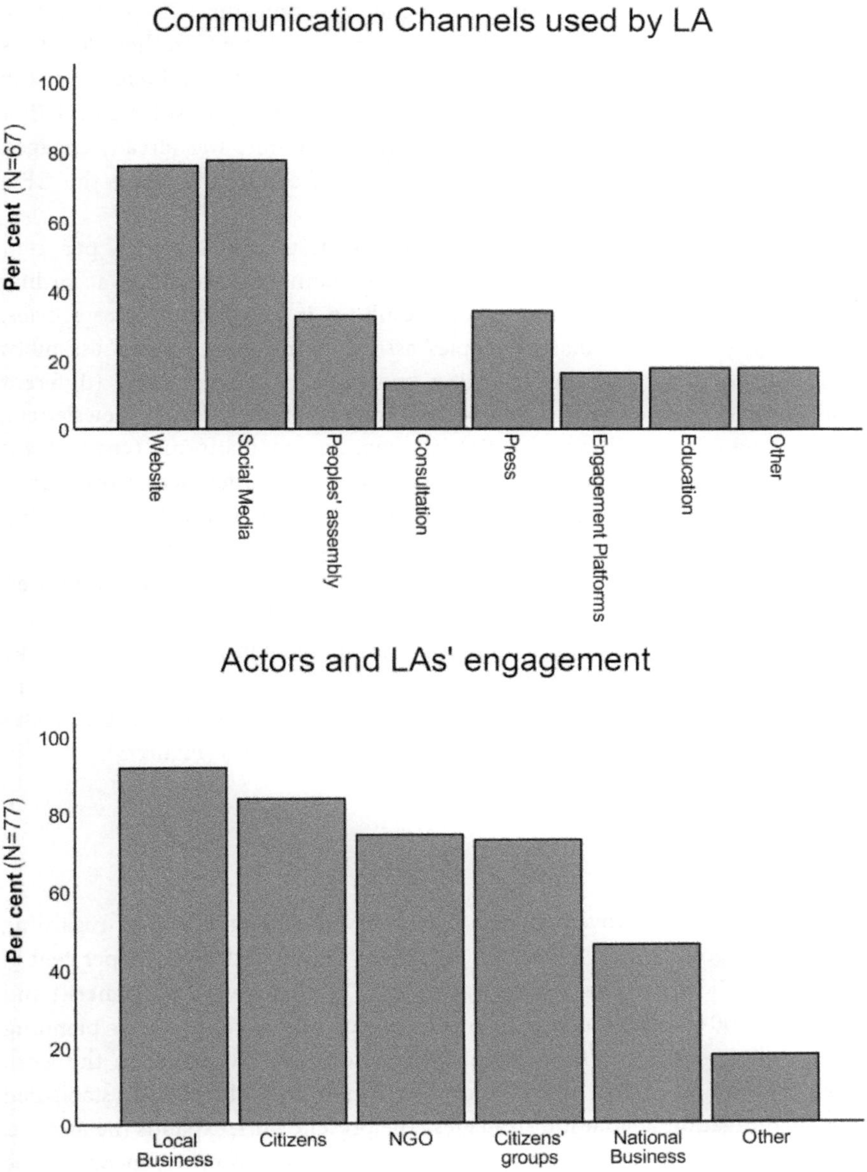

Source: Produced by the author.

a small extent for 26.4 per cent (N=19) of respondents, and to some/moderate extent for 54.1 per cent (N=39). There seemed to be a positive correlation (r=0.321, p=0.008, N=68) between the influence of civil movements in CEDs and the increase in the role of community in climate action since CEDs, indicating that LAs which attributed more influence to civil movements in their decisions to declare a climate emergency also experienced a posterior increase in the role of community. Additionally, there was a fairly strong positive correlation between the perception about how much the community was already engaged in climate action and the increase in the role of community since the CED (r=0.439, p=0.000, N=72).

When asked if the LA communicated with the public, 87.3 per cent (N=69) responded yes. The communication channels were coded according to the answers to an open question, resulting in the following categories: (a) website; (b) social media; (c) peoples' assembly (including citizens' assembly, neighbourhood forums and working groups); (d) consultation (different consultation channels and surveys); (e) press (press releases, newsletters, emails, traditional and local media); (f) engagement platforms (engagement events, festivals, campaigns); (g) education (webinars, conferences, workshops); (h) other (includes reports, private meetings, youth parliaments and steering groups). The most used communication channels were social media and websites, appearing in 77.6 per cent (N=52) and 76.1 per cent (N=51) of responses, respectively. The remaining channels are described in Figure 5. Despite the large percentage indicating that the community should be highly involved in climate action, only 58.2 per cent (N=46) responded that they had initiatives with non-governmental actors. The actors LAs mostly engaged with were local businesses (88.3 per cent – N= 68) and citizens (79.2 per cent – N=61) (Figure 5).

4. DISCUSSION

An encouraging improvement can be observed among UK LAs regarding climate change action. In 2002, an LGA survey indicated that only 4 per cent of LAs in the UK had climate change strategies,[46] and the work of Demeritt and Langdon (2004)[47] showed that 51.6 per cent of LAs were taking or planning to take climate actions. The percentage was considerably higher in the work of Heidrich et al. (2013), where 25 of 30 urban areas analysed had established climate mitigation/adaptation strategies. The present work expands the number of LAs analysed in comparison with Heidrich et al., showing an optimistic broader picture of the UK's LAs: 68.5 per cent of the sample already had CAPs

46 *Porter, Demeritt and Desai*, supra, note 23.
47 *Demeritt and Langdon*, supra, note 24.

or similar initiatives, and from the total number of respondents (80), only one LA did not intend to have one.

The rise in local government engagement was also attested by the great number of CEDs (93.8 per cent), aligned with the existence of more ambitious targets than those presented in the past,[48] since the majority of LAs analysed had set a net-zero target for 2030. Both figures were influenced by social movements and scientific reports: the survey suggests a considerable influence from these external factors in CEDs, where LAs pledged to achieve net-zero emissions targets. These observations are reinforced when examining the dates of CEDs (Figure 3), since many of the declarations were made around March and July 2019, when school strikes mobilised nearly 1 million students in protests around the world against government inaction on climate change (15th of March, 2019),[49] and Extinction Rebellion carried out protests in different UK cities, in what was called the "summer uprising" (July 2019).[50] In addition, the dates of production of CAPs or similar initiatives (Figure 3), the majority between 2019 and 2020, might indicate changes in the paradigm of climate action, driven by CEDs. "Climate emergency mode" demands action outside business-as-usual approaches, with crucial deployment of economic and social capital.[51] The analysis of documents containing CEDs indicated a potential shift, since many cited the 2018 IPCC Report,[52] highlighting the need for urgency in climate action, for example Swansea,[53] Blackpool[54] and Rotherham.[55]

This type of arrangement from local governments involves institutional capacity and proper policies to offer guidance and responses, considering that other sectors might not engage entirely with costs and responsibility.[56] The survey revealed that the percentage of LAs with CAPs was higher among those with specific departments for climate action, with the same true for the presence

48 *Demeritt and Langdon*, supra, note 24.

49 *A. Evans, H. Ellis-Petersen and N. Zhou*, "Climate strikes held around the world – as it happened", *The Guardian*, 15 March 2019, available at <https://www.theguardian.com/environment/live/2019/mar/15/climate-strikes-2019-live-latest-climate-change-global-warming>.

50 *M. Blackall*, "Extinction Rebellion protests block traffic in five UK cities", *The Guardian*, 15 July 2019, available at <https://www.theguardian.com/environment/2019/jul/15/extinction-rebellion-protests-block-traffic-in-five-uk-cities>.

51 *Davidson et al.*, supra, note 12.

52 *Masson-Delmotte et al.*, supra, note 10.

53 *Swansea Council*, "Notice of Motion on Climate Emergency", 27 June 2019, available at <https://democracy.swansea.gov.uk/documents/s57602/NOM%20on%20Climate%20Emergency.pdf?LLL=0>.

54 *Blackpool Council*, "Declaring a Climate Emergency", 26 June 2019, available at <https://democracy.blackpool.gov.uk/mgAi.aspx?ID=20236>.

55 *Rotherham Council*, "Notice of motion – Climate Change Emergency", 30 October 2019, available at <https://www.rotherham.gov.uk/energy-climate-change/responding-climate-emergency>.

56 *Davidson et al.*, supra, note 12.

of GHG emissions targets. In this context, many of the sampled LAs in the UK (33.7 per cent of the valid responses) still needed to create departments dedicated specifically to climate change, creating the opportunity for connecting different sectors in local government and maximising collaboration co-benefits.[57] Survey respondents seemed already to understand the problem, considering, for example, the data for the West Midlands Region, where only 40 per cent of the LAs had a designated department, and 80 per cent of respondents considered lack of staffing and lack of expertise to be significant hurdles in tackling climate change.

Despite the concern with measures able to constrain global warming and meet GHG emissions reduction targets, most CAPs or similar initiatives were still in the discussion phase (42.5 per cent), precluding a deeper analysis regarding priorities. The perception of respondents, however, did not appear to show a pattern (Table 2). The results differ from those obtained by Heidrich et al.,[58] where the analysis focused on LAs' climate change documents. There, transport and waste management ranked among the highest priorities (93 per cent and 96 per cent, respectively), which might indicate that respondents preferred not to commit with specific sectors in their answers to the questionnaire. Another possibility for the absence of a particular set of priorities lies in the existence of differences in territorial emissions, derived from variations in the economic roles of LAs in production networks, along with social, institutional and environmental factors specific to each area.[59] Previous works have demonstrated that different lifestyles, taking into consideration income and education, for example, have an important role in CO_2 emissions derived from consumption in the UK.[60] The GHG emissions reports produced by local governments indicate these discrepancies. For example, while in the UK as a whole the highest emissions come from the transport sector – 24 per cent in 2019[61] – Cambridge's Annual Update Report showed that the city's largest source of emissions was from industrial and commercial properties (49 per cent in 2017).[62] In Stockton-on-Tees,

57 *Heidrich et al.*, supra, note 26.

58 *Heidrich et al.*, supra, note 26.

59 *J. Minx et al.*, "Carbon footprints of cities and other human settlements in the UK", *Environmental Research Letters*, 2013 (3), 035039; *D. Reckien et al.*, "The Influence of Drivers and Barriers on Urban Adaptation and Mitigation Plans – An Empirical Analysis of European Cities", *PLoS ONE*, 2015 (10), e0135597.

60 *G. Baiocchi, J. Minx and K. Hubacek*, "The Impact of Social Factors and Consumer Behavior on Carbon Dioxide Emissions in the United Kingdom: A Regression Based on Input – Output and Geodemographic Consumer Segmentation Data", *Journal of Industrial Ecology*, 2010 (1), 50.

61 *Committee on Climate Change*, "Reducing UK emissions. 2020 Progress Report to Parliament", Committee on Climate Change, 2020.

62 *Cambridge Council*, "Annual Climate Change Strategy, Carbon Management Plan and Climate Change Fund Update Report", Cambridge Council, 3 October 2019, available at <https://www.cambridge.gov.uk/media/7731/climate-change-strategy-progress-report-2018-19.pdf>.

the same sectors were responsible for 69 per cent of emissions in 2013.[63] Such results reveal the importance of personalised solutions and localised initiatives, since achieving net-zero targets will be more difficult for some LAs than others. In response to this, many LAs are joining forces and building closer relationships, generating multi-agency groupings in a collaborative climate action effort.[64]

Although the UK Localism Act 2011 approved, for LAs, a "general power of competence", enabling some of these measures, the focus of top-down accountability was shifted to financial conformance,[65] resulting in an austerity localism, whereby there is a reallocation of obligations from national to local level, but without a corresponding redistribution of funding and authority.[66] Furthermore, the absence of direct guidance may relate to the high percentage of respondents (47.3 per cent) that saw lack of support from central government as an important hurdle, considering that climate governance at the national level impacts on climate plans at the lower administrative levels.[67] Similarly, according to Eyre and Killip,[68] the Clean Growth Strategy from 2017 presents restricted direct policies for energy efficiency, zero-carbon housing, and clean heat/transport, areas where LAs are requested to act on. This issue was also observed in previous surveys, indicating that the problem persists, along with lack of funding, which was also cited as a recurring hurdle, in this and other works.[69] This austerity localism approach not only assigns responsibility to local government, but also to the private sector and the community, and while it might encourage a depoliticised and voluntaristic spirit, it can also develop opportunities for civic engagement and resilience, to build alternative projects.[70]

The idea that public engagement is essential for local governance is reinforced by the answers of LAs' officers regarding community involvement in climate

---

63 *Stockton-on-Tees Council*, "Climate Change Strategy for Stockton-on-Tees: 2016–2021", Stockton-on-Tees Council, April 2016, available at <https://cape.mysociety.org/media/data/plans/stockton-on-tees-borough-council-aee34a7.pdf>.

64 *P. Gudde et al.*, "The role of UK local government in delivering on net zero carbon commitments: You've declared a Climate Emergency, so what's the plan?", *Energy Policy*, 2021 (154), 112245.

65 *L. Ferry and P. Eckersley*, "Budgeting and governing for deficit reduction in the UK public sector: act three 'accountability and audit arrangements'", *Public Money & Management*, 2015 (3), 203–210.

66 *S. Davoudi and A. Madanipour*, "Localism and neo-liberal governmentality", *Town Planning Review*, 2013 (84), 551–562; *Q. Bradley*, "Bringing Democracy Back Home: Community Localism and the Domestication of Political Space", *Environment and Planning D: Society and Space*, 2014 (32), 642–657; *J. Morris et al.*, "Energy policy under austerity localism: what role for local authorities?", *Local Government Studies*, 2017 (43), 882–902.

67 *Heidrich et al.*, supra, note 21; *Tingey and Webb*, supra, note 26.

68 *N. Eyre and G. Killip*, *Shifting the focus: energy demand in a net-zero carbon UK*, Centre for Research into Energy Demand Solutions, 2019.

69 *Demeritt and Langdon*, supra, note 24; *Porter, Demeritt and Dessai*, supra, note 23.

70 *A. Williams, M. Goodwin and P. Cloke*, "Neoliberalism, Big Society, and progressive localism", *Environment and Planning A*, 2014 (46), 2798–2815; *Bradley*, supra, note 66.

action. There were no answers ranking this below moderate, with 86.3 per cent believing such involvement should be to a great or very great extent. Despite this orientation, the number of initiatives with non-governmental actors was considerably lower – 58.2 per cent, and the increase in the role of community since CED had only been small to moderate, for the majority of respondents (80.5 per cent). Therefore, LAs' actions must focus on expanding the opportunities for public engagement, and work on policies that allow material participation.

Regardless of unfavourable public behaviour acting as a barricade to transitioning to a low-carbon economy,[71] the current landscape suggests that the public is open to talking about climate action, with recent research suggesting an increase in public engagement with climate change, particularly after mid 2018.[72] Furthermore, despite the characteristics presented by Connelly et al.[73] for social movements – constructed hierarchically and using institutional channels for communication – in recent social movements, such as Extinction Rebellion and school strikes, these features have not been prevalent. The groups have been formed mainly by students (both at school and university), with education about climate change, an understanding of science, and a great concern with the necessity of immediate action[74] perhaps indicating a change in patterns of action.

Regarding the channels of communication used by the UK LAs sampled, the research presented here found that websites and social media were the preferred means, with both chosen by more than 76 per cent of respondents. Although Internet media constitutes an up-to-date vehicle of climate communication for reaching the novel types of social movements discussed above, LAs must develop spaces not only to communicate their actions, but to involve the community in the process of climate mitigation/adaptation, since a low-carbon economy can benefit from a bottom-up approach.[75] Therefore, channels of communication such as citizen's assemblies and forums offer an opportunity to hear the community, and to build urban governance through hybrid arrangements made up of multiple actors (the business sector, public–private partnerships, civil society organisations and community groups).[76] Moreover, intermediate players, such as local universities and non-governmental organisations (NGOs),

71 *Dasgupta and De Cian*, supra, note 14.

72 *YouGov*, "Concern for the environment at record highs", YouGov, 5 June 2019, available at <https://yougov.co.uk/politics/articles/23691-concern-environment-record-highs>; *Thackeray et al.*, supra, note 9.

73 *Connelly et al.*, supra, note 24.

74 *BBC*, "Greta Thunberg quotes: 10 famous lines from teen activist", BBC, 25 September 2019, available at <https://www.bbc.co.uk/newsround/49812183>; *Thackeray et al.*, supra, note 9.

75 *P. North*, "The Politics of Climate Activism in the UK: A Social Movement Analysis", *Environment and Planning A* 2011 (7), 1581–1598.

76 *H. Bulkeley et al.*, *Transnational Climate Change Governance*, Cambridge University Press, 2011; *Broto*, supra, note 30.

can act as bodies for dissemination of knowledge, and narrow the gap between public and government, thus enhancing climate governance.[77] Initiatives such as participatory budgeting – a successful participatory tool invented in Porto Alegre (Brazil) more than 25 years ago, and still in use – offer an example of measures available to include the community and provide them with an active role.[78] In Europe, Dutch municipalities have adopted neighbourhood governance, through establishment of neighbourhood budgets or grounds for public participation in a network structure.[79] Some LAs in the UK are starting this process, as the survey showed that almost 40 per cent of respondents were using citizens' assemblies, consultation channels or similar fora. CAPs and similar initiatives are also incorporating the strategy: Wirral's climate strategy refers to the organisation of a public annual climate emergency forum;[80] London has launched a Community Energy Fund (LCEF) to support the development of community energy projects;[81] and South Tyneside has promoted consultation activities to inform its strategy and action plan.[82] Tactics such as these facilitate public dialogue, and might act as drivers of engagement within local governance.[83]

Irrespective of the progress achieved so far, the perceptions of LAs' officers about the COVID-19 pandemic are negative, with a major belief that it will impact climate action at least to some/moderate extent. The open-ended questions about negative effects of the pandemic were aligned with other hurdles indicated by LAs, considering that the main adverse effects were financial impacts, and delays in implementing climate actions. The economic forecast is also inhospitable, with an expected contraction of world gross domestic product (GDP) of between 8 and 15 per cent, linked to the social consequences of prolonged closures of venues for social interactions and education.[84]

---

77 *M. Kwon, H.S. Jang and R.C. Feiock*, "Climate Protection and Energy Sustainability Policy in California Cities: What Have We Learned?", *Journal of Urban Affairs*, 2014 (36), 905–924.

78 *Y. Sintomer, C. Herzberg and A. Röcke*, "Participatory Budgeting in Europe: Potentials and Challenges", *International Journal of Urban and Regional Research*, 2008 (32), 164–178.

79 *J. Bakker et al.*, "Citizens' Initiatives: How Local Governments Fill their Facilitative Role", *Local Government Studies*, 2012 (38), 395–414.

80 *Wirral Council*, "A strategy for Wirral in the face of the global climate emergency", Wirral Council, 18 December 2019, available at <https://www.wirral.gov.uk/sites/default/files/all/About%20the%20council/climate%20change/Cool2-Strategy-2020.pdf>.

81 *Greater London Authority*, "London Environment Strategy: One year on report", Greater London Authority, December 2019, available at <https://www.london.gov.uk/sites/default/files/les_one_year_on_2019_0.pdf>.

82 *South Tyneside Council*, "Sustainable South Tyneside 2020–2025", South Tyneside Council, 1 May 2020, available at <https://publications.southtyneside.gov.uk/strategies/climate-change-2020/>.

83 *R.J. Romsdahl*, "Deliberative framing: opening up discussions for local-level public engagement on climate change", *Climatic Change*, 2020 (162), 145–163.

84 *D.D. Sarma*, "COVID-19 and the Climate Crisis: Challenges and Opportunities ('The Times They Are A-Changin')", *ACS Energy Letters*, 2020 (5), 2916–2918.

Nonetheless, similarly to what has been observed about COVID-19, numerous studies suggest that climate change mitigation is more efficient than adaptation, from an economic perspective.[85] According to Hepburn et al.,[86] the COVID-19 recovery response can be used as an opportunity for policymakers, by implementing green fiscal recovery packages, to focus on long-term solutions to climate change, decoupling economic growth from GHG emissions, as well as addressing welfare inequalities aggravated by the pandemic. Manzanedo and Manning[87] also stress that policies should change the perspective, to communicate climate change prevention as an investment (using the same logic applied to personal health insurance), while building public confidence in science, and keeping communication clear and consistent about the consequences and risks of the climate crisis, similarly to the strategy adopted by countries that effectively contained the worst scenarios of the pandemic. Although COVID-19 has slowed the climate action "momentum", the very outcomes of the pandemic could be used to drive a new impetus. Analysis of the positive aspects of the COVID-19 pandemic observed by LAs' officers suggests that new ways of living are possible. The increase in active travel, with an attendant reduction of traffic, as well as improvements in air quality due to reductions in emissions, were the most common answers, but a new appreciation of nature, and willingness/resilience to change, were also described. Hence, the idea of social mobilisation being built by community empowerment, aligned with education through climate "truth-telling", gains material support.

The limitations of the results involve sample size, particularly regarding Scotland, Northern Ireland and Wales. Although Wales's and Northern Ireland's numbers of responses achieved the minimum of 20 per cent of the national population proposed by Eurostat Urban Audit Methodology,[88] Scotland's achieved only 18.64 per cent. Additionally, the number of LAs sampled in the three countries was small. Nevertheless, regarding the UK as whole, and England specifically, there are still useful insights for future research with a larger range of LAs. Additionally, because of the method used for sending the questionnaires – through EIR – some LAs' officers did not answer opinion-based questions. The number of these, however, was small, compared with the total number of respondents. Future research could benefit from combined

---

85 *M. Burke, S.M. Hsiang and E. Miguel*, "Global non-linear effect of temperature on economic production", *Nature*, 2015 (527), 235–239; *N. Glanemann, S. N. Willner and A. Levermann*, "Paris Climate Agreement passes the cost-benefit test", *Nature Communications*, 2020 (11), 1–11; *Y.-M. Wei et al.*, "Self-preservation strategy for approaching global warming targets in the post-Paris agreement era", *Nature Communications*, 2020 (11), 1–13.

86 *Hepburn et al.*, supra, note 38.

87 *Manzanedo and Manning*, supra, note 37.

88 *Eurostat*, supra, note 43.

investigations of specific actors and the public view, as well as analysis of the role Brexit will play in future policies.

5. CONCLUSION

The role of LAs in relation to climate action remains open for definition, since they are expected to deliver the material task of implementing climate policies, but the power and financial means to do so are not always present. This contribution indicates that the analysed UK LAs are continuing on a progressive path of climate action, showing advances in quantitative involvement, and suggesting a potential paradigm change compatible with the urgency recognised in CEDs. The adoption of CAPs and GHG emissions reduction targets is higher among LAs with a specific department dealing with climate change, confirming the importance of expertise for dealing with the matter. In general, the survey does not demonstrate a clear set of priorities, with many LAs understanding them as inapplicable. Additionally, analysis of the priorities in the strategies is hindered by the stages CAPs are at, since many are still in the discussion phase, despite the ambitious net-zero targets proposed. The hurdles faced by LAs, however, are consistent with what has been observed in the literature, positioning lack of funding as a significant challenge – an issue accompanying the austerity localism agenda. In this context, public engagement in climate action gains importance, especially considering the high level of community involvement that survey respondents deemed necessary in this matter, and the influence attributed to social movements in CEDs. Because the level of public engagement after these actions remains below the levels expected from LAs, a community role, via different participatory tools, should be a pivotal aspect of future climate policies.

APPENDIX

Table 4. Hurdles separated by England's regions

Expertise	0 (N=1)	1 (N=13)	2 (N=16)	3 (N=3)	4 (N=5)	5 (N=11)	6 (N=7)	7 (N=7)	8 (N=8)
N/A		7.7%				9.1%	16.7%		
1=Smallest		15.4%	7.7%	33.3%		9.1%			16.7%
2	100%	7.7%	7.7%	33.3%	20%	27.3%		71.4%	33.3%
3		38.5%	30.8%			27.3%	16.7%	14.3%	
4		15.4%	30.8%	33.3%	40%	18.2%	50%	14.3%	33.3%
5=Biggest		15.4%	23.1%		40%	9.1%	16.7%		16.7%

(continued)

Table 4 *continued*

Funding	**0 (N=1)**	**1 (N=13)**	**2 (N=16)**	**3 (N=3)**	**4 (N=5)**	**5 (N=11)**	**6 (N=7)**	**7 (N=7)**	**8 (N=8)**
N/A						9.1%	16.7%		
1=Smallest			7.7%						16.7%
2			7.7%			9.1%			33.3%
3		15.4%			20%	27.3%	16.7%	57.1%	16.7%
4		38.5%	23.1%	33.3%	20%	27.3%	33.3%	14.3%	33.3%
5=Biggest	100%	48.2%	61.5%	66.7%	60%	27.3%	33.3%	28.6%	

Jurisdiction	**0 (N=1)**	**1 (N=13)**	**2 (N=16)**	**3 (N=3)**	**4 (N=5)**	**5 (N=11)**	**6 (N=7)**	**7 (N=7)**	**8 (N=8)**
N/A		23.1%	15.4%			9.1%	16.7%		
1=Smallest		23.1%	15.4%		40%	9.1%		33.3%	
2		7.7%	38.5%			9.1%	33.3%		
3		23.1%	23.1%	100%	20%	36.4%	16.7%	16.7%	16.7%
4		23.1%	7.7%		40%	9.1%	33.3%	50%	50%
5=Biggest	100%					27.3			33.3%

Central Governance	**0 (N=1)**	**1 (N=13)**	**2 (N=16)**	**3 (N=3)**	**4 (N=5)**	**5 (N=11)**	**6 (N=7)**	**7 (N=7)**	**8 (N=8)**
N/A		7.7%				10%			
1=Smallest		30.8%			20%	10%			33.3%
2		15.4%	7.7%			10%	33.3%	16.7%	
3		15.4%	30.8%	66.7%	40%	20%	16.7%		16.7%
4		15.4%	38.5%	33.3%	20%	50%	33.3%	16.7%	50%
5=Biggest	100%	15.4%	23.1%		20%		16.7%	66.7%	

Staffing	**0 (N=1)**	**1 (N=13)**	**2 (N=16)**	**3 (N=3)**	**4 (N=5)**	**5 (N=11)**	**6 (N=7)**	**7 (N=7)**	**8 (N=8)**
N/A						9.1%			
1=Smallest		15.4%	16.7%			9.1%		33.3%	50%
2		15.4%	8.3%	66.7%	20%	18.2%	16.7%	16.7%	
3	100%	30.8%	16.7%			27.3%	33.3%	16.7%	33.3%
4		15.4%	33.3%	33.3%	40%	27.3%	50%		
5=Biggest		23.1%	25%		40%	9.1%		33.3%	16.7%

Note: Valid percentage. 0 = Greater London Authority; 1 = North East; 2 = North West; 3 = East Midlands; 4 = West Midlands; 5 = East; 6 = South East; 7 = South West; 8 = Yorkshire and the Humber.

Source: Compiled by the author.

Table 5. Answers to open-ended questions regarding positive and negative effects of COVID-19

	POSITIVE EFFECTS
Nature	Increased appreciation of nature and green spaces; increase in biodiversity.
Travel	Increase in active travel (walking/cycling); reduction of traffic, due to fall in domestic travel and motor vehicle usage; deployment of active transport measures (cycle lanes, pedestrian spaces, lowering road speeds).
Work	Increase in remote working, agile working, and inter-departmental working; less business travel; review of working practices.
Emissions	Improved air quality, due to reduction of emissions (from transport, from reduced building consumption), carbon and energy savings from less estate occupancy.
Behavioural Change	Increase in sense of community; community resilience; people shopping locally, and using local district centres; increased awareness about the importance of nature; seeing the two crises (COVID-19 and climate) as interlinked; desire for a green recovery.
Green Recovery	Use of recovery fund for green measures; funding for low-carbon investments; opportunity to reaffirm council's commitment to green recovery; central government-driven green recovery.
Other	Capitalise on positive changes made by people and businesses; transition in the wider economy; reduced waste arising from offices and schools; technological advances to enable service delivery; increased levels of flexibility within the workforce.
	NEGATIVE EFFECTS
Delay	Climate action has been delayed and focus diverted.
Financial	Lack of resources; concerns about financial support.
Waste	Increases in domestic waste and single-use plastic, and fly-tipping.
Staff	Reprioritisation of staff resource to pandemic response.
Energy	Increase in energy use in homes, due to remote work; less efficient heating for staff; instability in energy prices.
Transport	Increased use of private vehicle instead of public transport.
Other	Health inequalities, risk of high-carbon approach to economic recovery, impact upon engagement and communities; impact upon household finances and well-being.

Source: Compiled by the author.

THE ROLE OF REGULATION IN STRENGTHENING CLIMATE RESILIENCE AND FOOD SECURITY IN NIGERIA

Erimma Gloria ORIE* and King James NKUM**

1. BACKGROUND

Climate change is the biggest environmental problem of our time, threatening the existence of people and the environment. It is a major threat to the agricultural system and food security in many sub-Saharan African countries (including Nigeria). Food security is attained when all people, at all times, have physical, social, and economic access to sufficient, safe and nutritious food that meets their dietary needs and food preferences, for an active and healthy life.[1] Climate change refers to all climate changes as a result of natural variations and human activities. The natural variation is due to the increasing concentration of carbon dioxide (CO_2) and other heat-retaining gases[2] in the atmosphere. These heat-retaining gases are known as greenhouse gases (GHGs) and occur naturally in the atmosphere. Greenhouse gases prevent the direct heat of the sun from warming the earth's surface, but allow enough heat to keep the earth warm enough for life to survive. An increased emission of CO_2 into the atmosphere leads to a depletion of the ozone layer, and thus to an increase in the Earth's surface temperature, due to direct heating of the Earth's surface by ultraviolet radiation from the sun.[3]

* FCArb; Head of Department, Private and Property Law 2016–20, Faculty of Law, National Open University of Nigeria, Lagos. ORCID: https://orcid.org/0000-0002-9577-2083; eorie@noun.edu.ng; mmaorie@yahoo.co.uk.

** Deputy Dean/Head of Private and Property Law Department, Faculty of Law, Taraba State University, Nigeria. Email: kingjamesnkum@gmail.com; Tel. +2348065319125.

1 FAO, *Food and Agricultural Organization Report of the World Food Summit.* Rome: FAO, 1996, <https://www.fao.org/3/w3548e/w3548e00.htm>.

2 Such as methane, ozone, nitrous oxide, carbon monoxide and water vapour.

3 See P.A. Bucklund et al., *The Effects of Climate Change on Agriculture, Land Resources, Water Resources, and Biodiversity in the United States. A Report by the U.S. Climate Change Science Program and the Subcommittee on Global Change Research*, Washington DC: U.S. Environmental Protection Agency, 2008.

Climate change is also caused by human activities, such as large-scale deforestation, widespread land use, overpopulation, reduced dependence on organic fuels, and accelerated uptake of fossil fuels. These activities result in higher emissions of greenhouse gases into the atmosphere, which in turn increases the average temperature of the Earth's surface.[4]

Climate change is a threat to food security, due to its impact on the agricultural system. Agricultural production in most of sub-Saharan Africa (including Nigeria) is climate-dependent. Climate change has a direct impact on the productivity of physical factors of production, such as soil moisture and fertility, and this affects agricultural production, which in turn has a negative impact on food security. In other words, a nation's food security depends on the stability and sustainability of sufficient food from the agricultural sector.[5]

Climate change is often largely and primarily caused by specific human influences. The public has also been blamed for their contribution to climate change affecting food security in Nigeria. In an attempt to meet their energy needs, Nigerians over-rely on fossil fuels, resulting in the release of toxic gases, such as greenhouse gases – mainly CO_2 and methane – into the atmosphere. The fertilisers used on Nigerian farms, to improve crop yields, are also petrochemicals that have a negative impact on the atmosphere. Excess fertiliser escapes from fields as gases into the atmosphere. The use of synthetic nitrogen fertilisers have accelerated the rise in nitrous oxide over the past few decades. Deforestation results in the emission of CO_2, which saturates the Earth's atmosphere, and consequently leads to thicker cloud layers, with adverse consequences for climate conditions in some regions.

All of these threaten food security in Nigeria, and require the urgent attention of the Nigerian government and people. Climate change triggered by global warming is having profound effects on seasonal cycle disruptions and the instability and predictability of ecosystems, with adverse impacts on agricultural production in general, and especially on water and food production.[6]

Changes in precipitation patterns disrupt seasonal planting cycles. Late or very early rains have affected the farming and planting seasons. This often results in an unusual order when planting and transplanting crops. Late or delayed rains usually prolong the dry season, leading to a delayed sowing season. The adverse effect of the weather goes beyond the impracticability of the extreme rainy

---

4 Ibid.

5 J.L. Gamble, K.L. Ebi, F.G. Sussman and T.J. Wilbanks, *Analyses of the Effects of Global Change on Human Health and Welfare and Human Systems. A Report by the U.S. Climate Change Science Program and the Subcommittee on Global Change Research*, Washington DC: U.S. Environmental Protection Agency, 2008.

6 J.A. Ayo, M.O. Omosebi and A. Sulieman, "Effect of climate change on food security in Nigeria", (2014) (3)(4) *Journal of Environmental Science, Computer Science and Engineering and Technology*, 1763–1778.

weather, and the changes in rainfall. It has a major impact on the availability of healthy food for humans and animals. This, in turn, will drive up food prices, and make it even more difficult for the poor to access food.[7]

This contribution attempts to explore vexing issues on climate change and food security. It also looks at the regulatory measures put in place, through the Climate Change Act of 2021, towards mitigating the effects of climate change on food security in Nigeria. The contribution concludes that the implementation of the relevant legal framework for climate change, towards effectively addressing the challenges of climate change adaptation, is essential, if Nigeria's quest for food security for its population of over 200 million is to be achieved.

2. NIGERIA'S EXPERIENCE WITH CLIMATE CHANGE IMPACT

Climate change is widely believed to be disproportionately affecting Africa, with the rates of temperature rise and associated impacts, such as desertification, coastal erosion, biodiversity loss and saltwater intrusion, increasing faster than the global average. In 2016, Verisk Maplecroft ranked Nigeria as the seventh-most vulnerable country in the world. Similarly, Nigeria's vulnerability to climate disasters and adaptability, in 2021, ranked 161 out of 182 countries assessed by the Notre Dame Global Adaptation Initiative (ND-GAIN).[8] Nigeria is particularly vulnerable due to its large population, long coastline, limited resources to adequately fund climate change mitigation from public and private bodies, and knowledge gap on how to adapt to climate impacts.[9]

The country is currently facing challenges in the form of complex direct and indirect impacts, such as food insecurity, forced displacement, conflict, negative health impacts, and more, which collectively represent barriers to climate action and economic growth. In particular, drought and desertification in the arid and semi-arid regions of northern Nigeria have disproportionately affected local rain-fed farming communities. Drought and desertification are causing several communities dedicated to livestock to move from north to south, clashing with indigenous communities dedicated to agriculture, with increasingly scarce

7 Ibid.

8 H.M. Butu, C.U. Okeke and C. Okereke "Climate Change Adaptation in Nigeria: Strategies, Initiatives, and Practices", African Policy Research Institute, 10 October 2022, <https://afripoli.org/climate-change-adaptation-in-nigeria-strategies-initiatives-and-practices>.

9 O.E. Ayinde, M. Muchie and G.B. Olatunji, "Effect of Climate Change on Agricultural Productivity in Nigeria: a Co-integration Model Approach", (2011) (35)(3) *Journal of Human Ecology*, 189–194; M. Berhanu and A.O. Wolde, "Review on Climate Change Impacts and its Adaptation Strategies on Food Security in Sub-Saharan Africa", (2019) (19)(3) *Agricultural Socio-Economics Journal*, 145–154.

resources. These nomadic herders also bring with them zoonotic diseases that may be exacerbated by climate change.[10]

As early as 2012, the country was already suffering from climate fluctuations and high-intensity precipitation events in its central and southern regions, which led to multiyear flood disasters with total losses of around US$16.9 billion. Currently, floods and other climate change-related disasters in the country are also leading to an increase in the incidence of diseases, mainly vector-borne diseases, which caused over 200,000 deaths.[11] For example, in 2021, 32 per cent of all malaria incidents worldwide affected a total of 60 million Nigerians, with huge death figures. There is also an increasing risk of water-borne diseases such as cholera. Elsewhere in the country, a combination of droughts, encroaching salt water and rising sea levels has negatively impacted crop yields and urban infrastructure, leading to higher food prices, higher development costs and other related impacts. Crop yields are particularly sensitive to climatic changes and variability, as they are affected by multiple factors, and agriculture is largely rain-fed; only 1 per cent of agricultural land nationwide is irrigated, and more than 70 per cent is devoted to subsistence farming, which accounts for almost 23 per cent of gross domestic product (GDP).[12]

Econometric analysis estimates that Nigeria could lose between N15 trillion (US$100 billion) and N69 trillion (US$460 billion) if it does not adequately adapt to climate change by 2050.[13] These vulnerabilities persist, harming the lives and livelihoods of Nigerians, despite Nigeria having signed the Sendai Framework for Disaster Risk Reduction 2015–2030 (SFDRR).[14] The SFDRR is a programme aiming to significantly reduce disaster risks and loss of life and livelihoods, improve the health of communities and countries, and build disaster resilience, by addressing priorities such as understanding disaster risk and strengthening and implementing disaster risk investments. Through these goals, it aims to reduce mortality and direct economic losses and damage to critical infrastructure, and to significantly improve global cooperation and access to early warning systems.[15] This discrepancy between ongoing vulnerabilities and the signing of the SFDRR seems to indicate a gap

10 M.J. Fasona and A.S. Omojola, "Climate Change, Human Security and Communal Clashes in Nigeria", a paper presented at an International Workshop, Human Security and Climate Change, held at Holmen Fjord Hotel, Asker, near Oslo, 21–23 June 2005; O. Folami, "Climate Change and Inter-Ethnic Conflict in Nigeria", (2013) (25)(1) *Peace Review* 104–110.

11 Ibid.

12 Ibid.

13 E.G. Orie, "Climate Change Adaptation Mechanism for Sustainable Development Goal 1 in Nigeria: Legal Imperative" in W.L. Filho, N. Oguge, D. Ayal, L. Adeleke and I. Da Silva (eds.), *African Handbook of Climate Change Adaptation*, Cham: Springer, 2020, https://doi.org/10.1007/978-3-030-42091-8_81-1, pp. 1–21, 7.

14 S.L. Okoye, "Effects of Climate Change", The Heinrich Boll Foundation Abuja, Nigeria, 2016, <https://www.emerald.com/insight/content/doi/10.1108/IJCCSM-11-2020-0119/full/html>.

15 Ibid.

between the agreements signed and the sufficiency of the projects designed and implemented across the country.

3. CLIMATE CHANGE AND FOOD INSECURITY IN NIGERIA

Food security means access to nutritious staple foods. According to the United Nations Committee on World Food Security, food security means all people having physical, social and economic access, at all times, to sufficient, safe and nutritious food to meet their nutritional preferences and nutritional needs for an active and healthy life.[16] Food security, as defined at the World Food Summit in 1974, means the availability, at all times, of sufficient supplies of basic foodstuffs to sustain steady expansions in food consumption, and to accommodate fluctuations in production and prices. According to the Food and Agricultural Organization (FAO), food insecurity exists when not all people have adequate physical, social or economic access to food.[17]

Nigeria has been identified as one of the sub-Saharan African countries vulnerable to changing climatic conditions. Some researchers have found that recurring environmental disasters in parts of Nigeria have exacerbated food productivity issues and human suffering over the past decade, including losses of lives, crops and livestock, and displacement of people.[18] Changes in environmental conditions caused by climate change affect Nigeria's six vegetation zones differently.[19] In the semi-arid region of Sudan, and the arid savannah of the Sahel, this is leading to reduced rainfall, drought and increased desertification. In the savannah belt of Northern and Southern Guinea, it causes changes in precipitation patterns – often late rains and a longer dry season – and places along the coasts experience severe flooding during the rainy season.[20] In the tropical forest zone, it causes delays in the onset of rains, a prolonged dry season, heatwaves and coastal flooding, while in the mangrove swamps it causes flooding in generally dry plains, and poses the risk of a continued rise in sea levels, threatening agricultural activities, and also affecting the rise in

16 FAO, IFAD, UNICEF, WFP and WHO, *The State of Food Security and Nutrition in the World 2017: Building Resilience for Peace and Food Security*, Rome: FAO, 2017; *The State of Food Security and Nutrition in the World 2018: Building Climate Resilience for Food Security and Nutrition*, Rome: FAO, 2018.

17 Ibid.

18 C.M. Ughaelu, "Contemporary Environmental Issues Respect to Food Production in Nigeria", (2017) (41)(2) *Journal of Environmental Management*, 108–117; T.C. Ogbuchi, "Quantitative Indicators of Production of Food Crops", (2020) (32)(1) *Journal of Tropical Agriculture*, 79–88.

19 Ibid.

20 T.U. Ikem, "Prospects of Food Self-Reliance in Nigeria" (2018) (56)(1) *Farming and Rural System Economics*, 112–120.

water temperature. Recent studies have shown that extreme weather conditions, manifesting as desertification, high rainfall and flooding, have very adverse consequences for food production.[21]

The reason for the food and security crises Nigeria is currently facing is not unclear; weather has been identified by researchers as a subtle causative factor. The continued decline in the precipitation gradient in parts of northern Nigeria has rendered the affected areas increasingly unsuitable for agricultural and livestock production using natural resources.[22] In addition, persistent flooding in coastal and extreme south Nigeria has resulted in crop damage, loss of soil fertility, soil toxicity and soil ecosystem disruption.[23] The World Bank and the FAO have warned, in their various publications, that climate change will continue to pose a serious threat to sustainable food production in Nigeria.[24]

A lot of research indicates that weather variability caused by climate change is negatively impacting agricultural productivity in Nigeria, and leading to a decline in manufacturing output. This situation has led to food shortages and disruption, leading to soaring food prices. The era of food insecurity is deepening in Nigeria, due to climatic factors that have limited agricultural productivity. Disturbances caused by climate change, such as droughts, heavy rains, flooding of farmland, increased temperature, increased soil aridity and acidification, changes in relative humidity, and increased evaporation, among others, are adversely affecting agricultural productivity and food systems in Nigeria. Adishi and Oluka found that climate change has become a daily reality in Nigeria, with increasing intensity, as a result of the frequency of environmental issues, such as floods, droughts, rising temperatures and extreme weather events, that disrupt productive agricultural activities.[25] Similarly, Onuoha and Ezirim found that "the livelihoods of some 15 million pastoralists in northern Nigeria are threatened by decreasing access to water and scarcity of grazing land associated with climate change".[26] Climate change is gradually exacerbating

21 M.C. Tirado et al., "Climate change and food safety: A review", (2010) (43)(7) *Food Research International*, 1745–1765.

22 U.I. Uwazie, "Consumption of different forms of fish in Abakaliki metropolis of Ebonyi State, Nigeria", (2020) (20)(2) *African Journal of Food, Agriculture, Nutrition and Development*, 15523–15537; T. Wossen et al., "Impacts of Climate Variability and Food Price Volatility on Household Income and Food Security of Farm Households in East and West Africa" (2018) (163) *Agricultural Systems*, 7–15.

23 O.O. Okorafor, C.O. Akinbile and A.J. Adeyemo, "Soil Erosion in South Eastern Nigeria: A Review", (2017) *Scientific Research Journal (SCIRJ)*, vol. V, issue IX, Sep. 2017, ISSN 2201–2796, <https://www.scirj.org/papers-0917/scirj-P0917431.pdf>.

24 FAO, IFAD, UNICEF, WFP and WHO (above, n. 15).

25 E. Adishi and N.L. Oluka, "Climate Change, Insecurity and Conflict: Issues and Probable Roadmap for Achieving Sustainable Development Goals in Nigeria", (2018) (4)(8) *International Journal of Social Sciences and Management Research*, 12–20.

26 F.C. Onuoha and G.E. Ezirim, "Climate Change and National Security: Exploring the Conceptual and Empirical Connections in Nigeria", (2010) (12)(4) *Journal of Sustainable Development in Africa*, 255–269.

food insecurity in Nigeria, particularly in areas currently at risk of hunger and malnutrition. Moreover, climate variability and extremes are likely to pose a greater challenge to food stability. In addition, persistently rising food prices in parts of Nigeria will make staple foods inaccessible to low-income people. Increasing aridity in the savannah regions of the Sahel and Sudan has rendered large areas of land unusable for agricultural productivity, with the consequent crisis of food security in the affected areas, which are densely settled.

In addition, the number of malnourished children in Nigeria is expected to increase steadily due to the threats of climate change. One of the main reasons climate change has remained a global problem is the threat it poses to agricultural production. Empirical studies have shown that the higher and more variable temperatures and rainfall patterns observed in Nigeria over the past decade are gradually changing traditional agricultural production patterns there. The recurrence of extreme climatic events such as droughts and floods has thrown the agricultural production system into crisis. In general, researchers believe that increasing desertification is leading to the loss of water bodies and aquatic animals. Another aspect of food production that is affected by climate change is the quality of the food. Some empirical studies have shown that variability in climatic conditions has serious consequences for the nutrient composition of food crops. Therefore, people may be exposed to the consumption of toxic foods, or may not be able to meet their recommended daily caloric intake, due to the reduced quality of the crop. Fluctuations in weather conditions also pose serious challenges for food storage.

The Nigerian Meteorological Agency (NIMET) has observed some changes in climate parameters, such as precipitation, temperature and extreme weather events. These changes, adversely affecting agricultural production activities, have been recorded in several ecological zones in Nigeria.[27]

The subtle nature of climate change hides its devastating impact on people's lives. Food insecurity is one of its main consequences. It has obvious physiological effects on crops and livestock, such as changes in soil nutrients, a decrease in water resources, a change in humidity, an increase in temperature, and an increase in weeds and pests. Climate change is causing conditions such as desertification, erosion and ecological destruction, which threaten human security in affected regions, and cause droughts, floods and extreme environmental conditions that limit agricultural production. Climate change continues to pose a threat to agricultural development in Nigeria, with the loss of arable land due to flooding and increasing drought in the Sahel vegetation

27 K.J. Ani, V.O. Anyika and E. Mutambara, "The Impact of Climate Change on Food and Human Security in Nigeria" (2021) 14(2) *International Journal of Climate Change Strategies and Management* <https://www.emerald.com/insight/content/doi/10.1108/IJCCSM-11-2020-0119/full/html>.

zones and Sudan having serious consequences for agricultural productivity. Poor agricultural production, as a result of climate change, constitutes a major food crisis in Nigeria. The pattern of food production and distribution has been continuously affected by climate change, and disruptions in the usual system of food production and distribution have contributed to food supply shortages and led to steadily increasing food prices. This condition is attributed to stress associated with climate change. Climate change is undermining the ability of developing countries to achieve agricultural production targets. The persistence of this deficit indicates an intense food-security crisis.[28]

Climate change is also affecting aquatic ecosystems. The warming of the sea, changes in its salinity, and the increase in its acidity, are some of the physical changes brought about by climate change. Several cases of aquatic mass extinctions in the Niger Delta are evidence of the dire consequences of climate change. Such losses threaten the livelihoods of riverine communities that depend heavily on food and trade.[29]

Food insecurity is one of the main consequences of climate change. Changing climatic conditions have had a lasting negative impact on agricultural production activity in Nigeria, making food production unstable and unsustainable. Some of the threats that climate change poses to food production in Nigeria include the fact that climate change has gradually altered the pattern of when rain starts and ends in parts of the country, altering the normal planting and harvest times. Changes in salinity, increased acidity and rising sea temperatures have adversely affected aquatic life. Massive fish kills have been recorded in the Niger Delta in the last ten years. Commercial fishing has been negatively impacted by climate change. Reduced yields from fishing activities pose a significant threat to food security and the livelihoods of households dependent on marine resources.[30] Overall, food security is crucial to the achievement of the United Nations Sustainable Development Goals (SDGs) at both the national and global levels, and demands apposite responses to tackle the issues described above.

4. GLOBAL TREND IN CLIMATE CHANGE REGULATION

Over the past few decades, there has been a significant proliferation of policies and laws responsive to climate change, as evidenced by the number of global climate change laws. However, it took more than 100 years, until the early 1990s, to develop an international scientific document and legal framework

[28] Ibid.
[29] Ibid.
[30] Ibid.

on climate change.[31] The Intergovernmental Panel on Climate Change (IPCC) was created as the main body to provide policymakers with regular assessments of climate change and its impacts and potential risks, and to recommend adaptation and mitigation options. It mainly identifies the areas where the scientific community agrees on the issue of climate change, and the areas where more research is needed. In this way, it develops a comprehensive report that is reviewed at different levels, and is of high relevance for policymakers. In 1990, the *First Assessment Report* (FAR) was published. The FAR was very effective in justifying the importance of climate change as a challenge with global consequences, and the need for international cooperation. It was also instrumental in creating the United Nations Framework Convention on Climate Change (UNFCCC) in 1992, which was signed by at least 166 nations at the Earth Summit in Rio de Janeiro, and came into force in 1994.[32]

The UNFCCC has provided important principles, all of which are critical to future international deliberations and processes on climate change. Its provisions include:

(1) Ways to stabilise the climate and prevent certain anthropogenic interventions in the climate system.
(2) Use of a time frame that allows natural areas to function without disruption to food systems and economic development.
(3) The importance of nations monitoring and reducing their greenhouse gas emissions.
(4) Concerns about the challenges that developing countries might face in monitoring and reducing their greenhouse gas emissions.
The need for precautionary measures in response to the adverse effects of climate change.[33]

In 1997, the Kyoto Conference approved the Kyoto Protocol, setting emissions targets for developed countries from 2008 to 2012. The agreement included mechanisms such as an emissions trading system, clean development, carbon credits for investment in emission savings in developing countries, and joint implementation for investments in emission savings in other countries.[34]

Discussions and negotiations on a Framework Convention on Climate Change (UNFCCC), held at the 1992 United Nations Conference on Environment and Development, can be seen as the beginning of climate change law. And

31 J. Peel, 'Climate Change Law: The Emergence of a New Legal Discipline', (2008) 32(3) *Melbourne University Law*, 922.

32 Ibid.

33 Ibid.

34 See United Nations Conference on Environment and Development, Rio de Janeiro, Brazil, 3–14 June 1992, <https://www.un.org/en/conferences/environment/rio1992>.

although the UNFCCC cannot be seen as a legal framework for tackling the global problems of climate change, it did place strong obligations on nations, in an attempt to reduce gas consumption, implying emissions, and so forged certain relevant standards for the international regulation of climate change, and also provided the necessary institutional funds for the operation and adaptation of the climate change system.

Thereafter, the countries endeavoured to pass national climate protection guidelines and laws. The efforts of the federal states resulted in about 60 climate laws by 1997. This number had increased to more than 1,200 by 2017, and more than 2,400 by 2021. The need to find a solution to the problem of climate change, combined with scientific evidence on climate change, has required countries to adopt different approaches to solving this problem. Countries are taking different approaches to addressing climate change, depending on their regulatory traditions and local context. While some adopt the legislative approach, others adopt executive directives, such as executive orders, decrees, policies and development plans, that describe the policy framework and the way forward. For example, in China, the executive, through the National Development and Reform Commission, is the dominant authority in developing climate policy, coordinating all government agencies involved, and leading the relevant reforms, while countries with a strong parliamentary system, such as the UK, have taken the legislative approach.[35]

The Paris Agreement, reached by 196 countries, recognises the importance of safeguarding food security and ending hunger, and the particular vulnerabilities of food production systems to the adverse impacts of climate change. More than 500 million small farms depend on agriculture for their livelihoods. These small farmers are key to global food security, and are responsible for up to 80 per cent of production in some regions. The Paris Agreement will mean that more finance will be made available for climate change adaptation by the international community. The global objective is to achieve US$100 billion per year in new and additional climate finance by 2020.[36]

With regard to climate adaptation policies in Africa, it has been submitted, in some quarters, that effective climate adaptation at scale is central to the future of Africa. To achieve this, Africa has established the Africa Adaptation Acceleration Program (AAAP). Through the AAAP, the Global Center on Adaptation (GCA) and the African Development Bank (AFDB) are currently mobilizing $25 billion by 2025, to accelerate adaptation action in Africa through interventions

[35] M. Nachmany et al., *The 2015 Global Climate Legislation Study: A Review of Climate Change Legislation in 99 Countries*, London: Grantham Research Institute for Climate Change and Environment, 2015, p. 13.

[36] J. Bos, L. Gonzalez and J. Thwaites "Are Countries Providing Enough to the $100 Billion Climate Finance Goal?", World Resources Institute, 7 October 2021, <https://www.wri.org/insights/developed-countries-contributions-climate-finance-goal>.

in four priority areas/pillars: food security; resilience infrastructure; youth entrepreneurship and job creation; and innovative climate adaptation finance. The AFDB committed $12.5 billion of its capital to the AAAP from its launch, with the proposed African Development Fund's climate action window set to provide additional dedicated, efficient and affordable climate finance to the African countries most vulnerable and least adaptive to climate change.

In addition, there is also the Climate Smart Digital Technologies for Agriculture and Food Security. The Pillar, hosted by the Global Centre on Adaptation (GCA), aims to increase access to climate-smart digital technologies and data-driven agricultural and financial services for at least 30 million African farmers and improve food security in 26 African countries. The Pillar, in partnership with AFDB's Digital Agriculture Flagship, will enhance the applicability, accessibility and affordability of climate-smart digital technologies such as climate-informed advisory services, Geographic Information Systems (GIS) and remote sensing for resource management, e-registration of farmers and pastoralists, and climate-smart solutions for farm operations. These technologies could improve productivity, market connectedness, profitability and sustainable use of natural resources. Activities focus on knowledge and analytics, last-mile capacity development, and investments in pro-poor scalable digital agriculture innovations.[37]

As climate change legislation covers activities in different sectors, and interacts with other policy priorities, such as energy, transport, industrial policy, forestry and land use, air quality, and poverty and food security, there is an interdependence between climate policy (mitigation and adaptation) and many other policy issues. Therefore, when enacting climate change legislation, countries may choose to include climate change considerations in a general environmental law, for example by passing legislation to encourage the use of renewable energy, or to formulate climate change-specific legislation that addresses some or all of these issues, such as the UK's Climate Protection Act 2008.[38]

Specifically for Nigeria, the government has established:

(1) The National Adaptation Strategy and Plan of Action on Climate Change for Nigeria (NASPA-CCN), which is the principal strategy and plan of its type for Nigeria. The objectives of the policy are to integrate climate change adaptation into national, sectoral, state and local government planning, and into the plans of universities, research and educational organisations, civil society organisations, the private sector and the media; to mobilise

---

37 J. Karugia, "Climate Smart Digital Technologies for Agriculture and Food Security Pillar of the AAAP", National Livestock Research Institute, 2022, <https://www.ilri.org/research/projects/climate-smart-digital-technologies-agriculture-and-food-security-pillar-aaap>.

38 J. Bos, L. Gonzalez and J. Thwaites (above, n. 38).

communities for climate change adaptation actions, through the provision of appropriate user-friendly information; and to reduce the impacts of climate change on key sectors and vulnerable communities, among others. Specifically, with respect to agriculture, the policy seeks to adopt improved agricultural systems for both crops and livestock, and to provide early warning/meteorological forecasts and related information.

(2) The National Policy on Environment, which supports "the prevention and management of natural disasters such as floods, drought, and desertification".
(3) Nigeria's Agricultural Policy, whose objectives include the protection of "agricultural land resources from drought, desert encroachment, soil erosion, and floods".
(4) The Nationally Determined Contributions (NDCs), which are Nigeria's determined contribution as regards its carbon emissions reduction target.
(5) Nigeria's Drought Preparedness Plan.
(6) The National Policy on Erosion and Flood Control.
(7) The National Water Policy.
(8) The National Forest Policy.
(9) The National Health Policy.
(10) Nigeria's Sovereign Green Bonds. Nigeria embraced the issuance of its sovereign green bonds as an innovative alternative way of raising finance both locally and internationally. This is a financing mechanism to facilitate and assist Nigeria in meeting its Nationally Determined Contribution target, and a low-carbon pathway for socio-economic development in line with the Economic Recovery Growth Plan (ERGP).
(11) Development of the Sectoral Action Plan for the Nationally Determined Contribution (NDC) implementation road map.

It has, however, been argued that the absence of a climate change adaptation law is a major setback in the fight against food insecurity in Nigeria. Such a law would be expected to set out standards, procedures and principles that must be enforced by the judicial system. It would give clear expectations of the government vis-à-vis other national policies, and efficient implementation mechanisms. In addition, it would appear that adaptation, in Nigeria, is not given similarly serious attention to that given to mitigation.

5. SIGNIFICANCE OF THE NIGERIAN CLIMATE CHANGE ACT IN STRENGTHENING CLIMATE RESILIENCE AND FOOD SECURITY IN NIGERIA

Prior to the passing of the 2021 Climate Change Act, there was no specific local legal framework for climate change in Nigeria. However, Nigeria ratified the

UNFCCC in 1994, and the goal of this convention was to stabilise concentrations of greenhouse gases in the atmosphere at levels that would prevent dangerous disruption of the climate system.[39] Nigeria is also a party to the Kyoto Protocol, negotiated at the 1997 Conference of the Parties (COP) or Conference on Climate Change[40] meeting in Kyoto, Japan, and has also ratified the Doha Amendment.[41] The Protocol sets binding emissions limits for signatories, but leaves these countries free to make their own decisions about how to reduce emissions. To strengthen its commitment to reducing greenhouse gas emissions, Nigeria also became a party to the Paris Agreement, in 2017. Nigeria aims to reduce greenhouse gas emissions by 20 per cent, by 2030. The goal is to limit global warming to well below 2 degrees Celsius, and preferably 1.5 degrees Celsius, compared with pre-industrial levels. Although Nigeria has ratified these conventions, treaties and protocols, they have remained inapplicable, due to their non-incorporation into local law.

With the Climate Change Act 2021, Nigeria is, therefore, taking domestic steps to consolidate the climate protection goals, and to create a mechanism to comply with them. The Act established a National Climate Change Council, to oversee and advance Nigeria's climate action plans. Among other things, the Council is to oversee the coordination of national climate action, the mobilisation of financial resources to support climate action, the management of a recently established climate fund, and the urgency of the climate project.[42]

Regarding the administration and control of the Council, the law establishes a secretariat, and designates it as the administrative, scientific and technical arm of the Council. The secretariat advises and supports the Council in fulfilling its tasks, roles and functions under the law. The secretariat is responsible, among other things, for checking and reporting on the extent to which the national emission profile is in line with the carbon budget. The secretariat is also empowered to work with civil society to further the Secretariat's goals.[43]

---

39 Federal Republic of Nigeria, *Adaptation Communication to the United Nations Framework Convention on Climate Change (UNFCCC)*, Abuja; Government of Nigeria, 2021, <https://unfccc.int/sites/default/files/resource/Nigeria-Adaptation-Communication-UNFCCC-2.pdf>.

40 The Conference on Climate Change (COP) is the highest decision-making body of the United Nations Convention on Climate Change, representing all Parties to the Convention. It reviews the implementation of the Convention and other legal instruments adopted by the COP, taking necessary decisions to promote its effective implementation. The COP reviews national communications and emission inventories submitted by Parties, assessing the effects of their measures and progress in achieving the Convention's objectives. The COP meets annually, unless Parties decide otherwise. The first meeting was held in Berlin in 1995, and the current location is Bonn, unless a Party offers to host the session.

41 Nigeria became the 144th member to ratify the Doha amendment: <https://climatechange.gov.ng/nigeria-became-the-144th-country-to-ratify-the-doha-amendment/>.

42 Climate Change Act 2021, s. 1.

43 Ibid., s. 2.

The Act also established the Climate Change Fund, for the purpose of financing climate protection measures and interventions in Nigeria, and this is financed from carbon tax revenues, emissions trading, fines and fraud fees, climate protection and adaptation commitments, international organisations, fees and charges for services provided by the Council, etc., and encourages public and private entities in their efforts to transition to clean energy and sustain a reduction in greenhouse gas emissions. The fund, managed by the Council, is a welcome development, and a boost to food security, as it ensures the availability of funds to further the goals of the law, and to achieve Nigeria's climate goals, provided that these are rigorously applied, and that resources are allocated appropriately to fulfil its purpose. Perhaps one of the most innovative features of the law is the introduction of a carbon tax and carbon trading. The legislation requires the Council to work with the Federal Ministry of Environment, to develop the mechanism for Nigeria's carbon tax, and to develop a mechanism for CO_2 emissions trading, in cooperation with the Federal Ministry of Finance.[44]

The carbon tax is a fee levied on the burning of carbon-based fuels. It acts as a brake on CO_2 emissions, by ensuring that users of CO_2 fuels take responsibility for the environmental damage caused by the release of CO_2 into the atmosphere, and the associated economic damage. The carbon tax, as long as it is relatively high, would serve to reduce carbon emissions in society, and also as a revenue stream that can be used directly for the government's clean energy transition. Carbon trading, on the other hand, is the buying and selling of credits that enable a company or other entity to emit a specified amount of CO_2 or other greenhouse gases. Here, the government sets a limit on the maximum allowable emissions for companies, and issues permits or allowances for each unit of emissions that can be traded by individuals and companies. As a result, organisations must choose between limiting their emissions to permitted levels or buying more permits from the government or other emitting companies. The carbon tax and carbon trading are powerful incentives that should facilitate rapid reductions in carbon emissions if properly implemented and used judiciously. The logic is that paying for emissions motivates companies to look for alternatives to fossil fuels. In this way, companies are charged for polluting more, and others are rewarded for lower emissions.

Another revealing feature of the law is the introduction of the carbon budget. The law instructs the Federal Ministry of Environment to work with the ministry responsible for national planning to draw up a carbon budget for Nigeria. The budget aims to keep the average global temperature rise within 2 degrees Celsius, and to continue efforts to limit the temperature rise to 1.5 degrees Celsius, in line with the Paris Agreement, to which Nigeria is a signatory, by limiting the amount of carbon that can be emitted in a period to

44 Ibid., ss. 1, 3, 7 and 15(a)(e).

a level which keeps global temperatures within safe limits. The consequence of excess budget is a global temperature rise. This would accelerate climate change, and greatly amplify its effects. Limiting further warming requires reducing human greenhouse gas emissions, and then reducing emissions to zero.

The law also provides for the formulation of a National Climate Action Plan, to be formulated or reviewed every five years by the secretariat, in cooperation with the Federal Ministries for the Environment and National Planning. The Action Plan is intended to serve as a basis for identifying activities to ensure that the national emissions profile is in line with carbon budget targets. The Action Plan will set out the road map for achieving Nigeria's climate change goals.[45] It is expected to include milestones, timelines for goal achievement, and forecast budget needs for project execution. The Action Plan will include an articulated carbon budget for the five-year cycle, and the years that make up the five-year cycle, propose incentives for public and private entities to achieve greenhouse gas emission reductions, etc.[46]

To ensure achievement of the goals, sections 22, 23 and 24 of the Act contain provisions for climate change-related commitments by government ministries, departments and agencies (MDAs), and private and public organisations. All MDAs are obliged to set up a climate protection office, which serves to ensure the integration of climate protection activities into their core mandate. MDAs must meet the nation's annual carbon emissions reduction goals, and ensure proper planning and budgeting for all carbon offset projects and activities. The importance of this is illustrated by the duty placed on the Department of Finance and Budget to ensure that all MDA budget proposals have been properly screened for climate change considerations. If an MDA fails to meet its commitment to reduce carbon emissions, the MDA and its officers may be subject to sanctions, upon review and investigation. The Council has the power to impose obligations related to climate change on any public body. Finally, all private companies with employees aged 50 and over must take action to achieve annual CO2 emission reduction targets in line with the Action Plan. Private organisations in this category are also required to appoint a climate action officer, who must submit an annual report to the Council on the organisation's efforts to meet its climate change goals.

In fact, education and awareness campaigns are some of the most viable ways to curb the ills in society. The law is not silent on this. Section 26 of the Act directs the secretariat to advise MDAs responsible for regulating the educational curriculum in Nigeria to integrate climate change into different disciplines at all levels of education. The secretariat may collaborate with the MDA in this regard, or sponsor scientific research and other projects.

45 Ibid., s. 19.
46 Ibid., s. 20.

In spite of the above benefits provided by Nigeria's law on climate change, the country would need to address some challenges in order to be able to strengthen its climate resilience and food insecurity. These issues include:

(1) Legal gaps: the legislation contains lapses, including the huge cost and bureaucracy created by the establishment of states and zonal offices.
(2) Weak implementation: the government lacks the political will to galvanise support for the implementation of the Climate Change Act and related laws and policies, for the rural population to enjoy the benefits of such laws.
(3) Lack of political will: the government has not demonstrated enough political will to fight food insecurity in the country. For example, Nigeria has consistently spent less than 5 per cent of its annual budget on agriculture, while Malaysia, for example, has achieved accelerated agricultural development through sustained annual expenditure of between 20 to 25 per cent of its budget, on agriculture, over the last three decades.[47] The result is poor and dilapidated infrastructure, an absence of improved agricultural technology, and, ultimately, a low harvest.

6. CONCLUSION AND RECOMMENDATIONS

With the government having taken necessary legislative steps to address climate change problems as they affect food security in Nigeria, including the passage of the Climate Change Act as recently as 2021, the next steps would be to take action to implement the provisions of the law. The law appears to be compliance-oriented, as it creates structures for enforcing its regulations. This is reflected in the establishment of an office dedicated to the implementation of the Climate Change Act, and the transfer of specific tasks to the Federal Ministry of Environment and the Ministry of Budget and Regional Planning. One starting point is the creation of the Action Plan. The law provides for a period of 12 months to draw up the pilot Action Plan. The mechanisms for carbon-tax calculation and carbon-trading approval should be developed seriously, so that public and private organisations can seriously comply with the provisions of the Act.[48]

Suggestions for policy direction addressing the problems that climate change poses to food security require more robust and comprehensive strategies that

[47] A. Olomola, et al., "Analysis of agricultural public expenditures in Nigeria: Examination at the federal, state, and local government levels", IFPRI Discussion Paper 1395, Washington, D.C.: International Food Policy Research Institute (IFPRI), 2014, <http://ebrary.ifpri.org/cdm/ref/collection/p15738coll2/id/128804>.

[48] See I.O. Adelekan, N.P. Simpson, E. Totin and C.H. Trisos, *IPCC Sixth Assessment Report (AR6): Climate Change 2022 – Impacts, Adaptation and Vulnerability: Regional Factsheet Africa*, 2022, <https://policycommons.net/artifacts/2264240/ipcc_ar6_wgii_factsheet_africa/3023294>.

address the root causes of vulnerabilities and emerging risks. Adaptability of agricultural practices to the changing environment and the regulation of anthropogenic factors that trigger climate change is also necessary.

To address the emerging risks posed by climate change in relation to nutrition and human food security, this contribution recommends the following actions and strategies:

(1) Implementation of all regulations and laws on climate change, including the Climate Change Act and relevant conventions, treaties and protocols. The step taken in enacting the Climate Change Act is a welcome development, as it sets the country in motion on the path to actualisation of a net-zero target by 2070. It will provide the needed resilience to climate change, and thus help to mitigate the effects of climate change on achieving food security in Nigeria.[49]
(2) Appropriate legal policies and measures must be implemented to ensure environmentally friendly practices. Practices such as gas flaring, deforestation, illegal construction of waterways, and illegal diversion of natural waterways, must be banned. Such a measure would help prevent further deterioration of the environment. Effective legislation would also ensure that conservative practices are maintained, and that anthropogenic factors contributing to climate change are minimised.
(3) More research in natural and climate sciences should be considered, to develop a more robust and beneficial alternative to the natural agricultural production pattern, to ensure adequate nutrition and sustainability. Research should be directed towards the development of short-maturing plant and animal varieties, to ensure that reduced rainfall events have minimal impact on plants.
(4) Smart food systems or climate-resilient farming practices need to be implemented, to ensure sustainable food security in Nigeria. Drought-resistant grasses should be introduced, and spread widely in drought-affected areas. This would not only reduce the wave of desertification from the north, but also the migration of pastoralists to the south, which has led to friction and clashes between pastoralists and local farmers.
(5) The government and other stakeholders should introduce alternative practices, such as irrigation and replenishment of the dwindling waters in the savannah regions of Sudan and the Sahel, to ensure that farmers reinvest in productive activities.

49 See Federal Ministry of Environment, *Nigeria's National Adaptation Plan Framework*, Abuja: Government of Nigeria, 2020, https://napglobalnetwork.org/wp-content/uploads/2020/06/napgn-en-2020-Nigeria-National-Adaptation-Plan-Framework.pdf.

PART VIII
BIODIVERSITY LOSS

THE PROGRAMMATIC APPROACH, UNCERTAINTY AND MONITORING IN THE HABITATS DIRECTIVE

The Precautionary Principle as a Pavlovian Reflex to Uncertainty?

Rogier KEGGE and Hidde KREMERS

1. INTRODUCTION

In 2018 the European Court of Justice (CJEU) ruled, in the *Dutch Programmatic Approach to Nitrogen (PAN)* case, that the Habitats Directive[1] does not preclude national programmatic legislation.[2] The assessment of the various projects based on the programmatic approach, however, must meet all requirements of Article 6(3) of the Habitats Directive. Procedures for surveillance and monitoring must also be suitable for the purpose of complying with Article 6(2) of the Habitats Directive, in addition to the preventive measures in the programmatic approach. This means that the CJEU places great emphasis on the precautionary principle and scientific certainty, prior to the authorisation of plans and projects, and to that extent, it does not accept a role for monitoring and adjustment. This raises the question of whether a programmatic approach, with monitoring as an inseparable part of the approach, can be compatible with the Habitats Directive, and, if so, under what conditions is monitoring allowed? In this context, this contribution will focus on the difference between prior scientific certainty, as required by the precautionary principle, and the role of *ex post* monitoring in a programmatic approach. Do the concepts of the precautionary principle and

1 Council Directive 92/43 EEG of 21 May 1992 on the conservation of natural habitats and of wild fauna and flora.

2 Joined Cases C-293/17 and C-294/17, *Coöperatie Mobilisation for the Environment UA a.o. v. College van Gedeputeerde Staten van Noord-Brabant*, ECLI:EU:C:2018:882 *(Programmatic Approach to Nitrogen)*.

adaptive management with monitoring refer to different types of uncertainty, and are these concepts compatible with each other?[3]

This contribution will first introduce the programmatic approach and its key elements (section 2), and then describe the Dutch Programmatic Approach to Nitrogen (PAN) (section 3). Subsequently, it will discuss the CJEU's judgment in the Dutch *PAN* case (section 4). Sections 5 and 6 will analyse the role of monitoring in the Habitats Directive and the case law of the CJEU. It will then turn to the concepts of adaptive management and the precautionary principle, linking these concepts to different types of uncertainties (section 7). The contribution will conclude by answering the above-mentioned questions (section 8).

2. THE PROGRAMMATIC APPROACH

What is a programmatic approach, and why has this tool become popular in the Netherlands? Characteristic of the programmatic approach is its flexibility and the possibilities it offers for deregulation. It has been used to overcome deadlock situations in which it had become increasingly difficult and burdensome to authorise new projects, such as housing or infrastructural projects.[4] It seeks to balance economic development with environmental goals, such as improving the air quality in general, or improving the conservation status of Natura 2000 sites. If the instrument is used to implement an EU directive, the degree of flexibility depends on the requirements of that directive. These requirements can limit the choice of form and methods of implementation given to the Member States.[5] Flexibility, in a programmatic approach, comes from the combination of different measures with an environmental goal to be achieved within a certain period of time. The results must be monitored, and, if necessary, the programmatic approach has to be adjusted. Sometimes programmes only function as policy instruments, but when a direct link is made between the measures and the authorisation of specific projects, the instrument also functions as a legal framework, and qualifies as a programmatic approach. Squintani and Van Rijswick distinguish, in this context, between programmatic approaches with or without a delinking effect between the measures and the authorisation of

---

3 W.E. Walker, P. Harremoës, J. Rotmans, J.P. van der Sluijs, M.B.A. van Asselt, P. Janssen and M.P. Krayer von Krauss, "Defining Uncertainty, A Conceptual Basis for Uncertainty Management in Model-Based Decision Support", *Integrated Assessment*, 2003, 4(1), 5–17.

4 H. Schoukens, "Nitrogen deposition, habitat restoration and the EU Habitats Directive: moving beyond the deadlock with the Dutch programmatic nitrogen approach", *Biological Conservation*, 2017, 212 485–487.

5 Art. 288 of the Treaty on the Functioning of the European Union.

projects.[6] The present authors only regard instruments with a direct link between the measures and the authorisation of projects as a programmatic approach, and regard instruments without a direct link as policy programmes. This means that, in this contribution, a programmatic approach is a legal framework consisting of several measures and a method of assessment and authorisation of projects. The degree of effectiveness of the measures is, therefore, decisive for the ways and extent to which projects are allowed, on the basis of the programmatic approach.

A programmatic approach must contain at least the key elements to function properly as a legal framework. Groothuijse and Uylenburg distinguished the first three key elements.[7] Firstly, there must be an achievable and verifiable objective. This objective can be an environmental quality standard, like limit values for PM10 or nitrogen dioxide, or some other environmental goal, such as the favourable conservation status of natural habitats and species, as per the Habitats Directive. Secondly, a legal obligation to carry out measures, and a direct link between the objective(s) and the measures in the programme, are required. Thirdly, a programmatic approach needs a system of monitoring and adjustment. Monitoring can even be seen as the backbone of a programmatic approach, as it should ensure that the effectiveness of the measures is monitored.[8] Effective and timely monitoring should also be able to result in adjustment of the programmatic approach, by changing or adding measures, or decreasing the fixed space or amount of rights, or, as a last resort, amending or revoking given authorisations. In addition to these three elements, three more key elements can be identified. The fourth key element is a limited time span within which the objectives are to be achieved. Boeve and Van den Broek conclude that a binding legal time span or deadline in a directive limits the discretion of Member States to choose the kinds of measures they adopt, because the effectiveness must be guaranteed. If a directive does not have a binding legal time span or deadline, as is the case with the Habitats Directive, the Member State has more discretion.[9] The fifth key element is a fixed and measurable baseline (or reference) situation. Without a clear reference situation, the impact of a programmatic approach cannot be determined. The last key element is optional, and only applies if the approach entails a system of issuance of environmental rights. In that case,

---

6 L. Squintani and H. van Rijswick, "Improving Legal Certainty and Adaptability in the Programmatic Approach", *Journal of Environmental Law*, 2016, 28, 443–470.

7 F. Groothuijse and R. Uylenburg, "Everything according to plan? Achieving environmental quality standards by a programmatic approach", in M. Peeters and R. Uylenburg (eds.), *EU Environmental Legislation: Legal Perspectives on Regulatory Strategies*, 2014, Cheltenham, Edward Elgar Publishing, 116–145.

8 B.A. Beijen, H. van Rijswick and H. Tegner Anker, "The Importance of Monitoring for the Effectiveness of Environmental Directives, A Comparison of Monitoring Obligations in European Environmental Directives", *Utrecht Law Review*, 2014, 10(2), 135.

9 M.N. Boeve and G.M. van den Broek, "The Programmatic Approach; a Flexible and Complex Tool to Achieve Environmental Quality Standards", *Utrecht Law Review*, 2012, 8(3), 74–85.

the approach needs a method of allocation of those rights. Without these key elements, the effectiveness of a programmatic approach cannot be verified, and it will entail the risk of allocating too many rights, with the result that the objective(s) will not be achieved within the required time span.

3. THE DUTCH PROGRAMMATIC APPROACH TO NITROGEN

The PAN was introduced in 2015, in the Netherlands, as a legal instrument to implement Article 6 of the Habitats Directive. The background of this instrument was that the authorisation process for projects was becoming more and more difficult, due to the high nitrogen overload of Natura 2000 sites in the Netherlands. The nitrogen overload on Natura 2000 sites is largely due to the large livestock sector in the Netherlands.[10] This situation led to a legal deadlock, because many permits for new projects had to be refused or annulled. The PAN was intended to resolve this deadlock, and had a twofold objective.[11] On the one hand, it aimed to reduce nitrogen deposition so that vulnerable Natura 2000 sites would be able to recover from enduring overload of nitrogen. Ultimately, this had to lead to the favourable conservation status, as contained in the Habitats Directive. On the other hand, the programmatic approach also aimed to facilitate decision-making, and promote economic growth in the vicinity of Natura 2000 sites. Thus, the PAN also sought to deregulate and facilitate new activities.

The PAN included site-specific restoration measures and source-directed measures. The site-specific restoration measures included hydrological measures, such as the raising of the water levels in and around Natura 2000 sites, and active vegetation management. The source-directed measures included the requirement for modern livestock stables with lower ammonia emissions, low-emission fertilisation methods, voluntary feed measures, and management measures. It was assumed, in the PAN, that the source-directed measures would cause a significant reduction of nitrogen deposition, in addition to the autonomous decrease of nitrogen deposition.[12] This reduction was quantified as "room for deposition". A substantial part of this room for deposition was used for new economic activities, referred to as "room for development". Instead

---

10 National emission registration database, nitrogen, www.rivm.nl/stikstof.

11 H. Schoukens, "The Quest for the Holy Grail and the Dutch Integrated Approach to Nitrogen: How to Align Adaptive Management Strategies with the EU Nature Directives?", *Journal for European Environmental and Planning Law*, 2018 (15), 187–189.

12 R. Kegge and A. Drahmann, "The Programmatic Approach: Finding the Right Balance between the Precautionary Principle and the Right to Conduct a Business", *Journal for European Environmental and Planning Law*, 2020 (17), 78–80.

of assessing each individual plan or project, in the PAN the total amount of nitrogen deposition was to be assessed. The PAN included three categories of projects. First, projects causing nitrogen deposition of less than 0.05 mol/ha/yr did not need to obtain any prior authorisation. Second, projects causing nitrogen deposition of more than 0.05 mol/ha/yr, but less than 1 mol/ha/yr, were also permitted without prior authorisation, but had to be notified. Finally, all projects causing nitrogen deposition of more than 1 mol/ha/yr required a permit. As long as there was sufficient room for deposition, projects could be allowed. This system meant that only authorised projects were registered by means of notification or permit. The projects under the threshold of 0.05 mol/ha/yr were not registered. It was assumed that these small projects, no matter how many, could not have a significant effect on the protected sites. The PAN had a time span of six years. During that period, the allocation of the available amount of nitrogen deposition was partially registered, and the effects on the Natura 2000 sites were monitored. If this annual monitoring showed that the objective of sufficient reduction of nitrogen deposition was at risk, the PAN could be adjusted by adding more measures, or by limiting the remaining room for development.[13] According to the PAN, this system of monitoring and adjustment safeguarded the functioning of the programmatic approach within certain embedded safety margins. Moreover, it did not compromise the conclusion of the appropriate assessment that the PAN would not adversely affect the integrity of the 160 sites concerned.

4. THE *PAN* CASE

In the landmark *PAN* case, the CJEU answered several preliminary questions from the Dutch Council of State, which arose after the PAN came into force in the Netherlands, in 2015.[14] One of the questions was whether Article 6(2) and (3) of the Habitats Directive preclude legislation which exempts, from the permit requirement, projects and other operations causing nitrogen deposition which do not exceed a threshold or a limit value, and which are, therefore, permitted without individual approval, proceeding on the assumption that the effect of all projects and other operations, taken together, which could make use of the legislation, had been appropriately assessed before the adoption of the legislation. The reason for this question was that the PAN was based on an appropriate assessment that had examined a total amount of nitrogen

13 Administrative Jurisdiction Division of the Council of State, 17 May 2017, ECLI:NL:RVS:2017:1259.

14 Joined Cases C-293/17 and C-294/17, *Coöperatie Mobilisation for the Environment UA a.o. v. College van Gedeputeerde Staten van Noord-Brabant*, ECLI:EU:C:2018:882 *(Programmatic Approach to Nitrogen)*.

deposition instead of individual projects. Another question was whether it was important that the results of the measures in the PAN were monitored, and that if monitoring indicated that the results were less favourable than assumed in the appropriate assessment, adjustments took place. The CJEU ruled that Article 6(3) of the Habitats Directive does not preclude national programmatic legislation that allows the competent authorities to authorise projects based on an appropriate assessment in which a specific overall amount of nitrogen deposition has been assessed. The CJEU even added that an assessment with an overall evaluation, such as the PAN, makes it possible to better examine the cumulative effects of various projects, but stressed that all the requirements of Article 6(3) of the Habitats Directive must still be met. These requirements are only met if the national court has carried out a thorough and in-depth examination of the scientific soundness of the appropriate assessment, and has reached the conclusion that there is no reasonable scientific doubt as to the absence of adverse effects of each plan or project on the integrity of the sites concerned, within the programmatic approach. In this context the CJEU referred to its case law, which has held that Article 6(3) of the Habitats Directive integrates the precautionary principle, and makes it possible to prevent, in an effective manner, adverse effects on the integrity of protected sites, as a result of plans or projects envisaged.[15] The CJEU added that both conservation measures, within the meaning of Article 6(1), and preventive measures, within the meaning of Article 6(2), of which the expected benefits are not certain at the time of the appropriate assessment, may not be taken into account in the appropriate assessment. The same applies for protective measures on the basis of Article 6(3). Thus, retrospective monitoring cannot replace the required prior certainty of the effectiveness of the measures within the programme. Procedures of surveillance and monitoring of farms whose activities cause nitrogen deposition are sufficient for the purpose of complying with Article 6(2), and these procedures might even lead to the closure of those farms, according to the CJEU, if the deterioration of habitats cannot be prevented otherwise. Although the CJEU does not preclude a programmatic approach based on the Habitats Directive, it has set a pretty high bar by holding on to its strict interpretation of the precautionary principle as described in Article 6(3), and the corresponding no-doubts criterion, and sees no role for monitoring here.[16] On the basis of the *PAN* case, the Council of State declared the PAN non-binding, because the effectiveness of the measures was too uncertain, and, therefore, Article 6(3) of the Habitats Directive had been violated.[17]

---

15 Case C-441/17, *Commission v. Poland*, ECLI:EU:C:2018:255 (*Bialowieza Forest*), para. 118.

16 See also L. Squintani, "Balancing nature and economic interests in the European Union: On the concept of mitigation under the Habitats Directive", *Review of European, Comparative & International Law*, 2020, 29, 129–137.

17 Administrative Jurisdiction Division of the Council of State, 29 May 2019, ECLI:NL:RVS:2019:1603.

5. MONITORING AND THE HABITATS DIRECTIVE

Many environmental directives, such as the Nitrates Directive, the Air Quality Directive and the Habitats Directive, provide for monitoring.[18] The monitoring requirements may serve different objectives. The first and most important objective is to check compliance in the Member States. A second objective of monitoring can be that frequent monitoring results allow the detection of changes in the environment. A third objective, related to the first and second objectives, is comparability between the Member States. Article 11 of the Habitats Directive states that Member States shall undertake surveillance of the conservation status of the natural habitats and species referred to in Article 2. Article 17 of the Habitats Directive requires Member States to report, every six years, about the progress made with the implementation of the Habitats Directive. The preamble also clearly states that a system should be set up for surveillance of the conservation status of the natural habitats and species, and that the implementation of the Directive will be monitored on the basis of the information sent to the European Commission by the Member States. This information from the national reports leads to a periodic report by the European Commission. The Habitats Directive, therefore, does provide for a system of feedback and monitoring on the status of Natura 2000 sites by the Member States.[19] In the Commission notice "Managing Natura 2000 sites", the European Commission explains that the effects of conservation and preventive measures have to be assessed and monitored.[20] The same applies for protective measures taken on the basis of Article 6(3) of the Habitats Directive, but *ex post* monitoring may not be used as a tool for assessing whether the project, with these measures, will not adversely affect the integrity of the site(s) concerned.[21] If a project is authorised on the basis of Article 6(4) of the Habitats Directive and compensation measures are required, the effectiveness of those measures also has to be monitored.[22] This shows that the main objective of monitoring, in the Habitats Directive, is the evaluation of the effectiveness of the Directive in the Member States. Another objective is comparability between the Member States. However, *ex post* monitoring is not intended as an instrument for authorising projects in advance.

18 B.A. Beijen, H. van Rijswick and H. Tegner Anker, "The Importance of Monitoring for the Effectiveness of Environmental Directives: A Comparison of Monitoring Obligations in European Environmental Directives", *Utrecht Law Review*, 2014, 10(2), 126–135.

19 See also L. Krämer, "Monitoring the Application of the Birds and Habitats Directives", *Journal for European Environmental and Planning Law*, 2013 (10), 209–232.

20 European Commission notice, "Managing Natura 2000 sites, The provisions of Article 6 of the Habitats Directive 92/43/EEC", 21 November 2018, C (2018) 7621 final, 20 and 30–32.

21 Ibid., 52.

22 Ibid., 65–66.

6. MONITORING IN THE CASE LAW

The CJEU has ruled several times on monitoring under the Habitats Directive. In the *Orléans* case, the CJEU ruled that any positive effects of the future creation of a new habitat, aimed at compensating the loss of area and quality of that same habitat type on a protected site, are highly difficult to forecast with any degree of certainty, and, in any event, will be visible only several years into the future, and that those effects can only be relevant in the context of Article 6(4) of the Habitats Directive.[23] This meant that the creation of a new area of habitat as compensation for the expansion of the port of Antwerp should not have been taken into account in the assessment of whether this project had had adverse effects on the integrity of the Natura 2000 site concerned, where the expansion had been partly planned. Moreover, before compensatory measures may be taken into account on the basis of Article 6(4), an appropriate assessment must demonstrate that those measures will be effective. The CJEU added, in the *Moorburg* case, that as regards multi-phase monitoring, such monitoring cannot be considered sufficient to ensure performance of the obligation laid down in Article 6(3) of the Habitats Directive.[24] In this case, a fish ladder was installed in the Elbe river, intended to compensate for fish killed during the operation of the cooling mechanism, which drew large quantities of water from the river in order to cool the Moorburg power plant. In the assessment, multi-phase monitoring was prescribed, in order to verify the effectiveness of this measure.

With reference to the precautionary principle, the CJEU recalled in the *PAN* case that an appropriate assessment carried out under the first sentence of Article 6(3) of the Habitats Directive cannot have lacunae, and must contain complete, precise and definitive findings and conclusions capable of removing all reasonable scientific doubt as to the effects of the plans or projects.[25] The CJEU added that the national court must ascertain that there is no reasonable scientific doubt as to the absence of adverse effects of each plan or project on the sites, and must carry out a thorough and in-depth examination of the scientific soundness of the appropriate assessment. Not only in the case of compensatory measures, but also in relation to conservation or preventive measures, the Court held that the expected benefits of those measures could only be taken into account in the appropriate assessment if those effects were certain at the time of that assessment. The CJEU also added that procedures for the surveillance and monitoring of

[23] Case C-387/15 and C-388/15, *Orléans a.o. v. Vlaams Gewest*, ECLI:EU:C:2016:583, paras. 52–61.

[24] Case C-142/16, *European Commission v. Federal Republic of Germany*, ECLI:EU:C:2017:301 *(Power station Moorburg)*, para. 43.

[25] Joined Cases C-293/17 and C-294/17, *Coöperatie Mobilisation for the Environment UA a.o. v. College van Gedeputeerde Staten van Noord-Brabant*, ECLI:EU:C:2018:882 *(Programmatic Approach to Nitrogen)*, paras. 132–137.

farms whose activities cause nitrogen deposition are sufficient for the purpose of complying with Article 6(2) of the Habitats Directive. This means that the CJEU allows monitoring to verify compliance with granted authorisations. However, monitoring cannot replace the prior scientific certainty required to grant authorisation for plans or projects on the basis of Article 6(3) and 6(4) of the Habitats Directive. To sum up, in light of the precautionary principle, the CJEU makes a clear distinction between the prior obligation to assess the effects of projects and the *ex post* monitoring of the effectiveness of measures. Before measures may be taken into account in an appropriate assessment, their effectiveness must be certain. This does not mean that the effectiveness of these measures may not also be monitored afterwards, but this does not detract from the required certainty in advance, if projects are authorised on the basis of Article 6(3) or (4) of the Habitats Directive.

7. ADAPTIVE MANAGEMENT VERSUS THE PRECAUTIONARY PRINCIPLE?

The PAN was considered a form of adaptive management in environmental law.[26] The *PAN* case showed that this Dutch interpretation of adaptive management was in breach of the precautionary principle, as integrated in Article 6(3) of the Habitats Directive. However, this does not mean that adaptive management instruments, in themselves, have to go against the precautionary principle.[27] This raises the questions of what adaptive management actually is, and what limits environmental law, and the Habitats Directive in particular, impose on it.

Without striving for completeness, this section will briefly explain adaptive management, because it is often seen as a promising and innovative approach for dealing with uncertainty in environmental law.[28] It is a conceptual framework to account for stability and change, in a complex system subject to uncertainty.[29] The key elements of an adaptive management strategy are the use of models that include assumption and prediction, identifying uncertainty, the implementation of policies while learning, monitoring the effects of those policies, and learning

26 L.S. Braaksma, "The Programmatic Approach to Achieving Sustainability in Environmental Law", in M. Boeve, S. Akerboom, C. Backes and M. van Rijswick (eds.), *Environmental Law for Transitions to Sustainability*, 2021, Cambridge, Intersentia, 36.

27 H. Schoukens, "Atmospheric Nitrogen Deposition and the Habitats Directive: Tinkering with the Law in the Face of the Precautionary Principle?", *Nordic Environmental Law Journal*, 2015:2, 49.

28 J. Jones, "Regulatory Design for Scientific Uncertainty: Acknowledging the Diversity of Approaches in Environmental Regulation and Public Administration", *Journal of Environmental Law*, 2007, 19(3), 347–365.

29 L.H. Gunderson and C.S. Holling, *Panarchy: Understanding Transformations in Human and Natural Systems*, 2002, Washington DC, Island Press, 14–15.

from the monitoring results.[30] By repeating this strategy uncertainty can be reduced, because the monitoring results may lead to adjustment of the policies. It functions as an adaptive cycle that keeps repeating itself, delivering increasingly better outcomes.[31] Monitoring plays multiple roles in this cycle, by providing information to underpin decision-making, facilitating evaluation and learning, and adjustment, after decisions are made.[32] This means that monitoring is at the core of adaptive management, and is essential in the adaptive cycle of ecosystems.

Adaptive management is, first and foremost, an approach increasingly being put into practice, and used in legal systems, with the aim of creating more flexibility in regulating complex systems prone to uncertainty. However, this flexibility is not unlimited. After all, the purpose of law is to establish and maintain a stable structure in which our social systems and ecosystems can operate over time.[33] Law is not usually well suited to combating uncertainty in complex systems. It is inherently reactive, and is often based on predictable linear causality. Courts engaging in judicial review will demand thorough prior research on the predicted effects of decisions, and will often require a causal link between the decision and the effects (or absence thereof), based on the applicable legal provision. For sound predictions of effects in complex ecosystems, complex and reliable models are required. And even those models will not be able to rule out all uncertainty. Complex (eco)systems are dynamic, continually changing and evolving, and are thus not susceptible to very precise prediction.[34] In complex (eco)systems, problems often arise as a result of non-linear interactions and tipping points.[35] The result is that many environmental risks can be very difficult to predict. Ruhl distinguishes between front-end decision methods based on predecisional assessments that depend on predictive models, and adaptive methods that also respond to changing conditions at the back end.[36] The precautionary principle fits into front-end decision methods, while adaptive management with monitoring focuses on the back end of the decision. However, this does not mean that the precautionary principle automatically excludes

---

30 L. Rist, B.M. Campbell and P. Frost, "Adaptive management: Where are we now?", *Environmental Conservation*, 2012, 40(1), 5–18.

31 C.R. Allen, D.G. Angeler, A.S. Garmestani, L.H. Gunderson and C.S. Holling, "Panarchy: Theory and Application", *Ecosystems*, 2014, 17, 578–589.

32 B.K. Williams and E.D. Brown, "Adaptive Management: From More Talk to Real Action", *Environmental Management*, 2014, 53, 465–479.

33 J.B. Ruhl, "Panarchy and the Law", *Ecology and Society*, 2012, 17(3), 31.

34 R. Cooney and A.T.F. Lang, "Taking Uncertainty Seriously: Adaptive Governance and International Trade", *European Journal of International Law*, 2007, 18(3), 523–551.

35 B.A. Cosens, J.B. Ruhl, N. Sioninen and L.H. Gunderson, "Designing Law to Enable Adaptive Governance of Modern Wicked Problems", *Vanderbilt Law Review*, 2020, 73:6, 1687–1732.

36 J.B. Ruhl, "General Design Principles for Resilience and Adaptive Capacity in Legal Systems – With Applications to Climate Change Adaptation", *North Carolina Law Review*, 2010–11, 89, 1373–1403.

adaptive management approaches with monitoring. In fact, the two concepts should be firmly linked.[37]

In this context, a distinction can be made between epistemic uncertainty and variability or aleatory uncertainty.[38] Epistemic uncertainty is due to the imperfection of our knowledge, and can be reduced through prior research. Aleatory uncertainty is due to the variability of complex systems, and cannot simply be reduced through prior research, since not all possible effects can be predicted in advance by models. Here, the distinction between the precautionary principle and monitoring becomes relevant, because the application of the precautionary principle usually focuses on epistemic uncertainty. This does not mean that the precautionary principle does not recognise aleatory uncertainty, but this type of uncertainty will have to lead to the conclusion that there will always be residual risks, to a greater or lesser extent. And this only applies to known unknowns, because unknown unknowns cannot be assessed in advance. Monitoring during and after activities can offer a solution to this problem, because unexpected effects can be identified in time. However, *ex post* monitoring is not without its limitations. Biber points out that the geographic and temporal scale, and the associated financial costs can be contraindications of effective monitoring.[39] This also involves the reaction times of protected habitats and species, and the possible causal relationship between activities and those habitats and species. The geographic and temporal scale should be chosen so that a reasonable connection can be made between the authorised activities and the effects on the protected habitats and species.[40] In addition, monitoring must take place before irreversible damage occurs. Otherwise, it is pointless in the context of nature protection.

Monitoring can be a valuable and useful addition to the precautionary principle, to combat uncertainty due to residual risks, but by its very nature it always works retrospectively, and cannot, therefore, replace the preventive effect of the precautionary principle. The two concepts to reduce uncertainty complement each other, but have different objectives.

8. CONCLUSION

The case law of the CJEU allows programmatic legislation to implement Article 6 of the Habitats Directive. But, at the same time, the CJEU upholds

37 A. Trouwborst, "The Precautionary Principle and the Ecosystem Approach in International Law: Differences, Similarities and Linkages", *Review of European Community and International Environmental Law*, 2009, 18(1), 27–37.

38 T. Aven, "On Different Types of Uncertainties in the Context of the Precautionary Principle", *Risk Analysis*, 2011, 31(10), 1515–1524.

39 E. Biber, "The Problem of Environmental Monitoring", *Environmental Law Reporter News & Analysis*, 8-2013, 43(8), 10695–10797.

40 E. Biber, "Adaptive Management and the Future of Environmental Law", *Akron Law Review*, 2013, 46(4), art. 5.

its strict application of the precautionary principle in authorising projects on the basis of Article 6(3) of the Directive. To that extent, there is no room for monitoring. There is much to be said for this strict application, but it assumes that a lot of prior scientific certainty can be given to the effects of plans and projects, and that, without this certainty, authorisation should be denied. In the case of epistemic uncertainty, this application of the precautionary principle is understandable. In the case of aleatory uncertainty, prior research will not be able to solve this type of uncertainty in a complex ecosystem. The CJEU seems to be aware of this, but rightly sees no reason, in this difference, for relaxing the authorisation criterion in Article 6(3) of the Habitats Directive. *Ex post* monitoring is allowed on the basis of Article 6(1) and (2) of the Habitats Directive, but cannot be a ground for the authorisation of projects and plans. It thus performs the function of verifying the effects of conservation measures and preventive measures. This is in line with the main objectives of monitoring in the Habitats Directive, which are to monitor the effectiveness of the Directive in the Member States over time, and to avoid the authorisation of projects whose effects remain unclear. The CJEU limits the possibilities for a programmatic approach, by demanding that all the requirements of Article 6(3) of the Habitats Directive must still be met. These requirements are only met if the national court has carried out a thorough and in-depth examination of the scientific soundness of this appropriate assessment, and has reached the conclusion that there is no reasonable scientific doubt as to the absence of adverse effects of each plan or project on the integrity of the sites concerned, within the programmatic approach. All expected benefits of the measures must be certain at the time of the appropriate assessment of the programmatic approach. A large-scale national programmatic approach, with a long time span, which authorises a multitude of projects on the basis of the effects of future measures, seems, therefore, impossible under Article 6 of the Habitats Directive. Programmatic approaches on a smaller geographical and temporal scale will probably be able to meet this level of certainty, and thus be compatible with Article 6 of the Habitats Directive. The application of the precautionary principle by the CJEU leaves room for adaptive management instruments with monitoring, and allows the two concepts to be linked, but does not allow Member States to anticipate the effectiveness of a programmatic approach by authorising projects where the effects of the measures remain uncertain; or, in other words, you cannot have your cake and eat it too. Keeping in mind that the main aims of the Habitats Directive are to maintain biodiversity, and to prevent further deterioration of protected habitats and species, the CJEU's strict application of the precautionary principle is not a Pavlovian reflex to uncertainty. It is a prudent and sensible way to combine the precautionary principle with new forms of adaptive environmental law, without compromising the high level of protection pursued by the Habitats Directive.

LEGAL CHALLENGES BEFORE ENGLISH COURTS UNDER ECOSYSTEM SERVICES PROTECTION

Merve Robson, Oliver J. Jarvis, Rina Cindrak, Tilak Ginige and Iain Green

1. INTRODUCTION

The awareness that humans benefit from the natural environment is not a new concept.[1] However, there is a growing recognition that the concept of sustainability supports some elements of natural capital, including ecosystem services (ES).[2]

Despite this growing recognition and mounting scientific evidence, the general tendency is to use substitutes (manufactured or human capital) when natural capital reduces.[3] The main problem is that such substitution is not possible in some cases, such as the loss of culturally important species.[4] Substitutions can also be economically impractical for the loss of some services, such as erosion control.[5] As the original public good is free, difficulties arise when using substitutes is too costly, or an available substitute for that particular service is absent.[6] Also, it is essential to note that many ES do not have feasible substitutes.[7] If these vital services become unavailable, human well-being will be compromised.

1 G. Daily and others, "Ecosystem Services Supplied by Soil" in G. Daily (ed.) *Nature Services: Societal Dependence on Natural Ecosystems* (Island Press, 1997).

2 F. Brand, "Critical Natural Capital Revisited: Ecological Resilience and Sustainable Development" (2009) 68 *Ecological Economics* 605.

3 R. Costanza and others, "The Values of the World's Ecosystem Services and Natural Capital" (1997) 387 *Nature* 253.

4 G. Daily, "Management Objectives for the Protection of Ecosystem Services" (2000) 3 *Environmental Science & Policy* 333.

5 Millennium Ecosystem Assessment Board, *Ecosystems and Human Well-being: A Framework for Assessment* (Island Press, 2003), 14.

6 Daily, "Management Objectives" (n. 4).

7 Costanza and others, "The Values of the World's Ecosystem Services" (n. 3).

Governments tend to invest in the protection of specific services if there is obvious information on their benefits, for example clean water.[8] However, some ES are overlooked and excluded from policymaking.[9] This general inclination must be switched to an alternative approach that aims to maintain natural resources for future generations, as a requirement of sustainable development and intergenerational equity, i.e. the notion of fairness or justice between generations.

Forty-four international legal instruments explicitly incorporate or reference the principle of intergenerational equity, or the need to preserve the rights and interests of future generations.[10] These rights and the principles of intergenerational equity, and their relation to environmental policies, are being recognised and embedded in a growing number of national constitutions.[11] A recent development is the recognition of a human right to a clean, healthy and sustainable environment, by the United Nations Human Rights Council (UNHRC), announced in October 2021; however, the UK withheld its support.[12] Furthermore, the UK does not have a constitution to offer this level of protection. This is an area that requires improvement. As the call for rapid action and adequate protection continues, it is fundamental that the UK incorporates and protects these rights explicitly.

Incorporating ES benefits into policymaking and decision-making also remains a difficulty, due to the lack of instruments integrating ES into policies.[13] Today, we are fully aware that these services will continue to diminish without legal protection, which can only be achieved by legislative underpinning, legal status,[14] and meaningful incorporation of the concept into a court–exploiter relationship. Failure to halt the decline in ES will fundamentally undermine efforts to realise sustainability and intergenerational equity.

---

8 H. Tallis and others, "An ecosystem services framework to support both practical conservation and economic development" (2008) 105 *Proceedings of the National Academy of Sciences* 9457.

9 K. Grunewald and O. Bastian, *Ecosystem Services – Concept, Methods and Case Studies* (Springer, 2015).

10 Center for International Environmental Law, "Submission to the UN Special Rapporteur on Human Rights and the Environment" (31 October 2017), <https://www.ohchr.org/Documents/Issues/Environment/SREnvironment/Child/CIEL.pdf>.

11 International Union for Conservation in Nature, "The Right to a Healthy Environment" (*IUCN*, 29 October 2021), <https://www.iucn.org/news/world-commission-environmental-law/202110/right-a-healthy-environment>.

12 E. Farge, K. Abnett and V. Volcovici, "Clean environment could become U.N. human right. Not so fast, say U.S., Britain" (*Reuters*, 5 October 2021), <https://www.reuters.com/business/environment/clean-environment-could-become-un-human-right-not-so-fast-say-us-britain-2021-10-05/>.

13 K.M.A. Chan and others, "Conservation Planning for Ecosystem Services" (2006) 4 *PLoS Biology* 2138.

14 B. Pardy, "'Goods, Services and Systems': Book Review: The Law and Policy of Ecosystem Services, by J.B. Ruhl, Steven E. Kraft and Christopher L. Lant" (2008) 46 *Osgoode Hall Law Journal* 445.

This contribution explains the concept of ES, and the motivation behind the efforts to protect these services. It critically analyses the general focus of environmental cases before English courts, and investigates whether there are any specific claims for, or emphasis on, ES. The contribution also examines previous case law in several jurisdictions, and discusses the potential of ES to become a material consideration before English courts. It suggests that, if ES protection is established as a ground of legal challenge, numerous issues within the sphere of environmental law could be addressed innovatively. The contribution concludes by presenting a number of recommendations to remedy the present situation.

2. THE NEED FOR PROTECTING ECOSYSTEM SERVICES

ES underpin basic human health and survival needs, as well as supporting commercial activities, the fulfilment of potential, and enjoyment of life.[15] Indeed, there are several reasons for protecting ES, including economic reasons. These reasons involve the valuation of these services by assessing trade-offs towards achieving a goal.[16] Although ES valuation is a highly debated subject, all decisions that involve trade-offs include valuation, either implicitly or explicitly.[17] When assessing trade-offs, the overarching aim must be clear. As ES are the benefits people derive from ecosystems, their value is the ecosystems' relative contribution to that goal.[18] There are multiple ways to assess this contribution, some of which are based on individuals' perceptions of the benefits they derive. However, the support of sustainable human well-being is a much larger goal,[19] and individuals' perceptions are limited, and often biased.[20]

It is also important to note that ecosystems cannot provide any benefits to people without the presence of people (human capital), their communities (social capital), and their built environment (built capital). The challenge, in ES valuation, is to assess the relative contribution of the natural capital stock in this interaction, and to balance our assets to enhance sustainable human well-being.

Most ES are public goods (non-rival and non-excludable) or common-pool resources (rival but non-excludable), which means that privatisation and conventional markets work poorly, if at all. In addition, the non-market values estimated for these ES often relate more to use or non-use values than to

15 B. Burkhard and J. Maes (eds.), *Mapping Ecosystem Services* (Pensoft Publishers, 2017).

16 S.C. Farber, R. Costanza and M.A. Wilson, "Economic and Ecological Concepts for Valuing Ecosystem Services" (2002) 41 *Ecological Economics* 375.

17 Robert Costanza and others, "Changes in the Global Value of Ecosystem Services" (2014) 26 *Global Environmental Change* 152.

18 Costanza and others, "The Values of the World's Ecosystem Services" (n. 3).

19 Costanza and others, "Changes in the Global Value of Ecosystem Services" (n. 17).

20 V. Mauerhofer, "The law, ecosystem services and ecosystem functions: An in-depth overview of coverage and interrelation" (2018) 29 *Ecosystem Services* 190.

exchange values.[21] Nevertheless, it is crucial to assess the value of ES, for their effective management, which, in some cases, can include economic incentives, such as those used in successful systems of payment for these services.[22] When there is a decision to be made concerning trade-offs, ES valuation is unavoidable. The problem is that the valuation is implicit in the decision and hidden from view. Improved transparency about the valuation of ES (while recognising the uncertainties and limitations) could support more sustainable decisions.

The ES concept makes it abundantly clear that the choice of "the environment versus the economy" is a false choice. If nature contributes significantly to human well-being, then it is a major contributor to the real economy,[23] and the choice becomes how to manage all our assets, including natural and human-made capital, more effectively and sustainably.[24]

All ecosystems deliver a broad range of services, some of which have particular economic or social value. However, many crucial ES are undervalued, or have no apparent economic value within the existing decision-making frameworks. For example, a forest is a significant store of carbon; a resource for industry, in the form of fibre or fuel; a regulator of the climate; a preventer of loss of soil and nutrients; an important regulator of hydrology; and a location for recreational activities. Most of the benefits above tend to be undersupplied, due to the emphasis on provisioning services, from which land managers can secure market returns, in this case timber, as a resource for industry. A comprehensive valuation framework would highlight the additional benefits that are made available by these ecosystems, and help protect these valuable services. Therefore, the concept of ES and their value should be integrated into decision-making and policymaking, through a substantial approach reinforced by a legal underpinning.

3. ENVIRONMENTAL CASES BEFORE COURTS

3.1. GENERAL FOCUS OF THE ENGLISH AND WELSH COURTS

To protect ES, it will be essential for the courts to deliver judgments in this area, so that those who pose a threat to ES protection can be effectively challenged.

21 C. Galler, C. Albert and C. von Haaren, "From regional environmental planning to implementation: Paths and challenges of integrating ecosystem services" (2016) 18 *Ecosystem Services* 118.

22 R. Lal, "Enhancing ecosystem services with no-till" (2013) 28 *Renewable Agriculture and Food Systems* 102.

23 Costanza and others, "The Values of the World's Ecosystem Services" (n. 3).

24 C. White and others, *Developing ecosystem accounts for protected areas in England and Scotland: Main Report* (2015), <http://sciencesearch.defra.gov.uk/Document.aspx?Document=13488_DevelopingecosystemaccountsforprotectedareasinEnglandandScotland-MainReport.pdf>.

It is particularly important to ensure that government actions are pertinently checked and balanced, since most events which affect the environment are a consequence of government decision-making.[25] ES protection can only become a reality in England and Wales if the courts adopt ES as an essential environmental principle. Therefore, it is crucial to examine other forms of environmental protection and environmental principles, and how these are integrated or enforced in the UK, to determine how ES protection can be properly adopted.

One such example is sustainable development (SD). This principle only started to become a consideration for the judiciary in international courts from 1997 onwards,[26] although its roots were developed from the eighteenth century onwards.[27] However, since the turn of the century, perhaps owing to the success of the international recognition of SD, there has been an increased focus, in the UK, on the implementation of policies and objectives such as the 2005 UK SD Strategy by the Department for Environment, Food and Rural Affairs (DEFRA),[28] and recent bills that have reached the report stage in the House of Commons.[29] Achieving this level of recognition should be the ultimate objective for efforts towards protecting ES.

To demonstrate the influence which SD is now beginning to have on judgments in English courts, we shall look at two recent conflicting judicial review cases. These conflicting judgements demonstrate that, even with regard to the principle of SD, its proper adoption within the UK National Planning Policy Framework (NPPF)[30] has been interpreted differently by different members of the judiciary, expounding the argument that it has quickly developed into an important consideration.

In the *Wychavon District Council Case*, of 2016,[31] it was concluded that a development proposal under paragraph 14 of the NPPF,[32] which sets out a presumption in favour of SD, could acquire this presumption elsewhere

25 N.A.F. Popovic, "The Right to Participate in Decisions that Affect the Environment" (1993) 10(2) *Pace Environmental Law Review* 683.

26 *Case Concerning the Gabcikovo-Nagymaros Project* (Judgment) [1997] ICJ Rep 7.

27 S. Lumley and P. Armstrong, "Some of the Nineteenth Century Origins of the Sustainability Concept" (2004) 6 *Environment, Development and Sustainability* 367.

28 Department for Environment, Food and Rural Affairs, *Securing the Future: delivering UK sustainable development strategy* (March 2005), <https://assets.publishing.service.gov.uk/government/uploads/system/uploads/attachment_data/file/69412/pb10589-securing-the-future-050307.pdf>.

29 Ibid.

30 Ministry of Housing, Communities and Local Government, *National Planning Policy Framework* (2021), <https://assets.publishing.service.gov.uk/government/uploads/system/uploads/attachment_data/file/1005759/NPPF_July_2021.pdf> (hereinafter "NPPF").

31 *Wychavon District Council v. Secretary of State for Communities and Local Government and Anor.* [2016] EWHC 592 (Admin).

32 NPPF (n. 30), para. 14.

throughout the Policy. Yet, on the same day, in the *Cheshire* case,[33] the opposite conclusion was reached: that a proposal is assessed as SD unless the planning harm significantly outweighs the planning gain, hence paragraph 14 is about the process.[34] The latter judgment was favoured by Green J in the later *East Staffordshire* case.[35] These cases show that, although they were both predominantly centred around the interpretation of government policy, the judiciary is willing to discuss SD and its role in the national framework. In fact, Jay J even went so far as to describe SD as "the bedrock of the NPPF",[36] emphasising the crucial role SD has gained within the national policy. These cases and commentary represent a discussion of SD that did not exist 25 years ago, which furthers the argument that ES protection has the potential to be treated as a principle in the English and Welsh courts.

The precautionary principle is another established environmental principle in international law.[37] The precautionary principle places the burden of proof of not causing avoidable danger on to any decision-maker seeking to introduce innovations, or new practices or technologies,[38] and is even cited in the noteworthy Rio Declaration.[39] The recent Supreme Court *Heathrow* case[40] discussed the precautionary principle stemming from the Strategic Environmental Assessment (SEA) Directive. This discussion overturned the Court of Appeal's decision, and deliberated this principle at some length in its judgment. Although, in this instance, this principle was not given significant weight in the Supreme Court's judgment, the UK has been seen to adopt this principle more recently, as evidenced by the Secretary of State for the Environment's decision to ban neonicotinoids in agricultural use, in an effort to protect bee populations.[41]

Ultimately, these examples evidence that there is a genuine discussion within the judiciary regarding important environmental principles, not only regarding the principle itself, but also its proper place and adoption within UK policy. However, this approach by the courts has not yet been established within the

---

33 *Cheshire East Borough Council v. Secretary of State for Communities and Local Government* [2016] EWHC 571 (QB).

34 Ibid., [25]–[26].

35 *East Staffordshire Borough Council v. Secretary of State for Communities and Local Government* [2016] EWHC 2973 (QB) 42 (Green J).

36 *Cheshire East Borough Council* (n. 33), p. 10 (Jay J).

37 GreenerUK, "Briefing on the precautionary principle" (4 October 2018), <https://greeneruk.org/sites/default/files/download/2019-01/Briefing_on_the_precautionary_principle.pdf>.

38 R. Reid and T. O'Riordan, "The Precautionary Principle Under Fire" (2017) 59 *Environment: Science and Policy for Sustainable Development* 4.

39 United Nations Conference on Environment and Development, Rio Declaration on Environment and Development (1992), UN Doc. A/CONF.151/26, Principle 5.

40 *R (on the application of Friends of the Earth Ltd. and others) (Respondents) v. Heathrow Airport Ltd. (Appellant)* [2020] UKSC 52.

41 A. Patterson and C. McLean, "The precautionary principle at work: The case of neonicotinoids and the health of bees" (2019) 46 *Science and Public Policy* 441.

case law pertaining to ES. Indeed, a search in case law databases for the term "ecosystem services" produced only four cases in England and Wales that mention this topic, all of which contain no explicit reference to, or discussion about, the concept, further than the fact that the term is simply quoted in the necessary sections of the planning policy.

Furthermore, a study conducted in 2018 highlighted how far behind England and Wales seem to be regarding ES protection through domestic courts, compared with other common-law jurisdictions. The researchers identified 51 cases in Canada, and 18 in Australia, over the same period. However, the concept of ES is rarely relied upon by the courts, which do not consider ES as the central issue in these cases. One reason why ES are rarely focused on is the limited land space in England and Wales, coupled with restrictions relating to private property, whereby private landowners might not accept or consider ES, as part of their land, to be important.[42] It will be necessary to determine how the judiciary may have interpreted or referred to ES in cases, to establish how ES can be better recognised and protected in the future.

3.2. PREVIOUS CASES WITH REFERENCE TO ECOSYSTEM SERVICES

As mentioned in the previous section, there has been little discussion of ES protection in the higher courts of England and Wales.

Gallagher Properties, in January 2016,[43] is the first case which referenced ES. As other cases will demonstrate further, this case did not discuss ES at any length, nor was it concerned with ES protection. The case related to an application, under section 188 of the Town and Country Planning Act (TCPA) 1990,[44] to quash the inspector's decision to dismiss the applicant's appeal against the local authority's rejection of planning permission on a greenfield site.[45] Lord Justice Collins[46] referred to paragraph 109 of the NPPF,[47] which states: "[t]he planning system should contribute to and enhance the natural and local environment by: Protecting and enhancing valued landscapes, geological conservation interests and soils; [and] [r]ecognising the wider benefits of ecosystem services." The NPPF is also silent as to how ES are defined, which further demonstrates that ES lack importance or weight within planning policy.

42 K. Miksa and others, "Ecosystem Services and Legal Protection of Private Property Problem or Solution?" (2020) 1 *Geography and Sustainability* 173.

43 *Gallagher Properties Ltd v. Secretary of State for Communities and Local Government* [2016] EWHC 674 (Admin).

44 Town and Country Planning Act 1990, s. 188.

45 *Gallagher Properties Ltd.* (n. 43), [2].

46 Ibid., [15]–[16].

47 NPPF (n. 30), para. 109.

Similarly, in the cases of *Cheshire East Borough Council*,[48] *Peel Investments*[49] and *Nixon*,[50] ES only appear within the wide search owing to the brief reference that each judge makes to the NPPF, as they would be obliged to do in cases concerning planning applications. These cases depend upon process and economic reasoning rather than the protection of ES. The fact that ES have not been used in the reasoning of the courts, or been directly referred to in any of these cases, highlights the important need for a change in policy, so that ES and the environment may be better protected in the future.

There are a few examples where cases might loosely refer to, or be influenced by, the inclusion of ES. One such example relates to inheritance tax reliefs under the Inheritance Tax Act (ITA) 1984,[51] in agricultural or rural land. These reliefs can vary depending upon the use and occupation of the land itself.[52] In the Northern Ireland case *McCall and Keenan*,[53] although the contentious points did not rely upon the determination or existence of ES *per se*, the deceased's representatives in the case attempted to rely upon an exclusion from section 105 of the ITA[54] to the effect that the property provided a service to graziers, by providing grass to cattle. It is widely accepted in environmental law that grasslands provide significant ES.[55] The facts and outcome of the case are not relevant to this contribution, but the case does demonstrate that ES, although not explicitly referred to, can be a source of influence or discussion in many different legal jurisdictions, and are not exclusive to environmental law.

4. DISCUSSION AND RECOMMENDATIONS

4.1. DISCUSSION

If there are no available mechanisms for similar claims, how can English law protect ES? To start with, the court–exploiter relationship can be a basis for ES claims or emphasis before the courts. It is interesting to view ES as a tool to

---

48 *Cheshire East Borough Council v. Secretary of State for Communities and Local Government and Harlequin (Wistaston) Limited* [2016] EWHC 694 (Admin).

49 *Peel Investments (North) Ltd v. Secretary of State for Housing, Communities and Local Government* [2019] EWHC 2143 (Admin).

50 *Nixon v. Secretary of State for Housing, Communities and Government* [2020] EWHC 3036 (Admin).

51 Inheritance Tax Act 1984.

52 Practical Law: Agriculture & Rural Land, "Natural capital and ecosystem services: practical considerations for agricultural and rural land" (*Thomson Reuters Practical Law*, 2022), <https://uk.practicallaw.thomsonreuters.com/w-032-5831>.

53 *McCall and Keenan v. HMRC* [2009] NICA 12.

54 Inheritance Tax Act 1984 (n. 51), s. 105.

55 J. Bengtsson and others, "Grasslands – more important for ecosystem services than you might think" (2019) 10(2) *Ecosphere* e02582.

reveal potential claims for environmental damages. It is argued that it could be useful to classify ES and relate any damage to an ecosystem to potential plaintiffs, assisting them in framing legal actions and claiming compensation.[56] This approach helps with identifying the people who suffer as a result of specific damage.[57]

Common law using ES can halt damaging activities through the use of injunctions, and if damage has occurred, costs can also be recovered.[58] Such a system reveals the direct use, indirect use and non-use values, which shows the actual monetary impact of an activity or practice.[59] ES help the consideration of temporal and spatial impacts on ecosystems, and can inform the law in this context. Our scientific understanding of ecological services should improve, to allow us to identify injuries in specific harms.[60] In the US, the Supreme Court deliberated about the potential degradation of a marsh's ability to filter and clean run-off, which resulted in a public nuisance.[61] In another case, the Court asserted that a dune's storm-protection benefits would provide a homeowner with a benefit that should be taken into account when considering losses and benefits.[62]

Civil liability is responsible for actions and practices that could damage others, and requires three conditions, i.e. an operative event, damage and causation. The integration of ES offers a new perspective for civil liability.[63] Legal standing, which is the right of a party to bring a lawsuit to court, comes across as an issue here, because plaintiffs who wish to advance an ES-based argument must first convince the court of their stake in the litigation.[64] This could be as a result of a certain proximity to a harmful activity. However, adopting an ecosystem nexus approach enables action where proximity is not satisfied, but causation is.[65] Thus, those who suffer from the consequences of an activity that is not in geographic proximity, but who are within the same ecosystem, or merely deriving services from the affected ecosystem, should be able to bring legal action.[66] It is argued that the harm is not crucial for certain types of environmental action.[67] This approach can be seen as a more advanced deterrent when integrated into law.

---

56 M. Everard and T. Appleby, "Ecosystem services and the common law: Evaluating the full scale of damages" (2009) 20(6) *Environmental Law and Management* 325.

57 Ibid.

58 Ibid.

59 Ibid.

60 James Salzman, "Valuing Ecosystem Services" (1997) 24 *Ecology Law Quarterly* 887.

61 J.B. Ruhl, "In Defense of Ecosystem Services" (2015) 32 *Pace Environmental Law Review* 306.

62 Ibid.

63 S. Jean, "The effect of ecosystem services on civil liability law" in C. Hermon (ed.), *Ecosystem Services and Soil Protection* (Université Toulouse 1 Capitole, 2018).

64 C. Adaire Jones and L. DiPinto, "The role of ecosystem services in USA natural resource liability litigation" (2018) 29 *Ecosystem Services* 333.

65 Salzman (n. 60).

66 Ibid.

67 Ibid.

What should also be considered is how future generations might be afforded such protection under this ecosystem nexus.[68] If important ES flows are threatened or permanently reduced, then future generations' rights and needs will also be impacted upon. This ecosystem nexus might allow future generational standing to be found, so that ES are protected in the interests of generations yet unborn. The *Philippines Children's* case,[69] and the more recent *Urgenda Foundation* case[70] judgment from the Netherlands, are two examples where the judiciary have considered the environmental impact on future nationals. In 2021, the District Court in The Hague handed down a landmark judgment in *Milieudefensie et al. v Royal Dutch Shell*,[71] ordering the respondent company to cut its global carbon dioxide (CO_2) emissions by 45 per cent by 2030, as compared with 2019 levels. The court found that "the common interest of preventing dangerous climate change by reducing CO_2 emissions can be protected in a class action", but held that the "interests of current and future generations of the world's population … is not suitable" for a class action under Dutch law.[72] However, the court also found that the interests of current and future generations of Dutch residents were sufficiently similar to be served by a class action, because climate change will affect all Dutch residents similarly.[73] These developments show that the judiciary globally have moved slowly towards accepting future generational standing.

A similar argument is that when considering some ES, such as carbon sequestration, it does not make any difference where this service is being provided, in addressing the global threat of climate change.[74] Under such circumstances, compensating these losses by counterbalancing their losses elsewhere can be a point of discussion.[75] However, it is also worth highlighting that such compensation does not make sense when considering some collective functions and services. For example, the loss of soil biodiversity in the UK cannot be compensated simply by working towards increased biodiversity in Latin America.[76]

Compensation and direct payment for ES are two feasible tools for financial institutions to profit from ES. The overarching environmental law principle for operationalising this tool is the "polluter-pays principle", or the broader

68 J. Liu, W. Yang and S. Li, "Framing ecosystem services in the telecoupled Anthropocene" (2016) 14(1) *Frontiers in Ecology and the Environment* 27.

69 *Minors Oposa v. Secretary of the Department of Environmental and Natural Resources* (1994) 33 ILM 173.

70 *The State of the Netherlands v. Urgenda Foundation*, The Supreme Court of the Netherlands (20 December 2019), case 19/00135.

71 *Milieudefensie et al. v. Royal Dutch Shell plc.*, C/09/571932 (The Hague District Court 2021).

72 Ibid.

73 Ibid.

74 P.C. Baveye, J. Baveye and J. Gowdy, "Soil 'Ecosystem' Services and Natural Capital: Critical Appraisal of Research on Uncertain Ground" (2016) 4 *Frontiers in Environmental Science* 1.

75 Ibid.

76 Ibid.

"exploiter-pays principle". These principles impose a financial liability on those who treat natural resources as merely instrumental, and to be consumed in the short term, and do not consider the ecosystem, the survivability of the resource, or future generations.[77] Proper implementation of these principles is required to hold individuals fully accountable for engaging with activities that damage ecosystems. It is worth mentioning that the financial sector is, increasingly, affected by the notion of "saving nature to trade it".[78] Thus, even a major environmental incident can be seen as a financial opportunity, in a market which is hungry for serious events.[79] Therefore, the utmost consideration should be given when using these legal and economic tools in an ES approach. The priority should not be shifted from achieving high-level environmental protection, to generating financial profit.

Furthermore, these principles would suffer from compliance issues without proper enforcement.[80] Enforcement can prevent harm to ecosystems, by deterring violations, and requiring violators to cease violations, to fix ecosystems that they have harmed, or to restore or remediate them.[81] The question is whether there is a role for enforcement mechanisms or reliefs for ES protection.[82] Integration of the core notion of "polluter pays" should be completed through proper enforcement mechanisms. It can be argued that the enforcement of relevant laws is the best approach for the proper incorporation of ES into the law.

4.2. RECOMMENDATIONS

Having discussed the existing court-environmental protection relationship, we aim to present a number of recommendations that would strengthen our arguments regarding the necessity to ensure legal protection for ES.

The surge in popularity of environmental courts and tribunals (ECTs), and the simultaneous benefits that have been experienced by stakeholders in jurisdictions that have established and utilised these specialised facilities,[83] have

77 G. Nagtzaam, "Chapter 5: Environmental exploitation: an analysis and taxonomy" in L. Leonard and J. Barry (eds.), *The Transition to Sustainable Living and Practice* (Emerald Group Publishing Limited, 2009).

78 S. Sullivan, "Banking Nature? The Spectacular Financialisation of Environmental Conservation" (2013) 45 *Antipode* 19.

79 M. Cooper, "Turbulent worlds: financial markets and environmental crisis" (2010) 27(2–3) *Theory, Culture & Society* 167.

80 D. Markell, "Is there a Possible Role for Regulatory Enforcement in the Effort to Value, Protect, and Restore Ecosystem Services?" (2007) 22 *Journal of Land Use* 549.

81 Ibid.

82 Ibid.

83 B.J. Preston, "Benefits of Judicial Specialization in Environmental Law: The Land and Environment Court of New South Wales as a Case Study" (2012) 29(2) *Pace Environmental Law Review* 396; U. Bjällås, "Experiences of Sweden's Environmental Courts" (2010) 3(1) *Journal of Court Innovation* 177.

led to debate in countries that do not have ECTs. For the most part, the debate about ECTs in these countries has concentrated on a single question: should ECTs be created?

As Pring and Pring observed in their comprehensive study, over 350 of these specialised courts and tribunals for resolving environmental disputes may now be found, in many countries, and in every region throughout the world.[84] ECTs are as different from one another as the countries that implement them. Environmental courts can range from fully developed and independent judicial bodies that include trained staff and well-funded budgets, down to small, simple, low-budget village environmental courts that handle environmental cases on a set day per month, with a rotating judge.[85] Environmental tribunals also implement a wide range of approaches. Some are complex administrative-branch bodies, chaired by previous Supreme Court judges, with legal judges and science, economics or engineering PhDs, while some are local community land-use planning boards with no legal judge's guidance.[86]

It has been noted that the creation of ECTs may not be an ideal solution for the improvement of environmental justice and the rule of law, where they are found to be lacking.[87] Although numerous specialised courts have existed for many years, such as family or criminal courts, specialised ECTs have only recently gained attention internationally.[88] Indeed, there are drawbacks and challenges to these specialised ECTs.[89]

On the other hand, it has been argued that ECTs have positive features. One such widely accepted feature is that they offer input from expert decision-makers. As they are specialised, they can improve efficiency, leading to quicker decisions and access to justice.[90] This, additionally, can lower expense for litigants and the courts. Furthermore, they usually allow the use of a broader range of dispute-resolution techniques.[91] The establishment of ECTs provides greater uniformity in decisions, and litigants are better equipped to know what to expect.[92] Some drawbacks have been raised by critics of specialisation of courts in general, however. For example, many argue that ECTs produce competing needs, can lead to marginalisation, that the cost of creating specialised courts can be high,

---

84 G. (R.) Pring and C. (K.) Pring, *Greening Justice: Creating and Improving Environmental Courts and Tribunals* (The Access Initiative, 2009), 1; N.A. Robinson, "Ensuring Access to Justice Through Environmental Courts" (2012) 29(2) *Pace Environmental Law Review* 363.

85 Ibid.

86 G. (R.) Pring and C. (K.) Pring, *Environmental Courts & Tribunals: A Guide for Policy Makers* (UNEP, 2016), <https://wedocs.unep.org/bitstream/handle/20.500.11822/10001/environmental-courts-tribunals.pdf?sequence=1>.

87 Ibid.

88 Ibid.

89 Ibid.

90 Ibid.

91 Ibid.

92 Ibid.

and that there can be a risk of judicial bias, as specialist judges may be advocates of, and biased in favour of environmental protections.[93]

Arguments have been responded to by Professor Richard Macrory, who argues that "environmental issues can get side-tracked down a specialist route when the environment should be integrated into all areas of legal decision-making; non-specialised but high-quality judges can bring fresh perspectives and insights; and … drawing clear demarcation lines between environment and non-environment cases is not easy."[94]

The drawbacks raised can be mitigated through implementation strategies, and best practices can and should be planned, to avoid these potential negative impacts, maximising access to justice, and the future benefits of specialised courts. These potential drawbacks can be used as warning signs, and kept in mind during the planning and implementation stages, to avoid them as much as possible.

Another interesting argument relates to amalgamations, which are the clustering or joining of multiple existing courts or tribunals, which can include some ECTs, into one "umbrella" or "super-tribunal",[95] while operating under a single administrative and budget structure. These bodies usually allow each tribunal to operate independently. However, there can be blurring and merging of the outlines of ECTs.[96] Super tribunals have already happened in Canada, England and Wales, New York, and some states in Australia. The Province of Ontario's Environmental and Land Tribunal (ELTO) is a good example of a cluster tribunal that has managed to uphold five environmental tribunals as specialised subsidiary bodies.[97] The use of amalgamated courts and tribunals is useful if multiple smaller bodies with compatible or overlapping subject matter already exist.[98]

The Land and Environment Court of New South Wales was the world's first ECT.[99] It opened in 1980, as a "one-stop shop" for environmental, planning and land disputes, designed to rationalise the hearing of such cases, which had previously been dealt with in a plethora of different tribunals and courts.[100] The Court has a broad environmental jurisdiction, which covers merits review, the enforcement of civil and criminal environmental laws, and an appellate function.[101] A combination of its jurisdiction, and the appointment of suitably

93 Ibid.
94 Ibid.
95 Ibid.
96 Ibid.
97 'Ontario Land Tribunal', <https://olt.gov.on.ca/>.
98 Pring and Pring, *Environmental Courts & Tribunals* (n. 86).
99 The Hon. Justice Brian J Preston SC, "Characteristics of Successful Environmental Courts and Tribunals", (2014) 26 *Journal of Environmental Law* 365.
100 Ibid.
101 Ibid.

qualified judges sitting alongside technical experts, was intended to provide the specialisation which was previously lacking.[102]

The Scottish government is required to consult on the establishment of an environmental court, no later than six months after Scotland's new watchdog, Environmental Standards Scotland, publishes its first strategy.[103] This consultation will take place by spring 2023, creating an important opportunity for reassessing how environmental disputes are dealt with in Scotland.[104]

As mentioned earlier, in England and Wales there are as few as four cases in which a reference to ES has been identified. It can be argued that these numbers reflect the fact that the existing courts lack focus, and technical and scientific expertise in the field. Despite the fact that there is an environmental tribunal in England and Wales, this tribunal only deals with appeals against fines or notices for environmental offences.[105] Arguably, the tribunal does not have the specific expertise and resources to calculate the present and future economic loss that a decline in ES causes.

An environmental court whose jurisdiction is wider, whose judges are experts in their fields, and in which participation is enabled and broadened, could potentially change these trends. Using the right arguments, the number of ES cases could be increased, especially if environmental groups, acting as claimants, could assist courts in the development of ES-incorporated law.[106] Such an approach would be influential, especially in common-law countries, where rulings become law, and past decisions typically serve as binding precedents or persuasive legal authorities.[107] This practice could be of major help in mainstreaming the ES concept, in the legal scene.

The need for such an environmental court is highlighted by the number of environmental judicial review cases, which has increased substantially over the last decade. Additionally, previous research on the potential impact of implementing a dedicated environmental court has suggested that it would increase government accountability, particularly in the case of a large infrastructure project that is not sustainable, and has the potential to disproportionately threaten ES.[108]

---

102 Environmental Rights Centre for Scotland, *Why Scotland needs an environmental court or tribunal* (October 2021), <https://www.ercs.scot/wp/wp-content/uploads/2021/10/ECT_report_Oct-2021-v2.pdf>.

103 Ibid.

104 Ibid.

105 HM Courts & Tribunals Service, "Environmental fines or notices: appeal against a regulator" (*GOV.UK*, 15 June 2021), <https://www.gov.uk/guidance/environmental-fines-or-notices-appeal-against-a-regulator>, 2.

106 F.H. Kistenkas and I.M. Bouwma, "Barriers for the ecosystem services concept in European water and nature conservation law" (2018) 29 *Ecosystem Services* 223.

107 O. Sharon and others, "Ecosystem services and judge-made law: A review of legal cases in common law countries" (2018) 32 *Ecosystem Services* 9.

108 M. Grant, *Environmental Court Project Final Report: Report to the Department of Environment, Transport and the Regions* (2000), <http://www.law.du.edu/images/uploads/library/evert/

Such a court could also reduce litigation costs.[109] However, it is possible that, owing to the "cost-in-the-cause" principle, which requires the losing party to pay the successful party's costs in an environmental judicial review claim, individuals with little financial backing or entitlement to legal aid might be deterred from bring such claims in the first place. This might also be the case for less well-funded non-governmental organisations (NGOs). This is particularly troublesome in environmental cases, as it has been found that only 7 per cent of environmental judicial review cases in the UK are successful.[110]

It can be argued that this issue could give rise to a lack of real access to justice, which has been guaranteed, under Article 9 of the Aarhus Convention,[111] since the UK ratified the Convention in 2005. Access to justice, public participation, and access to information in environmental matters, particularly with regard to ES, could be properly implemented through the introduction of an environmental court. Citizens would be able to challenge potentially harmful projects and actions efficiently, and at a lower cost than under the current system. England and Wales would not only benefit from stronger protection of their crucial ES, but would also become more Aarhus-compliant, allowing greater public participation in environmental decision-making. Solidifying the three pillars of the Aarhus Convention could improve the legitimacy of decisions made by those in power,[112] and, crucially, encourage those decisions to take into account important localised information,[113] which should assist in further protecting ES.

5. CONCLUSION

Ecosystems offer countless benefits to humans, and being disconnected from nature has blurred our vision about how our and future generations' survival and well-being are dependent on nature, eventually leading to a situation in which we are failing to protect these benefits of nature. It is now clear that the

---

environmentalcourtprojectfinalreport2000.doc>; R. Macrory, "The Long and Winding Road: Towards an Environmental Court in England and Wales" (2013) 25 *Journal of Environmental Law* 371.

109 N. Parpworth and K. Thompson, "Establishing a Specialist Environmental Tribunal: The Implications for Magistrates" (2003) 167 *Justice of the Peace* 888.

110 R. Macrory and M. Woods, *Modernizing Environmental Justice: Regulation and the Role of an Environmental Tribunal* (Faculty of Laws, University College of London, 2003), 22.

111 Convention on Access to Information, Public Participation in Decision-Making and Access to Justice in Environmental Matters (entered into force 30 October 2001), 2162 UNTS 447 (Aarhus Convention), Art. 9.

112 M. Lee and C. Abbot, "The Usual Suspects? Public Participation Under the Aarhus Convention" (2003) 66(1) *Modern Law Review* 80.

113 E. Mostert, "The Challenge of Public Participation" (2003) 5(2) *Water Policy* 179.

concept of ES should be mainstreamed in policy and decision-making, and that this approach should be supported by a legal underpinning.

Offering legal protection for ES does not mean that the existing and established strategies should be abandoned. In fact, ES protection requires a holistic framework involving a number of disciplines, such as science, economics and law. Although there are a number of soft-law instruments that emphasise the importance of protecting ES and natural capital, these remain as guidance without enforcement. It is argued here that a robust legal perspective that includes court proceedings and enforcement could help ES protection to become established as a legal principle.

A dedicated, cost-effective environmental court may result in an increase in the number of environmental claims from those who might have ordinarily been dissuaded from pursuing them, under the current system. Moreover, the three pillars of the Aarhus Convention would be further enhanced in England and Wales, further promoting public participation. The success of this approach has been witnessed in other common-law jurisdictions, such as Australia, which have implemented this type of court. Undeniably, the protection of ES would benefit from the introduction of a specialist environmental court, if they become a material consideration for the judiciary in the future.

STRATEGIC CLIMATE CHANGE LITIGATION AND THE EU HABITATS DIRECTIVE

What Lessons can be Learnt from the Recent Case Law Developments in the United States?

Hendrik SCHOUKENS*

1. INTRODUCTION

Climate change is one of the most existential threats to the long-term survival of life on our planet today. In March 2022, both the North and South Poles had record temperatures, with thermometers recording a massive 15 degrees Celsius hotter than the previous all-time record at the Vostok station, about 1,300 kilometres from the geographical South Pole. At the North Pole, similar astonishing events were recorded.[1] Recent reports show the existence of a large emission gap, with the signatories to the Paris Agreement's current pledges only capable of reducing carbon emissions by about 7.5 per cent by 2030,[2] while the Intergovernmental Panel on Climate Change (IPCC) has indicated that emission reduction ranges to meet the internationally agreed climate targets should be around 45 per cent by 2030, compared with 2010.[3] However, the parties to the Paris Convention must redouble their climate efforts if they are to reach the overarching goal of limiting the global temperature rise to 2 degrees Celsius – ideally 1.5 degrees Celsius – by the end of the century.[4] Against the backdrop of rising temperatures, climate change lawsuits have recently emerged as a new

* This contribution is up to date as of mid-2022.

1 Donna Lu, "Extremes of 40C above normal: what's causing 'extraordinary' heating in polar regions?", *The Guardian* (London, 21 March 2022).

2 United Nations Environment Programme, *The Heat Is On: A world of climate promises not yet delivered* (Emissions Gap Report, 2021).

3 International Panel on Climate Change, *Climate Change 2022: Mitigation of Climate Change (Working Group III Contribution to the Sixth Assessment Report of the IPCC, 4 April 2022).*

4 Ibid.

lever, in order to step up compliance.[5] As of today, the majority of these strategic lawsuits, such as *Urgenda* in the Netherlands,[6] have been based upon tort law and human rights duties, given the major impact unhalted climate change would have on the survival chances of future generations of *humans*.

However, many terrestrial, as well as marine, ecosystems are also at risk from the global rise in temperatures, including in Europe. In 2019, the IPBES *Global Assessment Report on Biodiversity and Ecosystem Services* revealed that almost 1 million species are currently at risk of extinction,[7] indicating that we might well be witnessing what some scientists have already dubbed a "sixth mass extinction event".[8] Most importantly, this study also identified climate change as one of the leading threats to the long-term survival of today's species and habitats.[9] Mountainous habitats, as well as arctic ecosystems, are principally affected, amongst other things by melting glaciers and thawing permafrost. Recent research has revealed that the continuing loss of Arctic sea ice is forcing the polar bear – the "poster child" of climate change – to use four times as much energy to survive, severely impacting its long-term survival chances,[10] whereas recent mass starvation events of reindeer are partly linked to climate change.[11] Yet, more comprehensive studies indicate that the threat related to climate change is not confined to arctic ecosystems; elsewhere in the world, habitats are also shifting and shrinking, which poses insurmountable challenges for an increasing number of vulnerable species.[12] While some flexible species might adapt, and migrate towards higher elevations and latitudes, other species lack this ability, or are hindered from migrating due to geographical conditions (for example, they live on islands) or human-induced habitat fragmentation. The IPBES study concluded that nearly half of threatened terrestrial mammals and a quarter of threatened bird species have already been adversely affected by climate change.[13] In 2016, the disappearance of the Bramble Cay melomys, whose habitat was exclusively located on an island in the Great Barrier Reef,

5 See, for an overview, Joana Sitzer and Catherine Higham, "Global trends in climate change litigation: 2022 snapshot" (Policy Report, June 2022).

6 *Urgenda Foundation v. State of the Netherlands* [2019] ECLI:NL:GHDHA:2018:2591.

7 Intergovernmental Science-Policy Platform on Biodiversity and Ecosystem Services (IPBES), *Global Assessment Report on Biodiversity and Ecosystem Services* (IPBES Secretariat, 2019).

8 Anthony Barnosky et al., "Has the Earth's Sixth Mass Extinction Already Arrived?" (2011) 473 *Nature* 51.

9 IPBES report, supra, note 7.

10 Cody J. Dey et al., "Increasing nest predation will be insufficient to maintain polar bear body condition in the face of sea ice loss" (2017) 23(5) *Global Change Biology* 1281.

11 Bruce C. Forbes et al., "Sea ice, rain-on-snow and tundra reindeer nomadism in Arctic Russia" (2017) *Biology Letters* 12:20160466, http://dx.doi.org/10.1098/rsbl.2016.0466.

12 Céline Bellard et al., "Impacts of climate change on the future of biodiversity" (2012) 15 *Ecology Letters* 365.

13 IPBES report, supra, note 7.

was regarded by some scientists as the first case of mammalian extinction linked to climate change.[14]

In spite of the existential threat climate change is posing for many ecosystems and species, limited attention has been paid to the intersection between biodiversity law and climate change, either in relation to climate mitigation or adaptation actions.[15] Even so, in recent decades, the United States (US) has served as an interesting laboratory for addressing climate change effects through the prism of national biodiversity law, in particular the 1973 Endangered Species Act (ESA).[16] To be more precise, the jurisprudential developments of the past few decades, which have featured, amongst others, the polar bear – the first species listed by the US Fish and Wildlife Service (FWS), under the ESA, as endangered due to climate change[17] – have seemingly opened up a new pathway for climate activists, in their efforts to both mitigate climate change and force authorities to lay down comprehensive plans which focus on climate change adaptation.[18]

Based on the most prominent jurisprudential developments regarding the intersection between climate change and the ESA, this contribution aims to address to what extent a similar shift in climate change litigation is also thinkable in the European Union (EU). In particular, this contribution explores to what extent the 1992 EU Habitats Directive,[19] which is to be regarded as the cornerstone of EU biodiversity law, could be used as a complementary instrument to mitigate future greenhouse gas emissions, or at least prepare ("adapt") ecosystems for the inevitable impact of climate change. Both climate adaptation and mitigation are addressed. Rather than analysing the need for a comprehensive revision of the EU Habitats Directive, against the backdrop of the ongoing climate emergency, this contribution outlines whether there exists room to reinterpret the existing protection and restoration duties, against the backdrop of the interface between climate science and nature conservation.[20]

---

14 Hannah Seo, "Extinction obituary: how the Bramble Cay melomys became the first mammal lost to the climate crisis", *The Guardian* (London, 1 June 2022).

15 See, for instance, Mackenzie Landa, "Species Protection as a Natural Climate Solution" (2020) 50(6) *Environmental Law Reporter* 10498.

16 16 USCA §1531 *et seq.*

17 See, more extensively, Lindsay Card, "Polar Bears: Climate Refugees Expanding and Protecting Designated Critical Habitat for Polar Bears Using the Endangered Species Act" (2018) 34(2) *Journal of Land Use* 168/9.

18 See also Andrew J. Coffey, "Feeling the Heat: The Endangered Species Act and Climate Change" (2020) 36(2) *Georgia State University Law Review* 347.

19 Council Directive of 21 May 1992 on the conservation of natural habitats and of wild fauna and flora [1992] OJ L 206/7.

20 For more on the topic of climate adaptation and the EU Habitats Directive, see Arie Trouwborst, "The Habitats Directive and climate change: is the law climate-proof?" in Charles-Hubert Born et al. (eds.), *The Habitats Directive in its EU Environmental Law Context: European Nature's Best Hope?* (Routledge 2016), 303.

2. A QUICK PEEK INTO THE ENDANGERED SPECIES ACT AND THE EU HABITATS DIRECTIVE

2.1. INTRODUCTION

As this contribution primarily opts for a comparative approach, whereby the ESA is used as a benchmark to check the climate potential of its EU counterpart, the EU Habitats Directive, it is necessary to sketch a summary of both legislative instruments.[21] Of course, the different legal contexts in which the ESA and the EU Habitats Directive operate must be recalled. The ESA is a concrete manifestation of the US federal government's primary responsibility to regulate endangered species and their associated habitat, to achieve conservation and recovery.[22] Whereas the role of the individual states, in the context of nature conservation, is not negligible, as the ESA authorises the Secretary of the Interior to enter into cooperative agreements with states that have established "adequate and active" programmes of protection, it is safe to say the ESA plays a prominent role as the backbone of nature conservation in the US.

As is well known, the EU is a supranational legal order, since its Member States have agreed, as a result of their membership, to transfer some of their powers to the EU institutions in specified policy areas, amongst which are environmental protection and nature conservation. Although some analogies might be drawn between US and European federalism, which fall squarely beyond the scope of this contribution, the basic principles of the EU legal order are divided into primary legislation (the treaties and general legal principles), secondary legislation (based on the treaties) and supplementary law. The EU Habitats Directive is to be regarded as a prime example of secondary environmental legislation, which Member States are required to faithfully transpose into their national legislation and apply accordingly. As "guardian of the treaties", the European Commission oversees the application and enforcement of EU law, including the EU Habitats Directive. The latter also features prominently in infringement proceedings launched by the European Commission before the Court of Justice of the EU (CJEU), which is the final arbiter when it comes to the application and interpretation of EU law.[23] In the wake of the ratification of

---

21 For a recent overview, see Valerie Fogleman, "A comparative analysis of the selection of species and the establishment of their natural habitats in the US and the EU" in Marlon Boeve et al. (eds.), Environmental Law for Transition to Sustainability (Intersentia 2021), 207.

22 Susan George and William J. Snape III, "State Endangered Species Act" in Donald C. Baur and Wm. Robert Irvin (eds.), *Endangered Species Act: Law, Policy, and Perspectives* (2nd ed.) (American Bar Association 2010), 345.

23 See: Ludwig Krämer, "Implementation and enforcement of the Habitats Directive" in Born et al. (eds.), supra, note 20, 229.

the 1998 UNECE Aarhus Convention,[24] national courts also play an increasingly important role in the application of the EU Habitats Directive in national or regional permitting policies, by quashing decisions that stand at odds with the protection prescription laid out by this instrument. National courts are obliged to set aside provisions of national or regional law that clash with the protection duties set out by the EU Habitats Directive.[25] In the wake of the ratification of the Aarhus Convention, non-governmental organisations (NGOs) have been granted a relatively broad standing in the enforcement of the EU Habitats Directive.[26]

2.2. OVERVIEW OF THE ESA

The ESA was passed in order to overcome the major deficiencies of the 1969 Endangered Species Conservation Act.[27] The ESA's clear goal was to allow the conservation of species that were in danger of extinction. However, the ESA's main objective is not limited to preventing the extinction of species. It also endeavours to let species recover to the point where they may be delisted.[28] To receive the protection provided by the ESA, a species must first be added to the federal lists of endangered and threatened wildlife and plants. A species is added to this list when the FWS determines that it has met the definition of endangered or threatened under the Act. Such decisions are based on a set of criteria set forth in the ESA.[29]

A first potent mechanism the ESA puts forward to protect species is the designation of so-called critical habitat.[30] This is to be done at the time of listing of a species, or within one year. However, there are circumstances in which there exists no duty to designate such habitat, including where the benefits of exclusion, including economic benefits, outweigh the benefits of such designation.[31]

Under section 7, federal agencies are required to consult with the FWS or the National Marine Fisheries Service (NMFS), to ensure that any actions taken

---

24 Convention on Access to Information, Public Participation in Decision-making and Access to Justice in Environmental Matters, done at Aarhus, Denmark, 25 July 1998 (1999) 2161 UNTS 447; 38 ILM 517.

25 See, for instance, Case C-127/02 *Waddenzee* (2004) ECLI:EU:C:2004:482, paras. 60 *et seq.*

26 See, for instance, Case C-240/09 *Lesoochranárske zoskupenie VLK I* (2011) ECR I-01255, paras. 49–52.

27 See, for more extensive information, M.J. Bean, "Historical Background of the Endangered Species Act" in Baur and Irvin (eds.), supra, note 22, 9 and 14.

28 *Gifford Pinchot Task Force v. US Fish and Wildlife Serv.* (2004) 378 F.3d 1059, 1070 (9th Cir. 2004).

29 For an overview, see John B. Ruhl, "Listing Endangered and Threatened Species" in Baur and Irvin (eds.), supra note 22, 16.

30 S.4(a)(3) US Endangered Species Act, supra, note 16.

31 Federico Cheever, "Critical habitat" in Baur and Irvin (eds.), supra, note 22, 41 and 56.

by the agencies do not jeopardise the existence of a threatened or endangered species, or cause the destruction of, or harmful modification to, a listed species' designated critical habitat. The notable 1978 Supreme Court ruling *Tennessee Valley Authority v. Hill* (*TVA*),[32] which revolved around the survival of a small endangered fish, the snail darter, exemplified the "strong teeth" of the procedural and substantial obligations laid down by section 7.

Section 9 of the ESA also applies to non-federal and private actions, and prohibits the "taking" of any species listed as "endangered" or "threatened" under the ESA.[33] By stretching the definition of "take" to include habitat modifications that actually kill or injure listed species, by significantly impairing essential behavioural patterns, including breeding, feeding or sheltering, section 9 can be used to restrict land use activities that are otherwise legal. In its notable 1995 decision *Babbitt v. Sweet Home Chapter of Communities for a Greater Oregon* (*Sweet Home*), the US Supreme Court reasserted the ruling of *Palila*,[34] giving section 9 and the corresponding definition of harm an expansive reading.[35] Under section 10(a)(1)(B), non-federal landowners who plan activities on their lands that may "incidentally take" a listed species may apply to the FWS for an incidental take permit that exempts the activity at issue from the prohibition against "taking".[36] The issuance of an "incidental take permit" has been made conditional on the creation of a Habitat Conservation Plan (HCP).[37]

2.3. OVERVIEW OF THE EU HABITATS DIRECTIVE

The EU Habitats Directive is, together with the earlier Birds Directive,[38] considered to be one of the hallmarks of EU environmental law. The general objective of the EU Habitats Directive, as stipulated in Article 2(1), is to contribute towards ensuring biodiversity, through the conservation of natural habitats, and of wild fauna and flora, in the European territory of the EU Member States to which the treaty applies. Measures taken pursuant to the Directive must be designed to maintain or restore, at favourable conservation status, natural habitats and species of wild fauna and flora of Community interest.[39] By requiring Member

---

32 437 US 153 (1978).

33 Patrick Parenteau, "The Take Prohibition" in Baur and Irvin (eds.), supra, note 22, 147.

34 *Palila v. Hawaii Dept. Of Land & Natural Res.*, 852 F.2d 1106, 1107 (9th Cir. 1991).

35 515 US 687 (1995).

36 See, for more extensive information, D.P. Wheeler and R.M. Rowberry, "Habitat Conservation Plans and the Endangered Species Act" in Baur and Irvin (eds.), supra, note 22, 222.

37 Shi-Ling Hsu, "The Potential and the Pitfalls of Habitat Conservation Planning Under the Endangered Species Act" (1999) 29 *Environmental Law Reporter* 10592.

38 Directive 2009/147/EC of the European Parliament and of the Council of 30 November 2009 on the conservation of wild birds (2009) OJ L 20/7.

39 Art. 2(2) of the EU Habitats Directive, supra, note 19.

States to take measures to maintain or restore natural habitats and wild species listed in the annexes to the Directive at a favourable conservation status, the Habitats Directive lays down a set of robust protection and restoration duties in relation to those habitats and species of European importance.[40]

The EU Habitats Directive is built around two pillars: the Natura 2000 network of protected sites, and the strict system of species protection. All in all, the Directive protects over 1,000 animal and plant species, and over 200 so-called "habitat types" (for example, special types of forests, meadows, wetlands, etc.) which are of European importance. The creation of an EU-wide network of protected sites is one of the core objectives of the Directive. Currently, the Natura 2000 Network covers 18 per cent of the EU's land area, and more than 8 per cent of its marine territory, thereby establishing the world's largest coordinated network of protected sites. Although the term "Natura 2000" was only coined with the adoption of the EU Habitats Directive in 1992, the 1979 EU Birds Directive already mandated the EU Member States to select and protect eligible habitats for certain endangered bird species. In one of the first landmark rulings regarding the designation duties under the EU Birds Directive, which revolved around the Santoña marshes in Spain, the CJEU, in 1993, held that, while Member States retain a certain margin of discretion as regards the choice of Special Protection Areas (SPAs), the classification of these sites is directly subject to ecological criteria.[41] Economic interests cannot interfere with the designation duties, a rationale which was later reiterated by the CJEU in proceedings with respect to the EU Habitats Directive.[42]

Once designated, the Natura 2000 sites are subject to the application of the three-tiered conservation duties set out in Article 6 of the EU Habitats Directive. First, Article 6(1) of the Directive lays down a binding legal duty on Member States to take proactive management measures, including restoration actions if need be, for the designated Natura 2000 sites on their territories.[43] Second, Article 6(2) provides for a non-regression obligation, stipulating that Member States need to take appropriate action to avoid the further deterioration of natural habitats and the disturbance of species. This provision is interpreted by the CJEU as an obligation of result.[44] The scope of the said provision is large, encompassing ongoing uses,[45] activities that are not subject to a prior notification[46] or permit, and recently authorised plans or projects.[47] It is to be

---

40 For an overview, see An Cliquet et al., "Restoring nature in the EU: the only way is up" in Born et al. (eds), supra, note 20, 265.

41 Case C-355/90 *Commission v. Spain* (1993) ECR I-4221, para. 26.

42 Case C-226/08 *Stadt Papenburg* (2012) ECLI:EU:C:2010:10, paras. 31 *et seq.*

43 Case C-848/19 *Commission v. Greece* (2020) ECLI:EU:C:2020:1047, paras. 49 *et seq.*

44 See, for instance, Case C-559/19 *Commission v. Spain* (2021) ECLI:EU:C:2021:512.

45 See, for instance, Case C-404/09 *Commission v. Spain* (2011) ECLI:EU:C:2011:768.

46 Case C-241/08, *Commission v France*, [2010] ECR I-01697, para. 62.

47 Case C-226/08 *Stadt Papenburg* (2012) ECLI:EU:C:2010:10, para. 49.

regarded as a catch-all provision, primarily aimed at achieving a standstill in terms of degradation of natural habitats.[48]

In contrast to Article 6(2) of the Directive, which leaves a relatively large leeway to the Member States when it comes to the precise choice of actions and instruments, Article 6(3) is more precise and concrete. This provision sets out the procedural and substantive criteria to be observed when permitting plans and projects which could impact on the integrity of Natura 2000 sites. These plans and projects first need to undergo a so-called appropriate assessment, which needs to have an exclusive ecological focus, detailing both the direct and indirect (cumulative) effects the purported activities might give rise to.[49] By means of exception, a derogation can be granted from the above-mentioned conservation duties, whenever certain strict conditions are fulfilled. If no other realistic and less harmful alternative exists, a plan or project to which an imperative reason of overriding public interest (IROPI) can be attributed can, nevertheless, be authorised. In addition, proactive compensation actions need to guarantee that the overall integrity of the Natura 2000 network is not compromised. For spatial developments, only imperative reasons of overriding public interest can be invoked.[50]

Article 12(1) of the Directive obliges the Member States to establish a system of strict protection for the endangered species listed in its Annex IV. This set of protection rules needs to include, amongst other things, a prohibition on all forms of deliberate killing of these species in the wild;[51] the deliberate disturbance of these species, particularly during the periods of breeding, rearing, hibernation and migration;[52] and the deterioration or destruction of breeding sites or resting places.[53] In its steadfast case law, which started with the breakthrough ruling in *Commission v. Greece (Caretta caretta)*, the CJEU has consistently reiterated that Article 12(1)(a) of the Directive not only requires Member States to faithfully and precisely implement the protection duties in their national or regional legislation,[54] but also obliges them to apply them effectively, for instance when assessing decisions on activities that might lead to a transgression of the protection duties.[55] Only under limited circumstances can

---

48 See, more extensively, Hendrik Schoukens, "Non-Regression Clauses in Times of Ecological Restoration Law: Article 6(2) of the EU Habitats Directive as Unusual Ally to Restore Natura 2000?" (2017) 13(1) *Utrecht Law Review* 124.

49 For a recent application, see, for instance, Case C-441/17 *Commission v. Poland* (2018) ECLI:EU:C:2018:255.

50 Case C-182/10, *Solvay* (2012) ECLI:EU:C:2012:82.

51 Art. 12(1)(a) of the EU Habitats Directive, supra, note 19.

52 Ibid., Art. 12(1)(b).

53 Ibid., Art. 12(1)(d).

54 See, for instance, Case C-6/04 *Commission v. UK* (2005) ECLI:EU:C:2005:626.

55 See, for instance, Case C-103/00 *Commission v. Greece* (2002) ECLI:EU:C:2002:60; Case C-340/10 *Commission v. Cyprus* (2012) ECLI:EU:C:2012:143.

a derogation be granted and the strict prohibitions bypassed. These justification grounds relate, for instance, to damage to crops or livestock,[56] research purposes, or the interests of other threatened species.

3. EXPLORING THE POTENTIAL FOR CLIMATE-BASED LITIGATION UNDER THE EU HABITATS DIRECTIVE

3.1. INTRODUCTION

Having briefly sketched out the main traits of both the ESA and the EU Habitats Directive above, this section explores the potency of these protection and conservation tools, in the context of the climate crisis, both with the aim of avoiding further direct or indirect carbon dioxide (CO_2) emissions (mitigation), and to streamline future adaptive scenarios (adaptation). In light of the general similarities between the protection schemes enshrined in both the ESA and the EU Habitats Directive, this analysis focuses on a non-exhaustive list of climate-related elements that have come to the fore in the U.S. case law, and which might also reverberate, in future years, within the EU.

3.2. DOES CLIMATE CHANGE FALL WITHIN THE REALM OF BIODIVERSITY LAW?

The starting question of our analysis of the intersection between climate change and biodiversity legislation is relatively straightforward: does addressing climate change fall within the realm of EU nature conservation law? The answer to this question might be relatively straightforward: yes, of course, given the significant impact that it generates on ecosystems. Yet, somehow, the reply also ties in with what is precisely meant by "addressing climate change". Some might submit that tackling global challenges, such as climate change, falls squarely outside the scope of biodiversity legislation, which is, or at least was, primarily aimed at addressing more direct threats to ecosystems, such as habitat destruction through development, or the adverse effects of land conversion for agricultural purposes. Moreover, it cannot be denied that climate change was not the primary objective when much of the existing biodiversity legislation, such as the ESA, or even the EU Habitats Directive, was adopted.[57] Habitat destruction and overhunting were more often cited as the usual suspects in this regard. In

56 Art. 16(1)(b) of the EU Habitats Directive, supra, note 19.

57 See, for the US, Barry Kellman, "Climate Change in the Endangered Species Act" (2016) *Environmental Law Reporter* 10845, 10854.

addition to this, one might contend that climate change is a notoriously complex topic, with many uncertainties when it comes to its exact ramifications.[58] Whereas science has established, with 100 per cent certainty, that there exists a causal link between the warming of the Earth and the sharp rise in CO_2 emissions due to human activities, the question of attribution, which also will pop up later in this contribution, might arise in this regard.[59] Is it really possible to attribute the current ecological damage to easily identifiable emitters? With billions of contributors to climate change, is it feasible to directly link the loss of one specific ecosystem to a specific actor? And if not, does that not render biodiversity legislation an ill-suited instrument for tackling climate change, especially since, both at the international and national levels, additional legal tools have been adopted to tackle climate change, and in particular the topic of CO_2 reductions, in a more direct manner?

Let us first address the topic from the angle of the ESA. Although the risks of climate change had already been popularised by significant scientific research conducted in the 1980s and 1990s, US agencies only started incorporating climate science in decision-making at the end of the 2000s. It has been suggested that they were forced to move in this direction by strategic lawsuits launched by environmental NGOs.[60] Even so, this rather lax attitude quickly shifted after 2010, when the FWS and other agencies no longer hesitated to acknowledge, albeit in general terms, that the changing climate was poised to threaten the survival of, and habitat for, some species.[61] The same goes for the amount of legal literature on the topic of the linkages between climate change and the ESA, which exploded after 2010.[62] It must be noted that the wording of that Act is notoriously broad, leaving ample room for bringing climate change into its substantive scope. For one, the overarching objective of the Act is "to provide a means whereby the ecosystems upon which endangered species and threatened species depend may be conserved", which does not explicitly rule out more global challenges, such as climate change. Seeing the mounting scientific evidence which points out that climate change has progressed to become one of the existential threats for

58 John B. Ruhl, "Climate Change and the Endangered Species Act: Building Bridges to the No-Analog Future" (2008) 88(1) *Boston University Law Review* 19–20.

59 See, on the topic of attribution and the ESA more extensively, Jessica Wentz, *Climate Attribution Science and the Endangered Species Act* (Sabin Center for Climate Change Law, 2021).

60 See Landa, supra, note 15, 10504.

61 See, more extensively, Michael C. Blumm and Kya B. Marienfeld, "Endangered Species Act Listing and Climate Change: Avoiding the Elephant in the Room" (2014) 20(1) *Animal Law Review* 277.

62 For an overview, see Congressional Research Service, *The Endangered Species Act and Climate Change: Selected Legal Issues* (2019, CRS Report).

most of the ecosystems in the US, it becomes clear that climate change can no longer be ignored when further implementing the ESA.[63] In this regard, it is also worth noting that the Supreme Court, in the aforementioned *Tennessee Valley Authority v. Hill* case, held that "[t]he plain intent of Congress in enacting this statute was to reverse the trend toward species extinction, whatever the cost".[64] This clearly hints at a more progressive approach, which also leaves ample space to focus on climate change when implementing the Act, even where such an approach might entail heavy economic consequences for existing industry and society.

A similar rationale seems to prevail when focusing on the EU Habitats Directive, as is underlined by its broad objective, which was referred to in section 2.3. Likewise, in the preamble, the *transboundary nature* of threats to endangered habitats and species in the EU is referred to as one of the primary justifications for passing an EU directive in this regard. Additional support for a broad reading of the EU Habitats Directive, in the face of the impending climate crisis, is also offered by the definition of the key concept of "conservation status" in its Article 1, where it is stated that the conservation status of a natural habitat has to be understood as "the sum of the influences acting on a natural habitat and its typical species that may affect its long-term natural distribution, structure and functions as well as the long-term survival of its typical species within the territory referred to in Article 2". Given that the EU Habitats Directive has the goal of conserving endangered species at a favourable conservation status, it now becomes clear that climate change cannot remain unaddressed there.

The recent case law developments before the CJEU underline the relatively broad range of the EU Habitats Directive. In its recent ruling on the Dutch policy approaches to nitrogen deposition in Natura 2000 sites, the CJEU indirectly accepted that nitrogen emissions, even though they can travel hundreds of miles before they actually create depositions on ecosystems, fall within the scope of Article 6 of the Directive.[65] Whereas CO_2 and other greenhouse gases do not create immediate adverse effects for local habitats, which still sets climate change apart from nitrogen deposition (which produces a more localised effect), this case law clearly hints that the substantive scope of the EU Habitats Directive is not restricted to direct impacts, such as habitat destruction. The simple fact that the Directive does not seem to exhaustively enumerate the threats to biodiversity it aims to constrain further supports this thesis.

63 Ibid., 1.
64 437 US 153 (1978).
65 Case C-293/17 *Coöperatie Mobilisation for the Environment UA* (2018) ECLI:EU:C:2018:882.

This progressive line of interpretation is further buttressed by the 2014 modification[66] of the EU Environmental Impact Assessment (EIA) Directive,[67] which, amongst other things, explicitly focused on highlighting the importance of climate change when carrying out environmental impact assessments. In the preamble to this Directive, it is recognised that "[c]limate change will continue to cause damage to the environment and compromise economic development. In this regard, it is appropriate to assess the impact of projects on climate (for example greenhouse gas emissions) and their vulnerability to climate change."[68] Although the EIA Directive is to be regarded as a procedural instrument with a different, less substantive focus than the EU Habitats Directive, it serves as another illustration of how climate change also has to be taken into consideration when implementing and applying more horizontal EU environmental instruments.

Of course, it could be argued that the need to address climate change in the context of the EU Habitats Directive would interfere with the existing climate legislation of the EU, such as the Emission Trading Scheme (ETS) Directive;[69] the Land Use, Land-Use Change and Forestry (LULUCF) Regulation;[70] and the EU Climate Law.[71] Along similar lines, one might argue that this is what distinguishes the regulatory context regarding climate change in the EU from the US, where the federal level has remained notoriously absent in addressing climate change through legislation.[72] Even while the implementation of former President Obama's Clean Power Plan, and the adoption of the Paris Agreement, seemed to foreshadow more progressive climate legislation in this area at the federal level, the majority of these modest steps forward were rolled back by the Trump administration.[73] This regulatory stalemate is starkly different from

66 Directive 2014/52/EU of the European Parliament and of the Council of 16 April 2014 amending Directive 2011/92/EU on the assessment of the effects of certain public and private projects on the environment [2014] OJ L 124/1.

67 Directive 2011/92/EU of the European Parliament and of the Council of 13 December 2011 on the assessment of the effects of certain public and private projects on the environment [2011] OJ L 26/1.

68 Consideration 13 to Directive 2014/52/EU (supra, note 66).

69 Directive 2003/87/EC of the European Parliament and of the Council of 13 October 2003 establishing a scheme for greenhouse gas emission allowance trading within the Community and amending Council Directive 96/61/EC [2003] OJ L 275/32.

70 Regulation (EU) 2018/841 of the European Parliament and of the Council of 30 May 2018 on the inclusion of greenhouse gas emissions and removals from land use, land-use change and forestry in the 2030 climate and energy framework, and amending Regulation (EU) No. 525/2013 and Decision No 529/2013/EU [2018] OJ L 156/1.

71 Regulation (EU) 2021/1119 of the European Parliament and of the Council of 30 June 2021 establishing the framework for achieving climate neutrality and amending Regulations (EC) No 401/2009 and (EU) 2018/1999 ("European Climate Law") [2021] OJ L 243/1.

72 Landa, supra note 15, 10502–10503.

73 Ibid.

the situation in the EU. Is it, against this backdrop, still sensible to tackle climate change through legal instruments that were not adopted for this purpose? What if national courts come forward with additional reduction targets which go beyond the already applicable EU reduction targets at Member State level? How should biodiversity legislation be used to protect species threatened by global threats? These questions merit further consideration. As a preliminary conclusion, however, it is safe to hold that the *lex specialis* argument does not appear persuasive in an EU context, and that the climate considerations definitely need to trickle down within the scope of the EU Habitats Directive. The precise repercussions of this finding are explored below.

3.3. LISTING PROTECTED SPECIES ON THE BASIS OF CLIMATE CHANGE?

Having determined that climate change falls squarely within the substantive scope of both the ESA and the EU Habitats Directive, the question now arises whether this entails that agencies need to envisage protecting more species that might be impacted by rising temperatures. Interestingly, the majority of recent lawsuits regarding climate change, in the context of the ESA, have focused precisely on the question of whether it is necessary to list a species as endangered or threatened because of climate change.[74] This is partially linked to the fact that, in contrast to the EU Habitats Directive, the ESA does not contain a fixed list of protected species. Instead, it lays out a listing process involving a detailed technical review that can be initiated by non-federal parties (including environmental NGOs) through a petition, or by FWS or NMFS on their own initiative. Most listings are the result of petitions initiated by environmental NGOs.

Pursuant to section 4(a)(1) of the ESA, it is for the FWS to determine whether any species is endangered or threatened because of any of the following factors:

1. The present or threatened destruction, modification, or curtailment of the species' habitat or range;
2. Overutilization of the species for commercial, recreational, scientific, or educational purposes;
3. Disease or predation;
4. The inadequacy of existing regulatory mechanisms; or
5. Other natural or manmade factors affecting the species' continued existence.

74 See, more extensively, Blumm and Marienfeld, supra, note 61.

In considering these factors, the FWS are, moreover, required to base their decisions on the best available science.[75] As rightly noted by Ruhl:

> [T]here could hardly be a more definitive mandate to consider the effects of greenhouse gas emissions and climate change on species. Greenhouse gases are unquestionably a "man-made" factor, and if, as abundant evidence suggests, they are contributing to climate change, they are potentially "affecting ... [the] continued existence" of climate-threatened species.[76]

Indeed, the question of attribution is, in the context of listing, less relevant; it cannot reasonably be denied that the effects of climate change comprehensively fall within the ambit of the listing criteria.[77]

In spite of the broad consensus in the legal literature,[78] the FWS hesitated to base new listing decisions on climate change-related factors. This led to legal battles in courts, with environmental NGOs pursuing legal review of the initial refusal on the part of the FWS to list the polar bear as a threatened species in 2003.[79] The Center for Biological Diversity (CBD) argued that the polar bear should be listed, since rising global temperatures had put the bears' habitat in jeopardy, and thus the bear faced a real likelihood of extinction in the near future.[80] At the time of the petition, researchers had not identified a significant decline in the number of polar bears. Yet it was assumed by the CBD that modelled population projects pointed towards a steep decline in the near future. After years of litigation, the FWS finally agreed to list the polar bear as an endangered species in 2008, making it the first species to be listed as threatened with endangerment, under the terms of the ESA, because of climate change.[81]

The decision to list the polar bear was based upon three main findings: (1) the polar bear is dependent on sea ice for its survival; (2) that sea ice is declining; and (3) climate change will likely continue to reduce the extent and quality of Arctic sea ice enough to endanger the polar bear population.[82] Interestingly, this decision was challenged in court, by environmental NGOs, as well as the state of Alaska and industries. Using a rather deferential review standard, the US Court of Appeals for the District of Columbia (DC) Circuit upheld the listing ruling, holding that the FWS had reached a reasoned determination, based on the

---

75 16 USC §1533(b)(1), (2).

76 Ruhl, "Climate Change and the Endangered Species Act", supra, note 58, 32.

77 Ibid.

78 See also, amongst others, Blumm and Marienfeld, supra note 61.

79 Card, supra, note 17, 174.

80 Landa, supra, note 15, 10504.

81 US Fish and Wildlife Service, Press Release: Secretary Kempthorne, Press Conference on the Polar Bear Listing (14 May 2008). See, more extensively, Maggie Kuhn, "Climate Change and the Polar Bear: Is the Endangered Species Act up to the Task?" (2010) 27(1) *Alaska Law Review* 138.

82 Congressional Research Service, supra, note 62, 5.

"best available science data", encompassing both studies on existing population figures, as well as predictions of future population trends. In appraising the appeals launched by state and industry petitioners against a previous rejection of their claims by the DC District Court,[83] the DC Circuit Court was asked to assess seminal and complex legal questions pertaining to the standards used by the FWS in its listing decisions. Most prominent was the DC Circuit Court's firm rejection of the proposition that the climate science was too uncertain to support listing the polar bear as a species that was likely to become endangered in the "foreseeable" future. In this regard, the FWS' approach of defining the "foreseeable future" as a 45-year time frame, i.e. between 2005 and 2050, was deemed reasonable.[84] While it was submitted that the 45-year time frame was capricious, the DC Circuit Court found that this amounted to state-of-the-art science.[85] The counterclaims were partly dismissed by the Court, as amounting "to nothing more than competing views about policy and science".[86] By upholding the FWS' appraisal of the concept of the "foreseeable future", which is not further defined in the law, the DC Court created a seminal precedent for future climate-based listing decisions.[87]

However, not all petitions to list species based upon climate projections have received a favourable treatment by the competent agencies. A listing petition for the ribbon seal, built on climate-based arguments, was initially rejected by the NMFS, since it reasoned that the adverse effects linked to the loss of spring and winter sea ice were merely "speculative", as the population might simply adapt its behaviour and shift its range accordingly.[88] This decision not to list the ribbon seal was subsequently upheld in a federal district court in California. Amongst other things, the court held that decisions on how to frame the "foreseeable future" fell squarely within the agency's expertise and discretion.[89] The court sided with the NMFS, and did not identify any major error or flaw in the NMFS' holding that climate models after 2050 were too uncertain and unreliable to base a listing decision upon.[90]

A novel insight into the integration of climate data in listing decisions was offered by the US Court of Appeals for the Ninth Circuit, in its decision on the validity of the listing of two populations of Arctic bearded seals, in *Alaska Oil & Gas Association v. Pritzker*. In its listing decision, the NMFS now explicitly used climate projections through until 2100, which, amongst other things, led it to

83 In re Polar Bear Endangered Species Act Listing and §4(d) Rule Litigation, 838 F. Supp. 2d 214, 218 (DDC 2011).
84 709 F. 3rd 1 (DC Cir. 2013), 15.
85 Ibid., 16.
86 Ibid., 9.
87 Landa, supra, note 15, 10504.
88 73 Fed. Reg. 79822 at 79826.
89 *Center for Biological Diversity v. Lubchenco*, 758 F. Supp. 2d 645 (ND Cal. 2010).
90 Ibid.

the conclusion that bearded seals were ultimately at a greater risk from climate change than ribbon seals, since bearded seals usually frequent areas further north.[91] Even when the NMFS opted only to list just a part of the population of ribbon seals, as threatened, industry groups still decided to challenge this decision in court. Initially, the legal challenges were successful. However, this critical take on the NMFS' listing decision was, ultimately, overruled by the Ninth Circuit Court of Appeals, which concluded that the NMFS' climate projections for the second half of the twenty-first century were reasonable, scientifically sound and sufficiently supported by evidence.[92] Also crucial was the NMFS' determination that bearded seals used the ice for critical life stages, such as mating and giving birth.[93]

From these recent case law developments, it might be inferred that there exists a broad discretion on the part of the competent agencies to appraise the available climate science, when assessing petitions to list species as threatened or even endangered, based upon climate change-related arguments. This can work in both directions, as the courts also deferred to the agency's experience when dismissing unreliable long-term climate projections.[94] Even so, the overall conclusion appears to be that climate projects can no longer be sidelined in the listing process, especially not when faced with listing petitions for Arctic species that will face the consequences of climate change in their immediate habitat in the medium term.[95] In addition, and possibly most importantly, the jurisprudence underlines the need to interpret the notion of "foreseeability" in a relatively broad manner, especially in the context of species whose survival chances appear directly or indirectly threatened by climate change. The importance thereof cannot be understated, since it limits the discretion on the part of agencies to use a more short-term interpretation of the "foreseeable future". If the narrower view of "foreseeability" had prevailed, this would have significantly compromised the suitability of the ESA as a tool to address the climate change threat to endangered species.

However, recent litigation trends have, increasingly, shifted the focus to the leeway given to the agencies to use scientific uncertainty as an argument not to list a species as threatened or endangered.[96] In this respect, recent jurisprudence clearly underscores the need for a sound justification as to how this uncertainty underpins a non-listing decision. Such justification was, for instance, absent in a case focusing on the delisting of the Yellowstone grizzly bear as a threatened species, since the FWS had failed to articulate why the decline in whitebark pine,

91 Fed. Reg. 76740 (28 Dec. 2012).

92 *Alaska Oil & Gas Association v. Pritzker*, 840 F.3d 671 (9th Cir. 2016), 680–681.

93 Ibid., 679.

94 Congressional Research Service, supra, note 62, 6.

95 Wentz, supra note 59, 26–27.

96 Congressional Research Service, supra, note 62, 7.

a main food source for grizzlies, and threatened by climate change, could not affect the populations of this animal species.[97] Along similar lines, the decision to withdraw the proposed listing of the North American wolverine was also quashed by an American court.[98]

That said, the progressive jurisprudential take on the "foreseeable future", outlined above, could be challenged in future years, partly because of the 2019 amendments to the ESA Regulations, which were adopted by the Trump administration.[99] In the amended text, it is now specified that "[t]he term foreseeable future extends only so far into the future as the Services can reasonably determine that both the future threats and the species' responses to such threats are likely". Some fear that the new rule, which has not been rescinded by the FWS, as of the time of writing, might curtail the leeway to use climate-based arguments for listing species as threatened or endangered. Still, this preliminary assessment appears to be too pessimistic, since the amendments have not hindered the FWS from using climate projections for new listings.[100]

In sharp contrast to the abundant case law developments in the US, in the context of listing decisions and climate change, little to no evolution is taking place at EU level in this regard. This can certainly be attributed to the very rigid procedures, which are set out in its Article 19, for amending the annexes to the Habitats Directive. Pursuant to Article 19(1) of the Directive, "[s]uch amendments as are necessary for adapting Annexes I, II, III, V and VI to technical and scientific progress shall be adopted by the Council acting by qualified majority on a proposal from the Commission". For amending Annex IV, a unanimous decision of the Council is required, which sets the bar relatively high. Whereas the listing procedure under the ESA is relatively open, since it allows any person or organisation to petition the FWS or NMFS to add species to the endangered or threatened species list, the amendment procedures set out by the EU Habitats Directive serve as an effective obstacle to litigation strategies similar to those that have emerged in the US during the past decade. It is a well-known fact that the Annexes to the EU Habitats Directive are, as a result of the complex procedures to list new species, relatively outdated, and also not fully representative of the wide array of species, amongst others insects, that are endangered on the European continent.[101] The Annexes have only been revised at times of the extension of the EU, as this was necessary to ensure the ecological underpinnings of the Natura 2000 network. In general, however, no one seems

97 *Greater Yellowstone Coal., Inc. v. Servheen*, 665 F.3d 1015 (9th Cir. 2011).

98 *Defenders of Wildlife v. Jewell*, 176 F. Supp.3d 975, 1011 (D. Montana 2016).

99 Endangered and Threatened Wildlife and Plants, Regulations for Listing Species and Designating Critical Habitat, Final Rule, 84 Fed. Reg. 45.020–45.052 (2019).

100 Wentz, supra, note 59, 55.

101 Pedro Cardoso, "Habitats Directive species list: urgent need of revision" (2012) 5(2) *Insect Conservation and Diversity* 169.

very keen to open this "Pandora's box", since the fear exists that many Member States might be eager to submit requests for the removal of some politically sensitive species, such as wolves, from the Annexes. The adoption of objective and transparent criteria for the listing of protected species, and regular updates and amendments to the lists, based on such criteria, appear crucial to addressing this flaw.[102]

In theory, however, the wording of Article 19 seems to imply that scientific progress should urge the Council to consider amendments to the Annexes, which leaves open the option to use climate data and projections in arguments to bring more species under the scope of the Directive. In the existing case law of the CJEU, it has already become clear that decision-making, in the context of the Directive, is to be based upon the best available science,[103] and this also seems to be reasserted in Article 19. Thus, one might envisage future lawsuits aimed at adding species that are vulnerable to extinction scenarios, as a result of the creeping sea-ice loss, to the annexes of the EU Habitats Directive. From a pragmatic perspective, the chances of adding the polar bear, which was the "poster child" for climate litigation under the ESA, do not seem realistic, since the species' habitat is not to be found on EU territory. Greenland, where the species still has a robust stronghold, is an autonomous territory within Denmark. Between 1973 and 1985, Greenland was part of the EU. Following a referendum, held in 1982, it withdrew from the EU, and is now associated with it under the Overseas Association Decision. Also, Spitsbergen, the Norwegian archipelago located about midway between the northern coast of Norway and the North Pole, still hosts a considerable population of polar bears. Yet Norway also is not currently a member of the EU. In addition, it would make no sense to ask for the listing of additional seal or whale species in the EU, since all of them already fall within the scope of the EU Habitats Directive.

Be that as it may, one way to circumvent the above-mentioned obstacles to listing other species that are threatened by climate change on EU territory, and which do not yet feature in the Annexes of the Directive, would be to launch an action for failure to act, based upon Article 265 of the Treaty on the Functioning of the European Union (TFEU). An action for failure to act is based on the premise that unlawful inaction on the part of an institution, such as the European Council, makes it possible, including for individuals, to bring an action before the CJEU. Even leaving aside the limited standing environmental NGOs enjoy before the CJEU,[104] case law also seems to indicate that a mere written reply

102 Ibid.

103 See, for instance, Case C-674/17 *Tapiola* (2019) ECLI:EU:C:2019:851.

104 Hendrik Schoukens, "Access to Justice in Environmental Cases after the Rulings of the Court of Justice of 13 January 2015: Kafka Revisited?" (2015) 31(81) *Utrecht Journal of International and European Law* 46.

from an institution has already been deemed, by the CJEU, to be sufficient proof that an institution has acted.[105] In other words, the chances that, in the EU, climate lawsuits might find fertile grounds in the context of amendments to the Annexes, remain relatively limited in the short term.

3.4. DESIGNATING NEW HABITATS FOR SPECIES AT RISK BECAUSE OF CLIMATE CHANGE?

Climate change is pushing several species to migrate to more northerly habitats because their current habitats are no longer functional in light of the rising temperature. This raises questions as to whether climate change-related risks are to be taken into account as a baseline when designating protected areas. The provisions dealing with the designation of protected or critical habitats, therefore, constitute a logical next step in this analysis. Does there exist a legal obligation to designate new areas in light of the rising temperatures, focusing both on existing and future needs for habitat?

Again, recent developments under the ESA might be instructive here. Initially, the ESA does not seem to contain any provisions aimed at the establishment of a network of protected sites. However, when the FWS lists a species, it must, in principle, designate the critical habitat of the said species. Pursuant to the provisions of the ESA, critical habitat should encompass the geographical areas occupied by the species at the time it is listed, which: (1) are essential to the conservation of the species; and (2) may require special management considerations or protection.[106] The best available science is also to be used as a benchmark here, by the competent agencies.[107] It is true that the economic impact of designation is a factor to be appraised when specifying any particular area as a critical area, yet such areas can only be excluded if the benefits of such exclusion outweigh the designation, and if this does not result in the extinction of the species concerned.[108]

The most noteworthy example of the application of the designation rules in the face of the current climate crisis is offered by the aforementioned polar bear litigation. In the wake of the listing of the polar bear in 2008, the FWS decided to designate critical habitat for the species, which covered a five-mile buffer of coastal zone and land outside the known denning areas. In doing so, the FWS aimed to anticipate the loss of denning sites due to coastal erosion and sea-ice loss, two factors that can be attributed to

---

105 Inga Daukšienė and Arvidas Budnikas, "Has the Action for Failure to Act in the European Union Lost its Purpose?" (2014) 7(2) *Baltic Journal of Law & Politics* 209.

106 16 USC §1532(5)(A)(i).

107 16 USC §1533(b)(1),(2).

108 Cheever, supra, note 31, 57.

climate change.[109] The FWS' decision to designate no fewer than 187,000 square miles as critical habitat for the polar bear was subsequently challenged in court by the oil industry. After an initial success for the oil industry, the Ninth Circuit upheld the designation decision, based on two vital findings.[110] First, the court decided that future climate change was an effective consideration when designating critical habitats, even when this included sites that were not currently being used by polar bears. Subsequently, the court reiterated that the ESA does not merely aim to preserve endangered species, such as polar bears, but also envisages the protection of the futures of such species. Limiting designation policies to the existing habitats of species might, ultimately, run counter to the overarching objective of the ESA.[111] Second, the court did not question the climate data used by the FWS to underpin its designation decision, pointing out that the available science is unequivocal in relation to the incremental loss of sea ice in the Arctic.[112] Shortly thereafter, new legal challenges emerged in relation to designation policies for other species that were based upon climate-consideration. For instance, a district court in Montana reasserted the FWS' refusal to designate additional habitat for the lynx in presently unoccupied areas. The court noted that the available science did not shed further light on the exact location of lynx habitat in the near future.[113] A second attempt to review a revised habitat designation by the FWS also failed, with the competent court once more deferring to the discretion of the FWS.[114] Interestingly, in the context of court proceedings where the designation of currently *unoccupied* habitat for the sage grouse was at issue, a district court in Colorado stated that the designation of critical habitat for the sage grouse, even in areas that are currently unsuitable as habitat for the said species, was justifiable in light of, amongst other things, the available climate science.[115] This case thus seemed to reassert the rationale used by the Ninth Circuit in the polar bear case, regarding the designation of unoccupied habitats. However, a recent decision of the Supreme Court, in *Weyerhaeuser Co. v. FWS*, in which it was held that even unoccupied habitat still needs to qualify as habitat, might restrict future policies of designation in light of rising temperatures.[116]

The focus on *unoccupied* habitats is, of course, very crucial in the context of climate change, since species threatened by climate change will see their habitats shift to other sites, because of changes in temperature and precipitation, and sea level rises. The aforementioned 2019 amendments to the Habitat Regulations

109 75 Fed. Reg. 76086.
110 *Alaska Oil & Gas Association v. Jewell*, 815 F.3d 544 (9th Cir. 2016).
111 Ibid., 55.
112 Ibid., 59.
113 *All. for Wild Rockies v. Lyder*, 728 F. Supp. 2d 1126, 1140–43 (D. Mont. 2010).
114 *WildEarth Guardians v. U.S. Dep't. of the Interior*, 205 F. Supp. 3d 1176, 1186 (D. Mont. 2016).
115 *Colorado by and through Colorado Dep't of Nat. Res. v. FWS*, 362 F. Supp.
116 *Weyerhaeuser Co. v. FWS*, 139 S. Ct. 361, 368 (2018).

seem to further restrict the potential for a more climate-friendly interpretation of the provisions on critical habitat designation.[117] For one thing, the revised regulations now urge the agencies, when determining whether an unoccupied area is essential, to establish that the occupied habitat of the species at the time of listing is inadequate to ensure the conservation of the species. In addition, the area in question needs to, with a reasonable degree of certainty, contribute to the survival of the species, and contain one or more of those physical or biological features essential for the conservation of the species.[118] It needs little explanation to understand that this move might prove disastrous for future climate-based critical habitat designations, as has also been highlighted in recent literature on the topic.[119]

Once more in sharp contrast to the US, in the EU there exist no cases (at least to the present author's knowledge) that focus on the intersection between climate change and the designation duties, including on the EU Habitats and Birds Directives. Even so, it can be entertained that climate change is eligible as a relevant criterion to consider when designating protected sites, under both the Birds and Habitats Directives. As previously mentioned, the EU Birds Directive requires the Member States to rely exclusively upon ecological criteria when selecting the most suitable habitats for birds, leaving no room for other economic considerations in this regard.[120] In fact, the presence of birds listed in Annex I to the Birds Directive, or migratory bird species, is to be regarded as the leading criterion in this respect. In its case law, the CJEU has repeatedly highlighted the importance of ecological studies, such as the *Inventory of Important Bird Areas in Europe (IBA)*, as a baseline to check whether Member States have designated a sufficient number of protected sites.[121] In recent case law, the CJEU has, moreover, underscored that this obligation is dynamic by nature, which entails that Member States are required to re-evaluate their designation policies in view of new monitoring results and emerging scientific studies.[122] In so doing, the CJEU underlined that no single provision in the Directive seemed to indicate that existing sites must not continuously be amended in light of recent ecological information.[123] Against this backdrop, it is not impossible to contend that climate-based observations should also be integrated into the continuous re-evaluation of the designated Natura 2000 sites for birds. For instance, when recent studies reveal that certain bird species are relocating to new areas because

117 Regulations for Listing Species and Designating Critical Habitat, supra, note 99.

118 Ibid., at 45.043.

119 Wentz, supra, note 59, 56–58.

120 Case C-44/95 *Regina v. Secretary of State for the Environment, ex parte Royal Society for the Protection of Birds* (1996) ECLI:EU:C:1996:297.

121 See, for instance, Case C-3/96 *Commission v. The Netherlands* (1998) ECLI:EU:C:1998:238; Case C-418/04 *Commission v. Ireland* (2007) ECLI:EU:C:2007:780.

122 Case C-209/04 *Commission v. Austria* [2006] ECLI:EU:C:2006:195, para. 37.

123 Ibid., paras. 42–43.

of rising temperatures, it can be maintained that Member States need to consider including these recently emerged suitable habitats in the Natura 2000 network.

A similar conclusion arises when it comes to the designation duties included in the EU Habitats Directive. Moreover, Article 11 of the Directive requires the Member States to undertake surveillance of the conservation status of the species and habitats referred to in Article 2. The Member States must, therefore, keep *all* natural habitats and *all* wild fauna and flora in their European territory under surveillance. Since climate change is a crucial factor for the long-term conservation of many species, it bears little doubt that climate science must also trickle down into the existing designation policies.[124] It is true that Annex III to the Habitats Directive, where the criteria for the selection of Natura 2000 sites are enumerated, contains no explicit reference to the topic of climate change. However, given the clear importance of climate factors for the conservation status of many species, this omission cannot be used as an argument to keep climate change-related considerations out of designation policies. Furthermore, Annex III contains interesting hints as to the inclusion of currently unoccupied habitats, which might turn out to be crucial for the survival of some species in a warmer climate. Such sites could, amongst other things, function as new habitats, or assist species by acting as corridors to new habitats, to offset the loss of sites that have become uninhabitable due to climate change.[125] In addition, Annex III explicitly points out that the restoration possibilities of a site also need to be taken into consideration when selecting potential Natura 2000 sites for protected natural habitats and species. This restoration rationale also seems to be buttressed by recent case law developments. In a landmark 2017 ruling on the declassification of a Dutch Natura 2000 site, the CJEU highlighted that Member States are required to take into account the potential for restoration of threatened natural habitats and species when designating and selecting Natura 2000 sites.[126] Currently unoccupied areas that might function as potential migration corridors against the backdrop of rising temperatures also need to be factored into designation policies.

3.5. PREVENTING FUTURE LOCK-INS AND NEW CO_2 EMISSIONS?

The last, and potentially most daunting, legal question to be tackled when discussing the intersection between climate change and biodiversity legislation relates to the role of the latter in regulating greenhouse gas emissions. On the

124 Trouwborst, supra, note 20, 315.
125 An Cliquet et al., "Adaptation to climate change: Legal challenges for protected areas" (2009) 5(1) *Utrecht Law Review* 158, 166.
126 Case C-281/16 *Vereniging Hoekschewaards Landschap* (2017) ECLI:EU:C:2017:774, para. 37.

surface, the protection schemes in both sets of legislation appear very suitable for addressing direct and indirect threats to endangered species and their habitats. Yet, do the protection tools discussed above also extend to CO_2-emitting activities that contribute to climate change? Are they broad enough also to halt plans and projects, based upon their climate change impacts?

In the US, there exists no real consensus in the legal literature on whether activities emitting greenhouse gas emissions fall within the material scope of section 9 of the ESA, which prohibits activities giving rise to an "unlawful" take vis-à-vis endangered species.[127] Even though the above-mentioned case law opted for a relatively broad interpretation of the notion of "taking", many scholars remain sceptical about extending the take prohibition to CO_2 emissions.[128] Amongst other things, scholars like Ruhl have pointed to the multitude of evidentiary obstacles that might arise, since proving a direct causal link between a certain CO_2-emitting activity and concrete damage to the habitat of a certain species would be hard.[129] Indeed, establishing a concrete causal link between specific CO_2-emitting activities and specific damage – for instance, sea-ice loss in polar bear habitat – would be a complex issue. As Ruhl put forward in 2008, there appears to be a clear distinction between macro and micro analyses of a scenario in which the ESA protection clauses were used to regulate greenhouse gas emissions.[130]

For sure, one might submit that, at a macro level, the emissions of a power plant contribute to global warming, which will eventually further degrade the habitat of threatened species, such as polar bears and bearded seals.[131] Even so, at a micro level, it would be hard to attribute current damage to an individualised power plant. As Ruhl concludes, the evidentiary burden for a plaintiff in such a case might appear insurmountable or, alternatively, it might be necessary to entertain the idea that the "take prohibition" is applicable to all sources of greenhouse gases, even smaller farms.[132] Other authors take a more favourable stance, and argue that all greenhouse emissions contribute to climate change, which harms species, and suggest that, while many practical and political objections might arise, applying species protection schemes to individualised CO_2 emissions appears not totally out of the question.[133]

---

127 See, for an overview of the arguments for and against the ESA's application to greenhouse gases, Kuhn, supra, note 81, 148–150.

128 See, most prominently, Ruhl, "Climate Change and the Endangered Species Act", supra, note 58, 1.

129 Ibid., 41.

130 Ibid., 46.

131 Ibid.

132 Ibid., 41.

133 See, amongst others, Dave Owen, "Sea-Level Rise and the Endangered Species Act" (2012) 73 *Louisiana Law Review* 140–142.

Once more, the litigation surrounding the listing of the polar bear offers further insights into the intersection between climate change and biodiversity protection. It is somewhat ironic to note that, precisely by granting protected status to the polar bear because of the threats caused by climate change, the FWS immediately highlighted the limited scope of the ESA for mitigating climate change. At the time of the listing of the polar bear as a threatened species, the FWS issued a press release in which it stated that "the ESA was not the right tool to set U.S. climate policy or regulate GHG emissions".[134] Shortly after the press release, this stance was effectively inserted into a rule, the so-called "blanket 4(d) rule", which clarified that it is not appropriate to prohibit activities outside the species' current range, such as greenhouse gas-emitting activities which might contribute to loss of sea ice, one of the core elements of the polar bear's habitat.[135] Some observers criticised the rule, holding that it was a "gift to Big Oil".[136]

Several environmental NGOs argued that specific prohibitions were still needed to protect polar bears, and launched a legal challenge. A district court in Washington DC dismissed this line of argumentation.[137] To be more precise, the court referred to the global nature of the climate change threat, which entitles the agency to great deference.[138] The court agreed with the FWS that, based upon the best available science, it was impossible to identify an individual greenhouse gas emission as the cause of a specific adverse effect on the polar bear or its habitat. Hence, the FWS could reasonably hold that the ESA was not a useful or appropriate tool to alleviate the particular threat to the polar bear from climate change caused by global greenhouse gas emissions.[139] Against the backdrop of this jurisprudence, and taking into account the rescission of the "blanket 4(d) rule" in 2019,[140] it appears unlikely that the FWS will prohibit greenhouse gas emissions, based upon the ESA, any time soon.[141]

A similar conclusion seems to arise when it comes to section 7's consultation requirement, which requires federal agencies to guarantee that any action authorised, funded or carried out by a federal agency is not likely to "jeopardise" the continued existence of any endangered or threatened species, or result in the destruction or adverse modification of the critical habitat of such species. As of today, there exists no administrative practice or jurisprudence which seems to support the contention that section 7 cannot be used as a tool to curb greenhouse

---

134 See, for the exact reference, Landa, supra, note 15, 10505–10506.

135 Endangered and Threatened Wildlife and Plants; Special Rule for the Polar Bear Under Section 4(d) of the Endangered Species Act, 3 Fed. Reg. 76,249 (16 December 2008).

136 For more background, see Landa, supra, note 15, 10505.

137 *In re Polar Bear Endangered Species Act Listing & §4(d) Rule Litigation*, 818 F. Supp. 2d. 214.

138 Ibid., 218.

139 Ibid.

140 Endangered and Threatened Wildlife and Plants; Regulations for Prohibitions to Threatened Wildlife and Plants, Final Rule, 84 Fed. Reg. 44,753, 44,753 (27 August 2019).

141 Landa, supra, note 15, 10510.

gas-emitting activities.[142] Also, in this specific context, the competent agencies have issued a general administrative opinion, in which it is stated that no section 7 consultation is mandated if no causal connection exists among the proposed federal action, a reasonably certain climate change effect, and the listed species.[143] Another blow was sustained by the proponents of a more climate-friendly interpretation of section 7 in 2019, when the amended ESA regulations specified that the concept "effect of the action" merely included all consequences to listed species or critical habitats caused by the proposed action.[144] In addition, it was specified that a consequence is "caused by the proposed action if it would not occur but for the proposed actions and it is reasonably certain it would occur".[145]

Be that as it may, the latter findings do not entail that climate change falls completely outside the scope of section 7 of the ESA. It can, indeed, play an indirect role as a baseline when carrying out ecological evaluations, to check whether or not the proposed activity is likely to jeopardise any listed species or adversely modify its critical habitat. In this regard, a string of recent decisions have underlined the importance of taking climate change effects or projections into account when discussing the impact of newly planned activities. For instance, in 2017 a Ninth Circuit decision accepted the claim that the NMFS had acted arbitrarily by failing to consider climate data when holding that fishery expansion would not adversely affect a loggerhead population.[146] Other judicial decisions have also highlighted the importance of climate data when assessing the concrete impacts of new plans and projects through the lens of section 7.[147]

It might be no surprise to note that the potential for using Article 6 of the EU Habitats Directive has, to date, remained largely unexplored in the literature. Yet this does not imply that there does not exist great potential for climate litigation in this regard. Contrary to the situation in the US, there are no rules or guidance which explicitly rule out the use of the protection duties in the context of climate mitigation. Moreover, in a 2006 ruling, the CJEU already hinted at the potency of the non-regression clause included in Article 6(2) in addressing more general threats to biodiversity. In scrutinising the UK's transposition of the provision, the court concluded that, "[i]n implementing Article 6(2) of the Habitats Directive, it may be necessary to adopt both measures intended to avoid man-caused impairment and disturbance and measures to prevent natural developments that may cause the conservation status of species and habitats

142 Congressional Research Service, supra, note 62, 14.

143 Ibid., 16.

144 Endangered and Threatened Wildlife and Plants; Regulation for Interagency Cooperation, Final Rule, 84 Fed. Reg. 44,976–44,978.

145 Ibid.

146 *Turtle Island Restoration Network v. Dep't. of Commerce*, 878 F.3rd 725 (9th Cir. 2017).

147 See, for more details, Congressional Research Service, supra, note 62, 15–16.

in SACs to deteriorate".[148] Given the already broad interpretation given to the non-regression obligation that is put forward by Article 6(2) in the recent case law of the CJEU, which also includes addressing multisource air quality threats, such as nitrogen deposition,[149] it does not appear far-fetched to entertain the possibility that this provision could also be used as a lever for climate mitigation. As such, it cannot be denied that climate change is man-made, and is effectively leading to the degradation of EU-protected nature. For one thing, in its 2018 guidance document, the European Commission hinted at least at addressing the consequences of climate change on Natura 2000 sites when applying Article 6(2):

> For instance, in the case of natural succession or of climate effects, measures would need to be taken to halt or counter this process if it is deemed to be negatively impacting on the species and habitat types for which the site has been designated. Accordingly, naturally dynamic situations, as well as modifications linked to climate change (e.g. sea level rise, disappearing or newly arriving species) should be assessed case-by-case.[150]

In this regard, it should also be noted that, in its jurisprudence, the CJEU has highlighted that, when enforcing Article 6(2), no strict evidentiary hurdles apply. Possibly inspired by the precautionary principle, the CJEU held that:

> [I]n order to establish an infringement of Article 6(2) of Directive 92/43, it is not for the Commission to establish the existence of a cause-and-effect relationship between the action or inaction of the Member State concerned and a significant deterioration or disturbance caused to the habitats or species concerned. It is sufficient for the Commission to establish that there is a probability or risk that that action or inaction might cause significant deterioration or disturbance to those habitats or to those species.[151]

While this jurisprudence related to, amongst other things, groundwater abstraction activities, it might also open up perspectives for climate-based claims. Such claims might not only ask agencies to do more to adapt existing Natura 2000 sites to man-made climate change, for instance by creating new corridors (climate adaptation), but also focus on curbing additional emissions (mitigation), since such emissions would undoubtedly render the existing climate crisis even worse. The broad material scope of Article 6(2) certainly lends itself to such claims.

Along similar lines, it also appears not totally out of the question to use Article 6(3) of the EU Habitats Directive, which sets out substantive and

148 Case C-6/04 *Commission v. UK* (2005) ECLI:EU:C:2005:626, para. 34.

149 See, more extensively, Hendrik Schoukens, "Atmospheric Nitrogen Deposition and the Habitats Directive: Tinkering with the Law in the Face of the Precautionary Principle" (2015) *Nordic Environmental Law Journal* 25.

150 European Commission, *Managing* Natura 2000 *sites: The provisions of Article 6 of the "Habitats" Directive 92/43/EEC*, (EU (Luxembourg) 2018), 26.

151 *Commission v. Spain*, supra, note 45, para. 155.

procedural requirements to be followed when authorising plans or projects with possible effects on Natura 2000 sites, as a legal instrument to limit CO_2 emissions caused by plans or projects. In its case law, the CJEU has consistently underlined that the competent authorities can only authorise such plans and projects when no reasonable doubt exists as to the absence of potential negative effects on the integrity of such sites.[152] Also, the CJEU has repeatedly underscored the importance of using the best available science in this regard,[153] as well as the necessity of addressing cumulative effects.[154] And, in a recent case on agricultural practices close to Natura 2000 sites, the CJEU stated that the notion of a "project" is to be interpreted broadly, going beyond the concept as it is defined in the EU EIA Directive.[155] Accordingly, all activities which give rise to significant effects might qualify as projects that are to be submitted as "projects", in the sense of Article 6(3) of the EU Habitats Directive.[156] In this light, it also appears perfectly possible to contend that greenhouse gas emissions are also captured by the provision, especially since such a rationale was already explicitly accepted in the 2014 revised EIA Directive. As noted above, the wording of the amended Directive highlights the importance of also addressing climate change in the context of environmental impact assessments. *A fortiori*, such an obligation might also arise in the context of the even more strictly formulated substantive protection duties laid out by Article 6(3) of the EU Habitats Directive.

A first illustration of this potent link between the substantive protection duty enshrined in Article 6(3) and climate mitigation has been offered in the Dutch case law. In a 2021 decision, a Dutch local court decided to quash a permit for the operation of a biomass power plant, partly because the impact of the additional CO_2 emissions on the Dutch Natura 2000 sites had not been taken into account in the appropriate assessment. The Dutch court held that climate change, and especially the rising sea level, might effectively threaten the integrity of many Natura 2000 sites in the Netherlands, amongst others the Biesbosch swamp, which is located partly below sea level.[157] In reaching this conclusion, the Dutch court partially based its rationale on the 2019 *Urgenda* ruling of the Dutch Supreme Court. In the latter ruling, in which the Dutch government was ordered to raise its CO_2-reduction targets, the Dutch Supreme Court held that, while climate change is a global problem, the Dutch government needs to play its part in protecting its citizens from climate change, acting upon its joint international responsibility to prevent dangerous climate

152 Cases C-387/15 and C-388/15 *Orleans* (2016) ECLI:EU:C:2016:583.
153 *Waddenzee*, supra, note 25, para. 54.
154 *Commission v. Ireland*, supra, note 121, paras. 240–245.
155 *Coöperatie Mobilisation for the Environment UA*, supra, note 65, paras. 66–71.
156 Ibid.
157 Court of Oost-Brabant (8 December 2021), ECLI:NL:RBOBR:2021:6389.

change.[158] Most importantly, the Dutch judges also addressed the so-called "drop-in-the-ocean argument", which was raised by the Dutch government in defence. The court underlined that the fact that current Dutch greenhouse gas emissions are limited on a global scale does not alter the fact that these emissions cumulatively contribute to climate change.[159] They affect the remaining carbon budget, the judges reasoned. Likewise, the Dutch Supreme Court also held that that there is a broad consensus in the international community, and in climate science, that if mitigating measures are delayed, a large risk of so-called "tipping points" (drastic changes in climate) might arise.[160] This approach was ultimately replicated by the Court of Oost-Brabant in the context of a Natura 2000-related case. Combining both Article 6(2) and 6(3) of the EU Habitats Directive with the *Urgenda* rationale might, indeed, give rise to a very powerful lever for the integration of climate mitigation into the context of planning and project permits, especially in the context of Natura 2000 sites.

Of course, this does not alter the fact that the same objections as were raised in the US will probably also feature in future EU climate cases that try to further utilise Article 6(2) and 6(3) as a means to reduce greenhouse gas emissions. Ultimately, one might expect that some national courts, when faced with such arguments, might refer the matter, via a preliminary reference, to the CJEU, and raise questions regarding the application of the need to assess cumulative effects in the context of greenhouse gas emissions. In particular, it remains unclear what baseline is to be used in this regard. Should future greenhouse gas emissions be added to all existing greenhouse gas emissions, both in the EU and beyond? Can greenhouse gas emissions themselves qualify as "projects" within the meaning of Article 6(3) of the EU Habitats Directive? In any such future decision, the CJEU might also clarify to what extent the application of Article 6(2) and 6(3) might interfere with CO_2 emissions that are covered by the EU emission trading scheme.[161] However, in the meantime, it has become abundantly clear that, as has been observed in the US, in the particular context of section 7 of the ESA, climate change data and projections are to play a crucial role when carrying out appropriate assessments for plans and projects under Article 6(3) of the EU Habitats Directive. Climate change projections are also relevant in relation to plans and projects that do not directly give rise to additional CO_2 emissions.[162] Likewise, it is necessary to integrate climate data into the establishment of the conservation objectives for Natura 2000 sites, as these are a crucial benchmark for assessing the compatibility of new plans and projects with the conservation objectives of Natura 2000 sites.[163]

---

158 *Urgenda*, supra note 6, para. 6.2.
159 Ibid., para. 7.6.
160 Ibid., para. 4.7.
161 See supra, note 69.
162 See also, in this direction, Trouwborst, supra, note 20, 315.
163 Ibid.

4. CONCLUSION

Climate change will be a determinative factor for nature conservation in the twenty-first century. This contribution has pointed out that it will also be such a factor for EU nature conservation law. The fact that the EU Habitats Directive stands out as a remarkably powerful instrument for protecting biodiversity against direct threats, such as habitat destruction and unsustainable hunting, raises hopes that it will also be instrumental in achieving the overarching greenhouse gas emission targets. The protection of natural habitats and species, by virtue of instruments such as the EU Habitats Directive, already indirectly contributes to the achievement of the global target of limiting warming to 2 degrees Celsius, since it serves as a protection of existing carbon sinks. Likewise, the restoration duties enshrined in Article 6(1) and 6(2) of the EU Habitats Directive might allow these habitats to sequester more carbon in the decades to come.[164]

However, the more pressing question that lay at the heart of this contribution was how climate change could trickle down into the application of the strict substantive conservation duties enshrined in the EU Habitats Directive. This contribution has used the recent climate change-based case law developments in the US, in relation to the ESA, as a benchmark to analyse to what extent a similar repurposing of the EU Habitats Directive is also possible, in light of climate change. While the institutional and regulatory contexts of both instruments are, of course, different, this contribution has demonstrated that both instruments contain, at least to some extent, remarkably similar protection schemes, underpinning the relevance of this comparative analysis.

A first conclusion appears to be that strategic litigation in the US has managed to force the competent agencies to start using climate science and data when implementing the conservation duties included in the ESA. When it comes to listing decisions, the designation of critical habitats and the application of the protection schemes, such as section 7, climate change data constitute a useful lever for climate adaptation. Even when the competent agencies and the courts have obstinately refused to use the ESA as a tool to regulate CO_2 emissions, and to curb additional greenhouse gas emissions, the major leap forward that has been taken in this respect by listing hundreds of species as threatened, on the basis of climate change, should not be understated. A 2020 court ruling, in which the Court of Appeals for the Ninth Circuit quashed the permit for a controversial offshore oil-drilling project, proves that the listing of species and subsequent habitat designation can also indirectly limit the leeway for authorising new carbon-based projects. In this decision, the court held that the Trump administration had failed to properly consider the climate impacts

164 See, in relation to the ESA, Landa, supra, note 15.

of the project, in line with the National Environmental Policy Act.[165] It also determined that the FWS had failed to sufficiently analyse the impact on polar bears, in violation of the ESA. The fact that the area itself was designated as a critical habitat for the polar bear played a seminal role in this regard.

At the time of writing, a similar picture has not emerged in the EU. To some extent, the different listing and designation procedures, which appear to leave less explicit room for environmental NGOs in the EU, can be blamed. However, certainly at the national level, environmental NGOs now enjoy relatively broad standing in environmental cases, which might open new pathways for strategic climate litigation based upon the robust conservation duties enshrined in EU nature conservation law. Until now, however, relatively limited attention has been paid, in the legal literature and in case law, to the intersection between the EU Habitats Directive and climate change. The EU Habitats Directive seldom features in strategic climate lawsuits in the EU. That said, this contribution has revealed the ample potency of EU nature protection law for both climate adaptation actions, and, in contrast to the ESA, mitigation actions. Whereas adapting the Annexes listing protected species to the EU Habitats Directive seems to represent an obstacle-ridden pathway, it is clear that addressing climate change, both when it comes to mitigation and adaptation, will be crucial for EU Member States if they want to observe their existing conservation duties. Strategic litigation could force EU Member States to fully integrate climate change data into their designation policies, which might lead to the creation of new protected zones, crucial for the adaptation of protected species to a European continent where temperatures have risen significantly. Climate adaptation will also be a key challenge when implementing the management and protection duties included in Articles 6(1) and 6(2) of the EU Habitats Directive for existing Natura 2000 sites, while climate projections will prove to be a crucial benchmark when evaluating the significant impact of future plans and projects, even when these would not be directly emitting CO_2. Remarkably, this fertile ground for climate litigation has not yet been exploited in the EU.

Perhaps the fact that the EU has implemented several directives and regulations which explicitly regulate CO_2 emissions explains the big gap, in terms of climate litigation, between the EU and the US. That said, additional greenhouse gas reductions will be crucial, including in the EU, in order to meet the overarching climate ambitions. In light of the multitude of unsustainable carbon lock-ins, additional mitigation instruments are certainly not superfluous in times of climate crisis. The question whether the EU Habitats Directive can also be used as a binding instrument to curb greenhouse gas emissions remains moot for now. The 2021 Dutch biomass power plant decision seems to indicate that is not at all far-fetched to use the EU Habitats Directive as a tool to regulate

165 *Center for Biological Diversity et al. v. David Bernhardt* (7 December 2020), Ninth Circuit.

CO_2 emissions. Whether such an approach makes sense, when there are many other instruments that address this topic, at EU and national level, is a question that will, undoubtedly, give rise to future case law developments in Europe in the coming decades. The fact that the 2016 evaluation of the EU Birds and Habitats Directives held that they remained "highly relevant" and "fit for purpose",[166] further underscores the premise that climate change, as the dominant existential challenge for mankind and nature in the twenty-first century, falls squarely within the scope of the EU Habitats Directive. The collapse of a glacier in the Italian Dolomites, at the beginning of July 2022, once more highlights the concrete impacts of climate change on Europe's most vulnerable ecosystems. It is only a matter of time before climate activists start using the EU Habitats Directive to litigate against possible new unsustainable carbon-based developments. The story is to be continued.

166 European Commission, Commission Staff Working Document Fitness Check of the EU Nature Legislation (Birds and Habitats Directives) Directive 2009/147/EC of the European Parliament and of the Council of 30 November 2009 on the conservation of wild birds and Council Directive 92/43/EEC of 21 May 1992 on the conservation of natural habitats and of wild fauna and flora (SWD(2016)472 final).

PART IX

GREEN INFRASTRUCTURE

UNCERTAINTY IN GREEN INFRASTRUCTURE DECISION-MAKING

Types, Consequences and Available Legal Tools

Yelena M. Gordeeva*

1. INTRODUCTION

"Uncertainty", and the "uncertain science" behind GI (green infrastructure), are among the obstacles to the elaboration of a robust framework on GI and its subsequent wider implementation.[1] According to Gregory et al., "uncertainty" refers to the situations and/or outcomes for which we lack information that we would like to have.[2] Conroy and Peterson defines uncertainty as "anything that falls short of absolute certainty".[3] Thus, there is uncertainty even if an event has a 99.9 per cent probability of occurring. "Uncertainty" is not only about what

* The research on legal tools to manage uncertainty in a GI infrastructure context was carried out under supervision by Professor Charles-Hubert Born (UCLouvain, Belgium), when Dr Yelena M. Gordeeva was working as a post-doctoral research fellow on an environmental law research project, part of an interdisciplinary research project on landscape connectivity for forest species (WOODNET) co-funded by the European Commission (BiodivERsA), (https://www.biodiversa.org/1026).

1 *Y.M. Gordeeva*, "Uncertainty and Multifunctionality: Legal Challenges and Opportunities for 'Green Infrastructure'", *Theoretical and Applied Ecology*, 2020, (3), pp. 217–233; *Woodnet*, "Webinar – Uncertainty and Multifunctionality: Legal Challenges and Opportunities for Green Infrastructure (GI) Policy", 28 April 2020, https://www.forestplatform.org/event/woodnet-seminar-uncertainty-and-multifunctionality-legal-challenges-and-opportunities-for-green-infrastructure-gi-policy/.

2 Adapted from *R. Gregory et al.*, *Structural Decision Making – A Practical Guide to Environmental Management Choices*, Wiley-Blackwell, 2012, pp. 123, 126. According to Gregory et al., "uncertainty" is widely used to refer to all the ambiguities and knowledge gaps that prevent a good understanding of the consequences of proposed actions. Unlike risk, which is generally understood to be a negative thing, uncertainty does not imply a negative consequences *per se*; we could be just as uncertain about beneficial aspects as about adverse or feared aspects.

3 For Conroy and Peterson, "uncertainty" is anything that falls short of absolute certainty; there is uncertainty even if an event has a 99.9% probability of occurring. See *M.J. Conroy and J.T. Peterson*, *Decision Making in Natural Resource Management: A Structured, Adaptive Approach*, Wiley-Blackwell, 2013, p. 192.

we do not know, but also about what we do not know *well*, and what can evolve without us knowing how or when.[4]

Assuming that GI design and implementation will always need to be based on less-than-complete knowledge and uncertain science, reducing our ability to make accurate predictions regarding the responses of species and ecological processes and/or other changes across GI areas, including climate change, as well as our ability to perform all steps from design to implementation of GI (for example, how should a protection be enforced if habitats are not mapped, or if a term in legislation is difficult to interpret?),[5] this contribution intends to provide the beginnings of an answer to the very complex question of how to manage uncertainty in GI design and implementation.

Firstly, this Introduction to the contribution sets out the policy context, defines the problem, and states the research question (section 1). Secondly, the "Understanding the 'Green Infrastructure' concept" section explores the concept of "GI", suggesting that there is already uncertainty associated with the understanding of the concept (section 2). Thirdly, section 3, on "Uncertainty in GI Decision-making Process: Typology and Consequences", investigates how uncertainty may manifest itself in the process of GI design and implementation (section 3.1.), and what the consequences are of uncertainty in GI decision-making processes? (section 3.2.). Finally, the conclusion (section 4) highlights that future research is needed to explore possible legal tools which may be used to respond to each type of uncertainty identified in this contribution.

2. UNDERSTANDING THE "GREEN INFRASTRUCTURE" CONCEPT

Although the idea of "utilising the beneficial influences of nature", *inter alia* through linking natural areas and parks, is not a new idea, and the roots of GI planning can be traced back to the early twentieth century (for example,

4 The meaning of uncertainty is more complex than might be apparent. Science and technology studies have shown that uncertainty can stem from more than a simple lack of data or inadequate models of risk assessment. Uncertainty might also exist in the form of indeterminacy (where we do not know all the factors influencing the causal chains), ambiguity (where there are contradictory certainties), and ignorance (where we do not know what we do not know): *European Commission, Science for Environmental Policy, Future Brief: The precautionary principle: decision-making under uncertainty*, EU Publications Office, 2017, p. 5.

5 *European Commission, Science for Environmental Policy, Multifunctionality of Green Infrastructure*, EU Publications Office, March 2012, p. 9; *L. Boitani et al.*, "Ecological Networks as Conceptual Frameworks or Operational Tools in Conservation", *Conservation Biology*, 2007, 21(6), pp. 1414–1422; *R. Vimal*, "The Changing Landscape of Ecological Networks", *Journal for Nature Conservation*, 2011, 20(1), pp. 49–55.

projects such as the Boston Fenways, by F.L. Olmsted in the US),[6] the term "GI" is relatively new and flexible, with no single definition.

Most commonly, the term has been used among natural resource professionals.[7] Thus, Benedict and McMahon define GI as "an interconnected network of green spaces that conserves natural ecosystem values and functions and provides associated benefits to human populations".[8] Pauleit et al. define the GI concept through a set of main principles for GI planning: (1) the principle of multifunctionality (i.e. a multifunctional GI seeks to combine different ecological, social and economic functions); (2) the principle of connectivity (highlighting the importance of connectivity between green spaces to enhancing species' dispersal and complementarity). Connectivity can be of a "structural" nature (i.e. habitat continuity) or a functional nature (i.e. how landscapes allow various species to move and expand to new areas, without necessarily being physically connected); (3) the principle of integration (integration of GI with other (infra)structures); (4) the principle of socially inclusive planning and management (GI includes various types of green spaces – public, institutional and private – and, as it interacts with other (for example, urban) structures, many stakeholders or actors are involved); and, finally, (5) the principle of a long-term strategy (GI is aimed towards achieving overall long-term goals, while at the same time allowing new inputs through ongoing learning and discussion between different actors).[9] Furthermore, GI is considered to consist of "multifunctional networks of green spaces",[10] which are

---

6 As long ago as 1903, a landscape architect, Frederick Law Olmsted, stated that "no single park, no matter how large and how well designed, would provide the citizens with the beneficial influences of nature". Instead, parks needed "to be linked to one another and to surrounding residential neighbourhoods". For further information, please see *M. Benedict and E.T. McMahon*, "Green Infrastructure: Smart Conservation for the 21st Century", *Renewable Resources Journal*, Autumn 2002, p. 13; *T.S. Eisenman*, "Frederick Law Olmsted, Green Infrastructure and the Evolving City", *Journal of Planning History*, 2013, 12(4), p. 295.

7 *M. Benedict and E.T. McMahon*, "Green Infrastructure: Smart Conservation", above n. 6, p. 13.

8 Ibid., p. 12. GI as a counterpart to grey infrastructure has been championed by many, though it could be said that few have done more to promote and define the scope of the concept than M. Benedict and E.T. McMahon of the US-based Conservation Fund. Since the early 2000s, this pair have paved the way for the universal understanding of the concept, culminating in their publication "Linking Landscapes and Communities". See *M. Benedict and E.T. McMahon, Green Infrastructure, Linking Landscapes and Communities*, Island Press, 2006.

9 Adopted from *S. Pauleit et al.*, "Multifunctional Green Infrastructure Planning to Promote Ecological Services in the City", in J. Niemela, *Urban Ecology, Patterns, Processes, and Applications*, Oxford University Press, 2011, pp. 273–275.

10 E.g. high biodiversity "hubs", such as protected areas (e.g. Natura 2000 sites), or areas outside protected areas, containing large healthy functioning ecosystems; natural or artificial features that enhance ecosystem services or assist wildlife movements (e.g. hedgerows, fish ladders, green roofs); buffer zones that are managed sustainably, and which help improve the general ecological quality and permeability of the landscape to biodiversity (e.g. multifunctional farming), etc.

"needed for environmental, social and economic sustainability".[11] More and more frequently, GI is appearing in policy documents all over the world, and some countries have taken steps towards systematic GI policies and legislation.[12]

In the EU, the Natura 2000 network, with its exclusive nature-conservation goals, may be considered as the first form of EU GI. Ever since its establishment, in 1992, the network has been the very core of EU GI.[13] Stretching over 18 per cent of the EU's land area, and almost 6 per cent of its marine territory, Natura 2000 is the largest coordinated network of protected areas in the world.[14] The aim of the Natura 2000 network is to ensure the long-term survival of Europe's most valuable and threatened species and habitats;[15] or, to use the wording of the Habitats Directive, the 2000 network "shall enable the natural habitat types and the species' habitats concerned to be maintained or, where appropriate, restored at a favourable conservation status in their natural range".[16] The EU Member States (MS) select Natura 2000 sites according to scientific criteria, under a specific selection procedure, depending on which of the two nature directives – the Birds Directive[17] or the Habitats Directive – warrants the creation of a particular site. Under the Habitats Directive, MS designate Special Areas of Conservation (SACs), to ensure the favourable conservation status of each habitat type and species throughout their ranges in the EU.[18] Under the Birds

---

11 *S. Pauleit et al.*, "Urban Landscapes and GI", in *Oxford Research Encyclopaedia of Environmental Science*, Oxford University Press, 2017, https://oxfordre.com/environmentalscience/view/10.1093/acrefore/9780199389414.001.0001/acrefore-9780199389414-e-23; *M. Benedict and E.T. McMahon*, "Green Infrastructure: Smart Conservation", above n. 6, p. 12.

12 *S. Borgstrom and F. Kistenkas*, "The Compatibility of the Habitats Directive with the Novel EU Green Infrastructure Policy", *European Energy and Environmental Law Review*, 2014, 23(2), p. 37.

13 *European Commission*, "Building a Green Infrastructure for Europe", 2013.

14 *European Commission*, "Environment – Natura 2000", https://ec.europa.eu/environment/nature/natura2000/index_en.htm.

15 *European Commission*, "Environment, Managing and Protecting Natura 2000 Sites", https://ec.europa.eu/environment/nature/natura2000/sites/index_en.htm.

16 Council Directive 92/43/EEC on the conservation of natural habitats and of wild fauna and flora, OJ 1992, L 206/7, Art. 3.

17 Directive 2009/147/EC of the European Parliament and of the Council on the Conservation of Wild Birds, OJ 2010, L 20/7.

18 The Habitats Directive provides for a procedural framework as to the selection and designation of the SACs. Under the three-tiered procedure set out by the Habitats Directive: (1) MS are required to draw up a proposal for a list of Sites of Community Interest (SCI) within their borders harbouring either Annex I habitat types or species listed in Annex II; (2) these lists must, in a second stage, be submitted to the European Commission, which scrutinises the list for each of the biogeographical regions in light of the criteria mentioned in Annex III, with the aid of experts from the MS (Art. 4.2. Habitats Directive); (3) in agreement with the MS, the European Commission thereafter adopts a final list of SCIs that reflect the most important areas for the listed habitats and species in the MS; (4) the Habitats Directive then grants the MS a period of six years in which to designate these sites, and to establish priorities for the most important species and habitats, in order to take action once the sites are designated (Art. 4.4, Habitats Directive). However, in the meantime, MS are required to

Directive, the network must include Special Protection Areas (SPAs), designated for 194 particularly threatened species, and all migratory bird species.[19]

Depending on their national circumstances and priorities, the EU MS have also taken steps towards conceptualising "GI", but with no single commonly accepted scope or definition. Similarly to Natura 2000, most GI in the EU MS was initially designed and implemented for pure nature conservation purposes (for example, *Trame verte et bleue*, with its core objective of stopping the decline of biodiversity (France); the Walloon Nature Network, which aims at strengthening nature conservation efforts in the Walloon region (Belgium); the Green Belt of Vitoria-Gasteiz, focusing on nature areas' restoration and recovery (Spain), etc.).[20] Today, the GI design and implementation practices in the EU MS have shown a greater diversity of concepts and objectives pursued, including biodiversity conservation and other ecosystem services provision[21] (for example, the Flemish

ensure that the SCIs are protected pursuant to Arts. 6.2, 6.3 and 6.4 of the Habitats Directive (Art. 4.5, Habitats Directive).

19 The Birds Directive provides that "MS shall classify in particular the most suitable territories in number and size as special protection areas for the conservation of [Annex I] species in the geographical sea and land area where this Directive applies" (Art. 4.1, Birds Directive). Site-specific data must then be transmitted to the European Commission. Based on the information provided by the MS, the European Commission determines whether the designated sites are sufficient to form a coherent network for the protection of these vulnerable and migratory species (Art. 4.3, Birds Directive). These sites then become an integral part of the Natura 2000 network.

20 *European Commission, DG Environment and European Environmental Agency (EEA), Biodiversity Information System for Europe (BISE)*, "Countries, GI Developments", https://biodiversity.europa.eu/countries.

21 Please note that the term "ecosystem services" can be defined differently by different observers, and in different contexts. A number of scientific scholars (e.g. Potschin and Haines-Young) have noted the problems of defining exactly what an ecosystem service is. For instance, the definition provided by the Millennium Ecosystem Assessment describes ecosystem services simply as "benefits that ecosystems provide to people". The guide on *The Economics of Ecosystem and Biodiversity (TEEB)* views ecosystem services as "direct and indirect contributions of ecosystems to human well-being". The European Commission adopts the definition of "ecosystem services" as "benefits that people obtain from ecosystems, or their direct and indirect contributions to human well-being. These include provisioning services such as food and water; regulating services such as flood and disease control; cultural services such as spiritual, recreational and cultural benefits. Since people do not directly use supporting services such as of nutrient cycling, they do not obtain benefits from them and they may not strictly be part of ecosystem services." According to Potschin and Haines-Young, "the multi-faced characteristic of the term becomes a disadvantage once we come to measure and monitor these things, called 'services': if we cannot agree what they are then people will not believe what is said about them or act on the evidence we collect. These problems of definition are amplified once we start to make a case for valuing or managing ecosystem services – that is to apply the concept in a normative way". See *M. Potschin and R. Haines-Young*, "Defining and Measuring Ecosystem Services", in *M. Potschin et al.* (eds.), *Routledge Handbook of Ecosystem Services*, Routledge, 2016, pp. 25–26; *W.V. Reid et al.*, *The Millennium Ecosystem Assessment, Ecosystems and Human Well-being*, Synthesis, 2005, p. V; *P. Kumar et al.* (eds.), *The Economics of Ecosystem and Biodiversity (TEEB): Ecological and Economic Foundations*, Routledge, 2010, p. 19; *European Commission, Commission Staff*

Ecological Network, which currently seeks, *inter alia*, to increase the amount, quality and linkages of nature into the built environment (Belgium); Urban Nature Labs, which aim to enhance, *inter alia*, the water resilience of cities (France); and the Grow Green project, which aims, *inter alia*, to deliver improvements in the social, environmental and economic performance of several cities (Spain)).[22]

EU policy first mentioned the term "GI" in 2009, as "the interconnected network of natural areas including some agricultural land, such as greenways, wetlands, parks, forest preserves and native plant communities, and marine areas that naturally regulate storm flows, temperatures, flooding risk, and water, air and ecosystem quality".[23] This shifted the focus of the EU GI from pure nature conservation (for example, Natura 2000), towards a core focus on "ecosystem services" (for example, regulation of flows, regulation of temperatures, prevention of flood risks, etc.). However, at the EU level, no single definition of "ecosystem service" has followed, leaving it uncertain what the consequences of the shift in the focus of the EU GI concept may be for GI design and implementation.

In 2013, the European Commission adopted a GI Strategy with a new "working definition" of the GI concept:

> GI is a strategically planned network of natural and semi-natural areas with other environmental features designed and managed to deliver a wide range of ecosystem services. It incorporates green spaces (or blue if aquatic ecosystems are concerned) and other physical features in terrestrial (including coastal) and marine areas. On land, GI is present in rural and urban settings.[24]

The GI Strategy stressed the need "to ensure that GI becomes a standard part of spatial planning and territorial development and that it is fully integrated into the implementation of the policies whose objectives can be achieved as a whole or in part through nature-based solutions".[25] Accordingly, a broad range of EU sectoral policies have identified the conservation and development of GI as one of their priorities and/or main means for implementation: for example, the EU Biodiversity Strategy to 2020,[26] the Roadmap to a Resource

Working Document, "Technical Information on Green Infrastructure (GI)", SWD (2013), 155 final, p. 12.

22 *European Commission*, "Countries, GI Developments", above n. 20.

23 *European Commission*, "White Paper: Adapting to Climate Change: Towards a European Framework for action", COM (2009), 147 final, p. 5.

24 *European Commission*, "Communication from the Commission to the European Parliament, the Council, the European Economic and Social Committee and the Committee of the Regions", SWD (2013), 155 final, COM (2013), 249 final, p. 3.

25 Ibid., p. 8. See also *European Commission*, "Communication: Review of progress on implementation of the EU GI Strategy", COM (2019), 236 final, p. 2.

26 *European Commission*, "Communication from the Commission to the European Parliament, the Council, the Economic and Social Committee and the Committee of the Regions, Our

Efficient Europe,[27] the Common Agricultural Policy,[28] the EU Strategy on Adaptation to Climate Change,[29] the Blueprint to Safeguard Europe's Water Resources,[30] the EU Forest Strategy[31] (especially relevant, since many GI green spaces are forest-based),[32] etc.[33] Natura 2000 is at the core of EU GI,[34] and the Birds and Habitats Directives are, naturally, important legal instruments contributing towards the protection of biodiversity and ecosystem services. Other instruments relevant for supporting GI within the EU include, *inter alia*, the Water Framework Directive,[35] the Marine Strategy Framework Directive,[36] and legislation on groundwater protection and flood-risk management. At the procedural level, the Environmental Impact Assessment (EIA) Directive,[37] and

---

Life Insurance, our Natural Capital: an EU Biodiversity Strategy to 2020", COM (2011), 244 final, Target 2, p. 5.

27 *European Commission*, "Communication from the Commission to the European Parliament, the Council, the European Economic and Social Committee and the Committee of the Regions, Roadmap to a Resource Efficient Europe", COM (2011), 571 final, pp. 6, 8–9.

28 *European Commission*, "The CAP towards 2020: Meeting the Food, natural resources and territorial challenges of the future", COM (2010), 672, 18.11.2010, p. 11.

29 *European Commission*, "Communication from the Commission to the European Parliament, the Council, the European Economic and Social Committee and the Committee of the Regions, An EU Strategy on Adaptation to Climate Change", COM (2013), 216 final, pp. 5, 13.

30 *European Commission*, "Communication from the Commission to the European Parliament, the Council, the European Economic and Social Committee and the Committee of the Regions: A Blueprint to Safeguard Europe's Water", COM (2012), 673 final, p. 12.

31 *European Commission*, A New EU Forest Strategy: for forests and the forest-based sector, COM (2013), 659 final, 20.09.2013, p. 9.

32 Forests play a particularly important role in the Natura 2000 network: they hold a significant proportion of Europe's threatened biodiversity, and cover around half of the total area of the network. In fact, in the 2013 Forest Strategy, "forest protection and enhancement of ecosystem services" is referred as one of its priorities, stating that MS "should achieve a significant and measurable improvement in the conservation status of forest species and habitats by fully implementing EU nature legislation and ensuring that national forest plans contribute to the adequate management of the Natura 2000 network by 2020". See ibid., p. 9; *European Commission, Natura 2000 and forests: Part I–II*, 2015, p. 19.

33 The EU GI Strategy provides that "regional or cohesion, climate change and environmental policies, disaster risk management, health and consumer policies and the Common Agricultural Policy, including their associated funding mechanisms, are the main policy areas through which GI is promoted". See *European Commission*, "Communication from the Commission to the European Parliament, the Council, the European Economic and Social Committee and the Committee of the Regions", above n. 24, p. 10.

34 *European Commission*, "Building a Green Infrastructure for Europe", above n. 13.

35 Directive of the European Parliament and of the Council 60/2000/EC establishing a framework for Community action in the field of water policy, OJ 2000 L 327.

36 Directive of the European Parliament and of the Council of 17 June 2008 establishing a framework for Community action in the field of marine environmental policy, OJ 2008 L 164/19.

37 Directive 2011/92/EU of the European Parliament and of the Council of 13 December 2011 on the Assessment of the Effects of Certain Public and Private Projects on Environment, OJ 2012 L 26/1.

the Strategic Environmental Assessment (SEA) Directive,[38] provide a basis for the integration of GI into the sectoral decision-making systems. Thus, today the EU GI has developed into a complex integrated "policy regime".[39]

Having considered the evolution of the GI concept, it may be suggested that the EU GI concept is associated with uncertainty and complexity. The concept continues to be defined differently by different stakeholders in different contexts (for example, the EU operates with a "working" definition of the GI concept, and the EU MS have developed their own national concepts of GI, with different backgrounds and different objectives pursued). Furthermore, whereas the initial focus of the EU GI concept was on nature conservation (for example, Natura 2000), and GI has had an important role in conserving biodiversity,[40] today the multifunctionality of GI is being highlighted more and more (for example, biodiversity conservation; climate change adaptation and mitigation; disaster risk management; water regulation; flood prevention; food provision; economic growth; recreation; health and well-being; and increased land and property values, among others).[41] The concept of "ecosystem services" has been introduced into the definition at the EU level. Yet, no clear definition of what an "ecosystem service" is has followed. This adds another layer of uncertainty and complexity associated with the EU GI concept, for example what might the consequences be of the focus on the multiple ecosystem services (versus pure nature conservation) in the context of GI design and implementation? Might it be that biodiversity conservation will no longer be the focus in the GI context? Might it lead to a situation where designing and implementing GI to meet its multifunctionality will involve value choices, and where the win-win situation for all of the multiple ecosystem services (with biodiversity conservation being one among many other ecosystem services) may no longer be possible? Might the complex and competing interrelations between nature conservation and other ecosystem services provision, in GI design and implementation, have a negative impact on the conservation of biodiversity? Currently, answering these complex questions involves uncertainty.

---

38 Directive 2001/42/EC of the European Parliament and of the Council of 27 June 2001 on the assessment of the effects of certain plans and programmes on the environment, OJ 2001 L 197.

39 *S. Borgstrom and F. Kistenkas*, above n. 12, p. 38.

40 In particular, GI has been considered the main instrument for the implementation of Target 2 of the EU 2020 Biodiversity Strategy, which aims, by 2020, to maintain and enhance ecosystems and their services by establishing GI and restoring at least 15% of degraded ecosystems.

41 *European Commission*, "Communication from the Commission to the European Parliament, the Council, the European Economic and Social Committee and the Committee of the Regions", above n. 24.

3. UNCERTAINTY IN GI DECISION-MAKING PROCESSES: TYPOLOGY AND CONSEQUENCES

There have been numerous attempts on the part of scientists from various fields (for example, ecologists, statisticians, economists, etc.) to develop a broadly accepted typology on uncertainty.[42] Yet, no single classification scheme perfect for all management situations has emerged, and typologies of uncertainties may differ, depending on the scientific domain. This contribution builds on the typology of uncertainties for structuring environmental management decision-making proposed by Gregory et al.[43] (Table 1). The typology distinguishes two major types of "uncertainties", namely: (1) the "epistemic uncertainties"[44] (i.e. those resulting from the lack of knowledge); and (2) the "linguistic uncertainties" (those resulting from communication failures). The present section of the contribution extends the typology on uncertainty, to include additional types of uncertainties which may be encountered in the context of GI decision-making.

3.1. TYPOLOGY ON UNCERTAINTIES IN GI DECISION-MAKING PROCESSES

The "epistemic uncertainties" (i.e. "knowledge-based" or "scientific" uncertainties) are particularly significant in the context of GI decision-making. GI is "set in a scientific framework and firmly based on knowledge, [but] currently it has [had] little hard quantitative evaluation and monitoring".[45] The "epistemic uncertainties" reflect the incomplete knowledge, and the limits of using scientific data to understand ecological processes and other parameters relevant for GI and its management. "Epistemic uncertainties" may arise as a "measurement error", "uncertainties due to the subjective nature of judgements", "aleatory uncertainties" or a "parametric uncertainty". Furthermore, various "epistemic uncertainties" may interact and form new groups of uncertainties (for example, "structural uncertainty",[46] and, moreover, "structural uncertainty interacting with management actions").

---

42 See, for instance, *M.J. Conroy and J.T. Peterson*, above n. 3; *R. Gregory et al.*, above n. 2; *B.K. Williams et al., Adaptive Management: The U.S. Department of the Interior Applications Guide*, US Department of the Interior, 2012, Uncertainty and learning, p. VI.

43 *R. Gregory et al.*, above n. 2, p. 123.

44 Episteme is a philosophical term, derived from an ancient Greek word, which can refer to knowledge, science or understanding.

45 *European Commission, Science for Environmental Policy*, above n. 5, p. 30.

46 Also referred to as "model uncertainty" and/or "system uncertainty". See *M.J. Conroy and J.T. Peterson*, above n. 3, p. 195.

"Linguistic uncertainty" is uncertainty due to imprecision of language. In a GI context, it may arise from the challenges in agreeing on common terms, concepts and/or definitions among the multiple "interdisciplinary" stakeholders involved in decision-making (for example, policymakers, scientists (of various disciplines), and other interested stakeholders; private, institutional and public actors, etc.). Quite often, the same term and/or concept can mean different things to different stakeholders (for example, as is the case for the "GI" concept itself, which is defined differently by different stakeholders).[47] "Linguistic uncertainty" is particularly problematic when identifying stakeholders' objectives. Words can have multiple meanings; hence, a single stakeholder objective can mean something different to each of the stakeholders involved in a GI decision-making process. On a very broad scale, "linguistic uncertainties" may arise due to "context dependency", "underspecificity" and "indeterminacy".

Finally, uncertainties may be "reducible", for example "partial observability" (uncertainty due to the inability to accurately assess the state of the resource system that is being managed), or "irreducible", for example "partial controllability" (uncertainty due to the inability to perfectly control the system of interest).[48] The terms "reducible" and "irreducible" highlight the idea that some sources of uncertainty (i.e. those that are "reducible") can be decreased through additional efforts by GI decision-makers (for example, through better data, measurement, analysis, etc.);[49] however, other sources of uncertainty are irreducible – they can be better understood, but not reduced.

Table 1. Uncertainty Terms relating to GI Decision-making[50]

Uncertainty Terms	Definition
Epistemic Uncertainty	Uncertainty arising from the limits of human knowledge. Often linked to aspects of data (for example, lack of data or imprecise measurements).
Measurement Error	Special case of "epistemic uncertainty": uncertainty which arises from the inability to measure things precisely (uncertainties associated with connectivity measurement, in a GI context).
Subjective Nature of Judgements	Special case of "epistemic uncertainty": uncertainty about the selection of appropriate data or analysis methods, and about how to interpret data or how to interpret modelling results.

(continued)

47 For more information on the definition of "GI", please see section 2 above. The scientific community is already warning that research into GI is hindered by its broad definition, both in terms of what comprises GI, and what functions it seeks to perform. Please see *European Commission, Science for Environmental Policy*, above n. 5, p. 31.

48 *B.K. Williams et al.*, above n. 42, Uncertainty and learning, p. VI.

49 Please note that, even then, the new information can reveal new uncertainties. See *C. Hanna et al.*, "The Uncertainty Contagion: Revealing the Interrelated Cascading Uncertainties of Managed Retreat", *Sustainability*, 2020, 12(2), 736.

50 A compilation from *R. Gregory et al.*, above n. 2; *B.K. Williams et al.*, above n. 42; and *M.J. Conroy and J.T. Peterson*, above n. 3.

Table 1 ***continued***

Uncertainty Terms	Definition
Aleatory Uncertainty	Special case of "epistemic uncertainty": uncertainty arising from inherent variability in random processes (for example, demographic stochasticity, or environmental and catastrophic stochasticity).
Parametric Uncertainty	Special case of "epistemic uncertainty": uncertainty about the value of parameters or empirical quantities.
Structural Uncertainty	Special case of "epistemic uncertainty": uncertainty about which factors (physical, chemical, biological, economic and social) or ecological mechanisms affect the outcome of a decision.
Extended Structural Uncertainty	Special case of "epistemic uncertainty": "structural uncertainty" extended to include not just the interactions of elements in the natural system, but also the interactions of management actions with those system elements.
Linguistic Uncertainty	Uncertainty linked to language: vague or ambiguous terms and/or concepts; terms/concepts that are context-dependent (for example, defining the term "GI" in various contexts).
Reducible Uncertainty	Uncertainty that can be reduced or resolved with additional effort (for example, "partial controllability").
Partial Controllability	Difference between the results intended by a given management decision and the results that actually occur.
Irreducible Uncertainty	Uncertainty that cannot be resolved (for example, "partial observability").
Partial Observability	Uncertainty due to the inability to accurately assess the state of the resource system that is being managed.

Note: The italicised terms in this table are the broader categories, with the non-underlined terms being subcategories.

3.2. CONSEQUENCES OF UNCERTAINTY IN GI DECISION-MAKING PROCESSES

Designing and implementing GI requires a significant knowledge base, and is now highly "knowledge-hungry". Any type of uncertainty identified in the research (for example, "linguistic", "aleatory", "reducible" or "irreducible") can emerge at any stage of a GI decision-making process. At the very beginning of the process, a "linguistic uncertainty" can flaw a GI strategy design, in particular during the problem-framing or objective-setting stages (for example, the GI concept definition causing challenges during the process of selection between GI areas management approaches). "Linguistic uncertainty" can also occur during the implementation stage, for example due to the failure to communicate precisely what is meant by a term and/or concept in protection and conservation measures. One of the prime examples is the use of the "significant effect" concept, under Article 6.3 of the Habitats Directive, discussed earlier in the contribution. Along similar lines to "linguistic uncertainty", "epistemic uncertainty", and the reducible and irreducible types of uncertainties, can also play their roles during the various stages of GI design and implementation.

The influence and the consequences of uncertainty for GI decision-making may vary, depending on the types of uncertainties, the context, and the objectives. The consequences may include, *inter alia*, ineffective and/or flawed decisions, conflicting stakeholder interests, and lengthy and costly litigation. Thus, for instance, uncertainty has already been ruled upon in a wide range of cases on implementation of the Birds Directive and/or the Habitats Directive by the EU Court of Justice, for example uncertainty in granting permission (e.g. to the performance of activities, like agriculture, fishing or water management),[51] uncertainty about the existence of a strict species-protection system,[52] uncertainty on deliberativeness in species killing/catching,[53] uncertainty on deliberativeness in species disturbance,[54] uncertainty about exceptions to strict species protection,[55] etc. Furthermore, for the cases in which uncertainty is involved, legal critics have drawn attention to the fact that judges, more and more often, manipulate scientific data and conduct scientific comparisons, which raises questions as to the capacity of judges to be the "judges of science".[56] For example, in the *Commission v. Ireland* case, in concluding that Ireland had not taken the necessary measures to safeguard a sufficient diversity and area of habitats for the red grouse, pursuant to the Birds Directive, the Court based its reasoning on scientific data submitted by the parties, and indicated that a "comparison of the two scientific works" had been conducted, despite the need for caution in comparing such data.[57] The influence and consequences of uncertainty in GI decision- making pose challenges for decision-makers, and tend to lead to the available legal tools for managing uncertainty in the process of GI design and implementation being resorted to.

---

51 Case C-127/02 *Landelijke Vereniging tot Behoud van de Waddenzee and Nederlandse Vereniging tot Bescherming van Vogels v. Staatssecretaris van Landbouw, Natuurbeheer en Visserij*; Case C-258/11 *Peter Sweetman and Others v. An Bord Pleanála.*

52 Case C-183/05 *Commission of the European Communities v. Ireland.*

53 Case C-221/04 *Commission v. Spain.*

54 Case C-103/00 *Commission v. Greece.*

55 Case C-674/17.

56 *E. Truilhe-Marengo*, "How to cope with the unknown: A few things about scientific uncertainty, precaution and adaptive management", in *C.-H. Born et al.* (eds), *The Habitats Directive in its EU Environmental Law Context: European Nature's Best Hope?*, Routledge, 2015, p. 329.

57 Case C-117/00, para. 17.

4. CONCLUDING REMARKS

Designing an enabling GI framework, and subsequently implementing it, require a significant knowledge base, including common indicators, and an assessment framework, at EU, national and local levels, etc. Yet, GI design and implementation also require the recognition of uncertainties and knowledge gaps, and assessing them in order to manage those gaps. This contribution investigated the types of uncertainties which may be encountered in GI decision-making processes, and suggested a typology on uncertainties. This typology may be helpful in future legal research on determining how to deal with each type of uncertainty in GI decision-making by means of the available legal tools.

The adaptive management approach may become one of the responses to uncertainties in the GI design and implementation process, as far as possible, and as far as compatible with legal principles (like the principle of legal certainty). Other possible responses may include the evidence-based approach, the science-based approach, the robust decision-making process, and more flexible (legal) concepts which allow for evolving interpretations (backed by a knowledge base) in changing contexts (for example, "good ecological status", "ecosystem integrity" or "significant effect"). Yet, further assessment of the identified types of uncertainties in GI decision-making processes, and the application of the available legal tools to manage various types of uncertainty, in a GI context, requires further research.

PART X

BUSINESSES

ENHANCING ENVIRONMENTAL SUSTAINABILITY THROUGH REFORMING CZECH CONTRACT LAW

Rita SIMON*

1. INTRODUCTION

Originally, European consumer law[1] was framed as being for boosting the internal market and welfare. The main aim of consumer legislation was "through the achievement of [a] high level of consumer protection, to contribute to the proper functioning of the internal market".[2] However, with the growing awareness of planetary boundaries and climate change, the negative impacts of consumerism have created an issue which European lawmaking is supposed to tackle. To ensure the European Union (EU)'s commitments towards the United Nations (UN) Sustainable Development Goals, a more sustainable single market for businesses and consumers was to be achieved. Thus, the first legislative packages on sustainable consumption and production solely targeted production, but sustainable policies slowly arrived in the field of consumer legislation. The Sale of Goods Directive, which should redraft and modernise consumer sales law,[3] was the first step towards enhancing environmental sustainability in consumption. Ensuring a longer durability of consumer goods[4] via longer

* Rita Simon is a scientific researcher at the Institute of State and Law of the Czech Academy of Sciences. This contribution was written as part of a project of the Institute supported by the Lumina Quaeruntur Prize, awarded by the Academy of Sciences of the Czech Republic.

1 REICH, N., MICKLITZ, H.W., ROTT, P. et al., *European Consumer Law*, Intersentia, Cambridge 2014.

2 Art. 1 of Directive 2011/83/EU of the European Parliament and of the Council of 25 October 2011 on consumer rights amending Council Directive 93/13/EEC and Directive 1999/44/EC of the European Parliament and of the Council and repealing Council Directive 85/577/EEC and Directive 97/7/EC of the European Parliament and of the Council.

3 Directive (EU) 2019/771 of the European Parliament and of the Council of 20 May 2019 on certain aspects of contracts for the sale of goods, amending Regulation (EU) 2017/2394 and Directive 2009/22/EC and repealing Directive 1999/44/EC (hereinafter "SGD").

4 Recital 32 of the SGD (above n. 3) uses the term "durability", whereas the Czech Civil Code uses "lifetime"; therefore, in this contribution, the term "durability" will be used in relation to the SGD.

guarantee periods and software updates, and enabling consumers to require repair,[5] are two mentioned aims of the Directive to encourage more sustainable consumption patterns and a circular economy. This contribution will investigate how far the Czech implementation has contributed to these aims. After a brief explanation of why promoting sustainability is a binding target for the European and national legislators (section 2), national best practices, designed to improve sustainability through contract law, in other European countries, will be presented (section 3); and, finally, it will be analysed how far the Czech transposition of the 2019/770/EU Directive ensures sustainability (section 4).

2. PROMOTING SUSTAINABILITY AS A BINDING TARGET

2.1. INTERNATIONAL AND EUROPEAN OBLIGATIONS

Achieving sustainable development is a universal call, which should be respected and enhanced through the national policies of United Nations countries. The concept of sustainable development was framed by the Brundtland's report *Our Common Future*,[6] in 1987, but it took 23 years until sustainable consumption achieved a status of a universal call, through a resolution of the General Assembly of United Nations.[7] Since then, "responsible consumption and production" has counted as the twelfth Sustainable Development Goal, which should be implemented in national governments' political frameworks, and achieved by 2030. The Czech government prepared its strategy in 2017,[8] but the document mentions only reduced resource exigency, and better protection of consumers through market surveillance,[9] through which sustainable consumption should be achieved.[10]

On the European level, promoting sustainable development is connected to environmental protection requirements, and must be integrated into the

---

5 Recital 48 of the SGD (above n. 3).

6 World Commission on Environment and Development, "Report of the World Commission on Environment and Development: Our Common Future", available at: https://sustainabledevelopment.un.org/content/documents/5987our-common-future.pdf.

7 United Nations, Resolution adopted by the General Assembly on 25 September 2015, "Transforming our world: the 2030 Agenda for Sustainable Development" (A/RES/70/1), available at https://www.un.org/sustainabledevelopment/development-agenda/.

8 The Czech government created its Agenda 2030 in 2017, available at https://www.vlada.cz/assets/ppov/udrzitelny-rozvoj/projekt-OPZ/Strategic_Framework_CZ2030.pdf.

9 Ibis., https://www.cr2030.cz/strategie/wp-content/uploads/sites/2/2018/05/Strategic_Framework_CZ2030_graphic2.compressed.pdf, p. 30.

10 Simon, R., "Spotřeba, udržitelnost a změna klimatu" in Müllerová, H. et al., *Klimatické právo*. Wolters Kluwer, 2022, 375.

definitions and implementation of all Community policies and activities. This claim was originally anchored by the Nice Treaty, from 2002, into Article 6 of the TEU[11] but later moved to Article 11 of the TFEU,[12] by the Lisbon Treaty.[13] Further, the TEU mentions sustainable development as a limit for promoting economic and social progress, in its preamble (9), interestingly in context of the accomplishment of the internal market, but also for the Union's external actions, through Article 21 (2) (f) TEU. This means that, concerning all internal and external policies and actions of the EU, sustainable development should be promoted.

2.2. MORE RESPONSIBLE PRODUCTION IN THE EU, BUT LOW FOCUS ON CONSUMPTION

Following these objectives, the EU is fully committed to playing an active role in maximising progress towards the Sustainable Development Goals.[14] However, while "responsible production" is fairly well integrated in European policies, it seems that the European legislator is still reluctant to nudge the consumer towards more sustainable behaviour.

Focusing on more sustainable production, the European Commission had already started, by 1992, to create voluntary Ecolabel schemes, and a couple of years later started to label the energy consumption of household appliances,[15] and then to regulate the necessary eco-design[16] of several products. In 2008, it proposed the first package on sustainable consumption and production and sustainable industry policy,[17] which stood for widening the scope of both pillars of more green production, the Eco-design[18] and the Energy Labelling

11 Art. 6, Treaty on European Union (consolidated version 2002), OJ C 325, 24.12.2002, 5–32.

12 Art. 11 TFEU (ex Art. 6 TEC), Treaty of Lisbon amending the Treaty on European Union and the Treaty establishing the European Community, signed in Lisbon on 13 December 2007, OJ C 306, 17.12.2007, 1–271: "Environmental protection requirements must be integrated into the definition and implementation of the Union's policies and activities, in particular with a view to promoting sustainable development."

13 Kodek, G. and Leupold, P., *Gewährleistungsrecht*, Manz, 2019, 38.

14 Eurostat, "Sustainable development in the European Union Monitoring report on progress towards the SDGs in an EU context", available at: https://ec.europa.eu/eurostat/documents/3217494/11011074/KS-02-20-202-EN-N.pdf/334a8cfe-636a-bb8a-294a-73a052882f7f?t=1592994779000.

15 Directive 92/75/EEC.

16 Directive 2005/32/EC.

17 European Commission, "Sustainable Consumption and Production and Sustainable Industrial Policy Action Plan", COM (2008) 397 final.

18 Directive 2009/125/EC of the European Parliament and of the Council of 21 October 2009 establishing a framework for the setting of ecodesign requirements for energy-related products.

Directive.[19] Both Directives gained new product categories. With the Green Deal, even more important expansion is planned. Besides energy-consuming goods, the requirement of the Eco-design Directive should be applied to the broadest possible range of consumer goods, including textiles, furniture and chemicals. Next to energy efficiency, resource efficiency and sustainability are the new flagships for all policy fields.

The first step towards integrating sustainability into consumption-related legislation was achieved by the modernisation of consumer sales law, in 2019, although these first directives – Directives 2019/771/EU on Sale of Goods[20] (hereinafter "SGD") and 2019/770/EU on Digital Content and Digital Services[21] (hereinafter "DCD") – showed low ambition towards this aim. The SGD refers only twice to sustainable consumption, first concerning durability of products,[22] and, second, requiring repairability;[23] the DCD does not mention these aims in its recitals. Nevertheless, some requirements of both Directives enhance sustainable consumption. The first novelty is that durability, functionality, compatibility – and, in the case of digital content, available updates – became objective criteria for conformity of goods, under Article 7(1) SGD and Article 8(1) DCD. This means that goods offered for sale should possess these features, in addition to complying with any subjective requirement, otherwise the seller's performance will lack conformity, and consumers will be entitled ask for remedies. Second, a two-year legal guarantee period was set out for digital content and services, under Article 11 DCD. Concerning new consumer goods, Member States gain the right

19 Regulation (EU) 2017/1369 of the European Parliament and of the Council of 4 July 2017 setting a framework for energy labelling and repealing Directive 2010/30/EU; Directive 92/75/EEC of 22 September on the indication of the consumption of energy and other resources on energy labelling of household appliances and standard product information; Directive 2010/30/EU of the European Parliament and of the Council of 19 May 2010 on the indication of the consumption of energy and other resources on energy labelling of energy-related products and standard product information; Regulation (EU) 2019/2013 on energy labelling of electronic displays and Directive 2009/125/EC on energy-related products; Commission Delegated Regulation (EU) 2019/2013 of 11 March 2019 supplementing Regulation (EU) 2017/1369 of the European Parliament and of the Council with regard to energy labelling of electronic displays and repealing Commission Delegated Regulation (EU) No. 1062/2010; Commission Implementing Regulation (EU) 2021/535 of 31 March 2021 laying down rules for the application of Regulation (EU) 2019/2144 of the European Parliament and of the Council as regards uniform procedures and technical specifications for the type-approval of vehicles and of systems, components and separate technical units intended for such vehicles with regard to their general construction and safety characteristics; and Commission Delegated Regulation (EU) 2019/2013 of 11 March 2019 supplementing Regulation (EU) 2017/1369 of the European Parliament and of the Council with regard to energy labelling of electronic displays and repealing Commission Delegated Regulation (EU) No. 1062/2010.

20 SGD (above n. 3).

21 Directive (EU) 2019/770 of the European Parliament and of the Council of 20 May 2019 on certain aspects of contracts for the provision of digital content and services.

22 Recital 32, SGD (above n. 3).

23 Recital 48, SGD (above n. 3).

to introduce longer guarantee periods than two years, according to Article 10(3) SGD, and in case of second-hand goods the liability period was prolonged to one year, according to Article 10 (6) SGD. A further requirement, which can support more durability in a practical sense, was prolonging the presumption period for lack of conformity until one year after sale, under Article 11 SGD and Article 12 DCD. Regarding this rule, in the first year after delivery, the seller should prove that any problem did not exist before selling the goods. Despite these positive improvements, the Directives, unfortunately, did not encourage more sustainable remedies, and this was criticised by numerous scholars.[24] Repair – the more sustainable remedy – was not privileged over replacement, and further relevant environmental issues, such as availability of spare parts, and sustainable delivery, were not touched upon. Further, the minimum lifespan regulation of the Eco-design Directive was not interlinked with durability requirements, which would have created a synergy between these disparate fields of law, clearly supporting longer lifespans of products. Some of these issues are mentioned in newer policies, for example in the Consumer Agenda Strengthening Consumer Resilience for Sustainable Recovery,[25] but it is still uncertain how quickly the European legislator will progress these matters.

3. BEST PRACTICES TOWARDS REPAIRABILITY AND DURABILITY IN EUROPE

Despite the issues discussed above, the European legislation was revised to create more sustainable solutions through contract law, upon the modernisation of consumer sales law; the national legislators were not hindered in enhancing higher level of sustainability. Not even the maximum-harmonisation approach of the Directives created obstacles, first because of the reluctance to generate rules on these issues; second, because the SGD included some opening rules, such as, for example, the introduction of longer guarantee periods under Article 10(3), or a longer reverse burden of proof under Article 11(2) SGD. Several Member States have created legal requirements which aim to expand the lifespan of products, or make spare parts available for repairs. Legislators in Nordic countries, such as Finland and Sweden, and also in France, the Netherlands, Spain and Portugal, count as pioneers.

From the perspective of the placement of sustainability-supporting rules, three different types of solution should be mentioned. Some of the Member

24 Gool, E.V. and Michel, A., "The New Consumer Sales Directive 2019/771 and Sustainable Consumption: a Critical Analysis", *EuCML*, 2021/1, 136–148.

25 Communication from the Commission to the European Parliament and the Council: New Consumer Agenda Strengthening consumer resilience for sustainable recovery, COM/2020/696 final.

States' legislators, for example those in the Netherlands, placed these rules in their contract law, but most put them into their *lex specialis* consumer law, for example those in Spain, Finland and Sweden; however, some of the sustainability-supporting rules were secured through circular economy rules, for example in France. The French Act relating to the fight against waste and the circular economy,[26] for instance, imposes information obligations on producers of certain products, regarding durability, reparability and environmental impact, and regulates the use of remanufactured (refurbished) products.

Concerning the legal guarantee period, it should be noted that six Member States used the option in Article 10(3) SGD, and created guarantee periods longer than two years, via their consumer or contract law. In Sweden, a general three-year period is applied,[27] as in Spain,[28] Portugal[29] and Finland.[30] Interestingly, common-law countries, such as the United Kingdom[31] and Ireland,[32] adopted much longer guarantee periods than those under the SGD. In these countries, the guarantee period, in general, is six years long. In Spain, the liability periods can be suspended in the event of repair or replacement,[33] which *de facto* implies the extension of rights. Another type of guarantee extension was used in France, where, in the event of repair, the guarantee period automatically prolongs by six months, and in case of replacement it renews.[34] In Finland, the liability period begins when the buyer becomes aware of the lack of conformity, and this can also extend the guarantee period. The most interesting approach was chosen by the Netherlands,[35] where legal guarantees are limited by the expected lifespan of the purchased goods. Consumers in the Netherlands may claim the non-conformity of the good, as long as the product should be attributed to wear and tear, due to expiration of the good's expected lifespan. This approach requires the court's interpretation on the expected lifespan of goods/products, but soft law can indicate expected lifespans for different product categories,[36] which does not seem problematic for courts. This solution tends to interlink the existing

---

26 Law of the French Republic Nr. 2020-105 of 10 February 2020.

27 §23, Konsumentköplag (1990:932).

28 Art. 120(1), Texto Refundido de la Ley General de Defense de los Consumidores y Usuarios.

29 Art. 48(1b), Lei n.º 24/96, que estabelece o regime legal aplicável à defesa dos consumidores.

30 §16, Kuluttajansuojalaki (1978/38).

31 In UK, the limitation period under the common law is six years, in general, and the Consumer Rights Act 2015 implies terms under common law. Therefore, the period for breach of contract is much longer than is stipulated by the SGD.

32 Statutory Instrument No. 11 of 2003.

33 Art. 122, Texto Refundido de la Ley General de Defense de los Consumidores y Usuarios.

34 Art 22, Law of the French Republic Nr. 2020-105 of 10 February 2020.

35 Arts. VII.17 (2) and VII.23, Burgerlijk Wetboek.

36 UNETO-VNI Table for average service life expectations (UNETO-VNI Tabel met gemiddelde gebruiksduurverwachtingen), available at: https://www.technieknederland.nl/onze-leden/waar-staan-onze-leden-voor/gebruiksduurverwachting.

requirements on minimum lifespan, delivered by the Eco-design Directive, to contract law, an approach supported by many academics.[37]

The hierarchy of remedies was not changed through the SGD, so repair and replacement of goods, in the event of a lack of conformity, stayed the primary remedy for consumers.[38] Several Member States have taken initiatives to position repair as a primary remedy, but mostly outside of the scope of contract law. Sweden, for example, has introduced tax reductions for repair and remanufacturing activities.[39] In Slovenia, Portugal and Spain, the availability of spare parts is regulated. In Slovenia,[40] spare parts for household appliances and vehicles should be available for at least three years after the lapse of the guarantee; in both Spain[41] and Portugal,[42] the producer should make spare parts available for all kind of products, for a period of 10 years after the last unit of the good has been placed on the market, which has been criticised by some as a heavy burden for producers. In January 2022, in France, an obligation on professionals who maintain and repair electrical and electronic appliances was introduced, to allow consumers to opt for spare parts which come from the circular economy, instead of new parts.[43]

4. LOW AMBITION TO PROMOTE SUSTAINABILITY IN THE CZECH REPUBLIC

The ambitions of the Czech legislator to enhance environmental sustainability and the circular economy by way of implementing the DCD and SGD seem to be very low. The legislator updated the objective requirements for conformity, but did not use the option, made available to the Member States, to prolong the liability period of sellers. Norms to ensure longer durability of goods, or to make spare parts available, were not created. And durability did not appear on the list of precontractual information requirements, next to functionality, compatibility

37 Zinner, M., "Nachhaltiges Gewährleistungsrecht – Reality Check" in Reiffeinstein, M. and Blaschek, B., *Konsumentenpolitisches Jahrbuch 2021*, Verlag Österreich, 2021, 27 and Gool, E.V. and Michel, A., above n. 24, 136–142.

38 Terryn, E.A., "Right to Repair? Towards Sustainable Remedies in Consumer Law", *European Review of Private Law*, 2019/4, 851–874.

39 European Commission, "Commission Staff Working Document: Impact Assessment Report, Accompanying the document Proposal for a Directive of the European Parliament and of the Council amending Directives 2005/29/EC and 2011/83/EU as regards the empowering consumers for the green transition through better protection against unfair practices and better information, Brussels, 30.03.2022, SWD(2022) 85 final, 147.

40 Ibid, 149.

41 Art. 127, Texto Refundido de la Ley General de Defense de los Consumidores y Usuarios.

42 Art. 21, Decree Law 67/2003.

43 Art. 19(II), Law of the French Republic Nr. 2020-105 of 10 February 2020.

and interoperability, under section 1820 (r) of the Czech Civil Code (hereinafter "CzCC").[44]

One positive is that the wording of section 2161 CzCC now reflects both the subjective and objective requirements for conformity laid down in Articles 6 and 7 of the SGD. The issue of "durability" has been transposed into section 2161, paragraph 2, which explicitly states that the item shall correspond, in terms of quantity, quality and other characteristics, including durability, functionality, compatibility and safety, to the usual characteristics of the same kind that the buyer can reasonably expect, including with regard to public statements made by the seller or another person in the same contract chain, in particular through advertising or labelling. Thus, durability is a general concept which will be interpreted as the general ability of the goods to maintain their required functions and performance throughout normal use, i.e. in conformity with the SGD. When interpreted, a strong emphasis is placed on the legal regulations and technical norms, which must be observed when assessing the item's suitability for purpose or use. Unfortunately, no regulation is explicitly provided, by the new amendments, to interlink expected durability provisions of technical norms[45] with contractual liability. Whether the Czech courts would, in the future, interlink the expected lifespan of purchased goods with contractual guarantees, as is practised in the Netherlands,[46] is disputed.

A further problem is that the Czech transposition (section 2161, para. 2, CzCC) did not name producers' statements as a binding objective requirement for conformity of goods, as mentioned in Article 7(1)(d) of the SGD. Regarding the Czech implementation, public statements made by the seller, or by another person in the same contractual chain, particularly in advertising or on labelling, are governed by the quantity, qualities and other features of the goods which the consumer may reasonably expect. Therefore, the ordinary courts will have the task of also including producers' statements, when these prove which qualities the product should have.

Concerning digital services and content, the same structure of subjective and objective requirements was established, by Articles 7, 8 and 9 of the DCD, as is applicable for usual goods; this was transposed into sections 2389c, 2389d and 2389i of the CzCC.[47] Further, section 2389c requires that the goods be free from defects, and that the provider must provide to the user the newest version of

44 Act No. 89/2012 Coll., Civil Code.

45 Directive 2009/125/EC was transposed into the Czech legal system by Act No. 406/2000 Coll., on Energy Management, and the particular provisions on eco-design are laid down in Decree No. 319/2019 Coll., which establishes binding requirements for labelling for consumers as well. However, no interlinking with contract law liability was established.

46 Gool, E.V. and Michel, A., above n. 24, 142.

47 S. 2389f regulates the provision of digital content that is provided all at once. Subjective and objective requirements are laid down in s. 2389i.

the digital content available at the moment of conclusion of the contract. Under Section 2389d, the provider must ensure that the user will get the contractually agreed updates of digital content, as well as necessary updates which ensure that the digital content remains without defects during the term of the contract, and that the user will be notified of these. The liability period of sellers, however, seems to be less problematic for digital content, because, due to the speciality of these kind of products and services in cases of continuous supply, the trader will be liable for a lack of conformity for the full duration of the commitment/obligation, according to section 2389c, paragraph 1 of the CzCC, in conjunction with section 2161b, paragraph 2. Where digital content is provided all at once, the liability period is, under section 2389k CzCC, two years from when it was made available.

The new amendments to section 2169 CzCC change the old hierarchy of remedies slightly, in the event of a lack of conformity. The new rules make replacement and repair clear first options of equal rank, with termination and price reduction being second-option remedies. This hierarchy was already given by the Article 3 of the older Directive 1999/44/ES,[48] but the Czech implementation was complicated and, in part, confusing. The conditions for the applicability of the first-option remedies are, according to section 2169, paragraph 1 of the CzCC, that the chosen method of eliminating the defect should not be impossible or unreasonably expensive.[49] Only if the chosen method is impossible or unreasonably expensive, can the seller refuse the performance of these first-option remedies.

Concerning second-option remedies (termination of the contract or price reduction), it is welcome that the new amendments, in section 2171 CzCC, now clearly state in which cases the buyer can make use of them. These two options are only available if: (a) the seller refused or failed to replace or repair the goods; (b) the defect has appeared repeatedly;[50] (c) the defect is a significant breach of contract; or (d) it is apparent from the seller's statement, or from the circumstances, that the defect will not be remedied without significant inconvenience to the buyer.[51] However, termination is only possible if the defect is not minor. The new rules bring two novelties: first, if the defect occurs repeatedly, the consumer may exercise their right not only to terminate the contract, but also to a price reduction; second, even more importantly,

48 Directive 1999/44/EC of the European Parliament and of the Council of 25 May 1999 on certain aspects of the sale of consumer goods and associated guarantees.

49 The general provisions of ss. 1923, 2106 and 2107 on rights arising from defective performance will not apply.

50 Under Decision of the Supreme Court File No. 33 Cdo 1323/2013 from 31.03.2011, if the defect has been removed twice but occurs again.

51 Tichý, L., "§2169" in Švestka J. et al., *Občanský zákoník. Komentář. Svazek V (§1721–2520, relativní majetková práva 1. Část*, Wolters Kluwer, 2014, 980.

there is a reversed burden of proof concerning the level of lack of conformity. Under section 2171, paragraph 3 of the CzCC, the seller must, in the future, prove whether the non-conformity is only minor. This means that, in cases of manipulated car software,[52] or other complex goods, the burden is on the seller to prove that the defect is *not* significant. This rule will definitely facilitate the enforcement of consumers' remedies in cases of non-conformity.

Despite these important novelties, enhancing consumer rights, it should be noted that the Czech rules do not nudge the consumer towards choosing the more sustainable remedy. Similarly, they do not require the seller to offer more sustainable remedies via commercial guarantees. The often-practised immediate replacement of defective goods with new products is not a sustainable option.[53]

5. CONCLUSIONS

Achieving sustainable development has been a universal call since the Nice Treaty, whereby, according to Article 6 of the TEU sustainable development should be promoted in all internal and external policies and actions of the EU. Following these objectives, "responsible production and consumption", as the twelfth Sustainable Development Goal, should be fairly well integrated into European policies. While the European legislator has made important steps towards more responsible production, it is still reluctant to nudge the consumer towards responsible consumption. In the modernisation of European consumer sales law, in 2019, the European legislator showed a low level of ambition towards this aim. Although long durability has become the objective criterion for conformity of goods, the minimum lifespan regulation of Eco-design directive was not interlinked with durability requirements, and repair was not made a prioritised remedy. But national legislators were not prevented from achieving a higher level of sustainability. Some pioneering legislators have created legal requirements which aim to expand the lifespans of products, or make spare parts available for repairs, but the majority of Member States are waiting on future requirements from Brussels.

The ambitions of the Czech legislator to enhance environmental sustainability and the circular economy by way of implementing the DCD and SGD seem to be very low. Although the legislator updated the objective requirements

---

52 Under CJEU decision C-145/20 *Porsche Inter Auto and Volkswagen*, Art. 3(6) of Directive 1999/44 must be interpreted as meaning that a lack of conformity, consisting of the presence, in a vehicle, of a defeat device, the use of which is prohibited under Art. 5(2) of Regulation No. 715/2007, is not to be classified as "minor" even where the consumer would still have purchased that vehicle if he or she had been aware of the existence and operation of that device.

53 Terryn, E.A., above n. 38, 861.

for conformity, and complemented these with durability, it did not use the option, offered to the Member States, to prolong the liability periods of sellers. Norms on the lifespan statements of producers or sellers were not interlinked with contractual liability. The availability of spare parts is not required, and information on product durability did not get on to the list of precontractual information requirements. The only positive novelty is the slight change to the old hierarchy of remedies, in the event of non-conformity. The new rules make replacement and repair clear first options of equal rank, and termination and price reduction second-option remedies.

FOREIGN DIRECT LIABILITY AS AN EMERGING NORM FOR THE ACCOUNTABILITY OF TRANSNATIONAL CORPORATIONS

The European Experience

Ikechukwu P. Ugwu*

1. INTRODUCTION

The roles of transnational corporations (TNCs) have transcended mere economic activities, to include roles in politics and becoming agents for social engineering.[1] While performing their major businesses and profit maximisation activities, TNCs engage in environmental and human rights violations, necessitating various attempts at holding them accountable. Even though some of these attempts are still in place, albeit largely ineffective, many were abandoned at some point. For instance, the Norms on the Responsibilities of Transnational Corporations, by the United Nations (UN) Sub-Commission on the Promotion and Protection of Human Rights (the Norms)[2] failed for many

---

* PhD researcher at the University of Silesia in Katowice, Poland. This research was funded entirely by the Polish National Science Centre, under grant number UMO-2021/41/N/HS5/01227.

1 Examples of where TNCs played significant roles in social changes include when the Ford Motor Company of South Africa initiated proactive measures to fight HIV/AIDS: see Robert J. Bies and others, "Introduction to Special Topic Forum: Corporations as Social Change Agents: Individual, Interpersonal, Institutional, and Environmental Dynamics" (2007) 32 *AMR* 788. Again, many companies support the fight against racism. See Fernando Duarte, "Big Brands have Spoken out in Support of Black Communities Following George Floyd's Killing. How as a Consumer do you know which Companies Genuinely Support the Cause?", *BBC*, 13 June 2020, https://www.bbc.com/worklife/article/20200612-black-lives-matter-do-companies-really-support-the-cause.

2 Sub-Commission on the Promotion and Protection of Human Rights, "Norms on the Responsibilities of Transnational Corporations and Other Business Enterprises with Regard to Human Rights", UN ESCOR, 55th sess., 22nd mtg., Agenda Item 4, UN Doc. E/CN 4/Sub 2/2003/12/Rev 2 (13 August 2003).

reasons, including the primacy of the role given to corporations,[3] which would have led to indirectly "privati[s]ing the enforcement of human rights laws".[4] The idea behind another UN instrument, UN Guiding Principles,[5] was to establish an instrument that would serve as an "authoritative global reference point for business and human rights",[6] through its "protect, respect and remedy" themes. The Norms, the UN Guiding Principles, and other attempts, are soft laws based entirely on voluntarism, and, as a result, are not legally binding. Business enterprises are free to either comply with or reject them.

Again, national and regional courts have tried to establish TNCs' accountability over time. For instance, the US Alien Tort Statute (ATS) allows a foreign victim to sue, in a US federal court, either a foreign or a US-based defendant, for violating the law of nations. In other words, it gives the US federal courts jurisdiction to hear lawsuits filed by non-US citizens for torts committed in violation of international law.[7] The use of the ATS over the years has moved from the days of its glory, starting with the case of *Filartiga v. Peña-Irala*,[8] to its restriction by the US Supreme Court. In 2021, the US Supreme Court, in the case of *Nestlé USA, Inc. v. Doe*,[9] rejected the applicability of the ATS jurisdiction to foreign businesses with a "mere corporate presence" in the US. The hope built on the usefulness of the ATS for environmental activists to hold TNCs accountable[10] seems to have been dashed, considering the narrow approach the US Supreme Court has recently applied, which has necessitated the need for an alternative.[11]

---

3 Pini Pavel Miretski and Sascha-Dominik Bachmann, "The UN 'Norms on the Responsibility of Transnational Corporations and other Business Enterprises with Regard to Human Rights': A Requiem" (2012) 17 *DLR* 5, 20.

4 Ibid.; Carlos Manuel Vázquez, "Direct vs. Indirect Obligations of Corporations under International Law" (2005) 43 *CJTL* 927, 929.

5 United Nations Human Rights Council, "Report of the Special Representative of the Secretary-General on the Issue of Human Rights and Transnational Corporations and other Business Enterprises, John Ruggie Guiding Principles on Business and Human Rights: Implementing the United Nations 'Protect, Respect and Remedy' Framework", 17th sess., Agenda Item 3, UN Doc. A/HRC/17/31 (21 March 2011).

6 United Nations Office of the High Commissioner for Human Rights, "New Guiding Principles on Business and Human Rights Endorsed by the UN Human Rights Council" (16 June 2011), https://media.business-humanrights.org/media/documents/files/media/documents/ruggie/ruggie-guiding-principles-endorsed-16-jun-2011.pdf.

7 Judiciary Act of 1789, ch. 20, §9(b), 1 Stat. 73,77. The ATS is also called the Alien Tort Claims Act (ATCA).

8 *Filartiga v. Peña-Irala* 630 F 2d 876 (2d Cir 1980).

9 *Nestlé USA, Inc. v. Doe* 593 US – (2021).

10 Hari M. Osofsky, "Environmental Human Rights under the Alien Tort Statute: Redress for Indigenous Victims of Multinational Corporations" (1996–1997) 20 *STLR* 335; Michael Koebele, *Corporate Responsibility under the Alien Tort Statute: Enforcement of International Law through US Torts Law* (Martinus Nijhoff Publishers, 2009).

11 Ikechukwu Ugwu, "Establishing Accountability for Human Rights Abuses by Multinational Corporations: Looking Beyond the US Alien Tort Statute" in Obiajulu Nnamuchi and

In recent years, European national courts have been moving towards foreign direct liability (FDL), to hold TNCs accountable. FDL includes civil lawsuits against corporate actors in the courts of other countries, where the corporate actors are mostly headquartered. The primary goal is to get money as a settlement.[12] This mechanism, applied a couple of times, by some European national courts, could be compared with the US ATS. It allows victims of corporate abuses to seek justice globally, especially in the home state of the TNC.[13] This contribution looks at the recent cases on the ATS jurisdiction, and how the US Supreme Court has narrowed its coverage; the FDL cases in European states' courts; the possible setbacks FDL might suffer in the future; and the way forward. It also looks at the recent Directive of the European Parliament and the Council on Corporate Sustainability Due Diligence, to discover whether FDL is about to be codified.

2. THE FAILURE OF ACCOUNTABILITY

The present author has previously written about the failure to hold TNCs accountable for either polluting the environment or human rights abuses. For instance, I argued that the failure of international legal instruments to hold TNCs accountable is due, among other factors, to TNCs' status under international law.[14] Even though TNCs are not yet subject of international law in the strictly traditional view,[15] they have at least become participants in international law.[16] They shape international law, contribute immensely to the global economy,[17] and abuse human rights and environmental standards,[18] and some have been accused of sponsoring terrorism.[19] However, various international law

Ndubuisi Nwafor (eds.), *Joys of Human Rights: Essays in Honour of Professor Joy Ngozi Ezeilo* (Malthouse, 2021), 202.

12 Lucas Roorda, "Jurisdiction in Foreign Direct Liability Cases in Europe" (2019) *ASIL Proceedings* 161.

13 Ibid.

14 Ugwu, "Establishing Accountability" (n. 11), 213.

15 Emeka Duruigbo, "Corporate Accountability and Liability for International Human Rights Abuses: Recent Changes and Recurring Challenges" (2008) 6 *NJHR* 222, 237; Alexander Orakhelashvili, *Akehurst's Modern Introduction to International Law* (9th ed., Routledge, 2018), 111.

16 José Alvarez, "Are Corporations 'Subjects' of International Law?" (2011) 9 *SCJIL* 1; Duruigbo (n. 15), 237.

17 C. Fritz Foley and others, "Multinational Activity in the Modern World" in C. Fritz Foley, James Hines and David Wessel (eds.), *Global Goliaths: Multinational Corporations in the 21st Century Economy* (Brookings Press, 2021), 1.

18 Subhan Ullah and others, "Multinational corporations and human right violations in emerging economies: Do commitment to social and environmental responsibility matter?" (2021) 280 *JEM* 1, 3.

19 See *Jesner v. Arab Bank, PLC* 138 S. Ct. 1386 (2018), where Arab Bank was sued in the US for allegedly aiding and abetting terrorism.

instruments on the accountability of TNCs are not binding, or, at best, give room for voluntary compliance by either a state or a TNC. They do not, for instance, provide for a commission or quasi-tribunal with the jurisdiction to entertain complaints against any TNC, or impose punishment for not complying with the instruments. Article 1 of the UN Guiding Principles provides that states must protect human rights, within their jurisdiction, against abuses by third parties like TNCs, by taking the necessary steps to prevent and punish such abuses. Article 11 provides that a business entity must respect human rights by avoiding the violation of human rights and redressing any adverse human rights impacts caused by its business activities. In remedying abuses, states are merely enjoined to take necessary steps towards giving victims access to an effective remedy.[20] These provisions are not binding, and voluntary provisions cannot achieve the need for an accountability mechanism without concrete and definitive punishment mechanisms. This is especially so when most of the countries where human rights and environmental abuses occur are developing economies, where the states are generally incapable of providing, or in some cases unwilling to provide, adequate access to remedy mechanisms.[21]

Voluntary or non-mandatory provisions are seen in other legal instruments on business and human rights. The Organisation for Economic Co-operation and Development (OECD) Guidelines for Multinational Enterprises[22] are suggestions on responsible business behaviour, by government adherents, to TNCs that operate in their states.[23] The OECD Guidelines provide that TNCs should "take due account of the need to protect the environment, public health and safety, and generally to conduct their activities in a manner contributing to the wider goal of sustainable development", in the countries in which they operate.[24] The OECD Guidelines require governments adhering to them to establish a National Contact Point (NCP) to oversee the implementation of the voluntary recommendations at the national level. The NCP has two main functions: (1) promoting OECD Guidelines compliance among businesses; and (2) handling complaints (known as "specific instances") against businesses that do not comply with the Guidelines.[25] Domenico Carolei believes that the OECD Guidelines do not present "an ideal accountability system", and that their voluntary nature presents enormous limitations.[26] The numerous underlying

20 The UN Guiding Principles (n. 5), Art. 25.

21 Roorda, "Jurisdiction in Foreign Direct Liability Cases in Europe" (n. 12), 161.

22 OECD, *OECD Guidelines for Multinational Enterprises* (11th ed., OECD, 2011), https://www.oecd.org/daf/inv/mne/48004323.pdf.

23 OECD, *Annual Report on the OECD Guidelines for Multinational Enterprises 2020: Update on National Contact Point Activity*, OECD, 2021, http://mneguidelines.oecd.org/2020-Annual-Report-MNE-Guidelines-EN.pdf.

24 *OECD Guidelines* (n. 22), 42.

25 Ibid., 71.

26 Domenico Carolei, "Accountability beyond Corporations: The Applicability of the OECD Guidelines for Multinational Enterprises to Non-profit Organisations" (2021) 13 *NPF* 31, 45.

flaws in the OECD Guidelines can be directly attributed to the fact that they are not legally enforceable, and that the NCPs do not have the power to impose sanctions on TNCs when they violate them.[27] The failure of these instruments to achieve the desired accountability gave rise to FDL.

3. EXAMINING FOREIGN DIRECT LIABILITY

As already stated, FDL cases are legal claims filed in the domestic courts of foreign countries, against corporate entities, with the expectation of obtaining monetary compensation as a remedy.[28] The claims are brought on behalf of victims, who have little or no recourse to justice in the state where the damaging activities occurred, of harmful activities done by subsidiaries or local contractors of TNCs.[29] Instead of pursuing the entire case in the alternative jurisdiction, these cases typically involve attempting to join non-EU-domiciled co-defendants to proceedings in the forum state, against the "anchor" EU-domiciled defendant.[30] As early as 2000, Halina Ward foresaw that FDL would, in the future, become a veritable mechanism for holding TNCs accountable for both human rights abuses and violations of environmental standards. For Ward, FDL cases are "a quiet revolution in corporate social responsibility".[31] From the definitions, four elements are associated with FDL: (1) foreign victims; (2) civil wrongs or torts; (3) the liability of TNCs for their activities abroad; and (4) financial compensation.

The ATS and FDL have many things in common. Some writers have argued that the ATS is part of FDL, since both address wrongdoings committed against foreigners. The ATS, enacted as early as 1789, as part of the US Federal Judiciary Act,[32] has been described as a "legal Lohengrin", since "no one seems to know whence it came" (or, more specifically, how it was intended to be interpreted). It provides that, "the district courts shall have original jurisdiction of any civil action by an alien for a tort only, committed in violation of the law of nations or a treaty of the United States".[33] There are three elements regarding the ATS

27 Jernej Letnar Černič, "Corporate Responsibility for Human Rights: A Critical Analysis of the OECD Guidelines for Multinational Enterprises" (2008) 4 *HLR* 71, 94.

28 Roorda, "Jurisdiction in Foreign Direct Liability Cases in Europe" (n. 12), 161.

29 Ibid.; Liesbeth F.H. Enneking, *Foreign Direct Liability and Beyond: Exploring the Role of Tort Law in Promoting International Corporate Social Responsibility and Accountability* (Eleven International Publishing, 2012), 91.

30 Rachel Widdis, "Constructing Accountability in Business and Human Rights: An Investigation of the Development of Foreign Direct Liability Litigation and Feasibility in Ireland" (PhD thesis, University of Dublin, 2021), 40.

31 Halina Ward, "Foreign Direct Liability: A New Weapon in the Performance Armoury?" (2000) *The Royal Institute of International Affairs* 1.

32 The US Federal Judiciary Act 1978, 28 United States Code §1350.

33 Ibid.

jurisdiction: (1) a foreigner sues; (2) for a tort only; and (3) based on a tort perpetrated in breach of a US convention or the law of nations.[34] The law remained unknown for up to 200 years, until it was revived in the 1980s, beginning with the case of *Filártiga v. Peña-Irala*.[35] In *Filártiga*, the ATS jurisdiction was utilised to bring to justice a former Paraguayan official, Americo Peña-Irala, for the wrongful death of Joelito Filártiga, which occurred in Paraguay. The US Court of Appeal held that foreign citizens who had been victims of international human rights breaches could sue their perpetrators in a US federal court, for a civil remedy, even where the breach had happened outside the US. The court based its decision on the fact that torture had become "a norm of customary international law", capable of triggering the ATS jurisdiction.

After this decision, foreign victims instituted many other cases in the US,[36] including against TNCs.[37] In *Doe v. Unocal*,[38] the ATS jurisdiction was invoked to hold accountable a Myanmar corporation, with its parent company in the US, for its role in displacing members of a village, and causing environmental damage, while building a gas pipeline in Myanmar. Even though the claims were eventually settled out of court, it established the possibility of bringing foreign-based corporations under the ATS jurisdiction. Also, for the first time, a human rights litigation against TNCs using the ATS led to victims being compensated.[39] But in *Kiobel v. Royal Dutch Petroleum Co*,[40] *Jesner*,[41] and, more recently, *Nestlé USA*,[42] the US Supreme Court has limited the usefulness of the ATS as a tool for FDL cases. This contribution will return to these limitations later, and consider how FDL cases in European Courts might suffer similar limitations in the future.

3.1. THE POSSIBLE LEGAL BASIS FOR FOREIGN DIRECT LITIGATION CASES IN EUROPEAN COURTS

Apart from case law, there are EU legal instruments that make FDL cases possible. Within the EU Member States, civil courts' jurisdiction over foreign

34 Ikechukwu P. Ugwu, "An Examination of Multinational Corporations' Accountability in the Light of Switzerland's Failed Responsible Business Initiative in the Covid-19 Pandemic Era" (2021) 13 *AMULR* 119, 142.

35 *Filártiga v. Peña-Irala*, 630 F.2d 876 (2nd Cir. (NY) 1980).

36 *Argentine Republic v. Amerada Hess Shipping Corp* 488 US 428 (1989); *Kadic v. Karadžić* 70F.3d 232, 241 (2nd Cir. 1995); *Sosa v. Alvarez Machain* 542 US 692 (2004).

37 *Kiobel v. Royal Dutch Petroleum Co.* 569 US 108 (2013); *Jesner* (n. 19).

38 *Doe v. Unocal* 395F.3d 932 (9th Cir. 2002).

39 Earth Rights International, "*Doe v. Unocal* – The First Case of its Kind: Holding a U.S. Company Responsible for Rape, Murder, and Forced Labor in Myanmar", *Earth Rights International*, https://earthrights.org/case/doe-v-unocal/; Ugwu, "Establishing Accountability" (n. 11), 218.

40 *Kiobel* (n. 37).

41 *Jesner* (n. 19).

42 *Nestlé USA* (n. 9).

direct liability cases is essentially established by the EU's Brussels I regime, which establishes an obligatory set of norms governing jurisdiction in transboundary civil and commercial cases.[43] The Brussels I regime consists of, among other legal instruments, the Brussels Convention[44] and the Brussels Regulation.[45] According to the Brussels I Regulation, "persons domiciled in a Member State shall, whatever their nationality, be sued in the courts of that Member State".[46] For natural persons, domicile is established according to domestic law, and Member States are free to establish their separate domicile criteria.[47] Article 63(1) of the Brussels I Regulation is relied upon to establish jurisdiction for legal persons, and it provides that the domicile of a company includes where they: (1) have their statutory seat; (2) have their central administration; or (3) have their principal place of business.[48] For claims against EU-domiciled defendants, and in matters relating to tort, delict or quasi-delict, the courts will have jurisdiction where the harmful event occurred, or may occur.[49]

These provisions imply that EU Member States' courts have jurisdiction over FDL cases made against the parent companies or subsidiaries of TNCs that have their statutory seat, central administration, or primary place of business in the forum country. However, the jurisdiction of EU Member State courts in FDL cases may be defined by rules different from those described above.[50] A special provision is made where the defendant is not based in the EU. Article 6(1) of the Brussels I Regulation provides that, in a case where the defendant is not based in a Member State, "the jurisdiction of the courts of each Member State shall ... be determined by the law of that Member State". For instance, this is the case when FDL cases are brought against non-EU-based firms in EU Member State courts. In such a scenario, subsidiaries, subcontractors, or business associates not located in any Member State can be sued in a Member State's court, together with the parent company located within the territories of a Member State.[51] For the most part, the applicable domestic rules on international civil jurisdiction will contain provisions on jurisdiction that are remarkably similar to those contained in the Brussels I Regulation. The implication is that jurisdiction would, in principle,

---

43 Enneking (n. 29), 145.

44 European Parliament and Council Convention Brussels Convention of September 27, 1968, on Jurisdiction and the Enforcement of Judgments in Civil and Commercial Matters, OJ 1998 C 27/1.

45 Regulation (EU) No. 1215/2012 of December 12, 2012, on Jurisdiction and the Recognition and Enforcement of Judgments in Civil and Commercial Matters (Recast), 2012 OJ (L 351) 1 ("Brussels I Regulation").

46 Ibid., Art. 4(1).

47 Ibid., Art. 62.

48 Ibid., Art. 63.

49 Ibid.; Roorda, "Jurisdiction in Foreign Direct Liability Cases in Europe" (n. 12), 163.

50 Enneking (n. 29), 146.

51 Ibid.

not be assumed over FDL claims against subsidiaries of TNCs that are domiciled in countries outside the EU.[52]

The Brussels I regime is exhaustive and mandatory. EU Member States are not allowed to deviate from it, because Member States are not permitted to rely on domestic doctrines, in cases within the regime's scope, if those domestic doctrines are inconsistent with the regime's provisions. For instance, in *Owusu v. Jackson*,[53] the European Court of Justice held that the English common-law doctrine of *forum non conveniens* could not be raised to challenge cases that fall under the ambit of the Brussels I regime, such as FDL claims. As a judge-made doctrine, *forum non conveniens* allows a judge to decline jurisdiction because another forum or court is more favourable for the interests of all parties, and for justice to prevail.[54]

The Brussels 1 regime laid the foundation for FDL cases in the EU Member States, and in the next section, this contribution will look at the recent decisions embodying FDL.

3.2. SELECTED FDL CASES IN THE EU MEMBER STATES

In *AAA v. Unilever*,[55] the claimants argued that Unilever PLC, a TNC registered in the UK, and its Kenyan subsidiary, Unilever Tea Kenya Limited, were individually liable to the employees and families of the Kenyan subsidiary for failing to provide adequate protection measures against violence. They argued that the failure to provide the necessary safeguards was a breach of the duty of care which both the parent and the subsidiary companies owed them. The High Court first dismissed the claim, because the case against Unilever Tea Kenya Limited lacked a reasonable possibility of success, and there was no real issue to resolve between the claimants and Unilever. The court reached this decision by relying on the case of *Caparo Industries Plc v. Dickman*,[56] where a three-test approach for satisfying the existence of a duty of care was established: (1) the damage must be foreseeable; (2) there should exist, between the party owing the duty and the party to whom it is owed, a relationship characterised by the law as one of "proximity" or "neighbourhood";[57] and (3) the situation should be one in which the court considers it fair, just and reasonable that the law should impose a duty of a given scope upon one party for the benefit of the other.[58] Also, the

---

52 Ibid.

53 Case C-281/02, *Owusu v. Jackson*, 2005 ECR I-1383.

54 Catherine Cervone, "Recalibrating the *Forum Non Conveniens* Analysis: The Effects of Technology on Transporting Evidence" (2020) 18 *NJTIP* 91, 91.

55 *AAA & Others v. Unilever PLC and Unilever Tea Kenya Limited* [2018] EWCA Civ 1532.

56 *Caparo Industries Plc v. Dickman* [1990] 2 AC 605.

57 Ibid.

58 Ibid.

court was guided by the case of *Chandler v. Cape*,[59] in establishing the facts that must be proved before a parent company could be held accountable for the acts of its subsidiaries. In other words, the following must be shown to exist:

> [T]he parent and subsidiary businesses are substantially identical; the parent has, or should have, superior knowledge in the particular industry; the subsidiary's system of work is unsafe, as the parent company knew or should have known; and the parent knew or should have anticipated that the subsidiary or its employees would rely on the parent's superior knowledge for protection.[60]

On appeal, while appreciating the criteria established in *Chandler*, the English Court of Appeal provided two more tests. It held that the parent–subsidiary relationship would be implied for FDL cases "(i) where the parent has in substance taken over the management of the relevant activity of the subsidiary in place of (or jointly with); or (ii) where the parent has given relevant advice to the subsidiary about how it should manage a particular risk".[61]

Vedanta v. Lungowe[62] also presents an opportunity to expand the FDL jurisprudence. The case was first filed at the UK High Court Division on 31 July 2015, by 1,826 Zambian citizens who sought redress for various acts of environmental damage, damage to property, and denial of the right to the enjoyment of land, in Zambia. Konkola Copper Mines, a subsidiary of Vedanta Resources plc, a UK-registered TNC, caused these acts. The claimants relied on the Brussels I Regulation to argue that the UK-based Vedanta was accountable for the acts of its subsidiary in Zambia. The claimants also argued that Konkola Copper Mines was a "necessary and proper" party, which would permit service of court processes outside of the UK. While dismissing the defendants' argument for the court to decline jurisdiction, the UK Supreme Court ruled that an EU Member State cannot decline jurisdiction where the defendant is a company domiciled in that Member State. Going further, the court found that there was a triable case, since Vedanta sufficiently intervened in the management of its subsidiary in Zambia, and, by implication, assumed a duty of care towards the claimants. The UK Supreme Court appreciated that, ordinarily, the Zambian courts should have been the proper fora for the case, but reasoned that there was a likelihood of denial of access to substantial justice to the victims.[63] The court arrived at the possibility of denial of access to substantial justice for the victims by examining the fact that the victims were indigent, and would not obtain local legal aid. They could not obtain the services of legal experts who were

59 *Chandler v. Cape* [2012] EWCA Civ 525.
60 Ibid., para. 80.
61 *Unilever* (n. 55).
62 *Vedanta Resources Plc and Konkola Copper Mines Plc v. Lungowe and Others* [2019] UKSC 20.
63 Ibid., para. 97.

knowledgeable enough to manage the scale and complexity of the case.[64] Being a jurisdictional judgment on an anchor defendant, the judgment hinged partly on Article 4 of the Brussels I Regulation. The court ruled that the fundamental rule in Article 4 of the Brussels I Regulation is intended to safeguard the EU domiciliary, and provide a claimant with reasonable certainty on the jurisdiction in which they may sue. For an anchor defendant to be liable for the activities of its subsidiaries abroad, there must be "an opportunity to take over, intervene in, control, supervise or advise the management of the relevant operations (including land use) of the subsidiary".[65]

The ruling was also based on the decision in *Owusu*. The court contended that *Owusu* granted any claimant (regardless of their domicile) the right to sue an English-domiciled defendant in England without facing a *forum non conveniens* challenge, even where the contending parties for jurisdiction were England and a non-Member State, such as Zambia, as in this case.[66] This judgment establishes the "four *Vedanta* routes" through which a parent company could owe a duty of care in circumstances where its foreign subsidiary had caused harm. This was an apparent rejection of the argument that a duty of care could only arise in exceptional circumstances, as in *Chandler*.[67] These routes are as follows:

1. A parent company takes over the management or joint management of the relevant activity of its subsidiary.
2. A parent company provides defective advice and/or promulgates defective group-wide safety/environmental policies that its subsidiary then implements.
3. A parent company promulgates group-wide safety/environmental policies and takes active steps to ensure its subsidiary's implementation of those policies.
4. A parent company holds out that it exercises a particular degree of supervision and control of its subsidiary.[68]

In 2021, the UK Supreme Court handed down another judgment regarding FDL cases, in *Okpabi and others v. Shell*.[69] On 12 February 2021, the UK Supreme Court defined the concept of parent company liability, in a decision involving two lawsuits taken against Royal Dutch Shell plc (RDS) and its Nigerian

---

64 Ibid., para. 95.

65 Ibid., para. 49.

66 Ibid., para. 16. See Pamela Towela Sambo, "*Vedanta Resources PLC and Konkola Copper Mines PLC v Lungowe and Others* 2019 UKSC 20" (2019) 2 *SAIPAR CR* 8.

67 *Chandler* (n. 59).

68 See Will Owen, "The *Vedanta* Route: *Okpabi vs Royal Dutch Shell Plc*', *Global Mining Review*, 9 March 2021, https://www.globalminingreview.com/mining/09032021/the-vedanta-route-okpabi-vs-royal-dutch-shell-plc/.

69 *Okpabi and others v. Royal Dutch Shell Plc and another* [2021] UKSC 3.

subsidiary, the Shell Petroleum Development Company of Nigeria (SPDC), by hundreds of Nigerian villagers. The UK Supreme Court determined that a real issue existed between the claimants and RDS that deserved to be resolved. Thus, the UK Supreme Court reiterated, and expanded on, its earlier ruling in *Lungowe* regarding parent company liability through FDL litigation.[70] The case consisted of two sets of litigation: one brought by around 40,000 people of the Ogale village in Rivers State, Nigeria, and another brought by 2,335 residents of the Bille community in Rivers State.[71] The claimants held both RDS and its Nigerian subsidiary SPDC accountable for environmental damage caused by oil spills from SPDC-operated pipelines and infrastructure, which they contended resulted from the operating company's poor pipeline maintenance and spill response. Additionally, they contended that RDS owed them a common-law duty of care, because it exercised significant control and direction over its subsidiary, including promulgating, monitoring, and enforcing group-wide health, safety and environmental policies and standards.[72] The defendants objected to the service of the claims on SPDC, outside of the UK, as a "necessary and proper party". They argued that there was no "real issue to be tried".[73]

While approving the four *Vedanta* routes, the UK Supreme Court made it apparent that they are not exclusive, and that the standard for parent company responsibility is broad and non-restrictive. It was decided that the enactment of group-wide policies and standards could trigger a duty of care in the operation of one of the parent company's subsidiaries, in line with *Vedanta*.[74] The UK Supreme Court also rejected the argument that there needs to be evidence that the parent company exercised "operational control" over its subsidiary, for liability to arise. Instead, the court held that "the extent to which, and the way in which the parent availed itself of the opportunity to take over, intervene in, control, supervise or advise the management of the relevant operations … of the subsidiary" should be the operative test for liability, rather than focusing "inappropriately on the issue of control".[75] A parent company could incur liability if it held itself out as providing supervision and control over its subsidiaries but omitted to do so. According to the court:

> [T]he parent may incur the relevant responsibility to third parties if, in published materials, it holds itself out as exercising that degree of supervision and control of its

70 See Leigh Day Legal Briefing, "Supreme Court clarifies parent company liability principles in claims by Nigerian communities against Royal Dutch Shell", *Leigh Day*, https://www.leighday.co.uk/media/3h1dsha4/shell-sc-judgment-legal-brief-120221.pdf.

71 *Okpabi* (n. 69), para. 3.

72 Ibid., para 7; Lucas Roorda and Daniel Leader, "*Okpabi v Shell* and *Four Nigerian Farmers v Shell*: Parent Company Liability Back in Court" (2021) 6 *BHRJ* 368, 370.

73 *Okpabi* (n. 69), para. 10.

74 Ibid., para. 143.

75 Ibid., para. 146.

> subsidiaries, even if it does not, in fact, do so. In such circumstances, its very omission may constitute the abdication of responsibility which it has publicly undertaken.[76]

The cases discussed so far are English cases, but current EU Member States have also allowed FDL cases as a mechanism for the accountability of TNCs. For instance, a Dutch Court of Appeal, in *Four Nigerian Farmers and Stichting Milieudefensie v. Shell*,[77] allowed an FDL case as a mechanism for accountability against RDS and its subsidiary in Nigeria. The claims are the same as in *Okpabi*, as they relate to three separate oil spills from Shell-operated pipelines in some communities in Nigeria. The victims sued RDS and SPDC as co-defendants, alleging that the oil spills were due to their failure to maintain their old pipelines. The oil spills damaged cultural farmlands and fishing grounds of the communities. The co-defendants contested the allegations, arguing that the spills resulted from sabotage. They claimed to have responded effectively to the spills by shutting down pipelines, sealing off leaking pipes, and cleaning up polluted lands. The Dutch Court of Appeal ruled that SPDC was strictly liable for damage caused by two spills, and had acted negligently in its initial response to those spills. The judgment is unique in many aspects. Firstly, the court relied on the common-law duty of care, and Nigerian legal instruments like the Oil Pipelines Act,[78] because Nigeria, as a common-law country, has common law as one of the sources of its legal regime. According to the court, the justification for this was Article 7 of the EU's Rome II Regulation, which provides that "the law of the country in which the event giving rise to the [environmental] damage occurred" shall be the applicable law.[79] Secondly, it is the first time a court in a TNC's home state has held a subsidiary outside its jurisdiction accountable for harmful activities.[80] The court determined that the company was subject to strict liability for damage caused by the spills, under Article 11(5)(c) of the Oil Pipelines Act of Nigeria, and that Shell had failed to prove "beyond reasonable doubt" that an exception to this strict-liability standard applied. Concerning the damage caused by the company's actions, the court determined that it had committed a tort of negligence under Nigerian common law.[81]

---

76 Ibid., para. 148.

77 *Four Nigerian Farmers and Stichting Milieudefensie v. Royal Dutch Shell Plc and another* [2021] ECLI:NL:GHDHA:2021:132 (Oruma), ECLI:NL:GHDHA:2021:133 (Goi) and ECLI:NL: GHDHA:2021:134 (Ikot Ada Udo).

78 Oil Pipelines Act of Nigeria, Cap. O7 LFN 2004.

79 Regulation (EC) No. 864/2007 of the European Parliament and of the Council of 11 July 2007, on the law applicable to non-contractual obligations (Rome II) L 199/40.

80 Both *Vedanta* and *Okpabi* were based on UK jurisdiction, while the US ATS cases were either settled or dismissed. See Lucas Roorda, "Broken English: A critique of the Dutch Court of Appeal decision in *Four Nigerian Farmers and Milieudefensie v Shell*" (2021) 12 *TLT* 144, 146.

81 *Four Nigerian Farmers* (n. 77); Roorda, "Broken English" (n. 80), 146.

Although not as recent, an FDL case has also been witnessed in Italy. In *Eni v. Ikebiri*,[82] ENI, an Italian TNC, and its Nigerian subsidiary, the Nigerian Agip Oil Company (NAOC), were sued in the Ordinary Court of Milan, for environmental harm that polluted the fishing ponds and trees essential to the local community's survival. In October 2018, NAOC achieved an out-of-court and confidential settlement agreement with the victims, after several months of discussion through negotiations parallel to the court proceedings.[83]

The French Supreme Court, in March 2022, handed down a ruling allowing non-governmental organisations (NGOs) Sherpa, and Friends of the Earth France, access to documents that would prove the role of Perenco SA, a French company, in the management of oil operations in the Democratic Republic of Congo (DRC). The facts of *Sherpa and Friends of the Earth France v. Perenco SA*[84] are that Perenco, an oil TNC, was accused of creating substantial environmental damage on numerous occasions in DRC. Numerous reports condemned the devastation caused by crude oil spills, toxic product discharge, and gas flaring under unsafe conditions. Perenco operates in the DRC through four different entities, and has connections with political power in the country.[85] Since it is a significant contributor to the DRC government budget, it argued that Congolese laws should be applicable instead of French law, which would have prevented them from being required to produce the requested documents. In granting the NGOs access to the documents, the French Supreme Court ruled that the possibility of filing the suit, and the nature of the request, could only be according to Article 145 of the French Code of Civil Procedure, and not foreign law.[86] This ruling can be contrasted with the Dutch Court of Appeal's decision in *Four Nigerian Farmers*,[87] because whereas the Dutch Court of Appeal relied on the positive laws of Nigeria, and common-law principles as applicable in Nigeria, the French Supreme Court rejected the argument that foreign law should be the appropriate law.

---

82 *Ododo Francis (Ikebiri Community' representative) v. ENI and NOAC (ENI Nigerian subsidiary)*. The court dismissed the proceedings; it is, therefore, not possible to provide a reference for the case.

83 See Alejandro García Esteban and Christopher Patz, *Suing Goliath: An Analysis of civil proceedings brought against EU companies for human rights abuses and environmental harm in their global operations and value chains, and key recommendations to improve access to judicial remedy* (European Coalition for Corporate Justice, 2021), 22–25.

84 *Sherpa and Friends of the Earth France v. Perenco SA*, Ruling of 9 March 2022, reported by the Business and Human Rights Centre on 10 March 2022: see https://www.business-humanrights.org/en/latest-news/french-high-court-rules-in-favor-of-ngos-in-perenco-environmental-case-for-alleged-harm-in-the-democratic-republic-of-congo/.

85 Esteban and Patz (n. 83), 27.

86 Sherpa and les Amis de la Terre France, "Victory over the Transnational Corporation Perenco: a step forward in the fight against opacity and for access to justice", *Sherpa*, 10 March 2022, https://www.asso-sherpa.org/victory-over-the-transnational-corporation-perenco-a-step-forward-in-the-fight-against-opacity-and-for-access-to-justice.

87 *Four Nigerian Farmers* (n. 77).

The above cases are evidence of the increasing possibility and willingness of European Member States' national courts to hold TNCs headquartered in their countries accountable for environmental pollution and other breaches, through FDL litigations. The next section will look at the setbacks suffered by the US ATS, as an FDL tool, and how FDL might suffer similar setbacks in Europe.

4. THE FAILING ATS AND LESSONS FOR FDL CASES IN EUROPE

It is imperative to start this section by highlighting that the US ATS and the various FDL cases in Europe share many similarities. For example, claims under both the ATS and FDL are brought on behalf of victims of harmful acts done by subsidiaries or local contractors of TNCs, where such victims have little or no recourse to justice in the state where the harmful acts occurred.[88] Some failed ATS cases were refiled in Europe, but the applicable laws were not the same in both situations. In ATS cases, victims must show that the harm committed is against the law of nations or any convention to which the US is a party.[89] All of the FDL cases in Europe have been based on ordinary tort law, and subject to the domestic law of either the country where the harm was committed – as in *Four Nigerian Farmers* – or the law of forum, as in *Sherpa and Friends of the Earth*.[90]

The US Supreme Court has continued to narrow the applicability of the ATS, to the extent that one can question whether it is still useful for victims of harm committed by TNCs, as an accountability mechanism. In *Kiobel*,[91] the Supreme Court gave a devastating disapproval to the use of the ATS to hold foreign corporations accountable. Rebuttal of the "presumption against extraterritoriality" was introduced as an element of the ATS in this case, where Shell was accused of using Nigerian military officers in the killing and torturing of, and causing environmental pollution to, the Ogoni community in Nigeria. By extraterritoriality, the court cited with approval the case of *Morrison v. National Australian Bank Ltd.*,[92] where it was held that the US Congress enacts a statute to apply only in the US. The court thought that the events in a Nigerian community did not "concern and touch the US with sufficient force."[93] Although the majority judgment did not disclose the circumstances in which a claim touches and concerns the US, Justice Alito, who concurred in part, opined that once conduct violates international law, it is conduct that touches and concerns

88 Roorda, "Jurisdiction in Foreign Direct Liability Cases in Europe" (n. 12), 161–162.
89 *Sosa* (n. 36).
90 Roorda, "Jurisdiction in Foreign Direct Liability Cases in Europe" (n. 12), 162.
91 *Kiobel* (n. 37).
92 *Morrison v. National Australian Bank Ltd.* 561 US 247, 255 (2010).
93 *Kiobel* (n. 37).

the US.[94] Scholars have rejected this as the most unlikely interpretation of the majority judgment.[95] Although the judgment was silent on whether a foreign TNC could be sued under the ATS at all, it has been described as the "first premature obituary"[96] of the ATS.[97]

In relation to the case of *Jesner*,[98] it has been said that the "immediate result of excluding foreign corporate liability places the ATS on life support",[99] and, for some other scholars, it is a complete exclusion of foreign TNCs from US federal courts.[100] In this case, a bank based in Jordan was alleged to have been a constructive partner in a series of acts of terrorism, by serving as a medium through which funds for the financing of terrorism were transferred. The only connection with the US was its branch in the US, where it was alleged that part of the money was transferred. The court decided that foreign TNCs cannot be sued in the US unless there is a satisfaction of the requirements in *Sosa*, i.e. that the alleged tort violates "a norm that is specific, universal and obligatory".[101] Another reason given by the court was that allowing such cases in the US would likely create diplomatic problems between the US and other countries, and that only the lawmakers and the executive could determine questions relating to diplomatic relations.[102]

Finally, *Nestlé USA*[103] was a class action against Nestlé USA, Inc., Cargill, Inc., and other companies, for aiding and abetting child slavery in Côte d'Ivoire and Mali. The US Supreme Court held that all the acts alleged to have been committed by the American companies were outside of the US, and that, based on *Jesner*, the ATS cannot have an extraterritorial application without a proper connection to the US. Finally, the court held that a "mere corporate presence" in the US was not enough to establish an extraterritorial connection.[104] The decision appears to end the *Filartiga* line of ATS claims against persons whose relevant conduct happens outside the US. Additionally, it appears to limit the ATS cause of action in relation to claims against US TNCs for behaviour occurring in the US that extends beyond decisions on operating operations abroad.[105]

---

94 Ibid., 1670 (Alito J, concurring).

95 Ralph G. Steinhardt, "Determining Which Human Rights Claims 'Touch and Concern' the United States: Justice Kennedy's *Filartiga*" (2014) 89 *NDLR* 1695, 1705.

96 Ibid., 1696.

97 Ugwu, "Establishing Accountability" (n. 11), where these cases are discussed.

98 *Jesner* (n. 19).

99 *Harvard Law Review*, "*Jesner v. Arab Bank, PLC*" (2018) 132(1) *HLR 397* (9 November 2018), <https://harvardlawreview.org/2018/11/jesner-v-arab-bank-plc/>.

100 Rebecca Hamilton, "*Jesner v. Arab Bank*" (2018) 112 *AJIL* 720–724.

101 *Sosa* (n. 36).

102 Ibid., 1405–1406.

103 *Nestlé USA* (n. 9).

104 Ibid., 5.

105 William S Dodge, "The Surprisingly Broad Implications of *Nestlé USA, Inc. v. Doe* for Human Rights Litigation and Extraterritoriality", *Just Security*, 18 June 2021, https://www.justsecurity.

In summary, the following setbacks suffered by ATS cases could surface in the future regarding FDL cases:

1. Extraterritoriality: in *Kiobel*, the court insisted that US laws only have effects within the US. If a US law is to apply to acts committed outside the country, the claimants must rebut the presumption against the extraterritorial applicability of the law. In *Sherpa and Friends of the Earth*, the defendants were unsuccessful in persuading the French Supreme Court that Congolese laws should apply instead of French laws since the acts complained of happened in DRC. Thus, another EU national court might be willing to adopt this reasoning in *Kiobel* to require that claimants must rebut the presumption against extraterritoriality.
2. Sovereign immunity: some TNCs are wholly or partly owned by states, and holding such corporations accountable might be against sovereign immunity. States enjoy state immunity from prosecution,[106] and this extends to state agents and businesses. The US Foreign Sovereign Immunities Act[107] provides that this immunity is waived when a state engages in commercial activities,[108] but determining when a state is engaging in commercial activities has always been difficult.[109] SPDC, a subsidiary of Shell plc (formerly known as the Royal Dutch Company), is partly owned by the Nigerian government, since it owns up to a 55 per cent share in the joint venture guiding the ownership structure of SPDC.[110] The implication is that, while holding parent companies and subsidiaries accountable through the FDL, a court of another country could be indirectly stepping on another country's sovereignty.
3. Foreign Policy Doctrine: among other reasons, *Jesner* failed because of the fear expressed by the court that holding a foreign corporation liable for breaches committed in other countries would significantly affect US relations with other countries.[111] Many developing economies depend on TNCs for revenue, and this has been suggested as one of the reasons why these countries may be unwilling to prosecute corporations for various

org/77012/the-surprisingly-broad-implications-of-nestle-usa-inc-v-doe-for-human-rights-litigation-and-extraterritoriality/.

106 Malcolm N. Shaw, *International Law* (6th ed., Cambridge University Press, 2008), 697.

107 Foreign Sovereign Immunities Act 28, §§1330 (1976).

108 Ibid., s. 1605(a)(2).

109 Sascha-Dominik Bachmann, *Civil Responsibility for Gross Human Rights Violations: The Need for a Global Instrument* (Pretoria University Law Press, 2007), 20; *Saudi Arabia v. Nelson* 507 US 349 (1993); *Cicippio v. Islamic Republic of Iran* (1994) 30 F.3d 164 (DC Cir.).

110 Shell plc, "Who we are: Shell in Nigeria", https://www.shell.com.ng/about-us/who-we-are.html#:~:text=Shell%20holds%20a%2025.6%25%20share,%25)%20and%20ENI%20(10.4%25.

111 *Jesner* (n. 19), 1405–1406.

breaches.[112] Thus, holding a corporation accountable for acts committed in a country unwilling to prosecute for economic reasons may trigger diplomatic issues.

A difference from the possible setbacks that have affected ATS litigation is that FDL cases in Europe are not based on a unified substantive law. The absence of such a legal regime means that FDL cases are based on tort law, according to each EU Member State's domestic legal system, and are thus subject to private international law applicable to other tort cases with transnational elements.[113] All the FDL cases discussed, and that the present writer is aware of, except *Four Nigerian Farmers*, are procedural. Even in *Four Nigerian Farmers*, which was the first time a court in a TNC's home state had held a subsidiary located outside of its jurisdiction accountable for harmful activities, the court misapplied the common-law principles. This could be because the judges were not experts in common-law principles.[114]

5. EUROPEAN COMMISSION PROPOSAL FOR A DIRECTIVE ON CORPORATE SUSTAINABILITY DUE DILIGENCE

The European Commission, on 23 February 2022, adopted a Proposal[115] aimed at imposing "obligations for companies regarding actual and potential human rights adverse impacts and environmental adverse impacts, with respect to their own operations, the operations of their subsidiaries, and the value chain operations carried out by entities with whom the company has an established business relationship".[116] Corporations would be required to monitor and optimise their performance on child labour, worker exploitation, safe and healthy working conditions, biodiversity loss and pollution. The Proposal applies to corporations formed under the legislation of a Member State, and which fulfil one of the following conditions:

- EU corporations with more than 500 employees and more than 150 million euros in global net turnover.

112 Photeine Lambridis, "Corporate Accountability: Prosecuting Corporations for the Commission of International Crimes of Atrocity" (2021) 53 *ILP* 144, 150.
113 Roorda, "Jurisdiction in Foreign Direct Liability Cases in Europe" (n. 12), 162.
114 Roorda and Leader (n. 72), 144–150.
115 European Commission Proposal for a Directive on Corporate Sustainability Due Diligence, Brussels, 23.02.2022 COM (2022) 71 final 2022/0051 (COD).
116 Ibid., Art. 1.

- EU corporations operating in high-impact sectors with more than 250 employees and more than 40 million euros in global net turnover.
- Non-EU corporations active in the EU, and generating turnover in the EU exceeding the thresholds mentioned above.[117]

The Proposal applies to subsidiaries of EU corporations, especially if they are "a legal person through which the activity of a 'controlled undertaking' … is exercised".[118] Such a subsidiary could likely be outside of the EU, in this case. Again, the turnover criteria create a territorial connection between non-EU countries and EU members,[119] and could serve as a basis for FDL cases in the future. The Proposal could be interpreted as a gradual attempt at codifying FDL principles, and creating a uniform law and grounds for FDL cases. When the Proposal finally comes into force, TNCs registered or operating in the EU, and their subsidiaries, could be held accountable for breaches committed abroad. One of the likely significant drawbacks is the thresholds it would create, with the consequence that many corporations that did not meet the thresholds would escape accountability. The Proposal clearly establishes the conditions for jurisdiction, and even though victims of TNCs' abuses would have to establish that those thresholds had been met or exceeded, it would be a more precise accountability mechanism than the ATS. It would positively create substantive and procedural aspects of TNCs' accountability, unlike the ATS, which is primarily based on the US Supreme Court's decisions.

6. CONCLUSION

The increasing impossibility of using the US ATS to hold TNCs accountable for environmental and human rights violations has shifted attention to FDL cases in the EU Member States. Even though it has already existed for some years now, FDL promises a viable alternative to the US ATS. FDL cases could encounter the same problems that have limited the usefulness of the ATS, however, so the EU should attempt to develop some substantive legislation that would guide future FDL cases. This will eliminate the problems of choice of law and applying an ununiform law. The wrong application of the common-law doctrine of negligence, as occurred in *Four Nigerian Farmers*, or the argument over whether Congolese or French law should apply, as in *Sherpa and Friends*

117 Ibid., Art. 2.
118 Ibid., Art. 3(d).
119 Ibid., Preamble, para. 24.

of the Earth, would have been avoided if there had been an existing substantive law on FDL litigations. Finally, the Proposal for a Directive is not yet in its final draft, and it is not certain when its implementation will start. Ultimately, it would strengthen FDL litigation in Europe by establishing substantive and procedural law on FDL litigations.

PART XI

ENVIRONMENTAL CRIMES

THE PROSECUTION OF ENVIRONMENTAL CRIMES THROUGH RESTORATIVE JUSTICE

The "Criminal Settlement Procedure" in the Italian System

Matteo RICCARDI and Paola MARTINO

1. INTRODUCTION

Italian legislation prosecutes "green" crimes through a gradual approach, up a kind of "criminal stair" that, from administrative offences, proceeds through misdemeanours, provided by Legislative Decree No. 152 of 2006 (the so-called "Environmental Code"),[1] to the most serious environmental crimes, introduced into the Criminal Code by Law No. 68 of 2015 on "ecocrimes".[2]

Law No. 68 of 2015, against the trend of punishment, introduced a novel instrument of criminal management – the "criminal settlement procedure" (CSP)[3] – which gives the offender the opportunity to extinguish some criminal offences provided by Legislative Decree No. 152 of 2006, by paying a fine and abiding by collaborative and reparative behaviours imposed by the public authority.[4] As a type of "diversion procedure", it aims to restore damages caused by less offensive environmental crimes, and to reduce the caseloads of courts, ensuring the certainty of environmental prosecutions, in terms of resilience of

---

1 *B. Romano (ed.), I reati ambientali alla luce del diritto dell'Unione Europea*, Cedam, 2013; *C. Bernasconi, Il reato ambientale. Tipicità, offensività, antigiuridicità, colpevolezza*, Edizioni ETS, 2008; *C. Ruga Riva*, "L'inquinatore nuovo tipo di autore", *Rivista italiana di diritto e procedura penale* (2/2020), pp. 1081 *et seq.*

2 On the reform process, see *A.L. Vergine*, "La strada dell'inferno è lastricata di buone intenzioni. A proposito del D.d.L. 1345/2014 sui delitti ambientali", *Rivista giuridica dell'ambiente* (5/2014), pp. 457 *et seq.*; *A.L. Vergine*, "I nuovi delitti ambientali: a proposito del d.d.l. n. 1345/2014", *Ambiente & Sviluppo*, (6/2014), pp. 443 *et seq.*

3 Please note that the phrase "criminal settlement procedure" (CSP) was coined by the authors and it is not provided by Law No. 68 of 2015, nor by other environmental legislation (such as the Environmental Code).

4 *M.C. Amoroso*, "La nuova procedura estintiva dei reati contravvenzionali previsti dal d.lgs. 152/2006. Quali direttive per gli organi accertatori?", *Diritto Penale Contemporaneo*, 2015.

the punitive system, and more generally to benefit the efficacy of environmental legislation.

The CSP has the potential to revolutionise the traditional concept of criminal justice, and represents a new model of environmental prosecution legislation, enhancing voluntary collaboration, that requires the offender to comply with some "criminal obligations", in order to restore the *status quo ante*.

Moreover, even though the CSP is intended to be applicable to individuals, it might potentially impact on legal entities – the most important perpetrators of environmental crimes – as Legislative Decree No. 231 of 2001 (Italian law on criminal corporate liability), as amended in 2011 to enforce Directive 2008/99/EC, also provides for the prosecution of legal entities for environmental crimes. Although the criminal corporate liability law does not actually provide an effective reward system of incentives, as will be seen below, courts' case law and legal doctrine are, nevertheless, starting to recognise that some legal measures, such as probation, can be applied in order to "re-educate" corporations.

The CSP, shifting the old paradigm, adds to the "sticks" of sanctions and punishments a virtuous system of "carrots", which, encouraging a restoration approach based on the concept of "prosecution through remediation", increases environmental protection, and alleviates the burden on the criminal courts.

The aim of this contribution is to highlight the positive effects of the CSP, and, more generally, of the instruments of restorative justice,[5] on the criminal justice system, and to consider whether, *de iure condendo*, the CSP can be applied more widely in the context of environmental crimes.

To this end, the criminal settlement procedures should, therefore, be promoted in the debate on the perspectives of criminal law, as legal instruments able to settle, "at the source", the conflict between the community and the authors of less serious infringements of environmental criminal law (or other sector-specific legislation, such as health and safety at work or food regulations), while, in the case of crimes, they could represent an additional sanction, combining the punitive and the restorative effect, as a deterrent to the commission of further offences.

2. ENVIRONMENTAL CRIMINAL LAW IN THE ITALIAN SYSTEM: OVERVIEW OF THE "CRIMINAL STAIR"

In the Italian system, the protection of the environment is based upon a strict permit and registration legislation, applicable to all activities that have, or can

---

5 For a general introduction to the theme of restorative justice in environmental criminal law, see *G. Mannozzi and V. Molteni*, "Restorative justice methods in conflicts related to environmental crimes", in *Associação dos Juízes Federais do Brasil – AJUFE (eds.), Restorative Justice and the Environment*, AJUFE, 2011, pp. 49–56.

have, adverse effects in relation to any of the environmental compartments – air, soil or water.

The relevant law is contained mainly in Legislative Decree No. 152 of 2006 (the "Environmental Code"), although the regulatory landscape is fragmented, and a large set of sectoral laws aimed at protecting the environment can be found in parallel regulations. This is the case, for example, of the legislation regarding landfill, the management of some particular waste streams (waste electrical and electronic equipment (WEEE),[6] end-of-life tyres,[7] end-of-life vehicles),[8] and some environmental authorisations (such as the Environmental Single Authorisation under Decree of the President of the Republic No. 59 of 2013).[9]

According to the Environmental Code, business activities that are likely to have significant effects on the environment are not "free", but are subject to prior authorisation or registration, to ensure their compatibility with sustainable development, to be granted only if special requirements and conditions established by the regulations to carry out the activity are met.[10]

However, once the authorisation has been obtained, business activities are still not "free", as they are also subject to rules, limits and case-by-case prescriptions that need to be complied with.

To this end, the Italian system provides several sectoral authorisations (for example, emissions-into-air authorisation, wastewater discharge authorisation, waste management authorisation), which, in some cases, and under some conditions, must or can be integrated into a single permit.[11]

For some of the most relevant, and potentially most impactful, activities specifically identified by law, the Environmental Code prescribes that an Environmental Impact Assessment (EIA (Italian acronym: VIA)), in implementation of Directive 2011/92/EU on the assessment of the effects of certain public and private projects on the environment) and/or an Integrated Pollution Prevention and Control permit (IPPC (Italian acronym: AIA)), in implementation of Directive 2010/75/EU on industrial emissions (integrated pollution prevention and control) must be obtained.

---

6 Legislative Decree No. 49 of 2014, implementation of the Directive 2012/19/EU on waste electrical and electronic equipment (WEEE).

7 Decree of the Ministry of the Environment and the Land and Sea Protection No. 182 of 2019.

8 Legislative Decree No. 209 of 2003, implementation of Directive 2000/53/EC on end-of life vehicles. On the criminal matters of the law, see *P. Fimiani*, "I reati in materia di veicoli fuori uso", *Rivista Rifiuti* (291/2021), pp. 5 *et seq.*

9 *S. Grassi and M.A. Sandulli, I procedimenti amministrativi per la tutela dell'ambiente, Trattato di diritto dell'ambiente, vol. II*, Giuffrè, 2014; *P. Dell'Anno, Diritto dell'ambiente*, Cedam, 2021.

10 *C. Vivani, Introduzione allo studio delle autorizzazioni amministrative. Tutela dell'ambiente e attività economiche private*, Giappichelli, 2020; *P. Fimiani*, "Il principio di precauzione nelle attività autorizzate", *Rivista Rifiuti* (247/2017).

11 *P. Dell'Anno and E. Picozza (eds.), Discipline ambientali di settore, Trattato di diritto dell'ambiente, vol. 2*, Cedam, 2013.

In addition to the obligation to obtain a permit for activities that have a potential impact on the environment, the Environmental Code imposes several further obligations (for example, obligations to report to the competent authority every change planned to installations by the operator and an obligation to supply the competent authority regularly with a set of data enabling it to verify that the business activity is being carried out in compliance with the law and the permit), in particular on those who carry out waste management. The Environmental Code, in fact, ensures traceability of waste from production to final destination, by imposing certain registration and reporting requirements on all waste handlers (see section Four of the Environmental Code).

Failing to comply with the above-mentioned provisions, set out in rules or authorisations, results in the imposition of penalties, which are determined according to the seriousness of the infringement and according to a gradual and integrated approach, as the same infringement can be punished with administrative, civil and criminal penalties.

Some cases that can be considered in relation to IPPC regulations are set out below.[12]

Any violation of the obligation to inform the competent authority of any "non-substantial" change in the nature or functioning of or an extension to the installation, which may have consequences for the environment, is subject to an administrative penalty (from 1,500 to 15,000 euros), while, if the change is "substantial", carrying it out without a permit incurs a fine of a criminal nature, from 2,500 to 26,000 euros (Art. 29-*quattuordecies*, paras. 5 and 6 of the Environmental Code).

Moreover, any breach of the permit conditions leads to the application of an administrative penalty, whereas if the breach relates to the management of waste, the penalty is of a criminal kind, even if still of a pecuniary nature (from 5,000 to 26,000 euros), and if the management of waste concerns hazardous waste, the criminal penalty involves a fine and imprisonment (Art. 29-*quattuordecies*, paras. 2, 3 and 4 of the Environmental Code).

For the same breach of the permit conditions, the responsible operator can also be punished with so-called "atypical" sanctions (Art. 29-*quattuordecies*, para. 9 of the Environmental Code).

The competent authority must proceed, according to the seriousness of the breach, to either:

- a warning, assigning a time limit within which the non-compliances must be eliminated, as well as a time limit within which all appropriate provisional or

12 For clarification on the application of the different types of infringements, as reconstructed by case law, see *G. Taddia*, "Le sanzioni in materia di Aia", *Rivista Rifiuti* (250/2017), and, more recently, *P. Fimiani*, "La violazione delle prescrizioni nell'esercizio degli impianti soggetti ad Aia", *Rivista Rifiuti* (293/2021), pp. 5 *et seq*. See also *P. Fimiani*, "Gli illeciti in materia di Aia dopo il Dlgs 46/2014", *Rivista Rifiuti* (218/2014).

complementary measures that the competent authority deems necessary to restore or provisionally ensure compliance must be applied; or
- a warning and the simultaneous suspension of the activity for a fixed period of time, where situations arise that constitute an immediate danger to human health or the environment or where violations are otherwise repeated more than twice in a year; or
- a revocation of the permit and the closure of the installation, in the case of failure to comply with the requirements imposed by the warning and in the case of repeated violations that result in situations of danger or damage to the environment.

It should also be noted that, in the Italian legal system, each kind of penalty listed above depends upon a very different standard of proof: the Italian system is based on the "more probable than not" principle for administrative/civil penalties and the "beyond any reasonable doubt" principle for criminal penalties.[13]

Even under the criminal law, "green" crimes are prosecuted through a gradual approach, up a kind of "criminal stair" that, from administrative offences, proceeds through criminal offences provided by the Environmental Code, to the most serious environmental crimes, introduced in the Criminal Code in 2015,[14] in implementation of Directive 2008/99/EC on the protection of the environment through criminal law.[15]

In 2015, more severe sanctions were, indeed, introduced for those environmental crimes which cause the most adverse effects arising in the environmental matrices,[16] such as environmental pollution, environmental disaster, and activities organised for illegal trafficking in waste.[17]

---

13 *D. Camici et al.*, *Bonifica dei siti contaminati*, Maggioli Editore, 2012; *M. Pelissero (eds.)*, *Reati contro l'ambiente e il territorio*, Giappichelli, 2013.

14 For a general overview of the crimes introduced by Law No. 68 of 2015, see *P. Fimiani*, *La tutela penale dell'ambiente*, Giuffrè, 2015; *C. Ruga Riva*, *Diritto penale dell'ambiente*, Giappichelli, 2021; *M. Telesca*, *La tutela penale dell'ambiente. I profili problematici della Legge n. 68/2015*, Giappichelli, 2021.

15 Note that, on December 2021, the EU Commission adopted a Proposal for a Directive of the European Parliament and of the Council on the protection of the environment through criminal law and replacing Directive 2008/99/EC, and the Communication to the European Parliament and the Council on stepping up the fight against environmental crime, COM(2021) 814 of 14 December 2021. On the prospects of reform of environmental criminal law, see *L. Siracusa*, "Prospettive di riforma della tutela penale dell'ambiente nel diritto europeo e sovranazionale", *Lexambiente – Rivista trimestrale di diritto penale dell'ambiente* (3/2021), pp. 1 *et seq.*

16 *L. Cornacchia and N. Pisani (eds.)*, *Il nuovo diritto penale dell'ambiente*, Giappichelli, 2018; *A. Galanti*, *I delitti contro l'ambiente*, Pacini Giuridica, 2021; *C. Ruga Riva (ed.)*, *La legge sugli ecoreati due anni dopo. Un dialogo tra dottrina e giurisprudenza*, Giappichelli, 2018.

17 It should be noted that the crime of "activities organised for illegal trafficking in waste" was originally provided by Art. 260 of the Environmental Code and, after being amended by Law No. 68 of 2015, it was moved in 2018, unchanged, into the Criminal Code (Art. 452-*quaterdecies*).

On a more serious level, there are also crimes against public safety, aimed at protecting the lives and physical integrity of an indefinite number of persons, such as "unnamed" environmental disasters and poisoning and contamination of water.

In general, it can be noted that these offences aim to ensure the exercise of control by the competent authorities over potentially environmentally hazardous activities, whereas the subject of the protection of the new crimes, introduced in 2015, is identified more properly with the environmental asset.[18]

The identification of the environment as an asset, to be protected "as such", and the consequent normative evolution, has been accompanied by a changed collective sensibility that found its culmination, in Italy, with the introduction, in 2022, of environmental protection within the Constitution (a protection that, in the absence of express provisions, had at first been guaranteed by the Constitutional Court, through an extensive interpretation of the different principles of protection of the landscape and human health).

Law No. 68 of 2015, as anticipated, represented a relevant step change in the criminal protection of the environment, by introducing, into the Criminal Code, crimes punished with severe and afflictive sanctions (not only detention, but also the confiscation of the profit of the crime). At the same time, the legislative reform provided, alongside the "ecocrimes", a set of legal instruments aimed at ensuring the remediation or restoration of the environment, in the form of an attenuating circumstance ("active repentance", including cooperation with the police or judicial authority), a case of exclusion of the confiscation (if the suspect or the defendant carries out safety, decontamination and environmental-reinstatement measures), a corollary of the criminal conviction ("restoration of the places"), or even a crime itself ("failure to restore the site", which punishes those who, being bound by the law, by a court order or by a public authority, do not proceed with the remediation or restoration of the site).

In this perspective, in line with Directive 2008/99/EC, which asks for proportionate and dissuasive criminal penalties, the reform also introduced a novel instrument of restorative justice – the environmental "criminal settlement procedure" (CSP) – governed by the provisions of a specific and dedicated section of the Environmental Code.

In summary, this discipline, which will be explained in detail in the next section, gives an offender the opportunity to extinguish some criminal offences provided by Environmental Code, by paying a fine and abiding by collaborative and reparative behaviours imposed by the public authority.

---

18 *A. Gargani*, "Jus in latenti. Profili di incertezza del diritto penale dell'ambiente", *Criminalia* (2019), pp. 111 *et seq.*; *F. Camplani*, "Tutela anticipata dell'ambiente e teoria del bene giuridico. Il ruolo fondamentale dei beni giuridici intermedi", *Lexambiente – Rivista trimestrale di diritto penale dell'ambiente* (3/2021), pp. 16 *et seq.*

CSP is based on three essential considerations:

(1) The inefficacy of the classic criminal approach towards less severe environmental offences.
(2) The need to guarantee a ready answer to the damages or dangers arising from environmental offences.
(3) The *favor rei* approach for those who, even if responsible for a crime, cooperate with the authority to eliminate the negative consequences for the environment.

From an examination of the environmental criminal penalty system, it appears that the Italian legislator favoured a restorative approach (through the application of CSP) for those offences considered less serious, while reserving a punitive response for those considered more serious.

3. THE DISCIPLINE OF THE DIVERSION PROCEDURE FOR ENVIRONMENTAL CRIMES (SECTION SIXTH-*BIS*, LEGISLATIVE DECREE NO. 152 OF 2006)

3.1. REGULATORY FRAMEWORK

The procedure set out in the Italian Environmental Code can be considered a restorative instrument of criminal management; that is to say, a way to manage circumstances, relevant for criminal law and criminal proceedings, aimed not at punishing those responsible, but primarily at remedying the damage caused by the offence.[19]

From the point of view of court procedure, the law provides a pre-trial diversion procedure, as it prevents prosecution by suspending the preliminary investigations for the time necessary for the suspect to carry out the required restorative measures. It could be considered, for all purposes, a special procedure (in the Italian Code of Criminal Procedure, a "*procedimento speciale*"), additional to those already provided in the Code, which presents many similarities with probation.[20]

It is a new approach in environmental law, but not unique in the Italian system, as the legislation on health and safety at work (Legislative Decree

---

19 *A. Martufi*, "La 'diversione' ambientale tra esigenze deflattive e nuove tensioni sistemiche", *Diritto penale contemporaneo – Rivista trimestrale* (1/2018), pp. 293 *et seq*.

20 For an introduction to the discipline of the CSP, see *F. Pomes*, "Procedura estintiva delle contravvenzioni ambientali e funzione ripristinatoria del diritto penale", *Lexambiente – Rivista trimestrale di diritto penale dell'ambiente* (4/2019), pp. 60 *et seq*.

No. 81 of 2008, known as the Consolidated Law on Safety) already provide a similar procedure for criminal offences, which has proved its worth in judicial application, even though the respective regulations differ on some points.[21] More recently, a very similar procedure has also been introduced in the Food Safety Law (Law No. 283 of 1962, as amended by Legislative Decree No. 150 of 2022, in the implementation of the enabling Law No. 134 of 2021, the so-called "*riforma Cartabia*", which brings the recent reform of the Code of Criminal Procedure), but with significative differences.[22]

As the legal discipline of the CSP is very concise, the legal literature and the Public Prosecutor's Offices (the latter through the issuance of "guidelines"), often with differing interpretations, tried to resolve the ambiguities of the law, in order to achieve a homogeneous application in the national territory.

However, the wide variety of interpretations of the Public Prosecutor's guidelines caused a difference in treatment between those suspected, on the basis of their place of business and, as a result, between companies operating in one or other territory or even between different plants of the same company located in different geographic areas.

Nevertheless, the inspection and environmental control bodies (i.e. the Regional Environmental Protection Agencies (Italian acronym: ARPA)) also contributed to the standardisation process, through "circulars" or guidelines, including the recent SNPA Guidelines (2021)[23] issued by the National System for the Protection of the Environment (Italian acronym: SNPA),[24] the body that brings together all the ARPAs.

In the past few years, the Italian Court of Cassation has also shown an interest in this matter, by giving rulings on offences for which the defendants claimed the application of the CSP.

---

21 On the "diversion procedure" in the legislation on health and safety on work, see *D. Guidi*, "Regime sanzionatorio e cause di estinzione degli illeciti sulla sicurezza del lavoro", in F. Giunta and D. Micheletti (eds.), *Il nuovo diritto penale della sicurezza nei luoghi di lavoro*, Giuffrè, 2020, pp. 935 *et seq*. The differences between the procedures are highlighted by Constitutional Court, Judgment N. 76/2019, on the assumption that "protection of the environment and safety of workers, both of constitutional significance, don't require an equal protection".

22 *M. Riccardi*, "Dall'archiviazione meritata all'oblazione alimentare: il procedimento delle prescrizioni e l'estinzione delle contravvenzioni nella riforma Cartabia", *Rivista Penale* (1/2023), pp. 28 *et seq*.

23 *SNPA*, "Linee Guida SNPA per l'applicazione della Procedura di estinzione delle contravvenzioni ambientali, ex parte VI-bis D.Lgs. 152/2006 – Aggiornamento 2021". On the SNPA Guidelines, see *M. Chilosi and M. Riccardi*, "La procedura di estinzione delle contravvenzioni ambientali nelle Linee Guida SNPA (2021). Analisi sistematica e spunti di riflessione", *Percorsi Penali* (2/2022), pp. 91 *et seq*. On the effectiveness of the SNPA Guidelines in enviromental matters, see *P. Fimiani*, "Linee guida SNPA e responsabilità penale", *Rivista Rifiuti* (282/2020), pp. 5 *et seq*.

24 For more information about SNPA, see *G. Battarino*, "Il Sistema nazionale a rete per la protezione dell'ambiente tra diritto e organizzazione", *Lexambiente – Rivista trimestrale di diritto penale dell'ambiente* (2/2019), pp. 1 *et seq*.

Moreover, even if the CSP is intended to be applicable to individuals, it might potentially impact on legal entities, the most important perpetrators of environmental crimes, as provided for in the above-mentioned Directive 2008/99/EC on the protection of the environment through criminal law.[25] It should be noted, as mentioned above, that Law No. 68 of 2015 did not establish a link between the CSP and the system of corporate criminal liability under Legislative Decree No. 231 of 2001.[26]

In the Italian system, corporate criminal liability is provided for by Legislative Decree No. 231 of 2001, which includes some environmental crimes and also some offences provided for by the Environmental Code, the latter subject to the CSP, as predicate crimes of company liability.

In summary, the law regulates the corporate liability of legal persons, companies and associations for crimes committed or attempted by their directors or employees, in the interests of or to the advantage of the entity. Corporate criminal liability for environmental crimes was introduced, after a certain delay, by Legislative Decree No. 121 of 2011, implementing the above-mentioned Directive 2008/99/EC, by inserting a new Article 25-*undecies* in Legislative Decree No. 231 of 2001, later updated by Law No. 68 of 2015 on "ecocrimes". The liability of the entity must be based on an expression of company policy – a so-called "organisational failure" (*colpa di organizzazione*) – and the company may be exempted from liability if it is able to prove that it had previously taken all necessary measures to prevent the predicate crime, also through the adoption and implementation of a compliance programme,[27] the appointment of a supervisory body (*organismo di vigilanza*) and the adoption of a disciplinary system.

In comparison to other legal systems, for example the US, where deferred prosecution agreements (DPAs) or non-prosecution agreements (NPAs) are used, the Italian criminal corporate liability law does not actually provide an effective reward system of incentives for companies. The courts' case law and the legal literature are, nevertheless, starting to recognise that some legal instruments, such as probation, can be applied in order to "re-educate" the corporation.

---

25 *A. Alberico*, "Obblighi di incriminazione e 'controlimiti' nell'adempimento della Direttiva 2008/99/ce in materia di tutela penale dell'ambiente", *Rivista trimestrale di diritto penale dell'economia* (2/2014), pp. 233 *et seq.*

26 *M. Bonsegna and S. Miceli*, "La responsabilità amministrativa degli enti e la nuova 'oblazione ambientale': problemi di coordinamento e punti oscuri", *La Responsabilità amministrativa delle società e degli enti* (2/2018), pp. 275 *et seq.*

27 The compliance programme to prevent environmental crimes could be based on some international technical standards, such as the environmental management systems UNI EN ISO 14001 and Regulation 1221/2009/EC (EMAS).

3.2. THE CSP PROCEDURE: CONDITIONS FOR THE APPLICATION

The procedure is based upon some essential requirements. First, the proceeding must concern a criminal offence (not a crime),[28] which must be provided for in the Environmental Code. Criminal offences set out in the Criminal Code or in other special laws dealing with the environment (different from the Environmental Code) are excluded. At the same time, there is no doubt that administrative offences fall outside the scope of the procedure, despite the fact that the heading of the section, due to an oversight of the legislator, also refers to these.

On the other hand, the law does not specifically provide whether the procedure may be applied to all the criminal offences provided for in the Environmental Code regardless of the penalties, which could range from a fine to imprisonment, either jointly or as alternatives to one another. This is a very critical point, as the Italian Environmental Code, in many cases (for example, in the case of illegal hazardous waste management or for specific infringements of the IPPC) in which the restoration of the environment should be possible, imposes a joint penalty: both detention and a criminal fine.

The prevalent opinion within the legal literature and the guidelines is that criminal offences punishable only with a fine or with a fine alternative to detention, can be extinguished by the procedure, whereas the provision of the detention, eventually joint to fine, excludes its application. The main argument underlines the lack, in section Sixth-*bis* of the Environmental Code – unlike the Criminal Code (Article 135) – of a criterion for converting detention into a fine, so that it would be impossible to impose, at the end of the procedure, only a financial penalty on the suspect, as the Environmental Code states that it will be "a quarter of the maximum fine provided for the offence".[29] However, some interpretations support the idea that all proceedings regarding environmental criminal offences, in the abstract, could be regarded as falling within the CSP, in order to avoid the risk of widespread non-application.[30]

---

28 The Italian Criminal Code distinguishes two types of "crimes", on the basis of the respective sanctions: "delitti" (here referred as "crimes"), which represent the most serious offences, and "contravvenzioni", which constitutes the less serious offences (here referred to as a "criminal offence").

29 *V. Paone*, "La prescrizione dei reati ambientali secondo la l. 68/2015: non mancano dubbi interpretativi", *Ambiente & Sviluppo* (7/2016), p. 499; *A. Scarcella*, "L'istituto della prescrizione amministrativa e la sua applicabilità ai reati commessi dall'ente", *La responsabilità amministrativa delle società e degli enti* (3/2016), p. 25; *P. Fimiani*, "Limiti applicativi del sistema estintivo delle contravvenzioni ambientali tramite prescrizioni (Titolo VI bis TUA)", in *C. Ruga Riva (eds.), La legge sugli ecoreati due anni dopo. Un dialogo tra dottrina e giurisprudenza*, Giappichelli, 2018, p. 119.

30 *A. Melchionda*, "La procedura di sanatoria dei reati ambientali: limiti legali e correzioni interpretative in malam partem", *Lexambiente – Rivista trimestrale di diritto penale dell'ambiente* (1/2021), pp. 4 *et seq.*

Nevertheless, it should be noted that the recent discipline of the CSP introduced in the Food Safety Law specified that, in this matter, the procedure is also applicable, on one hand, to the offences provided for by special laws (on food and beverage hygiene, production, traceability and sale) and, on the other, to offences punishable with a fine together with detention.[31] The above differences in the legal discipline of the Environmental Code could raise, in the context of a criminal proceeding for an environmental offence, an issue of constitutionality before the Italian Constitutional Court for the violation of the principle of equality (Article 3 of the Constitution).[32]

The Environmental Code states that the application of the procedure is subject to another requirement, dealing with the lack of "damage or of concrete and actual danger for environmental, urban and landscape resources", which marks the difference between the environmental diversion procedure and the similar procedure provided for in the health and safety offences.[33] It represents a "quality" criterion, subsequent to the "punishment" criterion, which perfectly suits the rationale of the discipline – that is, to decriminalise only the less offensive infringements of environmental law – as it allows the "filtering" of offences whose effects on environment could be effectively restored.[34]

A strict interpretation of this condition would narrow the scope of the law, as the criminal offences of the Environmental Code are, in most cases, crimes "of abstract danger",[35] i.e. crimes punishing facts that, for the legislator, constitute, in themselves, a danger for the value protected (*bene giuridico*). On this view, as the danger would be "presumed", the procedure would never be applicable. Moreover, the common experience shows that every crime or offence determines

---

31 The different approach in the discipline of the "food safety CSP" is an express aim of the Italian legislator, which – as stated in the Explanatory Memorandum to Legislative Decree No. 150 of 2022 – justified this choice on the basis of the purposes of the legislative reform: to deflate criminal proceedings, to reduce cases in which the prosecution is time-barred and to increase the protection of certain legal assets, by promoting restorative behaviours.

32 *M. Riccardi*, "Dall'archiviazione meritata all'oblazione alimentare: il procedimento delle prescrizioni e l'estinzione delle contravvenzioni nella riforma Cartabia", *Rivista Penale* (1/2023), p. 31.

33 *V. Paone*, "Dopo tre anni dall'entrata in vigore della l. n. 68/2015, persistono dubbi e criticità in tema di estinzione delle contravvenzioni ambientali", *Lexambiente – Rivista trimestrale di diritto penale dell'ambiente* (1/2019), pp. 80 *et seq.*; *P. Fimiani*, "Gli aspetti problematici nel sistema di estinzione dei reati ambientali previsto dal titolo VI-bis del T.U.A.", *Lexambiente – Rivista trimestrale di diritto penale dell'ambiente* (4/2019), pp. 27 *et seq.*

34 *M. Poggi D'Angelo*, "La procedura estintiva ambientale: l'idea dell'inoffensività/non punibilità in ottica riparatoria e deflattiva", *Lexambiente – Rivista trimestrale di diritto penale dell'ambiente* (1/2022), pp. 37 *et seq.*; *M. Caterini*, "Le implicazioni sistematiche della nuova causa di estinzione delle contravvenzioni del Testo Unico dell'ambiente", *Rivista trimestrale di diritto penale dell'economia* (3–4/2016), pp. 579 *et seq.*

35 *A. Manna*, "Struttura e funzione dell'illecito penale ambientale. Le caratteristiche della normativa sovranazionale", *Giurisprudenza di merito* (10/2004), pp. 2162 *et seq.*; *L. Ramacci*, "I reati ambientali ed il principio di offensività", *Giurisprudenza di merito* (4/2003), pp. 817 *et seq.*

a minimum change to the environmental matrices, so that the "quality criterion" would exclude such infringements from the scope of the CSP.

The judicial practice and the above-mentioned guidelines, in order to ensure a broad application of the procedure, refer to the so-called "prescription purpose principle", according to which the procedure should be applied in all cases where the negative effects of the offence can be removed by the good environmental behaviour of the suspect, even when his criminal action has had a minimal impact on the environment. The SNPA Guidelines recognise the applicability of the CSP not only "when the prejudice for the environment could be remedied by measures having this effect and to which the suspect is entitled". In detail, the Guidelines support a "case-by-case" approach, through the "reversibility of the effects" criterion, on the basis of which the CSP should be able to ensure the "complete reversibility of the effects", to "easily and quickly remove" (in a time frame conducive to the criminal proceedings) those effects, and to "restore the site". The Guidelines, to corroborate this thesis, also state that not every crime causes "environmental damage" in a strict sense, which would preclude the CSP from applying to such crimes, as confirmed by the systematic analysis of the environmental legislation (see the concept of "environmental damage" under Article 300 of the Environmental Code) and the environmental criminal law (in particular, the crime of "environmental pollution" provided for in Article 452-*bis* of the Criminal Code), which refer only to "significant" and "measurable" changes of environmental matrices.[36] From this perspective, in accordance with the Guidelines, it would be possible to distinguish between "crimes that produce effects on the environment (to be remediated through the procedure) and crimes that produce an environmental damage for which the procedure is not applicable".

In the opinion of the present authors, the requirements explained above should be interpreted in line with the spirit of the reform, through a systematic approach to the CSP, extending the procedure's field of application to criminal offences punishable with a joint fine and detention, and, in order to ensure that circumstances causing a serious prejudice to the environment are prosecuted under the "ordinary" proceedings, "tightening the belt" on the interpretation of the requirement relating to damage to, or concrete danger for, the environment.

3.3. THE PROCEDURE: A "BRACKET" IN THE CRIMINAL PROCEEDING

The procedure consists of several steps, involving both administrative and criminal law authorities and the suspect. The first phase starts when the

36 On this issue, see also Court of Cassation, third section, Judgment N. 25528/2021; Court of Cassation, third section, Judgment N. 1131/2021.

police or environmental control bodies (ARPAs), when it is considered that an environmental criminal offence has been committed, lay down technical prescriptions to be complied with by the suspect within a mandatory time limit. The ARPAs are often involved during an administrative inspection (for example on the compliance with the permit) and have the same powers as the police.

The prescriptions can consist, for example, in the case of uncontrolled storage of waste, in the removal of waste, the subsequent recovery or disposal of waste after its classification with the appropriate waste code (EWC) and the transmission to the police of the documents relating to this transportation. In other cases, for example exceeding the emissions limit stated by the law or by an environmental permit, the suspect must draft a report on the causes of the exceedance and adopt adequate technical measures to avoid the repetition of the infringement. The statement of prescriptions can also include a set of urgent measures to stop dangerous situations or hazardous activities.

A different scenario can also occur, as the law provides for the cases where the reporting of a crime is submitted to the public prosecutor by an individual or by an official other than an ARPA officer (such as an official of the integrated water service provider). In such a case, the public prosecutor notifies the police or the inspection and control bodies, in order to start the procedure.

A special feature of the environmental CSP is that the prescriptions, to ensure their compliance with the environmental law, must be certified (with a "technical asseveration") by an environmental supervisory authority. This authority is not defined by the Environmental Code, but it is commonly identified with ARPA's officers.

The statement of prescription is notified not only to the suspect, but also, when the offence is related to the activity of a company, to its legal representative (for example, the chief executive officer, for an offence committed by the plant director). The company, even if it is not considered legally responsible for the payment of the fine, could contribute – as often occurs – to the remedial measures imposed, by arranging a specific budget, and could possibly pay the fine, in order to extinguish the offence.

In this phase, after the drafting of prescriptions, the police give the public prosecutor notice of the crime, for it to be recorded on the criminal register, while the law states that the criminal proceeding is suspended until the communication of the police about the compliance with (or breach of) the prescriptions. Nevertheless, the public prosecutor is allowed to carry out some urgent acts of criminal investigation, such as seizures (of the corpus delicti; or the profit of the crime) or evidence-gathering. Finally, the public prosecutor could also file a dismissal request, deciding not to prosecute the suspect, if the notice of crime is unfounded. The suspect (or the company on his behalf), as already said, has to comply with the prescriptions within the mandatory time limit fixed by the authorities, so that, in the event of a delay, the prescriptions will not be considered complied with and the suspect will not benefit from the procedure, with the sole exception of an extension, allowed by the police, upon an application by the suspect himself. Moreover, the Environmental Code, in the event of a late compliance that could be considered "reasonable" or a remediation achieved in a different way, recognises that the suspect could be allowed to pay a fine anyway, under Article 162-*bis* of the Criminal Code, but with a lower penalty reduction.

In a second step, the police check the implementation of the prescriptions and, in the event of an unsuccessful outcome, give notice of the procedural failure to the public prosecutor, who can now restart the prosecution of the suspect. If, however, the check has a positive outcome, the police issue the suspect with a statement of "admission to payment", in which the authority determines the amount of the penalty to be paid in order to extinguish the offence, warning the suspect that the payment must be made within a mandatory time limit (30 days from the notification). Any delay in payment leads to closure of the procedure and to the restarting of the criminal proceeding.

It has been debated whether the suspect should also be admitted to the procedure in two special cases: "voluntary restoration", when police do not provide prescriptions; and the "exhausted conduct" offence, which means that the offence has not produced negative effects to be removed. In such cases, in accordance with the case law,[37] the suspect can benefit from the procedure through the special mechanism called prescriptions "both then and now" (*ora per allora*),[38] which allows the police, in the first case, to "ratify" the actions carried out by the suspect on their own initiative and, in the second case, to admit the suspect to payment in the absence of any environmental restoration.

Partly related to that theme is the issue of the "formal" offence, widely diffused among the crimes provided by the Environmental Code; that is to say, an environmental offence consisting of a breach of the environmental legislation (for example, the lack of a permit or failure to renew a permit; or an infringement of obligations on traceability of waste),[39] which does not produce damage or a concrete danger for the environment. The SNPA Guidelines take a stand on this topic, arguing that the CSP could be applied in these cases, and they define a set of standard prescriptions which could be imposed on the suspect, such as, in more serious cases, the full or partial suspension of the activity subject to the permit; or, in a case of failure of notification (provided in Italy, instead of the permit, within the "simplified regime" for waste recovery), the notification to the competent authority; or, when the permit renewal has not been applied for, an application for the permit.

---

37 Court of Cassation, third section, Judgment N. 36405/2019.

38 Constitutional Court, Judgment N. 19/1998.

39 *A.R. Di Landro, La responsabilità per l'attività autorizzata nei settori dell'ambiente e del territorio. Strumenti penali ed extrapenali di tutela*, Giappichelli, 2018.

Regarding sanctions, it should be noted that the suspect, as in the case of a bargaining plea or sentence in a summary trial, obtains a considerable penalty reduction. The final penalty, equal to a quarter of the maximum fine provided for the criminal offence, represents a significant benefit for the suspect, bearing in mind that environmental crimes often incur high fines, in order to deter people from committing violations of legislation regarding waste, soil, water and air. For example, the fine (*ammenda*) imposed for the illegal management of non-hazardous waste amounts to a maximum of 26,000 euros, so that the suspect, after obtaining the permit, could extinguish the offence paying a reduced penalty of 6,500 euros. The CSP legal discipline states that the suspect must pay an "administrative fine" instead of a criminal penalty, making it debatable whether the law provides a depenalisation of the offence in the strict sense of the word, from criminal to administrative.

There is also a debate under way as to whether this "administrative fine" could represent a criminal sanction under the European Convention of Human Rights (ECHR), in light of the well-known "Engel criteria", with reference to the *ne bis in idem* principle, as the environmental law, as mentioned in the introduction, provides for different types of sanctions (administrative, criminal and restorative) to punish different aspects of violation relating to the same fact.[40] The issue involved is the lawfulness, pursuant to the ECHR, of the "twin track" deriving from the combined application, in different time frames, of different sanctions that, in spite of their "label", could be defined as "criminal".

It may be an "administrative" fine (as a result of the environmental CSP, representing, for all purposes, a phase of a criminal proceeding) and/or an administrative warning from the public authority (prescribing some mandatory obligations) and/or a "criminal" fine (which could be applied, for instance, for a different crime that does not fall under the scope of the CSP and is charged in a separate or in the same criminal proceeding), in relation to the same fact and against the same person (*idem factum*).

In such cases, according to the case law of the European Court of Human Rights, the judge should verify the "sufficiently close connection in substance and time", between the different proceedings and sanctions, and determine whether they correspond to an "integrated punitive approach" of the Italian legislator.

It should also be noted that, in contrast with other summary proceedings, at the end of the procedure the suspect is not formally convicted, but the case is closed by a request for dismissal by the public prosecutor, and by the subsequent dismissal decree of the judge, as the offence is extinguished.

40 For an overview of the expansive effects of the *ne bis in idem* principle inItalian case law, in light of the European legislation, see *M. Riccardi*, "Le frontiere mobili del ne bis in idem europeo come rimedio al doppio binario sanzionatorio: l'effetto red shift, dai crimini dei colletti bianchi verso il diritto penale 'comune'", *Bocconi Legal Papers* (14/2020), pp. 301 *et seq*.

That said, the legal discipline raises several problematic questions, whose resolution shapes the "borders" of the CPS in its concrete application. Firstly, it is not clear whether the commencement of the procedure by the police is compulsory or whether the police retain the discretion to determine whether or not the procedure should be applied: in other words, whether the environmental CSP is a "right" of the suspect, whose violation can be claimed in the subsequent phases of the criminal proceedings before the judge. The case law of the Court of Cassation currently states that the procedure, far from being a condition of criminal prosecution, is not mandatory, as the inspection and control body or the police can lawfully decide not to give prescriptions.[41] Likewise, the law does not specify whether, and under which circumstances, the police or the inspection and control body have to give reasons for the non-application of the procedure or even for the contents of the prescriptions. The SNPA Guidelines adopt a compromise approach, stating that the officers, in the notice of crime, have to provide "adequate and detailed reasons in those cases in which the procedure is considered not applicable", while, in cases of admission to the procedure, the reasons are usually implicit in the text of the statement. In the present authors' opinion, the obligation to state the reasons represents an essential guarantee of the procedure, including in cases of admission, as the suspect has an actual and concrete interest in knowing the legal and technical reasons at the basis of the prescriptions, in order to appeal the statement.

A similar question concerns the technical asseveration of the prescriptions, as some guidelines consider the certification unnecessary in certain cases (for example, when the prescriptions are given by a specialised body or they do not entail any technical evaluation), despite the law always requiring the asseveration. The SNPA Guidelines underline the relevance of the asseveration as an instrument that should ensure the pertinence and effectiveness of the prescriptions given to the suspect, their adequacy and legal or technical feasibility, also with reference to the time limit fixed in the statement, and their correspondence with standards. The law does not specify the role and the "powers" of the expert who certifies the prescriptions. On this point, ARPAs guidelines deny the expert the ability to modify or integrate the set of prescriptions, while the Public Prosecutor's Offices afford the expert a wider power to modify the contents of the statement.

The legal discipline of the CSP does not clarify how to manage the relationship between the criminal proceeding in which the CSP has started and the various administrative proceedings (for example, a warning from the public authority or remediation of the site) that could impose on to the responsible

41 Court of Cassation, third section, Judgment N. 7286/2022; Court of Cassation, third section, Judgment N. 19986/2021; Judgment N. 7220/2019; Judgment N. 49718/2019; Judgment N. 38787/2018.

prescriptions similar to those given in the criminal proceeding (for example, in the case of remediation, the obligation to start the preliminary investigation aimed at verifying a possible contamination of the site deriving from pollutants exceedance in soil and water). It is evident that a lack of coordinate between the two sets of proceedings can lead to a duplication of activities imposed on the suspect/responsible party, with the concrete risk of a "restorative" *bis in idem*.[42] It is not disputed that the prescriptions cannot be appealed before the administrative courts, as they constitute, for all purposes, an act of the police,[43] to be appealed in the criminal proceeding before the judge.

Another key point is to determine the phase of the criminal proceeding in which the procedure can be applied. Pursuant to the law, the procedure is started by the police at the beginning of the preliminary investigations, by giving prescriptions in the statement notified to the suspect. The Italian Constitutional Court recently ruled that the procedure can be started no later than the criminal prosecution.[44] The present authors believe, on the contrary, that the procedure could also be compatible with the preliminary phase of the trial, as recently recognised by the Court of Cassation,[45] at least in the above-mentioned cases of "voluntary restoration", which does not lead to an excessively long interruption of the trial (as the restorative activities have already been carried out), and suits the need to speed up the trial itself. On this specific point, it should be noted that such a solution is not uncommon, as the Italian criminal legal system already provides, in the probation procedure, a case of suspension of the trial, to allow the defendant to realise voluntary activities, so the CSP could be seen as a sort of an "environmental probation", requiring restorative measures in favour of the environmental matrices.[46]

Finally, another key point of the discipline is the role of the public prosecutor in the procedure, as the CSP seems to be a "procedure of the police", who start the procedure and manage every phase, whereas the public prosecutor is formally extraneous to this stage of the preliminary investigation.[47] Nevertheless, the most

---

42 *M. Chilosi*, "Estinzione delle contravvenzioni ambientali", in C. Ruga Riva (eds.), *La legge sugli ecoreati due anni dopo. Un dialogo tra dottrina e giurisprudenza*, Giappichelli, 2018, p. 133.

43 Council of State, Opinion N. 314/2019; Regional Administrative Court – Tuscany, Judgment N. 770/2015.

44 Constitutional Court, Judgment N. 238/2020. On the decision, see *D. Franzin*, "La procedura estintiva delle contravvenzioni ambientali al vaglio della Corte costituzionale: limiti e ragionevolezza della deroga del principio della retroattività della lex mitior", *Lexambiente – Rivista trimestrale di diritto penale dell'ambiente* (4/2020), pp. 91 *et seq.*

45 Court of Cassation, third section, Judgment N. 25528/2020.

46 *M. Riccardi*, "L'irretroattività 'attenuata' della procedura di estinzione delle contravvenzioni ambientali, tra procedimento e processo. La deflazione 'vince' sulla riparazione?", *Cassazione Penale* (2/2021), pp. 525 *et seq.*

47 Court of Cassation, third section, Judgment N. 25528/2021.

recent guidelines drafted by Public Prosecutor's Offices claim a "strong role" for the public prosecutor, who is entitled to verify the content of the prescriptions and also to have a "dialogue" with the suspect and his lawyer on the controversial issues of the criminal proceedings and, obviously, on the activation of the CSP procedure (power of veto).

4. CONCLUSIONS

The CSP adds, to the "sticks" of the sanctions provided by the environmental criminal law, a virtuous system of "carrots", which, by encouraging a restoration approach based on the concept of "prosecution through remediation", increases environmental protection and alleviates the burden on criminal courts.

In light of the above, the CSP procedure has the potential to revolutionise the traditional concept of criminal justice and represents a new model of environmental prosecution legislation, through means of voluntary collaboration, requiring the offender to comply with some "criminal obligations". It represents a form of criminal settlement whereby the state, in response to violations that cause minimal offence to the environment, forgoes trial and punishment, in return for the removal of danger or damage to the environment and payment of a penalty, which, although reduced, could be of a very large amount.[48] In short, the Italian legislator, in this specific context, seems to be moving away from the general environmental "polluter-pays principle", according to which the costs of measures to deal with pollution should be borne by the polluter, to the alternative approach of "who doesn't pollute pays". The latter means that criminal offences which have a minimal impact on the environment, in terms of danger or damage, and do not cause "pollution" in a strict sense, can ultimately be extinguished by paying a financial penalty, thus allowing the suspect to "settle the score" with criminal justice.

In this perspective, the CSP fits perfectly with the spirit of the law on criminal liability of corporations, especially in the case of environmental offences, as the purpose of Legislative Decree No. 231 of 2001 is not only to punish the corporation for its "organisational failure" in not taking the necessary preventive measures to reduce the risk of commission of a crime, but also to induce the corporation to repair damages and start a process of internal reorganisation. From this point of view, when an environmental crime is committed, with some negative consequences for the environment, corporations, due to their human and economic resources, are the main actors on the stage, as they can effectively remediate environmental damage. However, as mentioned above, the law does

48 V. *Dini*, "La mediazione penale ambientale: scenari non troppo futuribili", *Ambiente & Sviluppo* (4/2018), p. 248.

not provide that the CSP could be applicable to companies[49] and, moreover, the case law states that the CSP carried out by the natural person (for example, the chief executive officer of the company), due to the principle of "autonomy", does not relieve the liability of the company itself.[50] The company, currently, can only comply with the prescription imposed on the natural person and possibly pay the reduced fine on behalf of their manager or employee, to ensure the extinguishing of the individual's offence. However, the only benefits of the CSP to the company could be the reduction of the fine and the exclusion of the interdictory sanctions, if provided for by the law and applicable, pursuant to the provisions on the so-called "restorative actions" *(condotte riparatorie)*, which include, *inter alia*, the elimination of the harmful or dangerous consequences of the crime (Articles 12 and 17 of Legislative Decree No. 231 of 2001).

The topicality of this theme has emerged in the recent legislative reform of the Code of Criminal Procedure, introduced by the enabling Law No. 134 of 2021 (the so-called *"riforma Cartabia"*, implemented by the above mentioned Legislative Decree No. 150 of 2022), which, among its guiding principles, lays down the need to provide, during the preliminary investigation phase, a general cause for extinguishment of offences, in exchange for compliance with some prescriptions and the subsequent payment of a reduced fine.[51] The preparatory work on Law No. 134 of 2021, on the basis of experiences in other European countries,[52] even proposed a new hypothesis of "deserved closure" *(archiviazione*

49 For a reform proposal on this point, see *M. Riccardi and M. Chilosi*, "Verso il diritto punitivo dell'ambiente, 'tra chi fa il lavoro in modo onesto e i criminali'. Le novità del disegno di legge 'Terra mia'", *Giurisprudenza penale trimestrale* (4/2020), pp. 48 *et seq.*

50 *S. Petella*, "Ecoreati e responsabilità degli enti. Criticità e prospettive", *Diritto penale contemporaneo – Rivista trimestrale* (1/2018), pp. 323 *et seq.*

51 *F. Palazzo*, "I profili di diritto sostanziale della riforma penale", *Sistema Penale* (2021), p. 7. See also *G. Mannozzi*, "Nuovi scenari per la giustizia riparativa. Riflessioni a partire dalla legge delega 134/2021", *Archivio Penale* (1/2022). Law No. 134 of 2021, once again, did not consider the punitive system of corporations, despite a public announcement made by the Minister for Justice about the appointment of a commission for the reform of Legislative Decree No. 231 of 2001, which should evaluate the introduction of a set of restorative measures also applicable to corporations, in order to avoid prosecution or conviction to sanctions.

52 E.g. the German Code of Criminal Procedure (*Strafprozessordnung*) provides a similar case of non-prosecution (Art. 153a), whereby the public prosecutor can impose conditions on, and issue directions to, the accused, if these are of such a nature as to eliminate the public interest in criminal prosecution, and if the degree of guilt does not present an obstacle, e.g. rendering of a specified service in order to make reparations for damage caused by the offence; payment of a sum of money to a non-profit-making institution or to the Treasury; rendering of some other service of a non-profit-making nature; compliance with duties to pay a specified amount in maintenance; or making a serious attempt to reach a mediated agreement with the aggrieved person (victim–offender mediation), thereby trying to make reparation for the offence, in full or to a predominant extent, or to strive therefor. Likewise, the French Code of Criminal Procedure (*Code de procédure pénale*) foresees a form of criminal settlement (*composition pénale* under Article 41-2) that the public prosecutor can propose to the suspect, consisting in one of more of the measures provided by the law.

meritata) of the criminal proceeding – defined as a "third way" – applicable in cases of less serious crimes and based upon a specific request for an early closure of the proceeding by the public prosecutor or by the suspect, subject to compliance with some prescriptions in favour of the victim.[53]

In light of the above, the CSP should be promoted in the debate on the perspectives of environmental criminal law, as a legal instrument able to settle, "at the source", the conflict between the community and the perpetrators of less serious infringements of environmental criminal law, by requiring offenders to bear a financial burden, and to play an active role in the restoration of the negative consequences of the crime, in return for a non-prosecution agreement or at least a deferred prosecution agreement.[54]

This model of criminal management should also be extended, in the present authors' opinion, either through reform, or by way of interpretation, to the legislation on corporate criminal liability, which is becoming increasingly important in Italian criminal policy, as an instrument to enforce a process of self-regulation on corporations[55] and definitely as an added value in the economic chain. The perspective of avoiding prosecution and trial is an essential goal for corporations, which could match, as a negotiating outcome, the public interest in the prompt restoration of damage to the environment.

---

53 "Commissione di studio per elaborare proposte di riforma in materia di processo e sistema sanzionatorio penale, nonché in materia di prescrizione del reato, attraverso la formulazione di emendamenti al Disegno di legge A.C. 2435, recante Delega al Governo per l'efficienza del processo penale e disposizioni per la celere definizione dei procedimenti giudiziari pendenti presso le corti d'appello", Relazione finale e proposte di emendamenti al d.d.l. A.C. 2435, 2021, *Sistema penale* (2021), pp. 21 *et seq.*

54 For a contribution on the theme of prescriptive sanctions with restorative content, for environmental crimes, see *M. Dova*, "Vi è spazio per una pena prescrittiva – reintegratoria in materia ambientale?", *Lexambiente – Rivista trimestrale di diritto penale dell'ambiente* (1/2021), pp. 18 *et seq.*

55 *F. Centonze*, "Responsabilità da reato degli enti e agency problems. I limiti del d.lgs.vo. n. 231 del 2001 e le prospettive di riforma", *Rivista italiana di diritto e procedura penale* (3/2017), pp. 945 *et seq.*

PART XII

ENVIRONMENTAL LIABILITY

SCIENTIFIC UNCERTAINTIES AND RESPONSIBILITY IN ENVIRONMENTAL LAW IN THE ENVIRONMENTAL LIABILITY DIRECTIVE

Mariusz BARAN*

1. INTRODUCTION

Environmental law is, on the one hand, the law of risk, and, on the other, the law of distribution and protection of common goods over which a multitude of interests related to their use prevail.[1] The combination of these areas is programmatic: the aim is to create a uniform and comprehensive regulatory structure that can provide the environment (understood as a structure of action) with adequate protection aimed at eliminating environmental damage, removing environmental risks, avoiding other environmental risks, and restoring the ability of the environment to function.[2]

Therefore, it may reasonably be assumed that any human behaviour causing a threat to, or a violation of, the state or quality of the environment is, at the same time, a threat or a violation of the individual and/or collective right to use the environment.[3] Thus, the use of the environment and disposal of its resources has been subject to legal regulation aiming at protecting the environment in accordance with the requirements of "sustainable development", and taking into account, among other things, the principle of precaution and prevention, on the one hand, and the principles of liability for damage, and polluter-pays, on the other.[4]

* This study was prepared as part of the scientific project carried out under the contract concluded with the National Science Centre in Krakow, Poland on the basis of agreement no UMO-2016/21/D/HS5/03841 (Research project registration number 2016/21/D/HS5/03841).

1 See E. Schmidt-Aßmann, *Ogólne prawo administracyjne jako idea porządku* [*General Administrative Law as an Idea of Order*] (C.H. Beck, 2011), pp. 144–145.

2 See ibid., pp. 145–146.

3 Ibid.

4 See ibid., pp. 145–148.

The liability mechanism introduced by Directive 2004/35/EC on environmental liability with regard to the prevention and remedying of environmental damage (ELD),[5] prompts attempts to find and resolve problems related to scientific uncertainty *(the state of scientific and technical knowledge)* in the context of environmental law liability, in terms of bearing this liability.

According to the classical principles of liability in law, understood as "bearing the negative consequences foreseen by law for events or states of affairs subject to negative normative qualification and attributed to a legally defined entity in a given legal order",[6] it is necessary to establish the existence of a causal link between the act (action/omission) and environmental damage.

Directive 2004/35/EC aims to establish a framework for environmental liability based on a high level of environmental protection and the precautionary and "polluter-pays" principles, in order to prevent and remedy environmental damage caused by economic operators.[7]

In accordance with Articles 4(5) and 11(2) of Directive 2004/35, read in conjunction with Recital 13 in the preamble thereto, the following elements are required for the enforcement of the liability mechanism provided for by the Directive:

(1) The identification of one or more polluters (offenders).
(2) The damage should be identified and quantified.
(3) There should be a causal link (to be identified) between the damage and the identified polluter(s).[8]

5 Directive 2004/35/EC of the European Parliament and of the Council of 21 April 2004 on environmental liability with regard to the prevention and remedying of environmental damage (OJ 2004 L 143, p. 56); see. G. Winter, J. H. Jans, R. Macrory and L. Krämer, "Weighing up the EC Environmental Liability Directive" (2008) 20 *Journal of Environmental Law*, pp. 163–191; K. De Smedt, *Environmental Liability in a Federal System. A Law and Economics Analysis* (Intersentia, 2007) pp. 111–144; U. Salanitro, *Directive 2004/35/EC on Environmental Liability* (EFFACE, 2015).

6 W. Lang, "*Struktura odpowiedzialności prawnej. Studium analityczne z zakresu teorii prawa*" [*The Structure of Legal Liability. Analytical study from the field of legal theory*] (1968) 31 *Zeszyty Naukowe UMK*, p. 12 (author's own translation).

7 Case C-297/19, *Naturschutzbund Deutschland*, ECLI:EU:C:2020:533, para 31; cf., similarly, Case C-129/16, *Túrkevei Tejtermelő Kft.*, ECLI:EU:C:2017:547, paras. 47, 53, and the case law cited therein.

8 See Recital 13, second sentence, of Directive 2004/35/EC: "[w]here it is not possible to link the adverse effects occurring in the environment to the acts or failures of certain individual actors, liability is not an appropriate instrument to use in relation to diffuse widespread pollution."

The concept of causation (causing the pollution), i.e. the existence of a causal link, is crucial for imputing liability to the operator, as is apparent from Article 8(3)[9] and Recital 20 of the Directive.[10]

The following are, therefore, incumbent on the national authorities, in the context of an objective liability mechanism (this applies to environmental damage caused by operators whose activities fall within Annex III to the Directive 2004/35/EC):

- The prior establishment of the causes of the pollution found, the national authorities having, in that regard, a margin of discretion as to the choice of the procedures necessary for the adoption of measures, and the duration of such an investigation, with such establishment being made in accordance with national procedural rules (rules of evidence).
- The demonstration, "in accordance with national rules on evidence, [of] a causal link between the activities of the operators at whom the remedial measures are directed and the pollution".[11]

Where the obligation to provide remediation is shared between several operators, based on their respective contributions (different degrees of contribution) to pollution or the threat of pollution, it is the responsibility of the national authority to determine, as far as possible, the extent to which each of these operators has contributed to the pollution that they are required to remedy, and to take into account, as required by Article 9 of Directive 2004/35, their respective shares of the remediation costs.[12]

---

9 See ibid., Art. 8(3): "[a]n operator shall not be required to bear the costs of preventive or remedial action taken pursuant to this Directive if he can prove environmental damage or an imminent threat of such damage:

(a) was caused by a third party and occurred despite appropriate security measures; or

(b) resulted from compliance with a compulsory order or direction from a public authority other than an order or direction consequent upon an issue or event caused by the operator's own activities."

10 Ibid., Recital 20: "[a]n operator should not be required to bear the cost of preventive or remedial action taken pursuant to this Directive in situations where the said damage or imminent threat thereof is the result of certain events beyond the operator's control. In situations where the damage in question is the result of an authorised emission or event or where the potential for damage was not known when the emission or event took place, Member States may allow that operators who are not at fault or negligent in respect of that event do not bear the cost of remedial measures."; Cf. M. Baran "'Causal link' as a condition of liability in the Environmental Law: the example of the liability mechanism in Directive 2004/35/EC" in B. Pozzo and V. Jacometti (eds.) *Environmental Loss and Damage in a Comparative Law Perspective* (Intersentia, 2020), pp. 71–86.

11 See Order in Cases C-478/08 and C-479/08, *Buzzi Unicem and Others*, ECLI:EU:C:2010:129, para. 45; cf. also judgment in Case C-378/08, *ERG and Others*, para. 65; Baran, above n. 10, pp. 71–86.

12 Order in C-478/08 and C-479/08, *Buzzi Unicem and Others*, above n. 11, para. 47.

In the context of the liability mechanism introduced by Directive 2004/35/EC, the question arises *whether there are situations where the operator may not be held liable under the Directive*, i.e. to what extent problems related to scientific uncertainty *(state of scientific and technical knowledge)* may justify a waiver of liability.

In order to provide an answer to the problem raised above, it is necessary to analyse the provisions of Directive 2004/35/EC, and the existing case law of the European Court of Justice interpreting its provisions.

2. LIABILITY REGIME UNDER DIRECTIVE 2004/35/EC

The scope of Directive 2004/35/EC is narrow: the activities causing environmental damage are listed in its Annex III,[13] which identifies significant potential or actual risks to health and the environment. According to Article 3(1), only damage caused by "occupational activities", as defined in Article 2(7), falls within its scope.[14] The scope of the Directive includes:

- "[E]nvironmental damage caused by any of the occupational activities listed in Annex III, and to any imminent threat of such damage occurring by reason of any of those activities."[15]
- "[D]amage to protected species and natural habitats caused by any occupational activities other than those listed in Annex III, and to any imminent threat of such damage occurring by reason of any of those activities, whenever the operator has been at fault or negligent."[16]

It may be asked why, in the definition of environmental damage, as regards damage to "protected species and natural habitats" Directive 2004/35/EC refers to Annex III and occupational activities (Article 2(1)(a)), but in another provision outlining the scope of the Directive, for the same type of damage, liability is extended to "any occupational activity" under the sole condition that fault or negligence of the operator can be demonstrated, even if it is not listed in Annex III (Article 3(b)). This is a kind of "artificial" extension of the scope of

---

13 The activities listed in Annex III, e.g. are: waste management operations, including collection, generation, transport, and disposal of waste and hazardous waste; incineration; discharge into water; manufacture, use, storage processing, filling, release into the environment and onsite transport of: (a) dangerous substances; (b) dangerous preparations; (c) plant protection product; (d) biocidal products; and transport of genetically modified organisms; and transport of genetically modified organisms.

14 See. L. Bergkamp and B.J. Goldsmith (eds.), *The EU Environmental Liability Directive: A Commentary* (Oxford University Press, 2013), p. 52–55.

15 Art. 3(1)(a) of Directive 2004/35.

16 Ibid., Art. 3(1)(b).

the Directive, since it gives the Member States the option of including activities other than those listed in Annex III, in the event of fault or negligence on the part of the operator.

Both of the above types of damage refer to two different situations (scopes), and relate to two different models of liability. In the first case, it is a regime of strict liability.[17] This is also supported by the fact that liability is regulated differently in the subsequent part of Article 3(1) of the Directive *a contrario*. The application of liability independent of culpability is appropriate in situations where the occurrence of damage is connected with the use of tools and equipment that pose a risk resulting from their nature (use of natural forces).[18] The European Union (EU) legislature has used a stricter liability regime, which allows for the prevention or indemnification of damage, in the case of activities that, by their very nature, pose a particular threat to the environment.[19] Moreover, strict liability is usually connected with giving a stronger incentive to act to limit the possibility of damage. Therefore, stronger theoretical reasons exist for applying this principle.[20]

The second situation is expressly linked to fault[21] or negligence,[22] which has become a prerequisite for liability. Admittedly, the ELD does not mention recklessness as a principle on which liability can be based. This cannot affect the interpretation of the Directive, since, in many legal systems, recklessness is the lightest form of fault. However, given the discretion left to national legislatures (by Article 16 of Directive 2004/35/EC) to maintain and introduce stricter rules

17 See. A. Schwartz "The Case Against Strict Liability" (1992) 60 *Fordham Law Review* 819, pp. 832 *et seq*.

18 See. Salanitro, above n. 5, pp. 12–15.

19 See. Opinion of Advocate General Kokott in Case C-378/08, *Raffinerie Mediterranee (ERG)*, ECLI: EU:C:2009:650, paras. 90–92; B. Rakoczy, *Ciężar dowodu w polskim prawie ochrony środowiska* [*Burden of proof in Polish environmental law*] (author's own translation) (Wolters Kluwer Polska, 2010), p. 40.

20 The fact that such a theoretical assumption may not fully correspond to reality is demonstrated by works devoted to the impact of *strict liability*, in the United States, on the frequency of occurrence of environmental damage and investment in protective measures. They show that there is no relation which would allow the assumption that strict liability favours protective measures. It is noticeable that such actions are taken, above all, by companies possessing adequate size and capital. On the other hand, it also favours the transfer of risky processes from larger companies to smaller ones, in order to take responsibility: See e.g. A. Alberini and D.H. Austin, "Strict Liability as a Deterrent in Toxic Waste Management: Empirical Evidence from Accident and Spill Data" (1999) *Journal of Environmental Economics and Management* 38(1), pp. 20–48, especially p. 21 and pp. 43–44.

21 Comparative legal research on the subject of liability for environmental damage based on the principle of fault shows that, although its application is common, it is characterised by specificity. In Finland and Sweden, for example, special regimes of liability for environmental damage have been introduced to replace traditional liability on the basis of fault: see M. Gimple-Hinteregge, *Environmental Liability and Ecological Damage in European Law* (Cambridge University Press, 2008), pp. 67–68.

22 See Bergkamp and Goldsmith, above n. 14, pp. 37–38, 62–65.

for preventing and remedying environmental damage,[23] both types of fault can constitute a principle of liability under national legislation.

Regarding the concept of "occupational activity", as the European Court of Justice (ECJ) pointed out in *Naturschutzbund Deutschland*, this "means an activity carried out as an economic activity, a firm or an undertaking, regardless of whether it is private or public, profit-making or non-profit-making".[24]

Having regard to the context and general scheme of the Directive's provisions, and the objectives[25] pursued by it, the ECJ states, first, that Annex III to Directive 2004/35/EC contains a list of the professional activities covered by that Directive. "That annex lists activities that, like waste management, are in principle carried out in the collective interest on the basis of a statutory assignment of tasks".[26] Second, it follows from a combined reading of Articles 2(6) and (7) of the Directive that the concept of "occupational activities" encompasses a wide conception of the term, and also includes public activities, exercised by public legal persons, which are not profit-making in nature.[27] As for the objectives pursued by Directive 2004/35/EC:

> [I]t is apparent from reading recitals 2, 8 and 9 together that the directive, pursuant to the 'polluter pays' principle, seeks to hold operators financially liable where, on account of occupational activities posing a potential or actual risk for human health or the environment, they have caused environmental damage, so as to induce them to adopt measures and develop practices to minimise the risks of such damage.[28]

3. EXCLUSION AND WAIVER OF LIABILITY UNDER DIRECTIVE 2004/35/EC

Directive 2004/35/EC "does not cover environmental damage, or an imminent threat of such damage, caused by [...] a natural phenomenon of an exceptional, inevitable, and irresistible character" (Article 4(1)(b)). The Directive does not apply to environmental damage, or an imminent threat of such damage, arising

---

23 B. Rakoczy argues that the EU legislature did not limit, in any way, the legislators of the Member States; therefore, they may adopt stricter solutions within the whole scope regulated by the Directive: see B. Rakoczy, above n. 19, p. 111; see Opinion of Advocate General Kokott in *Raffinerie Mediterranee (ERG)*, above n. 19, paras. 47–52; Judgment of the ECJ in Case C-378/08 *Raffinerie Mediterranee (ERG)*, ECLI: EU:C:2010:126, paras. 65 and 68; Opinion of Advocate General J. Kokott in Case C-534/13, *Fipa Group*, ECLI: EU:C:2014:2393, paras. 46–54; ECJ Judgment in Case C-534/13, *Fipa Group*, ECLI:EU:C:2015:140, para. 61; *Túrkevei Tejtermelő KFT*, above n. 7, paras. 64–66.

24 *Naturschutzbund Deutschland*, above n. 7, para. 40.

25 Case C-395/18, *Tim*, ECLI:EU:C:2020:58, para. 36, and the case law cited therein.

26 *Naturschutzbund Deutschland*, above n. 7, para. 72.

27 Ibid., para. 73.

28 Ibid., para. 74.

from an event falling within the scope of the international conventions listed in Annex IV, including any future amendments thereof, which are in force in the Member State concerned (Article 4(2) and (3)).

Article 4 of the Directive implicitly excludes from its scope damage and an imminent threat of damage resulting from climate change, where a causal link cannot be established, thus excluding these cases of "diffuse pollution" (also known as the "concept of remoteness of the damage" or "long-distance pollution").[29] Such exclusions are not "optional" like the other exclusions indicated in Article 8 of the Directive – the "exemption from liability" rationale.

Finally, exclusions of liability relate to situations of environmental damage, or imminent threat of such damage, arising from:

(1) "acts of armed conflict, civil war, or natural phenomena" (Article 4(1)(a));
(2) the actions of "a third party, provided that the operator has taken appropriate preventive measures" (Article 8(3)(a));
(3) "compliance with a compulsory order or instruction emanating from a public authority" (Article 8(3)(b)).

In addition, the Directive, in its Article 4, provides for other exemptions in the case of oil spills and nuclear disasters. However, these exemptions apply only on the condition that the international instruments listed in Annex IV are in force in the Member States concerned. It is worth noting that these international agreements are not a satisfactory alternative to the liability mechanism introduced by Directive 2004/35/EC. The remedies provided for in these agreements are much less sophisticated with regard to: (a) the nature of the measures that should be taken; (b) the issue of who bears the costs; and (c) the level of remedies.

The second type of exclusion is the possibility of release from responsibility. This differs in nature from the exemptions referred to above. Member States can make use of the "discharge of liability" option in *two cases*, where environmental damage was caused by:

- "an emission or event expressly authorised by, and fully in accordance with the conditions of, an authorisation conferred by or given under applicable national laws and regulations which implement those legislative measures adopted by the Community specified in Annex III, as applied at the date of the emission or event";[30]

29 See S. Cassotta, *The transposition of the Environmental Liability Directive: the concept of threshold, the scope of application and defenses, Abstract from European Parliament, Public Hearing on the Environmental Liability Directive*, distinguished Key Note Speaker, Brussels, Belgium (2017).

30 Art. 8 (4)(a) of Directive 2004/35/EC.

- "an emission or activity or any manner of using a product in the course of an activity which the operator demonstrates was not considered likely to cause environmental damage according to the *state of scientific and technical knowledge* at the time when the emission was released or the activity took place."[31]

Individual Member States may also adjust the liability mechanism by introducing exculpatory grounds. Article 8(4) of the Directive allows Member States to modify strict liability by introducing a subjective element. In turn, the reference in these provisions to fault-based liability makes it possible for the operator to obtain further grounds for exculpation. It should be stressed that the grounds indicated in Article 8(4) of the Directive relate only to bearing the costs of remedial actions, and thus do not include preventive actions.

The second possibility for exemption from liability is for the operator to prove that, according to the state of scientific and technical knowledge, it was improbable for the damage to have occurred as a result of the emission, event, or use of the product.[32] In other words, environmental damage, according to scientific and technical knowledge, should not have occurred. Which means that there were no objective substantive data confirming the risk of harm. Thus, objective substantive criteria set the reference level of knowledge (its quantum) that the operator should have to avoid liability. The subjective lack of fault in the operator's achievement of that level of knowledge should not be relevant in assessing this condition. However, it would appear that the level of scientific and technical knowledge should refer to information that is inherent in a widely accessible scientific exchange.

The possibility of escaping liability is based on the operator's burden of proof, i.e. they must prove, in the first case, that the environmental damage was caused by the authorised emission or event, and that it complies with that authorisation. In the second case, it must prove that it was improbable, according to the state of scientific and technical knowledge, that the damage would have been caused by the emission, event, or use of the product. In other words, the environmental damage was, according to scientific and technical knowledge, unlikely to occur, and there were no objective data allowing the damage to be foreseen.

The construction of Directive 2004/35/EC provides for a large number of exemptions from liability, which must be criticised, because it leaves Member States with too much discretion in their application.[33] In this sense, the negative effect of introducing the possibility of exemption from liability, on the basis of Article 8(4) of the Directive, will be that some Member States will extend the

---

31 Ibid., Art. 8(4)(b) (emphasis added).

32 Cf. Cassotta, above n. 29; Salanitro, above n. 5, pp. 15–17.

33 See Casotta, above n. 29.

exemptions' scope of application and others will not, which will increase the disparity in the liability regime and the lack of harmonisation.[34]

4. AVAILABLE SCIENTIFIC AND TECHNICAL DATA, PRECAUTIONARY AND PREVENTIVE PRINCIPLES AND THE POLLUTER-PAYS PRINCIPLE

According to Article 191(2) of the Treaty on the Functioning of the European Union (TFEU),[35] EU policy on the environment should aim at a high level of protection, taking into account the diversity of situations in the various regions of the Union. Based on the precautionary principle,[36] and on the principles that preventive action should be taken, environmental damage should be rectified as a priority at the source, and the polluter should pay for this. This provision relates not only to the manner in which environmental legislation is established, and to its content,[37] but also to the standard for assessing the compatibility of secondary legislation with the rules of the Treaty on environmental policymaking,[38] and action by Member States to implement secondary legislation.[39]

Directive 2004/35/EC is a legislative implementation of the environmental policy of the EU, with its foundations in Article 191(2) TFEU, based on the principles of prevention and precaution and the generally relevant polluter-pays principle.[40] This approach is confirmed by the case law of the Court of Justice of the European Union and opinions of Advocates General. These indicate that the polluter-pays principle is a fundamental principle of Directive 2004/35/EC,

34 Ibid.

35 Consolidated version of the Treaty on the Functioning of the European Union, OJ C 202, 7.6.2016, p. 132–133.

36 The precautionary principle is, alone among the principles enshrined in Article 191(2) TFEU, recognised as a general principle of EU law: cf. Joined Cases T-74/00, T-76/00, T-83/00, T-84/00, T-85/00, T-132/00, T-137/00 and T-141/00, *Artegodan and Others v. Commission*, ECLI:EU:T:2002:283, para 184: "[i]t follows that the precautionary principle can be defined as a general principle of Community law requiring the competent authorities to take appropriate measures to prevent specific potential risks to public health, safety and the environment, by giving precedence to the requirements related to the protection of those interests over economic interests."

37 See. A. Epiney, "Environmental Principles" in R. Macrory (ed.), *Reflections on 30 Years of EU Environmental Law* (Europa Law Publishing, 2006), pp. 21–23.

38 See. Case C-293/97, *Standley and Others*, ECLI:EU:C:1999:215.

39 On the other hand, individuals do not have the right to rely on the principles set out in Art. 191(2) TFEU in order to request the non-application of Acts of national law: Joined Cases C-379/08 and C-380/08, *ERG and Others*, ECLI:EU:C:2010:127, para 39.

40 See. L. Kramer, "Environmental Principles and the EU Court of Justice" in M. Faure (ed.), *Elgar Encyclopedia of Environmental Law* (Edward Elgar, 2018), pp. 587–598.

which is intended to give a concrete form to that principle.[41] Furthermore, it is also intended to give a concrete expression to the other principles of Article 191(1) TFEU, i.e. the principles of preventive action, and remediation of damage primarily at the source.[42]

The above principles of environmental policy may be analysed from the perspective of lawmaking and its application, as confirmed by the wording of Article 8(4)(b) of Directive 2004/35/EC, since, if the operator proves that, "according to the state of scientific and technical knowledge at the time of the emission or activity, it was not considered likely that it could give rise to environmental damage", they might not bear the costs of the remedial measures taken pursuant to the Directive and, furthermore, demonstrate that the environmental damage is not connected with their fault or negligence. This places the issue in the context of the importance of the precautionary principle and the polluter-pays principle.

The precautionary principle implies that protective action should also be taken where the existence of a risk to the environment and human health is possible but not fully proven.[43] Applying the precautionary principle means using scientific evidence directly in the decision-making process. The precautionary principle responds to the impossibility of obtaining scientific proof to justify preventive measures in all situations. The application of the precautionary principle should be consistent with the principle of proportionality.[44] The precautionary principle is not only important in the development of secondary legislation, but also to national administrations and courts, indicating how secondary legislation, and the national legislation implementing it, should be interpreted.[45]

---

41 See Opinion of Advocate General Kokott in Case C-378/08 *Raffinerie Mediterranee (ERG)*, above n. 19, paras. 84 and 94; Case C-378/08 *Raffinerie Mediterranee (ERG)*, above n. 23, para. 67; Opinion of Advocate General J. Kokott in Case C-534/13 *Fipa Group*, above n. 23, para. 54; Opinion of Advocate General J. Kokott in Case C-129/16 *Túrkevei Tejtermelő KFT*, ECLI:EU:C:2017:136, para. 27.

42 See Opinion of Advocate General J. Kokott in Case C-378/08, *Raffinerie Mediterranee (ERG)*, above n. 19, para. 67; Opinion of Advocate General J. Kokott in Case C-534/13, *Fipa Group*, above n. 23, paras. 55–57.

43 The precautionary principle was introduced into EU legislation by the Maastricht Treaty; thus, it was not among the first principles for the conduct of environmental policy, which were adopted in 1987 with the Single European Act (OJ L 169, 29 June 1987, p. 1). Moreover, at the initial stage of application, the significance of the precautionary principle was also strongly influenced by acts of international law (1992 Rio Declaration, UNFCCC, A_CONF.151_26_Vol.I_Declaration). The importance of the precautionary principle in EU law has been developed by the jurisprudence of the ECJ since the late 1990s, and by the European Commission in a Communication issued in 2000 (COM(2000) 1 final, Communication from the Commission on the precautionary principle, Brussels, 02.02.2000 (COM:2000:0001:FIN:en:TXT)).

44 Case C-78/16, *Pesce and Others*, ECLI:EU:C:2016:428, paras. 48 and 56.

45 Case C-1/03, *Van de Walle and Others*, ECLI:EU:C:2004:490; cf. N. de Sadeleer, "Liability for Oil Pollution Damage versus Liability for Waste Management: the Polluters Pays Principle

The doctrine has pointed out that the precautionary principle is a response to uncertainty, which occurs in the face of threats to the environment, as well as to human health, and refers to the probability, causality and magnitude of the threat.[46] Components of this principle have also been identified, such as anticipatory action, calculation of costs and effectiveness of action, preservation of ecological space, legitimacy of the status of intrinsic values of natural systems, shifting the burden of proof to show that there is no probability of danger to the undertaking, planning activities on a medium-term scale, and repayment of past ecological debts for projects undertaken without due diligence in the assessment of risks.[47]

Therefore, not every risk will qualify as one which creates a likelihood of actual harm. Accordingly, full scientific proof of the genuinely harmful nature of the activity in question is not necessary, as the purpose of applying the precautionary principle is to avoid risks of a potential nature.[48] Furthermore, the likelihood of harm justifies taking action even when it is not possible to establish the existence or extent of the risk, due to inconclusive, insufficient or inaccurate findings.[49] Therefore, there is no single universal threshold of acceptability for environmental improvement measures motivated by the precautionary principle. Each case must be assessed on its own merits, but as Advocate General Bobek states, "the most important thing is that there must be at least some ascertainable risk based on scientific grounds".[50] The precautionary principle cannot be used to justify measures with respect to risks which may be merely hypothetical in nature[51] – a mere fear of danger.

The precautionary principle applies in all cases where a threat exists, where the possibility cannot be excluded, on the basis of objective circumstances, that the activity to be regulated will significantly affect the level of environmental protection.[52] This means that full scientific proof of the existence of a threat to the values covered by the scope of protection is not always required for the introduction of the desired legal measure. The absence of an absolute degree of certainty as to the realisation of the risk of negative effects on environmental protection is what distinguishes the precautionary principle

---

at the Rescue of the Victims", (2009) 21(2) *Journal of Environmental Law*, p. 299; A. Bleeker, "Does the Polluter Pay? The Polluter-Pays Principle in the Case Law of the Court of Justice", (Dec. 2009) *European Energy and Environmental Law Review*, p. 289.

46 See T. O'Riordan and A. Jordan, "The Precautionary Principle in Contemporary Environmental Politics", (1995) 4(3) *Environmental Values*, pp. 195–198.

47 Ibid.

48 See J.H. Jans and H.H.B. Vedder, *European Environmental Law: After Lisbon* (Europa Law Publishing 2012) p. 43.

49 Case C-41/02, *Commission v. Netherlands*, ECLI:EU:C:2004:762, para 54.

50 Opinion of the Advocate General M. Bobek in Case C-528/16, *Confédération paysanne*, ECLI:EU:C:2018:20, paras. 52–53.

51 Case T-229/04, *Sweden v. Commission*, ECLI:EU:T:2007:217.

52 See Opinion of Advocate General J. Kokott in Joined Cases C-105/09 and C-110/09, *Terre wallonne ASBL*, ECLI:EU:C:2010:120, para. 89.

from the principle of prevention.[53] Without the precautionary principle, taking action in the field of environmental protection would be possible only on the basis of the principle of prevention, i.e. the existence of negative effects of an activity covered by the scope of environmental regulation would have to be proven each time.[54] Presumably, this would only be possible as a result of the materialisation of the risk that environmental legislation is intended to counteract. This would fundamentally distort the fundamental purpose of environmental regulation, which is to protect and improve the existing state of the environment. Moreover, it is very difficult to fully prove that it is a particular activity that is harming the environment in an unacceptable manner, in a case of complexity and multiple sources of pollution. Consequently, relying only on the prevention principle could significantly hamper the development of environmental legislation.

The application of the precautionary principle is facilitated where the good to be protected is human health, in which case, as the case law of the ECJ indicates, a lighter version of the requirement for sufficient scientific proof of risk[55] should be applied. The cost–benefit analysis carried out for the application of the precautionary principle should also take into account non-economic aspects: after all, the main purpose of the precautionary principle is not economic in nature.[56]

The second principle relating to the legal instruments of environmental policy is the principle of prevention.[57] The aim of the prevention principle is to prevent the occurrence of negative environmental effects before they are caused by the entity whose activity is covered by the scope of environmental regulation. Therefore, the principle of prevention is based on the assumption that preventive action is a much more effective form of environmental protection than subsequent action. The characteristic that distinguishes the prevention principle from the precautionary principle is that the knowledge of the occurrence of negative effects of a certain activity must be certain.[58] The difference between the

53 Cf. N. de Sadeleer, *Environmental Law Principles: From Political Slogans to Legal Rules* (Oxford University Press, 2002), p. 74.

54 Ibid.

55 See K. Garnett and D.J. Parsons, "Multi-Case Review of the Application of the Precautionary Principle in European Union Law and Case Law", (2017) 37(3) *Risk Analysis*, p. 513.

56 See J. Zander, *The Application of the Precautionary Principle in Practice: Comparative Dimensions* (Cambridge University Press, 2010), p. 99.

57 See G. Bándi, "Principles of EU environmental law, including the objective of sustainable development" in M. Peeters and M. Eliantonio (eds.), *Research Handbook on EU Environmental Law* (Edward Elgar, 2020), p. 43–44.

58 In view of the fundamental difficulty in distinguishing between the practical application of the precautionary and preventive principles, the ECJ does not always consistently distinguish between the two, e.g. Case C-501/04 *Agrarproduktion Staebelow*, ECLI:EU:C:2006:30, para. 39. The ECJ case law indicates that the principle of proportionality must also be applied in

application of the precautionary principle and the application of the prevention principle, therefore, concerns the degree of certainty about the existence of a threat to the environment.[59] In a case where the negative effect of carrying out a certain activity can be regarded as certain, the action should be based on the principle of prevention. Therefore, the principle of prevention is aimed at preventing the occurrence of scientifically confirmed adverse environmental effects of a given activity. The principle of prevention, like the other principles of environmental policy, is concretised by individual Acts of secondary law, for example directives. Therefore, there is no "one-size-fits-all" approach as to how to implement the prevention principle in the various fields of environmental policy.[60]

The "polluter-pays" principle is also linked to the prevention principle: it is the polluter who is in the best position to take the most effective measures to avoid later liability.[61] The application of the "polluter-pays" principle further strengthens the precautionary principle by preventing any avoidance of financial liability if the anticipatory measures prove to be inadequate. The principle of prevention is also subject to the principle of proportionality: preventive measures should not go beyond what is necessary and appropriate to achieve the objective pursued.[62] References in secondary legislation to the "polluter-pays" principle imply an obligation to interpret acts adopted directly on the basis of the provisions of the Treaty concerning environmental policy in the

---

the application of the polluter-pays principle: cf. the judgment in *Standley and Others*, above n. 38, para. 54. The tendency to attribute the entire responsibility for environmental pollution only to industrial installations is, to some extent, justified by the fact that, thanks to the legal regime of granting permits, the activities of industrial installations are relatively easy to control: cf. *Van de Walle and Others*, above n. 45, paras. 57–58; Case C188/07, *Commune de Mesquer*, ECLI:EU:C:2008:359, para. 78; C-104/17, *Cali Esprou*, ECLI:EU:C:2018:188, para. 22; Opinion of the Advocate General J. Kokott in Case C-534/13, *Fipa Group*, above n. 23, para. 54.

59 See N. de Sadeleer, *"Environmental Principles"*, above n. 53, p. 74.

60 See N. de Sadeleer, "The principles of prevention and precaution in international law: two heads of the same coin?" in M. Fitzmaurice, D.M. Ong and P. Merkouris (eds.), *Research Handbook on International Environmental Law* (Edward Elgar, 2010), p. 196.

61 Opinion of the Advocate General J. Kokott in Case C-534/13, *Fipa Group and Others*, above n. 23, para. 55. As is the case with other environmental policy principles, the principle of obligations flowing from the "polluter-pays" principle requires concretisation in a piece of secondary legislation (giving normative meaning in a specific piece of legislation). In Case C-104/17 *Cali Esprou*, ECLI:EU:C:2018:188, the ECJ confirmed that the "polluter pays" principle can be understood more broadly than just the liability of the party responsible for the end result of the harmful activity. It may extend to a wider range of actors involved in the pollution, e.g. also to those who contribute to the production of waste of packaging waste, including importers and distributors of packaging (see para. 22).

62 See V. Fogleman, "The duty to prevent environmental damage in the environmental damage directive; a catalyst for halting the deterioration of water and wildlife", (2019) 20(2) *ERA Forum*, p. 707.

light of that principle.[63] The scope and normative content of the EU "polluter-pays" principle give rise to many doubts.[64]

The "polluter-pays" principle should, therefore, lead economic operators to internalise the environmental costs of their activities, which, if the principle were not applied, would be borne by the public authorities; that is, indirectly by society as a whole.[65] Therefore, it is essential, for the effectiveness of the principle, to establish a causal link between the operator's activities and the environmental damage or an imminent threat of such damage.[66]

The purpose of the "polluter-pays" principle is to ensure that an entity deriving a profit from an activity that is harmful to the environment will also contribute financially to reducing the expected negative effects of this economic activity, which is most often expressed through a system of fees for the use of particular environmental components (for example the emission of dust into the air or emission of waste water into water or the ground)[67] (*ex ante* application of this principle).[68] As de Sadeleer points out, the second element of the "polluter-pays" principle is the responsibility of entities for the environmental damage they cause (*ex post* application).[69]

Of the three principles analysed above, it is the precautionary principle and the prevention principle that should be given particular importance. The application of the best available techniques[70] to set a standard for the determination of pollutant emissions in the integrated permit (i.e. permit required by Directive 2010/75/EU) for larger industrial plants in the EU, by setting emission limits that reflect an appropriate balance between benefits and costs, should be regarded as a manifestation of the precautionary and

63 Opinion of Advocate General J. Kokott in Case C-129/16, *Túrkevei Tejtermelő Kft.*, ECLI:EU:C:2017:136, para. 38.

64 Ibid.

65 N. de Sadeleer, "The polluter-pays principle in EU law – Bold case law and poor harmonisation" in I.L. Backer, O.K. Fauchald and C. Voigt (eds.), *Pro Natura: Festskrift til H.-C. Bugge* (Universitetsforlaget, 2013) p. 408.

66 *Túrkevei Tejtermelő Kft*, above n. 7, paras. 47–48; B. Pozzo, B. Vanheusden, L. Bergkamp and E. Brans, "The Remediation of Contaminated Sites and the Problem of Assessing the Liability of the Innocent Landowner: a Comparative Law Perspective", (2015) *European Review of Private Law*, p. 1071; S. Varvaštian, "Environmental liability under scrutiny: The margins of applying the EU 'polluter pays' principle against the owners of the polluted land who did not contribute to the pollution", *Environmental Law Review*, (2015) 17(4), p. 270.

67 In a model approach, the funds raised in this way should be used by public authorities for environmental mitigation and compensation measures.

68 Notwithstanding this, the ECJ has accepted such national solutions imposing an obligation to pay charges, regardless of the absence of a real link between the rates and the actual pollution caused by those liable to pay: see judgments of the ECJ in Case C-686/15, *Vodoopskrba i odvodnja*, ECLI:EU:C:2016:927, para. 24; Joined Cases C-497/15 and C-498/15, *Euro-Team Kft*, ECLI:EU:C:2017:229, para. 56.

69 De Sadeleer, "The polluter-pays principle in EU Law", above n. 65, p. 412.

70 According to the definition in Art. 3 point 10 of Directive 2010/75/EU on industrial emissions (integrated pollution prevention and control).

prevention principles.[71] The negative effects of carrying out a given industrial activity cannot be fully predicted.

5. "STATE OF SCIENCE AND TECHNOLOGY" AS A KEY CONCEPT IN ENVIRONMENTAL LAW

Article 191(3) TFEU requires the Union (when adopting EU environmental law) and Member States (when adopting national environmental law) to take the utmost account of the criteria listed in that provision for the development of EU environmental policy.[72] However, as underlined by the ECJ in its *Safety Hi-Tech* and *Bettati v. Safety Hi-Tech* judgments, Article 191 TFEU contains objectives, principles and criteria which must be respected in the implementation of EU environmental policy. In order to ensure a balance between them, and to achieve them as fully as possible, all the objectives, principles and criteria must be treated as equally important, and be taken into account as far as possible.[73]

The criterion of available scientific and technical (S&T) data should be understood as an obligation to use scientific and technical information already obtained and available in the regulated area, in formulating EU environmental policy, without carrying out new research. It is not necessary to prove that regulations adopted on the basis of such data will be effective. It should also be emphasised that, in the case of the precautionary principle and the prevention principle, even provisional and approximate data may be used as a basis for taking or refraining from taking measures which could cause environmental damage. It is important to emphasise the link between this criterion and the precautionary principle.

The concept of available S & T data is also worth considering in the context of the concept of optimal available technologies. This concept exists in two variants: BAT (best available technology, best available techniques)[74] and BATNEEC (best available technology not entailing excessive costs).[75] In the first variant, the

---

71 According to Nicolas de Sadeleer (ibid.), prevention is not precaution. However, this view does not seem to be fully justified.

72 See A. Sikora, *Constitutionalisation of Environmental Protection in EU Law* (Europa Law Publishing, 2020), pp. 74 *et seq.*

73 Case C-284/95 *Safety Hi-Tech p. S. & T.*, ECLI:EU:C:1998:352, paras. 36–37 and Case C-341/95 *Bettati v. Safety Hi-Tech*, ECLI:EU:C:1998:353, paras. 34–35.

74 The concept of BAT emerged as the concept of "best available technology" in Community law, for the first time, in Directive 76/464 on discharge of dangerous substances into water (OJ L 129, 18.5.1976, p. 23-29). The Directive introduced the obligation to set limit values for such discharges, on the assumption that the best available technology would be used to reduce them.

75 However, the BAT concept, appearing later and in other Acts, did not receive a more precise definition, and its next variant, developed in a certain evolution of the way of approaching

latest processes, methods and means of operation that can be used, in practice, to prevent or minimise harmful impacts are taken into account. In the second case, such processes, methods and measures should be used which to the highest extent reflect the current state of scientific and technical development, but whose application, at the same time, does not entail excessive costs.[76]

The concept of BAT was referred to in 1996 by Directive 96/61/EC on integrated pollution control and management (IPPC Directive). The requirement to use, when carrying out protective tasks, measures and methods resulting from the current state of knowledge, and ensuring the maximum effectiveness of protection, currently stems from Directive 2010/75/EU (IED).[77] "Best available techniques" are defined as:

> [T]he most effective and advanced stage in the development of activities and their methods of operation, which indicates the practical suitability of particular techniques for providing the basis for emission limit values and other permit conditions designed to prevent and, where that is not practicable, to reduce emissions and the impact on the environment as a whole:
>
> (a) "techniques" include both the technology used and the way in which an installation is designed, built, maintained, operated and decommissioned;
> (b) "available techniques" means those developed on a scale which allows implementation in the relevant industrial sector, under economically and technically viable conditions, taking into consideration the costs and advantages, whether or not the techniques are used or produced inside the Member State in question, as long as they are reasonably accessible to the operator;
> (c) "best" means most effective in achieving a high general level of protection for the environment as a whole.[78]

---

the issue, became the BATNEEC concept. This is the concept of "best available technology not entailing excessive (unjustified) costs". The concept was first included in Directive 84/360 (OJ L 188, 16.7.1984, p. 20-25) on combating air pollution from industrial plants. The Directive established the obligation to take all appropriate preventive measures, including the best available technology, provided that their application does not entail excessive costs (Art. 4). Also amended in 1991, Directive 75/442 (OJ L 194, 25.7.1975, p. 39-41) on waste obliged the Member States of the EU to organise an integrated and tailor-made network of disposal installations, taking into account the best available technology not involving excessive costs (Art. 5). And this concept has not subsequently been defined in a precise way: see L.S. Braaksma and H.D. Tolsma, "Integrated Pollution Prevention and Control: A critical legal perspective on all-inclusive integration" in Peeters and Eliantonio (eds.), above n. 57, pp. 317–318.

76 See F. Oosterhuis and M. Peeters, "Limits to Integration in Pollution Prevention and Control" in M. Peeters and R. Uylenburg (eds.), *EU Environmental Legislation* (Edward Elgar, 2014), pp. 91–115, and references therein.

77 Directive 2010/75/EU of the European Parliament and of the Council of 24 November 2010 on industrial emissions (integrated pollution prevention and control) (OJ 2010 L 334, p. 17).

78 Ibid., Art. 3(10).

In the context of the possibility of "exemption from liability" provided for in Article 8(4)(b) of Directive 2004/35/EC – that is to say, an emission or activity, or the use of a product in any way in the course of an activity, for which the operator proves that, according to the state of scientific and technical knowledge at the time of the emission or activity, it was not considered likely to cause environmental damage – it should be pointed out that, since there is a condition excluding liability (exception), the reference level of knowledge which the operator should have had must, therefore, be construed as being as high as possible.[79] The subjective lack of fault of the operator in acquiring this level of knowledge should not affect the assessment of this condition. However, it appears that the level of scientific and technical knowledge should refer to information which is within the scope of ordinary scientific exchange, and to which access is possible. It cannot be applied to knowledge that has been developed but not yet disclosed (for example, knowledge used for military purposes that may later be transferred to civil use).

The possibility of exemption from liability depends on the operator proving that the conditions in Article 8(4) of Directive 2004/35/EC apply. This raises the question of how to understand the burden of proof, i.e. the obligation of the operator to prove that these circumstances exist. Some arguments are provided by the principles of prevention, precaution and polluter-pays. Looking at the issue in question from the perspective of these principles allows for the formulation of guidelines as to how the concept of burden of proof should be understood, in the context of conditions relieving operators from liability under Article 8(4) of the Directive.

The principles of prevention and precaution support solutions that impose the burden of proof on the business entity. The principles of prevention lead to the conclusion that the entity is obliged to prove that its activities do not have a negative impact on the environment (the lack of such evidence should lead to the conclusion that there is a negative impact, and that the entity is obliged to take preventive measures).

The principle of precaution,[80] in turn, is connected with the obligation on the individual to take "all possible precautionary measures". Following the precautionary principle allows one to free themselves from liability in the situation of proving that actions were taken in compliance with the precautionary

79 Salanitro, above n. 5, pp. 16–18.

80 See O'Riordan and Jordan, above n. 46, pp. 195–198; Janina Ciechanowicz-McLean and Maciej Nyka note that the precautionary principle is extracted, by some doctrine representatives, from the principle of prevention, as referring to the threats that have not yet been fully recognized, in J. Ciechanowicz-McLean and M. Nyka, "Nowe instrumenty administracyjnoprawne w ochrony środowiska" [New administrative law instruments in environmental protection] in M. Rudnicki, A. Haładyj and K. Sobieraj (eds.), *Dekada harmonizacji w prawie ochrony środowiska* [*A decade of harmonisation in environmental law*] (author's own translation) (Wydawnictwo KUL, 2011), p. 136.

principle (connected with due diligence, i.e. the average measure of diligence that a party is obliged to exercise).[81] It would appear that the precautionary principle does not require "all possible precautions" to be taken. At its most general level, the precautionary principle does not provide interpretative guidance as clear as that provided by the prevention principle.

The third of the principles, the polluter-pays principle, is, therefore, fundamentally applicable to the implementation of liability in environmental law.[82] As such, it functions in a sphere that is characterised by a clear shift of the burden of responsibility towards the administrative bodies that enforce obligations (in the objective aspect of the burden of proof). Only in practical terms, from the point of view of its own interests, should a party take the initiative of proof to demonstrate that it has acted on the basis of, and within the limits of, the law. In terms of subject matter, this rule may have the effect of limiting the elements to be proved. In particular, this concerns the element of unlawfulness of an act, because "unlawfulness" has the character of "objectivising administrative liability".[83] Specific solutions implementing this principle are of fundamental importance to determining the consequences of not establishing the person responsible. This substantive aspect of the proof is particularly important in the case of liability under Directive 2004/35/EC.

Failure to prove the prerequisites for the operator's liability will result in the administrative body needing to take preventive and corrective actions.[84] In such a case, the authority will bear the negative consequences of failing to meet the burden of proof, and so it can clearly be seen that it is in the interests of the authority to provide evidence imputing liability to the relevant entities.[85]

The EU's construction of the "best available technique" was, and is, of a more universal nature: the definition may be applied in all cases where reference is made to BAT, not necessarily only in connection with integrated (IED) permits. This is important in so far as references to the "best available technique requirements" under various specific provisions occur relatively often, and refer to various activities, not only those connected with operating an installation which requires an integrated permit.

---

81 On the subject of the burden of proof in the context of the principles of prevention and precaution, cf. B. Rakoczy, above n. 19, pp. 91–94.

82 See A. Lipiński, *Prawne podstawy ochrony środowiska* [*Legal basis for environmental protection*] (author's own translation) (Wolters Kluwer Polska, 2010), p. 31.

83 B. Rakoczy, above n. 19, p. 137.

84 See Order of the Supreme Administrative Court of 20 January 2012, II OW 97/11; M. Sieradzka, *Działalność stwarzająca ryzyko szkody w środowisku. Glosa do postanowienia NSA z dnia 20 stycznia 2012 r., II OW 97/11*, LEX/el. 2015 [*Activity Creating a Risk of Environmental Damage. Commentary to the decision of the NSA of 20 January 2012, II OW 97/11*, LEX/el. 2015] (author's own translation).

85 Cf Art. 6(3) of Directive 2004/35/EU; B. Rakoczy, above n. 19, pp. 199–201.

In this context, it is also worth noting Recital 21 of Directive 2010/75/EU, which states that, "in order to take account of developments in best available techniques or other changes to an installation, permit conditions should be reconsidered regularly and, where necessary, updated, in particular where new or updated BAT conclusions are adopted". This shows that the EU legislator is aware of the rapid technological changes that are taking place, with an obligation of the Member States (and the national authorities) to monitor this progress. Similarly, in the case of the "most efficient installations", explicitly prejudging which installations are the "most efficient" will make it impossible to respond to technological progress on an ongoing basis. This also confirms that it is the responsibility of the Member States, who monitor their markets, and the technologies that can be used there, to determine the understanding of the term "most efficient installations" within their territories.[86]

6. SUMMARY

It seems that the grounds for exemption from liability provided for in Article 8 of the Directive are justified by arguments founded on the principle of equity, but it is also about balancing the rationale between growth and economic interests, and environmental protection requirements.[87]

On the one hand, it is difficult to consider it fair to impose an obligation to compensate for damage resulting from an action if, at the time the action was taken, the (potential) damage was unknown. But, on the other hand, if the operator is exonerated from liability in such a situation, there will be no incentive for it to cease the potentially polluting activity, and to conduct the business activity in line with the precautionary principle.

86 The right of Member States themselves to define which installations will be regarded as the "most efficient", as mentioned above, does not deprive the European Commission of the right to control the criteria applied by Member States under Art. 258 TFEU. In this context, it is worth recalling the judgment of the ECJ of 7 July 2005 in Case C-364/03, *Commission v. Greece*, ECLI:EU:C:2005:433. In those proceedings, brought by the European Commission under Art. 258 TFEU, the Commission requested a "declaration that, by not determining the policies or strategies for progressively adapting to the best technology available the steam turbine units and gas turbine units of the power station operated by Dimosia Epicheirisi Ilektrismou, situated in Linoperamata on the Island of Crete (Greece), the Hellenic Republic has failed to fulfil its obligations under Article 13 of Council Directive 84/360/EEC of 28 June 1984 on the combating of air pollution from industrial plants (OJ 1984 L 188, p. 20)" – replaced by the Directive 2008/1. The Commission complained to Greece that the plant was operating on the basis of outdated and highly polluting technology which could not be regarded as "best available technology". The Court, after carrying out a "test" of the Greek installation (paras. 31–40), found that Greece had infringed the provisions of the Directive on the combating of air pollution from industrial plants.

87 See Cassotta, above n. 29.

Directive 2004/35/EC leaves too much discretion to Member States as to whether to use the possibilities provided for in that Directive to allow the operator to escape liability. Member States could even use these instrumentally, so that operators do not have to bear the costs of remedial measures in the event of pollution. It is somewhat paradoxical that the possibility of exoneration under Directive 2004/35/EC is provided for in Article 8 of the Directive, which is intended to implement the "polluter-pays" principle.

In this sense, the possibility of exoneration should also be seen as an obstacle to the implementation of this principle, since in the case of environmental damage, no economic operators should be exempted from liability, even in the absence of fault, and damage should always be compensable. Also, "development risk" should be covered by liability, but Directive 2004/35/EC does not include it. This type of damage indicates that the operator may be liable if there is a risk that the activity may be polluting, or if there is a risk that the polluting effects of the activity may become apparent over time.[88]

As a separate aspect, the possibility of exoneration, provided for in Article 8 of Directive 2004/35/EC, weakens the framework for environmental liability, and highlights the disparities between Member States in the way that liability for environmental damage is attributed.[89] The grounds for exoneration provided by the Directive leave too much discretion to the Member States in their application, and, therefore, increase the differences between the national rules of the Member States, instead of enhancing harmonisation.

88 Ibid.

89 See. B. Pozzo, "Environmental liability: the difficulty of harmonizing different national civil liability systems" in Peeters and Eliantonio (eds.), above n. 57, pp. 231–239.

PART XIII

JUDICIAL REVIEW

ELABORATING ON THE SCIENTIFIC EVIDENTIARY REQUIREMENTS OF THE PRECAUTIONARY PRINCIPLE

Rhoda JENNINGS*

1. INTRODUCTION

Scientific evidence is an essential element of environmental law. Science is required to inform the environmental legislative and regulatory decision-making process.[1] Scientific data is complex, uncertain and ambiguous.[2] Complexity and uncertainty are, therefore, a common feature of environmental decision-making and environmental law. The precautionary principle is one of a myriad of methods designed to incorporate scientific evidence into policy and law.[3] The principle provides a methodology for dealing with scientific uncertainty in regulatory decision-making. It provides regulators with a protocol for making decisions in the face of uncertainty, allowing regulation to progress. It is one of the foundations of EU environmental policy, supporting the aim of achieving a high level of environmental protection.[4] All EU environmental legislation is based on the principle.[5]

* EPA Irish Research Council Postgraduate Scholar, School of Law, University College Cork, Ireland: rjennings@ucc.ie. The research conducted in this contribution was funded by the EPA, through the Irish Research Council. I am grateful to Professor Owen McIntyre for his valuable comments on earlier drafts of this contribution. Any errors remain my own.

1 *A. Stirling*, "On 'Precautionary and Science Based' approaches to Risk Assessment and Environmental Appraisal" in A. Stirling (ed.), *On Science and Precaution in the Management of Technological Risk, vol. II, Case Studies* (An ESTO Project Report Prepared for the European Commission, JRC Institute Prospective Technological Studies Seville, 2001), Report EUR 19056/EN/2. Case studies conducted by Ortwin Renn, Andreas Klinke (CTA, Stuttgart), Andrew Stirling (SPRU, University of Sussex), Arie Rip (CSS, Twente) and Ahti Salo (HUT, Helsinki).

2 *Science Advice for Policy by European Academies (SAPEA)*, "Making sense of science for policy under conditions of complexity and uncertainty", Berlin: SAPEA, 2019, p. 44.

3 Ibid., p. 44. Other examples include integrated assessment or the consensus approach, which is employed by the IPCC.

4 See, e.g. Case C 217/19 *European Commission v. Republic of Finland* [2020] EU:C:2020:291, para. 91 and the case law cited therein.

5 See, e.g. Commission Notice, "Assessment of plans and projects in relation to Natura 2000 sites – Methodological guidance on the provisions of Article 6(3) and (4) of the Habitats Directive 92/43/EEC" (2021/C 437/01), para 2.2.

This contribution will discuss the scientific evidentiary base of the precautionary principle at an EU level, and the role played by the Court of Justice of the European Union ("CJEU" or "Court")[6] in defining the principle in terms of scientific evidence. It will first discuss the definition of the principle, and the central function ascribed to the scientific evaluation in instigating and substantiating precautionary decision-making. The contribution will then explore the legitimating power of scientific evidence in the application of the principle, before examining the approach of the Court to the scientific evidentiary base of precautionary decision-making in certain key decisions in environmental law.[7] The contribution will conclude by considering the role played by scientific advisory bodies and the scientific evaluation in precautionary decision-making, and whether the Court is best placed to elaborate on the definition of a principle such as precaution, which has a complex scientific and policy-specific foundation to its use.

2. DEFINING THE PRECAUTIONARY PRINCIPLE

The precautionary principle is not easily defined. From an international law perspective, the concept was first recognised in the World Charter for Nature.[8] The best-known formulation of the principle is that contained in Principle 15 of the Rio Declaration, from which the principle gained universal recognition:[9]

---

6 The CJEU is made up of the Court of Justice (CJ), previously known as the European Court of Justice (ECJ), and the General Court (GC), previously known as the Court of First Instance (CFI). The Treaty of Lisbon entered into force on 1 December 2009, and introduced a new institutional framework for the EU, renaming the court system. For ease of review, the terms CJ and GC will be used throughout this contribution, irrespective of whether a case was heard pre- or post-Lisbon.

7 A broad approach to environmental law is taken in this context, referring to interconnected issues, such as the protection of human, plant and animal health. There is a large amount of EU case law on the precautionary principle, and a full review is beyond the scope of this contribution. Key cases have been identified which demonstrate the Court's approach to the scientific evidence base of the principle.

8 UN General Assembly Resolution 37/7 on a World Charter for Nature, 28 October 1982. Adopted by the UN General Assembly in 1982. The UN World Charter for Nature, at Article 11(b), states that "[a]ctivities which are likely to pose a significant risk to Nature shall be preceded by an exhaustive examination; their proponents shall demonstrate that expected benefits outweigh potential damage to Nature, and where potential adverse effects are not fully understood, the activities should not proceed": *O. McIntyre and T. Mosedale*, "The Precautionary Principle as a Norm of Customary International Law", *Journal of Environmental Law*, (1997) 9(2), p. 221.

9 *N. de Sadeleer*, "The Precautionary Principle" in N. de Sadeleer, *Environmental Principles: From Political Slogans to Legal Rules*, Oxford: Oxford University Press, 2002.

> Where there are threats of serious or irreversible damage, lack of full scientific certainty shall not be used as a reason for postponing cost-effective measures to prevent environmental degradation.[10]

From an EU perspective, the principle was introduced by the Maastricht Treaty into Article 191(2) of the TFEU.[11] In order to give substance and clarity to the application of the principle at the EU level,[12] and in response to declining public confidence in EU regulatory decisions,[13] the Commission drafted a non-binding communication paper on the principle ("the Communication").[14]

The definition of the precautionary principle set out in the Communication is considered to be one of the "most nuanced and balanced".[15] This is perhaps because the Communication does not define the principle; instead, it gives broad guidelines as to its application, stating that it is of a "general scope".[16]

It could be argued that the lack of a definition prohibits any meaningful application of the principle. Equally, the lack of a definition may enable the precautionary principle to remain politically viable.[17] The Communication, however, is not "the last word" on the principle, but, rather, a starting point for discussion.[18] It places responsibility on the CJEU to "flesh out the principle."[19] The principle has been left vague by design, to allow the judiciary to define its boundaries.[20] In areas of ambiguity, it is common for the CJEU to be tasked with interpreting legal concepts.[21] In the case of the precautionary principle,

---

10 A/Conf.151/26 (Vol. I), Report of the United Nations Conference on Environment and Development (1992).

11 Consolidated version of the Treaty on the Functioning of the European Union, OJ C 326, 26.10.2012, pp. 47–390. Originally Art. 174, EC Treaty. The principle was introduced alongside other principles, such as prevention, damage to be rectified at source, and the polluter-pays principle.

12 *R. Lofstedt*, "The precautionary principle in the EU: Why a formal review is long overdue", *Risk Management*, (2014) 16(3), p. 137.

13 Due to issues such as the beef hormones dispute. For a detailed discussion of this area, see *E. Stokes*, "Liberalising the Threshold of Precaution – Cockle Fishing, the Habitats Directive, and Evidence of a new Understanding of 'Scientific Uncertainty'", *Environmental Law Review*, (2005) (1), p. 206.

14 European Commission, Communication from the Commission on the precautionary principle, Brussels, 02.02.2000, COM(2000) 1 final.

15 *J.B. Wiener and M.D. Rogers*, "Comparing precaution in the United States and Europe", *Journal of Risk Research* (2002) 5(4), p. 317.

16 Supra, note 14, p. 21.

17 *G.E. Marchant and K.L. Mossman*, *Arbitrary and Capricious: The Precautionary Principle in the European Union Courts*, Washington DC: The AEI Press, 2004.

18 Supra, note 14, p. 21.

19 Ibid., p. 9.

20 Ibid.

21 See, e.g. the role of the court in interpreting Directive 92/43/EEC on the conservation of natural habitats and of wild fauna and flora (OJ L 206, 22.07.1992, p. 7) (Habitats Directive), and the application of precautionary decision-making: *European Commission, Nature and*

it is recognised that its application will reflect trends in case law, which in turn reflect social and political values,[22] an area which the Court is best placed to adjudicate on.

3. EMPHASIS ON SCIENCE AND SCIENTIFIC DATA

The Communication places an emphasis on the role that science and scientific data play in the application of the precautionary principle. The first step in the precautionary process is a scientific evaluation.[23] The evaluation is a central and key aspect of the process, providing a factual basis to precautionary decision-making.[24] The evaluation identifies the scientific uncertainty that exists, so providing an objective and informed basis on which a precautionary decision can be made.

Some commentators suggest that the importance of science in the application of the principle is overstated, and that the political aspect is more important.[25] Early commentators pitted science against the precautionary principle,[26] contending that the principle was "anti-science and unscientific".[27] It was viewed as embodying the opposite of what science was trying to achieve; through a scientific evaluative process, results are obtained, which lead to transparency and a degree of certainty.[28] The precautionary principle, however, symbolised uncertainty, as it was seen as feeding on the fear of the unknown, giving policymakers an avenue to shift burden and blame on to industry, and so on to scientists.[29] The precautionary principle was viewed as replacing a science-based approach with an administrative procedure.[30] Increasingly, however, the relationship between science and the precautionary principle has come to be viewed in a more positive manner. The precautionary principle is an essential feature of "science-based" regulation.[31] Precautionary decisions

---

Biodiversity Cases – Ruling of the European Court of Justice, Luxembourg: EU Publications Office, 2006, p. 4.

22 Supra, note 14, p. 9.

23 Ibid., pp. 3 and 16: "The implementation of an approach based on the precautionary principle should start with a scientific evaluation, as complete as possible, and where possible, identifying at each stage the degree of scientific uncertainty."

24 *E. Fisher*, *Risk Regulation and Administrative Constitutionalism*, Oxford: Hart Publishing, 2007, p. 228.

25 *P. Jiang*, "A Uniform Precautionary Principle under EU Law", *PKU Transnational Law Review* (2014) 2(2), p. 490.

26 Supra, note 10.

27 *M.W. Brombacher*, "The Precautionary Principle Threatens to Replace Science", *Pollution Engineering*, Summer 1999, p. 32.

28 Supra, note 9.

29 Supra, note 27.

30 Ibid.

31 Supra, note 1.

are premised on a scientific foundation. Equally, the evolution of the principle has influenced the role of science in EU decision-making.[32] The precautionary approach is considered to be a broad and inclusive method, resulting in a scientific approach to risk regulation.[33]

4. LEGITIMATING PRECAUTIONARY DECISION-MAKING

The precautionary principle governs legitimate regulatory action where scientific uncertainty exists.[34] As the central activity of the precautionary process is a scientific evaluation, the legitimacy of a decision is contingent on this evaluation. Scientific evidence legitimates decisions by providing a vital objective basis for decision-making.[35] The legitimacy of a precautionary decision, therefore, depends on the characteristics of the scientific evidence used in the evaluation, and how this evidence is applied. The science that feeds into the evaluation must have objective and well-defined parameters. The evaluation itself must also adhere to procedural safeguards.

As the Communication places responsibility for defining the boundaries and application of the precautionary principle on the CJEU, the Court has a pivotal role in elaborating on the type and standard of scientific evidence used in the scientific evaluation. It also has a role in clarifying the scope of the evaluation, and how it is applied in the decision-making procedure. The Court has a role in ensuring that precautionary decisions are taken on a legitimate basis, underpinned by objective scientific evidence.

The Court is not expected to engage in a debate as to whether the science and scientific evaluation used in a precautionary decision are correct or not, but it does have a role in establishing the factual basis behind a decision. Broad discretion is granted to the EU institutions, especially in areas deemed to be complex and technical, such as environmental law.[36] The judicial review of

---

32 *B. Ballantine*, *Enhancing the role of science in the decision-making of the European Union*, EPC Working Paper No. 17, Brussels: European Policy Centre, 2005.

33 *A. Stirling and D. Gee*, "Science, Precaution, and Practice", *Public Health Reports*, (2002) (117) (6), p. 521.

34 Supra, note 27, p. 7.

35 *D. Bodansky*, "Legitimacy" in *D. Bodansky, J. Brunnée and E. Hey* (eds.) *The Oxford Handbook of International Environmental Law*, Oxford: Oxford University Press, online publication date: Sep. 2012.

36 See, e.g. Opinion of Advocate General Mischo in Case C-241/01, *National Farmers' Union and Secrétariat général du gouvernement*, EU:C:2002:415, [2002] ECR I-9108, para. 75; Case T-392/02, *Solvay Pharmaceuticals v. Council*, ECLI:EU:T:2003:277, [2003] ECR II-4559, para. 126.

regulatory decisions is limited to an assessment of the facts.[37] The Court has a duty to establish whether the evidence relied on in a precautionary decision is factually accurate, contains all the relevant information, and substantiates the conclusions reached.[38] Therefore, in cases concerning the application of the precautionary principle, the Court must examine the evidence put forward, to determine whether it substantiates the precautionary action taken. This type of assessment requires the Court to review the scientific data.[39] The Court can review scientific evidence without substituting its own assessment for that of a scientific body, or assuming the role of the legislature.[40] Sulyok sees this as a hybrid form of legal reasoning, bridging scientific and legal parameters.[41] There is scope, within the constraints of the separation of powers, to examine the scientific evidence. In carrying out a review of a precautionary decision, the Court can remain within EU judicial thresholds while also assessing the scientific data presented.[42] The Court is not required to determine the appropriate course of action, but to ensure procedural conformity by balancing the evidence presented.[43]

The review carried out by the Court, of the scientific evidentiary base underpinning a precautionary decision, is vital to ensuring the legitimacy of such a decision. The approach of the Court, as it elaborates on the definition of the principle, through the perspective of science, contributes to the application and legitimacy of the precautionary principle.

The next section will identify a selection of key decisions, in the broad area of environmental law, where the CJEU has engaged in an evaluation of scientific data in the context of precautionary decision-making. As the CJEU has been tasked with elaborating on the definition of the principle contained in the Communication, the analysis will compare the approach of the CJEU with

---

37 See, e.g. Case C-269/90, *Technische Universität München*, [1991] ECR 1-5469, para. 14; Case C-77/09, *Gowan Comércio Internacional e Serviços Lda v. Ministero della Salute*, EU:C:2010:803 [2010] ECR I-13533 (*Gowan*), para. 56.

38 See, e.g. Case C-12/03 P, *Commission v. Tetra Laval*, [2005] ECR I-987, para. 39; Case C-326/05 P, *Industrias Químicas del Vallés v. Commission*, [2007] ECR I-6557, para. 76; supra, note 37 *(Gowan)*, para. 57.

39 *K. Sulyok*, *Science and Judicial Reasoning: The Legitimacy of International Environmental Adjudication*, Cambridge: Cambridge University Press, 2020, p. 327.

40 The Court has acknowledged that it cannot substitute its own assessment for that of a scientific body, as it does not have the necessary expertise. See, e.g. Joined Cases T-74/00, T-76/00, T-83/00, T-84/00, T-85/00, T-132/00, T-137/00 and T-141/00, *Artegodan GmbH and Others v. Commission of the European Communities*, EU:T:2002:283 [2002] ECR II-04945 (Artegodan), para. 200.

41 Supra, note 39, p. 327.

42 *M. Eliantonio*, "The Impact of EU Law on Access to Scientific Knowledge and the Standard of Review in National Environmental Litigation: A Story of Moving Targets and Vague Guidance", *European Energy and Environmental Law Review*, (2018) 27(4), p. 115.

43 *A. Alemanno*, *European Legal Integration: The New Italian Scholarship: The Shaping of European Risk Regulation by Community Courts*, Jean Monnet Working Paper 18/08, New York: New York University School of Law, 2008.

the detail of the Communication, and discuss how this has impacted on the definition and application of the principle.

5. JUDICIAL REVIEW OF THE SCIENTIFIC ELEMENT OF PRECAUTIONARY DECISION-MAKING

5.1. ATTRIBUTES OF THE SCIENTIFIC DATA

The Communication notes that the scientific assessment should be undertaken based on the "available data",[44] and requires the scientific data to be "reliable".[45] From a scientific point of view, reliability denotes that the data are based on close observation, derive from a reputable methodology, are reproducible,[46] and have been subjected to an appropriate statistical analysis.[47] In order to be effective, scientific data must be reliable.[48]

In this context, the CJEU often refers to making decisions in light of the "best scientific information available" or "most reliable scientific data available".[49] This reflects the interpretation of scientific evidence adopted by many guidance documents and legislative instruments, such as the methodological guidance on the application of appropriate assessment under the Habitats Directive,[50] or, at a global level, the Paris Agreement.[51]

---

44 Supra, note 14, p. 13.

45 Ibid.

46 *P. Grandjean*, "Science for precautionary decision-making" in European Environment Agency (eds.), *Late lessons from early warnings: science, precaution, innovation*, EEA Report No. 1/2013, Luxembourg: Publications Office of the European Union, 2013, pp. 623–643.

47 *T.F. Lüscher*, "Good publishing practice", *European Heart Journal*, (2012) 33(5), p. 557.

48 Supra, note 46.

49 See, e.g. Case T-13/99, *Pfizer Animal Health SA v. Council of the European Union*, [2002] EU:T:2002:209 *(Pfizer)*, para. 158; Case C-192/01, *Commission of the European Communities v. Kingdom of Denmark*, [2003] EU:C:2003:492, ECR I-09693 *(Denmark)*, para. 51; Case C-236/01, *Monsanto Agricoltura Italia SpA and Others v Presidenza del Consiglio dei Ministri and Others*, [2003] EU:C:2003:431 *(Monsanto)*, para. 113; Case C-41/02, *Commission of the European Communities v. Kingdom of the Netherlands*, [2004] EU:C:2004:762 *(Dutch Vitamin Case)*, para. 53; Case C-127/02, *Landelijke Vereniging tot Behoud van de Waddenzee and Nederlandse Vereniging tot Bescherming van Vogels v. Staatssecretaris van Landbouw, Natuurbeheer en Visserij*, [2004] EU:C:2004:482, para. 54; Case C-343/09, *Afton Chemical Limited v. Secretary of State for Transport* [2010] EU:C:2010:419 *(Afton)*, para. 60; Case C-282/15, *Queisser Pharma GmbH & Co. KG v. Bundesrepublik Deutschland*, [2017] EU:C:2017:26 *(Queisser)*, para. 56; Joined Cases C-487/17 to C-489/17, *Criminal proceedings against Alfonso Verlezza and Others*, [2019] EU:C:2019:270 *(Verlezza)*, para. 57; Case C-616/17, *Criminal proceedings against Mathieu Blaise and Others*, [2019] EU:C:2019:800 *(Blaise)*, para. 46.

50 Supra, note 5, pp. 30 and 43.

51 *UN Framework Convention on Climate Change (UNFCCC)*, "Annex to the Report of the Conference of the Parties on its twenty-first session, held in Paris from 30 November to

The Court has given examples of how the criteria of "reliable" or "best" evidence may be met, referring to recommendations set out in legislation. The Court has referred to using data from peer-reviewed articles. This ensures, as far as possible, that the data meet current methodological and technical standards.[52] Officially recognised tests and analyses could be used,[53] which links into the scientific requirement for a reputable methodology. Further, the evaluation should be based on scientific principles, and be made with the benefit of expert advice.[54]

There are, however, shortcomings with this approach. Peer review may not be an adequate standard for assessing the credibility and reliability of scientific data.[55] There are inherent personal and systematic biases in the peer-review process, which affect the quality of the research published.[56] Professional and funding pressures demand an increased publication output from scientists. Publications are required in order to advance professionally, and to secure funding.[57] This means that the quality of output is not always of an adequate standard. More significantly, the peer-review process is susceptible to manipulation, and can be undermined by the selective use of data.[58]

The use of expert advice is also not infallible. The value of an expert opinion is premised on the assumption that the best person has been chosen to provide the expert input.[59] Experts are open to bias, whether conscious or subconscious,[60] and any conclusion involves an element of subjective judgement.

It is arguable that the attributes of the scientific data to be used to substantiate the precautionary process can only be elaborated on at a procedural level, and not at a judicial level. The standards to be employed are subject-specific,

13 December 2015", UN FCCC/CP/2015/10. The Paris Agreement refers to undertaking rapid reductions in greenhouse gas emissions in accordance with "best available science" (Art. 4).

52 Opinion of Advocate General Sharpston, Case C-616/17, *Criminal proceedings against Mathieu Blaise and Others*, [2019] EU:C:2019:190, paras. 64–75, referring to the requirements under the Plant Protection Regulation and EFSA guidance documents; See also *T.F. Lüscher*, "Quality and integrity in the preparation and publication of scientific results", *Herz*, (2014) (39), p. 551.

53 Supra, note 49 *(Blaise)*, para. 85.

54 Ibid., para. 90.

55 Supra, note 39, p. 346.

56 *S. Jasanoff*, *The Fifth Branch: Science Advisers as Policymakers*, Cambridge, MA: Harvard University Press, 1994, pp. 61–79.

57 Supra, note 52 *(Lüscher)*.

58 *L.B. McHenry*, "The Monsanto Papers: Poisoning the scientific well", *International Journal of Risk & Safety in Medicine*, (2018) 29(3–4), pp. 193–205.

59 *D. Bodansky*, "The Legitimacy of International Governance: 'a Coming Challenge for International Environmental Law?", *American Journal of International Law*, (1999) 93(3), p. 596.

60 *W.D. Ruckelshaus*, "Risk, Science and Democracy", *Issues in Science and Technology*, (1985) 1(3), p. 19.

and depend on the protocols adopted and followed in individual policy areas. In pesticide regulation,[61] for example, the European Food Safety Authority (EFSA) has compiled extensive guidance on the submission of scientific peer-reviewed open literature, for the approval of active substances. The guidance attempts to counteract any possible publication bias by recommending that an extensive literature search is carried out, so ensuring that the "best available science" is consulted.[62] The concept of "best available scientific evidence", in the context of appropriate assessment under the Habitats Directive, refers to the requirement to carry out field surveys or desk studies.[63] In terms of global greenhouse gas emissions, the best available science is compiled and synthesised by the Intergovernmental Panel on Climate Change (IPCC), and the parameters are defined in line with comprehensive methodological guidance.[64]

It appears, therefore, that while the Court has been tasked with elaborating on the definition of the precautionary principle, it is more appropriate for the attributes of scientific data to be elaborated on at a policy-specific level, having regard to particular procedural requirements. This requires input from the relevant scientific bodies. The Court has limited scope for developing the meaning of reliable science.

5.2. AVAILABILITY AND TEMPORAL QUALITY OF DATA

The Communication specifies that the scientific data to be used in the scientific evaluation is the data that is "available".[65] A second strand of the Court's requirement for a decision to be made in light of the "best scientific information available" is for the decision to be "based on the most recent results",[66] or that

61 Commission Regulation (EC) No. 1107/2009 concerning the placing of plant protection products on the market and repealing Council Directives 79/117/EEC and 91/414/EEC, OJ L 309.

62 *European Food Safety Authority (EFSA)*, "Submission of scientific peer-reviewed open literature for the approval of pesticide active substances under Regulation (EC) No 1107/2009, OJ L 309, 24.11.2009, pp. 1–50", *EFSA Journal*, (2011) 9(2), 2092 (available at www.efsa.europa.eu), p. 17. The guidelines, however, acknowledge that language barriers may limit the extent of the search. Therefore, measures can be taken to limit weaknesses such as publication bias, but such matters cannot be eliminated entirely.

63 Supra, note 5, pp. 30 and 43.

64 See, e.g. *M.D. Mastrandrea et al.*, "Guidance Note for Lead Authors of the IPCC Fifth Assessment Report on Consistent Treatment of Uncertainties", Intergovernmental Panel on Climate Change (IPCC), 2010, available at http://www.ipcc.ch.

65 Supra, note 14, p. 13.

66 See, e.g. supra, note 49 *(Pfizer)*, para. 158; supra, note 49 (*Denmark*), para. 51; supra, note 49 *(Monsanto)*, para. 113; supra, note 49 *(Dutch Vitamin Case)*, para. 53; supra, note 49 *(Afton)*,

the data must originate from "current scientific and technical knowledge".[67] There is a temporal requirement to the data. The reference to the "most recent" or "current" results signifies that the most up-to-date and relevant evidence should be taken into account in precautionary decision-making. This position is also reflected in legislation. The Plant Protection Regulation[68] specifies that an active substance is to be assessed in "light of current scientific and technical knowledge".[69] From a scientific viewpoint, however, this temporal approach also has its weaknesses.

Scientific research often replicates existing studies, rather than forging new research paths. This mirrors the traditional science paradigm, which requires replication and verification.[70] Replication is also linked to funding structures. Studies may be repeated, rather than new avenues explored, as researchers follow funding sources, creating a "science bubble".[71] This means that the scientific information that is available and most recent may not be the information that is required or needed by society,[72] but, rather, by industry. Replication is also favoured due to the uncertainty involved in starting a new project, and fears over the ability to achieve meaningful results.[73] This indicates that the "most recent" available research is not necessarily the research that is required to adequately inform all aspects of the scientific evaluation.

Arguably, such issues are linked to the scientific method, and cannot be solved at a judicial level. These issues are central considerations in determining how science is interpreted for policy, and open up a broader debate on the science-policy interface. It is not the role of the Court to remedy such an inherent problem. This role lies with the legislature, and how the relationship between science and policy in regulatory decision-making is structured and interpreted.

5.3. MINORITY AND CONTRADICTORY SCIENCE

The Communication specifies that due account is to be taken of minority and contradictory science, in any scientific evaluation.[74] When reviewing

---

para. 60; supra, note 49 *(Queisser)*, para. 56; supra, note 49 *(Verlezza)*, para. 57; supra, note 49 *(Blaise)*, para. 94.

67 Supra, note 49 *(Blaise)*, paras. 64–75, referring to the Plant Protection Regulation, supra, note 61.

68 Supra, note 61.

69 Ibid., Art. 4(1).

70 Supra, note 46.

71 *D.B. Pedersen and V.F. Hendricks*, "Science Bubbles", *Philosophy & Technology* (2014) 27(4), p. 503.

72 Supra, note 46.

73 Ibid.

74 Supra, note 14, p. 16. Contradictory evidence can be viewed as a subset of minority science. This is on the condition that the credibility of the minority science is recognised.

the application of the precautionary principle, the standard, set by the Court and legislation, of consulting the "best scientific information available",[75] and the "most recent results", ostensibly restricts the consultation of minority or dissenting views, as these may not be readily accepted or published in mainstream research. The importance of such science cannot be underestimated. Minority science is a key factor in horizon scanning, acting as an early warning system for human and environmental risks. It was minority science that indicated the risk of BSE to consumers,[76] and suggested that bisphenol A, a component of plastics, was an endocrine disruptor.[77]

The traditional science paradigm relies on repetition and a narrow research focus, to reduce uncertainty.[78] This approach leads to reductionism,[79] learning more and more about less and less. This standard is reflected in the scientific articles published. The articles tend to focus on the same issues taken from a different angle, or the articles are updated in line with technological development.[80] Studies on emerging risks are not as prevalent, or as accepted, in mainstream scientific publications; therefore, they would not necessarily fall within the category of the "best scientific information available" nor the "most recent results."

The use of such terms may also inadvertently favour certain studies over others. The Plant Protection Regulation[81] is underpinned by the precautionary principle.[82] Under the Regulation, the burden of proving the safety of a pesticide rests with industry. The safety of a product must be demonstrated before the

---

The Communication also refers to the World Trade Organization (WTO) Appellate Body Report on EC Measures Concerning Meat and Meat Products (Hormones) AB-1997-4, para. 194. which notes that divergent views are also to be taken into account, as they can be an indication of scientific uncertainty.

75 And the various other derivatives of this term.

76 Bovine Spongiform Encephalopathy (BSE). *P. van Zwanenberg and E. Millstone*, "Mad cow disease 1980s–2000: how reassurances undermined precaution" in P. Harremoës *et al.* (eds.), *Late lessons from early warnings: the precautionary principle 1896–2000*, EEA Report No. 22/2001, Luxembourg: Publications Office of the European Union, 2001, pp. 157–166.

77 *A. Gies and A.M. Soto*, "Bisphenol A: contested science, divergent safety evaluations" in *Late lessons from early warnings: science, precaution, innovation*, EEA Report No. 1/2013, Luxembourg: Publications Office of the European Union, 2013, pp. 215–240.

78 Supra, note 46.

79 Ibid.

80 Ibid. Grandjean carried out a survey of articles published over the years 2000–09, and found that the same chemicals analysed during the past 100 years are still the main chemicals being analysed today, making up the majority of publications in the area of chemical analysis, while very few studies had been carried out on chemicals identified as emerging risks. This research may have evolved since, due to legislation such as the Regulation (EC) No. 1907/2006 concerning the Registration, Evaluation, Authorisation and Restriction of Chemicals (REACH), OJ L 396, 30.12.2006, pp. 1–849. The research is indicative, however, of the potential shortcomings with the traditional science paradigm.

81 Supra, note 61.

82 Ibid., Art. 1(4).

product can be placed on the market. When presenting corroborating scientific evidence, emphasis is placed on good laboratory practice standards and the reproducibility of results.[83] Reference to the best scientific information available will potentially favour standardised industry studies over independent and minority investigations, which often take a more novel approach to research.[84]

As with the attributes and availability of scientific evidence, it is not the role of the Court to identify minority science, and to give it a place in the application of the precautionary principle. This role rests with the decision-makers, and the scientific agencies tasked with carrying out the scientific evaluation. It also depends on the policy area and context in which the evaluation is being conducted.[85] Unlike elaborating on the attributes and availability of scientific evidence, however, which may be viewed as a scientific task, the Court does have a role in ensuring that the evidence presented before it justifies a precautionary decision.[86] As the Communication requires minority evidence to be given due consideration, it is arguable that the Court has a role in ensuring that minority science is adequately assessed. It is often the case that the Court takes a limited approach to the judicial interpretation of scientific evidence in areas where minority or dissenting views exist.[87]

This approach was evident in the Court's decisions in the wake of the BSE crisis.[88] When reviewing the validity of decisions under the Plant Protection Regulation, which is often a contentious area,[89] the Court also carries out a limited review. The Court focuses on procedure rather than a review of the substance

---

83 *S. Rottger-Wirtz*, "Case C-616/17 *Blaise and Others*: The precautionary principle and its role in judicial review – Glyphosate and the regulatory framework for pesticides", *Maastricht Journal of European and Comparative Law*, (2020) 27(4), p. 529.

84 Ibid. The author notes, however, that this is a difficult issue to address as, in this case, the Court was dealing with an abstract review of the regulatory framework rather than a review of the approval decision process.

85 E.g. in the approval of active substances for use in pesticides, the applicant must submit regulatory studies sponsored by industry, following good laboratory practice standards and open scientific literature, as analysed by Member State and EFSA experts (see, generally, supra, note 61), while in an appropriate assessment carried out under the Habitats Directive, the scientific evaluation is compiled by scientific experts, and assessed by the relevant competent Member State authority. See, generally, supra, note 5, and the updated guidance, European Commission, "Assessment of plans and projects in relation to Natura 2000 sites – Methodological guidance on the provisions of Article 6(3) and (4) of the Habitats Directive 92/43/EEC" 2021/C437/01.

86 See, e.g. supra, note 40, para. 200.

87 See, e.g. *A. Donati*, "The Glyphosate Saga, A Further but Not a Final Step: The CJEU Confirms the Validity of the Regulation on Plant Protection Products in Light of the Precautionary Principle", *European Journal of Risk Regulation*, (2020) 11(1), p. 148.

88 See, e.g. Case C-1/00, *Commission of the European Communities v. French Republic*, EU:C:2001:687 [2001] ECR I-09989.

89 Supra, note 87.

of the decision.[90] The Court refrains from elaborating on the precautionary evidentiary requirements of the Regulation, even though there is scope under the Regulation to adopt a more expansive evidentiary interpretation.[91]

It is understandable that the Court may want to remain detached from divisive areas, so that it is better able to conduct a review of the evidence in an impartial manner. Arguably, however, it is especially in a situation where the science is contested that the Court should assess the reasoning behind a decision. The Court does not need to decide which data are correct, but it has a role in enforcing the requirements of the precautionary principle. The Court has a role in ensuring that all views, especially minority and contradictory views, are adequately considered. Looking at scientific facts is not an adversarial exercise but a balancing exercise.[92] The Court has been tasked with elaborating on the definition of the principle, and creating space for minority and dissenting science is a central element of the principle.

5.4. ROLE OF THE SCIENTIFIC EVALUATION AND THE SCIENTIFIC COMMITTEE

Scientific evidence should be independent and disinterested.[93] The Court has identified independence as a vital procedural guarantee in precautionary decision-making.[94] While independence may be an essential attribute of the data used to inform precautionary decisions, independence cannot always be guaranteed.

Many scientific projects are either funded by industry or driven by an academic agenda.[95] The results of such research are interpreted by an expert, and conclusions drawn. The interpretation of scientific data for policy is an empirical–hermeneutical task.[96] The conclusions are interpreted in light of the

---

90 Supra, note 83.

91 *C. Sobotta*, "Recent applications of the precautionary principle in the jurisprudence of the CJEU – a new yardstick in EU environmental decision making?", *ERA Forum*, (2021) 21(4), p. 723. This approach can be compared with the approach of the Court in its interpretation of the Habitats Directive where it takes an expansive approach to interpreting scientific evidentiary requirements.

92 Supra, note 39, p. 347.

93 *R.K. Merton*, "Priorities in Scientific Discovery: A Chapter in the Sociology of Science", *American Sociological Review*, (1957) 22(6), p. 635.

94 Supra, note 49 *(Pfizer)*, para. 172; Cases T-429/13 and T-451/13, *Bayer CropScience AG and Others v. European Commission*, [2018] EU:T:2018:280 *(Bayer 2018)*, para. 147; supra, note 52 *(Blaise)*, para. 66, referring to the Plant Protection Regulation, supra, note 61.

95 Supra, note 46.

96 To borrow the phrase from *H.J. Lauth*, "Legitimacy and Legitimation" in *D. Berg-Schlosser, B. Badie and L. Morlino* (eds.), *The SAGE Handbook of Political Science*, London: SAGE Publications Ltd., 2020, as it was used in the analysis of legitimation.

original hypotheses and agenda. The output will be skewed towards the initial question, and will, possibly, be value-laden.[97]

As part of the precautionary decision-making process, and to ensure the independence and quality of the scientific evaluation, the Commission often relies on expert advisory bodies, risk assessment agencies and scientific committees to carry out scientific evaluations on questions with regard to consumer safety, public health and the environment.[98] The risk management process must take into account the results of the evaluation and "in particular" the opinion of such bodies.[99] The advice given must be based on excellence, independence, impartiality and transparency.[100]

While the Commission may engage, or be obliged to engage, an agency to carry out a scientific evaluation in the form of a risk assessment, it is not bound to accept the opinion that the agency comes to.[101] Decisions are often made contrary to the recommendation of a scientific evaluation, or in the absence of an adequate scientific evaluation.

Two of the early seminal cases on the precautionary principle, *Pfizer* and *Alpharma*, demonstrate the contradictory approach to the conclusions of scientific evaluations. In *Pfizer*,[102] the EU institutions acted contrary to the recommendation contained in the opinion of the Scientific Committee on Animal Nutrition (SCAN), and upheld a ban on the use of certain antibiotics as animal growth promoters. The General Court (GC) clarified that a statement of reasons for disagreeing with the SCAN opinion must be provided, and must be on the same scientific level as the SCAN opinion. This may either be via a supplementary opinion from the same committee, or via evidence of a similar quality.[103] The examination should be carried out on all aspects of the individual case.[104] Therefore, to act contrary to an opinion issued by SCAN (and, arguably, any scientific evaluation), an equivalent independent report must be provided, to support the decision of the particular EU institution. The GC, however, further clarified that, while an alternative opinion would be helpful, there is no obligation to draw up such a report.[105] This negates the comment that an

97 Supra, note 59.

98 See for e.g. Regulation (EC) No 178/2002 of 28 January 2002 laying down the general principles and requirements of food law, establishing the European Food Safety Authority and laying down procedures in matters of food safety OJ L 31.

99 Ibid., Art 6(3).

100 Ibid., Art. 6(2).

101 Supra, note 49 *(Pfizer)*, para. 196; see also Case C-3/00, *Denmark v. Commission*, [2003] ECR I-2643, para. 114; Opinion of Mr Advocate General Poiares Maduro in Case C-41/02, *Commission of the European Communities v. Kingdom of the Netherlands*, [2004] EU:C:2004:520 *(Dutch Vitamin Case)*, fn. 52.

102 Supra, note 49 *(Pfizer)*.

103 Ibid., para. 199.

104 Ibid., para. 203.

105 Ibid., para. 208.

alternative opinion is required, as it is open to the EU institutions to act contrary to the view of the scientific committee, as long as they give their own adequate reasoning for doing so.

In *Alpharma*, the GC clarified that the scientific committees are "purely advisory bodies", and that the EU institutions are not bound by their findings.[106] It found, in this case, that the EU institutions were not required to rely on a SCAN opinion in coming to a decision. Yet at the same time, in *Alpharma*, the institutions justified their decision partly by reference to the results of the SCAN opinion from the *Pfizer* case.[107] This approach has been identified as a pattern of "confirmation plus qualification".[108] It brings no coherence to the role of the scientific evaluation or the risk assessment bodies.

This contradictory approach is also evident in the more recent case of *Bayer*.[109] In this case, the Commission prohibited the domestic use of certain neonicotinoids as pesticides, in the absence of an EFSA risk assessment. The Commission is not obliged to refer such an authorisation to EFSA for its opinion.[110] In this situation, the Commission carried out an assessment of the relevant data itself. Advocate General Kokott considered that the Commission had failed to adequately assess the available scientific evidence in coming to its decision, and alluded to the fact that the decision had been based on conjecture.[111] The Court did not agree with this interpretation, however, and upheld the ban on the neonicotinoids, referring to the high degree of toxicity of the substances,[112] and deferring to the discretion of the Commission.

In cases where precautionary measures are adopted in contravention of, or in the absence of, a scientific evaluation,[113] the EU institutions are potentially implementing precautionary measures in the absence of adequate supporting scientific evidence. The Court, in upholding such decisions, is weakening the

---

106 Case T-70/99, *Alpharma Inc. v Council of the European Union*, [2002] EU:T:2002:210 *(Alpharma)*, para. 237.

107 This is in reference to relying on certain information from the SCAN report from *Pfizer*, which said that, in certain circumstances, virginiamycin was safe to use. However, the antibiotic at issue in the *Alpharma* case was bacitracin zinc.

108 *V. Heyvaert*, "The changing role of science in regulatory decision-making in the European Union", paper presented at the fifth biennial Encounters in Citizen Science Association (ECSA) conference, 29 May–1 June 1997, Seattle, USA; *E. Vos*, "Antibiotics, the Precautionary Principle and the Court of First Instance," *Maastricht Journal of European and Comparative Law*, (2004) (11), p. 187.

109 Case C-499/19-P, *Bayer CropScience AG and Bayer AG v. Commission*, [2021] ECLI:EU:C:2021:367 *(Bayer 2021)*, paras. 79 and 115.

110 Supra, note 61, Art. 21(2).

111 Opinion of AG Kokott in Case C-499/18 P, *Bayer CropScience AG and Bayer AG v. European Commission* [2021] ECLI:EU:C:2020:735, para. 167.

112 Supra, note 109 *(Bayer 2021)*, para 158. This was specifically in relation to the private use of pesticides containing the contested neonicotinoids.

113 See, to that effect, supra, note 49 *(Pfizer)*; supra, note 106 *(Alpharma)*; supra, note 37 *(Gowan)*; supra, note 49 *(Afton)*; supra, note 109 *(Bayer 2021)*.

role that is played by scientific data in triggering and validating precautionary measures. This indicates that the scientific evaluation, and by association scientific data, are not central tenets of the precautionary principle, but data that are to be used when appropriate to justify the measures that have been invoked. It relegates the role of the scientific evaluation to a secondary role, which is not the intention of the Communication.[114]

5.5. MEMBER STATE DISCRETION AND VARIABLE PRECAUTION

The Communication requires the scientific evaluation to be "as complete as possible",[115] but also acknowledges that it is not possible, in all cases, to complete a comprehensive assessment of risk.[116] This has been reiterated by the Court, which has stated that the scientific risk assessment should be carried out as thoroughly as possible.[117] These comments reflect the inherent uncertainty that exists in science. Even if the scientific evaluation is incomplete, in the sense that there are uncertainties and gaps in the knowledge, there must still be enough information, however, for the competent authorities to be in a position to decide on the best course of action.[118]

The Court has not always held the EU institutions to this evidentiary standard. This is evident from the *Pfizer* and *Alpharma* cases, in which the EU institutions adopted precautionary decisions in conflict with the recommendations of scientific evaluations, and these were upheld by the Court. This is also evident in *Gowan*.[119] In this case, several scientific committees carried out research on the use of fenarimol as a plant protection product, and concluded that the risk was acceptable.[120] The Commission, however, over the course of negotiations with Member States, imposed a restriction on its use, based on "intensive consultation" with "experts".[121] No alternative risk assessment was carried out to justify the restrictions imposed. Nonetheless,

114 Supra, note 14, p. 16.
115 Ibid.
116 Ibid., p. 13.
117 See, e.g. supra, note 49 *(Pfizer)*, para. 162.
118 Case T-257/07, *French Republic v. European Commission*, [2011] ECR II-05827, para 77; see also supra, note 49 *(Pfizer)*, paras. 160 to 163; supra, note 106 *(Alpharma)*, paras. 173 to 176; supra, note 94 *(Bayer 2018)*, para. 118.
119 Supra, note 37 *(Gowan)*.
120 Ibid. The results were validated by the evaluation working group of the Standing Committee on the Food Chain and Animal Health, and certain questions were considered by the Scientific Committee on Plants.
121 Ibid., para 38.

the Court of Justice (CJ) accepted the Commission's reasoning, on the basis that there was scientific uncertainty.

In comparison, a higher standard has been applied by the CJEU to the scientific evaluations carried out by Member States. The reasoning often given is that the review is connected to the single market and trade restrictions, and so a more stringent application of the precautionary principle is warranted.[122] This approach was evident in a case concerning an action taken by the Commission against the Netherlands, for refusing to allow certain cereals fortified with vitamins to be sold in the Netherlands.[123] The GC stated that the proper application of the precautionary principle requires the identification of potentially negative consequences, and a "comprehensive risk assessment."[124] This can be compared with the acceptance by the Court, in cases such as *Gowan*, of a Commission decision in the absence of a single coherent risk assessment.

The Court has echoed the Communication's requirement that a full scientific evaluation of risk is not necessary to trigger precautionary measures. The Court, however, has been inconsistent in its application of this recommendation. It appears to grant more leniency to the EU institutions, justifying the lack of scientific evaluation by reference to the broad discretion enjoyed by the legislature.[125] In comparison, it applies the requirement for a scientific evaluation in a strict sense when dealing with Member States and possible restrictions on trade.[126] It seems to be the case, therefore, that the Court defines the need for, and parameters of, the scientific evaluation in a variable manner. The Court is not guided by the level of detail and scientific content of the evaluation, but by reference to the facts of, and the parties to, the case. This, again, places scientific evidentiary requirements into a secondary role.

5.6. SCIENTIFIC EVALUATION AND POLICY

While scientific evidence is a key aspect of precautionary decision-making, recourse to the precautionary principle cannot be based on science alone; there needs to be a policy dimension.[127] The Communication notes that, in applying the precautionary principle, general risk-management measures also need to

122 Supra, note 101 *(Opinion in Dutch Vitamin Case)*, para. 30.
123 Supra, note 49 *(Dutch Vitamin Case)*.
124 Ibid., paras. 53–55.
125 See, to that effect, supra, note 49 *(Pfizer)*; supra, note 37 *(Gowan)*; supra, note 49 *(Afton)*.
126 See supra, note 49 *(Dutch Vitamin Case)*.
127 Supra, note 101 *(Opinion in Dutch Vitamin Case)*, para. 32. Although, in this opinion, AG Maduro generally questions the role of science in the precautionary principle.

be taken into account, including, *inter alia*, a cost–benefit analysis.[128] It has been established that environmental protection and the protection of public health take precedence over economic concerns,[129] however there is also a point at which risk prevention potentially becomes economically and politically unfeasible.[130]

The position of the Court was summarised in *Pfizer*, where the GC noted that "scientific legitimacy is not a sufficient basis for the exercise of public authority".[131] An insight into the viewpoint of the Commission is evident in *CEVA Santé Animale*, where it stated that it must balance:

> [A]ll the scientific information available, taking into account scientific uncertainty, consumers' concerns, ethical or moral considerations or other legitimate factors and the precautionary principle.[132]

In *Zoofachhandel*,[133] which concerned the importation of wild birds into Europe, the Court reiterated the broad discretion that the legislature has under the Common Agricultural Policy, and noted that the political choice determining the appropriate level of protection for society lies with the EU institutions, and not with the scientists.[134] In the exercise of its discretionary power, it is for the legislature to "anticipate and evaluate ecological, scientific, technical and economic changes of a complex and uncertain nature".[135]

Similarly to the approach adopted by the Court when considering minority and dissenting science, where policy issues appear to be a defining factor in a precautionary decision taken by the Commission, the Court defers to institutional discretion. This, however, is not helpful when attempting to define the parameters of the precautionary principle. In such situations, policy, instead of the scientific evidentiary base, appears to be the factor that justifies a precautionary decision.

---

128 Supra, note 14, p. 19.

129 See, e.g. supra, note 40 *(Artegodan)*, para. 184; Case T-584/13 *BASF Agro BV and Others v. European Commission* [2018] EU:T:2018:279, para. 168; supra, note 94 *(Bayer 2018)*, paras. 106 and 109, and the case law cited therein; Ibid, p. 4.

130 Supra, note 17, p. 29.

131 Supra, note 49 *(Pfizer)*, para. 201.

132 Joined Cases T-344/00 and T-345/00, *CEVA Santé Animale SA and Pharmacia Entreprises SA v. Commission of the European Communities*, [2003] ECR II-00229 *(CEVA Santé Animale)*, para. 66.

133 Case T-817/14, *Zoofachhandel Züpke GmbH and Others v. European Commission*, [2016] EU:T:2016:157 *(Zoofachhandel)*.

134 Ibid., para. 42.

135 Ibid.

5.7. THE ROLE OF SCIENCE AND SCIENTIFIC ADVISORY BODIES IN DEFINING THE PRINCIPLE

While the Court has been given a central role in elaborating on, and defining, the boundaries of the precautionary principle, it may not be best placed to develop the evidentiary parameters of the principle. The principle has an intrinsically scientific nature, and a scientific evidentiary basis. In defining the attributes of the scientific data that inform precautionary decision-making, it is arguable that a more effective method is for such attributes to be defined at a procedural level, and to be policy-specific. The precautionary principle is applied in different policy areas in different ways, and so can only be defined within the context of each policy area.[136]

Some commentators recommend that the Court should assert more control over the scientific process at the evaluation stage, and become involved in how the results of the evaluation are translated into precautionary measures.[137] It is submitted, however, that the definition of the precautionary principle, for each policy area, may be better addressed by policy-specific scientific advisory bodies at the pre-legislative stage, or by means of guidance documents defining the scientific evidentiary requirements.[138] The Court will then be in a position to adopt a clarificatory role in areas of ambiguity, elaborating on an already-defined scientific evidentiary base.

As is evident from the sample of cases discussed above, it is often the case that the role of scientific evidence has been relegated to a secondary consideration in precautionary decision-making. This has the effect of weakening the legitimacy of the precautionary decision, as scientific evidence provides the objective and factual basis on which a decision is taken. In order to increase the legitimacy of precautionary decision-making, a clearly defined role should be attributed to science and scientific bodies, in the decision-making process. The precautionary principle is regarded as legitimising science, and it is acknowledged that science plays a vital role in implementing the principle.[139] Input from scientists is necessary to adequately define the acceptable parameters of the principle, in terms of the scientific evidence. Clear protocols need to be put in place outlining how scientific data is to be incorporated into a decision, or how, if the data is disputed or rejected, alternative data is to be sourced, evaluated and incorporated.

---

136 Supra, note 24, p. 7.

137 *A.M. Janssen and N.F. Rosenstock*, "Handling Uncertain Risks: An Inconsistent Application of Standards?", *European Journal of Risk Regulation*, 2016 (1), p. 144; supra, note 43.

138 As has been carried out, to an extent, under the Habitats Directive, supra, note 21, and the Plant Protection Regulation, supra, note 61.

139 Supra, note 9, p. 179.

There is an argument that increasing the role of scientists and scientific advisory bodies in a regulatory matter, such as contributing to the definition of a principle, may lead to legitimacy issues. These bodies lack democratic legitimacy. It could be interpreted that giving these bodies greater power may feed into the creation of a technocratic governance structure. It is not the intention, however, to create a technocracy, but to assist in the development of a reasoned approach to precautionary decision-making, based on scientific evidence. Scientific advisory bodies do not have democratic legitimacy or political responsibilities, but they have scientific legitimacy.[140]

A collaborative approach, whereby scientists have a role in policy, has also been criticised by members of the scientific community. It is considered that, when questions relating to society and society's values are posed to scientific agencies rather than elected officials, the scientific assessment suffers.[141] A solution, however, is needed to address the subordinate role that is often ascribed to science in precautionary decision-making. It adopts an ancillary position, behind matters such as policy. A solution is also needed to the silo mentality that exists in precautionary decision-making, whereby science takes an empirical, informative role, rather than an active role in finding a solution. A collaborative approach may not translate easily into a regulatory framework, but it more accurately reflects the interconnected nature of precautionary decision-making, combining science and policy.[142]

6. CONCLUSION

The CJEU has been tasked with defining the precautionary principle at an EU level. Due to the scientific nature of the principle, it may be more appropriate for certain elements of the scientific evidentiary requirements to be addressed and defined by scientific advisory bodies at a policy-specific level. The definition of the principle is linked to the more intrinsic question of how science is interpreted in EU regulatory instruments. There is a disjointed approach to incorporating scientific evidence into EU legislation.[143] This can only be addressed by a re-evaluation of the relationship between science advice and policy, at the EU level.

A definitive definition of the precautionary principle may be difficult to achieve, considering the complexity and scale of the application of precaution

---

140 Supra, note 49 *(Pfizer)*, para. 201. The GC noted, in relation to SCAN, that "scientific legitimacy is not a sufficient basis for the exercise of public authority."

141 *B. Url*, "Don't attack science agencies for political gain", *Nature*, (2018) (553), p. 381.

142 *E. Fisher*, "Framing Risk Regulation: A Critical Reflection", *European Journal of Risk Regulation*, (2013) 4(2), p. 125.

143 Supra, note 2, p. 110.

in policy. It is recognised that it may be difficult for the Court to reconcile its role as an impartial assessor with the role it has been assigned under the Communication, of "super-expert and risk assessor".[144] In the context of the scientific evidentiary requirements of the principle, however, clear parameters and protocols are vital, to ensure that the principle occupies a central and legitimate role in the risk-analysis procedure of the EU. Instead of requiring the Court to adopt a clarificatory role in a complex area that is policy-specific and in constant flux, it may be more efficient to consider the role that scientific advisory bodies and the scientific evaluation can play, setting out a clear protocol for science-based precautionary decision-making at the policy level.

144 *E. Vos*, "EU risk regulation reviewed by the European Courts" in M.B.A. van Asselt, M. Everson and E Vos (eds.), Trade, Health and the Environment: The European Union Put to the Test, Oxford: Earthscan/Routledge, 2014, p. 213.

PART XIV
RUSSIAN ENVIRONMENTAL LAW

LEGAL RISKS AND LEGAL UNCERTAINTIES IN RUSSIAN ENVIRONMENTAL LAW

Nikolay KICHIGIN

1. INTRODUCTION

The problems of legal uncertainties and legal risks are becoming an increasingly relevant topic of scientific research.[1] This trend is objective, as it is caused by the extremely high level of uncertainties and risks that exist in almost all spheres of modern life: technological, social, economic and political. The COVID-19 pandemic has significantly increased the level of all types of uncertainties. The level of uncertainty has also significantly increased in the context of global climate change.

The uncertainties of the surrounding world have a direct impact on the law, which is used as a mechanism for preventing and minimising uncertainties and risks: in property transactions, in political activities, and in inter-state relationships. In turn, law, as a social regulator, is also experiencing an increasing influence from the uncertainties of the surrounding world. Legal uncertainties become a threat to the stability and certainty of legal regulation, as they generate legal risks, gaps and conflicts. To combat legal uncertainties and risks, it is necessary to develop our own mechanisms to counteract them.

---

1 Micklitz, H.-W. and Tridimas, T. (eds.), *Risk and EU Law*, Edward Elgar Publishing, 2015; Miscenic, E. and Raccah, A., *Legal Risks in EU Law: Interdisciplinary Studies on Legal Risk Management and Better Regulation in Europe*, Springer, 2016; Steele, J., *Risks and Legal Theory*, Hart Publishing, 2004; Tikhomirov, Yu.A. and Shakhray, S.M., *Risk and Law: Scientific Publication*, Moscow University Press, 2012; Lyakhov, Yu.A., "Legal uncertainty in criminal proceedings", *Russian Justice*, 2009, no. 11. pp. 49–51; Li, S., *The Legal Environment and Risks for Foreign Investment in China*, Springer-Verlag, 2007; Aryamov, A.A., *General theory of risk (Legal, economic, and psychological analysis)*, 2nd ed., Wolters Kluwer, 2010; Tikhomirov, Yu.A., "Forecasts and risks in the legal sphere", *Journal of Russian Law*, 2014, no. 3, pp. 5–16; Vlasenko, N.A., "Uncertainty in law: the nature and forms of expression", *Journal of Russian Law*, 2013, no. 2, pp. 32–44; Vlasenko, N.A., "Legal understanding in the light of categories of certainty and uncertainty", *Journal of Russian Law*, 2014, no. 2. pp. 37–44; Vlasenko, N.A., *Problems of legal uncertainty: a course of lectures*, INFRA-M, 2015; Kryuchkov, R.A., "Risk in law: genesis, concept and management: abstract", Dis. cand. jurid. sciences, Nizhny Novgorod, 2011.

Legal uncertainties are the subject of scientific research in the theory of law. The problems of legal risks have been studied to the greatest extent in the science of civil and criminal law.[2] In the science of environmental law in Russia, the study of legal uncertainties and risks has not yet received proper development. Taking into account the above-mentioned situation, the purpose of this study is to analyse the concepts of "legal uncertainties" and "legal risks", to determine their specifics in environmental regulation, the impact of legal uncertainties and risks on the efficiency of environmental law, and means of minimising legal uncertainties and risks in environmental law. As a part of this study, the environmental legislation of the Russian Federation and legal literature will be considered.

The goal of the study of the concepts of "legal uncertainties" and "legal risks" is to describe the means of dealing with these concepts to improve the quality of legal regulation and prevent its disadvantages.

2. THE CONCEPT OF "LEGAL UNCERTAINTY IN ENVIRONMENTAL LAW"

The term "uncertainty" is used in certain Russian federal laws (Federal Constitutional Law No. 1-FKZ of 21.07.1994, "On the Constitutional Court of the Russian Federation"), but most often it is used in judicial acts. The judicial acts of the Constitutional Court of the Russian Federation, which is the highest judicial body of constitutional control in the Russian Federation (Article 1 of Federal Constitutional Law No. 1-FKZ, dated 21.07.1994, "On the Constitutional Court of the Russian Federation"), use the terms "uncertainty" and "legal uncertainty". When considering specific legal situations, the Constitutional Court of the Russian Federation overcomes legal uncertainties by interpreting the Constitution of the Russian Federation.[3]

In the judicial acts of the Constitutional Court of the Russian Federation, the content of the concepts of "uncertainty" and "legal uncertainty" is not disclosed. Therefore, there is a need for a scientific analysis of these terms, in order to develop definitions, and approaches to their identification, as well as to eliminate or minimise their consequences.

---

[2] Aryamov, above n. 1; Martirosyan, A.G., *Risk Theory in the Civil Law of the Russian Federation* Prospekt, 2017; Goryachkina, D.A., "On the issue of the category 'risk' in the theory of civil law", *Bulletin of Perm University. Juridical Sciences*, 2011, no. 3(11), pp. 90–92; Grinberg, M.S., "Risk in criminal law", *Bulletin of Omsk University*, 2006, no. 3; Baburin V.V., "Risk as a basis for differentiation of criminal responsibility", Dis. doct. jurid. sciences, Omsk, 2009.

[3] See, in more detail, Ivanova, E.A., "Some aspects of the interpretation of the concept of 'uncertainty' as grounds for applying to the Constitutional Court of the Russian Federation", *Lawyer*, 2009, no. 6; Zhigachev, A.V., *Uncertainty of the tax norm as a basis for its appeal by taxpayers to the Constitutional Court of the Russian Federation*, SPS ConsultantPlus, 2010.

In legal literature, legal uncertainties are usually considered a defect of legal regulation. Uncertainty in law refers to the construction and operation of a legal system in which there are legal conflicts and contradictions between levels and forms of legal regulation.[4]

Uncertainty in law is a phenomenon of the imperfection of legal regulation caused by objective and subjective factors of legal education. It denotes inaccurate, incomplete and inconsistent consolidation and implementation of the normative legal will in law. In addition, uncertainty in law is considered to be a technical and legal defect of the text of law, as an external written form of its expression. Uncertainty, as a technical and legal defect, represents logical and linguistic deviations and deformations in the construction and expression of legal norms, manifested in the absence of an accurate, complete normative legal establishment, which inevitably leads to a decrease in the regulatory properties of law, complicating the interpretation of its norms, and hindering their effective implementation.[5]

At the same time, some scientists have put forward the thesis that legal uncertainties may not only be negative, but may also have a positive effect. Negative legal uncertainties are defects of legal regulation and are subject to elimination. Positive legal uncertainties, on the contrary, provide flexibility of legal regulation, allowing the use of judicial discretion.[6] It is necessary to agree with this approach, since it takes into account various manifestations of legal uncertainty.

In the present author's opinion, legal uncertainty in environmental law is a state of environmental regulation that is characterised by a lack of clarity in the choice or application of a specific norm of environmental law, and may generate legal and other risks for the subjects of legal relationships (legal and natural persons).

3. THE CONCEPT OF "LEGAL RISK IN ENVIRONMENTAL LAW"

In our proposed definition of legal uncertainty, legal and other risks act as integral criteria for the existence of legal uncertainty. In the present author's opinion, it is the legal risk itself that serves as a criterion for distinguishing negative legal uncertainties from positive ones. Negative legal uncertainties may cause various negative consequences: holding companies or individuals legally responsible (e.g. through fines), refusal to grant permission to users of natural resources (cancellation of the subsoil use license, termination of the water use agreement),

---

4 Tikhomirov and Shakhray, above n. 1, p. 11.

5 Nazarenko, T.N., "Uncertainty in Russian law", Abstract, Dis. cand. jurid sciences Moscow, 2006, pp. 7–8.

6 Vlasenko, N.A., *"Problems of legal uncertainty: a course of lectures"*, above n. 1, p. 176.

and receiving a negative conclusion from state environmental expertise (e.g. the prohibition of the planned economic activity). Positive legal uncertainties do not create such consequences.

Positive legal uncertainties provide flexibility in legal regulation, and the possibility for the subjects of legal relationships (legal and natural persons) to act more freely. Most legal uncertainties have a negative character, but sometimes we encounter the phenomenon of positive legal uncertainty. For example, Federal Law No. 248-FZ of 14 July 2022, adopted in 2022, "On by-products of animal husbandry and on amendments to certain legislative acts of the Russian Federation", allows legal and natural persons to classify, on the basis of certain conditions, substances formed during the maintenance of farm animals, as by-products of animal husbandry, or as waste.

There are a lot of definitions of the concept of "risk" in the legal, economic and technical literature. The category of "risk" is a universal interdisciplinary concept. One of the founders of risk theory in Western humanities is sociologist Ulrich Beck.[7] This theory has become widespread in various scientific fields.[8] Climate risks are becoming increasingly important, and in the future may become global in nature, and have an impact on all spheres of human activity.[9]

In Russian legal science, the problem of risk has, traditionally, been considered in the context of civil and criminal law. However, recently, a lot of academic publications have been published on the topic of risk within various branches of law and legislation,[10] which indicates the extreme degree of relevance of this topic as a subject of scientific analysis. In this regard, Tikhomirov notes that, in fact, all branches of law "react" to risks, as a "shadow satellite" of law in different spheres, and it is necessary to see the interrelationships of risks in different industries – their peculiar "movements".[11]

---

7 Beck, U., *Risk Society: Towards a New Modernity*, SAGE Publishing, 1992.

8 Roeser S., Hillerbrand, R., Sandin, P. and Peterson M. (eds.), *Essentials of Risk Theory*, Springer, 2013.

9 Nobre, C.A., Marengo J.A., Soares, W.R. (eds.), *Climate Change Risks in Brazil*, Springer, 2019; Nadin, R., Opitz-Stapleton S. and Yinlong, X. (eds.), *Climate Risk and Resilience in China*, Routledge, 2016.

10 See, e.g. Meitardjian, D.A., "The concept and signs of risks in the sphere of budgetary legal relations", *Financial Law*, 2017, no. 9, pp. 22–27; Mikhailova, A.S., "On the importance of taking into account 'risk' as an object for determining the content of the 'compliance control' function", *Lawyer*, 2017, no. 18, pp. 20–24; Istomina, E.A., "Prevention of occupational risks: the French experience of labor law regulation", *Labor Law in Russia and Abroad*, 2017, no. 3, pp. 54–57; Sogiyainen, A.A., "Legal risks of medical activity in modern conditions", *Law in the Armed Forces*, 2017, no. 4, pp. 35–42; Kostyuk, M.F. and Kosheleva, M.V., "Banking risks and their legal consequences", A Russian Investigator, 2017, no. 6, pp. 24–27; Lipatov, E.G., "Corruption risks of legal regulation: experience of positive analysis", *Administrative Law and Process*, 2017, no. 2, pp. 26–31; Bolobonova, M.O., "The concept of civil risk", *Law and Economics*, 2016, no. 10, pp. 13–20.

11 Tikhomirov, Yu.A., "Risk in law: nature and causes", *Law and Modern States*, 2016, no. 6, p. 13.

Analysis of both Russian and foreign sources allows us to conclude that the concept of "risk" means the probability of occurrence of any negative consequences, for a certain subject (life, health, property of an individual or a legal entity) or object (the environment as a whole, individual components of the natural environment).

A variety of risks are legal risks. In the present author's opinion, legal risks are risks caused by the presence of legal uncertainty which implies the occurrence of negative legal consequences. Other categories of risks may also be a consequence of legal uncertainty. Thus, in the legal literature, managerial risks, budget risks, entrepreneurial risks, and risks in the field of labour relations are distinguished. Federal Law No. 7-FZ of 10.01.2002, "On Environmental Protection" (hereinafter referred to as the "Law on Environmental Protection"), provides for the term "ecological risk".

According to this law, ecological risk means the probability of an event having adverse consequences for the natural environment, having been caused by the negative impact of economic and other activities, natural and man-made emergencies. It may be supposed that the ecological risk and legal risk in environmental law may occur simultaneously. For example, carrying out economic activities using unauthorised technology, or without obtaining the necessary permits, may create a risk of causing harm to the environment, exposing the enterprise to legal responsibility, in the form of compensation for environmental damage, in cash, or through the remediation of the environment.

The differences between ecological risk, and risk in environmental law, lie in the origins and nature of such risks. The source of ecological risk is exclusively the economic activity of economic entities. Legal risk in environmental law may arise not only as a result of economic activity, but also as a result of the adoption of environmental laws and standards. In addition, environmental risks, unlike legal risks in environmental law, do not have a direct legal basis. The objects of ecological risk are narrower in comparison with the risk in environmental law: the environment and its components. The objects of legal risk in environmental law are much broader: the environment, legal entities and individuals, and the rights and legitimate interests of these entities and individuals.

According to researchers, the institute of risk is an institute of legal theory, which is being developed and specified both in the sectorial legal institutions of risk, and in complex institutions. The law performs such functions in relation to risk as the legal recognition and assumption of risks, the establishment of means of preventing and minimising risks, and the definition of liability measures, as well as the functions of compensatory means.[12]

---

12 Tikhomirov and Shakhray, above n. 1, p. 10.

Article 3 of the Law on Environmental Protection establishes the presumption of environmental danger of planned economic and other activities as a principle of environmental protection. Article 3 of Federal Law No. 174-FZ of 11/23/1995, "On Environmental Expertise", provides for the presumption of potential environmental hazards of any planned economic and other activities as a principle of environmental expertise.

Thus, the environmental legislation assumes that any planned economic and other activities carry potential danger or threat to the environment. Volkov, in this regard, notes that, in a broad sense, all legislation in the field of environmental protection is aimed at preventing and minimising the negative impact of economic and other activities on the environment, including, in particular, environmental damage.[13]

Based on the above, we can attempt to define the concept of "legal risk in environmental law". In the theory of law, the risk, from the viewpoint of jurisprudence, is generally considered to be the objectively existing probability (specific to human activities and, within certain limits, capable of being assessed and intently regulated), which is associated with negative consequences due to various negative occurrences connected with different prerequisites (risk factors). Risks are subdivided depending on their legal consequences, the level of legal regulation, industry affiliation, and stages of the legal regulatory mechanisms.[14] Tikhomirov understands legal risk as a probable unlawful deviation from the legal model, and existing legal Acts, and their drafts,[15] as well as a probable unlawful deviation from legal decisions and Acts, entailing negative consequences that need to be foreseen and prevented.[16]

The present author believes that legal risks do not only arise as a result of violations of the law. This is quite obvious: in the event of violation of legislation or other mandatory requirements, there is a legal risk of punishment or other negative consequences. But legal risks may also arise as a result of negative legal uncertainties, which, in turn, can be incorporated into legislation, as well as into law enforcement practice.

Considerable attention is paid, in foreign literature, to the study of the category of legal risk.[17] In particular, it is assumed that risk is a combination of the probability of an event and its consequences. A risk is a legal risk if its source

---

13 Volkov, G.A., "Prevention and minimization of environmental harm" in Minina, E.L., Bogolyubov, S.A., Tikhomirov, Yu.A, et al. (eds), *Legislative support for the protection of wildlife*, Law Institute of MIIT, 2016, p. 97.

14 Kryuchkov, above, n. 1, p. 27.

15 Tikhomirov, Yu.A., "Risk in law", above n. 11, p. 12.

16 Ibid., p. 10.

17 Mahler, T., "Defining Legal Risk", Proceedings of the Conference "Commercial Contracting for Strategic Advantage – Potentials and Prospects", Turku University of Applied Sciences, 2007, pp. 10–31, https://papers.ssrn.com/sol3/papers.cfm?abstract_id=1014364.

includes legal norms. The risk must serve as a manifestation of the potential harm of the legal norm. It is proposed to distinguish two types of legal risk inherent in environmental law: instrumental risk, and legal risk as a consequence of legal or factual uncertainty.[18]

Taking into account the above-mentioned approaches, it is proposed to understand legal risk in environmental law as a kind of legal risk: the likelihood of negative legal consequences for the environment, and for legal entities (the state, legal entities and individuals), in the legal regulation, in the process of planning and carrying out economic activities in the field of environmental management. For example, the legislative reduction of the special protection regime in relation to specially protected natural territories creates legal risks for such territories, such as development, reduction of areas, etc.

The greatest number of legal risks in environmental law arise at the stage of operation of objects of economic activities. However, legal risks in environmental law that are not minimised at an early stage may be impossible to mitigate or eliminate later. That is why the preamble of the UNECE Convention on Environmental Impact Assessment in a Transboundary Context (Espoo Convention)[19] stresses the need to pay close attention to environmental factors at an early stage of the decision-making process. Article 6(4) of the UNECE Convention on Access to Information, Public Participation in Decision-making and Access to Justice in Environmental Matters (Aarhus Convention)[20] prescribes that each party should ensure public participation at the earliest stage, when all opportunities are open to consider various options, and when effective public participation is guaranteed.

Among the legal risks in environmental law that arise during the planning and implementation of economic activities in the field of environmental management, the following can be outlined: incurring legal liability for committing an environmental offence (for example, paying an administrative fine); obtaining a negative conclusion from the state environmental experts; refusal to issue permits (permits for emissions and discharges, waste disposal production and consumption); suspension or termination of the right to use natural resources (land use, water use, subsoil use), cancellation of licences; liability to pay compensation for environmental damage; prohibition of economic activity; seizure of land.

---

18 Post, H.H.G., "Legal Risks in European Environmental Law and Policy" in Miscenic and Raccah, above n. 1, p. 221.

19 UNECE Convention on Environmental Impact Assessment in a Transboundary Context, https://unece.org/fileadmin/DAM/env/eia/documents/legaltexts/Espoo_Convention_authentic_ENG.pdf.

20 UNECE Convention on Access to Information, Public Participation in Decision-making and Access to Justice in Environmental Matters, https://unece.org/DAM/env/pp/documents/cep43e.pdf.

4. FEATURES OF LEGAL UNCERTAINTIES AND ENVIRONMENTAL RISKS IN ENVIRONMENTAL LAW

In the environmental sphere, legal uncertainties and risks are specific, which is due to the following circumstances: firstly, the specifics of ecological and legal relationships, as well as the peculiarities of the objects of environmental law. Environmental components, natural resources, environmental information, rights to natural resources: the inclusion of these objects within the sphere of legal regulation determines the peculiarities of the terminology used, ensures the "binding" of legislation to the laws of nature, and specifies the mechanisms used.[21]

The difficulty of using legislative techniques to describe and properly reflect the laws of nature in legislation distinguishes environmental legislation from other branches of law and legislation. It can be stated that the laws of nature and the laws of society do not coincide in their content and orientation, and often even contradict each other.

Secondly, legal risks in environmental law, and in environmental legal relationships, are caused by the presence of specific environmental risks, the nature of which is so specific that, even at the current level of development of science and technology, it is impossible not only to absolutely prevent, but even to identify and assess, all possible risks to the environment as a result of planned economic and other activities.

This issue is also reflected in the Russian legislation: Article 77 of the Law on Environmental Protection establishes the obligation of full compensation for environmental damage, which is expressed in the fact that environmental damage caused by the subject of economic and other activities should be compensated, even if the project obtained a positive conclusion from the state environmental experts.[22] Federal Law No. 174-FZ of 11/23/1995, "On Environmental Expertise", establishes the principle of presumption of potential environmental hazards of any planned economic and other activities.[23]

A similar situation has developed with regard to risks to human health, since environmental risks threaten the lives and health of citizens. Therefore, according to Article 79 of the Law on Environmental Protection, the damage caused to the health and property of citizens by negative impacts on the environment, as a result of economic and other activities of legal entities and individuals, is subject to compensation in full.

---

21 See, for more details, Brinchuk, M.M., *Environmental law: Objects of environmental relations*, Moscow, IGP RAN, 2011.

22 See, for more details, Bogolyubov, S.A. and Khludeneva, N.I., *Commentary to Federal Law No. 7-FZ of January 10, 2002 "On Environmental Protection" (article by article)*, Justicinform, 2009.

23 See, for more details, Brinchuk, M.M. (ed.), *Commentary to Federal Law No. 174-FZ of November 23, 1995 "On Environmental Expertise"*, Wolters Kluwer, 2011.

The scientific literature notes that, in 2019, global pollution was responsible for approximately 9 million premature deaths. Air pollution (both household and ambient air pollution) remains responsible for the greatest number of deaths, causing 6.7 million deaths in 2019. Water pollution was responsible for 1.4 million premature deaths. Lead was responsible for 900,000 premature deaths. Toxic occupational hazards, excluding workplace fatalities due to safety hazards, were responsible for 870,000 deaths.[24]

Thus, the federal legislator, following the science, presumes the impossibility of guaranteeing the complete environmental safety of any particular project, or that the project that has passed all the verification procedures established by law will not, ultimately, harm the environment.

Thirdly, legal uncertainties and risks in environmental law are caused by the relative youth of the branch itself. Environmental law, as a branch of law, is still in the phase of its active formation and scientific understanding.

Under these conditions, the emergence of legal uncertainties and risks in environmental law is an objective phenomenon. Therefore, an important task of increasing the efficiency of environmental law should be the study of the problem of legal uncertainty and legal risks, in relation to this branch of law and legislation.

Thus, the presence of legal uncertainties, and legal risks generated by them, is a permanent feature of environmental law, due to the specifics of the public relationships it regulates in the field of environmental protection. The main causes of legal risks in environmental law are legal uncertainties generated by the lack of clear rules of conduct, which, in turn, are due to the lack of complete and exhaustive knowledge about human impact on the environment.

5. IDENTIFICATION AND ASSESSMENT OF LEGAL RISKS AT THE STAGE OF DEVELOPMENT OF THE DRAFT REGULATORY LEGAL ACT

The tasks of the legislator and law enforcement authorities are to minimise the number of negative legal uncertainties and risks, since legal uncertainties are often the product of subjective factors in the development of legislation. It is precisely due to the incorrect formulation of legal norms that legal uncertainties and risks arise.

How can legal risks in environmental law be assessed at the stage of development of a regulatory legal Act, taking into account that they are approximate in nature, as the projected legal norm has not yet entered into

---

24 Fuller, R. (et al.), "Pollution and health: a progress update", *Lancet Planet Health*, 2022, vol. 6, p. e536.

force? On the one hand, it is very difficult to comprehensively assess legal uncertainties and risks in environmental law at this stage. On the other hand, identifying potential legal uncertainties and risks at the earliest stage of legal regulation makes it possible to minimise them in the most efficient way, since it is, by definition, easier to correct a draft regulatory legal Act than to initiate amendments to an already adopted Act, especially a federal law.

The following mechanisms for preventing and minimising legal uncertainties and risks in legislative activity can be specified:

(1) legal assessment of regulatory legal Acts;
(2) anti-corruption assessments;
(3) regulatory impact assessments;
(4) public discussions of draft laws, in the Public Chamber of the Russian Federation;
(5) conducting an experiment (legal experiment);
(6) developing a legal model of future legal regulation; working out the effect of the projected regulatory legal Act.

It should be emphasised that, although these mechanisms for analysing and evaluating draft laws work in Russia, they currently do not directly provide for the identification and minimisation of legal uncertainties and risks; in other words, this task is not directly articulated in the legislative process.

Let us assess the potential of some separate mechanisms, in the context of identifying and minimising legal uncertainties and risks.

5.1. CONDUCTING AN EXPERIMENT (LEGAL EXPERIMENT)

The Russian Federation has adopted Federal Law No. 34-FZ, dated 06.03.2022, "On conducting an experiment to limit greenhouse gas emissions in certain subjects of the Russian Federation", which provides that, in order to create the necessary conditions for reducing greenhouse gas emissions and increasing their absorption, subjects of the Russian Federation have the right to conduct an experiment on limiting greenhouse gas emissions on their territories, in accordance with this Federal Law and the legislation of the subjects of the Russian Federation in the territories in which the experiment is being conducted. The experiment is planned to be conducted in the territory of the Sakhalin Region, from 1 September 2022 to 31 December 2028, as well as on the territories of other subjects of the Russian Federation included in the experiment. As a part of this experiment, it is planned to work out a mechanism for providing and selling greenhouse gas emission quotas, similar to the European greenhouse gas emissions trading system (EU Emission Trading System). This experiment started last year, so currently there is none of the data necessary for legal analysis. It can, however, be stated that the necessary regulatory framework has been formed at the federal level, for the implementation of this experiment.[25]

5.2. DEVELOPMENT OF A LEGAL MODEL FOR FUTURE LEGAL REGULATION

The legal model is the predicted variant of optimal legal regulation of future phenomena and processes, which determines the goals and means of forming a new legal state, and allows calculation of the real results associated with it.[26] The concept of a legal model is that any law or other regulatory legal Act lays down a certain model of public relations as optimal and desirable. However, in real life, this model may not coincide with factual public relations. In this case, there are deviations of factual public relations from the proposed legal model. The task of the legislator is to monitor such deviations, on the basis of which a decision can be made to correct the proposed legal model itself, or to take additional measures to implement this model in factual public relations.

Risk assessment is a necessary element of social management, which is of fundamental importance in predicting the consequences of decisions taken. Modelling of risks in general, and legal risks in particular, is a separate, dynamically developing section of theoretical modelling, characterised by its

---

25 Resolution of the Government of the Russian Federation No. 708, dated 04/20/2022 "On Determining the coordinator of an Experiment to Limit greenhouse Gas Emissions on the Territory of Certain Subjects of the Russian Federation"; Resolution of the Government of the Russian Federation No. 1441, dated 08/18/2022 "On the rate of Payment for Exceeding the greenhouse Gas Emissions Quota in the framework of an experiment to limit greenhouse gas emissions on the Territory of the Sakhalin Region"; Resolution of the Government of the Russian Federation No. 1390, dated 05.08.2022 "On Approval of the Rules for Calculating and Charging Fees for Exceeding the Greenhouse Gas Emissions Quota as Part of an Experiment to Limit Greenhouse Gas Emissions in the Sakhalin Region"; Order of the Ministry of Economic Development of the Russian Federation No. 247, dated 06.05.2022 "On Approval of the Procedure for Classifying Legal Entities and Individual Entrepreneurs as Regional Regulated Organizations within the framework of conducting an experiment to limit greenhouse gas emissions in certain subjects of the Russian Federation"; Order of the Ministry of Economic Development of the Russian Federation No. 340, dated 06/29/2022 "On Approval of the Procedure for Submitting by the authorized body a report on the results of Monitoring the Implementation of the experiment Program to Limit Greenhouse Gas Emissions in Certain Subjects of the Russian Federation and the Form of such a Report"; Order of the Ministry of Economic Development of the Russian Federation No. 452, dated 08/24/2022 "On Approval of the Methodology for Determining Projected Greenhouse Gas Emission Quotas within the framework of the experiment to limit greenhouse Gas emissions. Greenhouse gas emissions in certain subjects of the Russian Federation".

26 Hakobyan, O.A., Vlasova, N.V., Gracheva, S.A., et al., *Legal Models and Reality* (Tikhomirov, Yu.A., Rafalyuk, E.E. and Khludeneva, N.I. (eds.)), Institute of Legislation and Comparative Jurisprudence under the Government of the Russian Federation: INFRA-M, 2014, p. 11.

special subject, methods and concepts. It can be said, with all certainty, that developments in the field of legal risk-modelling will only increase.[27]

To build a legal model for future legal regulation, the developers of the draft law form separate elements of such a model, united by a common idea, and coordinate them. The developed legal model can be formalised in the shape of a concept of a draft federal law. Within the framework of the legal model, the main mechanisms of future environmental legal regulation can be worked out, including the revealing of legal uncertainties and risks in environmental law.

5.3. WORKING OUT THE EFFECT OF THE PROJECTED REGULATORY LEGAL ACT OF ENVIRONMENTAL LAW

In order to work out the effect of the projected regulatory legal Act, its developer presents how the legal structures developed would work in practice. At the same time, legal risks, gaps and conflicts can be identified. The use of such a tool is especially effective in the framework of "business games", in which all interested persons can participate: users of natural resources, representatives of state authorities, the general public, and experts. Within the framework of the "business game", procedures are worked out, while requirements are clarified. In Russian environmental practice, there are examples of such "business games", aimed at working out procedures for obtaining complex environmental permits. These were attended by representatives of economic entities, as well as interested state authorities.[28]

This experience should be evaluated positively and recommended for promotion; however, it should be noted that such "business games" were held after the adoption of Federal Law No. 219-FZ, dated 21.07.2014, "On Amendments to the Federal Law 'On Environmental Protection' and Certain Legislative Acts of the Russian Federation", which introduced a mandatory requirement to obtain comprehensive environmental permits for Category I facilities.[29] Under such conditions, business games could not directly affect

---

27 Salygin, E.N., "Modelling in Law: Challenges and Prospects", *Zhurnal Vysshei shkoly ekonomiki (Journal of the Higher School of Economics)*, 2013, no. 3, p. 16.

28 A business game was held at the water supply company, on the procedure for issuing a comprehensive environmental permit of the South-Western sewage treatment plants (Saint-Petersburg): http://www.vodokanal.spb.ru/presscentr/news/v_vodokanale_proshla_delovaya_igra_po_procedure_vydachi_kompleksnogo_ekologicheskogo_razresheniya_yuzos/.

29 Category I includes facilities that have a significant negative impact on the environment (coke production; production of crude oil and (or) natural gas, including natural gas processing; production of petroleum products; extraction and (or) enrichment of iron ores, etc.).

the content of the already-adopted regulatory legal Act. Naturally, holding "business games" will not be a necessary step for each draft of a regulatory legal Act, but for important legal novelties, such a step can be beneficial.

The legal risks in environmental law identified at the stage of development of a regulatory legal Act are approximate and unclear, but their elimination will not entail the need for a complex and lengthy procedure for making amendments to an already-adopted legal Act. Currently, the tools described above for identifying and preventing legal risks in environmental law are practically unregulated, and if applied, then in an informal manner. It should be noted that the assessment of potential legal risks in environmental law is an element of the expert analysis of the draft law. When analysing the draft law, the expert mentally tries to evaluate the projected mechanism of legal regulation. However, such an analysis is not comprehensive, since it is carried out by one person, and interested legal entities often do not participate in the process of "debugging" the legal model of future regulation.

6. IDENTIFICATION AND ASSESSMENT OF LEGAL UNCERTAINTIES AND LEGAL RISKS IN ENVIRONMENTAL LAW AT THE STAGE OF IMPLEMENTATION OF A REGULATORY LEGAL ACT

At the stage of law enforcement activities, the task of identifying and eliminating legal risks in environmental law also remains relevant, since it is necessary to monitor potential legal risks in environmental law that were identified at the stage of developing a regulatory legal Act. In addition, at the stage of developing a regulatory legal Act, it is not always possible to identify all legal risks in environmental law. Therefore, it is necessary to continue working on identifying and minimising these risks.

Thus, the mechanism for identifying, eliminating and minimising legal risks in environmental law acts as a universal platform aimed at ensuring the efficiency of environmental and legal regulation.

At the stage of law enforcement activities, the identification of legal risks in environmental law arising as a result of the adoption of a regulatory legal Act is possible within the framework of law enforcement monitoring. The legal basis for monitoring law enforcement is the Decree of the President of the Russian Federation No. 657, dated 20.05.2011, "On Monitoring Law Enforcement in the Russian Federation". Paragraph 2 of the Regulation on the Monitoring of Law Enforcement in the Russian Federation, approved by this Decree, establishes that monitoring includes comprehensive and planned activities carried out by federal executive authorities and state authorities of the subjects of the Russian

Federation, within their powers, to collect, summarise, analyse and evaluate information, in order to ensure the adoption (publication), modification or invalidation (cancellation) of legislative and other regulatory legal Acts of the Russian Federation and its subjects. The legal basis of this type of monitoring has been studied in detail in the legal literature.[30]

Resolution of the Government of the Russian Federation No. 694, dated 19.09.2011, approved the Methodology for Monitoring Law Enforcement in the Russian Federation (hereinafter referred to as "the Methodology"). In accordance with paragraph 2 of the Methodology, constant and operational types of law enforcement monitoring are carried out. A wide range of regulatory legal Acts at the federal and regional levels are subject to law enforcement monitoring: federal laws, and subordinate regulatory legal Acts of the President of the Russian Federation or the Government of the Russian Federation, and Acts of federal executive authorities.

Paragraphs 8 to 10 of the Methodology establish indicators (markers) that are identified in the process of monitoring law enforcement, which include, for example, non-compliance with the guaranteed rights, freedoms and legitimate interests of a person and citizen; the presence of corruption-causing factors in a regulatory legal Act; the presence of errors of a legal and technical nature; and the presence of duplicate legal norms in regulatory legal Acts.

Paragraph 8 of the Methodology lists the indicators that are subject to law enforcement monitoring. These indicators include, in particular: the presence of corruption-causing factors in a normative legal Act; incompleteness in the legal regulation of public relationships; conflicts of law; and distortion of the meaning of the provisions of a normative legal Act in its application.

At the same time, the Methodology does not provide for the identification of gaps in legal regulation, only conflicts of law (subparagraph (h) of paragraph 8), which seems to be a disadvantage of the Methodology. In addition, it does not provide for the identification of legal risks and legal uncertainties.

Taking into account the above-mentioned factors, the monitoring of law enforcement, in the present author's opinion, should be aimed (in addition to identifying legal conflicts) at finding and identifying legal gaps, legal risks and legal uncertainties, including those in environmental law. When conducting such analyses, it is important to consider those legal and other risks that were identified at the stage of developing the concepts of draft federal laws and their texts, and which are reflected in the concept of the draft law, and in the explanatory note to it.

---

30 Tikhomirov, Yu.A. and Gorokhov, D.B., *Legal monitoring: Scientific and practical*, Yurisprudenciya, 2009; Pavlushkin, A.V., *The mechanism of legal monitoring: Scientific and practical manual*, IZiSP, 2012.

7. MEANS OF MINIMISING LEGAL UNCERTAINTIES AND LEGAL RISKS IN ECONOMIC ACTIVITY

Legal risks in environmental law, at the stage of law enforcement activities, can be identified not only directly when analysing the provisions of a regulatory legal Act, but also when analysing the economic activities of users of natural resources. In Chapter VII of the Law on Environmental Protection, environmental requirements are established for various stages of the life cycle of capital buildings: during architectural and construction design, construction, reconstruction, major repairs, commissioning, operation, decommissioning and demolition.

The identification of legal risks in economic activity allows a conclusion to be drawn about the quality of a regulatory legal act, and the need to adjust it, if other ways of eliminating or minimising associated risks cannot solve the problem. The results of using these tools to identify, eliminate and minimise legal risks in environmental law complement the data obtained during the monitoring of law enforcement.

Identification of legal uncertainties and risks in environmental law, arising in the course of economic activity, can be carried out through the following tools and procedures: environmental audits, environmental insurance, environmental and legal consulting, assessment of the impact of the planned activity on the environment, environmental expertise, explanations of public authorities, judicial practice, and project financing.

Some of these tools are provided by environmental legislation. Other tools have been developed in practice. It is also important to note that these means of identifying legal uncertainties and risks in environmental law make it possible to take measures to minimise or eliminate them. Let us now consider the application of these tools to identify and minimise legal uncertainties and risks in environmental law in more detail.

7.1. ENVIRONMENTAL AUDIT

The legal institute of environmental audit, which has been thoroughly researched in the legal and economic literature,[31] is practically unused in Russian

[31] Zaslavskaya, N.M., "Environmental audit: history and modern legal regulation", Environmental Law, 2015, no. 6., pp. 3–11; Ponomarev, M.V., "The legal mechanism of environmental audit", *Journal of Russian Law*, 2010, no. 8, pp. 106–110; Iutin I.G., "Environmental audit: role, essence and issues requiring legal regulation", *Journal of Russian Law*, 2008, no. 2; Kichigin, N.V. and Maryin, E.V., *Legal regulation of environmental audit: A scientific and practical guide*, Jurisprudence, 2010; Kichigin, N.V. and Egiazarov, V.A., "Environmental audit: prospects of legislative regulation", *Journal of Russian Law*, 2011, no. 4, pp. 11–18.

environmental practice, except in cases of implementation of large international projects financed by foreign banks. One of the reasons for this is the lack of clear legislative regulation of the organisation and conduct of environmental audits.

Environmental audits are a very promising means of identifying, minimising and eliminating legal risks in the field of environmental law. According to the legal definition of the concept of "environmental audit", given in Article 1 of the Law on Environmental Protection, an environmental audit includes an assessment of compliance, by a legal entity or an individual entrepreneur, with environmental requirements, when carrying out economic activities, and the preparation of recommendations to improve such activities. Environmental risks, legal risks in environmental law, and other risks – for example, environmental risks of privatisation programmes – should be identified in the process of conducting an environmental audit.[32]

Abroad, banks use environmental audits in order to reduce the risk of non-repayment of loans.[33] The environmental auditor not only records the presence of the relevant risk, but should also, in its audit report, give recommendations on how to eliminate or minimise it. The issue of including the assessment of environmental risk, and the risk of human activities, in the environmental audit of a particular enterprise, should be decided by the customer and the auditor, in accordance with the audit programme.[34]

There was a legal incident with environmental audit in the Russian Federation: Article 1 of the Federal Law "On Environmental Protection" establishes the definition of the concept of "environmental audit"; however, during the consideration of the draft law "On Environmental Protection", in the State Duma of the Federal Assembly of the Russian Federation, an independent article on environmental audit was excluded from its text. As a result, there are no relevant procedural norms in the current law with reference to the term "environmental audit", which in itself creates a situation of legal uncertainty.

In the present author's opinion, the introduction of environmental audits into environmental practice should begin with the regulation of voluntary environmental audits, since civil-law regulation, in the case of voluntary environmental audits, is not enough for their active application. This is because civil legislation cannot determine the legal status of the environmental audit report, the requirements for environmental auditors, or the obtaining of the right to carry out environmental audit activities.

---

32 Gogaeva, M.T., "Improving the legal foundations of environmental audit as a necessary element of the mechanism for making environmentally significant decisions", *Environmental Law*, 2010, no. 5, pp. 18–25.

33 Iutin I.G, above n. 30; Maryin, E.V., "Legal problems of environmental audit in Russia", *Environmental Law*, 2008, no. 1.

34 Serov G.P., *Environmental audit. Educational and practical manual*, M.: Eksamen, 1999, p. 60.

It is not clear from the definition of the concept of environmental audit that it is aimed at preventing or minimising legal risks in environmental law; however, when determining the assessment of compliance, by a user of natural resources, with environmental requirements, environmental and legal risks of economic activity are also identified. Proposals for minimising and preventing legal risks in environmental law are included in recommendations for improving such activities, which are an integral part of the concluded environmental audit report.

7.2. ENVIRONMENTAL INSURANCE

Another potentially efficient means of minimising and preventing legal risks in environmental law is environmental insurance. Environmental insurance is aimed at securing property risks in the implementation of economic activities, in the field of environmental management. The literature suggests that there is no voluntary environmental insurance market in Russia, as such, for a number of reasons, in particular due to the scale of environmental risks, and insufficient economic and legal incentives, including the inability to recognise the insurance premium in income tax expenses, etc. Voluntary types of environmental insurance are practically unused; even large insurers do not always have the appropriate rules.[35]

Repeated attempts to adopt a special federal law "On Mandatory Environmental Insurance" have also failed.[36] In the present author's opinion, the reason for this is that the developers of the draft law sought to introduce mandatory environmental insurance for users of natural resources. Meanwhile, experiences in foreign countries show that environmental insurance has developed there as voluntary insurance of risks arising in the field of environmental management.

We should agree with Novikova's opinion that voluntary environmental insurance is an effective tool for financial coverage of imminent residual environmental risks, which is confirmed by the experience of both developed (United States) and developing (People's Republic of China) countries. Foreign experience is also based mainly on voluntary, rather than compulsory, insurance.[37]

For example, in the United States, environmental insurance is formally voluntary, but in fact no major project in the field of environmental management

35 Novikova, E.V., "Institute of Environmental Insurance as an element of environmental safety", *Environmental Law*, 2018, no. 6, pp. 16–22; 2019, no. 1, pp. 8–12.

36 Motkin, G.A., "Political and economic barriers in the development of environmental insurance", *Environmental Law*, 2006, no. 3.

37 Novikova, E.V., "Modern economic and legal mechanisms of prevention and minimization of environmental harm", *Pravovedenie*, 2018, vol. 62, no. 4, pp. 625–639.

will be able to get a bank loan without obtaining such insurance coverage. In addition, multi-million-dollar claims for compensation for environmental damage caused as a result of economic activity have become an impetus for the development of voluntary environmental insurance abroad. As a result, users of natural resources themselves are interested in sharing their own financial risks with insurance companies (hedging risks). It is advisable to follow a similar path in Russia, creating an economic interest for users of natural resources in the implementation of voluntary environmental insurance.

The situation with the legal regulation of environmental insurance in the Russian Federation resembles the situation with environmental audits, described above. On the one hand, Article 18 of the Law on Environmental Protection is dedicated to environmental insurance, according to which mandatory state environmental insurance can be conducted in the Russian Federation, while environmental insurance has been conducted in accordance with the legislation of the Russian Federation; on the other, there is no special legislation on environmental insurance in the Russian Federation.

A draft law on environmental insurance has been developed in Russia, which, like the draft law on environmental audit, has not been adopted. One of the reasons for this, in the present author's opinion, is that the developers of the draft law sought to introduce mandatory rather than voluntary environmental insurance. This approach has caused the anticipated resistance from business, which fears that the introduction of mandatory environmental insurance will increase the cost of production, and reduce its competitiveness in the market.

In the present author's opinion, it is still necessary to regulate voluntary environmental insurance at the level of federal laws. It should be noted that it is not necessary to adopt a separate federal law for this. At the same time, it is important to develop measures to economically stimulate business entities to conclude voluntary environmental insurance contracts, for example by reducing payments for negative environmental impacts.

As we know, insurance activity is inextricably bound with minimising and preventing risks. In accordance with Article 929 of the Civil Code of the Russian Federation, the following property interests may, in particular, be insured under a property insurance contract: (1) the risk of loss, shortage or damage to certain property; (2) the risk of liability for obligations arising as a result of harm to life, health or property of other persons, and, in cases prescribed by law, contractual liability or the risk of civil liability; and (3) entrepreneurial risk. According to Article 931 of the Civil Code, the risk of liability of the policyholder themselves, or another person to whom such liability may be assigned, may be insured under the contract of liability risk insurance, for obligations arising as a result of harm to the life, health or property of other persons.

It seems that the liability risk insurance contract is quite suitable as a model of voluntary environmental insurance. When carrying out insurance activities, insurers should monitor how policyholders comply with environmental legislation in their activities. As part of the insurance, legal risks in environmental law can be assessed, among other things, which will directly affect the sum paid by the policyholder for the insurance.

7.3. ENVIRONMENTAL AND LEGAL CONSULTING

Legal regulation of environmental and legal consulting is provided by civil legislation. It can be carried out through the provision of services or works on the basis of relevant civil-law contracts. The environmental sphere does not impose any special conditions. Environmental and legal consulting can be carried out as part of a set of works (environmental audits, due diligence), or provided as an independent service. The task of environmental legal consulting is to identify and assess legal risks in environmental law, and prepare recommendations for their reduction or elimination.

7.4. ASSESSMENT OF THE IMPACT OF THE PLANNED ACTIVITY ON THE ENVIRONMENT

The purpose of the environmental impact assessment is to prevent or mitigate the impact of planned activities on the environment and related social, economic and other spheres. As part of the environmental impact assessment process (hereinafter referred to as the "EIA"), among other things, the environmental impacts of the planned economic and other activities are assessed (the likelihood of risk, and its degree, nature, scale and distribution zone, as well as the prediction of environmental and related social and economic consequences). Environmental risk assessment (ERA) has become widespread abroad.[38] In Russia, this type of EIA is not regulated by law, but it can be carried out, at the request of the customer, within the EIA procedure.

Within the framework of the Russian EIA procedure, an assessment of the compliance of the planned economic activity with the requirements of the current legislation is also carried out. Thus, legal risks in environmental law are also identified. If any are discovered, then means should be offered, in the EIA materials, to minimise or eliminate them. That is why the EIA can be considered a means of minimising and preventing legal risks in environmental law. Unfortunately, the EIA mechanism in Russia, unlike the similar EIA procedure

---

38 Galatchi, L.D., "Environmental Risk Assessment" in Simeonov, L. and Chirila, E. (eds.), *Chemicals as Intentional and Accidental Global Environmental Threats*, Springer, 2006, https://doi.org/10.1007/978-1-4020-5098-5_1.

in foreign countries, has not received proper recognition, and is, therefore, often treated as a formality.[39]

7.5. ENVIRONMENTAL EXPERTISE

According to Federal Law No. 174-FZ of 11/23/1995, "On Environmental Expertise", environmental expertise is aimed at establishing the compliance of documents and/or documentation justifying planned economic and other activities with environmental requirements. On the one hand, according to the regulations, legal risks in environmental law are not identified and eliminated within the framework of environmental expertise; on the other, state environmental experts cannot ignore the legal risks of the planned economic activity. Consequently, as a result of the environmental assessment, legal risks in environmental law are minimised or prevented, since, in the event of non-compliance with mandatory requirements, a negative environmental assessment conclusion must be prepared. In the event of such a negative conclusion, the implementation of economic and other activities is not allowed.

7.6. JUDICIAL PRACTICE

Judicial practice is a universal and quite effective way to identify and eliminate legal risks in environmental law. The court, considering the specific circumstances of the case, gives a judicial interpretation of legal norms. Judicial interpretation makes it possible to clarify the content of the disputed legal norm, not only for the parties to the case, but also for other persons who have access to the relevant court decision. Even in the absence of officially recognised judicial precedents, judicial acts of the Constitutional Court of the Russian Federation and the Supreme Court of the Russian Federation have a significant impact on the formation of law enforcement practice, reducing the legal risks for users of natural resources.

7.7. EXPLANATIONS OF PUBLIC AUTHORITIES

It should be recognised that even the presence of court decisions cannot answer all the questions facing users of natural resources. This is especially true in

---

39 Kichigin, N.V., "Legal regulation of environmental impact assessment in Russia and abroad", *Journal of Foreign Legislation and Comparative Jurisprudence*, 2016, no. 5, pp. 117–123.

the sphere under consideration, since environmental and legal regulation contains many specific technical requirements: standards of permissible impact; parameters of objects; and environmental and other features of territories. Legal regulation in these conditions cannot objectively reflect and take into account all situations that might arise in practice, without exception.

In practice, this situation is resolved by preparing and issuing explanations of a particular controversial situation. These clarifications may be mandatory for the territorial bodies of the federal executive authority, or contain the opinion of the authorised body on a specific situation. In any case, written explanations should be of a recommendatory nature for users of natural resources, and should not replace or substitute the provisions of legislation.

Unfortunately, the use of explanations is currently ineffective, since there is no systematised database with explanations, within the public reach. In addition, public authorities are forced periodically to respond to the same types of requests. In view of the above-mentioned factors, it seems necessary to introduce a register of explanations of federal executive authorities, on the most important issues. The register would allow the systematisation of mandatory requirements. It is necessary not only for users of natural resources, but also for the public authorities themselves, since very often they have to give answers to appeals for which there are already relevant explanations. In the event of a new appeal, the state authority could provide a reference to the previously given explanation. The database should be periodically reviewed, and explanations that are irrelevant, or contrary to the law, should be excluded. This will keep the database up to date.

7.8. PROJECT FINANCING

Project financing could, in the future, become an effective way to identify and minimise legal risks in environmental law. International financial institutions, when deciding on the provision of credit funds, require an environmental assessment (environmental audit) to be conducted according to international standards, within the framework of which, among other things, various risks of the planned activity are studied.

7.9. THE USE OF THE CONCEPT "ACCEPTABLE RISK" IN ENVIRONMENTAL LAW

Thus, legal uncertainties and risks in environmental law are not only scientific terms, but also have important practical significance: they act as a universal tool for evaluating a regulatory legal act at all stages of its development and implementation. For the effective application of this mechanism, it is necessary to improve legislation, as well as to develop a methodology for identifying, and preventing or minimising, legal uncertainties and risks in environmental law.

The tools considered here for minimising or preventing legal uncertainties and risks in environmental law, applied in combination with one another, are capable of, if not eliminating the relevant risks completely, then reducing them to an acceptable level. In scientific works on risk theory, the concept of "acceptable risk", which was proposed in the 1980s by academician Valery Legasov, is used to assess and grade risks. By acceptable risk, he understood "a risk that is indistinguishable by a person against the background of other risks to which he is exposed in normal living and working conditions".[40]

It seems that the category of "acceptable risk" can also be applied to minimise legal risks in environmental law. This approach finds support in the scientific literature. Thus, Begak and Kodolova note that the prevention of unacceptable risks and unacceptable harm is the responsibility of the state, and is guaranteed by its institutions. At the same time, acceptable risk is a conventional concept. Its value is determined by public institutions.[41]

8. MINIMISATION OF LEGAL RISKS IN ENVIRONMENTAL LAW ON THE CORRELATION BETWEEN STATE LAND SUPERVISION AND MUNICIPAL LAND CONTROL

As a rule, if it is discovered that there is a negative legal uncertainty in environmental law that generates corresponding risks, then the federal legislator eliminates the legal uncertainty as the cause of the legal risk. However, there is an example, in Russian land legislation, where the legislator has actually recognised the existence of negative legal uncertainty, and has not eliminated it, but has still minimised legal risks.

The land legislation (Articles 71 and 72 of the Land Code of the Russian Federation (hereinafter referred to as the RF Land Code)) provides for state land supervision and municipal land control, which can be conditionally associated with the concept of "public land control (supervision)".

The analysis of the subjects of state land supervision and municipal land control, as provided for by Articles 71 and 72 of the RF Land Code, allows us to conclude that the subjects of these types of public land control (supervision) are not properly differentiated among themselves, which inevitably leads to a

40 Begak, M.V. and Kodolova, A.V., "The National strategy of environmental safety of Russia: problems and prospects", *Eurasian Legal Journal*, 2016, no. 2, p. 227.

41 Ibid., p. 228.

situation of negative legal uncertainty; the risk of duplication of control checks, both on the side of land users, as well as public land control (supervision) bodies; and other legal risks.

Most often, legal uncertainties in legislative Acts are eliminated either by amending the relevant law, or by specifying provisions at the level of subordinate rulemaking, by adopting a decree of the Government of the Russian Federation or a departmental regulatory legal Act.

However, in order to eliminate this negative legal uncertainty, the Government of the Russian Federation has applied a fundamentally different approach: a special procedure has been established for the interaction of state land supervision and municipal land control bodies with each other, in order to prevent duplication of inspections.

The Rules of interaction of federal executive bodies exercising federal state land control (supervision) with bodies exercising municipal land control (hereinafter referred to as the "Rules of Interaction") were approved by Decree of the Government of the Russian Federation No. 2019, dated 24.11.2021.

Thus, a rather unique situation has developed in which negative legal uncertainty is not actually eliminated, although its presence has been recognised. At the same time, an attempt is being made to normatively minimise the consequences of such uncertainty: the risk of duplication of types of public land control (supervision).

The Rules of Interaction provide a separate procedure for approval of draft annual plans for municipal control (supervisory) measures by the state land supervision authorities. Joint meetings are also held, among other things, in order to eliminate drawbacks. On the one hand, this refers to the possible duplication of control checks. On the other hand, land users may not be included in both inspection plans. There is also uncertainty about which body of land control (supervision) should conduct unscheduled land control (supervision).

Thus, in accordance with the Rules of Interaction, in the "manual mode", objects of state land supervision and municipal land control are differentiated annually. "Manual mode" means that the differentiation of objects of land control (supervision) is carried out without established criteria, by annual approval of plans for scheduled inspections. It is difficult to agree with such an approach, since it allows for the arbitrary formation of annual inspection plans, and does not contain the necessary criteria for distinguishing objects, which, in turn, does not allow for unambiguous identification of either objects of state land supervision or objects of municipal land control.

Taking into account the above-mentioned issues, it seems necessary to legally distinguish the subject and (or) objects of public state land control (supervision), in Articles 71 and 72 of the RF Land Code, in order to eliminate the identified duplication, as well as negative legal uncertainties and risks.

9. CONCLUSIONS

The research conducted allows a few conclusions to be drawn. The presence of legal uncertainties and legal risks in environmental law is due to a number of objective factors: the specifics of environmental and legal relationships, and features of environmental law objects; the presence of environmental risks; the youth of environmental law, as a branch of law; and the process of its active formation.

Legal uncertainties in environmental law can be understood as such a state of environmental regulation, which is characterised by a lack of clarity in the choice or application of a specific norm of environmental law, and which may generate legal and other risks for the subjects of legal relationships. Positive and negative legal uncertainties can be distinguished.

Legal risks in environmental law are a type of legal risk: the likelihood of negative legal consequences for legal entities (the state, business entities and individuals) in the process of planning and carrying out economic activities in the field of environmental management. Legal risks in environmental law are criteria for identifying negative legal uncertainties.

The means of identifying and minimising legal uncertainties and risks in environmental law at the stage of drafting regulatory legal Acts may be: legal assessment of regulatory legal Acts; anti-corruption assessments; regulatory impact assessment procedures; public discussions of draft laws in the Public Chamber of the Russian Federation; conducting an experiment (legal experiment); development of a legal model of future legal regulation; and working out the effect of the projected regulatory legal Act. These means are not developed in the current legislation of the Russian Federation at all, and do not work effectively to prevent the occurrence of legal uncertainties and risks in environmental law, at the stage of drafting regulatory legal Acts. That problem has a broader character, and also concerns other branches of Russian legislation, not only environmental law.

The means of minimising legal uncertainties and risks in economic activity are environmental audits; environmental insurance; environmental and legal consulting; assessment of the impact of planned activities on the environment; environmental expertise; explanations of public authorities; judicial practice; and project financing. The situation with minimising legal uncertainties and risks in economic activity is certainly better than the situation in relation to drafting regulatory legal Acts.

Environmental audits are not regulated in environmental legislation, except for the notion of the environmental audit itself. But legal risks may be an object of a voluntary environmental audit. Auditors can consider such types of risks, along with ecological and other risks.

Environmental insurance is regulated in the Law on Environmental Protection, but this almost entirely fails to work in practice. Nevertheless, voluntary environmental insurance might potentially work, and counter legal uncertainties and risks in environmental law.

Environmental and legal consulting, explanations of public authorities, judicial practice and project financing are not the objects of environmental legal regulation, but nevertheless these mechanisms work in practice, and counteract legal uncertainties and risks in environmental law. Environmental expertise and the assessment of the impact of planned activities on the environment are regulated in environmental legislation, but do not provide analysis of legal uncertainties and risks in environmental law.

This study demonstrates the necessity to develop a legal doctrine of elimination or minimisation of legal uncertainties and risks in environmental law, and its implementation in the lawmaking process and law enforcement practice.

www.ingramcontent.com/pod-product-compliance
Ingram Content Group UK Ltd.
Pitfield, Milton Keynes, MK11 3LW, UK
UKHW051918100926
8556IPUK00021B/1240